Effective Surveillance for Homeland Security

Balancing Technology and Social Issues

Multimedia Computing, Communication and Intelligence

Series Editors: Chang Wen Chen and Shiguo Lian

Effective Surveillance for Homeland Security: Balancing Technology and Social Issues
Edited by Francesco Flammini, Roberto Setola, and Giorgio Franceschetti
ISBN: 978-1-4398-8324-2

Music Emotion Recognition
Yi-Hsuan Yang and Homer H. Chen
ISBN: 978-1-4398-5046-6

Optimal Resource Allocation for Distributed Video and Multimedia Communications
Yifeng He, Ling Guan, and Wenwu Zhu
ISBN: 978-1-4398-7514-8

TV Content Analysis: Techniques and Applications
Edited by Yiannis Kompatsiaris, Bernard Merialdo, and Shiguo Lian
ISBN: 978-1-4398-5560-7

Effective Surveillance for Homeland Security

Balancing Technology and Social Issues

Edited by

Francesco Flammini • Roberto Setola • Giorgio Franceschetti

CRC Press
Taylor & Francis Group
Boca Raton London New York

CRC Press is an imprint of the
Taylor & Francis Group, an **informa** business

CRC Press
Taylor & Francis Group
6000 Broken Sound Parkway NW, Suite 300
Boca Raton, FL 33487-2742

© 2013 by Taylor & Francis Group, LLC
CRC Press is an imprint of Taylor & Francis Group, an Informa business

No claim to original U.S. Government works

Printed on acid-free paper
Version Date: 20130401

International Standard Book Number-13: 978-1-4398-8324-2 (Hardback)

Library of Congress Cataloging-in-Publication Data

Effective surveillance for homeland security : balancing technology and social issues / editors,
    Francesco Flammini, Roberto Setola, Giorgio Franceschetti.
    pages cm. -- (Multimedia computing, communication and intelligence)
    Includes bibliographical references and index.
    ISBN 978-1-4398-8324-2 (hardcover : alk. paper)
    1. Electronic surveillance. 2. Video surveillance. 3. Privacy, Right of. 4. National security. I.
Flammini, Francesco. II. Setola, Roberto. III. Franceschetti, Giorgio.

TK7882.E2E42 2013
363.325'1630973--dc23   2013008817

Visit the Taylor & Francis Web site at
http://www.taylorandfrancis.com

and the CRC Press Web site at
http://www.crcpress.com

To Liana, Lucia, and Giuliana:

amare et sapere vix deo conceditur.

Contents

Foreword

The September 11, 2001, terrorist attacks shocked the entire world—the scale of devastation inflicted by this horrific attack still evokes a spine-chilling reaction today! More than a decade later, the events on that day still impact us in various ways and at different levels—from our increased awareness of the threat in our day-to-day lives to the augmented security measures, known and unknown, that are in place to protect us. The recognition that the threat of terrorism can range from the macro to the micro scale has changed how homeland security forces in different countries think about interdiction and the way in which governments, business, and insurance industry manage potential loss as a result of any terrorist activity.

The threat of terrorism persists with us, despite the formation of an alliance of the Western nations to eradicate it completely, and it is an unfortunate reality that this threat will continue in some form for many years to come. The security and counterterrorism intelligence alliance of the Western countries has played a crucial role in controlling the frequency of the attacks and minimizing their impact in the United States and Europe. Unfortunately, in other countries, especially those in the Asian and African continents, terrorism still rages with less interdiction success, and more than 25,000 people worldwide are estimated to have died in militant Islamic terrorist attacks since the catastrophic attack on 9/11.

The sheer scale and magnitude of the 9/11 attacks, executed by a network of terrorists intent on triggering simultaneous events causing mass destruction and loss of human lives, stunned the entire world and moved the threat of terrorism to the top of security priorities in many countries around the globe. In addition to causing significant loss of life and physical destruction, the attacks also resulted in one of the most costly insurance events in the history of the world.

In a presentation to the South West Regional Chapter of the INMM (Institute of Nuclear Materials Management) in 2002, Sig Hecker of Los Alamos National Laboratory characterized the tragedy of 9/11 as the third seminal event in the history of mankind—the first being the dropping of atomic bombs on Japan, and the second the fall of the Soviet Union. Hecker believed that the world's response to 9/11 would be our "third chance" to create a promising future for mankind. However, he also pointed out that if the right actions are not properly taken, the event might plunge the world into a detrimental future. He hoped that using various tools of scenario planning, a future world could be created that would provide the environment for strategic discussion among global leaders, so that even more significant events than 9/11 could be prevented or mitigated.

Dr. Hecker was not wrong in his observation. In the aftermath of the 9/11 attack, infrastructure security has become the top priority of the governments of all countries and many commercial organizations. The most critical infrastructures include banking and finance, telecommunications, energy (gas and electricity), water distribution, transportation, emergency services, and essential government services. Any damage or destruction of these critical infrastructures would have a crippling effect on the defense and economic security. Moreover, these infrastructures are so interconnected that the failure of one will adversely affect the operations of the others. Hence, safety and security of these infrastructures have become extremely critical after the deadly attack on 9/11. As rightly predicted by Hecker, meeting the test of terrorism today requires a proactive approach to the technological innovation—consolidating on the present and betting on the future: formulating clear requirements, prioritizing the needs, establishing cooperative means to foster the development of technologies, and building the human and financial capital program necessary to transition and sustain them as effective antiterrorism tools.

It is not very difficult to understand that technology is not the only answer to address the devilish specter of transnational terrorism. However, it is a hard truth that the technological answers we have today are inadequate to deal with the scope and potential severity of the threat that pervade us. Instead of merely adapting technologies to keep pace with the evolving dangers and changing tactics of terrorism, what is needed is to develop more powerful and overmatching security systems to get ahead of the terrorists. Adoption of a proactive and well-thought security strategy can only ensure that the public is protected, their liberties are safeguarded, and commerce, business, and critical emergency operations can continue unhindered. Developing technologies that leap ahead of those in the hand of the terrorists requires vision and strategy, and a good strategy requires hard choices. Adopting some of the current technologies is also important for this purpose. Some of the existing information-searching and analytical approaches that can be adopted to counterterrorism domain are (i) the use of the existing general-purpose and meta-search engines, (ii) terrorism research centers' portal, (iii) information analysis techniques, (iv) social network analysis, and (v) chatterbot techniques. However, the research on certain technologies can lead to the development of novel techniques to counterterrorism such as (i) biometrics, (ii) development of nonlethal weapons, (iii) data mining and link analysis technologies, (iv) nanotechnologies, (v) image and video processing, (vi) intrusion detection and access control, and (vii) directed-energy weapons.

However, mere adoption of current technologies is not enough. We need innovations for developing new technologies to counterterrorism. For example, in addition to traditional biometric techniques such as iris recognition, hand geometry analysis, fingerprint recognition, face recognition, voice recognition, and DNA matching, some novel biometric techniques may be used, such as odor sensing, blood pulse measurements, skin pattern recognition, nail bed identification, gait recognition, and ear shape recognition.

Development of nonlethal weapons can be a new addition to the armory of counterterrorism mechanisms. These weapons should be explicitly designed and deployed to incapacitate or destroy terrorists or dangerous materials while keeping their impact on the facilities and the environment at a minimum. Research conducted by the US military has shown that there are four promising areas in the development of nonlethal weapons: (i) calmatives for controlling crowds and clearing facilities, (ii) directed-energy systems that work on high-power microwave for stopping potentially dangerous vehicles or vessels, (iii) novel and rapidly deployable marine barrier systems, and (iv) adaptation of unmanned or remotely controlled platforms and other sensors for application of nonlethal weapons.

Design of advanced data mining algorithm for carrying out complex analytics on the humongous volume of historical and current online data to identify patterns and anomalies is an important direction of research for counterterrorism mechanism development. Link analysis is another analytical approach that can be gainfully exploited in developing counterterrorism systems. While data mining attempts to identify anomalies in large volume of information, the objective of link analysis is to search for commonalities among the datasets. In identifying terrorist activities, link analysis is used to analyze the data surrounding the suspect relationships to determine how they are connected—what links them together. The research on data mining and link analysis needs to be augmented to handle unstructured and disparate data consisting of a mix of text, image, video, and sensor information. In addition, new algorithms need to incorporate knowledge of human experts into their derivation patterns.

Development of nanoscale sensors is another emerging area of counterterrorism applications. Nanodevices can be used to design fast, cheap, and accurate sensors and actuators that can be used for a wide range of forensic activities.

Active defenses such as directed-energy weapons could provide protection to the critical infrastructures. In contrast to conventional weapons that rely on kinetic or chemical energy of a projectile, directed-energy weapons can hit a target with subatomic particles that can travel at the speed of electromagnetic waves. These weapons generate very high power beams and typically use a single optical system for tracking a target and for focusing the beams on the target in order to destroy it.

There are daunting barriers to the creation of an arsenal of counterterrorism technologies that are efficient, yet cost-effective, and that can overpower the threat of terrorism in the twenty-first century. However, it is mandatory to create a vision of these future technologies, implement initiatives that broaden the market of these technologies and make them more dependable, and develop policies that would help in overcoming the barriers to innovation and research. In this way, these technologies can be harnessed to the future needs of law enforcement and countering terrorism.

The objective of this book entitled *Effective Surveillance for Homeland Security: Balancing Technology and Social Issues*, edited by Francesco Flammini, Roberto Setola, and Giorgio Franceschetti, is to discuss the various technological aspects related to homeland security solutions. It also focuses on privacy and other related social issues, which are of conflicting interests with the surveillance operations necessary for working of homeland security solutions.

The book is especially useful for engineers and researchers working in the area of homeland security solution design and development, people working in the law enforcing agencies, operators of critical infrastructures, and researchers and people who are in the decision-making position for establishing security policies and infrastructures for safety and security of citizens and critical infrastructures. It is also useful for graduate students and faculty members working in graduate schools and universities.

Jaydip Sen
Senior Scientist
Tata Consultancy Services Ltd.
Kolkata, India

Preface

It is a common feeling for people living in developed countries that their privacy is being increasingly threatened by surveillance and tracking technologies. The fact that surveillance is essential to reduce criminal acts is only partially supported by evidence, and that raises big questions about the effectiveness of technologies and of how they are managed.

This book, *Effective Surveillance for Homeland Security: Balancing Technology and Social Issues*, addresses two aspects of surveillance: (i) advances in technology developments and (ii) their social impact in terms of privacy and human-related factors.

Quite obviously, when monitoring public areas, Internet usage, or working personnel, increasing surveillance means decreasing privacy. Therefore, the challenge is twofold:

1. To provide evidence that technology is actually effective for deterrence, prevention, and timely reaction
2. To make technology as much as possible noninvasive and respectful of privacy, ergonomics, and wellness

The issue becomes even more delicate when surveillance aims at addressing the complex and multifaceted problem of homeland security.

Most developed countries addressed the issue of privacy by appropriate laws and norms. As an example, the Data Protection Directive (officially Directive 95/46/EC on the protection of individuals with regard to the processing of personal data and on the free movement of such data) regulates the process of acquisition, management, and storage of personal data within the European Union (EU), being an important component of EU privacy and human rights law. Most of us are aware of the impact of such laws on our everyday life, since they define many rules on video surveillance installations (e.g., mandatory signs and constraints on watched areas) and on the management of personal data (e.g., when registering on websites).

At the same time, as legislation defines appropriate regulations about surveillance, tracking technologies have advanced in such a way as to be able to control the behavior of millions of people 24 h a day: it suffices to think of high-resolution satellite imaging, people scanning, RFID tagging, intelligent multimedia (audio–video) analytics, web surfing monitoring, etc.

With this background in mind, it is easy to imagine the importance of a book addressing the often neglected aspects of advanced surveillance, filling a gap existing in the related literature between technology developments and the delicate issues related to their social impact.

The book consists of 21 chapters written by experts in different aspects of homeland security. These chapters deal with three broad areas: (i) surveillance technologies; (ii) legislative and social aspects of homeland security operations; and (iii) advanced issues on surveillance operations, such as advanced analytics and multimodal surveillance.

Book Structure

According to a scheme that is unusual in technical books on security and surveillance, Part I—Surveillance and Society is not dedicated to technological aspects, focusing instead on the societal dimension of surveillance. This choice stresses the importance of societal acceptability as a precondition to any surveillance system.

Starting from that general picture, Part II—Physical and Cyber Surveillance focuses on advanced technologies for surveillance. Most of those developing technologies are part of a framework whose aim is to move from a simple collection and storage of information toward proactive systems, able to fuse several information sources in order to detect relevant events in their early incipient phase. Such a trend leads to security information management systems that are increasingly smart.

Finally, some relevant applications of surveillance systems used in the framework of homeland security are collected in Part III—Technologies for Homeland Security in order to show via real-world case studies how innovative technologies can be used to effectively improve the security of sensitive areas without violating the rights of involved people.

In what follows, a more detailed description of the parts of the book, providing insights on the content of the chapters is provided.

Part I: Surveillance and Society

In Chapter 1, "An Ethics for the New (and Old) Surveillance," Marx discusses how various types of surveillance can be analyzed. More specifically, the author stresses on the ethical evaluation of surveillance systems that involves (i) initial policies, procedure, and capabilities of the surveillance systems; (ii) characteristics of surveillance tools; (iii) goals of the system; (iv) fitness between means and goals of the system; (v) data collection and analysis involved in the system; (vi) rights and resources of the surveillance subjects; and (vii) protection and fate of the collected data.

These concepts are extended by Haemmerli et al. in Chapter 2, "Trust Networks among Human Beings: Analysis, Modeling, and Recommendations," where the authors analyze the issues related to the problem of trust in worldwide connected networks (like the Internet), providing basic definitions, reference models, and practical guidelines for trust development. The chapter also stresses the importance of taking into account cultural diversities and national laws, surveying current frameworks and tools.

In Chapter 3, "Art of Balancing Utilities: Privacy and Video Surveillance in Sweden," Björklund discusses how public video surveillance systems have been finding increasing deployments, with relatively less concern being shown by the public on its associated privacy violation issues. The author argues that the Swedish approach toward homeland security may be described as consistently utilitarian and as a manifestation of a proactive welfare state legacy.

The same topic is addressed by Leese in Chapter 4, "Perceived Threat: Determinants and Consequences of Fear of Terrorism in Germany," presenting the results of a survey conducted in Germany on "fear of terrorism." The study shows that there is an increasing shift in the citizen's mind from the issues of civil liberties to acceptance of different security and surveillance measures introduced by the Government of Germany for prevention of any attack.

Moving a step toward the optimal trade-off between security and privacy, Paruchuri et al., in Chapter 5, "Preserving and Managing Privacy Information in Video Surveillance Systems," propose a privacy-preserving video surveillance system that can help to protect privacy-sensitive information by using a rate-distortion optimized data-hiding scheme. This scheme allows retrieval of private data with a robust, yet anonymous, authentication module that utilizes encrypted biometric signals.

A very similar topic is further investigated in Chapter 6, "Objective and Subjective Evaluation of Content-Based Privacy Protection of Face Images in Video Surveillance Systems Using JPEG XR," where Sohn et al. use both objective and subjective assessments to analyze the level of privacy protection achieved by a layered scrambling technique, developed by the authors for video surveillance systems. Experimental results have been analyzed to show and judge the strength of privacy protection provided by different approaches for different use cases.

Part II: Physical and Cyber Surveillance

In the cyberphysical surveillance framework, the very first element is the capability of the system to detect events of interest. The issue is described by Atrey in Chapter 7, "Event Representation in Multimedia Surveillance Systems." The framework proposed by the author defines events at three levels of a hierarchical structure: transient, atomic, and compound. The events at the lower level are mapped into those at the higher ones by a clustering technique. The framework also analyzes the relationships between various events from three dimensions: temporal, causal, and spatial.

In Chapter 8, "Challenges and Emerging Paradigms for Augmented Surveillance," Flammini et al. identify several components of "augmented surveillance systems," such as (i) improved sensor technology; (ii) use of combined and diversified sensing technologies, leading to multimodal distributed surveillance; and (iii) proactive and early detection of events by superior situation awareness and decision support capabilities. The authors also describe how such an augmented surveillance system can be realized in practice and deployed in real world.

In Chapter 9, "Pervasive Surveillance System Management," Hilal and Basir discuss the various issues and challenges in designing sensor-based intelligent systems management framework for carrying out a pervasive and ubiquitous surveillance operation. The authors present a detailed survey on the state-of-the-art sensor management architectures and strategies for deployment in real-world surveillance systems.

How information collected by sensors can be merged in order to assess the actual situation and to predict near-future evolution is addressed by Digioia et al. in Chapter 10, "Moving from Measuring to Understanding: Situation Awareness in Homeland Security." This chapter presents a critical review of various existing methodologies and schemes for fusion of data from multiple and heterogeneous sources to obtain a high-level pattern, or behavior detection and prediction, and to achieve situational awareness in the context of homeland security. The authors have also discussed some popular and widely used mechanisms for extraction of high-level information from raw data gathered by heterogeneous sensors.

In Chapter 11, "Ergonomic Design and Evaluation of Surveillance Systems," Coelho and Nunes present the ergonomical and human-related factors in designing surveillance systems. The authors present a survey on the various human factors for achieving an effective human–system coupling in a surveillance system, with particular attention on perception and modes of control, as well as on information processing. The authors also focus on an evaluation framework for surveillance systems based on ergonomic considerations, such as usability and user-centered design, as well as from an operational efficiency perspective.

Moving to the cyberspace domain, whose surveillance is nowadays essential to prevent possibly disruptive cyberattacks, in Chapter 12, "Awareness, Assessment, and Reduction of Web Application Vulnerability," Ward and Cavestro analyze the threats in the World Wide Web, which are especially important when these applications are used in business-critical domains (e.g., finance). The chapter also presents the future trends in web applications and the related societal and legislative issues.

In Chapter 13, "Distributed Framework for Cybersecurity of Critical Infrastructures," D'Antonio et al. present various challenges in detecting different attacks in SCADA network systems. The identification of potential attacks requires that the information is gathered from several different sources and diverse geographical locations, and there are no general locality principles that can be gainfully applied for detecting such attacks. The authors also propose a distributed framework for SCADA system security, which consists of a number of modules whose operations are integrated and coordinated in unison, so as to achieve overall protection of the SCADA system itself.

In Chapter 14, "Modeling and Counteracting Virus Diffusion in Sensor Networks for Net-Centric Surveillance Systems," Battistelli et al. discuss the issue of the adverse impact of malicious viruses and other malwares on the operations of surveillance systems based on wireless sensor networks. The authors present a detailed study on various models for virus diffusion, and their detrimental effects on network connectivity, and other network operations. Simulation results are presented to show how the spreading of virus affects in-network information fusion, causing serious disruption in monitoring activities.

Part III: Technologies for Homeland Security

In the context of developing software solutions for homeland security applications, Chapter 15, "GEPSUS GEOINT Applications for Homeland Security," by De Amicis et al., addresses the important roles being played by geospatial technologies. As a specific case study, the authors present the details of the project GEPSUS (Geographical Information Processing for Environmental Pollution-Related Security within Urban Scale Environments) to show how geographical intelligence (GEOINT) technologies can significantly help in designing solutions for enhancing the security of humans and infrastructures against human-launched or natural disasters. The chapter also illustrates a simulation framework for natural emergencies such as landslides, floods, and human-made disasters such as intentional release of toxic and poisonous gases.

In Chapter 16, "Omnidirectional Human Intrusion Detection System Using Computer Vision Techniques," Wong et al. discuss how a system can be designed to detect human intrusions using the techniques of computer vision. The authors defined such a system as "omnidirectional," since it is capable of carrying out surveillance over a full area under its coverage, without leaving any blind spot. For designing a system of this kind, the authors have used vision spectrum and infrared imaging: in particular, for intrusion detection, a "partitioned region of interest" algorithm and a "human head curve" algorithm are utilized.

In Chapter 17, "Wireless Sensor Networks and Audio Signal Recognition for Homeland Security," Martalò et al. propose a security solution using audio signal pattern recognition techniques over a wireless sensor network. The authors propose a signal pattern recognition mechanism based on a simple time-domain approach, and they show how this approach can be utilized in a commercial application using unattended ground sensors. The mechanism is further enhanced by using a hybrid time-frequency approach for achieving higher accuracy in the results.

In Chapter 18, "Dynamic Bayesian Multitarget Tracking for Behavior and Interaction Detection," Marcenaro et al. propose the use of a joint human tracking and human-to-human interaction recognition system in video surveillance. Although effective tracking is a fundamental building block for video analytics in surveillance applications, it is challenging to design tracking algorithms that effectively operate in crowded public places. The proposed tracking algorithm recursively works between time slices and makes use of a forward–backward message passing within each time slice under a probabilistic graphical model framework.

In Chapter 19, "Imaging Tunnels and Underground Facilities Using Radio-Frequency Tomography," Lo Monte et al. present a discussion on the surveillance mechanism of targets, which are hidden such as under a tree, inside a building, or below the ground. The authors argue that the design of underground imaging facilities is of critical importance for the protection of international borders and sensitive areas. For achieving effective remote sensing and detection of events, the authors propose radio-frequency, tomography-based remote sensing that utilizes randomly deployed transceivers, which communicate with base stations over the ground, in case the anomaly is detected underground.

In Chapter 20, "Surveillance Framework for Ubiquitous Monitoring of Intermodal Cargo Containers," Varma et al. discuss various issues in designing a global seamless cargo monitoring system and present relevant protocols and existing standards for this purpose. The authors also propose a framework for containerized cargo monitoring system, which integrates the existing resources for container monitoring with advanced geospatial threat detection using global data. This framework is particularly relevant in today's world since the security of ports and intermodal cargo containers is essential for protecting nations against potential threats of terrorism.

Finally, in Chapter 21, "Model-Based Control of Building Evacuation Using Feedback from Sensor and Actuator Wireless Networks," Lino et al. focus their attention on an important issue related to human security—safe evacuation of a large number of humans from buildings or open-air environment—in the event of an attack or an unforeseen incident. The authors propose a supervisory model-based controller for designing an evacuation system, operating on the data coming from a distributed sensor network. The control actions of the system are coordinated to reduce the human egress time so that safe dynamics of the crowd are guaranteed.

MATLAB® is a registered trademark of The MathWorks, Inc. For product information, please contact:

The MathWorks, Inc.
3 Apple Hill Drive
Natick, MA 01760-2098 USA
Tel: 508-647-7000
Fax: 508-647-7001
E-mail: info@mathworks.com
Web: www.mathworks.com

Francesco Flammini
Roberto Setola
Giorgio Franceschetti
Editors

Acknowledgment

The editors would like to warmly thank all the outstanding experts, serving as chapter authors and/or members of the editorial board, who have contributed to make this book an essential reference source in its area.

Editors

Francesco Flammini got with honors his laurea (2003) and doctorate (2006) degrees in computer engineering from the University of Naples Federico II. Since October 2003, he has worked in Ansaldo STS (Finmeccanica) on the safety and security of rail-based transportation infrastructures. He has taught computer science and software engineering as an adjunct professor at the University of Naples, as well as seminars on computer dependability and critical infrastructure protection in postdegree courses on homeland security. He has coauthored several books and more than 50 scientific papers published in international journals and conference proceedings. He has served as the chairman, a PC member, and an editor for several international conferences and journals. He is a senior member of the IEEE, an ACM Distinguished Speaker, and the vice-chair of the IEEE Computer Society Italy Chapter. He is also member of the European Workshop on Industrial Computer Systems Reliability, Safety and Security (EWICS TC7), FME (Formal Methods Europe), ERCIM WG on Formal Methods for Industrial Critical Systems (FMICS), ESRA TC on Operational Safety & Security of Interconnected Critical Infrastructures, and IEEE SMC TC on Homeland Security.

Roberto Setola obtained his master of science in electronic engineering (1992) and PhD in electronic engineering and computer science (1996) from the University of Naples Federico II. He currently serves as a professor of automatic control at University CAMPUS BioMedico and head of the COSERITY Lab (Complex Systems & Security Lab). He is also the director of the master's program for "Homeland security, systems and methods and tools for security and crisis management." Formerly a member of the Italian Prime Minister's Office (1999–2004), Setola was the coordinator of the working group on critical information infrastructure protection established by the Italian Prime Minister (2003–2004), a member of the G8 Senior Expert CIIP Group (2002–2006), and an affiliate of the G8 working group on High-Tech Crime (2002–2004). Since 1992, Roberto, in collaboration with several universities and research centers, has presented numerous studies on many topics related to modeling, simulation, and control of complex networks and systems and the protection of critical infrastructures. In addition, he has been the coordinator of the EU DG JLS project SecuFood on the security of the food supply chain and coordinator of the EU DG HOME project FACIES on the automatic identification of failure/attack in critical infrastructures. Moreover, as leader of a specialized unit, Setola was involved in more than 12 national and international projects related to critical infrastructure protection and homeland security. Throughout his career, Roberto has coauthored

3 books, edited 3 books, been a guest editor of 3 special issues on international journals, been an editor in chief of 2 magazines, and coauthored roughly 130 scientific publications. Setola is a founding member and current general secretary of the "AIIC—Associazione Italiana esperti in Infrastrutture Critiche", senior member of the IEEE, and founding member of the IFIP 11.10 working group on critical infrastructure protection.

Giorgio Franceschetti is emeritus professor, University of Naples Federico II, and distinguished visiting scientist, JPL. He has been adjunct professor, UCLA (1992–2008), visiting professor in many European and U.S. universities, and lecturer in China, India, and Somalia. He is the author of 12 books and of about 200 papers in international journals of recognized standard in the area of basic and applied electromagnetic theory, remote sensing, signal processing, and homeland security. He is also a life fellow of the IEEE and member of the Electromagnetic Society. Among many outstanding awards, he is recipient of the Gold Medal of the Italian Republic President (2001); the Marconi (1975), Philip Morris (1990), IEE London Mountbatten (1998), and IEEE AP-Society (1999 and 2008) Schelkunoff Prizes; and the IEEE GRS-Society (2007), the NASA Cassini Radar Team (2009), and the IEEE APS-Society (2010) Distinguished Achievement Awards. As honorary positions, he has been appointed Officer of the Italian Republic (2003) and Bruno Kessler Honorary Chair, University of Trento, Italy (2010).

Contributors

Pradeep K. Atrey
Department of Applied Computer Science
University of Winnipeg
Winnipeg, Manitoba, Canada

Ronald D. Barnes
School of Electrical and Computer
    Engineering
University of Oklahoma
Norman, Oklahoma

Otman A. Basir
Department of Electrical and Computer
    Engineering
University of Waterloo
Waterloo, Ontario, Canada

Giorgio Battistelli
University of Florence
Florence, Italy

Fredrika Björklund
School of Social Sciences
Södertörn University
Huddinge, Sweden

Jessica Cavestro
Jessoftware
Fontaneto, Italy

Sen-Ching S. Cheung
Department of Electrical and Computer
    Engineering
University of Kentucky
Lexington, Kentucky

Luigi Chisci
University of Florence
Florence, Italy

Michał Choraś
ITTI Sp. z o.o.
Poznań, Poland

and

Institute of Telecommunications
University of Technology and Life Sciences
Bydgoszcz, Poland

Denis A. Coelho
Department of Electromechanical Engineering
University of Beira Interior
Covilha, Portugal

Giuseppe Conti
Fondazione Graphitech
Trento, Italy

Luigi Coppolino
Department of Technology
University of Naples "Parthenope"
Naples, Italy

Salvatore D'Antonio
Department of Technology
University of Naples "Parthenope"
Naples, Italy

Raffaele De Amicis
Fondazione Graphitech
Trento, Italy

Wesley De Neve
Department of Electrical Engineering
Korea Advanced Institute of Science
    and Technology
Daejeon, Republic of Korea

Alberto Debiasi
Fondazione Graphitech
Trento, Italy

Giusj Digioia
University of Roma Tre
Rome, Italy

Danilo Erricolo
University of Illinois at Chicago
Chicago, Illinois

Alfonso Farina
Selex Electronic Systems S.p.A.
Rome, Italy

Gianluigi Ferrari
Department of Information Engineering
University of Parma
Parma, Italy

Francesco Flammini
Ansaldo STS
Naples, Italy

Chiara Foglietta
University of Roma Tre
Rome, Italy

Giorgio Franceschetti
University of Naples Federico II
Naples, Italy

Antonio Graziano
Selex Electronic Systems S.p.A.
Rome, Italy

Bernhard Haemmerli
Gjovik University College, Norway
Lucerne, Switzerland

Allaa R. Hilal
Department of Electrical and Computer
    Engineering
University of Waterloo
Waterloo, Ontario, Canada

Rafał Kozik
ITTI Sp. z o.o.
Poznań, Poland

and

Institute of Telecommunications
University of Technology and Life Sciences
Bydgoszcz, Poland

Dohyoung Lee
Department of Electrical and Computer
    Engineering
University of Toronto
Toronto, Ontario, Canada

Matthias Leese
Section Security Ethics
International Centre for Ethics in the Sciences
    and Humanities
University of Tuebingen
Tuebingen, Germany

Alessio Liburdi
Selex Electronic Systems S.p.A.
Rome, Italy

Way Soong Lim
Faculty of Engineering and Technology
Multimedia University
Melaka, Malaysia

Paolo Lino
Department of Electrical and Electronics
    Engineering
Technical University of Bari
Bari, Italy

Lorenzo Lo Monte
University of Dayton Research Institute
Dayton, Ohio

Chu Kiong Loo
Faculty of Computer Science and Information
  Technology
University of Malaya
Kuala Lumpur, Malaysia

Ying Luo
Department of Electrical and Computer
  Engineering
University of Kentucky
Lexington, Kentucky

Daniele Magliocchetti
Fondazione Graphitech
Trento, Italy

Bruno Maione
Department of Electrical and Electronics
  Engineering
Technical University of Bari
Bari, Italy

Guido Maione
Department of Electrical and Electronics
  Engineering
Technical University of Bari
Bari, Italy

Claudio S. Malavenda
Selex Electronic Systems S.p.A.
and
Sapienza University of Rome
Rome, Italy

Lucio Marcenaro
Department of Electrical, Electronic,
  Telecommunications Engineering
  and Naval Architecture
University of Genova
Genoa, Italy

Marco Martalò
School of Engineering
E-Campus University
Novedrate, Italy

and

Department of Information Engineering
University of Parma
Parma, Italy

Gary T. Marx
Department of Urban Studies and Planning
Massachusetts Institute of Technology
Cambridge, Massachusetts

Giovanni Mugnai
University of Florence
Florence, Italy

Konstantinos N. Plataniotis
Department of Electrical and Computer
  Engineering
University of Toronto
Toronto, Ontario, Canada

Isabel L. Nunes
Faculdade de Ciências e Tecnologia
Department of Mechanical and Industrial
  Engineering
University Nova de Lisboa
Caparica, Portugal

Gabriele Oliva
Complex Systems and Security Laboratory
Campus Bio-Medico University
Rome, Italy

Stefano Panzieri
University of Roma Tre
Rome, Italy

Alfio Pappalardo
Ansaldo STS
Naples, Italy

and

University of Naples Federico II
Naples, Italy

Jithendra K. Paruchuri
Department of Electrical and Computer
   Engineering
University of Kentucky
Lexington, Kentucky

Stefano Piffer
Fondazione Graphitech
Trento, Italy

Federico Prandi
Fondazione Graphitech
Trento, Italy

Margrete Raaum
Gjøvik University College
Gjøvik, Norway

Carlo S. Regazzoni
Department of Electrical, Electronic,
   Telecommunications Engineering
   and Naval Architecture
University of Genova
Genoa, Italy

Yong Man Ro
Department of Electrical Engineering
Korea Advanced Institute of Science
   and Technology
Daejeon, Republic of Korea

Roberto Setola
Complex Systems and Security Laboratory
Campus Bio-Medico University
Rome, Italy

Andrej Škraba
University of Maribor
Kranj, Slovenia

Hosik Sohn
Department of Electrical Engineering
Korea Advanced Institute of Science
   and Technology
Daejeon, Republic of Korea

Francesco Soldovieri
Consiglio Nazionale delle Ricerche
Rome, Italy

Mauricio Soto
Department of Electrical, Electronic,
   Telecommunications Engineering
   and Naval Architecture
University of Genova
Genoa, Italy

Radovan Stojanović
University of Montenegro
Podgorica, Montenegro

Diego Taglioni
Fondazione Graphitech
Trento, Italy

Monte Tull
School of Electrical and Computer
   Engineering
University of Oklahoma
Norman, Oklahoma

Yogesh Varma
School of Electrical and Computer
   Engineering
University of Oklahoma
Norman, Oklahoma

Valeria Vittorini
University of Naples Federico II
Naples, Italy

David Ward
Security Technology Assessment Unit
Joint Research Centre
Ispra, Italy

Michael C. Wicks
University of Dayton Research Institute
Dayton, Ohio

Wai Kit Wong
Faculty of Engineering and Technology
Multimedia University
Melaka, Malaysia

SURVEILLANCE AND SOCIETY

Chapter 1

An Ethics for the New (and Old) Surveillance*

Gary T. Marx

Contents

* This article draws from G.T. Marx, *Windows into the Soul: Surveillance and Society in an Age of High Technology*, University of Chicago Press, forthcoming.

If it doesn't look right, that's ethics.

Popular expression

I'm in computer science. I took this class because eventually I want to do the right thing.

MIT student

New surveillance technologies such as the matching of computer databases, monitoring, profiling, tracking internet use, videocams, enhanced undercover activities, infrared and other searches, biometric and drug testing, and various forms of electronic location monitoring raise important social, political, and cultural questions.* In articles at www.garymarx.net, I have pursued an interest in the topic in a variety of contexts—the state, work, consumption, entertainment, and families—and identified key analytic elements such as surveillance structures and processes and means, goals, types of data, and culture.

In this work I suggest concepts to order the rich variation the topic offers across kinds of tools for collecting personal information and across various contexts regardless of whether they involve national security, work, commerce, family, or friends.

Underlying the research and interlaced with the empirical questions are moral concerns. Is a given practice good or bad, desirable or undesirable? These questions are at the core of new technologies for surveillance as a contemporary issue. However, posing questions in such a general

---

* For a sampling of the many discussions of the new surveillance and related themes, see Marx (1988, 2002, and 2012), Lianos (2001), Lyons (2007), and Norris and Wilson (2006). The term "new surveillance" refers to the technologically enhanced forms that extend our unaided senses ("the old surveillance") and cognitive abilities and that have expanded in power and scale so significantly in the last half-century.

way is not helpful. The only honest answers are "yes and no," "sometimes," and "it depends." The empirical and normative task for etiquette, policy, and law is to suggest what the evaluation of surveillance does, and should, depend on.

This article stresses the contingent nature of ethical evaluation based on answers to a series of questions designed to capture the rich variation in surveillance behavior and settings. *Surveillance (or in the case of most of the chapters in this book security) is neither good nor bad, but context and comportment make it so.* Tools of course have distinctive characteristics such as the ability to see from great distances, through walls or in the dark. But whether these are right or wrong depends on the setting and goals (e.g., voyeurism, industrial espionage, legitimate law enforcement).

This chapter is organized around a series of questions for ethical evaluation that involve (1) the initial policies, procedures, and capability conditions of surveillance; (2) the characteristics of the surveillance tool; (3) the goals of surveillance; (4) the fit between means and goals; (5) data collection and analysis; (6) the consequences; (7) the rights and resources of surveillance subjects; and (8) the protection and fate of the data collected. The chapter ends with a consideration of stages of the surveillance process that the questions can be applied to.

The rich variation in surveillance across methods, goals, settings, relationships, time periods, and specific applications illustrates the importance of making distinctions—whether for purposes of social science or judgment. A situational approach to ethics is needed, rather than one emphasizing a technology or behavior in isolation from its setting or an overarching first principle to judge everything.

In studying undercover police practices for the purpose of reaching policy and ethical conclusions, I stressed the importance of rules and less formal expectations in specific contexts, rather than anything inherent in the tool (Marx 1988). This also holds for other forms of surveillance.

In writing about privacy, Nissenbaum (2010) creatively develops ideas of contextual integrity. This perspective can be applied beyond privacy to the more encompassing concept of surveillance as well.*

Simply having a technique that is morally acceptable is obviously not a sufficient condition for its use anymore than a good goal is justification for using a morally challenged or unduly risky or costly means. But even with appropriate means and ends, ethical concerns can also arise at other points such as collection, analysis, data protection, and data fate. The ethical status can vary from cases in which the means, goals, conditions of use, and consequences are wrong or even abhorrent, to those in which they are all acceptable or even desirable, to varying combinations. A more precise and richer analysis is possible when judgments are related to such distinctions.

Most contemporary disputes over domestic practices do not involve the means as such; rather they are more likely to be found in a disjuncture between the context and the means and/or the goal or to involve concern over the absence of, or failure to follow, appropriate standards for collection, analysis, and data protection. Or they involve disagreements about how a technique should be defined—is an e-mail best seen as a postcard or a first-class letter? Is a noninvasive search by a dog or a machine the same as a search by a person?

---

* A good summary of United States thought as of 2009 on privacy is in Waldo et al. (2007), a report of the National Academy of Sciences.

International public opinion polls consistently show that a very large percentage of citizens are concerned about security, privacy, and surveillance issues (Zureik et al. 2010). But the elements of this are rather muddled, muddied, and inconsistent. Many persons feel a sense of discomfort in the face of indiscriminate drug testing, hidden video cameras, electronic work monitoring, airport screens, and the collection and marketing of their personal information—even as they favor security, responsible behavior, efficiency, economic growth, and credit card-aided consumption. Given the newness of the technologies, opinion here is less well defined and coherent than is the case for many more settled issues.

Persons often have trouble articulating what seems wrong with a surveillance practice beyond saying that privacy is invaded. The narrower concept of privacy is almost as confusing. What's the fuss all about? What is it about the new technology that is troubling? By what standards should we conclude that a given practice is right or wrong or at least desirable or undesirable? How should surveillance activities be judged?

Formal and abstract definitions of ethics can of course be offered based on ontological and denological principles for judging behavior. But for public policy purposes, I prefer to interrogate meanings seen in popular culture such as "if it doesn't look right that's ethics" and "you don't treat people that way." Data gathering and protection efforts imply ethical assumptions that are often unstated. In what follows, I suggest an ethical framework for thinking about the surveillance of individuals whether involving the new or traditional means (e.g., such as informing and eavesdropping). At a very general level, there are shared expectations in Western and industrial–capitalist cultures (and perhaps beyond), whose violation underlies the discomfort, or at least ambivalence, experienced in the face of many personal border crossings.

This chapter suggests some basic questions that can help identify the major factors that would lead the average person to feel that a surveillance practice is wrong or at least questionable—whether in general or in a given case. Table 1.1 lists the subjects of the questions.

I draw from examples in the literature, my interviews, and participation in various policy inquiries, court cases, and mass media accounts. The disparate violations or intrusions can be systematically located within a broader, real-world field corresponding to the surveillance occasion and context.

The analysis emphasizes the watchers rather than the watched, avoiding harm, the borders of the individual rather than the group, the short rather than the long run and domestic, and non-crisis uses rather than exceptional and emergency uses. However, many of the ideas can be applied more broadly.

The argument applies to conventional domestic settings in a democratic society for those with full adult citizenship rights. In situations of extreme crisis such as war and pandemic or when dealing with very different countries or cultures, the incompetent and dependent, or those denied juridical rights such as prisoners, a somewhat different discussion is needed and the lines in some ways will be drawn differently. The rhetoric of states of exception (Agamben 2005) or of persons of exception of course calls for extreme vigilance.

In most cases the questions are structured so that answering "yes" is likely to be supportive of a broader value and related principle. Given variation and complexity, no simple additive score is possible. Much depends. Yet other factors being equal, the more these questions can be answered in a way that affirms the underlying principle (or a condition supportive of it), the more ethical and wise the use of a tactic is likely to be.

Questions are organized according to the following categories: initial conditions; means, goals, and connections between them; data collection and analysis; consequences for subjects and others; data protection; and fate.

Table 1.1   Questions for Judging Surveillance

Formal procedure and public input in the decision to adopt
Role reversal
Restoration
Unwanted precedents
Symbolic meaning
Reversibility
Agency competence and resources
Validity
Human review
Alternative means
Appropriate goals
Goal clarity
Unitary usage
Goodness of fit between means and goals
Inaction as action
Proportionality
Criteria for subject selection
Minimization
Border crossings
Violation of assumptions
Harm in collection
Disadvantage
Unfair strategic advantage
Manipulative advantage
Restrict social participation
Damage to reputation
Betrayal of confidence and trust violation
Intrusions into solitude
Not sharing the wealth
Right of inspection

(*continued*)

Table 1.1 (continued)   Questions for Judging Surveillance

Right to challenge and express a grievance
Redress and sanctions
Equal access to surveillance tools
Equal access to neutralization tools
Harm to agents
Spillover to uninvolved third parties
Periodic review
Data fate

1.1 Initial Conditions: Policies, Procedures, and Capabilities

1.1.1 Formal Procedure and Public Input in the Decision to Adopt

Does the decision to apply a potentially sensitive technique result from an established review procedure in which affected parties (whether within or beyond the organization) are consulted?* In deciding whether or not to adopt, the procedure needs to give attention to questions involving role reversal, restoration, unwanted consequences, symbolic meaning, and reversibility. These broader factors stand apart from the specifics of the tactic such as its effectiveness.

1.1.2 Role Reversal

Would those responsible for the surveillance (both the decision to apply it and its actual application) agree to be its subjects if roles were reversed? This is an aspect of the golden rule, but one restricted to an imagined shift in the organizational role played. It relates to Kant's consistency or reciprocity principle, which asks more broadly, "what if everyone used the means?"†

1.1.3 Restoration

Does the proposed technique radically break with traditional protections for personal information? Can, and should, these be reestablished through other means (whether legal or technical)? If they can't be reestablished, are new accountability procedures adopted?

Consider, for example, caller ID in potentially ending the anonymity of the caller and infrared or x-ray means that "see" through walls, clothes, and skin. Under some conditions restoration may not be desirable or possible, but then it is incumbent upon advocates to make the case for why undermining or outright destruction of the status quo is appropriate.

---

* For a careful examination of doing this through privacy impact assessments, see Wright and de Hert (2012). Many other impacts can be noted in equivalent assessments as well.

† Other strands of a broader equality question: "Are the tools equally available to all in situations where reciprocity is appropriate?" or "Is the tool applied equally to all subjects?"

1.1.4 Unwanted Precedents

Is the tactic likely to create precedents that will lead to its application in undesirable ways? What unwanted consequences might the tactic have for subjects, agents, third parties, and society more broadly? How might traditional liberties and basic democratic values be affected? Will a tactic lead opponents to turn to the same tactic?

1.1.5 Symbolic Meaning

Do the tool and the way it is applied communicate a view of citizens with rights appropriate for a democratic society? Or is the individual subject viewed as an object without rights who must be subservient to the interests and greater power of an organization entitled to indiscriminately apply invasive and even degrading techniques? The standards for assessing symbolic communication are more subjective than for many of the other questions.

1.1.6 Reversibility

If subsequent experience were to suggest that the tactic is undesirable, how easily can it be ended in the face of large capital expenditures and vested interests backing the status quo?

1.1.7 Agency Competence and Resources

Does the organization have the resources, skills, and motivation to appropriately and effectively apply, interpret, and use the tactic? Does it engage in critical self-reflection in the use of sensitive techniques? For example, in the case of undercover police practices that can be effective, the discussion is not about the worth of the tactic but whether the risks it brings can be adequately managed given the agency's policies and resources. Similarly some of the criticism of the United States' Transportation Security Administration is not about its technology but about whether the agency's personnel have adequate training and competence to apply it.

1.2 Means

1.2.1 Validity

Is the tactic valid with respect to both its potential for accurate measurement and a given application?—a valid tactic can be wrongly applied or in error or the tactic can be insufficiently reliable. How much agreement is there among specialists about the merits of a tactic? Validity is in part a socially constructed concept. As the philosopher Alfred Whitehead observed, "Everyway of seeing is also a way of not seeing." Awareness of this brings the question, "Say's who?" How are claims of validity defined—what degree of certainty is deemed necessary for strong conclusions and actions based on the results? How are the lines drawn between "acceptable" and "unacceptable" levels of proof?

1.2.2 Human Review

Are there means to verify results and periodic checking on the tool itself? Is there human review of machine-generated results—both basic data and (if present) automated recommendations for action? In many settings, human checking of automated findings and recommendations is vital given the acontextual nature of the data and risks of hardware and software failure.* Generally, individuals as interpreters of human situations are far more sensitive to nuance than are computers, even if they are more expensive and corruptible.

1.2.3 Alternative Means

Is this the best available means? How does it compare to other tools with respect to ethics, ease of application, validity, costs, risks, and measuring outcomes? Is there a tilt toward counting (in both senses) what can most easily and inexpensively be quantitatively measured, rather than toward what is more directly linked to the goal?

1.3 Goals

1.3.1 Appropriate versus Inappropriate Goals

Are the goals of the data collection legitimate and consistent with the information expectations of the setting? Is there a strong rational for pursuing the surveillance goal within the environment in question?

Relatively noncontroversial, positive goals such as health and protection are easier to identify than their opposites. The latter, by their very nature, are likely to be hidden under the camouflage of acceptable goals.

A data collection goal acceptable in one context may be unacceptable in another. Consider the following contrasting cases:

- Drug testing school bus drivers versus junior high school students who wish to play in the school band (as has happened in the United States)
- Electronic eavesdropping carried out by a national security agency subject to strong policy and law versus that done by a domestic political party against its opponents (as was the case with President Richard Nixon in the Watergate scandal)
- A doctor asking patients about sexually transmitted disease, birth control, and abortion history in a clinical setting versus asking this of all female employees (as one large U.S. airline did) without indicating why the information was needed

But even when the goal is right for the setting, if results of the surveillance spill over into other settings, controversy is likely. For example, is it appropriate to use a pulmonary lung test to measure whether employees are in conformity with a company's nonsmoking policy? Employees are told that this is a necessary health and cost-saving measure—good for the company, the other workers, and the employee. But some employees see this as wrong because it seeks to control their behavior away from the job—behavior they have a legal right to engage in.

---

* For example, in an early Massachusetts computer matching case, a list of those on welfare was compared to a list of those with more than $5000 in the bank (the cutoff point for being on welfare). Those on both lists had their welfare payments automatically terminated with no further checking (Marx and Reichman 1984).

1.3.2 Clarity in Goals

Is the goal(s) clearly stated, justified, and prioritized (if more than one)? Where secrecy is appropriate and the goals are not publicized, have they been clearly defined within the organization? Is there broad consensus on the goals?

1.3.3 Unitary Usage

Are data used for the purpose for which they were collected consistent with the subject's understanding (and where appropriate agreement)? Do the data remain with the initial agent/owner or migrate? If the latter, is this because of a failure to maintain confidentiality and security of the data? In the United States to a much greater extent than in Europe, second, third, fourth, and more users and uses are common. Combining data from different sources gathered for different reasons through computer matching, profiling, and mining can yield information in which the sum exceeds the individual elements. As such it constitutes a new kind of involuntary search not envisioned by traditional human rights protections against unreasonable searches and seizures and requires careful debate.

1.4 Connections between Means and Goals

1.4.1 Goodness of Fit between the Means and the Goal

Is there a clear link between the information sought and the goal to be achieved? How well a test measures what it claims to—truth telling, drug and alcohol use, miles driven, or location—can be differentiated from second-order inferences made about goals only indirectly related to the actual results of the measurement such as risk predictions. A measure can be valid in its immediate empirical results without being effective with respect to a goal.*

As we move from the direct results of a measure that is immediately meaningful given the goal (e.g., heat or location data from a sensor to more removed goals based on probabilistic inferences about future behavior) as with profiles, usefulness of the data often lessens. A profile such as one used to predict airline highjacking (young males buying one-way tickets paid for with cash) involves very accurate data but a very weak correlation to subsequent incidents.

Urine drug tests, when properly done and backed by a second confirming test, show high validity. Yet some research suggests that drug tests may not be associated with the employment performance behaviors they are presumed to predict. In that regard, drug tests based on manual dexterity for drivers of trucks, buses, and taxis may offer a better fit than the more inferential urine drug tests.

1.4.2 Inaction as Action

Where the only available tool is costly and/or risky or weakly related to the goal because what is of interest is difficult to detect or statistically very unlikely to occur, has consideration been given

---

* Valid that is in what it measures. It can also be effective but not valid via the mechanisms claimed. Note the polygraph that "works" when individuals confess in the belief that the machine can tell if they are lying.

to taking no action or to redefining the goal? For example, the arguments for decriminalizing marijuana point to the failure of enforcement efforts and the many unwanted consequences.

1.4.3 Proportionality

Do means and ends stand in appropriate balance? This requires attention to the potential problems and gains from the means and the importance of the goal. A sledge hammer should not be used to crack open a nut, nor a sprinkling can to put out a house fire. Hanging them all will likely get the guilty, but unduly stringent restrictions will mean subjects deserving of scrutiny (and worse) may escape.

1.5 Data Collection and Analysis

1.5.1 Criteria for Subject Selection

Are universalistic standards applied? Where there are no grounds for treating persons differently, are all subject to surveillance or do all have an equal chance of being surveilled, even if few are actually chosen?* For example, contrast categorical scrutiny within a group, as with checking names of all flyers against no fly lists, against selecting a few subjects for an intensive customs border search based on a table of random numbers. When there are no easily identifiable correlates of what is looked for, preliminary superficial screening of everyone may be used to identify cases for a more intensive gander.

1.5.2 Minimization

Is there an effort to minimize the invasiveness of the tactic and the extent of personal and personally identifiable information collected? This cuts across other questions such as alternative means, goals, specificity in subject selection and data collection, and the related ability to control spillover. Other factors being equal, a less invasive tactic is preferable, only personal information directly related to the goal should be collected and then no more than is required.

1.5.3 Border Crossings

Does the technique cross a potentially perilous personal boundary without notice or permission (whether involving coercion or deception or a bodily, relational, spatial, or symbolic border)? If consent is given, is it genuine?

1.5.4 Violation of Assumptions

Does the technique violate assumptions that are made about the conditions under which personal information will be collected? This can involve standard, often tacit, cultural expectations such as that persons are who they claim to be, that conversations will not be secretly reported, that confidences will be respected, or that there will be no secret government blacklists. It can also involve

---

* The consistency principle here, which asks whether the tactic is applied to everyone, is different from asking what if everyone applied it.

failing to honor explicit policies or promises such as that data will be destroyed or not shared or used only for purposes consistent with stated intentions.*

1.5.5 Harm in Collection

Does the act of data collection involve physical or psychological harm? Some interrogation tactics (e.g., as against passive data collection) are based on the creation of fear and threats to inflict harm as a bargaining tool. Torture is the obvious example. But a data collection, particularly in face-to-face settings, need not involve the threat of violence to be stressful or ethically questionable.

Interviews, psychological tests, drug tests, and searches can be done to minimize or maximize discomfort. Being questioned about sensitive subjects and having personal data gathered may necessarily involve some feelings of embarrassment, shame, discomfort, powerlessness, and recalling or reexperiencing painful memories. The agent's manner and the conditions of data collection however can exacerbate these. The agent may go farther than is required or than has been publicly announced (and perhaps agreed to by the subject). Consider intentionally inflicting pain in drawing blood (e.g., in the mandatory AIDS tests required of those in prison and the military) or added stress in the application of the polygraph (e.g., by making the cuff tighter than necessary).

1.6 Consequences

1.6.1 Disadvantage

Are the results used to cause unwarranted disadvantage or harm to the subject, the agent, and the third parties? There is of course much room for debate over this and whether it should be defined in objective or subjective terms and whether the intentions of the agent should be considered apart from measurable consequences.

Some common forms include the following:

1. *Unfair strategic advantage* in discovering information the subject wishes to withhold in situations where there is a legitimate conflict of interest. Consider a bugged car sales waiting room, which permits the seller to learn a customer's concerns and maximum payment or corporate espionage.
2. *Manipulative advantage* in persuading or influencing a subject whether involving consumption or politics. At the extreme is blackmail and intimidation. But consider the more benign form of a candy company mailing a special discount offer to a list of diet workshop participants it had purchased.
3. *Restrict social participation* or otherwise unfairly treat persons based on information that is invalid, irrelevant, acontextual, or discriminatory. Many examples are in health insurance, banking, housing, employment, and even chances for consumption. Oscar Gandy (1993) has noted how market research on consumption behavior can work to the disadvantage of the least privileged.

---

* This is particularly likely to be an issue for political databases. Consider the case of Greece (Samatras 2004), for example, where government claims to have destroyed prohibited political databases were reputed to simply have been transferred to private holders. The failure to create documents—for example, not having audiovisual equipment on or failing to record and save when the rules require—presents an opposite problem.

4. *Damage to reputation* as a result of unwarranted publication or release of personal information that causes embarrassment, shame, humiliation, or otherwise puts a person in a negative light.*

5. *Betrayal of confidence and trust violation* may occur (even if the information is neutral or positive for the subject). This is distinct from hurtful content, procedural violations, and exaggerated claims. Trust is a central element in spontaneity, sociability, and communality. Its absence makes cooperative group action difficult. A belief that one is continually monitored can inhibit innovation and experimentation and eliminate risk taking.

6. *Intrusions into solitude* as a result of the collection and use of surveillance data may deny the individual the ability to control the access others have to them. The act of data collection may perturb the individual's sense of personal space and expectation of being left alone. The indiscriminate use of discriminate results may result in targeted marketing via uninvited use of the subject's communication resources (fax, phone, computer) and time.

7. *Not sharing the wealth*—is the additional benefit or profit a company or a data warehouse gains from selling an individual's personal information shared with the subject? Has the individual given permission for the reuse and sale of the data?

1.7 Agents and Third Parties

1.7.1 Harm to Agents

Does the tactic avoid harm to the agent? Are there undesirable impacts on the values and personality of the surveillance agent? Can the risks be reduced or mediated? Consider super electronic sleuth Harry Caul in the film "The Conversation." Over the course of his professional career, Caul becomes paranoid, devoid of personal identity, and desensitized to the ethical aspects of his work. Undercover police agents face a variety of risks from attack to crime temptations to psychic and family costs. There is some evidence that police who use radar guns in traffic enforcement have higher rates of testicular cancer.

1.7.2 Spillover to Uninvolved Third Parties

Can the tactic be restricted just to subjects? Can undesirable effects on others be avoided? How focused and contained is the tactic? Audio- and videotaping may record the behavior of subjects as well as that of their family and friends; DNA may offer information on family members whose DNA was not collected.

1.8 Data Protection and Fate

1.8.1 Periodic Review

Is the system regularly reviewed for effectiveness, efficiency, fairness, and operation according to policies (or the need for new or revised policies)? Are there audit trails and inspections?

---

* The embarrassment caused by the falsely accused is a rarely considered form—for example, an invalid result such as having an alarm go off by mistake as one walks through a detection device in a store or library or the rejection of a valid credit card.

1.8.2 Data Fate

Are there rules regarding the retention, conditions for sharing, and destruction of the data, and are these honored?

1.9 Rights and Resources of Subjects

Right of inspection: Are subjects aware of the findings and how they were created? Fundamental aspects of procedural justice involve the right to know and challenge the evidence in the face of the haze of bureaucracy experienced by Franz Kafka. In the case of government, the right to have access to one's file is related to a broader principle that, absent special conditions, there should be no secret personal databases in a democratic society.

Right to challenge and express a grievance: Are there procedures for challenging the results and for entering alternative data or interpretations into the record?

Redress and sanctions: If the individual has been wronged, are there means of discovery and redress and, if appropriate, for the correction or destruction of the record? Are there means for minimizing or preventing such problems? Are there audits and sanctions to encourage responsible surveillant and fair and just outcomes?

Unlike Europe and Canada where there are official data commissioners who may actively seek out compliance, in the United States, it is generally up to individuals to bring complaints forward. But in order for that to happen, they must first be aware that there is a problem and that there are standards.* Internal agents such as inspector generals, auditors, and public interest watchdog groups are other means of identifying problems. The development of privacy officers within organizations is a recent tool. How independent and effective they can be given their host is a challenging organizational question.

Equal access to surveillance tools: In settings of reciprocal (or potentially reciprocal) surveillance, are the means widely available or disproportionately available (or restricted) to the more privileged, powerful, or technologically sophisticated? Contrast the ability to use satellite imagery with the cell-phone camera. Must doctors reveal personal information (e.g., investigations by professional boards) to patients, just as patients may have to agree to a search of a database to see if they have ever sued a doctor?

Equal access to neutralization tools: In settings where neutralization is legitimate (whether because the rules permit it or because unwarranted agent behavior may be seen to justify it), are the means widely available or limited to the most privileged, powerful, or technologically sophisticated? Some means of maintaining control over personal information such as providing a false name and address when the request is irrelevant (as when paying with cash at a store) or free anonymous e-mail forwarding services are available to anyone. In other cases, protecting information may require technical skills or come with a price, as with the purchase of a shredder, an unlisted phone number, or otherwise purchasing a higher level of privacy.

---

* This is the discovery of dirty data issue. Among common means of discovery are accidents, tests, informers, and deduction (Marx 1984).

1.10 Questions about Questions

As suggested, the more the principles implied in these questions are honored, the more ethical the situation is likely to be, other factors being equal—which of course they rarely are given, among many other concerns, the importance of prioritizing and weighing values. The questions require several kinds of evaluation.

Are there procedures and policies covering the basic areas? Questions can then be asked about substance—are they good policies? Are the policies followed in practice? Does the organization (or others) regularly check on itself through audits and inspections? Is the subject likely to be aware when a policy fails?

Inquiring if the policies are followed can be looked at across all, or a sample of cases, as well as in any given case. For example, the validity and consequences of a specific type of drug testing as a class can be considered. But questions can also be asked about the application in a given case.

Distinctions are also needed between rejecting, limiting, or revising a tactic such as the polygraph because of questions about its efficacy, as against rejecting a particular flawed application of an otherwise acceptable tactic.

When failings are identified, it is vital to know if they are idiosyncratic and seemingly random or are systemic. Is it the apple or the barrel? How often do individual problems have to appear before it is concluded that the problem is in the system rather than an unfortunate, but tolerable, occurrence? If it is the former, can it be fixed?

If answers to the earlier questions are supportive of adopting a new technique, it is then necessary to ask about the presence of policies and resources for managing it. Are there policies and procedures for guaranteeing the integrity, fairness, and effectiveness of the system? The ability and will to develop such policies should be a necessary condition for adoption of an otherwise acceptable technique. Policies will cover who agents and subjects are; their rights and responsibilities; how and when data are to be collected, merged, altered, analyzed, interpreted, evaluated, used, communicated, protected, updated, or purged; and internal and external oversight.

1.10.1 Surveillance Stages

An additional analytic perspective is provided by identifying stages of activity. Table 1.2 lists seven kinds of activity called *surveillance strips* that follow each other in logical order. The strips are temporally, conceptually, empirically, and often spatially distinct.

Table 1.2   Seven Surveillance Strips

1	Tool selection
2	Subject selection
3	Data collection
4	Data processing/analysis (raw data) numerical/narrative
5	Data interpretation
6	Uses/action—primary, secondary uses/users and beyond
7	Data fate (made public, restricted, sealed, destroyed)

Over time, the distinct action fragments of these stages combine into stories about personal data and illustrate the emergent character of surveillance and privacy as multifaceted abstractions made up of many smaller actions. These are not unlike the frames in comic books (although not intended to be entertaining and the patterns are more like the fluid, jumpy sequences of cyberspace explorations than the rigid frame ordering of the comic book).

When viewed sequentially and in their totality, these elements constitute *surveillance occasions*. A surveillance occasion begins when an agent is charged with the task of gathering information. Following that, the seven phases in Table 1.2 can be considered.* Studying the behavioral sequences of tool selection, subject selection, data collection, data processing, interpretation, resulting action (or inaction), and fate of the data offers a way to order the basic behaviors occurring within the family of direct surveillance actions.†

The questions in Table 1.1 may cut across various stages of the surveillance process or be restricted just to one. Awareness of the sequential stages of data generation and use can help anticipate and locate problems. The stages are the direct pressure points where most problems will be found and questions can be asked about ethics for each.

The kind of problem may differ by stage—thus violations of consent are likely at data collection, of fairness and validity at processing and interpretation, of discrimination at use, and of confidentiality at data fate.

It would be useful to have a checklist of problems that can occur and (when possible) of ways of avoiding them or ameliorating them when they can't be prevented. As implied by the questions earlier, the list would include various kinds of physical, psychological, and social harm and unfairness in application and use; minimizing invalid or unreliable results; and not crossing a personal boundary without notice or permission (whether involving coercion or deception or a body, relational, spatial, or symbolic border). Other problems to be avoided involve violating trust and assumptions that are made about how personal information will be treated (e.g., no secret recordings, respect for confidentiality, promises for anonymity, for the compartmentalization of kinds of data, and for their protection or destruction).

Awareness of the stages can direct research on the correlates and location of particular kinds of problems. This can contribute to assessing the seriousness and likelihood that a risk will occur and the costs of prevention (whether by not using, regulating, or amelioration after the fact).

The likelihood of prevention is also greatly affected by the stage. Just saying "no" to a data collection request (if honored) is the ultimate prevention. But as the process moves from collection to the final fate, controls become more challenging. In the initial stages, the relevant actors and locations for accountability are known—but over time, if the information spreads out in wider circles and is combined with other data, as often happens, control weakens. The form of the data matters as well—type of format, encryption, self-destroying, and identity masking—in a single highly secure file or a more open system.

---

* Decisions about *who* is responsible for doing the surveillance and the design of the technology could be treated as the initial strips as well. However, attention here is on the next stage directly associated with doing the surveillance.

† This is said mindful of the fact that it is always possible to make ever greater differentiations within the categories identified and to push the causal chain back farther. For example, with respect to the data collection phase, contrasts can be made based on the tool, the sense involved, the kind of activity, or the goal. Yet I think Table 1.2 captures the major natural breaks in activity once a problem in need of surveillance is identified.

1.11 Conclusion: Complexity Yes, Abstention No

In the best of all possible planets, for the philosopher an ethical theory needs to be grounded in a formal normative argument that offers justifications for its principles, indicates their logical implications, and leads to clear conclusions. Such an argument would anticipate and respond to likely objections and would be consistent across types of justification (e.g., it would not mix arguments based on categorical first principles with those based on empirical consequences as is done here).

Like a kaleidoscope with a unifying light source, an integrated ethical theory should illuminate and link the varied shapes of surveillance.* It would be nice if the world had been created such that a simple deductive Rosetta stone for judging surveillance was possible. But given the world in which we live, such an effort would need to be so general and banal as to be of modest interest or use ("do good, avoid harm").

The alternative offered here—an inductive approach that asks about the ethics of heterogeneous settings and behavior—also has limitations. A comprehensive consideration of the myriad factors that can go wrong or right with surveillance may overwhelm the observer. Casting such a wide, yet thinly meshed, net brings the risk of being unwieldy and unrealistic, let alone unread.

This can easily lead to the search for quick solutions ignoring complexity and moral conflicts. There is the danger of denying the requirements of the "dirty harry problem" in which there are costs associated with whatever action is taken (Klockars 1980). There is also the risk of accepting the fallacy of quantification—falling back on automatic bureaucratic decision making based on ethics by the numbers (e.g., simply counting up the "yes" and "no" answers to the questions in Table 1.1 and declaring the majority wins).

I have sought an intermediate position—casting a net broad enough to capture the major sources of variation and filtering these through some basic values. This chapter's emphasis on surveillance agents reflects concern over the abuses that can be associated with the tilted nature of private sector, organizational and authority playing fields, and unequal access to surveillance resources. Yet the demonology and glorification involved in viewing data gatherers as invariably up to no good and surveillance subjects as helpless victims whose rights are always trampled need to be avoided.

We all play multiple roles and rotate between being agents and subjects. Organizations and those in positions of authority are prone to give greater emphasis to their rights to gather and use personal information than to their duties or to the rights of subjects. Subjects generally show greater interest in protecting their own information than in the informational rights of others and are relatively unaware, or uninterested, in the information of organizations.

Under appropriate conditions, agents have a right and even an obligation to surveil, but they also have a duty to do it responsibly and accountably. Reciprocally, those subject to legitimate surveillance have obligations as well (e.g., not to distort the findings or threaten agents), even as they also have rights not to be subjected to some forms of surveillance.

In spite of all the factors (whether contextual or inherent in values) that work against broad generalizations about the ethics of surveillance, some moral threads that swirl within and between the questions can be noted.

---

* Thus, it would need to take account of the behavior of individuals, organizations, states, and the international order as these involve crossing borders to impose upon and to take from subjects; the rights and obligations of various parties; the ethical meanings of doing good and avoiding harm; and various levels of analysis such as kinds of institutions and roles, the cross-cultural, and the short and long run.

Some values are desirable as ends in themselves (e.g., honesty, fairness). But values may also be a means to some other ends (e.g., democracy as a support for legitimacy, privacy as a support for intimacy or political organization, transparency as a support for accountability).

In democratic societies operating under the rule of law, a cluster of value justifications underlie the questions raised. The most overarching and important is the Kantian idea of respect for the dignity of the person and respect for the social and procedural conditions that foster a civil society.

References

Agamben, G. 2005. *States of Exception*. Chicago, IL: University of Chicago Press.

Gandy, O. 1993. *The Panoptic Sort*. Boulder, CO: Westview Press.

Klockars, C. 1980. The dirty harry problem. *The Annals* 452: 33–47.

Lianos, M. 2001. *Le Nouveau Controle*. Paris, France: L'Hamilton.

Lyons, D. 2007. *Surveillance Studies: An Overview*. Cambridge, U.K.: Polity Press.

Marx, G.T. 1984. Notes on the discovery, collection, and assessment of hidden and dirty data. In *Studies in the Sociology of Social Problems*, Eds. J. Schneider and J. Kitsuse. pp. 78–114. Norwood, NJ: Ablex.

Marx, G.T. 1988. *Undercover: Police Surveillance in America*. Berkeley, CA: University of California Press.

Marx, G.T. 2002. What's new about the 'new surveillance'?: Classifying for change and continuity. *Surveillance and Society* 1(1): 9–23.

Marx, G.T. 2012. 'your papers please' personal and professional encounters with surveillance. In *International Handbook of Surveillance Studies*, Eds. D. Lyon, K. Ball, and K. Haggerty.

Marx, G.T. and Reichman, N. 1984. Routinizing the discovery of secrets: Computers as informants. *American Behavioral Scientist* 27(4): 423–452.

Nissenbaum, H. 2010. *Privacy in Context: Technology, Policy, and the Integrity of Social Life*. Palo Alto, CA: Stanford University Press.

Norris, C. and Wilson, D. 2006. *Surveillance, Crime and Social Control*. Hampshire, U.K.: Ashgate.

Samatras, M. 2004. *Surveillance in Greece*. Pellas, NY: Pella Press.

Waldo, J. et al. 2007. *Engaging Privacy and Information Technology in a Digital Age: Issues and Insights*. Washington, DC: National Academies Press.

Wright, D. and de Hert, P. 2012. *Privacy Impact Assessments Engaging Stakeholders in Privacy Protection*. Dordrecht, the Netherland: Springer.

Zureik, E. et al. (Ed.). 2010. *Privacy, Surveillance and the Globalization of Personal Information: International Comparisons*. Montreal, Quebec, Canada: McGill-Queen's University Press.

Chapter 2

Trust Networks among Human Beings: Analysis, Modeling, and Recommendations*

Bernhard Haemmerli, Margrete Raaum,
and Giorgio Franceschetti

Contents

---

* This chapter is based on the research of Margrete Raaum for her master thesis at University College Gjovik.

2.1 Introductory Considerations

In the olden days, our social life was essentially confined to the αγορά (agorà) or *village square*. The social bonds might have been trusted or distrusted, but the nature of bonds was known and stable variables. All participants were tightly socially connected, often even at the level of being relatives, with the additional important advantage that people spoke the same language.

Just 30 years ago, virtual communication was to the public only restricted to telephony and mail, and no virtual *village squares* were offered. The situation is now quite different: we live in a global village where each electronic forum is a place for socializing and the electronic network carries an endless amount of messages in discussions at all levels of secrecy. This virtual connectivity is still evolving in the meeting arena, as companies and cooperatives are becoming still more international at the same time as family and environmental awareness drive us toward less traveling. The technological advancements on areas of virtual socialization are also progressing, and this may complicate matters even more. As a consequence, nowadays, there are issues of trust in the global village that should be examined with deeper detail. These are questions that may become even more urgent, as technology advances, and the new generations take advantage of this evolution. The challenges are of both technical and social nature. First, we comment on the technical aspects of the challenges, and then we concentrate on the social ones.

Nowadays, operational roots of our society, and the way of living, are totally dependent on the Internet, our everyday connecting network (CN). This CN allows for fast, and assumed reliable, operational information exchange, interconnecting everything from private people's mailboxes to critical systems, as electricity, transportation, banking, telecommunication, health care, and all other critical sectors. The critical infrastructure (CI)—the sum of all critical systems—is not isolated, but the elements are interconnected with all the rest of the CN, which leads to a robust operational network, but it leaves the single service vulnerable. Our society and economy are now totally dependent upon CI services, as they play an important role in making our life safe and productive. Their operations are realized via a sophisticated connection through the cyber world, which can be either misused or violated. Hence, it is vital to protect them and assure their cyber security against their unintentional or intentional human misuse. In particular, we should prevent intrusions by anticipating attacks, and we should be able to detect intrusions and limit the damage, in the event of an incident. The CI must be designed to be trustworthy. The CI is the collection of systems, a *system of systems* that operates the fundamental building blocks of society, which should adequately be functioning, despite environmental disruption, human errors, or even attacks by hostile parties. Their continuous and uninterrupted service requires first of all implementation of a number of technical improvements in order to render the CI and its *system controlling systems* resilient, but this is not the final solution to the problem. An additional issue should be accounted for, as discussed in the following.

The amount of damage that can be inflicted on society by cyber attacks is proportional to the value, or the information, carried by the system: as these features increase, the need to protect the networked asset becomes more and more acute. The motives for the attack's perpetrators can be economical, like fraud, blackmail, and theft, or it can be idealistic, or political, like espionage or sabotage. There are different approaches to implement valid defense against these cyber crimes. Protecting the assets and hardening the systems, in order to try to prevent the attackers from reaching their target, are important and the best option for the defense. The second best option is to prepare reaction (if we cannot avoid malware) and to implement quick detection of security breach or attack, so that appropriate manual and/or organizational measures can be taken to counteract its effects.

In order to properly counteract the attacks, one must be able to predict its type and features, that is, one needs information about previous security incidents. Having sources of such information, from outside your own network, is a great advantage, when assessing the threats. There are several initiatives to enable sharing of relevant information, like experiences from break-ins or logs of observed attacks. Obviously, this information sharing is a convenient tool for cyber criminals also. It has been known that in many cases they are well organized and have an international network, with effective information-sharing procedures.

The relevance of information sharing in safe operation of the CN is apparent, but the cyber security assessment of the CN remains incomplete: incomplete because there are indirect risks in addition to the CN-related risks. The CN is already today the backbone of our society as a whole (everybody is using Internet), and indirect consequences of cyber security incidents should be assessed. These indirect consequences are today treated mostly in the frame of impact assessment on society and economy in sector studies.* Consider the case where a large industrial company is dispersed over a wide number of branches, localized in many countries all over the world. Efficient and effective cooperation among these branches needs exchange of information. The problem is that being employed in the same company is not a sufficient motivation to be willing to share sensitive and delicate information with colleagues that belong to a nonfamiliar nation, or another culture, people they have not met that do not speak the same language or share the same perceived values.

There is a key ingredient to implement real information sharing, leading to effective cooperation: however, it is not easy to individuate and properly define this constituent. Possibly, its best approximation is the existence of trust, implying faith, confidence, and reliance, among the interacting people. It should be noted that we are not yet at the level to define the word *trust* with a mathematical model, because it does not represent a physical object, but rather the behavioral attitude of human beings toward their human counterparts. In spite of the unavoidable intrinsic ambiguity of the term, there is no doubt that it plays a fundamental role in the establishment and performance of operations, in the frame of a human network. In the subsequent sections of this chapter, we try to define at our best the meaning of this term and investigate its role in the performance of the CN. Rules and techniques exist in the frame of physical networks but should be reinvented in the psychological ones. Some preliminary attempts along this direction have been initiated.

2.2 Preliminary Trust Definitions

Trust is a group phenomenon, but the decision to trust is individual, and the factors that influence decision processes are complex and not even always conscious. Zucker postulates that trust is based on the process of exchange [1], that is, characteristics of partners and societal institutions

---

* http://www.gao.gov/new.items/d08113.pdf

participating in the exchange. Doney concludes that trust is a set of beliefs or expectations and the willingness to act along those beliefs, judged from the individual's subjective evaluation of the probability of success [2].

Humans want to trust, because it makes life easier and in general more joyful. The more verification and securing techniques are applied, the less trust is necessary. To circumvent the uncomfortable trust reduction techniques, humans balance belly feeling and rational mind in a kind of risk assessment procedure, resulting in personal level of trust willingness and finally in the personal lifestyle.

2.2.1 Basic Trust Properties Applied in Information Sharing

The fact that information sharing increases with trust, as well as positive collaboration in incident handling, indicates that trust is experience based and therefore necessarily personal. Trust in collaborative situations may well be a group phenomenon, but the decision to trust remains individual, and the factors that influence these decision processes are complex and for sure not always conscious. There is always some risk involved: if not, no need for trust would be necessary. And the reward for trusting is easier interaction, more efficiency, and better feelings. However, trust does not reduce the consequence of a breach of confidence, but it does decrease the likelihood of a breach happening—because of the will of each counterpart to be trustworthy and accepted in the trust circle.

There is a certain degree of transitivity in trust relationship, as one is inclined to listen to recommendations from someone whom one trusts sufficiently. *Sufficiently* is in this case a variable that is linked to the nature of the situation, the sensitivity of the material, and the robustness of the trust link to the subject making the recommendation. Figure 2.1 demonstrates how C is willing to trust A, because C received a positive recommendation from B, which trusts A. The general principle is to trust friends of friends: generally, friends share common values, and it is very likely that friends of friends share the same values as well.

Figure 2.2 shows the case where the new person is related via two friends of friends, which means that the ties are more loosely coupled. The transitivity chain increases, and these links

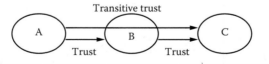

Figure 2.1   Trust has boundaries. In trust transitivity, trust propagates through trust actors by proxy.

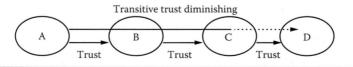

Figure 2.2   There are limits to how long transitive trust links can be; as with growing number of links, the trust propagation effect bandwidth will gradually approach decrease to zero.

become less robust [3]. You would trust less someone if the link degree or link distance away from the recommended person is increasing. Generally, it would become a problem if the link number or distance exceeds three.

Only subjective/personal trust holds the quality of transitivity, and, as it is experience based, even if via proxy building, the individual trust links take time. Rational trust is built on facts only, hence is not transitive. A form of rational trust is the confidence that a party is properly authenticated and that the integrity of the data is sound, as this can be fairly easily proven.

2.2.2 Human Trust Decision

Personally perceived trust can be broken down into several dimensions. The modified Cosimano model [4] is centered on the trustee's characteristics, more specifically the trustee's ability, integrity, and benevolence, all of which are determined from experience. As experience is growing, continuous adaption and fine-tuning of trustee's ability, integrity, and benevolence will take place. On the left side of Figure 2.3, there are two boxes: individual predisposition to trust and relation to team and other authorities, the collective culture background of values norms and assumptions. With the background of predisposition, the trustee will perform risk evaluation by making scenario predictions (what could happen if …) and assigning the associated risks. The evaluation of risks consisting of scenario prediction and risk assessment could be based on signals, which are conscious and rational or unconscious, which is often named *belly feeling*. The result of the risk assessment is the individual's trustee's perceived trust (this may be for each trustee different and has not a direct association to rational risk assessment) in relation to sharing decision: the three options for the decision are as follows: share secret information, make some rumor around the topic but don't talk so much that one reaches vulnerable state, or just be quiet (which means don't share information). Being helpful is to understand "trust in intent" (see definition in the following), which is actually the result of the processing in Figure 2.3, to correctly predict the actions of the truster, hence to make a correct risk assessment about the intent.

Trust is influenced by the truster's perceived risk in exposing vulnerabilities to the trustee. This means that the truster must believe that the trustee is benevolent and be able to predict how the trustee will act, which is difficult to judge if one does not understand the relevant—and always changing—microclimate values and norms in the specific scenario. The ability to predict such behavior decreases as the cultural distance increases.

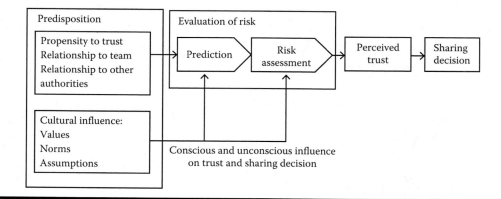

Figure 2.3   Cultural influences on the sharing decision.

2.2.3 Types of Trust

Many factors influence a truster's decision whether to share information or not, the risk assessment being heavily influenced by cultural aspects and the person's ability to understand and interpret the behavioral pattern of the trustee. Some standard trust patterns are

- *Trust in intent*: The belief that the other person's intentions are good. This trust is personal and based on experience, and, from the first personal meeting, it takes time for trust to settle at a given level, depending on a number of factors. The trust in intent is a compound quality of experience, reputation, scenario-based or setup-based trust conditions (kind of general background), and social compatibility, factors that are not easily manipulated.
- *Rule-based trust*: There is a rule, which is recognized, and everyone is assumed to comply with it (for instance, driving left or right according to national rules).
- *Deterrence-based trust* is based on the assumption that fear of punishment, or fear of potential negative reaction, creates a compliance behavior aimed at avoiding the enforcement of sanctions. As an example, motor traffic obeys to rules, among them speed limits, and drivers usually comply with rules, even if they think that they would be able to manage higher speed. Accordingly, in a sense drivers trust the rules: in general, all penalty law-related rules have a component of deterrence-based trust.
- *Trust bandwidth*: The amount of experience-based trust shared by the parties. The bandwidth will normally increase over time but will decrease when breaches of trust occur.

2.3 Basic Trust Role in the Network

A trust network can be anything from a family to a group of friends, or international trust networks, and cyber-based trust networks are not a novel thing, since for decades communities of peers on the Internet have been already operating. Trust networks can be consciously formed and managed, or they can be more informal, just emerging from working groups (WG). To be able to go from single trust relationships to trust networks, there should be a structure in place, to shorten and strengthen the transitive trust links. The smaller, informal networks exhibit recommendation, as well as activity level rules, more stringent than the larger, more formal networks. As a matter of fact, it becomes unmanageable to impose strict rules on personal relationships, in a large trust network.

2.3.1 Voluntary versus Mandatory and Sector-Wise Trust

Trust network participation can be either voluntary or mandatory, but in a mandatory network, there is a likelihood of lower trust level, as personal trust cannot be commanded. If the conditions are right, a fruitful trust network might emerge, but nurturing trust in a mandatory network is far more complicated than in a voluntary network. This is a bad news for the creation of protective collaboration networks for CI, as these are often mandatory. Another complicating element in the creation of CI-networks is the *isolation* industry practices. A main CI-network usually splits up into sector networks. In the main sector, you potentially get an insight into what that particular type of industry/organization sees as its threats and receive information about current relevant attacks toward that particular sector. However, it is usually difficult for a particular sector to have enough competence in all cyber security areas; even to build up and maintain enough competence in few cyber security areas is often very hard: to build up and maintain cyber security in a few areas is obviously insufficient for reaching holistic and good cyber security, but it is still by far better than "not focusing at all" on cyber security.

Trust groups where the members have little obvious similarities sector-wise (i.e., in the core business), or culture- or competence-wise, might have a hard time to develop trust. However, when focusing on similarities in cyber challenges rather than on differences, a trust spirit can develop, for example, by agreeing on common goals, methods, and vision.

2.3.2 Creation of Subgroups in the Network

To discuss Figure 2.4, in the first paragraph just issues related to hub, hub representative, and the trust links between are raised; in the second paragraph, the trust between representative and ordinary member; and in the third paragraph, we look at real situations, where the trust links between representatives are of different quality.

Consider an umbrella trust network, as graphically represented in Figure 2.4. The umbrella trust networks consist of several hubs (represented by circles with trust links to the other hubs, named member hubs in the figure, subsequently just named "hub"), which are interlinked among them with trust links. Each hub has a representative, which fulfills the fiduciary responsibilities associated with the role "representative." For the representative, we argue the question

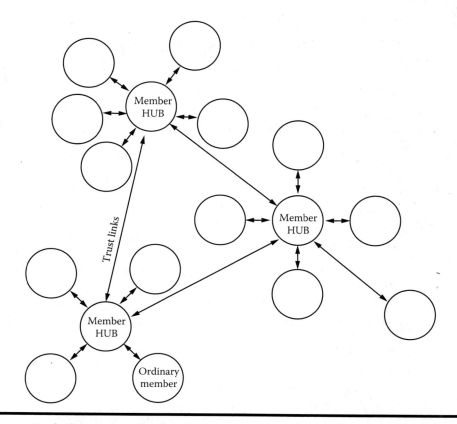

Figure 2.4 Scale-free trust network with (human) hubs.

on how much trust is related to the person and how much trust is in the role. On the one hand, the hub representative must exchange confidential information among themselves to perform the job. However, this works only when role and person of the representative are trusted. And the attributes of the representative must be trustworthy, knowledgeable, and competent, as well as sufficiently long in the network and accepted. This means that in many cases only a few members of hub may fulfill the requirements to be representative. If the election or nomination of an appropriate representative fails, the hub does not work properly and may disturb the whole umbrella network.

Each member hub consists of the representative and has several ordinary members (empty circles), which collaborate on specific incidents and technical issues. For proper collaboration, the trust level between the ordinary members must be rather high, and between the representatives as well as between ordinary member and representative, trust must be even higher.

In reality, the trust links between hubs exhibit different trust levels (as a result of combination of role based and representative's personal trust) and are therefore called *scale-free*. In scale-free networks, the goal should be to develop deep trust such that the network is better functioning and has therefore better performance.

Creation of new links and strengthening of existing links in the networks are important. In the beginning, the network is just a framework for new members to be included in a trust mesh, but relationships, learning, and sharing basic network qualities become rewards and incentives. Any trust network should at any time strengthen the network robustness, by encouraging the creation of new connections within the network or strengthening existing links. In practice, this would mean keeping up activity, additionally providing social activity, or initiating collaborations between members of the network, where there has been little previous contact. Normal evolution in a trust network will converge toward a scale-free structure, as some participants are natural hubs (team leader) where some members feel attracted either by the social behavior or by an attractive knowledge and competence of the unofficial team leader.

2.3.3 Trust Types and Level in Organized Networks

Trust networks are worthless, even counterproductive, if the general trust level is too low and likewise if the competence level sinks too low. The former situation can be corrected to some extent by increased information sharing, but if there are no obvious data to share, obstacles to information sharing may be present and should be examined. The members might develop a *sharing standoff* similar to "the prisoner's dilemma," where everybody holds off, waiting to see if anybody else decides to share their data. The sharing standoff, or other organizational barriers, may be rectified if correctly handled. Lack of information sharing may even be due to the replacement of the network function by other structures, hence rendering the network superfluous. This would be worth exploring and identifying.

We understand that previously mentioned reasoning and considerations are dispersive and difficult to organize in a logical fashion. We try to summarize hereafter trust and trust network aspects.

Trust is a group phenomenon, but most trust is personal. By *real* trust or *personal* trust, most people mean *experience-based* trust. This coincides with the terms *history-based* trust and *relational* trust, used in the literature. *Transitive trust* is *experience-based* trust via proxy.

Organizational or system-based trust (subsequently named *institutional trust*) is a group phenomenon that some argue to evolve when experience-based trust (i.e., faith in the continuation of proper application of rules) reaches a certain level or there is enough trust *bandwidth* (experience).

This statement is related to rule-based trust. Explanation: if persons have a high level of trust in institutions, this trust is not continuously reevaluated but rather a general presumption. An example would be a society and a government, well trusted, that emanate laws; as a consequence, these rules and laws are automatically trusted. This kind of trust depends heavily on cultural factors, as some cultures allow stronger system-based trust than others.

2.3.4 Issues with Network Size

Large networks with many members tend to be too big for trusted information exchange: therefore, such networks, also called umbrella or backbone networks, are often split up into smaller groups (also called inner circles), with the goal of having real interpersonal trust between all members. In general, the role of the umbrella or backbone trust network is setting strategic targets and facilitating in-depth technical or strategic collaboration in smaller groups (hubs, Special Interest Groups [SIGs]). Often initial trust relations of a new member are established in the umbrella or backbone, and later the new member registers for working in SIG.

In general, delegated work from the umbrella network to SIG will be executed in the SIG, and results elaborated in SIG will be prepared (neutralized, simplified) such that results can be fed back to the umbrella network, where the members will understand it and can take decisions based on this new knowledge.

2.4 Trust Development

The trust level in a group or network is never static. As shown in Figure 2.5, incident handling (common activities foster trust), no specific activity (trust is passing away because there is no interaction), changing of its members (new members must first be integrated before the trust decreases), vetting (transparent check of new and/or existing members increases trust), breach of trust (a trust shock: trust decreases), planned repair process (very cautious regeneration of trust), low activity (trust is passing away because there is low interaction), and exercises (common activities build trust) all affect the trust level in the group. And remember, building trust takes time and has to follow a natural development. Additionally, Figure 2.5 has presumed that a specific network has a "sustainable trust level," which is the minimum trust level, which must be reached in order to be operational. If real trust is lower than sustainable trust, creating actions (repair, exercise) must be invoked. Temporarily, trust level might be higher or lower, but the sustainable level is necessary for well functioning, which means that sharing of information is lived reality, and the network has sufficient activity.

The network trust level is the sum of all the joint trust of all members. When representatives have changed or a breach of confidence happened or a successful cooperation handling an incident took place, the trust level will change. The desired situation is to have the highest possible trust level, but this may not actually be the most stable and predictable situation.

There are several options to repair trust: exercises, socializing, discussions on rules and regulations, etc. However, parties can be forced to cooperate, but if this is mere cooperation, this is not the same as trust. One may say that trust is the replacement of control and command. Deterrence-based trust cannot be considered real trust, as one never knows whether someone has good intentions or just wants to avoid punitive actions. It is easier to tear down rather than to build trust, and the goal in governing a group should be to keep the trust level as steady as possible and to create predictability.

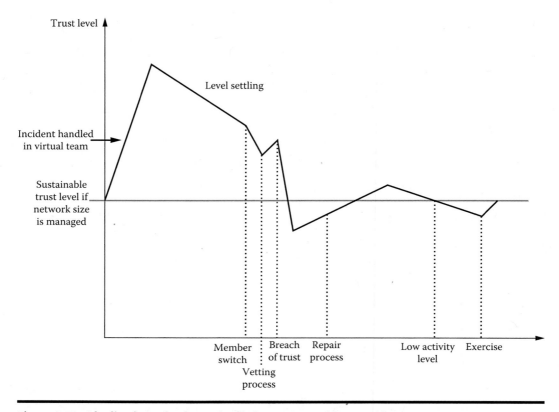

Figure 2.5 Idealized graph of trust level change caused by specific events.

Introducing new members in a group may diminish the trust level: for instance, if someone is representing a company and a new representative is sent to the group, because there was a role change in the company. All trust networks have some kind of recommendation function: the smaller the networks are, the more the vetting is trusted, as the links are stronger and the network more robust.

In the event of a breach of confidence in the network, restoring trust to the same level as before the breach is probably impossible. But, if the evidence for the breach is weak, or the breach is merely based on lack of competence, the level might be possibly restored. Leadership, and coaching of the parties involved in the breach, is extremely important, as well as having a sufficiently transparent process to avoid speculations. But, at the end of the day, the fate of the changes in trust level is in the hands of the offended party: if this member leaves the network because of distrust, it could lead to dissolution of the whole network. A trust network, in which considerable amount of distrust appears, has a hard time to complete the given task. Remediation is necessary for refinding trust.

The leadership role should be defined to suit each network type, as some networks may benefit from defining different leading roles for different tasks. Existing networks have different policies on how the leading persons/group/committees are chosen and whether the leadership is rotating, even from continent to continent. The important thing is that the members not only accept but also support the method.

2.4.1 Vetting and Recommendations

To avoid the decrease in trust level at network when members change, or even just to lower the cost for building trust for the birth of a trust relationship, vetting or recommendations are good tools (see Figure 2.6). The assumption in the figure is that A is trusting B and B is trusting C, as well as A is trusting E and F, which is discussed later (solid arrows for a settled trust relationship). New member "D" is entering the trust network, and E, F, and C are trusting D (solid links). What we discuss is the development of trust of A in D (because it is transitive trust and not settled, the trust links from A to D are drawn in Figure 2.6 with arrows starting solid and turning to dotted). Vetting is used in many of the branches of CI, as well as an elaborate background check. Except for some cases that are economically or politically sensitive, visibility in vetting increases trust link transparency and enables new trust link creation. Recommendation, for example, introducing or sponsoring a friend to another friend, creates a sound immediate trust level. To reinforce the trust of A in D, additional and direct recommendation of E and F are supportive (feasible only, when A is trusting in E and F). With the growing number of recommendation (dotted links, A receives recommendation of E and F directly and of C indirectly), trust credit of member A to D is increased. Recapitulation: closeness of recommendation and number of recommendation positively influence trust credit to a new member.

Vetting shortens the transitive trust links and can be seen as experience-based trust by proxy. However, one recommendation, even if in the right context, does not constitute a robust link, as the vetting party, or the recommender, is an isolated element of strength: if this is the case and the vetting party somehow disappears, the link is totally destroyed. Many trust networks demand vetting from several existing members in order to make the network more robust. This would render the network more resistant to single failures or attacks.

The value of a recommendations, hence the robustness of the resulting link, depends on the strength of the link between the recommended and the recommender and also on the link between the recommender and the party considering to base a trust link on the recommendation. This can be accomplished by personal relationships but also reputation based. The more trustworthy the vetting, the stronger the tie is. The vetting process is not without risk for the recommender, because reputation is at stake if the recommended party is dishonest or lacking the promised competence or resources.

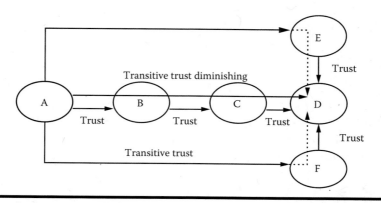

Figure 2.6   Vetting shortens the trust distance and eliminates long, transitive links.

2.4.2 Incentives to Trust Building and Information Sharing

The network should exhibit a perceived valuable incentive for potential members to join the trust networks and for existing members to implement an active participation. When the member (employed by a specific company) individuates a positive value, then its counterpart costs, either time or money, should be justified to the company or to the organization leadership. The process of weighing potential negative consequences versus positive gains exhibits several facets.

In general, this conflict is resolved as follows: IT security and cyber security are defined as a noncompetition domain; meanwhile, potential competing enterprises are represented in trust groups. Why is this useful? An example is given. An incident suffered by one financial institution (for instance, a bank) is in the public perception all over other far away countries, often associated to all the institution of the financial place where the incident did happen. Accordingly, the incident is perceived far away as a problem of the associated financial place (for instance, London or Zurich) and not of the specific suffering institution. Therefore, the common interest of avoiding incidents is prevailing, in comparison of having a market advantage because the other institution is suffering. Therefore, collaborative effort of sector members is taken for avoiding as much incidents as possible by creation of higher resilience and cyber security.

One of the main incentives for companies to be part of a trust network, or information-sharing initiatives, is of course the expectation that the shared data contain useful information. The smaller companies, or organizations, would potentially benefit more compared to the huge ones because the smaller have less data to analyze and learn from and naturally less data to share. Lack of data can be compensated in other ways, for instance, by sharing their expertise. If a company is low on expertise, as well as data, it is very likely that its ability to efficiently utilize the received information is low too. Several networks offer tutoring and education for such *low-level* teams in order to enable them to rise to an acceptable degree of competence.

Cost saving is an incentive of high importance. In a well-functioning network, this is quite visible. The savings can originate from

- Shared development of tools
- Reasonable and targeted education
- Increased detection of malicious activity, hence incident prevention
- Faster incident analysis, hence shortening the recovery time

The network members, who have been in a situation where the previously mentioned detection and prevention of malicious activity has been experienced, that is, underwent some kind of attack that was at least partly resolved, tend to be more active, as well as more inclined afterward to trust their peers in the network.

Network membership and activity can also function as an improver of reputation, not only signaling that the member has competence and is considered important enough for membership but also signaling power, because he is in power to handle resources and possesses enough control and self-confidence to share data. The influence of network membership on reputation is bilateral. The individual member can affect the network's reputation as well, both negatively and positively.

A possible strategy that has been voiced for governments is to create incentives, in the form of tax or other forms of benefits, for those who join the network. But in any case, a necessary prerequisite is that the person should be willing to join the network and is perceived from the network member as good and trustworthy. In addition, the incentive should not be purely monetary. As a matter of fact, if the driving factor of a network is a personal financial benefit for its members, the motivation of an individual to join could be driven by financial advantage and not to collaborate with the trustworthy in resolving challenges. Therefore, also other types of individuals may be attracted, those with doubtful trustworthiness and intentions.

Not all networks that are formed to protect CI are focused on the establishment of trust relations at all. This might be a mistake, as trust itself is an advantage in the network government, and fewer members are likely to withhold information to protect their reputation in a network of trusted relations.

There are always costs involved in the memberships. Some organizations have yearly fees, some are government financed, and yet others are based on a shared cost model. In the latter case, each member covers some specific cost in the network, like hardware, meeting costs, and others.

Joining as a sharing member can be a fundamental decision, just like agreeing to insurance contract (e.g., personal, home, or car insurance). Fundamental decisions for security expenses indicate sufficient wealth to agree on contracts beyond cost–benefit analysis.

Benefits to becoming sharing members of networks would be weighed by most people against the related costs (cost–benefit analysis). The economic challenges are more acute in some countries rather than in others, and not only membership fees and investments would be an obstacle but also traveling to meetings would be impossible. If the trust networks do not consider solutions to this issue, the networks would in reality be limited to the wealthier countries. This is absolutely not a desirable situation: many security incidents, especially fraud cases, have perpetrators located in poorer countries. On the other hand, the same countries have more potentially vulnerable victims, although the information and money finally are stolen in the rich countries. It is highly desirable to have well-connected teams in as many countries as possible, and especially in the poor countries, where attackers use nodes to hide their identity. To support the goal of wide distribution, the network itself could raise money or dedicate an amount of the membership fee to sponsor teams, although this would certainly raise some controversy. As governments have the duty to care for security, they often are interested in improving security and reaction capabilities by joining global networks. As a consequence, political bodies and governments that might benefit by the cooperation with the members from poor regions may sponsor or cosponsor participation of poor countries. Even so the funding or sponsoring of poor regions creates discussion: these challenges must be addressed and resolved for working effectively, especially in case of investigations and prosecution.

2.4.3 Trust Supporting Tools

Trusted security information sharing usually starts in person at meetings. The usual next step is the wish to share information in between meetings. Such exchanges may be enabled by a secure electronic platform. However, this secure electronic platform is not enough [5]: secure technology is presumed to ensure integrity, identity, and confidentiality in trusted information sharing. However, secure technology platform is useless if the members using the platform are not allied up front and have defined faith and trust in each other.

There are sound frameworks and technical solutions for information sharing, like the framework developed by the Telecommunication Standardization Sector (ITU-T) (CYBEX) or the frameworks developed in the CERT communities.

Typical areas to be covered by such frameworks are (for complete catalogue, see CYBEX [6])

- Structuring cyber security information for exchange purposes
- Identifying and discovering cyber security information and entities
- Requesting and responding with cyber security information
- Exchanging cyber security information
- Enabling assured cyber security information exchange

Again, technical frameworks do not address the issues of interpersonal trust and group trust. Technical trust, trust in the technical framework, and secure electronic identities are comparatively easy to obtain. However, personal and community trust must be established up-front, otherwise no trusted exchange on secure electronic communication platform will take place. In other words, solid foundation for trusted information sharing should be based upon a sound technical framework, which is necessary but not sufficient, and complete, to create interpersonal trust. This framework should not be complicated, as complicated solutions are often left unused. The framework should assure to the participants the necessary confidence in the secure data transfer all over the information-sharing process.

2.4.4 Encryption and Trusted Third Parties

Pretty Good Privacy (PGP) allows visible trust, for the link between a PGP member and its electronic identity, by secure electronic signing the link, which means that the signing person confirms knowing this PGP member. Therefore, PGP is starting at *distrusting* new members and after many signatures leading to ultimate *trust* in the link of new member's electronic identity to its owner. This framework is based on personal trust of members of the community and confirming others' identity as they know these people. Confirmation of the new member's identity is implemented by signing new member's key. The larger the number of existing PGP members confirming the identity of the new member, the bigger is the trust: the electronic identity of the new member is correct and really represents the new member.

A public-key infrastructure (PKI) enables the acquisition of certificates that warrant the authenticity of the person or company. On this basis, a private- and public-key pairs for encryption, or digital signing of communication, could be implemented. However, a certificate does not state anything about the holder's policies, intentions, integrity, competence, or quality of service, and this is true for both public and private keys. A trusted encryption scheme should be in place, if information sharing is to be trusted. Similarly, a PGP-signed network can be a trust network with visible vetting, if the signed keys are uploaded to a key server. However, as with information-sharing networks, these are mechanisms to support a communication based on already developed links of experience-based personal trust.

2.5 Trust and Network

There are a number of potential barriers to trust implementation and information sharing, both pertaining to build new and maintain existing "trust relationships." Some of these barriers are paradoxically a result of the network itself.

2.5.1 Network Size

Trust network size introduces an impact on trust. As a group size enlarges, it becomes increasingly difficult to know all the group members personally, which is a prerequisite to experience-based trust, if not by proxy. Smaller groups tend to be more effective and include members in a tighter fashion. They also generally exhibit a higher activity level, which in turn is likely to increase group trust, as a continuous improvement loop. The larger networks may struggle to meet these standards but have a range of advantages. The bigger networks have international participation, disparate knowledge bases, and more resources.

Size and growing issues in the larger networks can be alleviated if growth issues are addressed early and continuously observed. The issue is not about stopping growth, since stopping the intake of new members, solely on the account of existing network size, would lead to a skewed network, consisting of people whose most important quality is that they were earlier accepted. Therefore, too large networks should subdivide in WG, or SIG, to reach operational size.

The trust level required to share information is closely interlaced with the nature and sensitivity of the information. For instance, the mission of a meta-network—a union of general members and members of deeply trusted subgroups—is to operate as a trust forger and enabler, introducing new participants that could later work in areas where deep trusting qualities are required. If new participants learn by experience, education of rules, and behavior of the culture of the trust network, they adapt and start to be ready for deeper involvement.

By rule-enforced reorganization of a trust network to enable better information sharing, a possible but well-recognized option—although very rarely applied in reality—could be limiting and organizing the number of members in trust groups or subgroups. Reorganization may mean generating hierarchical structure of subgroups or defining loosely a couple of groups interacting informally or according to a specific rule set. The reason why such formal reorganization is rarely applied is that individuals might feel separated from other friends that interacted deeply with them up to that moment. One might think that hierarchy is a good structure for enforcing policies and rules, as well as keeping the size down, but historical experience shows the opposite: the reason is that trust is not commendable and hierarchy has a lot to do with command and following commands. Therefore, professionals tend to react negatively to hierarchical organization, and this directly affects the sharing efforts.

An option is to observe well an existing large network, fostering the natural-grown scale-free approach by enabling the option of formalized hubs.

A typical topology of hierarchical networks is given in Figure 2.7, where each circle represents a person, and the arrow between the circles (i.e., nodes) shows the information flow. The nodes at the bottom of the figure (leaf nodes, which have no successor in the hierarchical chain) represent experts in incident handling (I = incident handler), and the nodes above them represent managers of the network (circles with M). Incident handlers are now organized in hierarchical structure, and this means that they talk not directly to each other, but they communicate via managers and managers of managers. This indirect communication may introduce relevant delay because each manager may need some time for propagation of information. This delay may be a serious obstacle for investigation and resolution of cases; in some situations, the delay may reach a level such that forensic evidence (traces necessary for the investigation) may have been erased in between, and a resolution of the case may be impossible. In Figure 2.7, we explore the number of transition nodes necessary for sharing information from the incident handler in the left lower leaf node I1, with the other three incident handlers I2–I4 depicted on the right side in the figure. Passing a single

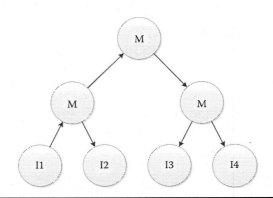

Figure 2.7   Hierarchical network with no horizontal information flow.

managerial node is necessary to transfer information to the second incident handler I2, whereas three and four managerial nodes must be passed to reach the incident handlers I3 or I4.

Bilateral trust between delegates, that is, trusted members and the other members of the network, is especially important in hierarchical organized networks. The previous members (constituents) must trust not only the delegate's intentions but also their capabilities and competence. The delegate may also meet situations where the views of the trust network are opposing to the general view of the constituency. This can be a challenge to both trust relationships.

Another challenge to hierarchical networks is the individual contributor's need to have strict control of their own data and take control of their information release. It is also important for contributors to be seen and to be given credit for contributions. Unfortunately, human's instinct is to trust on their own abilities and intentions and setting them above the abilities and intentions of others; this automatic routine pattern makes complicated such participation by representation.

A hierarchical structure, organized with only one exclusive point of contact (POC), for instance, per country or per sector, is an entirely different matter and does not require such a complex internal trust structure. This solution may be judged an appealing idea to large technology companies operating worldwide. However, complications can arise also in these situations, because usually an incident does not limit itself to a single geographical area (e.g., Europe) or a particular network provider. Trickling down the incident information to the appropriate parties may not be straightforward. Mapping out the information flow structure in these structures are scenarios suitable for incident exercises.

A hierarchical network is more prone to having a single point of failure than mesh networks, which consists of multiple couple nodes, where the coupling is determined according the need of information flow. If a representative, or the top leader, is somehow compromised, there must be a contingency plan.

Another way of dealing with large umbrella networks is to tone down the sensitivity level by moving the more detailed work and more sensitive data sharing to smaller groups, referred to as SIGs. In Figure 2.8, the large circle represents the networks of many nations, here for simplicity limited to four countries only. Each country may have several members, and a connection is implemented to the network umbrella, represented by connected black rectangles in the Figure 2.8. The four countries delegate according to agreed network's rule (as example, in Figure 2.8 one respectively two member) into the SIG. The SIG is charged to perform a given task, and after execution results are transferred in suitable form to the umbrella network.

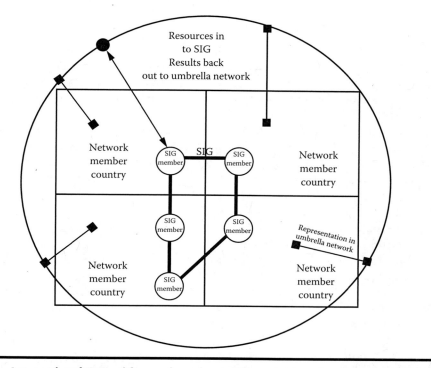

Figure 2.8 **International SIG with members from different countries that are represented in the international umbrella network. The "umbrella" network supports the SIG and gets results back out.**

In general, larger networks can delegate tasks to smaller networks, for example, for experts with special competence in the relevant area, and could enforce mini joint ventures with smaller existing networks inside or outside the umbrella network. In general, smaller groups tend to inspire professionals because of the topic-related dialogue. Additionally, they have more mutual commitments and fewer internal conflicts. Another advantage of SIG is that their vocabulary is more uniform, creating fewer misunderstandings. It is likely that people in SIG are at approximately the same level of competence in the relevant area, hence be able to create a shared identity in the umbrella network by supplying homogeneous results at their level of expertise.

There is need for transparency between the umbrella and the smaller networks, enough to provide assurance to the members of the umbrella network (shown as the surrounding circle in Figure 2.8) that the work in the smaller groups (bold links) is worthwhile to be supported and that tasks are appropriately addressed. However, this should not turn into strict control mechanisms that become a strain because of excessive reporting, thus limiting network creativity. Even though the network depicted here might seem similar in structure with hierarchical networks, there is a difference: even if smaller WG may have someone responsible for keeping in touch with the umbrella network, there is not a *chain of command* implemented or expected. It is rather an open exchange, and the groups share information according the estimated need to inform other groups; with sharing, value is created, and it will lead to more security by fostering the exchange process.

There are numerous other ways to structure a trust network, but most of them are not specifically designed to meet the challenges of large, international networks.

2.5.2 Cultural Differences

As trust networks are increasingly expected to function across national borders, cultural differences, sectors, and company cultures, that is, a number of barriers, are present and should be considered.

Competition between members in a trust network can be a barrier. Whether it is market-driven competition, frictions between publicly funded authorities, or just plain human nature competitiveness, the result can lead to withholding of information, aimed at inflicting to the other members a disadvantage and preventing network transparency all together. This is difficult to avoid. Sector-based networks may be a good way to individuate the particular threats to a certain industry, but it inevitably brings cooperative challenges on account of competitive issues between the members. These competitive barriers can and should be fairly strictly regulated. These barriers are predictable areas that are normally governed and addressed anyway: accordingly, predicting most potential conflicts of interest should be feasible. However, agreements and rules should be assessed, and trust members are presumed to honor them.

The national laws of different countries and the lack of international legislation are barriers. For one thing, the ownership right to data differs, and the right for the national authorities to access/read data that flow within the borders differs too. Another matter is whether the individual member has an obligation to report potential *illegal data* to the national authorities, especially taking into account that the data are not necessarily illegal in the country where the data originated.

This would certainly be an issue for law enforcement or legislative institutions. It should be assured that nobody shares information at an extent wider than all group members have agreed upon. However, this is a real minefield, and agreements would have to be updated continuously. For example, if a country should outlaw encryption in country or cross-borders, this would constitute an impenetrable barrier to electronic information sharing.

One of the large trust networks, Organization of the Islamic Conference CERT (OIC-CERT),* is in effect built on a religious basis, as the member countries are mainly in the Organization of Islamic Cooperation. This might seem unusual, but as religion is a large part of everyday culture in many countries, this may be a natural coalition: looking more deeply in this matter, deeper trust is found along Christian and Jewish, as well as Islamic and Confucius predominant countries. Of course, political and religious–political conflicts build obstacles to trust and to share, as well as expensive and long interregional traveling for face-to-face meetings.

2.5.3 National Culture and Identity

The key trust element in a multinational network is to acknowledge and respect cultural differences: many of these differences are to the network's advantage, not disadvantage. Differences that pose a problem for the functioning of the network should be met, not necessarily avoided. Networks can easily end up adopting a culture of misunderstood political correctness, where everybody should be treated equally: however, in reality, this equal treatment is not met. This may leave some experts in a situation where they are not treated as they would like or expect. However, there is no need to focus particularly on the differences themselves, it is much more important to focus on the similarities between the members, such as security challenges and goals.

---

* http://www.scribd.com/doc/15231860/OICCERT-OIC-Computer-Emergency-Response-Team, http://itlaw. wikia.com/wiki/Organisation_of_the_Islamic_Conference-CERT

The term culture has many aspects, namely, the culture of an academic education like security engineers or even more specific cyber security engineers; the culture of dressing, in some specific countries; and the culture of trusting and bargaining cultural habits and expectations in the communication process. The non-education-based culture differs between countries, religious and political groups, and law frameworks.

Networks' rules and best practices are often created by a fairly culturally uniform subgroup; a broader cultural view could help to overcome unwanted consequences, such as alienation and misunderstandings. The consideration of noneducation culture must be decided on for each situation, whether to honor differences or not. If some experts feel their culture not sufficiently respected, they can accept better if the process is *transparent*, and they feel oneself anyway as a member of the group. There is no need to understand each little element of all cultures: just a few important ones—relevant for the network communication—makes the difference.

An important cultural difference to consider is clarity in messages, rules, and structure. In some cultures, the roles are traditionally well defined, while in others they are made up as they go. As an example, if the members just expect per default a *leader role* in a network, they expect also a behavioral set of leader qualities and leader responsibilities. If this set does not meet these member's expectations, they might perceive the situation as chaotic and probably have the wish of withdrawing their membership. Therefore, the reactions are different and may include disappointment, confusion, and deeming the leader incompetent for not fulfilling what they expect to be the leader's duties.

Some cultures are individualistic, and some are more collectivistic, where the collectivistic ones are more group aware, with a high degree of mutual assurance and perceived stability [7]. Examples for collectivistic cultures are family clans (smaller groups), and for large groups, it could be the collectivistic part of a nation's culture. The type of culture (individualistic or collectivistic) naturally affects trust. Collectivistic cultures are more skeptical to strangers from a foreign culture, compared to the individualistic ones. On the other hand, the former are more trusting to strangers within their own culture than are the latter [8].

If possible, the best approach would be to accommodate the culture that most easily finds a situation offensive. Most cultures are more skeptical to outsiders, some more than others. If possible, when dealing with new network members or negotiating with external parties, it is convenient that someone from a similar culture takes care of the negotiating issue or the membership discussions, so that the process could be smoothened out.

A variety of elements may be valued as important in a negotiator or communicator, like his or her education, work position, or gender. In the interaction with this person, it is impossible to account for and accommodate with all these features at the same time. One might want to focus on the culture, as much as possible, when negotiating or discussing on their turf. However, if the network is multinational and multicultural, one must consider the work within the network to be as neutral as possible. Even if it sounds a little bit ridiculous, one should respect clothing or symbols of cultural (including religious) belongings, without attempting to create regulation. This type of open-minded and respectful culture will automatically lower conflicts.

Overgeneralization of cultural or national issues is unfortunate, and it can be perceived as offensive and prejudicial. Stating that a whole country is attacking some facility not only is incorrect but brings people from the *accused* country on the defensive. These details are important to make multinational communication more constructive. People tend to forget or ignore national pride before making statements that may be perceived as accusations.

Problematic situations such as countrywide distrust, or disturbances, should be addressed. There are cultural variations in political loyalty, but this has to be considered at membership acceptance. A change in trust situation along common network activities could happen due to particular political moment. A sudden change in government could lead to doubts, whether the trust network member was compromised or in some way forced. This should be cleared up as quickly as possible. There might be a need for a (possible temporary) suspension of the member, or conversely there may be a need for the network to reach out support for the fellow member. The teams in the multinational networks are often concerned and look after each other, offering their help, in the event of political unrest or natural catastrophes, for instance, the Arab Spring and the earthquake/tsunami in Japan. Conversely, local teams often volunteer providing information to keep the trust network updated.

The language barrier is a big challenge, not only intercontinent but also intracontinent. It is important that information is kept in a fairly easily accessible language, for example, having active instead of passive form of a sentence and using shorter periods and simpler language. *Simpler language* does not mean less technical; on the contrary, it must be at the appropriate technical level for the group in question. The language barriers in groups of limited size are smaller, as the participants are likely to be at similar technical level, and the group consists of fewer nationalities. Bringing up the language barrier explicitly can be controversial, as admitting lack of knowledge of languages can both be subjective and a question of honor.

All cultures have a fear of reputation loss, but some more than others. Fear of reputation loss can be a barrier in several settings: a member might be afraid to share data from break-ins, since the organization may appear inadequately secured. Or the member may be afraid that the shared information looks uninteresting, or wrongly interpreted, so that the organization appears to be ignorant. Such issues are not really a national cultural barrier, but rather a matter of trust network culture, and must be addressed as a part of the network governance. In any interaction, there is always the possibility that the counterpart is more knowledgeable, so there is no reason to be ashamed. On the contrary, one should embrace the advantages of being exposed to extra expertise reasoning, and even if the data may be trivial to some, this should not constitute a problem if the intentions behind sharing are good. The natural feeling of shame, when confessing an incident, must be overcome. There are two arguments to overcome this potential shame: first, there are other organizations that suffer worse incidents (this gives the sharing party the feeling of being less stupid than others and reduces therefore the feeling of shame), and, second, the other members usually respect the case, especially when they learn the lessons identified by the case. Naturally, experts presenting a case gain profile and authority. However, experts tend to talk (chat) more favorably about each other (socializing and getting trust to each other) than the work of information sharing would need. Furthermore, experts learned that the actual value of the shared information can truly be assessed locally only and ex posterior. This means that chatting and sharing very seldom lead to loss of reputation. Important exceptions are sharing of somebody else's information or sharing information of an inappropriately high sensitivity level. With an increased transparency in all processes of the network, these problems could be counterfought.

One is always more skeptical toward people that are different from oneself, especially nowadays, where nationalism is on the rise in many countries [9,10]. These are barriers, but they can be mitigated by promoting and sustaining a sharing culture. All experiences show that trust and information sharing increase with activity level. Some cultures feel more comfortable having rules and regulations and show stronger faith in institutions. To accommodate a sustaining sharing culture for both interacting parties and to implement a solid foundation for trusted information sharing, a sound technical framework, transparent processes, and clear and consistent rules of engagement are highly desirable or even necessary. The chosen framework should be appropriate for the network type, in complexity and form.

2.6 Temporal Dynamics

Any trust network must face a number of situations and accommodate its performance during its life. A number of cases are discussed hereafter with some detail.

2.6.1 Activity Level

Activity in a trust network is important. The network needs to continuously acquire full information about the dynamics of its member's teams. Each team should be functional and governed as safely as it was at the time of its association; no exchange of trusted members took place without notifying the network; the contact remained unchanged and so on. If a member is active, this kind of information is naturally updated, as the member is reminded to check team/member information. Sharing information keeps up reassurances about the individual member's benevolence, which is imperative in the calculation of risk before making a shared decision. Conversely, the one that participates silently begins to lose trustworthiness, until there is no real trust left.

The sensitivity level of data shared must be adjusted to the network: everybody shares at the level that was established for the considered particular network. There is a fine line between sharing too much and too little. If information is shared just to look active and the data are essentially worthless (old, not interesting, etc.), the other members would conclude that this happening is an attempt to receive information without disclosing anything; it follows that this sharing behavior is counterproductive. On the other hand, if the sensitivity level of the shared information is unnaturally high, this results in a negative impact on the trust level in the network. The reason is that this unnatural behavior of the member is perceived as lacking experience in the sharing business, which again leaves doubt within the individual team, whether their shared data would be treated appropriately.

If a network member is to share with members that have not yet shared anything, they can insist on mutual sharing, halting the process until the information flows bilaterally. Conversely, they can be "the bigger person," to seek to avoid a "standoff" (the prisoner's dilemma).

The process of judging other member's trustworthiness is a combination of evaluating the expected behavior and activity from these members. The process of judging starts with assurance and vetting to finally reach a critical point where people feel comfortable sharing information. Approaching this final situation may take some time but can certainly be reached faster if the new member shares, too, and is otherwise an active part of the network. Figure 2.9 graphically shows the positive and encouraging feedback loop, at time of well functioning of the network: trust stimulates information sharing, which produces increased network well functioning (capability) and spreads out improved reputation; this is again an enabler for more trust. This chain of facts is called *positive trust feedback loop*.

2.6.2 Incident Handling

Several past incidents, which have been handled internationally, support the necessity and convenience of good information sharing. Both the attacks on Estonian[*] Government and later on the Georgian[†] one strongly validate the earlier statement. The existing information sharing via channels and networks enabled efficient information sharing about malware, as well as attacking hosts and networks.

---

[*] http://en.wikipedia.org/wiki/2007_cyberattacks_on_Estonia
[†] http://en.wikipedia.org/wiki/Cyberattacks_during_the_2008_South_Ossetia_war

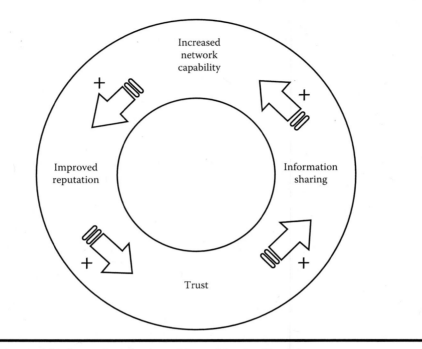

Figure 2.9 Trust and information sharing with positive feedback loop.

Information sharing and international collaboration has also been invaluable in the resolution of several computational GRID-related incidents. The nature of computational GRID (large collection of decentralized computer resource collaborating to perform computation intense tasks), renders it more vulnerable to attackers, as the GRID is only as secure as the least secure participating facility. The fact of least secure facility and vast computing resources defines the GRID as an attractive target. However, the information sharing between the participating facilities significantly improves the detection rate and enables proactive securing of sites. The recovery time from detection to resolution can decrease from weeks to days if the communication channels and the trust level enable information sharing.

Example: an investigation of the break-ins in several European institutions—led by the Dutch National Cyber Police in the worldwide network of experts—ended happily with the arrest of a perpetrator in the Netherlands on March 2012. However, a strong collaboration with Australia was necessary, and an interim arrest happened in Australia. These arrests were enabled by the trust and informal cooperation by worldwide partners.

Paradoxically, not only does trust enable information sharing, but this sharing fosters trust. There is an initial perception of the trustworthiness of the other party, but after a close cooperation, these expectations are either confirmed or refuted. Hence, future collaboration attempts result at a much lower cost in terms of collaboration strategies; the only important aspect left would be the mutual authentication.

2.6.3 Training Exercises

Apart from encouraging members to share information, exercises bring some information into the network veins. Real incident handling is the best way to test the network functionality, but waiting for real incidents is suboptimal; one should ideally be trained before incidents hit. Also, incidents include a random part of the network, and statistically the attack rate in the network is not uniform, as well as its knowledge distribution. An exercise can be tailored to show a variety of scenarios and knowledge centers, allowing everyone to contribute. The efficiency of exercises is debatable. First of all, it takes much work, and collecting detailed information about possible scenarios, to design a realistic exercise. Then, perhaps the most important challenge is rendering the participants aware of the value of the exercise. In principle, this is the responsibility of all the representatives in the network, but if the whole member teams should be involved, reaching a common understanding of the importance of the exercise is the responsibility of the team leader. It is all a waste of time if some parties go through the exercise with an attitude of nonchalance and superiority. Not only do they not follow the defense procedures, thus loosing the training to face a real incident, but also the other participating members do not learn anything about their capabilities. In addition, this kind of attitude spreads quickly: *it is only an exercise.*

When people are asked about the efficacy of an exercise, their judgment is based not only on their experience but also on the comments from trusted colleagues: if the samples are few, the result can be somewhat random. If the ones asked are also the same organizing the exercise, it would be difficult not to be biased, and if the participants are being judged on the exercise, it may be difficult not to become defensive. Exercises, if successful, create an increased data flow in the network and provide to the participants, at some extent, a clearer view of the abilities, goodwill, and methods of response of the other members, thus promoting the team building. Exercises are also suitable for testing with virtual crisis scenario (created for exercising purposes), the crises team setup (i.e., the crisis team's organization), and the defined operational rules applied during crises.

2.7 Building Trust Networks for the Future

All community members agree that sharing security information, and in particular security incident information, is essential to increase preparedness and to battle cyber crime. However, the decision of with whom to share is complex. The key element is trust, and—as stated before—trust cannot be forced or commanded.

The trust decision does not become less complex when we want to share it with many members in a trust network. When the network grows larger, neither sufficient direct, experience-based trust nor short-chained transitive trust will be present to trigger positive sharing decisions. Network participants seem to favor smaller WG surrounding a larger network, keeping the trust level high in the smaller WG. A small-group support for a hierarchical structure could also be a way to improve vertical communication, since this can be a problem area. An important factor is that the groups need clear goals and milestones and may need support in the form of technical frameworks, secretarial services, etc., which should be provided by the larger network, especially if the smaller network is expected to produce something of value to the community. The trust level could and should be kept at a high level in all involved networks, but the type of trust, hence the shared information, becomes context dependent.

The important thing when creating or revising a network would be to prepare for a large-size network, to agree on the purpose of the network, and to take appropriate measures to support the growth. This could consist of analyzing the dynamics, creating supporting trust structures within, or surrounding (socializing, common fun activity) the network, as well as setting up mechanisms and activities to enhance trust. The need for vetting and face-to-face meetings in the "mainframe" network is still important. First of all, a certain trust level should be assured in order to make participants willing to contribute in any way to the network development. Furthermore, in a crisis where immediate collaboration is required, the members are likely to take a slightly higher risk, letting transitive trust be sufficient for even deep-level information sharing: you need to trust someone purely on recommendation, and this is easier to accomplish if the parties have already met before, even though just briefly.

However, irrespective of the capabilities of a trust network leader and its members, the mutual trust is essential prerequisite and differentiator of these network types. The trust level itself is dynamic, which is an important aspect to take into consideration. The trust level in a group can be disrupted by a breach of confidence or by a simple thing like an individual's change of employment situation or a new person being brought into the group. Trust level in a group may change for a variety of reasons, and some fluctuations must be acceptable, especially in a backbone network. If these fluctuations are acknowledged rather than ignored, the trust level can—to some extent—be rendered predictable, which is a key element in trust decision making. It is important to prepare for the inevitable trust fluctuations caused by new members, breaches of confidence, etc.

Compliance to guidelines, rules, and regulations presumes that network members know their rules; therefore, educating network members in the governing guidelines, rules, and regulations is imperative to avoid breaches caused by mistakes. Members cannot avoid pitfalls if it is not clear what should be avoided and how to implement it.

Clear statements about the policy for breaches of confidence should be present. In the case of a breach, the gravity of the incident should be established according to the data owner. An explanatory meeting with the parties and a mediator could clarify the circumstances. When the matter is resolved, the network should be informed to avoid rumors. It is important to examine the reason for the breach, as it might be a symptom of something else.

A vital component in a network is its activity, and steps should be required to govern the activity level to some extent in order to avoid a dwindling of the trust level. The members are the only ones who can create activity, but a framework of support with meetings and exercises could be created to ensure a sustained level. The effect of social events in trust network meetings is of paramount relevance. Exercises are useful to verify that the information-sharing framework is understood and functioning, to be assured that teams have exchanged current keys, or simply to see that teams actually respond on the given contact addresses. Another important aspect of exercises is the building of the virtual team to give an idea of what the virtual incident response work would be like as well as to create a sense of togetherness. Nothing builds a team like to operate on a real incident, but also some appropriate exercise is a good tool, along the line to create the framework for the virtual team to be prepared for incidents.

A culture of giving feedback should be nurtured, as feedback promotes initiative. Nothing is as uninspiring as total silence after posing a question. Even content of little informational level should receive feedback. The sharing ones need feedback to be encouraged to share more, whereas the ones who have not shared yet need stimulation to overcome anxiety to share because they could feel violated, inferior, or unprofessional while sharing.

If a certain activity level is expected, it should be clearly stated, providing appropriate guidelines for activity level and meeting attendance. The variation of the desired activity level may be huge: from contributing one email per month up to define mandatory numbers of yearly meeting attendance (e.g., visiting 75% of the scheduled meetings). One must consider the members' economic situation and proximity to the meetings before demanding attendance. A simple thing like setting up a meeting schedule well in advance can help keep costs down and promote predictability.

The organizational form of a trusted group might be, for instance, *association*. However, it should be up-front well defined, which types of members (individual, institutional, etc.) are foreseen, and what are their membership fees. If there is a reason to include members who need financial assistance to participate, seeking solutions like having a common funding arrangement, or finding sponsors should be well organized.

Cultural diversities should be addressed if there is a desire to keep networks multinational. Political correctness can be a threat to trust in this context, in the sense that relevant cultural differences are ignored. Involving members from multiple cultures to form the network, for instance, inviting them to write, or revise guidelines, striving to focus on common visions and individual assets, would ensure—in spite of a certain level of diversity—a productive and united network, hence a trustful network. It is important to create an environment that does not alienate anyone, limit the perceived differences, and work together toward a common vision and common goals. This may be easier if the creation or revision process is done by a multinational set of experts. It can ensure that appropriate respect for cultural differences is adhered to. Anything from avoiding enforcing insensitive dietary decisions to ignore time zone differences, when setting up online or telephone meetings and similar apparently marginal issues, should be avoided.

We recognize that trust is the vital component in these networks, and the support of a framework for communication and information sharing is important. As a matter of fact, this and unambiguous rules and guidelines support the growth of trust in a cultural diverse network and prevent potential problems with conflict of interest. It is important to make sure that the rules and regulation function are implemented as a support for the trust network and not as a straitjacket, in which case these would become an inhibitor of information sharing and hence trust.

A network should have clear acceptance rules, including the vetting ones. Potential members should be strongly encouraged to be frank about what they believe to bring to the table, as information, knowledge, and experience. Tabs should be kept on members to make sure they have not interchanged personnel, whether all members still have other member's willingness to vet them and whether they still deliver the same services. This could easily be set up with an ongoing vetting process, making sure no member is left without support or some degree of supervision. The vetting process may very well be transparent and open and visible to the network members, in some cases also to external persons, for justification of the seriousness of the network.

Rules and expectations for activity level and visibility in a network should also be clearly stated. This can be anything from requirements for visibility on an email list to a demand for meeting participation, the latter being more complicated, as discussed earlier, taking the variance in global economy into account. The rules for breaches of confidence should be clearly stated, but the information owner is always the one who can judge the real seriousness of the breach.

There are a number of benefits by setting up clear written rules from the beginning, as (but not limited to) the following ones:

■ Avoiding the possibility of breaking domestic laws
■ Eliminating difficult situations where members would be forced to break their domestic laws
■ Controlling misunderstandings, breaches, and repercussions due to cultural, religious, or other personality backgrounds
■ Decreasing the likelihood of disputes
■ Better understanding of their own and other members' needs

As a consequence, it is expected that the following results are met:

■ Likely increase of the system trust, which again works as a support for personal trust
■ Trust increase and respect by other similar communities in the network performance
■ Improved data protection for the individual member
■ Likely increased data sharing and other activity level
■ Ultimately, increased trust level between members

For each type of network, one has to identify a suitable governance model and a method of obtaining leaders. These could be appointed via a regular voting process or by implementing another nominating scheme, for instance, per country or per industry. Should rotating leadership be implemented, then define frequency of leadership change, nomination procedure of leaders and other practicalities. Some national cultures are hierarchically oriented, and others more individualistic. This would lead to complications in choosing a good governance model to cater all needs, but it can be done by either creating a hierarchical model with a good support network to ensure good information flow in the network, or defining a mesh network with good role descriptions to remove insecurity in the leadership, or governing roles.

Many of the elements that are perceived as barriers of information sharing are actually lack of trust. For instance, *fear of leaks* would not even be present if the members trusted each other. Other perceived barriers, like *group size* or *type of participants*, are dependent on management, that is, how the network is defined, regulated, and governed.

2.8 Measures to Make Trust Networks Well Functioning

Years of experience have shown stereotypical pattern of barriers (obstacles) in information sharing in the frame of a trust network. These barriers have been presented and discussed in the previous sections of this chapter.

An overview on the barriers in information sharing and recommend techniques in running the network (governance) is depicted in a condensed form under Table 2.1. From Table 2.1 the issues less deeply treated in the earlier sections are better explained:

■ National laws may contradict each other in a way that some actions of trust networks could lead to compliance violations. Such situations let the participant feel bad and discourage the information sharing. By addressing all potential issues and agreeing on the way to handle it, the participants get security and allow freedom to share.
■ Lack of information sharing is killing the network's purpose. As earlier written, the activity of the network is the health indicator. Oversized network can be split into subgroups to reactivate participants in a trustful and more homogeneous group, where sharing feels more natural.
■ The quality of shared information is too low or questionable. This is a delicate situation to be addressed because the feelings of the sharing experts might be hurt, and then all sharing will stop as other participants will not like to be in a comparable situation. By creating frameworks, using tools and education, the issue can be addressed on a general and "not personal" level.

Table 2.1 Trust and Governance: Barriers and Supporting Measures

Barriers in Information Sharing	Governance Measures
Contradicting national laws	Identify all the potentially interfering laws, and make agreements around this for trustworthy handling of confidential information
Insecurity in trust issues in larger networks	Strong and transparent vetting process, define smaller subgroups, for example, *SIG* for deeper trust—when appropriate
Oversized network resulting in lack of information sharing	Delegate responsibility to subgroups (hubs) of fine-tuned size to the task to be performed
Questionable information quality	Identifying other areas of information to share, for example, tools and educational frameworks
Administrative overhead	Create smaller WG, so that people of the same technological and administrative level can directly cooperate
Insecurity in network policy and rules	Have an internationally diverse committee, identifying shortcomings and confusion in the network rules and practices; reconfirm the rule set; and educate members
Breaches of trust: fear of promiscuous information sharing	Have clear rules with stated repercussions, and govern the process of resolving the breaches
Cultural barriers	Promote *culture of respect*, clearly identify barriers, and address these with best practices
Language barriers	Identify problem level, promote a culture of simplification and tolerance of language, and create awareness on the issue
Variance in members' funding	Explore possibilities of sponsorships, virtual meetings, cooperation within geographical regions, changing of meeting locations, etc. Important: bring the discussion on the table!

- Technician never loves administration! In small teams, the administrative share is lower, and experts restart to work.
- Insecurity in network policy and rules: obviously, when members are changing and memories of rules are decaying, then it is time to check on rules and reconfirm. As precaution, an international committee can periodically (e.g., each year) verify and recap on rules.

2.9 Conclusions

The key issues considered in the previous sections of this chapter are summarized hereafter and briefly commented.

CN (Connected Networks, e.g., Internet) needs strong security because it is now diffused over the everyday life of citizens, being also an integrative part of nearly all CIs.

Most of the effort in securing networks is in the hands of IT staff running the daily operation. In case of need, there is usually a second-level support and/or a related Computer Emergency Response Team (CERT). Most failure and attacks may be resolved on site. Two approaches are recommended to resolve remaining issues:

1. CERT, which runs on technical and operational level and supports forensics investigation with the police.
2. Information Sharing and Analysis Centers (ISACs), which have the primary target of strategic information exchanges on risks, threats, and attacks. Participants in ISACs are usually working in higher hierarchical layers and care for strategic security and impact management, within those critical sectors, which may be affected by reduced or no service.

Both CERT and ISAC are trust networks, where sharing experts need a feeling of security and benevolence to overcome the real and justified fear of misusing the shared information by others. The agony of selecting between exposing oneself in a risky situation and "not exposing" because of fear has been successfully analyzed and modeled. Interviews with key experts running such networks, and some experience of the authors, lead to identification of the barriers—no matter whether those are in initiating phase, in operational phase, or in dynamic situations—as well as proven concepts of countermeasures, overcoming fear in finding or refinding trust to the sharing partners.

Major issues are

■ Perceiving others and trust: "Interpersonal relationships begin with the perception of others" [11]. From initiating relationship, trust is built one step at a time, which is for both general personal contacts and contacts in trust networks.

■ Activity (information sharing and socialization) is trust building: Promoting socialization and information sharing in trust networks enforces intermember links and increases trust network robustness, so that confidence develops to plentiful level, and trust bandwidth as well as tolerance against failures grows [12]. As trust bandwidth increases, information sharing is supported by a positive feedback loop.

■ Governance for managing trust variation over time: Fluctuations in trust level and variation of trust bandwidth are justifiable concerns, which can be alleviated by conscious trust governance. A crystal clear governance regime would also help the trust level to overcome potential barriers, such as culture and different educational background.

■ Transparency of trust level and rules is key to success: Each network should identify the expected trust and information-sharing levels to be as close to reality as possible in order to create predictability—as this is a key ingredient in risk assessment—and hence the principal fundament of trust. The decision to share or not is binary. But foundations for the trust decision are far more complex, based on rational, intuitive, and emotional components, interacting in the individual in a not totally predictable fashion.

■ Multiple network membership and national sector networks: Different networks have different characteristics, and for participation, membership, and activity in more than one network, experts must be very aware of differences in network culture. Additionally, joining national sector-specific network is a desirable goal to leverage impact.

References

1. Zucker, L. G., Production of trust: Institutional sources of economic structure, *Research in Organizational Behavior*, 8, 1986, 53–111.
2. Doney, P. M., Cannon, J. P., and Mullen, M. R., Understanding the influence of national culture on the development of trust, *The Academy of Management Review*, 23(3), 1998, 601–620.
3. Jøsang, A., Hayward, R., and Pope, S., Trust network analysis with subjective logic, *Proceedings of the 29th Australasian Computer Science Conference*, Hobart, Tasmania, Vol. 48, 2006, pp. 85–94.
4. Cosimano, T. F., Financial institutions and trustworthy behavior in business transactions, *Journal of Business Ethics*, 52(2), 2004, 179–188.
5. Kimble, C., Barlow, A., Li, F., Effective virtual teams through communities of practice, Strathclyde Business School Management Science Working Paper, No. 2000/9.
6. Editors of the CYBEX Correspondence Group, CYBEX, 2010, Draft recommendation itu-t x.1500: Cyber security information exchange framework, study group 17, Telecommunication Standardization Sector.
7. Kramer, R. M., Trust and distrust in organizations: Emerging perspectives, enduring questions, *Annual Review of Psychology*, 50, 1999, 569–598.
8. Yuki, M., Maddux, W. W., Brewer, M. B., and Takemura, K., Cross-cultural differences in relationship- and group-based trust, *Personality and Social Psychology Bulletin*, 31(1), 2005, 48–62.
9. Schmidt, V., The unfinished architecture of Europe's economic union, *Governance*, 23(4), 2010, 555–559.
10. Rosecrance, R., Capitalist influences and peace, *International Interactions: Empirical and Theoretical Research in International Relations*, 36(2), 2010, 192–198.
11. Shaw, M. E., Group dynamics, *Annual Review of Psychology*, 12, 1961, 129–156.
12. Rosseau, D. M., Sitkin, S. B., Burt, R. S., and Camerer, C., Not so different after all: A cross-discipline view of trust, *The Academy of Management Review*, 23(3), 1998, 393–404.

Chapter 3

Art of Balancing Utilities: Privacy and Video Surveillance in Sweden

Fredrika Björklund

Contents

Video surveillance of public spaces is a feature of modern societies that has expanded rapidly during the last decades. This chapter concerns the expansion of video surveillance in Sweden and the comparatively weak opposition to this activity. In some national contexts, for example, Germany (Hempel and Töpfer 2004), video surveillance has been quite contested, both by the public and by privacy protection commissioners. In Sweden, however, concern for video surveillance as violation of privacy has been rather limited. Public video surveillance continues to expand without causing much contestation. In this chapter, it is suggested that the weak attention to privacy has its roots in a utilitarian approach both to this notion and to monitoring as such. Thus, in general terms, the study illustrates the rationale behind this kind of approach to video surveillance.

Certainly, a proper regard for privacy is demanded from Swedish legislators and policymakers when legal acts involving extended surveillance are proposed and/or such policies initiated. In Sweden as elsewhere, there is a conflict of social values involved in technical supervision.

In democracies, public authorities and politicians concerned with this policy field must pay attention to them. Therefore, the academic literature often tends to approach the social and moral aspects of technological surveillance as globally uniform issues, and while this is partially true, it is not exclusively so. This study shows that the values and value conflicts involved in public surveillance look different in different national contexts (Raab 1999: 68; Bennett and Raab 2006: 6). For example, this is true as regards the conflict between claims about privacy and the quest for security and crime prevention. I will argue that the Swedish approach can be described as extremely consequentialist; Swedish authorities' characterization of the task can be summarized as one of balancing equivalent *utilities*. Accordingly, the rights perspective, that is, privacy defined as a right, which is the common and internationally accepted way to comprehend the notion of privacy, is neglected. Ultimately, the Swedish approach has significance for how the relationship between the state and the citizen is understood. It is characteristic of a protecting state, that is, a manifestation of a strong welfare state legacy. The close relationship between the political and judicial "discourses" signifies a value consensus that benefits the Swedish model, possibly to the detriment of an unbiased debate.

The focus of this chapter is public video surveillance in Sweden and the way in which privacy is attended to and weighed against other values in legal documents, policy documents, and parliamentary debates. A critical idea analysis is used to substantiate the claims. Where applicable, references are made to other national contexts and international documents.

Why should we pay special attention to the Swedish case? While technology itself, for example, surveillance technology, is not culturally or socially sensitive, the application of it is. The introduction of surveillance techniques may create tensions in social and legal practices. These tensions and the efforts to resolve them are often nationally specific. On the one hand, the consequentialist—or utilitarian—approach is fairly well established internationally as one way to handle conflicts between privacy and demands for new surveillance technologies that threaten to intrude on it. Weighing the pros and cons is a common and often-used approach. On the other hand, Sweden is an exceptional case due to its very consistent reliance on a utilitarian course of action. This contrasts with the traditional liberal individualist approach to privacy issues, which in this chapter is exemplified by Poland, and with the more collectively oriented approach, which is represented by Germany. Thus, if we are interested in the social and legal aspects of surveillance, there is something to learn from the Swedish case.

3.1 Privacy and Surveillance Studies

Why does privacy matter as an issue of academic interest? There is no doubt that concerns about privacy define a well-established and productive research area (Bennett and Grant 1999; Bennett and Raab 2006; Rule 2007; Nissenbaum 2009). Nonetheless, devoting academic interest to this concept is not an uncontested issue. Over the past 10 years, the scholarly field that takes privacy and privacy protection as a platform for the study of surveillance has been subjected to a good deal of criticism (Bennett 2011). Although it should not be exaggerated, some kind of antagonism has developed between scholars who assert the significance of privacy and the academic field that is referred to as surveillance studies (Bennett and Raab 2006: 22). It is argued that the notion of privacy is too vague (Stadler 2002), narrow, legalistic, and hyper-individualistic (Gilliom 2011) to serve as an intellectual tool for analyzing the implications of surveillance. In particular, critics claim that the notion of privacy fails to grasp one very fundamental feature of surveillance, that is, the practice of exclusion. Privacy ignores the fact that surveillance is an instrument of control primarily directed toward groups traditionally equipped with limited social resources. Thus, it is argued that surveillance should be analyzed as a matter of social sorting (Norris and Armstrong 1999; Lyon 2003; Gandy 2006) rather than as a menace that affects all people equally and in the same way.

Hence, it has been suggested that the concern for privacy is based on an academic legacy of traditional liberal values that is heavily normatively charged. Within this tradition, privacy represents nothing more than the individual control of a personal space that may not be interfered with in the name of some social good (Stadler 2002). Thus, it is argued that a concern for privacy is exclusively in the interest of established social elites, that is, those in society who have the most to gain from public noninterference. But, although it is correct that studies focused on privacy often have a normative point of departure, this does not mean that privacy must be defined solely as a traditional negative liberal freedom. During the last decades, the field of privacy studies has expanded to also include contextual and social aspects of privacy (Regan 1995; Nissenbaum, 2009). In addition, private versus public is still a distinction frequently referred to in contemporary public debates (Vogel and Passerin d'Entrèves 2001; Gallagher 2004). Privacy is something that concerns politicians, and it is a matter of public policy (Bennett 2011: 488). It is an important concept in both national and international discourses, which means that it is a value of great political, and academic, significance. The academic literature includes a number of policy-focused studies on the regulation of privacy, and international efforts in this field have generated special interest (Flaherty 1989; Bennett 1992; Newman 2008; Rule and Greenleaf 2008; Goold and Neyland 2009). Despite this, privacy as national discursive marker is an understudied aspect of surveillance. A deeper knowledge about how privacy is conceptualized may tell us important things about the social control mechanisms within a society. That is, empirical studies on approaches to privacy reveal something about the relationship between the state and the citizens.

3.2 Rise of Video Surveillance in Sweden

Sweden is one of the camera densest countries in the world. Video surveillance has been used since the Second World War, but initially it was exclusively used by the security police to detect possible threats to state security. In the 1970s, video surveillance emerged on the political agenda as an instrument of general crime prevention, but at the time, it was primarily used by financial institutes and within the banking sector. It was not until the beginning of the twenty-first century that the massive expansion of technological supervision began. Certainly, the World Trade Center attacks in 2001 and subsequent acts of international terrorism motivated efforts to find effective measures to combat such threats in all countries, Sweden included. But it was not as a means to fight terrorism that video surveillance became so prevalent in Sweden. A more important justification was monitoring public space in order to protect law and order in general. Public spaces such as public transportation, stores, and shopping malls were increasingly equipped with video cameras. Sometime later, cameras also increasingly appeared in schools, taxicabs, and public squares. The quest for surveillance was usually pursued by private or local initiatives rather than state authorities. However, because the latter often benefited from the actions of the former, increased surveillance was also in the interest of the state, in particular the police and legal system.

Despite a massive deployment of cameras in Sweden, video surveillance has never been a hot issue in public debate. Rather, debate during the last 10 years has been rather modest, both on the Internet and in more traditional mass media channels, and there is no civil society organization with video surveillance high on its agenda. In newspapers, journalistic interest is mostly limited to reporting about specific incidents, for example, when cameras are deployed in new areas or when there is technological progress in surveillance techniques. Reporting rarely takes a critical perspective. In the political arena, one might have expected that the recently established Pirate party (Piratpartiet), which has had seats in the European parliament on Swedish mandates since 2009, would have put criticism of technical visual supervision high on its political agenda. The party set itself up as a kind of interest organization focused on matters related to the free use of Internet sources. It subsequently broadened its focus to include general issues of privacy protection, but video surveillance does not seem to be a priority issue. Nor has the issue of public video surveillance inspired Internet activity of the kind that occurred in 2008 in connection with the introduction of a controversial act on phone tapping (the so-called FRA act).

The general public seems to be quite content with the new "security-reinforcing" measures of monitoring. Public opinion is largely supportive of the use of technological surveillance to monitor public places. In a survey conducted by researchers at Gothenburg University in 2008, 61% of respondents said that video surveillance of public places should always be allowed. This is an increase from 2002, when 47% supported video surveillance (Bjereld and Demker 2009). It is interesting to note that opinions about video surveillance deviate from opinions on other measures that potentially violate privacy. As regards the latter, the public seems to be more skeptical. In sum, the attitude to video surveillance in Sweden can be characterized as somewhat disinterested and, in general, fairly favorable.

3.3 Legal Regulation of Public Video Surveillance

While Sweden has invested quite heavily in video surveillance, it is also ahead of most countries in legally regulating the field. Thus, Sweden has a specific legal act covering video surveillance. However, this does not automatically mean that the legal instruments in the act are particularly restrictive about when and where video surveillance is permitted. Somewhat paradoxically, it seems as if the readiness to legally regulate goes hand in hand with the introduction of video surveillance in new social contexts, that is, the law to a large extent confirms an already ongoing development rather than slowing down or restricting it.

The Act on Public Video Surveillance (Lagen om allmän kameraövervakning 1998:150) came into force in 1998 and replaced the 1990 legislation on video surveillance cameras (Lagen om övervakningskameror m. m. 1990:484). However, the first legal act dates back to 1977 and addressed the monitoring of television (Lagen om TV övervakning 1977:20). Technological progress in the field and its possible implications for violations of privacy led to the revision of the first act (Government bill 1989/90:119). An examination of the written documentation that constitutes the preparatory work for both the first and second legal acts reveals that there was genuine skepticism about the implications of the new technology. The risk of misuse was thoroughly discussed, but ideas about possible applications of the new technique were rather vague. In the preparatory work that preceded the enactment of the present legislation, the word "public" was added to the name, and a new type of argument was introduced. According to the government bill proposing the law, the main intention was to regulate the use of video surveillance so that it could be used as an efficient instrument of crime prevention while also safeguarding privacy protection in a satisfactory way (Government bill 1997/98:64). Thus, with the 1998 revision, a positive end—crime prevention—was attributed to video surveillance, and its usefulness was regarded as a variable to be considered when evaluating requests for permission to use the technique.

The current legal act on public video surveillance says that surveillance of public spaces in Sweden is allowed if certain conditions are met. Normally, the installation of a surveillance camera requires authorization from the County Administrative Board (Länsstyrelsen). Public institutions and private companies that want to set up video surveillance apply for permission to do so. The main role of the county boards is to rule on the applications, that is, to license video camera monitoring. Under certain circumstances, for example, in banks and specified areas in stores, no permission is needed. In these cases, it is sufficient that the board is notified. There are also exceptions for police surveillance for specific purposes and for some other public authorities, for example, the National Road Administration. As a rule, where surveillance cameras are installed, there must be a sign informing people about them; however, there are also some exceptions to this requirement. A comparison of the three acts on video surveillance indicates that the list of exemptions from the requirement that the County Administrative Board must grant formal permission has grown gradually since 1977. In practice, permission increasingly tends to be given more or less automatically in the form of renewals of previous authorizations. Besides licensing, the 21 county administrations also oversee the observance of the law on video surveillance of public spaces.

The chancellor of justice (Justitiekanslern) may appeal decisions of the County Administrative Board in the Administrative Court in order to protect public interests. However, the results of doing so have been quite meager. One illustrative case from 2007 involved the chancellor of justice's appeal, in the Administrative Court of Appeals (Kammarrätten), of a verdict from the County Administrative Court (Länsrätten). The police had requested permission to install cameras in a number of public places and streets in central Stockholm that they argued were characterized by high rates of crime. The County Court approved the request. The chancellor of justice objected to the decision and therefore appealed it on the grounds that, in making its decision, the County Administrative Court had failed to properly consider the privacy (personal integrity) of individuals. The Administrative Court of Appeals dismissed the chancellor's argument. The case was eventually appealed to the Supreme Administrative Court (Regeringsrätten), but it was dismissed there as well. The court concluded that, in accordance with the information and reasoning contained in the preparatory work to the Act on Public Video Surveillance, licensing was to be less restrictive if its purpose was to prevent crimes and accidents (Regeringsrätten lawsuit no. 7873, 10-02-11).

Amendments to the current act on video surveillance have been continuously discussed since 1998. The government initiated an evaluation in 2001, which resulted in the Video Surveillance Report (SOU 2002:110). The report called for certain modifications of the law, for example, that victims of illegal video surveillance should be awarded compensation. Another suggestion concerned weakening the restraints on the authorization of police video surveillance and surveillance by storeowners. The proposals in the report did not lead to any revisions of the law, and in 2008, a new expert commission was appointed to look over the legislation. This committee's report, entitled *A New Video Surveillance Act*, was published in October 2009. It included proposals about fees for damages for unjustified violations of privacy, but also proposed prolonging the length of time that data from monitoring could be retained (SOU 2009:87).

The law on video surveillance of public spaces does not, in fact, cover all areas of technological monitoring of the public. The installation of cameras in what are referred to as semipublic spaces, for example, workplaces, living areas, and schools, is not regulated by the act. Instead, the Data Protection Act (Personuppgiftslagen 1998:204) is applicable, and the Swedish data protection authority, the Data Inspection Board (Datainspektionen), is the supervising authority. The Data Inspection Board may demand changes if it determines that filming constitutes an unjustified violation of privacy. However, video surveillance in this context is not strictly understood as a form of personal data registration. As long as the footage is what is known as "unstructured"—which it usually is— the legal demands are milder than those normally prescribed in the law. The decisions of the Data Inspection Board may be appealed in the Administrative Court.

One influential case worth mentioning concerns surveillance in schools. In 2008, the Data Inspection Board ruled that the Stockholm School Board had to ensure that all indoor video surveillance in one of the secondary schools in Stockholm was stopped. The Data Inspection Board argued that, given its stated purpose, which was to prevent theft and vandalism, video surveillance was not a proportional measure because the negative consequences for pupils' privacy were too great (Datainspektionen Dnr.742-2008). The school board appealed the decision to the County Administrative Court, but without success. It also lost a second appeal to the Administrative Court of Appeals.

Video surveillance is well regulated in Sweden, and the same is true for data protection in general. The first Swedish Data Protection Act (Datalagen 1973:289) is of early date. It originates from 1973 and was one of the first acts in the world dealing with the protection of privacy. In the late 1990s, the European Union Directive (95/46/EC) required all EU nations to set up data protection acts, so Sweden's was adapted to meet the demands of European coherence. In most countries, the national Data Protection Act is the main document for the regulation of video surveillance, although restrictions are also often found in other national legal documents. The Swedish Act on Public Video Surveillance may thus be regarded as a reinforcement of privacy protection for this specific field, a kind of protection that is rarely found elsewhere. Sweden thus has two legal acts applicable to video surveillance. In addition, the control function is shared between the Data Inspection Board, which takes action on the basis of the Data Protection Act, and the county administrative boards, which base their decisions on the Act on Public Video Surveillance.*

Nonetheless, in 2007, Privacy International ranked Sweden as second from the bottom among EU countries as regards attending to the privacy of its citizens, and nothing indicates that there have been any changes since then. In the national ranking, Sweden is categorized as a country with "systemic failures to uphold safeguards" (Privacy International 2007). Despite extensive legal regulation, privacy is still not satisfactorily protected. On the one hand, the Swedish state is committed to regulating. On the other hand, it nevertheless fails to substantially protect privacy in legal documents.

3.4 Crime Prevention

Why, in a European comparative perspective, is there weak concern for privacy in Sweden? Certainly, there is more than one possible explanation. One that seems plausible, however, is that there are other values at stake, ones that potentially conflict with attention to privacy and that are regarded as more important. The rival objective pursued with the use of video surveillance is the prevention of crime.

In the 1998 legal act and the preparatory work to it (Government bill 1997/98:64), crime prevention was identified as an explicit object of video surveillance for the first time. In other

---

* However, this is not obviously the most efficient organizational and legal structure, and it has been discussed and criticized from time to time. In fact, the 2009 report mentioned earlier suggested that the overall oversight function should be assigned to the Data Inspection Board in order to secure national uniformity in decisions.

words, from this point on legal regulation of the technique was a direct application of the politically expressed ambition to combat crime with specific instrument. The legal text says that, when deciding whether to grant permission to use video monitoring, particular attention should be paid to the question of whether surveillance is needed to prevent crime (6 §). The legislation seeks to limit the installation of cameras for all sorts of nonproductive reasons and to give county administrative boards clear guidelines on which to base decisions. Video monitoring should be reserved for very important social objectives such as crime reduction. At the same time, as a result of the act, the idea that video surveillance is an efficient measure to reduce crime is legally sanctioned. The intention behind legislation is to regulate and restrict; yet because of the way in which the main objectives of video monitoring are specified, the legal document actually legitimates increased video surveillance. Combating criminal offenses is a worthy cause that should not be dismissed. In fact, the political investment in video surveillance as an efficient means to increase crime prevention has been very great. Despite this, crime prevention is not a completely uncontested ambition in this context, and the reason for this has to do with efficiency—or, more correctly, lack of demonstrated efficiency.

Before discussing the political promotion of video surveillance as an efficient means of crime prevention, some comments about the concept of prevention are in order. Video surveillance is usually categorized as a type of situational prevention (Waples et al., 2009). The literature discriminates between situation-directed measures of prevention and socially directed ones (Garland 2000: 4; Fussey 2008: 129). The purpose of the latter type is to improve social conditions for people in the risk zone for criminality or to help former criminals return to a normal life. In contrast, the former type of prevention is directed at specific situations in which crimes are likely to be committed. These different types of prevention approach individuals, or rather prospective offenders, in different ways. Focusing on situations directs attention to opportunities available to individuals rather than on risk categories. Crime is assumed to be a rational choice based on a cost/benefit analysis by the potential offender. (Fussey 2008: 123). Theoretically, situational prevention does not discriminate between groups; every citizen is a possible offender, as well as a possible victim (Duff and Marshall 2000: 27). Naturally, this premise does not mean that every citizen is constantly of equal interest to the police. Nonetheless, situational prevention represents a view of man and society that, on the one hand, equalizes human beings—everybody could have shady intentions—and, on the other hand, expands the total magnitude of distrust (Lodge 2003; Goold 2009). Crimes will be committed unless the price, that is, the risk of detection, is too large. The chance of being detected by a camera adds to the cost side of the calculation; this is the significance of video monitoring. It is obvious from the Swedish discourse that this is the expectation associated with technological monitoring; criminality is defined as a rational activity (SOU 2002:110:98). An additional positive outcome of video surveillance that is sometimes mentioned is the possibility of identifying offenders after a crime has been committed. If the perpetrator is caught on video film, it makes the legal process easier. This argument is made in the Swedish public debate (Motion bill 2011/12:Ju 209 and 2011/12:M852) and also appears in official documents. However, while it has become more frequent, it has nonetheless been subordinated to the situational prevention argument (SOU 2009:87).

The term "public" in the Act on Public Video Surveillance clearly refers to situational prevention. In the same year that crime prevention was introduced as the primary aim of video surveillance, that is, 1998, the additional specification of "public" turned up in the legal discourse. When video surveillance was established as an important measure of crime prevention, its field of application was also generalized. "Public" in this context refers both to public as "the people" and to public as a spatial qualifier, that is, public places or, in legal terms, "places that the public has access to." At the time, video surveillance had certainly expanded into a public matter simply by virtue of its extension, but the term public also opened up the possibility of a general use of cameras for the purpose of maintaining social order.

Situational prevention directed toward the public is a perfect means of control in a neoliberal society. The neoliberal idea is to leave all moral deliberation to the rational atomistic individual who makes his or her choice in a market of different options in order to optimize his or her cost/benefit calculus. The state–citizen relationship in this context is not one of direct government, but rather indirect insofar as it operates by governing the preferences of the individual citizen (Björklund 2011). At the same time, this kind of indirect governance is not at odds with a protecting state such as Sweden's welfare state. With video surveillance, it distributes equal security to the citizens in a way that is in keeping with the traditional welfare state, but—it is argued—more efficiently than before. However, when the benefits of video surveillance are advertised in the Swedish discourse, the value of crime prevention, a clearly measurable utility, is emphasized over the notion of increased security.

In fact, however, both Swedish and international studies have called into doubt the merits of video surveillance in crime prevention (Brottsförebyggande rådet 2003, 2009; Welsh and Farrington 2007). The conclusion that is drawn is that video surveillance may work under certain specified circumstances, in specific locations such as parking places and places with a high level of criminality or against property crimes such as planned burglary. According to the Swedish Crime Prevention Board (Brottsförebyggande Rådet), video surveillance is not a universal panacea for reducing crime. It works best in combination with other measures (Brottsförbyggande Rådet 2009). Still, despite research on the topic, in the political arena, prevention has continued to be heavily emphasized as an argument for video surveillance (Justitiedepartementet 2008:22).* This is so regardless of the political orientation of the government, and it has been a widely accepted argument in the parliament during the past decade. Of course, it has not been possible to completely ignore the not-so-encouraging research results about video surveillance as a crime prevention measure. Nonetheless, the argument has persistently been used as the most important justification for surveillance. When facts spoke against the program, favorable evidence to the contrary was sometimes actively sought. Because video surveillance did not achieve the expected positive results, the public committee (SOU) appointed in 2001 was instructed to include in its report suggestions about *how* camera surveillance could be used effectively and strategically for crime preventive purposes (Justitiedepartementet 2001:53).

The preoccupation with video surveillance as crime prevention is important, but it does not fully explain the lack of attention to the risks of privacy violation. The weak attention to privacy in Sweden is due primarily to factors other than the simple assumption that values such as crime prevention or protection outrank privacy. How privacy is treated in the context of video surveillance has to do with more fundamental properties characterizing the values involved and the manner in which they are weighed against each other. It is here that ideas about privacy, its definition, and its urgency are set.

---

* See also the instructions regarding the evaluation of the Act on Public Video Surveillance from the Ministry of Justice (2001:53), Parliament protocol (2006/07:132), Parliament protocol (2006/07:1463), Parliament protocol (1997/98:86), Motion bill (2005/06:Ju275), Motion bill (1997/98:Ju21), and Motion bill (1997/98:Ju910). Certainly there have also been skeptical voices; see, for example, Parliament protocol (1997/98:86) and Motion bill (1997/98:Ju20).

3.5 Balance Metaphor

The Swedish approach to privacy is characterized by vagueness, a practice of primarily relating to privacy in contrast to something else—that is, to other values in an act of balancing and an unwillingness to define privacy as a right. Privacy turns out to be a loosely defined interest of an undefined subject.

In the Swedish discourse, privacy is seldom mentioned as a self-contained and independent concept. It appears almost exclusively as an additional and conflicting value when the objectives of video surveillance are discussed. Privacy is defined in relation to a competing goal that must be achieved. In the Act on Public Video Surveillance (§6), this relational conception of privacy is inscribed in the rules about granting permission to conduct surveillance: "The license granting permission to engage in public video surveillance must be issued if the value of such surveillance weighs heavier than the individual's interest in not being monitored" (author's translation).

In the legal vocabulary, this reasoning reflects the "the proportionality principle"—the surveillance measures must be proportional to the injuries inflicted on privacy. The act assumes a conflict between the gains from public surveillance and the individual's interest in not being filmed. These gains are specified later in the law text, which states that in assessing the benefits of surveillance, special attention should be paid to the need to prevent crimes and accidents. The interest of not being videotaped is not clearly specified. Despite the vague definition of privacy, the two goals are supposed to be balanced against each other in order to determine which one weighs heaviest in a specific case. The idea of a balancing act appears frequently in public reports and political debate, although the competing interests or goals may be expressed in slightly different ways.

The image of a balance that involves different *interests* is widely used both in documents prepared by the government and the Ministry of Justice and in parliamentary debate. (Justitiedepartementet 2001:53; 2008:22).* The government bill proposing the 1998 legislative act sketches a potential conflict between the interest of combating and investigating crime and the individual's interest in the protection of privacy. In public video surveillance, these two interests must always be balanced against each other (Government bill 1997/98:64). However, the balance is sometimes also expressed in terms of conflicting needs. Answering an interpellation about a proposed revision in the video surveillance law during a parliamentary debate in 2006, the minister of justice spoke about the need for efficient measures and individuals' contradictory need for protection of privacy (Parliament protocol 2006/07:132).

In the act of balancing, the value of privacy is constantly made relative to the benefits of video surveillance. The balance between the two is presented as an ongoing and case-dependent process that involves constant adjustment between the value of surveillance and the protection of the privacy of the individual. According to the minister of justice, this must be done on a case-by-case basis—which interest weighs heaviest cannot be established once and for all (Parliament protocol 2006/07:1463). While this opinion seems reasonable, too much relativism risks depriving privacy of every form of consistent protection. Temporary circumstances may instantly alter the balance.

The legal establishment, assumed to be a protector of the right to privacy, also embraces the idea of a balance. In an interview in November 2008, the chancellor of justice expressed disappointment in the ruling made by the Administrative Court of Appeal on police monitoring in the inner city of Stockholm. The chancellor stated that he had hoped that the court would have a different opinion about the balance between the interest of surveillance and the interest of privacy

---

* See also Parliamentary Standing Committee on the Administration of Justice (2006/07:JuU8) and Parliament protocol (1997/98:86).

(Tidningarnas Telegrambyrå 2008).* In general, when the chancellor of justice has initiated a legal process against the use of video surveillance, the main arguments used in the case have been based on the balance of interests. A feature of these processes is the effort to convert both the interest of surveillance and the interest of privacy into concrete measurable entities that make it possible to determine which one of them is most pressing.†

The chief inspector at the Data Inspection Board also subscribes to the balance principle. The fact that the chief inspector, unlike the government, is more skeptical to the entire issue of video monitoring seems to be of less importance. In a newspaper article in 2005, the chief inspector argued that video surveillance is an expansive field that involves privacy violation. The article offered no concrete suggestions about how to approach the issue; rather, a balancing of interests was referred to (Gräslund 2005). A doctrine of balancing interest has guided the activity of the Data Inspection Board ever since. In fact, Flaherty noticed as early as 1989 that the Swedish data protection agency was engaged in balancing social interests rather than prioritizing the articulation and protection of privacy (Flaherty 1989: 106–107). In this process, the social interest of security tends to be perceived as a collective interest, while privacy is defined as an individual one that is less urgent for society, and this is certainly not beneficial for privacy. Although it might be argued that the balance doctrine to some extent is a general guide for all European data protection commissioners, there may well be important variation nonetheless. What characterizes the Swedish balance doctrine is a focus on social interests and the inclusion of privacy in them, that is, privacy itself has no special status.

In Sweden, the idea of a balance is accepted not only by surveillance advocates but also by those who are critical to expanded video surveillance. Although the privacy argument has been discussed by critical columnists in Swedish newspapers, even in these columns, there is support for the idea of a balance in which privacy is one of the values. The utility of video surveillance is questioned with the argument that using it is costly and leads to a loss of privacy, without necessarily bringing about an increase in crime prevention (Kjöller 2008).‡

Certainly, the balance metaphor is a construction where two desirable but seemingly incompatible aims—the aim of security/crime prevention and the aim of privacy—both seem to be achievable in a less conflicting way than would otherwise be possible. By balancing them, there is no need to choose, both can be attained to an appropriate extent. Obviously, the idea of a balance is especially attractive to politicians. In fact, balancing security and civil liberties is a universal metaphor widely used in both the legal and the political discourses (Liberatore 2007: 114). That is because it is essentially both a neutral and constructive endeavor; nobody can be against it. "The term 'balance' tends to disarm opponents because it has no tenable antithesis: nobody would stand up and argue for imbalance, or indeed for disproportionality" (Ashworth 2007: 208).

Thus, the balance or proportionality principle is not an exclusively Swedish invention; the doctrine of a balance is the generally prevailing model in the privacy protection context (Raab 1999: 69). Indeed, it represents a kind of consequentialist thinking that is widespread in the security discourse. Despite this, it has been heavily criticized among privacy scholars. Gallagher (2004: 287)§ argues that the idea of a balance inevitably means that an individual right will be

---

* See also Łambertz (2008).
† See, for example, Regeringsrätten (the Supreme Administrative Court), lawsuit no. 6572-98, on video surveillance in taxicabs 00-09-29; lawsuit no. 5767-02, on video surveillance in a hospital, 04-03-09; and lawsuit no. 7873-08, on video surveillance on streets and in public squares, 10-02-11.
‡ See also Weiss (2008).
§ See also Ashwood (2007: 209).

intruded upon in the name of the public good. In addition, it is very difficult, probably impossible, to objectively determine the moment at which a reasonable balance has been achieved (Bennett and Raab 2006: 13). Yet there are also more fundamental objections to this type of calculating activity. Zedner (2005: 516) argues that balancing presumes that the goods at stake are commensurable and that it is possible to convert them into comparable scales. It is highly questionable if this is the case when privacy is weighed against the effects on crime prevention. Nonetheless, as shown by the Swedish case, the conditions for balancing may be better or worse depending on the character of the values included.

As in the Swedish case, and for various reasons, the values involved in balancing exercises are often used in an imprecise way. This is inherent in political rhetoric, but it also conceals the problematic aspects of the practice. Nonetheless, the idea of a balance is extremely powerful in Sweden because of a lack of elements of rights reasoning. In the Swedish debate, the conflict between values is very rarely presented as one between video surveillance and the individual's right to protection of his or her privacy. Somewhat remarkably, the rights perspective is articulated almost exclusively by debaters on the left (Motion bill 1997/98:Ju22), who ought to be suspicious of the liberal worldview to which rights originally belong.

Privacy conceptualized as an interest or a need is a fundamental feature of the Swedish discourse. Thus, privacy is defined as a utility rather than a right. Balancing utilities against one another is much easier if rights are not involved, because rights have a more inviolable and absolute character. Utilities (privacy and prevention) are more easily balanced because utility itself is something relative. Understanding privacy as a right, on the other hand, complicates balancing and strengthens its value in the balancing exercise (Bennett and Raab 2006: 48).

3.6 Swedish Conception of Privacy

The Swedish utilitarian position can be described as a political approach, in contrast to a legalistic one. It is political in the sense that the focus is on compromise, and this then defines the attitude taken toward the values involved, including privacy. Still, the Swedish discourse is not only about pragmatism; utilitarianism is a prudent and deliberate way of reasoning that stands in contrast to other ways of reasoning about, in this case, privacy.

Although, most people, including utilitarians, would agree that privacy is an important aspect of human life, it is anything but a straightforward and uncontroversial concept. From the academic debate, it is possible to construct at least three differences of opinion or controversies. First, as a kind of basic issue with ontological connotations, we have the question of whether privacy is a human right worth recognition. Second, if it is argued to be such a right, what exactly does that mean in terms of inviolability? Third, does this right exclusively adhere to individuals, or is privacy also a value of concern for the larger collective, for example, citizens as a group? On these questions, as is true of many other issues of a political theoretical nature, the deepest antagonism is between the liberal and communitarian schools. The liberal idea of privacy defined as a human right is dismissed by the latter. It is argued that privacy often represents a self-interest that is hardly compatible with communitarian values of the common good. In other words: "Privacy is one good among other goods and should be weighted as such" (Etzioni 1999, 2007: 115). The value of privacy is dependent on whether it is perceived to be important in a given social context.

The communitarian view of privacy is certainly consistent with other, basic conceptions associated with this tradition of thought. It is fully in line with the communitarian approach to liberal, context-independent values in general. The utilitarian position (Rule 2007: 10–13) resembles the communitarian, but a utilitarian approach to privacy does not involve the culturalist condition, the common good of a specific historically emerged society, upon which communitarians base their analysis. Utilitarianism is also about value relativism, balancing goods against each other, but the utilitarian solution to value conflicts is not preconditioned by cultural or specific social factors. Rather, the conflict involves culturally neutral individuals or aggregates of individuals.

The opposite extreme to communitarian and utilitarian relativism is the natural law position, forcefully advocated by Dworkin (2009). In principle, rights are inviolable and must not be context sensitive because they are strongly associated with the fundamental condition that humans are entitled to equal respect. The international discourse of conventions and declarations on human rights, including privacy, is constructed around this idea of absolute inviolability. Yet this absolutist position is not very common in the literature, or, to be more exact, the main argument has not concerned whether or not the right to privacy is absolute. Rather, it has been about the purposes for which it is justifiable to infringe on privacy. Still, in speaking about rights, we are usually thinking about things that are more or less stable and inviolable or at least costly to violate. In fact, this is what motives the extensive literature on the topic.

Assuming that we conceive of privacy as a right, the main issue of concern has been whether it is linked only to the individual or whether it also has a social value that goes beyond protection of the individual's sphere. The traditional liberal definition of privacy is as a negative right, that is, the right to be left alone and to not be interfered with—normally by the state. This is privacy as an individual property right, distinctly associated with the position that there is and should be a clear separation between state and civil society. This approach still has a strong position in the privacy literature (Bennett and Raab 2006: 17) and among the public, but privacy conceived in this manner has attracted massive debate in the last several years. The negative rights construction can reasonably be said to be partly outdated in the information era, where it is hard to delineate a private space in terms of something that resembles an individual property. Also, it has been argued that it is a rather passive notion. The information society demands an understanding of privacy that concerns the possibility to control the use of information (Rule and Hunter 1999; Solove 2004; Rule 2007), rather than to merely withhold information about oneself. Privacy should thus be understood as control over the distribution of information about the individual. In addition, the idea that privacy should be understood exclusively as an individual asset has been disputed. A loss of control over information about themselves, besides damaging the privacy of individuals, might also have negative social consequences. Privacy serves public and collective ends and is indispensable in a well-functioning society. "Instead of being derived from an aggregation of individual preferences, the importance of privacy derives from a sense of connection and mutuality" (Regan 1995: 243). Lack of privacy might negatively affect free opinion and eventually even democratic systems (Schwartz 1999: 1647). It should be noted that this discussion of the social benefits of privacy arises primarily from the liberal rather than communitarian discourse. Also utilitarianism is a liberal position that is concerned with democracy, but, in this context, democracy is the input rather than the outcome of attention to privacy. Utilitarians are not primarily concerned with whether or not a lack of privacy impairs democracy. Instead, privacy is the focus insofar as it is a manifestation of the public will.

The Swedish utilitarian position should be considered in the light of a broader discursive environment and has its roots in Swedish legal and social traditions. Before discussing this issue, however, another discursive condition will be addressed: the peculiarities of the Swedish language. In fact, Swedish does not contain any specific word for privacy, something which Flaherty pointed out in his 1989 study on privacy and surveillance in five states. Yet this does not mean that there is no conception of privacy. For the most part, "integritet" is the Swedish word used to mean privacy. The meaning of "integritet" encompasses both the English words privacy and integrity (decent, honorable). Commonly, it is used synonymously with privacy, sometimes with the adjective personal, that is, "personlig integritet."

Linguistic formations certainly affect and interact with the way in which we think about different things. However, although the human language sets the limits of imagination, the fact that Swedish lacks a word for privacy should not be exaggerated. The political significance of this condition is not obvious because there are related expressions at hand. Still, it is interesting to note that the expression that is used, that is, "integritet," opens up the possibility of trading on the concept of privacy. Integrity (privacy) and security might be defined as the same thing. In this case, the conflict between the two can be resolved. Thus, embedded in the Swedish language is a solution to the balance equation. The balance is manifest more in the form of a paradox than a genuine contradiction.

The solution to the balance paradox is illustrated by the comments of a member of parliament presented in the following. First, security is defined as a component of privacy (den personliga integriteten), that is, an important aspect of privacy is not being afraid: "To be able to move around freely is to a very large extent a part of peoples' privacy" (Motion bill 2007/08:Ju417) (author's translation).

Video surveillance increases the possibility for people to move around freely without being exposed to threats. Second, it is argued that the violation of an individual's security, that is, being a victim of a serious crime, is an important violation of privacy: "The most severe violation of privacy is to be exposed to serious crime" (Motion bill 2007/08:Ju417) (author's translation).

Almost the same wording appears in a joint article by the prosecutor general, the national police commissioner, and the director general of the Swedish Secret Security Police (SÄPO). In the article, it is argued that to be a victim of crimes or terrorist attacks is an invasion of privacy (Strömberg et al. 2006). In an interview, the director of the Public Prosecution Authority took the argument a step further, arguing that video surveillance actually increases privacy because it makes people feel more safe and taken care of (Molin 2005). The radical conclusion of this is that failing to deploy cameras threatens both security and privacy. A more nuanced way to formulate it is to counterpose one kind of violation of integrity with another. This was what the Ministry of Justice did in 2001, in its instructions to the committee appointed to evaluate the law: "The invasion of privacy (integritet) that video surveillance implies must also be weighed against the invasion of privacy (integritet) caused by not being able to freely move about due to fear of being exposed to crime" (Justitiedepartementet 2001:53) (author's translation).

In the Swedish case, obscuring the difference between privacy and security is fundamental to legitimizing surveillance, and it substantially weakens critical arguments. It would be going too far to say that the perception of privacy as identical with security is the commonly accepted view, but it is common (Motion bill 2011/12:M24), including in statements from the government. The minister of justice argued in the parliament in 2008 that it is important that video monitoring is done openly, in the interest of citizens' security (Parliament protocol 2007/08:69). At issue was the need for signs in places where cameras are deployed in order to make people aware that they are being watched. Intuitively and most commonly, the demand for signs and transparency about video surveillance belongs to the privacy protection argument. The minister was speaking about security, but in this sentence, the word security could be exchanged for privacy, and the meaning would be the same. It should be said that the minister of justice was not the only participant in the parliamentary debate who explained the rational for signs in this way (Parliament protocol 2005/06:82).

There is a built in ambiguity in the Swedish vocabulary concerning the notion of privacy. From a discourse analytical point of view, this is certainly relevant to the position and quality of this value in Swedish legal acts. Privacy protection is given sparse attention in the Swedish legal framework. In addition, when the term privacy (integritet or personlig integritet) appears, its status is weak. Neither in the Act on Public Video Surveillance nor in the Swedish Act on Data Protection is anything said about the right to privacy. The Act on Data Protection does not mention privacy as a right that may be claimed; the purpose of the law is said to be to protect people from suffering violations of their personal integrity. Thus, the Swedish act differs from, and in this respect is weaker than, corresponding acts in other European states. One example of this is the way that data subjects are approached in the German (Bundesdatenschutzgesetz) and Polish (Ustawa o Ochronie Danych Osobowych) data protection acts. In these, the data subject is a person with rights to be protected. The Data Protection Act in Sweden is a subsidiary law; if it conflicts with another act, then the latter takes precedence. This is also the case in other countries. However, an ambitious video surveillance regulation policy such as Sweden's may in fact erode rather than support the privacy protective ambitions of the Data Protection Act. It might be argued that the Swedish Act on Video Surveillance works proactively to extend surveillance because it gives recognition to the idea of video monitoring as an effective method of crime prevention. Privacy is treated poorly when weighed against other social goods in this context.

Turning to the Swedish constitution, the protection of privacy there is not very strong when compared with those of other democratic states or with formulations in international conventions. According to the second chapter, 6§ in the recently amended Instrument of Government Act (Regeringsformen), every citizen should be protected against significant invasions of personal integrity if it is not based on consent and implies surveillance or mapping of the individual's personal circumstances. This paragraph is a reinforcement of the protection of privacy, which was previously taken into account only in an indirect way. Still, there is not now nor has there ever been any general protection of privacy in the Swedish constitution. Chapter 2 is entitled Basic Freedoms and Rights, but the right to privacy is never mentioned explicitly. Since 1995, the European Convention on Human Rights (ECHR), including its privacy prescriptions, has been incorporated into the Swedish legal system and can be referred to in Swedish court decisions. Nonetheless, the Swedish Data Inspection Board is not guided by any *national* legal document that explicitly refers to the right of privacy protection.

In international legal frameworks such as the ECHR, the Universal Declaration of Human Rights, and the International Covenant on Civil and Political Rights, privacy is addressed primarily as an individual property right to be protected from abuse perpetrated by the state and private business. The European convention states that: "Everyone has the right to respect for his private and family life, his home and his correspondence" (ECHR 3.8.1).

Privacy is not an unconditional matter in this act, and it may be restricted for different reasons, for example, security and democratic necessity. Despite this, it is established as a right. The right to protection of personal data is enshrined in the Council of Europe Convention No. 108, which establishes respect for rights and fundamental freedoms, among them the right to privacy with regard to automatic processing of personal data (art. 1).

When the Swedish constitution is compared with the constitution of Poland, which is one of Europe's recently democratized states and which has largely incorporated the European approach to privacy rights in it legislation, we find obvious differences. Privacy is addressed in a much more thorough way in the Polish constitution. The right to privacy is protected in article 47, which states that there is a right to legal protection of private and family life as well as the individual's honor and good reputation. In addition to the Data Protection Act, the Polish inspector general of Data

Protection (Generalny Inspektor Ochronie Danych Osobowych) is guided by the Polish constitutional right of protection of personal data and by the Polish Civil Code, which refers to a list of personal civil rights such as personal dignity, freedom of conscience, secrecy of communication, and the inviolability of the home. The Polish legislation follows international legal documents in defining privacy as property right. However, this does not automatically mean that privacy, in practice, is more strongly protected in Poland than Sweden.

The property rights conception of privacy can, as mentioned earlier, be considered incomplete in a modern society based on the efficient flow of information. By stressing the subject's right to access the data gathered about himself or herself (art. 12) and the importance of his or her consent to their use and storage (art. 7), the EU Data Privacy Directive (95/46/EC) is an adaptation to this condition. However, the German conception of privacy is even further ahead in this respect, because it contains a clear ambition to define privacy in a positive and substantial way that goes beyond the traditional liberal definition found in international conventions. As early as 1983, the Federal Supreme Constitutional Court (Bundesverfassungsgericht), in a case concerning a planned, but controversial, national census, interpreted the two core articles on privacy in the constitution—the "right to free development of one's personality" and the "right to human dignity"—as implying a right to "informational self-determination" (Informationelles Selbstbestimmungsrecht). The court regarded self-determination as an essential condition of a free democratic society based on every citizen's capacity to act and cooperate (DeSimone 2010: 295). Everyone should therefore have the right of access to and control over stored data about himself or herself (Kilian 2008: 80–81). A fear that personal information might be collected and stored ought not to hinder people from using their basic freedoms and democratic rights. As is true elsewhere, the German right to informational self-determination is not absolute. Limitations are accepted on the grounds of collective social interests that are perceived as having priority (Lepsius 2004). Nonetheless, the protection of informational self-determination is at the center of German discourse on surveillance and privacy, a hub around which debate takes place. Both those who favor expanding video surveillance and critics of it must relate to this principle.

In the Swedish legal context, privacy is discussed neither as a democratic concern, as in Germany, nor as a more or less absolute individual property right, as in Poland. In the context of video surveillance, as well as more generally, the term signifies instead a vaguely specified utility. It is neither a value of high priority in itself nor instrumental to any social end. By extension, the utility perspective may lead to privacy being treated as a *subjective* need, that is, an approach to privacy involving a very far-reaching type of relativism. The argument on video surveillance put forth by the chancellor of justice in November 2008 illustrates this development. Explicitly referring to the balance between the need for surveillance and privacy, he argued: "The legal protection of privacy first and foremost concerns those who really feel discomfort with surveillance. We who are not so much affected have to remember that" (Lambertz 2008)* (author's translation).

Equating the need for protection of privacy with a feeling of discomfort would be almost impossible if privacy was regarded as a right. In addition, reducing privacy to a subjective feeling does not guarantee it a strong position in any balancing decisions, not at present or in the future.

The unwillingness to consider privacy as a right distinguishes the Swedish approach to this value from those of other European states as well as from the international discourse on privacy. It is productive to discuss the Swedish understanding of privacy as a product of a broader Swedish historical discourse in which social democracy has played a central role. The Social Democratic Party has been very influential in modern Swedish political history, and while social democracy

---

* The Data Inspection Board also subscribes to a subjective kind of relativism (Datainspektionen 2012).

may no longer have a hegemonic position in Sweden, there is reason to believe that it still influences the understanding of normative issues such as privacy. Historically, social democracy was less attracted to the idea that liberal individual rights defined as negative freedoms might interfere with the state's ambition to promote social equality. Such rights were regarded as infringements on democracy conceptualized as the realization of popular will. Democracy defined as the satisfaction of demands of equal standing is a utilitarian idea that does not automatically support privacy rights (Rule 2007: 11). A doctrine of legal realism (i.e., the doctrine of Scandinavian legal realism) was established very early in Sweden. This doctrine completely dismissed notions of idealism and absolute rights. In addition to a scientifically inspired positivism, Scandinavian legal realism took, to some extent, a utility perspective on the law, implying that in the making and practicing of law, the social good must be considered. The doctrine was formulated by scholars, some of whom were more or less associated with the Social Democratic Party and their program. They had a great impact on the party's policy between the First and the Second World Wars (Nordin 1984).

Viewing privacy as utility rather than as a right undoubtedly has consequences for how the value should be treated by the state. Privacy as utility, interest, or need is something to be distributed in appropriate proportions to concerned individuals or groups of individuals. Rights, on the other hand, are something to be legitimately claimed against the state. In fact, rights have this nature irrespective of whether they are understood in Dworkin's absolute sense or as inviolable in a less strict way and regardless of whether they are a matter of individual or collective value. It is true that interests are also something to be claimed, but they are not, per definition, legitimate in the way that rights are.

The degree of general legitimacy that privacy is afforded affects the position and strength of privacy protection institutions. Two Swedish institutions have a special responsibility for acting against violations of privacy, the Data Inspection Board and the chancellor of justice. They are strongly integrated in the same discursive practice about the utility of privacy that characterizes the approach of government policymakers and parliamentarians. The task of the Data Inspection Board is to supervise the protection of privacy and scrutinize the practice of the public bureaucracy, among other institutions. However, the chief inspector of the Data Inspection Board fully approves of the utility perspective (Gräslund 2008); therefore, the board's focus is not entirely on privacy. Arguments in favor of stronger privacy protection are a matter of paying greater attention to this value than to other ones when making judgments about what is a proper balance (Datainspektionen Dnr 742-2008). There is no qualitative difference in the argumentation found in the political sphere and that made by the Data Inspection Board; differences are rather a matter of emphasis. On an Internet site maintained by the board to provide information to the public about video surveillance, the argument about privacy appears even more dependent than usual on the outcome of a calculation of competing interests. In fact, it is established that if the weighing of different values is done correctly, then there should be no violation of personal integrity. In order for video surveillance not to violate privacy, the purpose of and need for video surveillance must weigh heavier than the individual's interest in the protection of personal integrity" (Datainspektionen 2012) (author's translation). This is the utilitarian rationale driven to its extreme.

3.7 Welfare State Legacy?

Providing security is a traditional responsibility of the state. In today's increasingly global security discourse, states have taken on new forms of responsibility for the safety of their people and have adopted new types of devices, for example, video surveillance, for exercising this responsibility.

Privacy, on the other hand, is traditionally understood as something that should be protected from state interference. Making privacy and security into equal entities of utility, that is, including them both under the umbrella of protection, invalidates the understanding of privacy claims as emanating from the individual or society and directed against the state. In the Swedish case, privacy is something more or less distributed by the state rather than something to be legitimately asserted against the state. The Swedish state takes responsibility for both the distribution of security and the distribution of privacy in adequate proportions. The idea of a balance between security (crime prevention) and privacy is the metaphorical depiction of the aggregation of different utilities.

It is obviously not particularly controversial to understand crime prevention/security as a publicly distributed utility. As regards the notion of privacy, the matter is more complicated. International legal documents favor the rights conception of privacy, and this is also the case in many—probably most—democratic states. Without making any normative judgment, it must be concluded that the Swedish utility approach weakens the idea of privacy. If privacy is regarded as something that should be distributed by the state rather than as something to be legitimately claimed against the state, then it will inevitably have a weaker position.

A relevant question is whether the utilitarian perspective is a better provider of equal consideration of privacy for people who are particularly strongly affected by surveillance, for example, socially marginalized and exposed groups, and people who are not well served by a property rights approach. This question cannot be answered within the scope of this study. In fact, however, the distribution of utilities is the usual way in which welfare state policy operates. Guided by traditional welfare state ambitions, the state takes responsibility for delivering privacy to its citizens in the same way as it supplies material needs. The Swedish discursive consensus around the utility perspective, which the legal establishment also adheres to, makes this task easier.

What is the future of the Swedish approach? Is it stable or the product of a defined and finite period of time? Because Sweden is definitely a part of the European community and norms and values tend to converge, it may be expected that Sweden will adapt more and more to the European conception of privacy as a right.* The reformation of the Swedish constitution mentioned earlier might be considered an example of this process. On the other hand, an alternative scenario is that European privacy policies will become increasingly utilitarian because, today, more explicit attention tends to be paid to state security and crime prevention at the expense of privacy.

References

Ashworth, A. 2007. Security, terrorism and the value of human rights. In *Security and Human Rights*, eds. B. J. Goold and L. Lazarus, pp. 203–226. Portland, Orlando: Hart Publishing.

Bennett, C. J. 1992. *Regulating Privacy. Data Protection and Public Policy in Europe and the United States.* Ithaca, New York: Cornell University Press.

Bennett, C. J. 2011. In defence of privacy: The concept and the regime. *Surveillance and Society* 8: 485–496.

Bennett, C. J. and R. Grant, eds. 1999. *Visions of Privacy: Policy Choices for the Digital Age.* Toronto, Ontario, Canada: University of Toronto Press.

Bennett, C. J. and C. Raab. 2006. *The Governance of Privacy: Policy Instruments in Global Perspective.* Cambridge, MA: The MIT Press.

---

* See also the Appendix to the public report SOU (1997:39), preparatory work on the revision of the Data Protection Act.

Bjereld, U. and M. Demker. 2009. Frihet och övervakning. In *I Europamissionens tjänst*, eds. C. Alvstam, B. Jännebring, and D. Naurin, pp. 241–250. Göteborg, Sweden: Centrum för Europaforskning.

Björklund, F. 2011. Pure flour in your bag: Governmental rationalities of camera surveillance in Sweden. *Information Polity* 16: 355–368.

Brottsförebyggande rådet. 2003. *Kameraövervakning i brottsförebyggande syfte*. Stockholm, Sweden: Fritzes.

Brottsförebyggande rådet. 2009. *Kameraövervaking i Landskrona. En utvärdering*. Stockholm, Sweden: Fritzes.

DeSimone, C. 2010. Pitting Karlsruhe against Luxemburg? German data protection and the contested implementation of the EU data retention directive. *German Law Journal* 11: 291–317.

Duff, R. A. and S. E. Marshall. 2000. Benefits, burdens and responsibilities: Some ethical dimensions of situational crime prevention. In *Ethical and Social Perspectives on Situational Crime Prevention,* eds. A. v. Hirsch, D. Garland, and A. Wakefield, pp. 17–36. Oxford, London, U.K.: Hart Publishing.

Dworkin, R. 2009, 1977. *Taking Rights Seriously*. London, U.K.: Duckworth.

Etzioni, A. 1999. *The Limits of Privacy*. New York: Basic Books.

Etzioni, A. 2007. Are new technologies the enemy of privacy? *Knowledge, Technology and Policy* 20: 115–119.

Flaherty, D. H. 1989. *Protecting Privacy in Surveillance Societies. The Federal Republic of Germany, Sweden, France, Canada & the United States*. Chapel Hill, NC: University of North Carolina Press.

Fussey, P. 2008. Beyond liberty, beyond security: The politics of public surveillance. *British Politics* 3: 120–135.

Gallagher, C. 2004. CCTV and human rights: The fish and the bicycle? An examination of Peck v. United Kingdom (2003) 36 E.H.R.R. 41. *Surveillance and Society* 2: 270–292.

Gandy, O. 2006. Data mining, surveillance and discrimination, in the post-9/11 environment. In *The New Politics of Surveillance and Visibility*, eds. K. V. Haggerty and R. V. Ericson, pp. 363–384. Toronto, Ontario, Canada: University of Toronto Press.

Garland, D. 2000. Ideas, institutions and situational crime prevention. In *Ethical and Social Perspectives on Situational Crime Prevention,* eds. A. v. Hirsch, D. Garland, and A. Wakefield, pp. 1–16. Oxford, London. U.K.: Hart Publishing.

Gilliom, J. 2011. A response to bennett's in defence of privacy. *Surveillance and Society* 8: 500–504.

Goold, B. J. 2009. Technologies of surveillance and the erosion of institutional trust. In *Technologies of Insecurity: The surveillance of Everyday Life*, eds. K. Aas et al., pp. 207–218. Oxon, England, U.K.: Routledge.

Goold, B. J. and D. Neyland, eds. 2009. *New Directions in Surveillance and Privacy*. Padstow, England, U.K.: Willan Publishing.

Gräslund, G. 2005. Likheten inför lagen ur spel av kameror för övervakning. Datainspektionens chef vill ha övergripande ansvar för att kameralagen tillämpas lika över hela landet. *Dagens Nyheter*, February 12.

Gräslund, G. 2008. Kameraövervakningen på skolor är olaglig. Datainspektionen sätter stopp för övervakningskameror på sju granskade skolor: Beslutet är vägledande för alla skolor i landet. *Dagens Nyheter*, October 2.

Hempel, L. and E. Töpfer. 2004. CCTV in Europe. Final Report. Working paper No. 15. Centre for Technology and Society, Technical University Berlin.

Kilian, W. 2008. Germany. In *Global Privacy and Protection: The First Generation*, eds. J. B. Rule. and G. Greenleaf, pp. 80–106. Cheltenham, England, U.K.: Edward Elgar Publishing.

Kjöller, H. 2008. Hur kunde något så dyrbart hanteras så billigt. *Dagens Nyheter,* January 16.

Lambertz, G. 2008. Lagen tillåter inte dagens kameraövervakning. *Dagens Nyheter*, November 29.

Lepsius, O. 2004. Liberty, security and terrorism: The legal position in Germany. *German Law Journal* 5: 435–460.

Liberatore, A. 2007. Balancing security and democracy, and the role of expertise: Biometrics politics in the European Union. *European Journal on Criminal Policy and Research* 13: 109–137.

Lodge, J. 2003. EU homeland security: Citizens or suspects? *Journal of European Integration* 26: 253–279.

Lyon, D, ed. 2003. *Surveillance and Social Sorting*. London, U.K.: Routledge.

Molin, K. 2005. Fyra frågor till Sven-Erik Alhem: Låt gå mentaliteten är det värsta som finns. *Dagens Nyheter*, August 19.

Newman, A. L. 2008. *Protectors of Privacy. Regulating Personal Data in the Global Economy*. Ithaca, New York: Cornell University Press.

Nissenbaum, H. 2009. *Privacy in the Context. Technology, Policy and the Integrity of Social Life*. Palo Alto, CA: Stanford University Press.

Nordin, S. 1984. *Från Hägerström Till Hedenius: Den Moderna Svenska Filosofin*. Bodafors, Sweden: Doxa.

Norris, C. and G. Armstrong. 1999. *The Maximum Surveillance Society: The Rise of CCTV*. Oxford, London. U.K.: Berg.

Raab, Ch. D. 1999. From balancing to steering: New directions for data protection. In *Visions of Privacy: Policy Choices for the Digital Age*, eds. C. J. Bennett and R. Grant, pp. 68–93. Toronto, Ontario, Canada: University of Toronto Press.

Regan, P. M. 1995. *Legislating Privacy: Technology, Social Values and Public Policy*. Chapel Hill, NC: University of North Carolina Press.

Rule, J. B. 2007. *Privacy in the Peril. How We are Sacrificing a Fundamental Right in Exchange for Security and Convenience*. New York: Oxford University Press.

Rule, J. B. and G. Greenleaf, eds. 2008. *Global Privacy Protection. The First Generation*. Cheltenham, England, U.K.: Edward Elgar.

Rule, J. and L. Hunter. 1999. Towards property rights in personal data. In *Visions of Privacy: Policy Choices for the Digital Age*, eds. C. J. Bennett and R. Grant, pp. 168–181. Toronto, Ontario, Canada: University of Toronto Press.

Schwartz, P. M. 1999. Privacy and democracy in cyberspace. *Vanderbilt Law Review* 52: 1609–1701.

Solove, D. 2004. *The Digital Person: Technology and Privacy in the Information Age*. New York: New York University Press.

SOU. 1997:39. Integritet, Offentlighet, Informationsteckning. Appendix 4. Stockholm, Sweden: Fritzes.

SOU. 2002:110. Allmän kameraövervakning. Stockholm, Sweden: Fritzes.

SOU. 2009:87. En ny kameraövervakningslag. Stockholm, Sweden: Fritzes.

Stadler, F. 2002. Opinion: Privacy is not the antidote to surveillance. *Surveillance and Society* 1: 120–124.

Strömberg, S., F. Wersäll, and K. Bergstrand. 2006. Sluta måla upp falska bilder över övervakarstaten. Riksåklagaren, rikspolischefen och Säpochefen: Vi behöver moderna verktyg för att bekämpa den grova brottsligheten. *Dagens Nyheter,* February 11.

Vogel, U. and M. Passerin d'Entrèves. 2001. *Public and Private: Legal, Political and Philosophical Perspectives*. Florence, KY: Routledge.

Waples, S., M. Gill, and P. Fisher. 2009. Does CCTV displace crime? *Criminology and Criminal Justice* 9: 207–224.

Weiss, L. 2008. Men kamerorna då? Lars Weiss om en växande övervakningsindustri. *Dagens Nyheter,* December 9.

Welsh, B. C. and D. P. Farrington. 2007. *Kameraövervakning Och Brottsprevention: En Systematisk Forskningsgenomgång*. Stockholm, Sweden: Brottsförebyggande rådet.

Zedner, L. 2005. Securing liberty in the face of terror: Reflections from criminal justice. *Journal of Law and Society* 32: 507–533.

Other Sources

Bundesdatenschutzgesetz (The German data protection act, BDSG).

Datainspektionen. Dnr 742-2008, Decision after inspection according to the Data Protection Act 1998:204 (Swedish data inspection board).

Datainspektionen. 2012. "Kameraövervakning"; http://www.datainspektionen.se/lagar-och-regler/ personuppgiftslagen/kameraovervakning/ (accessed February 15, 2012).

Government Bill 1989/90:119 (Swedish government).

Government Bill 1997/98:64 (Swedish government).

Justitiedepartementet. Instruction 2001:53 (Swedish ministry of justice).

Justitiedepartementet. Instruction 2008:22 (Swedish ministry of justice).

Lagen om allmän kameraövervakning 1998:150 (The act on public video surveillance).

Lagen om övervakningskameror 1990:484 (The act on surveillance cameras).

Lagen om TV övervakning 1977:20 (The act on TV surveillance).

Personuppgiftslagen 1998:204 (The Data Protection Act).

Regeringsrätten. Lawsuit no 5767-02, on video surveillance in a hospital, 04-03-09.

Regeringsrätten. Lawsuit no 6572-98, on video surveillance in taxicabs, 00-09-29 (The Supreme Administrative Court).

Regeringsrätten. Lawsuit no 7873-08 on video surveillance on streets and in squares, 10-02-11.

Parliament protocols and Parliament Motion Bills 1997-2011. http://www.riksdagen.se/sv/Debatter—beslut/

Privacy International. 2007. "PHR 2006 – Kingdom of Sweden" December 18; http://www.privacyinternational.org/article.shtml?cmd[347] = x-347-559487.

Tidingarnas Telegrambyrå. 2008. Rätten sa ja till kameraövervakning på Stureplan. *Dagens Nyheter,* November 11.

The Council of Europe Convention No. 108 for the Protection of Individuals with regard to Automatic Processing of Personal Data.

The EU Data Privacy Directive 95/46/EC.

Ustawa o ochronie danych osobowych (The Polish data protection act).

Chapter 4

Perceived Threat: Determinants and Consequences of Fear of Terrorism in Germany*

Matthias Leese

Contents

4.1 Introduction

Security and surveillance measures nearly almost create an impact that lies far beyond their usually narrow technological scope. For this matter, not only technical disciplines but also scholars of law and the social sciences are involved in critically examining the societal consequences of surveillance, for example, regarding privacy and social interaction. This chapter strives to examine the connection between the fear of terrorism, general attitudes of the German population, and the acceptance of security and surveillance measures. The data set originates from the research project "The transparent citizen between apathy and resistance—the genesis of new governmental surveillance technologies and their effects on attitudes and behavior of the population" at the *Institut für*

---

* In memory of Christian Lüdemann.

Sicherheits-und Präventionsforschung (Institute for security and prevention research)* in Hamburg, funded by the DFG (German research foundation).

When speaking about terrorism in the aftermath of 9/11, one has to be aware of the fact that terrorism, especially religious terrorism, does not pose a new form of threat to societies or cultures (Daase 2001; Frey et al. 2007; Münkler 2002). After the events of 9/11, however, the perception of the terrorist threat has risen to a new level. This increase is mainly due to the dislocated and global structure of today's terrorist networks, sending out one crucial message: attacks might happen anywhere and at any given time; there is no absolute safety for anybody (Karstedt 2002, 124f.; Müller 2008; Münkler 2002). To understand this matter properly, Section 4.3 is dedicated to the theoretical foundations of terrorism and its psychological effects. Then, a model representing the relations between the perception of threat, the fear of terrorism, the assessment of security measures, and other variables are introduced and discussed.

When correlating the fear of terrorism with new security measures, the implications of surveillance and control on societal dynamics also have to be considered. Security legislation almost always carries a curtailment in civil liberties in order to work effectively (Schulte 2008, 227). After 9/11, public debates about the balance between the two sides have been controversial. The academic dimension has not only been limited to legal aspects but also involved the social sciences. Surveys have shown that populations seem to be undecided about the best compromise between civil liberties (like privacy and data protection) and the effectiveness of security and surveillance measures. The assessment of risk and threat depends on individual factors as well as on the local and temporal context (Davis and Silver 2004, 28).

The basic concept of a trade-off is simple. Civil liberties are an important prerequisite for the (possible) self-realization of the citizens. By imposing restrictions on these liberties, security measures potentially violate the principles of liberal political systems. Hassemer claims that civil liberties represent intrinsic social values, whereas security would only serve as a condition for realizing those values (Hassemer 2002, 10). Public debates often tend to overemphasize conflicting positions, which leads to strongly opposed points of view. Academically, though, a logical priority of one over the other cannot be derived (Bauman 1999, 25).

Besides these theoretical considerations, the trade-off can be approached empirically. Based on empirical data, Viscusi and Zeckhauser have shown that the balance in the trade-off between the needs of security and the protection of civil liberties depends on individual preferences and the temporal context (Viscusi and Zeckhauser 2003, 100). The changed individual perception of terrorism expresses itself in a changed relation between civil liberties and security. After terrorist attacks, the respondents' estimated number of victims was significantly higher than before, while the level of civil liberties was maintained. In order to reduce the estimated number of victims of terrorism, respondents showed willingness to cut back civil liberties, providing a higher level of perceived security.

Reflecting the considerations up to this point, it is necessary to analyze the political (and social) consequences of higher levels of fear. A diagnosis of the German constitution shows that security is not mentioned explicitly as a public good or a positive externality (Callies 2002, 2). On the other hand, terrorist attacks make modern societies aware of their own vulnerability, therefore requesting a higher need for security. Böckenförde diagnosed that liberal political systems cannot guarantee their own prerequisites without denying their very goals (Böckenförde 1976, 60). Societies based on liberal values require a strong basic consensus on the importance of civil liberties that is prone to being unbalanced by external threats easily.

---

* http://www.isip.uni-hamburg.de

Following the 9/11 attacks, several new laws were passed in Germany, introducing a number of security and surveillance measures. The data set includes seven of them, not providing a complete listing but representing some of the most controversially discussed measures. They are as follows: (1) the introduction of biometric passports and biometric identity cards; (2) granting law enforcement agencies online access to digital images in biometric passports or biometric identity cards of suspects; (3) granting police, tax authorities, employment agencies, and social welfare offices online access to personal bank records of suspects; (4) instructing telecommunication providers to retain data for a period of 6 months; (5) permitting governmental security agencies to search suspects' personal computers; (6) the establishment of an anti-terror database; and (7) gathering and passing on of air and ship passenger data to the federal German police.

From a liberal point of view, those security measures have been intensely criticized (see Callies 2002; Hoffmann-Riem 2002). But a changed constellation featuring higher levels of threat also carries consequences for a general understatement of security. After 9/11, concepts of homeland security and international security clearly have become blurred (Lüdtke et al. 2003, 11). Homeland security has become strongly related to an external enemy, which has been framed as terrorist threat.

For the social sciences, more important than an (questionable) increase of threat by terrorist attacks is the increase of subjectively perceived risk (Slovic and Weber 2002). When trying to analyze and evaluate the societal consequences of new surveillance and security measures, the increased perception of risk plays a key role. Mainly two consequences can be derived from higher levels of perceived risk or threat. On the one hand, individuals feel less safe and tend to overestimate risks. Therefore, the level of fear increases to new heights. On the other hand, political systems react to a terrorist threat with security legislation, expanding the powers of law enforcement authorities and demonstrating the ability to deal with all kinds of hazard. Most of the time, technological solutions are deployed in order to solve problems such as terrorism or crime. It will be argued here that the higher the level of the fear of terrorism, the more accepted new security measures will become. This chapter does not necessarily claim to provide new findings on the consequences of the fear of terrorism and perceived threat, but rather aims at critically analyzing the German situation and the societal consequences of the implementation of concrete surveillance and control measures. This seems necessary since studies examining determinants and consequences of terrorism fear are not available for Germany in comparable quantity as they are for the United States (see Brück and Müller 2009; Drakos and Müller 2010; Lübcke and Irlenkaeuser 2006; Müller 2008).

For this purpose, this chapter analyzes empirical data from a representative, standardized telephone survey in Germany ($N = 2176$). It will be argued that the reasons for fear of terrorism are to be found in the individual perceptions of threat, which may vary strongly and are influenced by cognitive processing as well as overestimation of risk. Regarding these factors, the perceived level of threat may be significantly higher than the actual level of security concerns issued by the authorities. Moreover, fear of terrorism does not seem to be not necessarily linked to knowledge or assessment of security measures. On the other hand, the consequences for threatened societies can be substantial. As the trade-off between security and civil liberties arguably shifted toward security following 9/11, security measures are likely to gain more and more acceptance by the population. Civil liberties might not be abolished by the implementation of surveillance and control measures, but restricted in several aspects. Most modern electronic security measures affect the entire population and not only specific subgroups that are suspected of crime or terrorism. In consequence, basically every citizen is turned into a suspect, and the classical concept of crime and prosecution is turned upside down.

By using up-to-date electronic data processing, it has furthermore become possible for law enforcement authorities to accumulate, connect, and analyze large amounts of data. From these data, complex profiles of mobility, consumption, or social activities can be derived. According to Garland's "New Culture of Control" (2001), criminological concepts tend to become rather preventive (or even preemptive) than repressive (Zedner 2007), which basically means that from an investigative point of view, all citizens have turned into potential offenders, posing a threat to public safety. In classical liberalism, the individual is to be protected from the state. But when in the actual contexts the state claims to protect the individual, some fundamental consensus of society is at stake. Consequently, this chapter aims at analyzing the beliefs, attitudes, and concerns of the population and presenting a model visualizing complex relations between perceived risks and threat, the fear of terrorism, and attitudes toward the state and new security measures. For the purpose of modeling, using structural equation modeling (SEM), some assumptions will be derived from the existing literature.

It has been shown that fear of terrorism can be identified as a result of underlying fears concerning general worries about human existence (Drakos and Müller 2010; Hirtenlehner 2006). According to that assumption, there is also a strong link between the fear of crime and the fear of terrorism, with the latter being regarded as a special form of the former (Brück and Müller 2009; Hirtenlehner 2006; Wehrheim 2004). In addition, it will be assumed that higher knowledge about security measures should lower reported fear of terrorism, arguing that people tend to feel safer when they know more about the powers of law enforcement authorities and government decisions.

Numerous studies have pointed out the link between the fear of terrorism and the acceptance of security measures curtailing civil liberties (Bozzoli and Müller 2009; Davis and Silver 2004; Huddy et al. 2003; Lübcke and Irlenkaeuser 2006; Viscusi and Zeckhauser 2003). According to attachment theory or evolutionary psychology theory, individuals are likely to seek shelter by looking for more powerful institutions (Sinclair and LoCicero 2010). In this case, the political system in the form of the government and legal authorities provides the power to fight a terrorist threat, leading to an increased system trust (Chanley 2002; Davis and Silver 2004; Huddy et al. 2003; Sinclair and LoCicero 2010). It can also be assumed that increased trust in the political system leads to higher acceptance of security measures, even if they imply restrictions on civil liberties (Davis and Silver 2004). This can be regarded as part of a general evaluation of government performance, which tends to be more positive if the level of trust in the political system is high.

Furthermore, this chapter argues that the better the knowledge of security measures is, the lower the fear of terrorist attacks will be. It is assumed that a high level of information on the competence of law enforcement authorities leads to the conclusion that these powers can be used effectively to prevent the risk of terrorist attacks. The fact that most modern security measures do focus not only on actual suspects but also on the entire population is not as important as a perceived lower level of threat by the citizens.

Concerning the question of how the abstract trade-off between security and civil liberties translates into everyday life, it can be assumed that the willingness to "pay" in any sense for security (with money, time, information costs, etc.) rises as the level of the fear of terrorism rises (Viscusi and Zeckhauser 2003). The survey specifically inquired how much more time passengers were willing to wait at the airport in order to submit to intensified security checks, leading to more (perceived) security on board. Incidentally, the amount of additional time should be positively influenced by the fear of terrorist attacks. As well as the willingness to pay in terms of additional time for security, the individually assessed probability of the future increase of fear is likely to rise dependent on the fear of terrorism (Huddy et al. 2003). Fear arguably leads to a higher individual detection of possible threats and works as a kind of self-fulfilling prophecy (Sunstein 2007).

4.2 Sample and Measurement of Variables

The representative telephone interviewing survey leading to the analyzed data set was conducted between October 5 and November 30, 2009. The population consisted of all German private households using a landline telephone connection. Only persons of the age of 18 and older were interviewed, leading to a data set of $N = 2176$. The sample was randomized on two stages (household and person within the household). The average length of the interviews was 28 min. In order to handle the missing values in the data set (which are almost common in social science surveys and may cause problems in SEM when analyzing covariance), a correlation matrix was produced using pairwise deletion and then processing the matrix in the software AMOS 17.0. By using pairwise deletion instead of listwise deletion or imputation, the structure of the data could be used in a more complete way, deactivating only those variables with missing values used for computing and leaving the rest of the data active (Byrne 2010).[*]

There are several arguments concerning the advantages and disadvantages of the use of SEM (Nachtigall et al. 2003). Generally speaking, SEM analyzes direct and indirect causal effects between variables (Backhaus et al. 2003, 334), giving the researcher the choice whether he or she wants to use it in a confirmatory way, test alternative theory-driven models, or generate (consecutive) models (Jöreskog 1993). SEM can be considered an integrative method, combining the advantages of path analysis, factor analysis, and regression analysis. Moreover, the methods grant the researcher a high degree of freedom in modeling causal relations.[†] In this chapter's theory-driven model, the following variables were used.

The *fear of terrorism* was measured directly. Since it is only partially based on rational situation analysis and known facts (Slovic and Weber 2002; Sunstein 2007), a direct question concerning the subjective fear was used for inquiry.

How afraid are you that there will be terrorist attacks in Germany? (1) not afraid at all, (2) little afraid, (3) fairly afraid, (4) very afraid.

The same type of direct measurement was used for the *fear of crime* (index, Cronbach's $\alpha = 0.86$),[‡] which was constructed using different types of crime.

How afraid are you of becoming (a) victim of a theft, (b) victim of a burglary, (c) victim of an assault? (1) not afraid at all, (2) little afraid, (3) fairly afraid, (4) very afraid.

Existential fears (index, Cronbach's $\alpha = 0.77$) are based on five questions about the possible loss of the economic and social status quo (Drakos and Müller 2010; Hirtenlehner 2006) and are regarded as the counterpart to life satisfaction.

How afraid are you of (a) falling seriously ill, (b) becoming unemployed, (c) lower standards of living in old age, (d) loneliness in old age, (e) needing nursing care in old age and being a burden on others? (1) not afraid at all, (2) little afraid, (3) fairly afraid, (4) very afraid.

The *trade-off* was inquired using an everyday example considering between security and civil liberties. Most people are familiar with the situation at airport security screening, making the example easily understandable (see also Viscusi and Zeckhauser 2003).

---

[*] Particularly three ways have been established to deal with missing values. Byrne (2010, 355f.) notes that imputation, as well as pairwise and listwise deletion, has specific advantages and disadvantages. In this study, pairwise deletion was the method of choice, since it allows for a better use of the data set as it only deactivates variables with missing values when they are not needed for calculation.

[†] For a detailed introduction on SEM, see, for example, Backhaus et al. (2003) or Byrne (2010). For a good practical guidance on application, see Jöreskog (1993).

[‡] Cronbach's α is a coefficient of reliability, used to ensure the internal consistency of an index on the basis of correlations between its items.

How much additional time would you be willing to wait at the airport if all passengers were to be checked more thoroughly? (1) no additional time, (2) 1–15 min, (3) 16–30 min, (4) 31–60 min, (5) 61–120 min, (6) more than 120 min.

The *knowledge about security measures* (index, Cronbach's $\alpha = 0.52$)* was measured in a dichotomous way, asking whether respondents had heard about the security measures or not.

Have you heard about (a) the introduction of biometric passports and biometric identity cards containing a digital image and two fingerprints; (b) granting law enforcement agencies like the police and traffic authorities (Bußgeldbehörden) online access to digital images in biometric passports or biometric identity cards of suspects; (c) granting police, tax authorities, employment agencies, and social welfare offices online access to personal bank records of suspects; (d) instructing telecommunication providers to retain the following data for a period of 6 months: data about telephone calls made and received, emails sent and received, and web sites visited; in the case of using mobile phones, the data enable the identification of the location of the mobile phone; (e) permitting governmental security agencies to search suspects' personal computers for evidence of illegal activities without their knowledge; and (f) the establishment of an anti-terror database to which 38 German law enforcement agencies have access. Information in this database includes name, address, religion, travel movements, bank details, or the possession of firearms, (g) gathering and passing on of air and ship passenger data to the federal German police (Bundespolizei)? (0) no, (1) yes.

The acceptance of those measures was conducted in the form of the *assessment of security measures* (index, Cronbach's $\alpha = 0.83$). Being a theoretical construct, acceptance is difficult to measure. When a security measure is positively assessed, though, it is concluded that the acceptance of the security measure is correspondingly positive.

Following the question about individual knowledge about the seven German security measures, the respondents were asked to give an assessment of each of the measures, thereby providing information about the general acceptance of security measures: (1) very poor, (2) poor, (3) good, (4) very good.

Just like fear, trust is a highly subjective emotion. *System trust* (index, Cronbach's $\alpha = 0.70$) was measured as the individual trust in the institutions of the state. Concerning the fear of terrorism, it can be assumed that trust derives from the citizen's ascription of powers to the authorities to deal with a perceived threat.

How high is your level of trust in the following state institutions? (a) the government (Bundesregierung), (b) the legal authorities, (c) the police: (1) very much, (2) much, (3) little, (4) very little.

Being a subjective assessment of future odds, *probability: increase of fear* reflects the individual judgment of the impact of security measures. The question here is whether the fear of terrorism and the fear of crime are likely to be reduced or whether they are to remain on the same level as before.

Do you think that based on the introduced security measures, the fear of crime and terrorism will increase? (1) no, not at all; (2) more likely not; (3) more likely yes; (4) yes, absolutely.

Likewise, *probability: prevention of terrorism* captures not the impact of security measures on the level of fear but the assumed effectiveness of those measures by the citizens.

Do you think that the introduced security measures will prevent terrorist attacks? (1) no, not at all; (2) more likely not; (3) more likely yes; (4) yes, absolutely.

---

* The quality here is to be assessed as acceptable, although α falls short of 0.70, which is usually agreed to be a cutoff value (Peterson 1994; Christmann and Van Aelst 2006). Since all of the security measures lie on the same dimension, it is assumed that the election campaign for the German Bundestag caused salience in the knowledge of the measures, being responsible for the low item correlation.

4.3 "New" Terrorism and Fear

In order to analyze terrorism fear properly, at least some attention should be on understanding both the terms terrorism and fear. For this matter, the following section is dedicated to briefly providing a theoretical basis for the statistical analysis. Much attention has recently been paid to "new" forms of terrorism (Crenshaw 2000; Hoffman 2006). But then, what exactly are the specific aspects that separate "new" terrorism from older forms of terrorism?

Considering empirical results, the intuitive assumption that the number of terrorist attacks has increased since 9/11 can be easily refuted. Data from the U.S. Department of State show that there is no clear trend in frequency (Frey et al. 2007; Sandler and Enders 2004). On the contrary, though, the number of victims has reached new peaks roughly since 2000. Of course, the attacks of 9/11 are responsible for a main part of this increase, but on the whole terrorist attacks seem to have gained greater efficiency in the last years (Frey et al. 2007, 3–4). At least, the incidents turned out to be fatal at a higher percentage. Karstedt even calls 9/11 cynically the "most successful" terrorist incident up to date (Karstedt 2002, 125). The explanation for this development is to be found in improved and more powerful weapons and strategies (Frey et al. 2007). Hijacking airplanes is not a new terrorist tool, but using them as weapons adds a new dimension to the existing arsenal. Another aspect of new terrorism is the seemingly higher percentage of Islamist attacks, aiming at indiscriminately killing the highest possible number of people who do not correspond to the terrorists' religious views. For the purpose of maximum media attention, new forms of terrorist attacks are staged according to all theatrical rules, looking to control their depiction and the media coverage as far as possible (Klimke 2002).

Thus, "new" terrorism is based on an exclusive and closed system of values and ideology, which provides its own definitions of moral values and justice. Religious motives are additionally replenished with new forms of hierarchy (shallow structures of command) and organization (Hoffman 2006, 430f.). Global networks function by providing operational autonomy to fragmented cells, acting within their respective local and cultural context. The organization remains decentralized, and attacks are planned and executed independently in different parts of the network. Those structures correspond with the most important aim of attacks, which still is the creation of fear. Terrorist attacks strive to implement a message of vulnerability and fear into the collective conscience of societies. The devices and methods may have changed over the years, yet the creation of perceived threat remains the ultimate goal and is far more important than the factual level of security concerns identified by the authorities.

The psychological processing of external threat is a key factor in understanding how to balance technological and social issues in security measures. As has often been argued, modernity has become a highly complex environment for the individual. Old patterns and habitual orientations have largely been replaced by the need to make decision with unpredictable outcomes, thus by insecurity. This complexity is likely to create a state of confusion, since the individual is not capable of processing the entity of incoming information (Bauman 2006, 96ff.; Zolo 1992).

Fear can thus be regarded as the logical counterpart of security or as insecurity (Bauman 2006), which can easily be evoked by the threat of a terrorist attack. Leaving the individual in a state of uncertainty remains the principle of terrorism. Therefore, this study concentrates on perceived threat rather than on empirical or measurable threat. Correspondingly, it does not matter how perceived threat comes into being—either by extensive media coverage, mediated by the political system aiming at passing security legislation and introducing new surveillance and control measures, or by any other form. The consequence remains the same—fear produces a distorted perception of threat, leading to a highly subjective evaluation of risk.

An often-used example for this kind of cognitive lapse is traffic. It is widely known that in terms of mortality rate, significantly more people are killed in traffic than in terrorist attacks (Johansson-Stenman 2008, 235; Viscusi and Zeckhauser 2003, 99). However, intuitively, no one would rate traffic as a more significant threat than terrorism. The reasons for such a differing evaluation are to be found in the acceptance of everyday risks. As fear is a highly selective emotion (Sunstein 2007, 328), extreme events such as the attacks of 9/11 create an outstanding psychological impact, leaving their indelible marks on the collective conscience (Kasperson et al. 1988). In contrast to clinical concepts, the social sciences define fear as prospective, thus referring to events that might happen in the future (Sinclair 2010, 104). It can be assumed that fear is not necessarily linked to the actual happening of the event: nonetheless a concrete terrorist attack certainly has several effects on the general perception of risk. After 9/11, an increased number of cases of post-traumatic stress syndrome (PTSS) had been diagnosed. Those cases were not only locally bound to the area of the attacks. In fact, all over the U.S. territory, the same diagnosis would be certified in weakened forms (Marshall et al. 2007, 304), hinting at a wide-scale spread of threat perception within whole societies.

A brief glance at risk assessment also provides helpful insights on perceived threat. In the social sciences, an empirical, quantitative risk assessment, based on technical knowledge and statistical calculations, is often rejected as too narrow a concept (Kasperson et al. 1988, 178). Following Weber (2003), the perception of risk is not exclusively based on rational considerations about possible consequences of actions, but also influenced by several other dimensions. For example, emotions have a considerable impact on the individual assessment of risk (Cacioppo and Gardner 1999, 201ff.; Lerner et al. 2003, 144; Loewenstein et al. 2001; Sunstein 2007, 98). Crucial for the rejection of rational choice concepts is the fact that an objective "calculation" would require a person to be extensively informed about the risk to be assessed. On the contrary, individuals often specifically do not want to be informed in detail, but rather trust in an intuitive assessment of threat or risk (Slovic 1987; Sunstein 2007, 106), even when there is information about objective probabilities available (Loewenstein et al. 2001, 207).

Speaking from a social sciences perspective, there cannot be a true, rational risk, and neither can there be a false, socially constructed risk (Kasperson et al. 1988, 181). Perceived threat, in the end, results from a combination of influences on the individual and is what must be taken into account concerning this chapter's analysis. Thus, it focuses on general judgments of the population, which are not necessarily based on rational calculations (Marshall et al. 2007, 307). Some scholars have described the fears of the population as bipolar, either underestimating or overestimating threat (Sunstein 2007, 309; see Cacioppo and Gardner 1999, 201ff.). In the data set, for those reasons, not the individual assessment of the objective probability of a terrorist attack was inquired, but the survey explicitly asked about the individual fear of such an attack. Subjective fear is already linked to individual risk assessment.

4.4 Data Analysis

Based on the theoretical assumptions introduced in Section 4.1, in this section, the SEM model will be presented and evaluated. Based on the arguments discussed up to this point, two general tendencies concerning the fear of terrorism have become apparent. On the one hand, fears are not based on rational information processing and are somewhat independent of statistical risks. On the other hand, an increased need for security strongly calls for legal consequences. In a situation of perceived threat, the assessment of recently introduced security measures, and the general

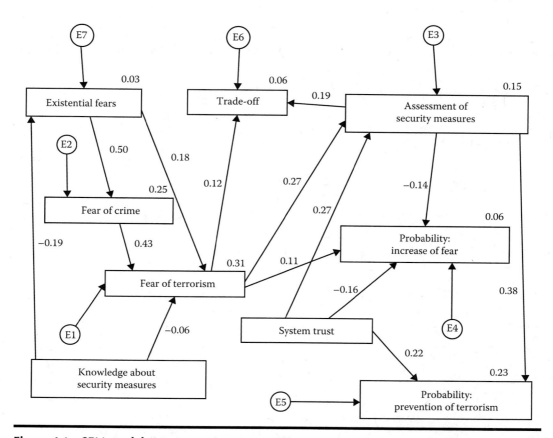

Figure 4.1 SEM model (N = 2174, χ² = 138.174, df = 22, p = 0.000, RMR = 0.018, RMSEA = 0.050, GFI = 0.986, NFI = 0.950). E1, E2, …: error terms; RMR, root mean square residual; RMSEA, root mean square error of approximation; GFI, goodness of fit index; NFI, normed fit index.

attitudes toward the political system tend to be much more positive than in a situation with no such perceived threat.

By modeling the theoretically assumed effects between the variables, this chapter seeks to identify determinants (independent variables) and consequences (dependent variables) of the fear of terrorism in Germany. Figure 4.1 shows the SEM model, representing the structure of the empirical data very well. The p level for the overall model is at 0.000, while the fit indexes root mean square residual (RMR, 0.018), root mean square error of approximation (RMSEA, 0.050), goodness of fit index (GFI, 0.986), and normed fit index (NFI, 0.950) all suggest a very good overall fit for the model (Blunch 2008; Schermelleh-Engel et al. 2003: 52). CMIN/df is 6.281, also indicating an acceptable fit. All in all, the assumed relations formulated on a theoretical basis are confirmed by the data. Table 4.1 specifies the parameters for every single path in the model, shifting the focus from overall fit to partial fit. All paths show a high level of significance (*** = $p \leq 0.01$). The standard error of estimation does not exceed 0.064, pointing to a reliable estimation of path coefficients. Additionally, the critical ratio goes beyond the cutoff value of 1.96 for all paths, and the matrix of residuals does not display any values exceeding 0.1. After all, not only the overall fit but also the partial fit of the model is to be assessed as very good.

Table 4.1 Standardized Regression Weights SEM Model

Dependent Variable		Independent Variable	Estimate	S.E.	C.R.	p
Existential fears	←	Knowledge about security measures	−0.187	0.061	−8.799	***
Fear of crime	←	Existential fears	0.497	0.020	26.487	***
Terrorism fear	←	Knowledge about security measures	0.062	0.064	−3.378	***
Terrorism fear	←	Fear of crime	0.432	0.024	20.849	***
Terrorism fear	←	Existential fears	0.180	0.026	8.566	***
Assessment of security measures	←	System trust	0.266	0.024	13.288	***
Assessment of security measures	←	Terrorism fear	0.274	0.016	13.722	***
Probability prevention of terrorism	←	System trust	0.219	0.032	11.138	***
Trade-off	←	Assessment of security measures	0.189	0.039	8.672	***
Probability increase of fear	←	System trust	−0.156	0.033	−7.177	***
Probability increase of fear	←	Assessment of security measures	−0.145	0.028	−6.380	***
Probability prevention of terrorism	←	Assessment of security measures	0.376	0.026	19.123	***
Trade-off	←	Terrorism fear	0.125	0.032	5.734	***
Probability increase of fear	←	Terrorism fear	0.114	0.022	5.236	***

$*p \leq 0.1$; $**p \leq 0.05$; $***p \leq 0.01$.

In order to be able to evaluate the quality of the modeled causal relations, it is necessary to take a closer look at the strength of the particular effects. Table 4.1 includes a complete listing of the standardized regression coefficients represented in the model. First of all, strong effects among the three types of fear (existential fears, fear of crime, fear of terrorism) confirm the assumption that the fear of terrorism is a special form of the fear of crime (0.432), and both types of fear originate from the same existential fears (0.492/0.180) (see Brück and Müller 2009; Hirtenlehner 2006; Wehrheim 2004). This can be considered as a clear hint for the hypothesis that, for a major part, reasons of fear are not created on a rational basis but rather influenced by other factors. Subjective selection of information prevents individuals from objective evaluation of risk or at least leads to distortion (Sunstein 2007; Tyler and

Tucker 1982). Considering the fact that everyday risks like smoking or car driving expose individuals to far greater threat than possible terrorist attacks (Johansson-Stenman 2008; Viscusi and Zeckhauser 2003), existential fears are the biggest influence factor of terrorism fear, which would not exactly be an intuitive association.

The knowledge about security measures introduced by the government, on the other hand, has only a small effect on the fear of terrorism (–0.062). Although the knowledge simultaneously moderates existential fears (–0.187), this more rational side influencing the fear of terrorist attacks is clearly weaker than the influence from other forms of fear. To sum up the first part of the hypothesis, arguing that the determinants for terrorism fear often remain relatively irrational and distorted, the fear of terrorist attacks is considered as a mixture of exaggerated threat perception and equally exaggerated risk assessment (see Slovic and Weber 2002; Sunstein 2007).

On the other hand, irrationality concerning the determinants of the fear of terrorism does not necessarily carry on regarding the consequences of the fear of terrorism. The second part of the hypothesis argues that increased fear of terrorist attacks would lead to more restrictive attitudes in the population, therefore contributing to a higher approval of security measures. Recent studies have shown that the trade-off between security and civil liberties changes according to the level of threat societies are confronted with (Viscusi and Zeckhauser 2003). While liberal political systems emphasize the freedom of the individual from the state, debates about security legislation are dominated by the emphasis of freedom granted (and simultaneously endangered) by the state. In the model, the concrete trade-off scenario is in fact positively influenced by the level of the fear of terrorism (0.125). Furthermore, the assessment of security measures has a positive effect on the willingness to pay for security (0.189).

Basically, security legislation can be regarded as a governmental reaction to an expressed need of protection by the citizens. The political system responds in a simple fashion: the temporal and factual connection of security measures to the addressed threat is of utmost importance (Schulte 2008). Of course, effectiveness and adequacy of the measures also do matter, but security legislation might be regarded primarily as a symbolic act, satisfying the needs for a perceived security in the population. Not surprisingly, cutbacks in civil liberties have been criticized relatively little by the population (Huddy et al. 2007) compared to the scholarly critique. According to a shift in the trade-off, security measures are assessed more positively depending on the level of the fear of terrorism. Within the structure of the data set, in addition to this effect (0.274), the assessment of security measures is also influenced by the trust in the political system (0.266). Likewise, the better the overall assessment of the included security measures is, the lesser the individual expectation of a further increase of fear (–0.145) and the higher the anticipated probability of preventing future terrorist attacks (0.376) will be. Both probabilities are also influenced by the trust in the political system. A higher level of trust in the institutions of the state causes an expected lesser probability of increased fear (–0.156) and an anticipated higher probability of future prevention of terrorist attacks (0.219).

Surprisingly, there is no effect of the fear of terrorism on the trust in the political system. Several studies have confirmed the assumption that a higher level of fear of terrorist attacks would lead to increased trust in the government or in the political system as a whole (Chanley 2002; Davis and Silver 2004; Huddy et al. 2003; Sinclair and LoCicero 2010). In the structure of the data set, though, neither an effect of the fear of terrorism on trust in the government nor an effect on system trust could be identified.

4.5 Discussion and Conclusion

Analogous to an increased citizens' need for security, concepts for security have changed. When facing external threat, preventive forms of security, though arguably having a negative impact on civil liberties, are evaluated far more positive than in times when there is no external threat. Modern security measures turn the sequence of criminal act, prosecution, and punishment upside down and shift the focus to investigations in the forefront of the concrete offense (Hassemer 2002). More distinguishing features of this shift are the lack of distinction between crime and terrorism and an increased feeling of insecurity (von Trotha 2010, 220). The lacking differentiation between crime and terrorism has especially led to the application of more rigid surveillance and control techniques, especially when methods derived from warfare can be applied to potential enemies inside of societies (Scheerer 2003, 93ff.).

The presented model shows that the security measures implemented by the German government are assessed positively by the citizens when the level of the fear of terrorism is high. Accordingly, the population is willing to support preventive forms of security. The assumption that the need for security has reached new heights, as well as the acceptance for modern security measures, could be confirmed. The output of the political system in form of security legislation is appreciated by the population. But surprisingly, the political system itself does not benefit from this output. Although several empirical studies have claimed a connection between the fear of terrorist attacks and the trust in the government, this assumption could not be confirmed by the data set. Linked closely to perceived threat and the assessment of security measures is the individual anticipation of the probability of future events. The model shows that the assessment of probabilities is highly consistent with the overall assessment of surveillance and control measures. But the evaluation of prospective probabilities also depends on the trust in the political system, meaning that in this case, there is no distinction between output and system.

The aim of this chapter was to provide a review of the German situation concerning the fear of terrorism, security legislation, and their societal consequences, using a powerful statistical method (SEM). Focusing on "new" forms of religious terrorism (Münkler 2002), it chose to have a closer look at determinants and consequences of the fear of terrorism. As a matter of fact, many findings from recent literature are supported by the representative survey data. In summary, it could be stated that determinants of the fear of terrorism are predominantly subjective, while the consequences of fear show a more rational structure. Setting the focus for a great part on modern security measures that became a product of post-9/11 security legislation in Germany, the analysis has shown that exaggerated perceptions of threat can easily lead to factual consequences for societies. In this way, risks that are objectively not bigger than other risks are potentially able to destabilize the common consensus of liberal political systems. A need for safety is expressed in the public's demand and acceptance of more and more technological solutions (e.g., security measures). This demand affects, as technological development goes on, not only parts of the German population but all of it. Finally, globalized forms of terrorism evoke new forms of legal reactions. The political system primarily addresses the needs of the population by turning to new concepts of security. This change has been accompanied by controversial debates that most likely will not subside for quite some time. But from a social science point of view, keeping in mind that in representative political systems power still derives from a mandate of the population, one should always be aware of the fact that laws are merely an expression of societal needs and therefore can be changed. Following this argument, if the trade-off between security and civil liberties should tilt toward security, eventually a stronger need for liberty would be formulated and expressed by the citizens.

What further starting points do evolve from these findings? Concerning the research design, any form of longitudinal data analysis would be highly desirable in order to examine if and how the findings of the existing literature would change over time (see Sinclair and LoCicero 2010). Cross-sectional data only represent the population's attitudes at the time of the survey. In addition, a comparative research design would be appropriate (Sjöberg 2005, 58). Since religious terrorism according to the definition applied in this chapter focuses mainly on Western societies, a study examining differences in the processing of terrorist threat in several EU member countries would also be fruitful. Much has been written about legal consequences of terrorist attacks, while societal reactions are still an important field to be further researched.

References

Backhaus, K., B. Erichson, W. Plinke, and R. Weiber. 2003. *Multivariate Analysemethoden: Eine Anwendungsorientierte Einführung*, 10th edn. Berlin, Germany: Springer.

Bauman, Z. 1999. Freiheit und Sicherheit. Die unvollendete Geschichte einer stürmischen Beziehung. In *Die neue Ordnung des Politischen. Die Herausforderungen der Demokratie am Beginn des 21. Jahrhunderts*, E. Anselm, A. Freytag, W. Marschitz, and B. Marte (Eds.). Frankfurt a.M., Germany: Campus-Verlag, pp. 23–34.

Bauman, Z. 2006. *Liquid Fear*. Cambridge: Polity.

Blunch, N. J. 2008. *Introduction to Structural Equation Modelling using SPSS and AMOS*. Los Angeles/London/New Delhi/Singapore: Sage Publications.

Böckenförde, E.-W. 1976. *Staat, Gesellschaft, Freiheit. Studien zur Staatstheorie und zum Verfassungsrecht*. Frankfurt a.M., Germany: Suhrkamp.

Bozzoli, C. and C. Müller. 2009. Perceptions and attitudes to a terrorist shock: Evidence from the UK. Economics of Security Working Paper 13, Berlin, Germany.

Brück, T. and C. Müller. 2009. Comparing the determinants of concern about terrorism and crime. DIW Discussion Papers 904, Berlin, Germany.

Byrne, B. M. 2010. *Structural Equation Modeling with AMOS. Basic Concepts, Applications, and Programming*. New York: Routledge.

Cacioppo, J. T. and W. L. Gardner. 1999. Emotion. *Annual Review of Psychology* 50: 191–214.

Callies, C. 2002. Sicherheit im freiheitlichen Rechtsstaat. Eine verfassungsrechtliche Gratwanderung mit staatstheoretischem Kompass. *Zeitschrift für Rechtspolitik* 35(1): 1–12.

Chanley, V. A. 2002. Trust in government in the aftermath of 9/11: Determinants and consequences. *Political Psychology* 23(3): 469–483.

Christmann, A. and S. Van Aelst. 2006. Robust estimation of Cronbach's alpha. *Journal of Multivariate Analysis* 97(7): 1660–1674.

Crenshaw, M. 2000. The psychology of terrorism: An agenda for the 21st century. *Political Psychology* 21(2): 405–420.

Daase, C. 2001. Terrorismus—Begriffe, Theorien und Gegenstrategien. Ergebnisse und Probleme sozialwissenschaftlicher Forschung. *Die Friedens-Warte. Journal of International Peace and Organization* 76(1): 55–79.

Davis, D. W. and B. D. Silver. 2004. Civil liberties vs. security: Public opinion in the context of the terrorist attacks on America. *American Journal of Political Science* 48(1): 28–46.

Drakos, K. and C. Müller. 2010. On the determinants of terrorism risk concern in Europe. Economics of Security Working Paper 36, Berlin, Germany.

Frey, B. S., S. Luechinger, and A. Stutzer. 2007. Calculating tragedy: Assessing the costs of terrorism. *Journal of Economic Surveys* 21(1): 1–24.

Garland, D. 2001. *The Culture of Control. Crime and Social Order in Contemporary Society*. Chicago, IL: University of Chicago Press.

Hassemer, W. 2002. Zum Spannungsverhältnis von Freiheit und Sicherheit. Drei Thesen. *Vorgänge* 41(3): 10–15.

Hirtenlehner, H. 2006. Kriminalitätsfurcht—Ausdruck generalisierter Ängste und schwindender Gewissheiten? *Kölner Zeitschrift für Soziologie und Sozialpsychologie* 58(2): 307–331.

Hoffman, B. 2006. *Terrorismus—der Unerklärte Krieg: Neue Gefahren Politischer Gewalt.* Bonn, Germany: Bundeszentrale für Politische Bildung.

Hoffmann-Riem, W. 2002. Freiheit und Sicherheit im Angesicht terroristischer Anschläge. *Zeitschrift für Rechtspolitik* 35(12): 497–502.

Huddy, L., S. Feldman, G. Lahav, and C. Taber. 2003. Fear and terrorism: Psychological reactions to 9/11. In *Framing Terrorism. The News Media, the Government, and the Public*, P. Norris, M. Kern, and M. R. Just (Eds.). New York: Routledge, pp. 255–280.

Huddy, L., S. Feldman, and C. Weber. 2007. The political consequences of perceived threat and felt insecurity. *Annals of the American Academy of Political and Social Science* 614(1): 131–153.

Johansson-Stenman, O. 2008. Mad cows, terrorism and junk food: Should public policy reflect perceived or objective risks? *Journal of Health Economics* 27(2): 234–248.

Jöreskog, K. G. 1993. Testing structural equation models. In *Testing Structural Equation Models*, K. A. Bollen and J. S. Long (Eds.). Newbury Park: Sage, pp. 294–316.

Karstedt, S. 2002. Terrorismus und "Neue Kriege". *Kriminologisches Journal* 34(2): 124–131.

Kasperson, R. E., O. Renn, P. Slovic, H. S. Brown, J. Emel, R. Goble, J. X. Kasperson, and S. Ratick. 1988. The social amplification of risk: A conceptual framework. *Risk Analysis* 8(2): 177–187.

Klimke, D. 2002. Zeichen des Terrors. *Kriminologisches Journal* 34(2): 89–97.

Lerner, J. S., R. M. Gonzalez, D. A. Small, and B. Fischhoff. 2003. Effects of fear and danger on perceived risks of terrorism: A national field experiment. *Psychological Science* 14(2): 144–150.

Loewenstein, G. F., E. U. Weber, C. K. Hsee, and N. Welch. 2001. Risk as feelings. *Psychological Bulletin* 127(2): 267–286.

Lübcke, B. and J. C. Irlenkaeuser. 2006. *Bedrohungsperzeption durch das Phänomen des Terrorismus und Bewertung der Gegenmaßnahmen der BR Deutschland.* Kiel, Germany: Institut für Sicherheitspolitik.

Lüdtke, A., M. Sturm, and H. Uhl. 2003. Ängste, Risiken, Sicherheit. *SoWi. Das Journal für Geschichte, Politik, Wirtschaft und Kultur* 32(2): 4–14.

Marshall, R. D., R. A. Bryant, L. Amsel, E. J. Suh, J. M. Cook, and Y. Neria. 2007. The psychology of ongoing threat: Relative risk appraisal, the September 11 attacks, and terrorism-related fears. *American Psychologist* 62(4): 304–316.

Müller, C. 2008. Sorgen um den globalen Terrorismus in Deutschland. Wochenbericht des DIW 37, Berlin, Germany.

Münkler, H. 2002. *Die neuen Kriege.* Reinbek bei Hamburg, Germany: Rowohlt.

Nachtigall, C., U. Kroehne, F. Funke, and R. Steyer. 2003. (Why) Should we use SEM? Pros and cons of structural equation modeling. *Methods of Psychological Research Online* 8(2): 1–22.

Peterson, R. A. 1994. A meta-analysis of Cronbach's coefficient alpha. *Journal of Consumer Research* 21(2): 381–391.

Sandler, T. and W. Enders. 2004. An economic perspective on transnational terrorism. *European Journal of Political Economy* 20(2): 301–316.

Scheerer, S. 2003. Einige definitionstheoretische Aspekte des 'Terrorismus'. In *Grenzenlose Konstruktivität? Standortbestimmung und Zukunftsperspektiven konstruktivistischer Theorien abweichenden Verhaltens*, B. Menzel and K. Ratzke (Eds.). Opladen, Germany: Leske + Budrich, pp. 85–98.

Schermelleh-Engel, K., H. Moosbrugger, and H. Müller. 2003. Evaluating the fit of structural equation models: Tests of significance and descriptive goodness-of-fit measures. *MPR-Online* 8(2): 23–74.

Schulte, P. H. 2008. *Terrorismus und Anti-Terrorismus-Gesetzgebung: Eine Rechtssoziologische Analyse.* Münster, Germany: Waxmann.

Sinclair, S. J. 2010. Fears of terrorism and future threat: Theoretical and empirical considerations. In *Interdisciplinary Analyses of Terrorism and Political Aggression*, D. Antonius, A. D. Brown, T. K. Walters, J. M. Ramirez, and S. J. Sinclair (Eds.). Newcastle, U.K.: Cambridge Scholars, pp. 101–115.

Sinclair, S. J. and A. LoCicero. 2010. Do fears of terrorism predict trust in government? *Journal of Aggression, Conflict and Peace Research* 2(1): 57–68.

Sjöberg, L. 2005. The perceived risk of terrorism. *Risk Management* 7(1): 43–61.

Slovic, P. 1987. Perception of risk. *Science* 236: 280–285.

Slovic, P. and E. U. Weber. 2002. Perceptions of risk posed by extreme events. Paper prepared for discussion at the conference '*Risk Management Strategies in an Uncertain World*', April 12–13, Palisades, New York.

Sunstein, C. R. 2007. *Gesetze der Angst: Jenseits des Vorsorgeprinzips.* Frankfurt a.M., Germany: Suhrkamp.

von Trotha, T. 2010. Vom Wandel des Gewaltmonopols oder der Aufstieg der präventiven Sicherheitsordnung. *Kriminologisches Journal* 42(3): 218–234.

Tyler, S. K. and D. M. Tucker. 1982. Anxiety and perceptual structure: Individual differences in neuropsychological function. *Journal of Abnormal Psychology* 91(3): 210–220.

Viscusi, W. K. and R. J. Zeckhauser. 2003. Sacrificing civil liberties to reduce terrorism risks. *Journal of Risk and Uncertainty* 26(2): 99–120.

Weber, E. U. 2003. Origins and functions of perceptions of risk. Presentation at *NCI Workshop on Conceptualizing and Measuring Risk Perceptions*, February 13–14, Washington, DC.

Wehrheim, J. 2004. Städte im blickpunkt innerer sicherheit. *Aus Politik und Zeitgeschichte* 44: 21–27.

Zedner, L. 2007. Pre-crime and post-criminology? *Theoretical Criminology* 11(2): 261–281.

Zolo, D. 1992. *Democracy and Complexity: A Realist Approach.* University Park, PA: Pennsylvania State University Press.

Chapter 5

Preserving and Managing Privacy Information in Video Surveillance Systems

Jithendra K. Paruchuri, Ying Luo, and Sen-Ching S. Cheung

Contents

5.1 Introduction

Video surveillance has become a part of our daily lives. Closed-circuit cameras are mounted in countless shopping malls for deterring crimes, at toll booths for assessing tolls, and at traffic intersections for catching speeding drivers. Since the 9-11 terrorist attack, there have been much research efforts directed at applying advanced pattern recognition algorithms to video surveillance. Specifically, searchable surveillance with the help of automatic event detection and human recognition had turned the once labor-intensive monitoring into powerful automated system that can quickly and accurately identify and track visual objects and events. For example, as reported in the Face Recognition Vendor Test (FRVT) in 2006, the best-performing algorithms have already exceeded human capability in face recognition, achieving a false rejection rate of 0.01 at a false acceptance rate of 0.001 [1]. Thus, it is unsurprising that the general public is increasingly wary about the possibility of privacy invasion with video surveillance systems. From the public outcry on the use of face recognition in public events [2] to the report by the American Civil Liberties Union (ACLU) on the surveillance systems' assault on public's privacy [3], privacy concerns about surveillance systems can rival those on sensitive financial and medical information. To mitigate these concerns and to facilitate continued development of surveillance technologies, it is imperative to make privacy protection a priority in current and future video surveillance systems.

In the United States, the constitutional theory of the right to privacy is expressed in various sections of the U.S. and state constitutions [4]. While there is no comprehensive framework on how privacy should be protected in video surveillance, there is widespread support for the technology. According a recent random phone survey we conducted on noninstitutionalized Kentuckians 18 years of age and older,* the solid majority expressed that they were interested in privacy-protecting video surveillance. Urban residents, those in higher income levels and those with advanced education attainment, all were more disposed to privacy-protecting video technology. Additionally, focus groups of law enforcement, first responders, hospitals, and public infrastructure managers have all reflected strong interest in privacy-protecting video technology. In this chapter, our goal is to outline the technological foundation for privacy protection in video surveillance, which could ultimately form the necessary foundation for future legislation.

There have been many recent works in enhancing privacy protection in surveillance systems [5–11]. Many of them share the common theme of identifying sensitive information and applying image-processing schemes for obfuscating that sensitive information. But the security flaw overlooked in most of these systems is that they fail to consider the security impact of modifying the surveillance videos. The key challenge facing any such system is to provide a balanced approach so that the need for privacy can be addressed without interfering with the intended purpose of providing security. As such, a privacy-enhanced surveillance system must provide a clear policy for retaining and accessing the privacy information for various purposes, for example, as evidence in

---

* The survey was a cooperative effort through the University of Kentucky annual Kentucky Survey, and the research was sponsored by a grant from the U.S. Department of Homeland Security through the National Institute for Hometown Security. The survey research was conducted utilizing a modified list-assisted Waksberg Mitofsky random-digit-dialing procedure for sampling, and the population surveyed was noninstitutionalized Kentuckians 18 years of age and older. The margin of error is 3.3% at the confidence interval. The respondents were asked, "Do you have a video security system that is used routinely?" The results reflected that employed Kentuckians have an operative video surveillance system at their workplace. We then asked of those employed, "Would you be interested in a video surveillance system at work if you knew it could protect an individual's privacy?"

a legal proceeding. While sophisticated privacy policy has been studied in the literature [12], the privacy visual information of an individual should be ideally treated in the same manner as any other personal information such as passport or credit card numbers. That is, every access of such information must require a full consent from the corresponding individual. To satisfy this goal, a privacy-protected surveillance system must be able to address two key goals:

1. *Privacy information preservation*: How to preserve and retrieve the privacy information?
2. PIM: Who can retrieve the privacy information?

This chapter addresses the first problem by using video data hiding to preserve the privacy information in the modified video itself in a seamless fashion. Using data hiding, we not only can provide access to the privacy data but also can conceal its existence. The video bit stream will be accessible for both regular and authorized decoders, but only the latter can retrieve the hidden privacy information. Also the use of data hiding for privacy data preservation makes it completely independent from the obfuscation step unlike in some other work [13,14].

The application of using data hiding for privacy data preservation is unique in the sense it requires huge amount of information to be embedded in the video without disturbing the compression bit syntax. Since data hiding disturbs the underlying statistical patterns of the source data, it adversely affects the performance of compression that is designed based on the statistical properties of the data. As such, it is imperative to design a data-hiding scheme that is compatible with the compression algorithm and at the same time introduces as little perceptual distortion as possible. In this work, we propose a novel compression-domain video data-hiding algorithm that determines the optimal embedding strategy to minimize both the output perceptual distortion and the output bit rate. The hidden data are embedded into selective discrete cosine transform (DCT) coefficients that are found in most video compression standards.

The second part of this chapter addresses the privacy information management (PIM) problem. Our goal here is to provide anonymous access to the individual his or her preserved privacy information. To satisfy this goal, the surveillance system must be able to reliably associate the identity of an individual to the visual information based on, for example, various forms of biometrics. Unfortunately, the combination of biometrics and visual information dramatically increases the privacy risk of the entire system as identity information will be directly linked to pixels. To address this problem, we propose a novel system that provides selective and anonymous access to the preserved privacy information in video surveillance systems using iris biometrics. There are two main components in our system. The first component is an anonymous biometric access control (ABAC) module that matches iris patterns in encrypted domain to determine whether an individual needs privacy protection. Our implementation of ABAC is based on Ref. [15]. The ABAC module allows the surveillance system to reliably discern whether a particular visual object needs to be redacted and preserved without knowing the true identity.

In the second component, we encrypt the private visual information using the iris pattern provided to the ABAC module. Specifically, our scheme is based on the key-binding iris template scheme proposed in Ref. [16]. Error correction coding (ECC) is used to allow small amount of variation between two different iris patterns from the same individual. A concatenated-coding scheme is adopted to correct two types of errors: Random errors brought by camera pixel noise and iris distortion are corrected by Hadamard code, while burst error introduced by undetected eyelashes and specular reflections are corrected by Reed-Solomon code.

The rest of this chapter is organized as follows: We first review related work in Section 5.2 and provide an overview of our proposed system in Section 5.3. The design of the optimized data-hiding module for privacy information preservation is presented in Section 5.4. Next in Section 5.5, we describe the two secure protocols used in our privacy data management system: the privacy information encryption and privacy information retrieval. In Section 5.6, experimental results are presented to show the efficiency of our data-hiding and information management schemes. Section 5.7 concludes this chapter by discussing future work.

5.2 Related Work

5.2.1 Privacy Information Preservation

In this section, we review existing work on visual privacy protection technologies followed by video data-hiding and privacy management techniques. There is a recent surge of interest in selective protection of visual objects in video surveillance. The PrivacyCam surveillance system developed at IBM protects privacy by revealing only the relevant information such as object tracks or suspicious activities [17]. Such a system is limited by the types of events it can detect and may have problems balancing privacy protection with the particular needs of a security officer. Alternatively, one can modify the video to obfuscate the appearance of individuals for privacy protection. In Ref. [5], the authors propose a privacy-protecting video surveillance system that utilizes RFID sensors to identify incoming individuals, ascertains their privacy preference specified in an XML-based privacy policy database, and finally uses a simple video-masking technique to selectively conceal authorized individuals and display unauthorized intruders in the video. While Ref. [5] may be the first to describe a privacy-protected video surveillance system, there are a large body of work that utilize such kinds of video modification for privacy protection. They range from the use of black boxes or large pixels in Refs. [6,7] to complete object removal as in Ref. [5]. New techniques have also been proposed recently to replace a particular face with a generic face [10,18] or a body with a stick figure [11] or complete object removal followed by inpainting of background and other foreground objects [19,20].

All the aforementioned work target only at the modification of the video but not at the feasibility of recovering original video securely. To securely preserve the original video, selective scrambling of sensitive information using a private key has been proposed in Refs. [13,14,21–23]. These schemes differ in terms of the types of information scrambled that leads to different complexity and compression performances—for example, spatial pixels are scrambled in Ref. [13] and DCT signs and Wavelet coefficients are used in Refs. [14,21], respectively. With the appropriate private key, the scrambling can be undone to retrieve the original video. These techniques have the advantages of simplicity with modified regions clearly marked. However, there are a number of drawbacks. First, similar to pixelation and blocking, scrambling is unable to fully protect the privacy of individuals, revealing their routes, motion, shape, and even intensity levels [10]. Second, as obfuscation is usually the first step in a complex process chain of a smart surveillance system, it introduces artifacts that can affect the performance of subsequent image processing. Lastly, the coupling of scrambling and data preservation prevents other obfuscation schemes like object replacement or removal to be used.

Using data hiding for privacy data preservation is more flexible as it completely isolates preservation from modification. Since our introduction of using data hiding for privacy data preservation in Ref. [24], there have been other works like Refs. [25–29] that employ a similar approach. Unlike other works, our contribution in the data-hiding algorithm is an optimization framework to combine both the distortion and rate together as a single cost function and to use it in identifying the optimal locations to hide data. This allows a significant amount of information to be embedded into compressed bit streams without disproportional increase in either output bit rate or perceptual distortion.

5.2.2 Privacy Information Management

There have been a number of work in providing information access to privacy data. One approach is to use a trusted centralized unit to act as a mediator between various parties [30,31]. However, this trusted mediator creates a single point of failure and is vulnerable to concerted attacks. Cheung et al. proposed a new management system within which the users and the client agents can anonymously exchange data, credential, and authorization information [32]. A mediator is still used in this architecture, but the users do not need to trust the mediator as plaintext videos are protected from the system. On other hand, anonymous access control is not implemented in the system, and the mediator can associate the encrypted videos with the identity of an individual.

As mentioned in Section 5.1, one approach to combine anonymity in biometric access control and privacy data management is to encrypt the privacy information using the biometric signal itself. Methods that use biometric to protect sensitive data are referred to as biometric cryptosystems [33]. They have been applied in a number of practical biometric systems [16,34–36] in which a random key is protected by a biometric signal to produce a privacy template [16,34] or helper data [35,36]. Such a privacy template or helper data can only be decrypted by another biometric sample from the same individual. The purpose of their proposed protocols is to protect the security of the biometric system against the attack to central server by replacing the raw biometric samples with these templates. For our application, we use biometric cryptosystems to protect the Advanced Encryption Standard (AES) keys that encrypt the privacy imagery. Specifically, our scheme is based on the key-binding iris template scheme proposed in Ref. [16], in which ECC is used to allow small amount of variation between two different iris patterns from the same individual.

5.3 Privacy-Protected Video Surveillance

In order to appreciate the role of privacy information preservation and management, it is imperative to understand how it fits into the overall architecture of a privacy-protected video surveillance system. A high-level description of our proposed system is shown in Figure 5.1. The three main processing units are the secure camera system, the subject identification module, and the privacy data management system. The secure camera system is similar to any smart camera system in that it contains the typical object identification and tracking functionalities. In addition, it also obfuscates the appearance of individuals who need privacy protection. The raw video objects are then encrypted and stored within the modified video via our secure data-hiding module. The detailed description of the data-hiding module can be found in Section 5.4.

The subject identification module uses anonymous biometric matching to identify and discriminate an authorized user from others. The two main processing units in this module are the biometric server and the biometric reader as depicted in Figure 5.2a. The server has a biometric database of M biometric signals $DB = \{\mathbf{x}_1, \ldots, \mathbf{x}_M\}$, where $\mathbf{x}_i = (x_1^i, \ldots, x_n^i)^T$ is the biometric signal of member i. The biometric reader is installed outside each entrance of the surveillance area. It is used to capture the biometric signal of every individual entering the area to validate their identity. In order to perform biometric signal matching in an anonymous fashion, we used the ABAC system described in Ref. [15] that performs the matching entirely in encrypted domain and reveals only a

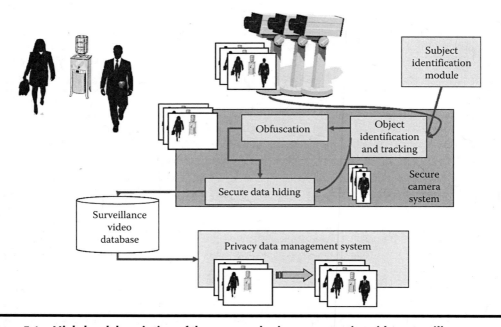

Figure 5.1 High-level description of the proposed privacy-protecting video surveillance system.

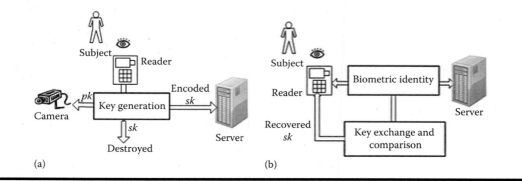

Figure 5.2 Privacy Information Management. (a) Encryption and (b) retrieval.

single bit that indicates a match to the server. We will not go into details of ABAC in this chapter, and interested readers should consult Ref. [15].

The reader also has a keypad for the user to enter a passcode that is needed for the key generation in PIM process. After capturing both the biometric signal and the passcode, the reader randomly generates a pair of public key (*pk*) and secret key (*sk*). *pk* is sent to the secure camera system that will use the key to encrypt all imageries associated with the individual, embed them into the modified video, and send them to the server. As for the secret key *sk*, the reader will apply an error correction code to it and encrypt the result using a combination of biometric signal and the passcode from the individual. This encrypted secret key will also be sent to the server and stored alongside with the privacy video of the same individual.

As we will demonstrate in Section 5.5, the server, even with access to all the biometric signals, cannot break the encryption due to the use of the secret passcode known only to the specific individual. When there is a request to retrieve the original imageries at a later time, the requester must demonstrate his or her identity by presenting both the biometric signal and the password to a reader, possibly different from the one used at the entrance. The aforementioned use of error correction code is designed to absorb the noise introduced by a different reader. As depicted in Figure 5.2(b), the passcode and biometric signal will be used to recover the secret sk. Using sk, the requester can use it to decrypt the videos and only those videos that correspond to the requester. The details of these procedures can be found in Section 5.5.

5.4 Data Hiding for Privacy Preservation

In this section, we describe the various components in our proposed data-hiding unit. Figure 5.3 shows the overall design of the data-hiding unit and its interaction with the video compression algorithm. Our data hiding is integrated with a typical motion-compensated DCT video compression algorithm such as ITU-T H.263. In Figure 5.3, the purple area contains the components of the data-hiding module, while the green area contains those of the compression module. There are two inputs to this combined unit: The first one is the privacy-protected video with the sensitive information already redacted. The second input is the compressed video bit streams of the privacy information, encrypted based on the approach described in Section 5.3. The goal is to hide the second input in the first input in a joint data-hiding compression framework. After the motion compensation process, the residue of the privacy-protected video is converted into the DCT domain. The embedding step is introduced between the final step of entropy coding and the DCT. This ensures that the decoder gets the same reference frame to prevent any drifting errors. The encrypted video stream is hidden, using a modified parity embedding scheme, in the luminance DCT blocks that occupy the largest portion of the bit stream. The positions of embedding are obtained using an R-D optimization framework to minimize the distortion and rate increase for a target-embedding requirement. The distortion is based on human visual system, and a perceptual mask in DCT domain is used to facilitate the calculation. The distortion and rate calculations for the R-D block, the embedding techniques, and the optimization algorithms are explained in the following subsections. Note that while the proposed data-hiding algorithm is general enough to be used in any video codec, the distortion and rate calculations are specific to an H.263 codec.

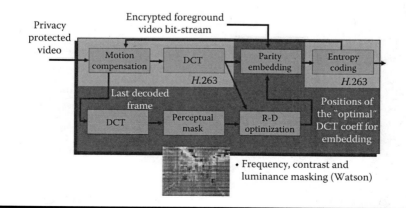

Figure 5.3   Schematic diagram of the data-hiding and video compression system.

5.4.1 Perceptual Distortion

To identify the embedding locations that cause the minimal disturbance to visual quality, we need a distortion metric to input into our optimization framework. Mean square distortion does not work for our goal of finding the optimal DCT coefficients to embed data bits—as DCT is an orthonormal transform, the mean square distortion for the same number of embedded bits will always be the same regardless of which DCT coefficients are used. Instead, we adopt the DCT perceptual model proposed by Watson [37], which has been shown to better correlate with the human visual system than standard mean square distortion. While there are other more sophisticated video-based perceptual models such as the one in Ref. [38], we adopt the Watson model for its simplicity to be included in our optimization algorithm.

The Watson model takes into accounts the overall luminance, contrast, and frequency of a coefficient and calculates a perceptual mask $s(i,j,k)$ that indicates the maximum just-noticeable change to $c(i,j,k)$, the (i,j)th coefficient of the kth 8×8 DCT block of an image:

$$s(i,j,k) = \max\left[t_L(i,j,k), |c(i,j,k)|^{0.7} \, t_L(i,j,k)^{0.3} \right] \tag{5.1}$$

where

$$t_L(i,j,k) = t(i,j)\left(\frac{c(0,0,k)}{c_0} \right)^{0.649} \tag{5.2}$$

for $i,j \in \{0,1,\ldots,7\}$. $t(i,j)$ is the frequency sensitivity threshold, $c(0,0,k)$ is the DC term of block k, and c_0 is the average luminance of the image [39]. The higher the mask value, the less distortion the corresponding coefficient will cost by embedding hidden data. As the embedding is performed in the quantized coefficient domain, it is convenient to normalize with the quantization step size and use the following distortion value instead:

$$D(i,j,k) = \frac{QP}{s(i,j,k)} \tag{5.3}$$

where
  QP is the quantization parameter
  $s(i,j,k)$ is the perceptual mask value as calculated in Equation 5.1

As a few highly distorted coefficients account for more distortion than many mildly distorted ones [39], an L_4 norm pooling is employed for calculating the total distortion over the entire frame:

$$D = \left(\sum_{i,j,k} |D(i,j,k)|^4 \right)^{1/4} \tag{5.4}$$

5.4.2 Embedding Process

To embed data in the compressed bit stream, we follow the *quantization index modulation* (QIM) approach in which quantization is altered based on the hidden data. Let $c(i,j,k)$ and $q(i,j,k)$ be the (i,j)th coefficient of the kth DCT block before and after quantization, respectively. They are related as in Equation 5.5 where QP is the chosen quantization parameter at the codec:

$$q(i,j,k) = \left\lfloor \frac{c(i,j,k) + QP}{2 \cdot QP} \right\rfloor \tag{5.5}$$

The maximum error due to the quantization will be QP as reconstruction values are centered in the quantization bins of width $2 \cdot QP$. To enable the data hiding, the quantization is made coarser with the finer levels reserved to represent the embedded bits. To embed an L-bit number V in a coefficient, the quantized coefficient can be altered in two different ways:

$$\tilde{q}(i,j,k) = \left\lfloor \frac{c(i,j,k) + 2^L \cdot QP}{2^{L+1} \cdot QP} \right\rfloor \cdot 2^L + V \tag{5.6}$$

or

$$\tilde{q}(i,j,k) = \left\lceil \frac{c(i,j,k) + 2^L \cdot QP}{2^{L+1} \cdot QP} \right\rceil \cdot 2^L + (V - 2^L) \tag{5.7}$$

The choice of embedding with (5.6) or (5.7) depends on which method produces a reconstructed value closer to the real $c(i,j,k)$. Hidden data extraction is straightforward—for an L-bit embedding in a particular coefficient, it is given as in Equation 5.8:

$$x = \tilde{q}(i,j,k) \bmod 2^L \tag{5.8}$$

This embedding, however, is not invertible. Since the quantization is altered to a coarser level as part of data embedding, it causes irrecoverable loss of data. For a single bit embedding, the maximum quantization noise doubles compared to that of without embedding. Besides the irreversible changes to the coefficient, the modified reference frame in the motion loop propagates the effect of data hiding into future frames, making the changes permanent. We can also use reversible embedding techniques [40] but usually at the expense of available embedding bit rate.

5.4.3 Rate Model

Data hiding affects the compression performance—simply choosing the distortion-optimal locations based on the perceptual model may increase the output bit rate manyfold. As surveillance video is typically quite static, many DCT blocks do not have any nonzero coefficients. Hiding bits into these zero blocks, while perceptual optimal, may significantly increase the bit rate.

This is caused by the fragmentation of the long run-length patterns that are assumed to be frequent by the entropy coder. One possible approach to mitigate this problem is to limit the number of blocks to be modified [24]. However, the fewer blocks used for embedding, the more spatially concentrated the embedding becomes that will make the distortion more visible. As such, we need to measure the increase in rate by different embedding strategies so as to produce the optimal trade-off with the distortion. The rate increase for a particular embedding is calculated using the actual entropy coder used for compression. As both the encoder and the decoder need to compute the rate function so as to derive the optimal data-hiding positions, the actual privacy data cannot be used as they are not available at the decoder. Instead, we approximate the embedding by assuming the "worst-case" embedding, that is, we choose the hidden bit value that causes the higher increase in bit rate.

5.4.4 Rate-Distortion Optimized Data Hiding

In our joint data-hiding and compression framework, we aim at minimizing the output bit rate R and the perceptual distortion D caused by embedding M bits into the DCT coefficients. By using a user-specified control parameter δ, we combine the rate and distortion into a single cost function as follows:

$$C = (1 - \delta) \cdot N_F \cdot D + \delta \cdot R \tag{5.9}$$

where N_F is a constant used to equalize the dynamic ranges of D and R so that varying δ translates to trading off between D and R. As such, N_F is not a free parameter and is determined based on the particular compression mechanism. On the other hand, the choice of δ depends on applications—it is selected based on the particular application that may favor the least amount of distortion by setting δ close to zero, or the least amount of bit rate increases by setting δ close to one.

In order to avoid any overhead in communicating the embedding positions to the decoder, both of these approaches compute the optimal positions based on the previously decoded DCT frame so that the process can be repeated at the decoder. In our data-hiding framework, the constrained optimization can be formulated as follows:

$$\min_\Gamma C(\Gamma) \text{ subjected to } M = N \tag{5.10}$$

where
  M is the variable that denotes the number of coefficients to be modified
  N is the target number of bits to be embedded
  C is the cost function as described in Equation 5.9
  Γ is any selection of M DCT coefficients for embedding the data

Lagrangian method turns a constrained optimization problem like (5.10) into an unconstrained one and is commonly used in rate-distortion optimized video compression. Using a Lagrange multiplier $\lambda \geq 0$, the constrained optimization problem introduced in Equation 5.10 can be turned into an unconstrained version:

$$\min_\Gamma \Theta(\Gamma, \lambda) \quad \text{with} \quad \Theta(\Gamma, \lambda) = C(\Gamma) + \lambda(M - N) \tag{5.11}$$

If the unconstrained problem (5.11) for a particular $\lambda \geq 0$ has an optimal solution that gives rise to $M = N$, this will also be a solution to the original constrained problem [41]. We can further simplify Equation 5.11 by decomposing it into the sum of similar quantities from each DCT block k:

$$\Theta(\Gamma, \lambda) = \sum_k C_k(\Gamma_k) + \lambda \left(\sum_k M_k - N \right) \tag{5.12}$$

$$= \sum_k \left(C_k(\Gamma_k) + \lambda \left(M_k - \frac{N}{L} \right) \right) \tag{5.13}$$

where
  Γ_k denotes the particular selection of M_k coefficient in the kth DCT block
  L is the total number of DCT blocks in a frame

The minimization can now be performed for each block at different values of λ so as to make $\sum_k M_k \doteq N$.

To prepare for the aforementioned optimization, we need to first generate the curves between the cost and the number of embedded bits for all the DCT blocks. The cost function, as described in Equation 5.9, consists of both the distortion and the rate. The distortion is calculated using an L_4 norm pooling of distorted coefficients as given in Equation 5.4. Rate increase is considerably more difficult as it depends on the run-length patterns. Embedding at the same coefficient may result in different rate increase depending on the order of embedding. While one can resort to dynamic programming techniques to compute the optimal curve, the computation time is prohibiting, and we approximate the rate increase function using a greedy approach by embedding at the minimum cost position at each step. As the decoder does not know the actual bit to be embedded, the worst-case scenario is assumed—both the distortion and the rate increase are computed by embedding the bit value at each step that leads to a bigger increase in cost. Once the cost curves are generated for all the DCT blocks, we can minimize the Lagrangian cost $\Theta(\Gamma, \lambda)$ for any fixed value of λ to find the distribution of embedding bits. λ value is chosen using the binary search such that the total bits over all the DCT blocks are just greater than or equal to the target-embedding requirement. At this optimal slope, we get the number of bits to be embedded as the value of N that minimizes the unconstrained equation.

5.5 Privacy Information Management

In this section, we describe the PIM module that supports anonymous authentication of privacy information retrieval using biometric signals. In a PIM system, the server (referred as Bob) has a database of video segments encrypted by the secure camera system (referred as Charlie) as described in Section 5.3. A user, through an iris reader (referred as Alice), will engage Bob in a protocol over a public network to retrieve an encrypted video segment. The security and privacy goals of a PIM system are listed as follows:

1. A user has access to all of his or her raw video segments.
2. A user does not have access to raw video segments of any other users.

3. Bob does not have access to any raw video segments and has no knowledge of the identity of the user associated to each video segment.
4. Bob must authenticate a user's identity using his or her biometric signals but cannot have access to the raw biometric signals.

The problem of designing a PIM system is similar to that of private information retrieval (PIR) [42]. Our design is in fact an adaptation of a PIR system to (1) allow variability in iris patterns between the time when the signal is first captured during identification and when retrieval request is made and (2) support low computation and communication overhead by using a surrogate data record. Our proposed design consists of two protocols: The first one is the encryption of the privacy imagery in video based on the iris pattern obtained during the subject identification process. The second protocol is invoked during the retrieval process when the user provides his or her iris pattern for decryption. These two protocols are described in the following.

5.5.1 Privacy Information Encryption

The privacy information encryption protocol shown in Protocol 1 involves three parties: Alice the iris scanner, Bob the server, and Charlie the camera. It is executed after Bob has ascertained that the subject entering the surveillance needs to be protected via the ABAC protocol [15]. At that point, Alice still possesses the iris pattern in plaintext. In addition, Alice has also acquired a passcode from the user. This passcode is not stored for identification purpose, but the combination of the iris pattern and the passcode is needed for later retrieval of the privacy information. Charlie is responsible for redacting pixels corresponding to the subject for privacy protection, encrypting the raw pixels of the subject and recording both the redacted video and privacy information to a database controlled by Bob. AES is used for encrypting the video because of its high efficiency in processing high bit rate videos. All three parties are assumed to be semihonest connected through a public network—they faithfully follow the protocol, but any data they received can be used to infer sensitive information about others. Furthermore, the public-key cipher $Enc(\cdot,pk)$ used in the protocol is assumed to be additively homomorphic—addition in plaintext can be computed directly using the ciphertext. An example of a popular additively homomorphic public-key encryption scheme is Paillier cryptosystem [43].

Protocol 1 Privacy Information Encryption

Require

Alice: Iris $\mathbf{q}$, passcode $\mathbf{p}$, and keys (sk,pk) used in ABAC

Bob: Encrypted probe $Enc(\mathbf{q},pk)$ and decision bit s from ABAC

Charlie: Video segment v containing the protected subject

Ensure

Bob stores the encrypted privacy video and auxiliary information that satisfy the security goals.

1. Bob sends the decision bit to Alice and Charlie. This protocol aborts if the subject requires no protection.
2. Alice sends the public key pk to Charlie.

3. Charlie randomly generates an AES key k and encrypts the privacy video v of the subject to $AES(v,k)$.
4. Charlie encrypts the AES key k with pk to create $Enc(k,pk)$.
5. Charlie sends his camera ID, time of day for the video, $AES(v,k)$, and $Enc(k,pk)$ to Bob.
6. Alice applies an error control code (ECC) to her secret key sk. The result is then exclusive-ORed with the concatenation of the iris probe $\mathbf{q}$ and the passcode p to create $ECC(sk) \otimes [\mathbf{q}\,p]$ that is then sent to Bob.
7. For each video v, Bob creates two data records. The first one is the video surrogate record:

$$\left\{ pk, ECC(sk) \otimes [\mathbf{q}\,p], \text{camera-ID}, \text{time-of-day} \right\}$$

and the second contains the actual video with other auxiliary information:

$$\left\{ AES(v,k), Enc(k,pk), Enc(\mathbf{q},pk) \right\}$$

Protocol 1 does not leak any private information among parties. First, Alice does not gain any information about the iris database or videos of other users as she only receives a single decision bit from Bob about the result of her protection status. Second, Charlie receives pk from Alice that is a randomly chosen public key and thereby gains no information about the subject. Charlie does not receive any information from Bob. Third, Bob receives data from both Alice and Charlie. These data include $Enc(k,pk)$, $AES(v,k)$, and $ECC(sk) \otimes [\mathbf{q}\,p]$. The video v is protected by k that in turn is protected by pk. Bob can decrypt these information if and only if he knows sk. sk is stored in $ECC(sk) \otimes [\mathbf{q}\,p]$. The use of ECC allows the decryption of sk provided that Bob has an approximate key $[\mathbf{q}'\,p']$ with hamming distance $d([\mathbf{q}\,p],[\mathbf{q}'\,p'])$ less than an error-correcting threshold T. As Bob owns the plaintext iris database, he can exhaustively test all of them for that part of the key. On the other hand, provided that the length of p is sufficiently larger than T, Bob's chance of decrypting sk can be made negligibly small. While a long passcode p may be difficult for the subject to remember, it can be generated using a pseudorandom number with a short random seed provided by the subject. Note that all the decrypting information is stored in $ECC(sk) \otimes [\mathbf{q}\,p]$ that is assumed to be significantly smaller than the encrypted video $AES(v,k)$. This surrogate data record allows a more efficient implementation of the retrieval process that we describe next.

5.5.2 Privacy Information Retrieval

The privacy information retrieval protocol in Protocol 2 is used when the user wants to retrieve his or her private information from the video database at Bob. The subject will accomplish this by providing his or her iris pattern $\mathbf{q}'$ and passcode p' to an iris scanner (Alice). Since this scanner will be different from the scanner used at the entrance, iris patterns from the same person obtained at the two scanners can be different, but their hamming distance is assumed to be within the error-correcting threshold T.

Protocol 2 guarantees that any video v_i retrieved by Alice must satisfy $sk' = sk_i$, which in turn implies that $d([\mathbf{q}_i\,p_i],[\mathbf{q}'\,p]) < T$. This condition restricts Alice's access to only those videos with a match in both Alice's passcode and biometrics. As the decryption of the correct sk' in step 4 already implies $d(\mathbf{q}_i,\mathbf{q}') < T$, it might seem redundant to perform an encrypted-domain comparison in step 7 and provide further protection on the AES key k_i in step 8. These steps, however, are important to counter a serious attack, which we call "fake surrogate attack," on the iris scanner. The fake surrogate attack works as follows: During the privacy information encryption process as described in Section 5.5.1, the scanner must provide a correct probe $\mathbf{q}_i$ to gain protection from the system. As such, the encrypted probe $Enc(\mathbf{q}_i, pk_i)$ must indeed correspond to a legitimate user. The surrogate record $ECC(sk_i) \otimes [\mathbf{q}_i\ p_i]$, however, is computed solely by the scanner without any validation from the server. A compromised scanner may replace it with a fake record and can gain access to all privacy information if Protocol 2 stops at step 4 with Bob handing over the AES key to Alice. Instead, steps 7 and 8 ensure that providing a surrogate record is not enough for retrieval. A live probe $\mathbf{q}'$ must be provided to demonstrate a match with $Enc(\mathbf{q}_i, pk_i)$ in order for Bob to release the true AES key. The comparison result is not disclosed to Bob but only used to add noise to the AES key if there is a mismatch. This is to prevent Bob from learning the true identity of the individual by comparing the encrypted probe with other irises in his database.

Protocol 2 Privacy Information Retrieval

Require

Alice: Probe $\mathbf{q}'$ and passcode p

Bob: Video database

Ensure

Alice obtains all v's whose corresponding biometric signals $\mathbf{q}$ satisfied $d(\mathbf{q}', \mathbf{q}) < T$.

1. Alice requests Bob to send over a set I_{match} of surrogate records that matches Alice's query on camera IDs and time of recording.
2. Alice sets a counter $i: = 1$.
3. Alice gets the *ith* surrogate record from I_{match}.
4. Alice XORs the $ECC(sk_i) \otimes [\mathbf{q}_i\ p_i]$ field with its own $[\mathbf{q}'\ p]$ and then applies ECC decoding to obtain sk'. $sk' = sk_i$ if and only if $d([\mathbf{q}_i\ p_i],[\mathbf{q}'\ p]) < T$.
5. Alice uses the public key pk_i field to encrypt her probe and form $Enc(\mathbf{q}', pk_i)$.
6. Alice sends $Enc(\mathbf{q}', pk_i)$ and $Enc(\mathbf{q}_i, pk_i)$ to Bob.
7. As $Enc(\otimes, pk_i)$ is homomorphic, it is possible for Bob, with access only to $Enc(\mathbf{q}', pk_i)$ and $Enc(\mathbf{q}_i, pk_i)$, to compute $Enc(c, pk_i)$ where $c = 0$ if $d(\mathbf{q}', \mathbf{q}_i) < T$ and 1 otherwise [15]. Note that the exact value of c is unknown to Bob.
8. Bob retrieves the encrypted AES key $Enc(k_i, pk_i)$ from the corresponding video record and conditionally randomizes it based on the result of c. Specifically, Bob exploits the homomorphism and computes $Enc(k_i + cr_i, pk_i)$ where r_i is a random number selected by Bob.
9. Bob sends $Enc(k_i + cr_i, pk_i)$ and the encrypted video $AES(v_i, k_i)$ to Alice.
10. Alice uses sk' to decrypt $Enc(k_i + cr_i, pk_i)$. The correct k_i will be recovered only if (a) $sk' = sk_i$ and (b) $c = 0$. Alice then uses the result to decrypt $AES(v_i, k_i)$.
11. Increment i and go back to step 4 until I_{match} is exhausted.

5.6 Experiments

In this section, we first present the experimental results to show the efficiency of our proposed R-D optimized data hiding. Greedy technique for selection and irreversible embedding are considered. We then present results on an iris biometric database to evaluate the effectiveness of the proposed PIM system.

5.6.1 Data Hiding for Preservation

We have tested our proposed schemes on two sequences using a variety of video obfuscation techniques. The two sequences are as follows:

Conference: Five persons sit around a conference table with two leaving one after the other (356 frames).

Hall: A standard sequence used in video compression (299 frames).

Both sequences are in CIF (352×288) format in YCbCr color space with 4:2:0 subsampling. For each sequence, privacy objects are extracted according to a separate segmentation mask calculated using the background subtraction and object segmentation schemes described in Ref. [20]. Three video obfuscation techniques are then applied after the privacy objects are removed. They are (a) silhouette in which the holes are replaced by black pixels, (b) scrambled in which the pixel values are exclusive-OR with a pseudorandom sequence, and (c) inpainted using an object-based video inpainting scheme from Ref. [20]. The data-hiding algorithm is implemented based on the TMN Coder version 3.0 of the ITU-T H.263 version 2 by University of British Columbia. Both sequences are compressed using a constant quantization parameter with the first frame intra-coded and the remaining inter-coded. The encoding performance is measured based on running the program on a Windows XP Professional machine with Intel Xeon processor at 2 GHz with 4 GB memory.

In the first experiment, we contrast the performances of the proposed data hiding over different privacy protection schemes. As one of the key advantages of data hiding for privacy data preservation is its universal applicability to different obfuscation schemes, it is of interest to consider their performances. We have run the greedy irreversible scheme with $QP = 10$ for both the videos at three different obfuscation schemes. Table 5.1 summarizes the results. The first row shows the luma peak signal-to-noise ratio (PSNR) of the sequences after the embedding and compression. The variations in PSNR can be better interpreted using the percentage drop as compared with those of the encoded sequences without hidden data. The percentage drop allows us to compare the impact of data embedding across different obfuscation techniques that produce very different video sequences. The lower PSNR drop in the scrambled versions compared with the other two is due to the concentration of the hidden data among the high spatial-temporal frequency-scrambled areas. In a typical residual frame, most DCT coefficients are close to zero, and those coefficients enjoy little distortion due to quantization. Hiding data in these zero coefficients statistically causes a higher relative decrease in PSNR when compared with nonzero coefficients. The scrambling process introduces many nonzero high-frequency coefficients that attract hidden data, thus reducing the amount of loss in PSNR as compared to the silhouette and inpainted schemes. These high-frequency coefficients are chosen because they introduce less perceptual distortion, as indicated in the measurements in the third row.

On the other hand, these high-frequency coefficients are very difficult to compress. The resulting bit rates after data hiding as shown in the fourth row clearly demonstrate this phenomenon. Similar to PSNR, we also consider the relative increase in bit rates as compared with those of compressing the modified videos and privacy data separately. While it is expected that the hidden data introduce minor or even negative bit rate increase in scrambled videos, there are significant increases in bit rate among silhouette and inpainted sequences—they range from 26% to more than 100%. These increases are more significant among the inpainted sequences than the silhouette sequences.

Table 5.1 Comparing the Performances among Different Video Obfuscation Schemes

Inpainted Sequences		Conference	Hall
PSNR-Y (dB)	Silhouette	35.72	35.15
	Scrambled	34.61	33.49
	Inpainted	34.96	33.43
PSNR-Y Drop %	Silhouette	2.4	3.8
	Scrambled	2.0	3.2
	Inpainted	2.5	3.6
Distortion	Silhouette	27.11	28.97
	Scrambled	19.30	20.35
	Inpainted	27.29	28.53
Bit rate (kbps)	Silhouette	145.2	315.0
	Scrambled	359.8	1113.0
	Inpainted	127.7	285.2
Bit rate Increase %	Silhouette	31.1	45.5
	Scrambled	−3.0	−4.1
	Inpainted	44.6	59.6
Mark-to-Work Bit rate	Silhouette	0.53	0.60
	Scrambled	0.12	0.08
	Inpainted	0.77	0.83

In the next experiment, we ran our data-hiding algorithm under varying design parameters like QP and δ. This is carried out on both sequences using inpainting as the obfuscation scheme. Four QP parameters are used (5, 10, 15, and 20), and three δ values are used (0, 0.5, and 1). QP defines the quantization parameter of the codec for compressing *both* the modified video and privacy information, while δ is the control parameter between rate and distortion during the optimization. $\delta = 0$ gives the distortion-based optimization ignoring rate increase, while $\delta = 1$ minimizes only the rate increase during the selection of embedding coefficients. Tables 5.2 and 5.3 summarize the results for both sequences. Finally, we tested our Lagrangian-embedding distribution strategy to naive equal distribution strategy across DCT blocks. To ensure a fair comparison, we fix the greedy approach with $\lambda = 0$ to enforce a full emphasis on minimizing the visual distortion. On average, there is a bandwidth savings of 47% when switching from equal distribution to the Lagrangian approach.

The notations R_o, R_p, and R_e denote the rates of obfuscated (inpainted) bit stream, privacy bit stream, and embedded bit stream, respectively. From the tables, we can observe, as expected,

Table 5.2 Rate and Distortion for Irreversible Embedding Hall-Monitor at Varying *QP* and δ Values

QP	R_o (kbps)	R_p (kbps)	δ	R_e (kbps)	Rate Increase %	PSNR-Y (dB)	PSNR-Y Drop %	Distortion
5	359.72	161.38	0	754.5	44.79	36.77	3.29	15.76
			0.5	698.04	33.96	36.76	3.31	21.06
			1	690.54	32.52	36.73	3.39	58.61
10	97.36	81.26	0	314.32	75.97	33.45	3.57	22.59
			0.5	285.15	59.64	33.43	3.63	28.53
			1	267.50	49.76	33.42	3.66	98.76
15	59.12	54.77	0	202.98	78.22	31.37	3.77	28.64
			0.5	186.38	63.65	31.42	3.62	34.95
			1	170.50	49.71	31.30	3.99	138.77
20	44.9	42.82	0	152.87	74.27	29.93	3.64	35.39
			0.5	141.9	61.76	29.97	3.51	41.92
			1	129.1	47.17	29.82	3.99	178.27

Table 5.3 Rate and Distortion for Irreversible Embedding for Conference at Varying *QP* and δ Values

QP	R_o (kbps)	R_p (kbps)	δ	R_e (kbps)	Rate Increase %	PSNR-Y (dB)	PSNR-Y Drop %	Distortion
5	122.42	76.17	0	309.27	55.73	38.29	3.28	18.02
			0.5	279.37	40.68	38.34	3.16	28.67
			1	275.02	38.49	38.29	3.28	60.38
10	49.81	38.44	0	135.50	53.54	34.94	2.57	28.16
			0.5	123.63	40.09	34.95	2.54	39.58
			1	120.93	37.03	34.84	2.84	94.18
15	36.41	28.66	0	94.12	44.64	33.19	2.35	39.99
			0.5	87.97	35.19	33.22	2.27	47.93
			1	85.87	31.97	33.05	2.77	134.61
20	30.33	23.96	0	74.23	36.73	31.89	2.39	51.33
			0.5	70.66	30.15	31.86	2.48	58.95
			1	68.41	26.01	31.85	2.51	161.62

that the rate increase reduces while the perceptual distortion increases with an increase in the control parameter δ. Despite the increase in the bit rates of the privacy streams, the percentages of bit rate increase in the embedded stream stay the same or drop at higher *QP*s due to the presence of more nonzero coefficients that are more suitable for hiding data. Also, the results from both the sequences confirm that PSNR is not a good measure for the cost computation as it doesn't vary much with parameter δ, while the perceptual distortion measure better correlates with it. Figure 5.4 shows a sample frame from Hall-Monitor sequence before and after irreversible embedding at variable values of *QP* and δ.

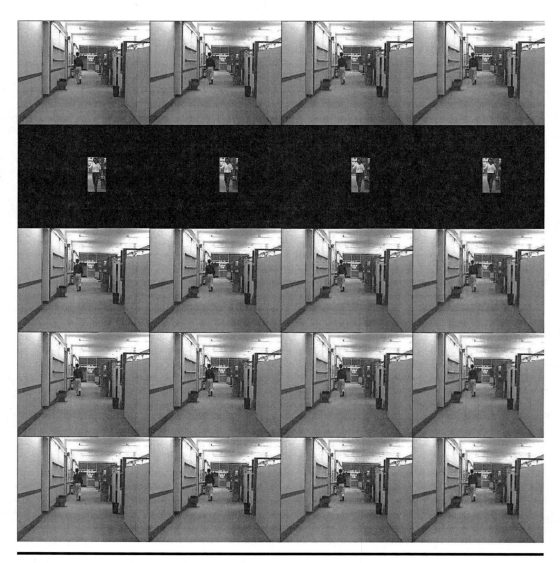

Figure 5.4 Sample frame (200th) from Hall-Monitor sequence—irreversible embedding at varying *QP* and δ. Rows from top to bottom: inpainted frame, privacy frame, and data-embedded frames with δ = 0, 0.5, and 1. Columns from left to right: *QP* = 5, 10, 15, and 20.

5.6.2 Privacy Information Management

For our experiments to evaluate the effectiveness of proposed PIM design, we use the Chinese Academy of Sciences Institute of Automation (CASIA) Iris database CASIA-IrisV3 [44], a common benchmark for evaluating the performance of iris recognition systems. We use CASIA-IrisV3-Lamp database containing 411 individuals with 16213 iris images. For the iris feature extraction, we use the MATLAB® code from Ref. [45] to generate both the iris feature vectors and the masks. Each iris feature vector is 9600 bit long. Similarity distance between iris patterns are measured by a modified hamming distance defined as follows [46]:

$$d_H(\mathbf{x},\mathbf{y})^2 := \frac{\left\| (\mathbf{x} \otimes \mathbf{y}) \cap mask_\mathbf{x} \cap mask_\mathbf{y} \right\|_2^2}{\left\| mask_\mathbf{x} \cap mask_\mathbf{y} \right\|_2^2} \tag{5.14}$$

where

$\otimes$ is the XOR operation

$\cap$ is the bitwise AND

$mask_\mathbf{x}$ and $mask_\mathbf{y}$ are the corresponding mask binary vectors that mask the unusable portion of the irises due to occlusion by eyelids and eyelash, specular reflections, boundary artifacts of lenses, or poor signal-to-noise ratio

As the mask has substantial variation even among feature vectors captured from the same eye, we assume that the mask vectors do not disclose any identity information.

We focus on the parameters needed to implement the PIM system as described in Section 5.5. The main parameter is the rate (n,k) of the ECC code used in protecting the private key sk, where n and k denote the output and input length. The rate determines the number of bits that can be corrected, which is directly related to the variability of biometric patterns. At retrieval, the operation $ECC^{-1}(ECC(sk) \otimes [b\ p] \otimes [\mathbf{q}'\ p])$ is performed to recover sk where $\mathbf{q}$ and $\mathbf{q}'$ are biometric signals captured at different time and p is the passcode. As such, ECC should be able to correct up to the number of bit differences equal to the maximum hamming distance T between two iris patterns from the same person. Furthermore, to prevent impersonation, hamming distance between iris patterns of different individuals should be much larger than T and cannot be recovered with the ECC.

Let us first determine T for our dataset. Note that hamming distance, rather than the default modified hamming distance, is used in the design of ECC. This modification excludes the use of masks and may adversely affect the matching process. In Figure 5.5, we plot the distributions of the normalized hamming distances for iris patterns from the same person and between different persons. Without mask codes, hamming distances between the same individuals are within the range of 0.08 and 0.29 with mean equal to 0.18. Hamming distances between patterns from different individuals are from 0.32 to 0.47 with mean equal to 0.41. Based on these results, we can set $T = 0.30$ that is sufficient to achieve perfect separation of the two groups.

The $T = 0.3$ or 30% bit differences between iris patterns, however, are not uniformly distributed over the entire pattern. We partition the 9600 bit pattern into 128 bit blocks and notice that 79% of the blocks have less than 25% of bit differences. This concentration of bit differences leads us to use a concatenation of two ECCs with the (128, 8) Hadamard code as the outer code to correct uniform random error and the (174, 128) Reed-Solomon code with 8-bit symbols as the inner code to correct burst errors. Exhaustive testings have been performed to confirm that such a design can cope with the variability of all patterns in our database.

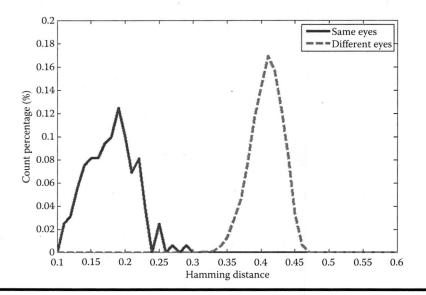

Figure 5.5   Distribution of minimum IrisCode hamming distances without masks.

5.7 Conclusions

In this chapter, we have presented a privacy information preservation and management system for privacy-protected video surveillance. Novel data-hiding methods have been proposed to securely preserve large amount of privacy information into the redacted video. An optimization framework has been proposed to identify DCT coefficients for hiding information that simultaneously minimize the perceptual distortion and the rate increase caused due to embedded information. In the second part, we have proposed a PIM system that uses the combination of iris pattern and passcode to provide authenticated and anonymous retrieval of private information. Error correction code is used in the encryption process to cope with the difference between the iris patterns captured at the time of surveillance and at the time of retrieval. We have demonstrated the security of the proposed encryption and retrieval protocols by proving that the subject cannot gain any information about other users and the system knows nothing about the identity of the subject in the video. Experimental results have been presented to demonstrate the efficient implementation of our proposed system. One weakness of our system is its reliance on continuous identification of the protected individual throughout the entire surveillance. Such an assumption may fail under heavy occlusion. We are currently extending our PIM system to other biometric modalities such as face and body features, which allows the system to resume tracking after occlusion while maintaining full anonymity.

Acknowledgments

Part of this material is based upon work supported by the National Science Foundation under Grant No. 1018241. Any opinions, findings, and conclusions or recommendations expressed in this material are those of the author(s) and do not necessarily reflect the views of the National Science Foundation.

References

1. P. J. P. et al., Frvt 2006 and ice 2006 large-scale results, National Institute of Standards and Technology, Technical Report NISTRI 7408, March 2007.
2. L. M. Brown, Tampa drops face recognition system, CNET, http://news.cnet.com/Tampa-drops-face-recognition-system/2100–1029_3–5066795.html?tag = nl, Technical Report, August 2003.
3. J. Stanley and B. Steinhardt, *Bigger Monster, Weaker Chains: The Growth of an American Surveillance Society*, New York: ACLU, 2003.
4. J. G. Frye and M. W. Hail, Seminole tribe of Florida v Florida, in *American Federalism: An Encyclopedia*, J. R. Marbach, Ed. Westport, CT: Greenwood Publishing, 2005.
5. J. Wickramasuriya, M. Datt, S. Mehrotra, and N. Venkatasubramanian, Privacy protecting data collection in media spaces, in *ACM International Conference on Multimedia*, New York, pp. 48–55, October 2004.
6. A. M. Berger, U.S. Patent 6,067,399: Privacy Mode for Acquisition Cameras and Camcorders, Sony Corporation, May 23, 2000.
7. J. Wada, K. Kaiyama, K. Ikoma, and H. Kogane, *Monitor Camera System and Method of Displaying Picture from Monitor Camera Thereof*, Osaka, Japan: Matsushita Electric Industrial Co. Ltd., April 2001.
8. J. Schiff, M. Meingast, D. Mulligan, S. Sastry, and K. Goldberg, Respectful cameras: Detecting visual markers in real-time to address privacy concerns, in *International Conference on Intelligent Robots and Systems (IROS)*, San Diego, CA, pp. 971–978, October 29–November 2, 2007.
9. D. Chen, Y. Chang, R. Yan, and J. Yang, Tools for protecting the privacy of specific individuals in video, *EURASIP Journal on Advances in Signal Processing*, 2007, Article ID 75 427, 9, 2007, doi:10.1155/2007/75427.
10. E. N. Newton, L. Sweeney, and B. Main, Preserving privacy by de-identifying face images, *IEEE transactions on Knowledge and Data Engineering*, 17(2), 232–243, February 2005.
11. H. Wactlar, S. Stevens, and T. Ng, *Enabling Personal Privacy Protection Preferences in Collaborative Video Observation*, NSF Award Abstract 0534625, http://www.nsf.gov/awardsearch/showAward?AWD_ID= 0534625&HistoricalAwards=false, accessed on July 15, 2011.
12. Y. Deswarte and M. Roy, Privacy-enhancing access control enforcement, in *W3C Workshop on Languages for Privacy Policy Negotiation and Semantics-Driven Enforcement*, Ispra, Italy, October 17–18, 2006.
13. T. E. Boult, Pico: Privacy through invertible cryptographic obscuration, in *Proceedings of Computer Vision for Interactive and Intelligent Environments: The Dr. Bradley D. Carter Workshop Series*, University of Kentucky, Lexington, Kentucky, pp. 27–38, November 17–18, 2005.
14. F. Dufaux and T. Ebrahimi, Scrambling for video surveillance with privacy, in *2006 Conference on Computer Vision and Pattern Recognition Workshop (CVPRW'06)*, Washington, DC, p. 160, 2006.
15. Y. Luo, S.-C. S. Cheung, and S. Ye, Anonymous biometric access control based on homomorphic encryption, in *IEEE International Conference on Multimedia & Expo*, Cancun, Mexico, June 2009.
16. F. Hao, R. Anderson, and J. Daugman, Combining cryptography with biometrics effectively, *IEEE Transactions on Computers*, 55(9), 1081–1088, 2006.
17. A. Senior et al., Blinkering surveillance: Enable video privacy through computer vision, IBM, Research Report, Technical Report, August 2003.
18. X. Yu and N. Babaguchi, Privacy preserving: Hiding a face in a face, in *Computer Vision—ACCV 2007, Proceedings of 8th Asian Conference on Computer Vision*, Tokyo, Japan, Part II; pp. 651–661, November 18–22, 2007.
19. S.-C. Cheung, J. Zhao, and V. V. M., Efficient object-based video in painting, in *Proceedings of IEEE International Conference on Image Processing, ICIP 2006*, Atlanta, GA, pp. 705–708, 2006.
20. M. V. Venkatesh, S.-C. Cheung, and J. Zhao, Efficient object-based video in painting, *Pattern Recognition Letters: Special Issue on Video-based Object and Event Analysis*, 30(2), 168–179, 2009.
21. K. Martin and K. N. Plataniotis, Privacy protected surveillance using secure visual object coding, *IEEE Transactions on Circuits and Systems for Video Technology*, 18(8), 1152–1162, 2008.
22. P. Agrawal and P. Narayanan, Person de-identification in videos, *IEEE Transactions on Circuits and Systems for Video Technology*, 21(3), 299–310, March 2011.

23. H. Sohn, W. De Neve, and Y. M. Ro, Privacy protection in video surveillance systems: Analysis of subband-adaptive scrambling in jpeg xr, *IEEE Transactions on Circuits and Systems for Video Technology*, 21(2), 170–177, February 2011.

24. W. Zhang, S.-C. Cheung, and M. Chen, Hiding privacy information in video surveillance system, in *Proceedings of the 12th IEEE International Conference on Image Processing*, Genova, Italy, Vol. 3, pp. II-868–II-871, September 11–14, 2005.

25. X. Yu and N. Babaguchi, Hiding a face in a face, *Lecture Notes in Computer Science*, Berlin, Germany: Springer, Vol. 4844, pp. 651–661, 2007.

26. G. Li, Y. Ito, X. Yu, N. Nitta, and N. Babaguchi, A discrete wavelet transform based recoverable image processing for privacy protection, in *International Conference of Image Processing*, San Diego, CA, pp. 1372–1375, October 12–15, 2008.

27. J. K. Paruchuri and S.-C. Cheung, Joint optimization of data hiding and video compression, in *Proceedings of IEEE International Symposium on Circuits and Systems (ISCAS 2008)*, Seattle, WA, pp. 3021–3024, May 18–21, 2008, http://www.vis.uky.edu/~jkparu0/ISCAS.pdf, accessed on July 15, 2011.

28. S.-C. Cheung, J. K. Paruchuri, and T. Nguyen, Managing privacy data in pervasive camera networks, in *Proceedings of IEEE Internal Conference on Image Processing (ICIP)*, San Diego, CA, pp. 1676–1679, October 12–15, 2008, http://www.vis.uky.edu/~jkparu0/ICIP.pdf, accessed on July 15, 2011.

29. P. Meuel, M. Chaumont, and W. Puech, Data hiding in h.264 video for lossless reconstruction of region of interest, in *Proceedings of EUSIPCO 2007*, Poznan, Poland. HAL—CCSD, 2007 [online]. Available: http://hal-lirmm.ccsd.cnrs.fr/lirmm-00192603/en/

30. D.-A. Fidaleo, H.-A. Nguyen, and M. Trivedi, The networked sensor tapestry (nest): A privacy enhanced software architecture for interactive analysis of data in video-sensor networks, in *VSSN '04: Proceedings of the ACM 2nd International Workshop on Video Surveillance & Sensor Networks*. New York: ACM Press, pp. 46–53, 2004.

31. G. V. L. et al., A middleware architecture for privacy protection, *Computer Networks: The International Journal of Computer and Telecommunications Networking*, 51(16), 4679–4696, November 2007.

32. S.-C. Cheung, M. V. Venkatesh, J. Paruchuri, J. Zhao, and T. Nguyen, Protecting and managing privacy information in video surveillance systems, in *Protecting Privacy in Video Surveillance*, A. Senior, Ed. New York: Springer, Vol. 50, pp. 11–33, 2009.

33. U. Uludag, S. Pankanti, S. Prabhakar, and A. Jain, Biometric cryptosystems: Issues and challenges, *Proceedings of the IEEE*, 92(6), 948–960, 2004.

34. A. Cavoukian and A. Stoianov, *Biometric Encryption: A Positive-Sum Technology that Achieves Strong Authentication, Security and Privacy*. Ontario, Canada: Information and Privacy Commissioner, 2007.

35. U. Uludag and A. Jain, Securing fingerprint template: Fuzzy vault with helper data, *Proceedings of CVPR Workshop on Privacy Research in Vision*, New York, pp. 163–170, 2006.

36. J. Linnartz and P. Tuyls, New shielding functions to enhance privacy and prevent misuse of biometric templates, in *Audio-and Video-Based Biometric Person Authentication*. J. Kittler and M. S. Nixon, Eds., *Proceedings of 4th International Conference, AVBPA 2003*, Guildford, U.K., pp. 393–402, June 9–11, 2003.

37. A. Watson, Dct quantization matrices optimized for individual images, in *Proceedings of SPIE Human Vision, Visual Processing, and Digital Display IV*, Vol. SPIE-1913, San Jose, CA, pp. 202–216, 1993.

38. K. Seshadrinathan and A. C. Bovik, A structural similarity metric for video based on motion models, in *Proceedings of IEEE International Conference on Acoustic, Speech and Signal Processing (ICASSP 2007)*, Honolulu, Hawaii, Vol. 1, pp. I-869–I-872, April 15–20, 2007.

39. I. Cox, M. Miller, and J. Bloom, *Digital Watermarking*. Burlington, MA: Morgan Kaufmann Publishers, 2002.

40. J. K. Paruchuri, S.-C. S. Cheung, and M. W. Hail, Video data hiding for managing privacy information in surveillance systems, *EURASIP Journal on Information Security—Special Issue on Enhancing Privacy Protection in Multimedia Systems*, Vol. 2009, Article No. 7, 2009.

41. Y. Shoham and A. Gersho, Efficient bit allocation for an arbitrary set of quantizers, *IEEE Transactions on Acoustics, Speech and Signal Processing*, 36(9), 1445–1453, September 1988.

42. W. Gasarch, A survey on private information retrieval, *Bulletin of the EATCS*, 82, 72–107, 2004.

43. P. Paillier, Public-key cryptosystems based on composite degree residuosity classes, *Proceedings of International Conference on the Theory and Application of Cryptographic Techniques (EUROCRYPT 99)*, Prague, Czech Republic, Vol. 1592, pp. 223–238, May 1999.

44. T. Tan and Z. Sun, Casia-irisv3, Chinese Academy of Sciences Institute of Automation, http://www.cbsr.ia.ac.cn/IrisDatabase.htm, accessed on July 15, 2011, Technical Report, 2005.

45. L. Masek and P. Kovesi, MATLAB source code for a biometric identification system based on iris patterns, The School of Computer Science and Software Engineering, The University of Western Australia, Technical Report, 2003.

46. J. Daugman, How iris recognition works, *IEEE Transactions on Circuits and Systems for Video Technology*, 4, 21–30, January 2004.

Chapter 6

Objective and Subjective Evaluation of Content-Based Privacy Protection of Face Images in Video Surveillance Systems Using JPEG XR

Hosik Sohn, Dohyoung Lee, Wesley De Neve,
Konstantinos N. Plataniotis, and Yong Man Ro

Contents

6.1 Introduction

Present-day video surveillance systems often come with high-speed network connections, high processing power, and plenty of storage capacity. These computational capabilities enable the deployment of sophisticated computer vision algorithms that make it possible to find people [1], detect faces [2], recognize faces [3], and analyze the activity of people [4]. As a result, video surveillance systems are increasingly getting better at detecting terrorists and acts of crime, enhancing our sense of security. However, the increasing ability of video surveillance systems to successfully identify people has raised several privacy concerns during the past few years. Indeed, such concerns have, for instance, been voiced with respect to the use of FR technology in public spaces, archiving face images for possible later use, the unauthorized addition of face images to watch lists, and power abuse by guards [5]. In addition, large-scale FR systems, possibly built by making use of face images and corresponding name labels shared on social media applications [6], have the potential to further intrude upon the privacy of individuals in the foreseeable future.

The privacy debate regarding the deployment of intelligent video surveillance systems has spurred the development of a plethora of tools for privacy protection [7–14], mainly focusing on concealing vehicle tags and the identity of face images. Both Refs. [15] and [16] provide a survey of the state of the art. However, little attention has thus far been paid to a rigorous and systematic evaluation of the level of privacy protection offered by these tools. Also, a protocol for evaluating the effectiveness of privacy protection tools has thus far not been standardized. Although a framework for assessing the capability of privacy protection tools to hide facial information has been proposed in Ref. [17], the framework in question addressed neither diverse experimental conditions that may cause privacy leakage nor a subjective evaluation of privacy protection tools.

The study presented in this chapter aims at furthering the understanding of experimental conditions that may cause privacy leakage and the effectiveness of already existing approaches for evaluating the level of security offered by privacy protection tools. To that end, we study the privacy-preserving nature of a subband-adaptive scrambling technique developed for the JPEG XR standard, previously proposed by the authors in Ref. [14]. This technique minimizes bit rate overhead and delay in order to allow for deployment in video surveillance systems that need to facilitate real-time monitoring in diverse usage environments. To investigate the level of privacy protection offered by the lightweight scrambling technique of Ref. [14], we make use of both objective and subjective assessments. In our objective assessments, we apply three automatic FR techniques to scrambled face images, taking advantage of domain-specific information (i.e., face information): principal component analysis (PCA) and eigenfeature regularization and extraction (ERE), which both extract global features, and local binary patterns (LBP), which extracts local features. Additionally, we apply three general-purpose visual security metrics to the scrambled face images used: the luminance similarity score (LSS) [18], the edge similarity score (ESS) [18], and the local feature-based visual security metric (LFVSM) [19]. Finally, we conduct subjective assessments to study whether agreement exists between the judgments of human observers and the output of automatic FR. Given the focus of this chapter on the use of thorough objective and subjective assessments for evaluating the effectiveness of privacy protection tools, we would like to make note that Ref. [14] only used a cryptographic security analysis and ad hoc visual inspection to determine the level of security of the scrambling technique proposed. Indeed, at the time of designing and testing the scrambling technique of Ref. [14], a rigorous and systematic evaluation methodology was not available yet.

Our results demonstrate that the scrambled face images come, in general, with a feasible level of protection against automatic and human FR. However, for video surveillance requiring a high level of privacy protection, our results indicate that the strength of the scrambling technique studied needs to be enhanced at low bit rates, that chroma information needs to be scrambled, and that the presence of eyeglasses and a low number of gallery face images may contribute to the success of a replacement attack. Our results also show that, compared to automatic FR, the general-purpose visual security metrics studied are less suited for detecting weaknesses in tools that aim at concealing the identity of face images. Additionally, our results show that our objective and subjective assessments are not always in agreement.

This chapter is organized as follows. We review related work and the layered scrambling technique of Ref. [14] in Sections 6.2 and 6.3, respectively. In Section 6.4, we investigate the privacy-preserving nature of the scrambling technique of Ref. [14] by means of both objective and subjective assessments. In Section 6.5, we propose and evaluate a number of improvements to the aforementioned scrambling technique, addressing the needs of video surveillance applications requiring a high level of privacy protection. Finally, we present conclusions in Section 6.6, as well as a number of recommendations that may assist in better evaluating the effectiveness of privacy protection tools.

6.2 Related Work

One of the main challenges of privacy protection in video surveillance systems can be found in the secure concealment of privacy-sensitive regions by invertible transformation of visual information at a low computational cost. In general, dependent on the location where scrambling or encryption is applied, three different approaches can be distinguished [20]: scrambling or encryption (1) in the uncompressed domain, (2) in the transform domain (before multiplexing), and (3) in the compressed bit stream domain (after multiplexing). Scrambling or encryption in the uncompressed domain has the advantage of being independent of the coding format used. Most scrambling and encryption techniques, however, operate in the transform domain in order to minimize the impact on the effectiveness of source coding. In addition, techniques operating in the transform domain are less sensitive to attacks that exploit the highly spatially and temporally correlated nature of video data [20].

The authors of Ref. [21] propose and evaluate a format-independent encryption scheme that operates in the uncompressed domain, randomly permuting pixel values in each macroblock (MB) before compression. The permutation-based encryption scheme tolerates lossy compression and is also robust to transcoding. The author of Ref. [22] makes use of cryptographic obscuration in order to conceal the identity of face images in surveillance video content, either using the Data Encryption Standard (DES) or the Advanced Encryption Standard (AES) in the uncompressed domain.

Most scrambling and encryption techniques, however, operate in the transform domain, for reasons pointed out in the introduction of this section. Random level shift (RLS), random permutation (RP), and random sign inversion (RSI) are for, instance, frequently applied after prediction and quantization of transform coefficients [20]. The authors of Ref. [9] discuss a scrambling technique that operates in the transform domain, concealing regions of interest (ROIs) by pseudorandomly flipping the sign of selected transform coefficients in video content compliant with MPEG-4 Visual. Similar approaches have also been studied in the context of H.264/AVC [23] and Scalable Video Coding (SVC), the scalable extension of H.264/AVC [12].

The authors of Refs. [9,24] introduce scrambling techniques that operate in the compressed bit stream domain (H.264/AVC and Motion JPEG, respectively), directly inverting sign bits of the compressed bit stream. The result of applying RSI in the compressed bit stream domain is theoretically identical to the result of applying RSI in the transform domain, but the approach is different from a system point of view. For example, scrambling at the level of the compressed bit stream is useful when having to apply privacy protection to the compressed output of IP-based surveillance cameras.

Finally, it is worth mentioning that privacy protection can also be ensured by means of data hiding. Given a video sequence, the authors of Ref. [25] first remove privacy-sensitive information and subsequently encrypt the removed information with DES. Next, the encrypted information is embedded in an H.263-compliant bit stream using a compressed-domain watermarking technique. To conceal the removal of privacy-sensitive information, the authors propose to make use of video obfuscation (e.g., in-painting). The authors of Ref. [26] also facilitate privacy protection by means of data hiding, taking advantage of the fundamental characteristics of the discrete wavelet transform (DWT) to realize data embedding.

6.3 Subband-Adaptive Scrambling in JPEG XR

In Ref. [14], we propose a scrambling technique that aims at concealing the identity of face regions in a JPEG XR-based video surveillance system, where the system used targets real-time monitoring in heterogeneous usage environments. Specifically, in Ref. [14], we propose a scrambling technique that is layered in nature, applying RLS to DC subbands, RP to low-pass (LP) subbands, and RSI to high-pass (HP) subbands. That way, a trade-off can be achieved between the visual importance of different subbands, the amount of coded data present in different subbands, the level of security offered by a particular scrambling tool, the effect of a particular scrambling tool on the coding efficiency, the computational complexity of the scrambling tools used, and the scalability properties of JPEG XR. Table 6.1 summarizes the scrambling technique proposed in Ref. [14].

6.4 Evaluation of the Privacy-Preserving Nature of Subband-Adaptive Scrambling in JPEG XR

We evaluate the privacy-preserving nature of subband-adaptive scrambling in JPEG XR by means of both objective and subjective assessments. Our objective assessments investigate to what extent subband-adaptive scrambling influences the effectiveness of three automatic FR techniques and three general-purpose visual security metrics, whereas our subjective assessments investigate whether agreement exists between the judgments made by 35 human observers and the output

Table 6.1 Overview of Subband-Adaptive Scrambling in JPEG XR

Subbands Used	Scrambling Tools Used	Cryptographic Security	Visual Effect
DC+LP+HP	No scrambling tools used	None	
DC	RLS	$(2^L+1)^N$	
DC+LP	RLS for DC subbands RP for LP subbands	$(2^L+1)^N + (15!/(15-K)!)^N$	
DC+LP+HP	RLS for DC subbands RP for LP subbands RSI for HP subbands	$(2^L+1)^N + (15!/(15-K)!)^N + (2^M)^N$	

N denotes the total number of MBs in an image, L denotes the level shift parameter used by RLS (see Ref. [14]), K denotes the number of nonzero LP coefficients in an MB, and M denotes the number of nonzero HP coefficients in an MB.

of automatic FR. Both our objective and subjective assessments make use of four experimental conditions that may cause privacy leakage:

Spatial resolution: In general, the higher the spatial resolution of face images, the better the overall effectiveness of FR [27]. Consequently, in order to facilitate a high level of privacy protection, the strength of scrambling needs to remain high when face images with a high spatial resolution are in use.

Visual quality: Video scrambling typically alters the signs (e.g., by means of RSI), indexes (e.g., by means of RP), and magnitudes (e.g., by means of RLS) of predicted transform coefficients in a pseudorandom way. Given that the visual significance of the transform coefficients decreases when the bit rate decreases, the aforementioned scrambling tools also become less effective when the bit rate decreases.

Replacement attack: Each type of subband in JPEG XR has a different level of visual significance. In addition, coding and scrambling dependencies between different types of subbands are limited in order to allow for scalability. As a result, an adversary aware of the compressed bit stream structure may try to attack a single type of subband, and thus a single scrambling tool, in order to circumvent the combined strength of incremental scrambling.

Nonscrambled chroma information: Given that luma information is more important to the human visual system than chroma information, tools for privacy protection may only focus on altering luma information in order to limit bit rate overhead. However, since nonscrambled chroma information is available to an adversary aware of the compressed bit stream structure, it is important to investigate whether subband-adaptive scrambling is still effective when both luma and chroma information are used by automatic FR. Indeed, previous research has demonstrated that the use of chroma information is capable of increasing the overall effectiveness of automatic FR [27].

6.4.1 Objective Assessments

This section discusses our objective assessments in more detail, studying the influence of the aforementioned four experimental conditions on the effectiveness of automatic FR applied to privacy-protected face images. In addition, we compare the output of automatic FR with the output of three general-purpose visual security metrics, for the following experimental conditions: a varying spatial resolution, a varying quality, and a replacement attack. We start by detailing our experimental setup.

6.4.1.1 Experimental Setup

6.4.1.1.1 Face Images Used

In our experiments, we made use of face images belonging to the Carnegie Mellon University (CMU) Pose, Illumination, and Expression (PIE) database [28]. In particular, to construct sets of training, gallery, and probe face images, we collected 3070 frontal face images of 68 subjects from the "talking" image set of CMU PIE. As such, we used 68 gallery face images, 340 training face images, and 2662 probe face images. Frontal face images from the "talking" image set only have slight variation in lip movement, thus allowing for a high effectiveness of automatic FR. This makes it possible to test the privacy-preserving nature of subband-adaptive scrambling in JPEG XR in a more rigorous way.

To generate privacy-protected face images, we inherited the settings used for the "ATM" [29] video sequence in Ref. [14]. In particular, given a quantization parameter (QP) value of 20, 35, and 80, we set the range of the shift value L, a parameter used by RLS, to 8, 8, and 3, respectively. In addition, based on empirical observations made for the face images present in the "ATM" video sequence [14], we used face images with a spatial resolution of 192×192, 96×96, and 48×48.

6.4.1.1.2 FR Techniques Used

In our experiments, we investigated the privacy-preserving nature of subband-adaptive scrambling in JPEG XR using the following FR techniques: PCA [30], ERE [31], and LBP [32]. PCA and ERE extract global facial features using unsupervised and supervised learning, respectively, whereas LBP extracts local facial features. Distance measurement for PCA-, ERE-, and LBP-based FR was done by means of the Euclidean, cosine, and chi-square distance metric, respectively [33]. Implementations of the aforementioned FR techniques are available online [34]. We normalized all face images following the recommendations made in Refs. [32,35]. Further, assuming that eye coordinates are known, we applied subband-adaptive scrambling after geometrical alignment. Also, assuming that an attacker does not have access to a tool that implements subband-adaptive scrambling, we did not scramble training and gallery face images. Indeed, in our research, we only scrambled probe face images, assuming that these probe face images represent face images that appeared in surveillance video content.

6.4.1.1.3 Measurement of FR Effectiveness

We plotted FR results on a cumulative match characteristic (CMC) curve [35]. In order to allow for a fair comparison, we adopted the best found correct recognition rate (BstCRR) for PCA- and ERE-based FR [36]. On the other hand, given that LBP-based FR does not make use of a projection matrix, we obtained the recognition rates for LBP-based FR for feature vectors with a maximum dimensionality.

Note that in Figure 6.1, and in all other figures used thereafter, the area shaded in gray represents the set of recognition rates that yield an ideal or asymptotical level of privacy protection, which is the probability of success of random guessing. In general, the recognition rate of random guessing at rank K is equal to K/N_s, where N_s denotes the total number of gallery face images used, that is, 1.47% (=1/68) in our experimental conditions.

6.4.1.1.4 Notation

Table 6.2 introduces a number of notations used throughout the remainder of this chapter. *DC*, *LP*, and *HP* denote a DC, LP, and HP subband, respectively. A first subscript is used to denote the incremental use of several subbands. Specifically, S_1, S_2, and S_3 represent the use of DC, $DC+LP$, and $DC+LP+HP$, respectively. A second subscript is used to denote the presence of luma and/or chroma channels. Finally, a prime is used to indicate the use of scrambling. As an overall example, $S'_{3,Y}$ indicates that the DC, LP, and HP subbands of the luma channel have been scrambled: $S'_{3,Y} = DC'_Y + LP'_Y + HP'_Y$.

6.4.1.2 Influence of Spatial Resolution

In this section, we evaluate the effectiveness of subband-adaptive scrambling when varying the spatial resolution of the probe face images. To that end, the experiment presented in this section makes use of probe face images having the following three spatial resolutions: 192×192, 96×96, and 48×48. Note that, before applying FR, we first rescaled the probe face images with a resolution of 96×96 and 48×48 to a resolution of 192×192 for normalization purposes. Also, we kept the spatial resolution of training and gallery face images fixed to 192×192. Further, we encoded all probe face images with a QP value of 20, irrespective of the spatial resolution used.

Figure 6.1a shows the effect of a varying spatial resolution on the effectiveness of PCA-based FR. The rank 1 recognition rate for nonscrambled probe face images is higher than 82%, regardless of the spatial resolution used. On the other hand, when using scrambled probe face images, the rank 1 recognition rate drops to less than 7% for the spatial resolutions used, showing that the influence of a varying spatial resolution on the effectiveness of subband-adaptive scrambling is limited.

Figure 6.1b shows the effect of a varying spatial resolution on the effectiveness of ERE-based FR. The CMC curve obtained for ERE-based FR is similar to the CMC curve obtained for PCA-based FR. The rank 1 recognition rate for nonscrambled probe face images is higher than 98%, regardless of the spatial resolution used. On the other hand, when using scrambled probe face images, the rank 1 recognition rate drops to less than 4% for all three spatial resolutions used.

Finally, Figure 6.1c shows the recognition rates obtained for LBP-based FR. Compared to PCA- and ERE-based FR, LBP-based FR shows a higher vulnerability against changes in spatial resolution. The rank 1 recognition rate is approximately 94% when the spatial resolution of the nonscrambled probe face images is 192×192, while the rank 1 recognition rate drops to 78% when

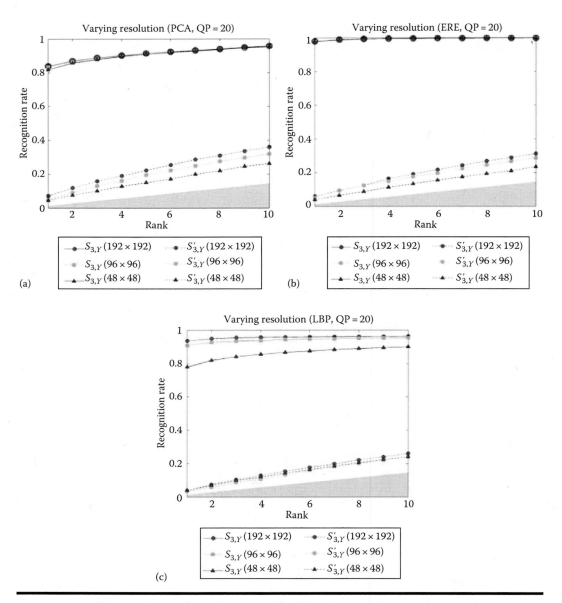

Figure 6.1 Influence of spatial resolution on the effectiveness of FR: (a) PCA, (b) ERE (PC = 1.0, RC = 0.99), and (c) LBP (PC = 0.99, RC = 0.83).

the spatial resolution of the nonscrambled probe face images is 48×48. In addition, the rank 1 recognition rate drops to approximately 3% when using scrambled probe face images, regardless of the spatial resolution used.

The caption of Figure 6.1 also reports the correlation between the rank 1 recognition rates of the three FR techniques applied. Specifically, using the effectiveness of PCA-based FR as a baseline, we computed the Pearson correlation coefficient (PC) and Spearman's rank order correlation coefficient (RC) between the rank 1 recognition rate of PCA-based FR and the rank 1 recognition

Table 6.2 Summary of Notations Used

Notation	Explanation
DC, LP, and *HP*	DC, LP, and HP subband
S_3	$DC+LP+HP$
S_2	$DC+LP$
S_1	DC
Subscripts (*Y, Co, Cg*)	Luma and chroma channels (Y, Co, and Cg)
Prime (')	Scrambled image data

rates of ERE- and LBP-based FR. We can observe that the correlation between the rank 1 recognition rate obtained for ERE- and PCA-based FR is higher than the correlation between the rank 1 recognition rate obtained for LBP- and PCA-based FR.

To summarize, given the three different FR techniques, LBP-based FR has the lowest overall recognition rates for both scrambled and nonscrambled probe face images. The relatively high vulnerability of LBP-based FR to subband-adaptive scrambling can be attributed to the fact that the construction of LBP feature vectors is highly dependent on adjacent pixel information. On the other hand, when making use of scrambled probe face images, the recognition rates obtained for PCA-based FR are the highest.

6.4.1.3 Influence of Visual Quality

In this section, we investigate the level of privacy protection offered by subband-adaptive scrambling in the context of a varying visual quality (i.e., when varying QP values are used), for face images with a spatial resolution of 192 × 192. Note that we did not vary the visual quality of the training and gallery face images (we used a fixed QP value of 20 to encode the training and gallery face images).

Given varying QP values, Figure 6.2a and b illustrate that the rank 1 recognition rate for nonscrambled probe face images is approximately 81% and 98% for PCA- and ERE-based FR, respectively. When subband-adaptive scrambling is used in combination with a QP value of either 20 or 35, the rank 1 recognition rate drops to less than 7% and 6% for PCA- and ERE-based FR, respectively. However, when the QP value is set to 80, the rank 1 recognition rate remains relatively high at around 20% and 13% for PCA- and ERE-based FR, respectively. This implies that subband-adaptive scrambling in JPEG XR becomes less effective when the bit rate of probe face images is low. Indeed, as the bit rate decreases, the visual influence of RP and RSI becomes insignificant since most of the LP and HP coefficients converge to zero (due to strong quantization). In addition, as the bit rate decreases, the range of the pseudorandom numbers (i.e., the shift value L) in the DC subband becomes smaller in order to avoid a significant amount of bit rate overhead [14]. This also contributes to a decrease in the effectiveness of scrambling at low bit rates (i.e., when a QP value of 80 is used). Consequently, for video surveillance applications requiring a high level of privacy protection, the results reported in Figure 6.2a and b indicate that the strength of subband-adaptive scrambling needs to be enhanced at low bit rates. This could simply be done by increasing L, albeit at the cost of a higher bit rate overhead (see Section 6.5.1).

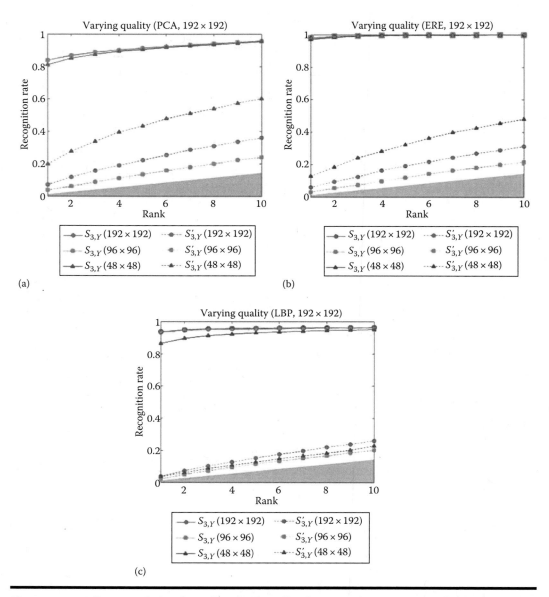

Figure 6.2 Influence of visual quality on the effectiveness of FR: (a) PCA, (b) ERE (PC = 1.0, RC = 0.99), and (c) LBP (PC = 0.99, RC = 0.93).

Figure 6.2c shows that the effectiveness of LBP-based FR behaves differently compared to the effectiveness of PCA- and ERE-based FR. Specifically, Figure 6.2c shows that when QP is set to 20, the rank 1 recognition rate for nonscrambled face images is 94% for LBP-based FR. On the other hand, at the lowest bit rate (i.e., for a QP value of 80), the rank 1 recognition rate obtained for LBP-based FR drops significantly, from 94% to 87%. This can again be attributed to a loss of adjacent pixel information caused by severe quantization. Further, LBP-based FR is ineffective in finding the identity of scrambled probe face images when a QP value of 80 is used. This is also due to information loss caused by severe quantization. Further, given the caption of Figure 6.2, we can observe that the correlation between the rank 1 recognition rate obtained for ERE- and PCA-based FR is higher than the correlation between the rank 1 recognition rate obtained for LBP- and PCA-based FR. This is in line with the observation previously made in Section 6.4.1.2.

6.4.1.4 Influence of a Replacement Attack

An adversary aware of the compressed bit stream structure may try to attack a single type of sub-bands, and thus a single scrambling tool, in order to circumvent the combined strength of incremental scrambling. To that end, an adversary may make use of a replacement attack [9], setting all transform coefficients to zero after entropy decoding, except for the transform coefficients the attacker is interested in. As an example, Figure 6.3c, which was obtained by setting the transform coefficients in the DC and HP subbands to zero, shows that stand-alone LP subbands of the luma channel of a nonscrambled probe face image already provide an adversary with sufficient visual information to determine the identity of the probe face image under consideration.

To investigate the robustness of subband-adaptive scrambling against a replacement attack, we extracted subbands from the luma channel of probe face images, all having a spatial resolution of 192×192 and encoded with a QP value set to 20. To that end, after entropy decoding, we replaced all transform coefficients with zero in the subbands different from the subbands extracted. We then decoded the resulting subbands to the spatial domain. Finally, we applied several FR techniques to the probe face images obtained.

Figure 6.4 shows the CMC curves obtained for PCA-, ERE-, and LBP-based FR. Our results demonstrate that stand-alone LP subbands of the luma channel of nonscrambled probe face images contain distinctive face information as rank 1 recognition rates are achieved in the range of 53%–84% for all FR techniques used. In addition, for DC subbands, the rank 1 recognition rate is 80% for PCA-based FR and 91% for ERE-based FR, whereas the rank 1 recognition rate is significantly lower for LBP-based FR (i.e., the rank 1 recognition rate is 1.2%). This substantial decrease can be attributed to the fact that distinctive pixel information in local regions is almost completely eliminated in DC subbands. Further, we can observe that stand-alone HP subbands are less useful than stand-alone DC and LP subbands for the purpose of automatic FR: the rank 1 recognition rates for PCA-, ERE-, and LBP-based FR are approximately 3%, 4.1%, and 2%, respectively.

We performed a similar evaluation for scrambled subbands. Figure 6.4 illustrates that the rank 1 recognition rate drops to less than 6% for all scrambled subbands, showing a near-ideal level of privacy protection. Also, given the caption of Figure 6.4, we can again observe that the

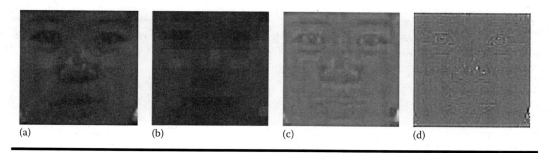

(a)   (b)   (c)   (d)

Figure 6.3 Visual significance of each type of subband in JPEG XR: (a) original image, (b) DC image of (a), (c) LP image of (a), (d) HP image of (a). Contrast has been enhanced for visualization purposes. Further, only luma information is visualized in (b) through (d).

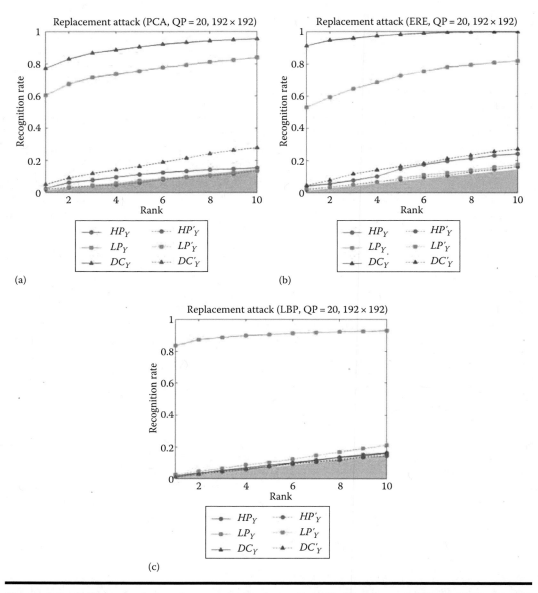

Figure 6.4 Influence of a replacement attack on the effectiveness of FR: (a) PCA, (b) ERE (PC = 0.98, RC = 1.0), and (c) LBP (PC = 0.50, RC = −0.37).

correlation between the rank 1 recognition rate obtained for ERE- and PCA-based FR is higher than the correlation between the rank 1 recognition rate obtained for LBP- and PCA-based FR.

6.4.1.5 Influence of Nonscrambled Chroma Information

In this experiment, we investigate whether subband-adaptive scrambling is still effective when both luma and chroma information are used by automatic FR. This assumes that an adversary aware of the compressed bit stream structure has access to nonscrambled chroma information.

In this experiment, all face images have a resolution of 192×192 and were encoded with a QP value set to 20. We fused the nonscrambled Co and Cg chroma channels with the scrambled Y channel by concatenating the feature vectors extracted from the different channels (feature-level fusion [37]). Note that JPEG XR by default makes use of the YCoCg color space. Also, note that we made use of YCoCg 4:4:4 (i.e., we did not subsample the chroma channels during encoding).

As shown in Figure 6.5, the recognition rates significantly increase when automatic FR makes use of both scrambled luma and nonscrambled chroma information, compared to the recognition rates obtained when automatic FR only makes use of scrambled luma information. In particular,

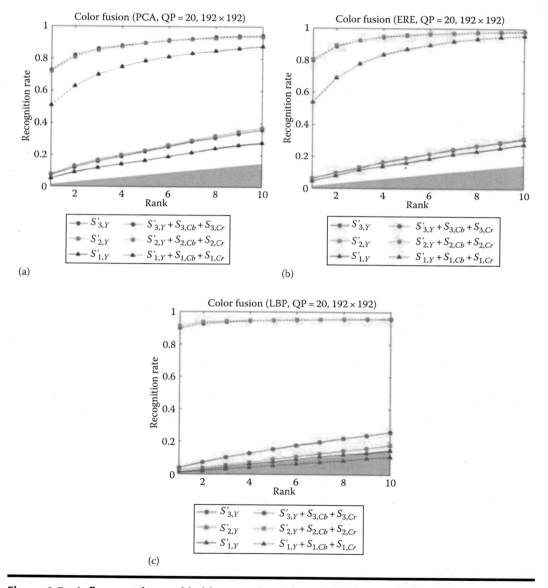

Figure 6.5 Influence of scrambled luma and nonscrambled chroma information on the effectiveness of FR: (a) PCA, (b) ERE (PC = 1.0, RC = 0.94), and (c) LBP (PC = 0.85, RC = 0.64).

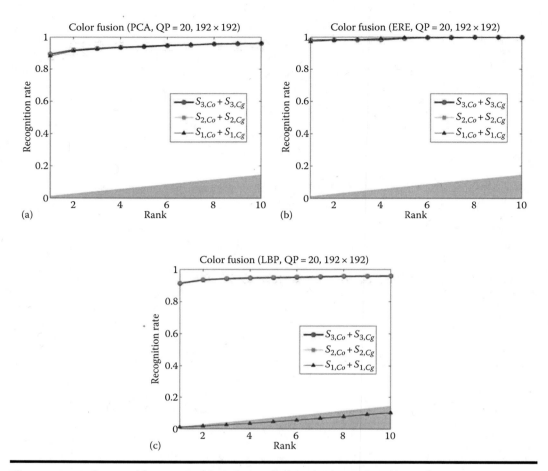

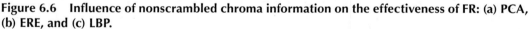

Figure 6.6 **Influence of nonscrambled chroma information on the effectiveness of FR: (a) PCA, (b) ERE, and (c) LBP.**

the rank 1 recognition rates increase with at least 46%, except when LBP-based FR is applied to DC subbands (as previously discussed, this is due to the elimination of distinctive pixel information in local regions). This implies that, when an adversary has access to the compressed bit stream structure, the presence of nonscrambled chroma information may reduce the effectiveness of a scrambling technique that only protects luma information. Moreover, Figure 6.6 shows that, when not making use of scrambled luma information, the stand-alone use of nonscrambled chroma information also results in relatively high recognition rates. Specifically, regardless of the FR technique used, the rank 1 recognition rate is higher than 88%, except when LBP-based FR is applied to DC subbands. Consequently, for video surveillance applications requiring a high level of privacy protection, our experimental results indicate that chroma information also needs to be scrambled (at the cost of a higher bit rate overhead; see Section 6.5.2 for a more detailed analysis).

6.4.1.6 Effectiveness of General-Purpose Visual Security Metrics

The development of general-purpose visual security metrics has recently attracted some research attention, given that these metrics can be evaluated automatically. In this experiment, we investigate the effectiveness of three general-purpose visual security metrics to assess the level of privacy protection offered by subband-adaptive scrambling: LSS [18], ESS [18], and LFVSM [19]. To measure the similarity between two images, LSS and ESS make use of luma and edge information, respectively, whereas LFVSM takes advantage of both local color moments and local edge features to estimate the level of security. We study the influence of the following three experimental conditions on the output of the aforementioned metrics: a varying spatial resolution, a varying visual quality, and a replacement attack. Similar to Refs. [18,19], our implementation of LSS, ESS, and LFVSM only makes use of luma information, thus leaving a study of the influence of non-scrambled chroma information as a future research item.

Similar to automatic FR, we represent the output of the three visual security metrics by making use of CMC curves. This is done by first applying PCA-based FR to scrambled face images and by subsequently computing and visualizing the average visual security of the scrambled face images obtained for each rank. As an example, an LSS value at rank 3 represents the average of the LSS values computed for the top three scrambled face images selected by PCA-based FR. Note that LFVSM values have been subtracted from one to simplify the visualization. That way, the following statement holds true for all of the visual security metrics used: the lower the values computed by the visual security metrics, the higher the visual security.

Given a varying spatial resolution, Figure 6.7 shows the effectiveness of LSS, ESS, and LFVSM in estimating the level of security provided. We can observe that, compared to automatic FR, the visual security metrics show different behaviors. Specifically, as the spatial resolution decreases, the visual security metrics indicate that the security of the scrambled face images decreases, whereas automatic FR indicates that the security of the scrambled face images increases. The behavior of the visual security metrics can most likely be attributed to the fact that face images with a resolution of 96×96 and 48×48 were rescaled to a resolution of 192×192 for normalization purposes, where interpolation decreased the strength of scrambling. Further, we can observe that, in contrast to automatic FR, the values computed by the visual security metrics are almost constant over the different ranks, implying that LSS, ESS, and LFVSM have less discriminative power than automatic FR (see Figure 6.1). Indeed, if the values computed by LSS, ESS, and LFVSM would well reflect the individual level of security offered by each scrambled face image, then the scores computed would decrease as the rank increases (given that automatic FR is able to correctly identify highly ranked face images with a higher probability than lowly ranked face images).

Figure 6.8 shows the effect of a varying visual quality on the effectiveness of the three general-purpose visual security metrics. We can observe that the lowest level of visual security can be found at the lowest bit rates (i.e., when using a QP value of 80). The latter observation is in line with the results obtained by automatic FR (see Figure 6.2). Similar to the results reported in Figure 6.7, the values computed by LSS, ESS, and LFVSM are almost constant over the different ranks.

Figure 6.9 shows the effect of a replacement attack on the output of the visual security metrics. With the exception of LSS, the visual security metrics indicate that the level of security is higher for subbands containing low-frequency transform coefficients, an observation that is not in line with the results obtained for automatic FR (see Figure 6.4). This is due to the fact that these subbands do not contain distinctive facial information (i.e., edge information), where the latter is mainly captured by the high-frequency transform coefficients. Again, similar to Figures 6.7 and 6.8, the values computed by LSS, ESS, and LFVSM are almost constant over the different ranks.

To summarize, with the exception of a varying visual quality, we could observe that the output of the general-purpose visual security metrics used is not in line with the results obtained for

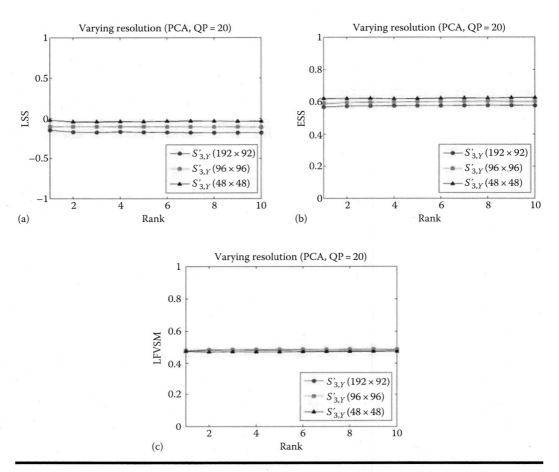

Figure 6.7   Influence of a varying spatial resolution on the output of the visual security metrics studied: (a) LSS, (b) ESS, and (c) LFVSM.

automatic FR. The latter can be considered more reliable than the former, given that the computation of the FR results made use of a ground truth that indicates whether or not a scrambled probe image was correctly identified. Also, given a particular experimental setting (e.g., face images all having the same visual quality), we could observe that the visual security metrics studied are not able to assess the individual level of security of scrambled face images.

6.4.2 Subjective Assessments

Objective results are not always consistent with the perception of human observers. This is, for instance, well known in the area of video quality assessment [38]. Consequently, we also conducted subjective assessments to investigate the level of privacy protection offered by subband-adaptive scrambling in JPEG XR, studying the influence of the following five experimental conditions: a varying spatial resolution, a varying visual quality, a replacement attack, the presence of nonscrambled chroma information (once with and once without scrambled luma information), and the presence of eyeglasses. We start by discussing our test methodology.

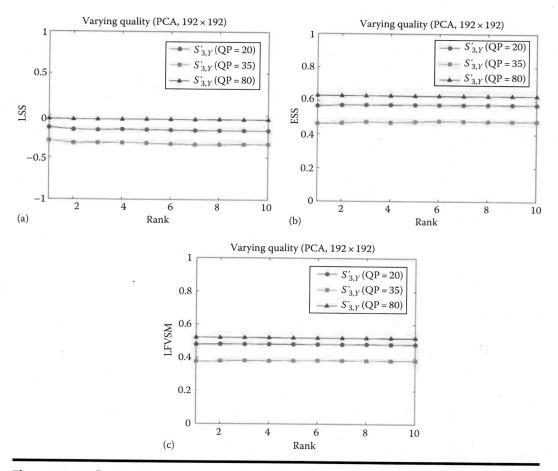

Figure 6.8 **Influence of a varying visual quality on the output of the visual security metrics studied: (a) LSS, (b) ESS, and (c) LFVSM.**

6.4.2.1 Test Methodology

Thirty-five human observers aged 22–38 participated in our subjective assessments. All of the observers did not have any expertise in the forensic identification of people. We made use of three probe face images for each parameter setting (e.g., a particular resolution or QP value). As a result, given the aforementioned experimental conditions, the human observers were presented with a total of 45 probe face images (five experimental conditions, three parameter settings per experimental condition, three probe face images per parameter setting). Given a probe face image, the human observers were asked to select the best matching face image from a set of 12 gallery face images. The observers were also able to indicate that a suitable match could not be found. The mere use of 12 gallery face images, part of the CMU PIE database and shown in Figure 6.10, allowed keeping the subjective experiments simple. This also made it possible to more rigorously test the privacy-preserving nature of subband-adaptive scrambling in JPEG XR.

Note that the identity of the privacy-protected face images shown from Tables 6.3 through 6.7 is the same as the identity of the face image shown in the top left corner of Figure 6.10. Further,

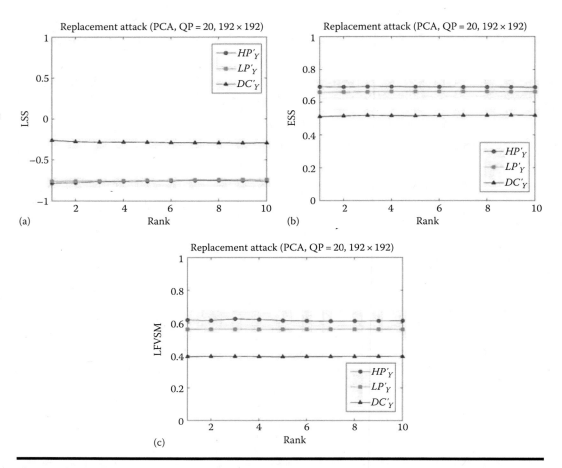

Figure 6.9 Influence of a replacement attack on the output of the visual security metrics studied: (a) LSS, (b) ESS, and (c) LFVSM.

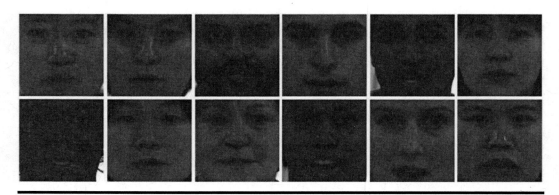

Figure 6.10 Gallery face images used in our subjective assessments.

Table 6.3   Influence of the Spatial Resolution ($S'_{3,Y}$, QP = 20)

Spatial Resolution	48×48		96×96		192×192	
Sample images						
SRR	0.04		0.03		0.03	
ORR	0.33		0.33		0.33	
SRR vs. ORR	Hit	Miss	Hit	Miss	Hit	Miss
	0.02	0.02	0.01	0.02	0.02	0.01

Table 6.4   Influence of the Visual Quality ($S'_{3,Y}$, 192 × 192)

QP Value	80		35		20	
Sample images						
SRR	0.03		0.01		0.01	
ORR	0.0		0.33		0.33	
SRR vs. ORR	Hit	Miss	Hit	Hit	Miss	Hit
	N/A	0.03	0.0	0.01	0.0	0.01

A value of "N/A" for "Hit" implies that none of the probe face images were correctly identified by automatic FR. On a similar note, a value of "N/A" for "Miss" implies that all probe face images were correctly identified by automatic FR.

note that we enhanced the contrast of the probe face images and that the human observers were also able to study the probe face images at different zoom levels. This reflects a real-world scenario in which an adversary has complete control over the scrambled face images in order to find a configuration that is visually optimal.

To facilitate a fair comparison of the subjective and objective results, we conducted additional objective assessments that are complementary to the subjective assessments, using common experimental settings. Note that the complementary objective assessments made use of

Table 6.5 Influence of a Replacement Attack (192 × 192@QP = 20)

Subband Used	DC'_Y		LP'_Y		HP'_Y	
Sample images						
SRR	0.02		0.03		0.03	
ORR	0.0		0.33		0.33	
SRR vs. ORR	Hit	Miss	Hit	Miss	Hit	Miss
	N/A	0.02	0.0	0.03	0.0	0.03

Table 6.6 Influence of Scrambled Luma and Nonscrambled Chroma Channels (192 × 192@QP = 20)

Subbands Used	$S'_{1,Y}+S'_{1,Co}+S_{1,Cg}$		$S'_{2,Y}+S'_{2,Co}+S_{2,Cg}$		$S'_{3,Y}+S'_{3,Co}+S_{3,Cg}$	
Sample images						
SRR	0.0		0.03		0.05	
ORR	1.0		1.0		1.0	
SRR vs. ORR	Hit	Miss	Hit	Miss	Hit	Miss
	0.0	N/A	0.03	N/A	0.05	N/A

PCA-based FR, given that PCA-based FR outperformed ERE- and LBP-based FR in terms of effectiveness in Section 6.3.1.

Also, we made use of the methodology outlined in Ref. [39] to fairly compare our subjective and objective results. Specifically, given that subjective and objective recognition rates (ORRs) are computed differently, we separately measured the subjective recognition rate (SRR) for the case where PCA-based FR was able to correctly identify a probe face image (denoted as a "Hit") and where PCA-based FR was not able to correctly identify a probe face image (denoted as a "Miss"). Indeed, for each parameter setting, we obtained the ORRs by counting the number of correctly

TABLE 6.7   Influence of Nonscrambled Chroma Channels (192 × 192@QP = 20)

Subbands Used	$S_{1,Co} + S_{1,Cg}$		$S_{2,Co} + S_{2,Cg}$		$S_{3,Co} + S_{3,Cg}$	
Sample images						
SRR	0.34		0.79		0.80	
ORR	1.0		1.0		1.0	
SRR vs. ORR	Hit	Miss	Hit	Miss	Hit	Miss
	0.34	N/A	0.79	N/A	0.80	N/A

identified probe face images over the total number of probe face images at rank 1, while we obtained the SRRs by counting the number of human observers reporting a correct identification over the total number of trials, thus making a direct comparison impossible. Given the use of 12 gallery face images, we would like to make note that the subjective and objective recognition rates should be lower than 0.08 (1/12) in order to achieve an ideal level of privacy protection.

6.4.2.2 Influence of Spatial Resolution

Table 6.3 shows the subjective and objective recognition rates obtained for probe face images that have been encoded with a fixed QP value of 20, also having a varying spatial resolution and a scrambled luma channel. The SRRs in Table 6.3 show that most of the human observers were not able to correctly identify the privacy-protected probe face images, given that the SRR for each parameter setting is lower than the ideal recognition rate of 0.08. In addition, as shown by the SRRs obtained for the cases "Hit" and "Miss," the subjective results are independent of whether automatic FR is able to correctly identify the privacy-protected face images or not.

6.4.2.3 Influence of Visual Quality

Table 6.4 shows the subjective and objective recognition rates obtained for probe face images that have been encoded with varying QP values, also having a fixed spatial resolution of 192 × 192 and a scrambled luma channel. Similar to Table 6.3, our results show that most of the human observers were not able to correctly identify the privacy-protected probe face images.

6.4.2.4 Influence of a Replacement Attack

As discussed in Section 6.4.1.4, an adversary may try to attack a single subband in order to thwart the strength of incremental scrambling. Table 6.5 shows the subjective and objective recognition rates obtained when applying a replacement attack to probe face images that have a spatial resolution of 192×192, where the probe face images under consideration have been encoded with a QP value of 20. We can observe that the visual effect of scrambling is sufficiently strong to conceal the identity of the probe face images present in each type of subband. Indeed, although the privacy-protected probe face images leak edge information around the eyes (see the sample probe face image for LP_Y') and visual information around the four corners of the probe face images (see the sample probe face image for LP_Y' and HP_Y'), the privacy leakage is such that it does not allow identifying the scrambled probe face images.

6.4.2.5 Influence of Nonscrambled Chroma Information

Table 6.6 shows the subjective and objective recognition rates obtained for probe face images having a scrambled luma channel and nonscrambled chroma channels. We can observe that the visual effect of subband-adaptive scrambling is sufficiently strong to conceal the identity of the privacy-protected probe face images. Indeed, as shown in Table 6.6, a scrambled luma channel significantly hampers the successful identification of probe face images when simultaneously visualizing luma and chroma information. Therefore, assuming that an adversary is not able to get access to the compressed bit stream structure, thus assuming that an adversary is only able to observe the visualized image data, it is not necessary to scramble chroma channels, mitigating bit rate overhead. However, when an adversary is able to get access to the compressed bit stream structure, Table 6.6 shows that automatic FR is able to successfully exploit nonscrambled chroma information, achieving perfect recognition rates.

Table 6.7 shows the subjective and objective recognition rates obtained for probe face images having nonscrambled chroma channels, not visualizing the scrambled luma channels. The SRR is approximately equal to 79% for $S_{2,Co} + S_{2,Cg}$ and 80% for $S_{3,Co} + S_{3,Cg}$, while the SRR is approximately equal to 34% for $S_{1,Co} + S_{1,Cg}$. The lower SRR for $S_{1,Co} + S_{1,Cg}$ can be attributed to the pixelated nature of the probe face images. For all of the three aforementioned cases, we found that human observers were able to correctly identify the probe face images by taking advantage of facial attributes such as the skin color, the shape of a face, the presence of four corners in the face images, and even the slight differences in the orientation of a face. Further, for all of the three aforementioned cases, we can observe that automatic FR is able to achieve perfect recognition rates. Both our subjective and objective experimental results thus indicate that, when an adversary has access to the compressed bit stream structure, nonscrambled chroma channels can be used to correctly identify privacy-protected face images. Consequently, for video surveillance applications requiring a high level of privacy protection, our results demonstrate that all chroma channels need to be scrambled.

6.4.2.6 Influence of the Presence of Eyeglasses

To investigate the influence of the presence of eyeglasses—a strong visual clue—on the effectiveness of automatic and human FR, we reconducted the previous experiments with gallery and probe face images all containing eyeglasses (in the previous experiments, gallery and probe face images did not contain eyeglasses). Figure 6.11 shows the gallery face images used.

For all experimental conditions, except when a replacement attack is applied, we found that both the subjective and objective results were not significantly different from the previously obtained results. Consequently, for reasons of brevity, we only present and discuss results obtained for the replacement attack in the remainder of this section.

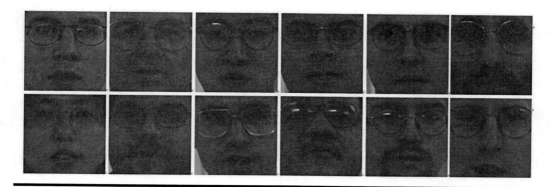

Figure 6.11 Gallery face images containing eyeglasses.

TABLE 6.8 Influence of a Replacement Attack (192 × 192@QP = 20)

Subband Used	DC_Y'		LP_Y'		HP_Y'	
Sample images						
SRR	0.0		0.01		0.42	
ORR	0.33		0.0		0.0	
SRR vs. ORR	Hit	Miss	Hit	Miss	Hit	Miss
	0.0	0.0	N/A	0.01	N/A	0.42

When making use of a replacement attack, Table 6.8 shows that several human observers were able to successfully identify probe face images by taking advantage of facial information available in HP_Y'. Figure 6.12 contains the HP_Y' probe face images used. In addition, Table 6.8 indicates that disagreement exists between the subjective and objective results obtained for the HP_Y' probe face images. Indeed, the SRR is 0.42, while the ORR is zero. The latter is also in line with the observations previously presented in Section 6.4.1.4.

6.5 Discussion

Our objective and subjective assessments allowed identifying and quantifying three weaknesses of the subband-adaptive scrambling technique originally proposed in Ref. [14]. In this section, we discuss solutions for these three weaknesses.

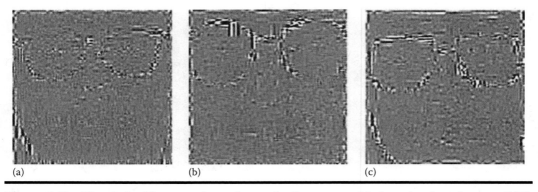

Figure 6.12 Visual significance of eyeglasses in three scrambled probe face images (HP'_Y, 192 × 192@QP = 20): scrambled HP subbands of the (a) fifth, (b) sixth, and (c) ninth face image in Figure 6.11 (counting face images in raster scan order).

6.5.1 Low Bit Rates

Throughout our study, we observed that subband-adaptive scrambling is not always able to offer an ideal level of privacy protection when using well-known FR techniques with state-of-the-art effectiveness. Indeed, when using PCA- and ERE-based FR, the ORR for scrambled probe face images mostly does not reach the ideal recognition rate, which is the rate obtained for random guessing. The aforementioned observation holds particularly true when studying Figure 6.2a and b, demonstrating that the subband-adaptive scrambling technique proposed in Ref. [14] is less effective at low bit rates (i.e., when QP has a value of 80).

As previously indicated, the robustness of subband-adaptive scrambling in JPEG XR can be improved by increasing the value of L when applying RLS to the DC subbands, albeit at the cost of a higher bit rate overhead. Therefore, to improve the strength of privacy protection at the level of DC subbands while minimizing the bit rate overhead, we propose to apply both RSI and RLS at the level of DC subbands. Since RSI does not affect the coding efficiency, its application at the level of the DC subbands helps to enhance the level of privacy protection without producing additional bit rate overhead:

$$DCcoeff''^e = \begin{cases} -DCcoeff^e, & \text{if } r = 1 \\ +DCcoeff^e, & \text{otherwise} \end{cases} \tag{6.1}$$

where $DCcoeff^e$ denotes a DC coefficient that has been scrambled using RLS.

Figure 6.13a shows the recognition rates obtained for PCA-based FR, making use of probe face images that have been scrambled using our improved approach. The face images have a resolution of 192 × 192, and the QP value was set to 80. In Figure 6.13a, $S^*_{3,Y}$ represents the case where the luma channel is scrambled up to the level of the HP subbands and where both RSI and RLS are applied to DC subbands. Our results demonstrate that the combined use of RSI and RLS significantly decreases the recognition rates (see $S'_{3,Y}$ and $S^*_{3,Y}$ when L is set to 3). In particular, the rank 1 recognition rate significantly drops from 20% for $S'_{3,Y}$ to below 2.3% for $S^*_{3,Y}$. This is close to the ideal rank 1 recognition rate of 1.47%.

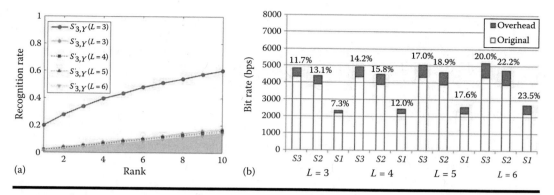

Figure 6.13 **Improved scrambling for DC subbands: (a) recognition rates and (b) bit rate overhead.**

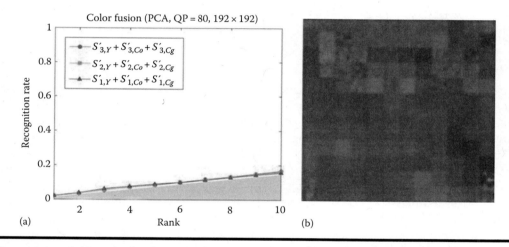

Figure 6.14 **Subband-adaptive scrambling of both luma and chroma channels: (a) Recognition rates and (b) a privacy-protected face image encoded with QP = 80 at the level of S_3.**

Additional decrements in the recognition rate can be achieved by further increasing L. However, these additional decrements in the recognition rate are not significant enough in order to justify the increase in bit rate overhead. This trade-off, is for instance, shown in Figure 6.14b, illustrating the bit rate overhead for varying values of L when scrambling up to the level of the DC subbands, up to the level of the LP subbands, and up to the level of the HP subbands. In particular, we measured the bit rate overhead of $S_{1,Y}^{*}$ relative to $S_{1,Y}$, of $S_{2,Y}^{*}$ relative to $S_{2,Y}$, and of $S_{3,Y}^{*}$ relative to $S_{3,Y}$ (measured over all 2662 probe face images). It should be clear that the bit rate overhead is lower when measuring this overhead relative to the whole image size (the whole image size includes all subbands and background information).

6.5.2 Nonscrambled Chroma Information

Both our objective and subjective results demonstrate that it is important to scramble the chroma channels in order to guarantee a high level of privacy protection. Indeed, automatic FR techniques

can take advantage of nonscrambled chroma channels (see Figures 6.5 and 6.6). This observation also holds true for human FR (see Table 6.7). To protect chroma information, we applied our improved subband-adaptive scrambling technique (see Section 6.5.1) to both the luma channel (i.e., Y) and the chroma channels (i.e., Co and Cg) of the probe face images. The resolution of the probe face images was fixed to 192×192, and the QP value was set to 80.
The face image to the right is the scrambled version of Figure 6.3a.

As shown in Figure 6.14a, the recognition rates obtained for PCA-based FR show that a higher level of privacy protection can be achieved by protecting chroma information. In particular, the rank 1 recognition rate is 2.1% for S_3^*, 2.0% for S_2^*, and 2.1% for S_1^*, nearing an ideal level of privacy protection. When using RLS, L was set to 3, 2, and 2 for the Y, Co, and Cg channels, respectively, resulting in a relatively high bit rate overhead of 26%, 29%, and 35% for S_3^*, S_2^*, and S_1^*, respectively (measured over all 2662 probe face images). However, bit rate overhead is inevitable when it is required to facilitate a high level of privacy protection. Figure 6.14b visualizes a privacy-protected face image, illustrating that the visual effect of subband-adaptive scrambling at the level of both the luma and chroma channels is sufficiently strong to conceal the identity of the face image.

6.5.3 Presence of Eyeglasses

The subjective results reported in Table 6.8 demonstrate that the presence of eyeglasses and the use of a low number of gallery face images may contribute to the success of a replacement attack. However, it should be clear that the chance of success of a replacement attack becomes lower as the number of gallery face images containing eyeglasses increases. In addition, when the use of intrablock-based scrambling tools cannot prevent privacy leakage, interblock-based scrambling tools [20] can be used. For example, interblock shuffling pseudorandomly permutes the locations of MBs within an image. That way, strong facial features can be spatially distributed over different locations, making these facial features less recognizable. However, the use of interblock-based scrambling tools may result in a substantial loss in coding efficiency. In addition, encoding and decoding delay may be introduced. Also, content-adaptive scrambling tools can be used in order to better conceal strong facial features, for instance, making the visual effect of scrambling stronger in heterogeneous regions in face images (at the cost of higher bit rate overhead) and making the visual effect of scrambling weaker in homogeneous regions in face images.

6.6 Conclusions

Little attention has thus far been paid to a rigorous and systematic evaluation of the level of security offered by privacy protection tools, thus leaving room for achieving a better understanding of experimental conditions that may cause privacy leakage and the effectiveness of already existing tools for evaluating the level of security offered by privacy protection tools. To that end, in this chapter, we investigated the privacy-preserving nature of a subband-adaptive scrambling technique developed for JPEG XR by means of both objective and subjective assessments. In our objective assessments, we applied three automatic FR techniques to scrambled face images, taking advantage of domain-specific information: PCA, ERE, and LBP. Additionally, we applied three general-purpose visual security metrics to the scrambled face images used: LSS, ESS, and LFVSM.

Finally, we conducted extensive subjective assessments to study whether agreement exists between the judgments of human observers and the output of automatic FR.

Our experimental results demonstrate that subband-adaptive scrambling of face images offers, in general, a feasible level of protection against automatic and human FR. However, for video surveillance requiring a high level of privacy protection, our experimental results indicate that the strength of subband-adaptive scrambling needs to be enhanced at low bit rates, that chroma information needs to be scrambled, and that the presence of eyeglasses and a low number of gallery face images may contribute to the success of a replacement attack. As a result of these observations, we additionally propose and evaluate a number of improvements to the scrambling technique studied in our research. Our experimental results also show that, compared to automatic FR, the general-purpose visual security metrics studied are less suited for detecting weaknesses in tools that aim at concealing the identity of face images. Specifically, given a particular experimental setup (e.g., face images all having the same resolution), we found that the general-purpose visual security metrics used do not allow comparing the individual level of security of the scrambled face images used. This implies that the general-purpose visual security metrics tested have less discriminative power than automatic FR. Finally, our experimental results demonstrate that our objective and subjective assessments are not always in agreement. For instance, when conducting a replacement attack, we observed that human recognition rates were higher than automatic FR rates due to the presence of eyeglasses and a watch list with a limited number of subjects.

With the aim of better evaluating the effectiveness of tools that aim at concealing identity, our experimental results allow making the following recommendations:

1. *Use of subjective assessments*: Given that objective and subjective results are not always in agreement, subjective assessments may help to reliably estimate the effectiveness of scrambling.
2. *Use of automatic FR*: Compared to general-purpose visual security metrics, automatic FR techniques are more effective in testing the level of security offered by scrambled face images. This observation holds particularly true for PCA-based FR.
3. *Use of a varying visual quality*: The visual effect of scrambling may become less pronounced when the bit rate of probe face images is low, due to strong quantization.
4. *Use of a replacement attack*: An adversary can make use of a replacement attack to selectively test the effectiveness of scrambling. This holds particularly true for scalable coding formats.
5. *Use of strong facial features*: The presence of strong facial features such as eyeglasses may result in privacy leakage, especially when the number of gallery face images is low.
6. *Use of color information*: The presence of nonscrambled color information may result in significantly higher automatic and human FR rates, especially when an adversary has access to the compressed bit stream structure.

Although our experimental study focused on evaluating the privacy-preserving nature of a subband-adaptive scrambling technique developed for video surveillance systems making use of JPEG XR, we believe that our test methodology can be applied to other scrambling techniques and coding formats in a straightforward way. Further, although our assessment of the privacy-preserving nature of subband-adaptive scrambling focused on the use of still images, we would like to point out that the effect of scrambling, and in particular its ability to conceal identity, may be different when applied to a video sequence, given that humans, for instance, have the ability to perceive and recognize faces by temporal integration of separated face parts [40].

Acknowledgment

This research was supported by the National Research Foundation (NRF) of Korea (grant: NRF-D00070).

References

1. D. Vaquero, R. S. Feris, L. Brown, and A. Hampapur, Attribute-based people search in surveillance environments, *Workshop on Applications of Computer Vision (WACV)*, December 2009, Snowbird, UT, pp. 1–8.
2. H. Kruppa, M. Castrillon-Santana, and B. Schiele, Fast and robust face finding via local context, *Joint IEEE International Workshop on Visual Surveillance and Performance Evaluation of Tracking and Surveillance (VS-PETS)*, Nice, France, October 11–12, 2003, pp. 157–164.
3. W. Zhao, R. Chellappa, P. J. Phillips, and A. Rosenfeld, Face recognition: A literature survey, *ACM Computing Surveys (CSUR)*, 35(4), December 2003, 399–458.
4. I. Haritaoglu, D. Harwood, and L. S. Davis, W4: Real-time surveillance of people and their activities, *IEEE Transactions on Pattern Analysis and Machine Intelligence*, 22(8), August 2000, 809–830.
5. K.W. Bowyer, Face recognition technology: Security versus privacy, *IEEE Society on Social Implications of Technology*, 23(1), (2004), 9–19.
6. Z. Stone, T. Zickler, T. Darrell, Toward large-scale face recognition using social network context, *Proceedings of the IEEE*, 98(8), August 2010, 1408–1415.
7. A.W. Senior, S. Pankanti, A. Hampapur, L. Brown, Y.-L. Tian, and A. Ekin, Blinkering surveillance: Enabling video privacy through computer vision, IBM Technical Report RC22886, 2003.
8. E.N. Newton, L. Sweeney, and B. Malin, Preserving privacy by de-identifying face images, *IEEE Transactions on Knowledge and Data Engineering*, 17(2), February 2005, 232–243.
9. F. Dufaux and T. Ebrahimi, Scrambling for privacy protection in video surveillance systems, *IEEE Transactions on Circuits and Systems for Video Technology*, 18(8), August 2008, 1168–1174.
10. K. Martin and K.N. Plataniotis, Privacy protected surveillance using secure visual object coding, *IEEE Transactions on Circuits and Systems for Video Technology*, 18(8), August 2008, 1152–1162.
11. A. Frome, G. Cheung, A. Abdulkader, M. Zennaro, B. Wu, A. Bissacco, H. Adam, H. Neven, and L. Vincent, Large-scale privacy protection in Google street view, *IEEE International Conference on Computer Vision (ICCV)*, 2009, Kyoto, Japan, pp. 2373–2380.
12. H. Sohn, E.T. Anzaku, W. De Neve, Y.M. Ro, K.N. Plataniotis, privacy protection in video surveillance systems using scalable video coding, *IEEE International Conference on Advanced Video and Signal Based Surveillance (AVSS), 2009*, Genova, Italy, pp. 424–429.
13. T. Winkler and B. Rinner, TrustCAM: Security and privacy-protection for an embedded smart camera based on trusted computing, *IEEE International Conference on Advanced Video and Signal Based Surveillance (AVSS), 2010*, Boston, MA, pp. 593–600.
14. H. Sohn, W. De Neve, and Y.M. Ro, Privacy protection in video surveillance systems: Analysis of sub-band-adaptive scrambling in JPEG XR, *IEEE Transactions on Circuits and Systems for Video Technology*, 21(2), February 2011, 170–177.
15. A. Cavallaro, Privacy in video surveillance, *IEEE Signal Processing Magazine*, 24(2), March 2007, 168–169.
16. A. Senior (ed.), *Protecting Privacy in Video Surveillance*, Springer, London, U.K., 2009.
17. F. Dufaux and T. Ebrahimi, A framework for the validation of privacy protection solutions in video surveillance, *Proceedings of IEEE International Conference on Multimedia & Expo*, 2010, Singapore, pp. 66–71.
18. Y. Mao and M. Wu, A joint signal processing and cryptographic approach to multimedia encryption, *IEEE Transactions on Image Processing*, 15(7), (2006), 2061–2075.
19. L. Tong, F. Dai, Y. Zhang, J. Li, Visual security evaluation for video encryption, *Proceedings of ACM International Conference on Multimedia*, 2010, Florence, Italy, pp. 835–838.

20. W. Zeng and S. Lei, Efficient frequency domain video scrambling for content access control, *Proceedings of ACM International Conference on Multimedia*, 1999, New York, pp. 285–294.
21. P. Carrillo, H. Kalva, and S. Magliveras, Compression independent reversible encryption for privacy in video surveillance, *EURASIP Journal on Information Security*, Vol. 2009, pp. 1–13, 2009.
22. T.E. Boult, PICO: Privacy through invertible cryptographic obscuration, *Proceedings of the Computer Vision for Interactive and Intelligent Environments*, 2005, pp. 27–38.
23. F. Dufaux and T. Ebrahimi, H.264/AVC video scrambling for privacy protection, *Proceedings of IEEE International Conference on Image Processing (ICIP)*, 2008, San Diego, CA, pp. 1688–1691.
24. K. Kuroiwa, M. Fujiyoshi, and H. Kiya, Codestream domain scrambling of moving objects based on DCT sign-only correlation for motion JPEG movies, *Proceedings of International Conference on Image Processing (ICIP)*, 2007, San Antonio, TX, pp. 157–160.
25. J.K. Paruchuri, S.S. Cheung, and M.W. Hail, Video data hiding for managing privacy information in surveillance systems, *EURASIP Journal on Information Security*, Vol. 2009, pp. 1–18, 2009.
26. G. Li, Y. Ito, X. Yu, N. Nitta, and N. Babaguchi, Recoverable privacy protection for video content distribution, *EURASIP Journal on Information Security*, Vol. 2009, pp. 1–18, 2009.
27. J.Y. Choi, Y.M. Ro, and K.N. Plataniotis, Color face recognition for degraded face images, *IEEE Transactions on Systems, Man, and Cybernetics, Part B: Cybernetics*, 39(5), October 2009, 1217–1230.
28. T. Sim, S. Baker, and M. Bsat, The CMU pose, illumination, and expression database, *IEEE Transactions on Pattern Analysis and Machine Intelligence*, 25(12), December 2003, 1615–1618.
29. IVY Lab video surveillance dataset, Available on: http://ivylab.kaist.ac.kr/demo/vs/dataset.htm, accessed on January 13, 2013.
30. M.A. Turk and A.P. Pentland, Eigenfaces for recognition, *Journal of Cognitive Neuroscience*, 3(1), (1991), 71–86.
31. X. Jiang, B. Mandal, and A. Kot, Eigenfeature regularization and extraction in face recognition, *IEEE Transactions on Pattern Analysis and Machine Intelligence*, 30(3), March 2008, 383–394.
32. T. Ahonen, A. Hadid, and M. Pietikainen, Face description with local binary patterns: Application to face recognition, *IEEE Transactions on Pattern Analysis and Machine Intelligence*, 28(12), December 2006, 2037–2041.
33. H. Sohn, D. Lee, W. De Neve, K.N. Plataniotis, and Y.M. Ro, Contribution of non-scrambled chroma information in privacy-protected face images to privacy leakage, *Proceedings of International Workshop on Digital-forensics and Watermarking*, October 2011, Atlantic City, NJ.
34. IVY Lab privacy evaluation tools, Available on: http://ivylab.kaist.ac.kr/demo/FR/sourcecode.htm, accessed on January 13, 2013.
35. P.J. Phillips, H. Wechsler, J. Huang, and P. Rauss, The FERET database and evaluation procedure for face recognition algorithms, *Image and Vision Computing Journal*, 16(5), 1998, 295–306.
36. J. Wang, K.N. Plataniotis, J. Lu, and A.N. Venetsanopoulos, On solving the face recognition problem with one training sample per subject, *Pattern Recognition*, 39(6), September 2006, 1746–1762.
37. A.K. Jain, K. Nandakumar, and A. Ross, Score normalization in multimodal biometric systems, *Pattern Recognition*, 38(12), December 2005, 2270–2285.
38. B. Girod, What's wrong with mean-squared error?, in *Digital Images and Human Vision*, A. B. Watson, Ed., Cambridge, MA: MIT Press, 1993, pp. 207–220.
39. A. Mike Burton, P. Miller, V. Bruce, P.J.B. Hancock, and Z. Henderson, Human and automatic face recognition: A comparison across image formats, *Vision Research*, 41(24), November 2001, 3185–3195.
40. D. Anaki, J. Boyd, and M. Moscovitch, Temporal integration in face perception: Evidence of configural processing of temporally separated face parts, *Journal of Experimental Psychology: Human Perception and Performance*, 33(1), February 2007, 1–19.

PHYSICAL AND CYBER SURVEILLANCE

II

Chapter 7

Event Representation in Multimedia Surveillance Systems

Pradeep K. Atrey

Contents

7.1 Introduction

Multimedia surveillance systems are designed and developed with the primary goal of detecting events occurring in a real-world environment [12]. Such systems consist of various multimedia sensors that are used to capture data. The sensory data are processed and analyzed to infer the events that occurred in the real world.

The events usually occur over a period of time; however, this time period could vary from event to event. There could be some events that occur for only a few seconds, while other events can occur over a longer period of time. For example, a "conference" as a whole could be considered as an event that runs for many days. Within this conference, there could be many technical keynotes. These keynote sessions could also be considered as events that run for a few hours within the conference event. At a finer granularity of time, that the keynote speaker spoke the word "multimedia" during his or her address could also be considered as an event that occurred for only a few seconds. Furthermore, multiple events can occur simultaneously. For example, in this conference event, many technical sessions may occur in parallel in different rooms. This establishes that the event is a complex phenomenon, which a machine may not recognize and cluster as easily as a human does [18].

From the perspective of humans versus machines, the events can be described at two levels: domain level and data level. Domain-level events are the events that are perceived at a high level by humans or the users of the system. Alternatively, data-level events are represented at a low level by the machine. For example, an event of "a person is walking through the subway" is a domain-level event. The equivalent data-level event for this domain-level event could be "a blob has the regular displacement of 20 pixels in the image plane."

Multimedia surveillance systems capture and process the sensory data to detect the occurrences of events at designated points over time. A meaningful domain-level event is constructed from the events detected at these points. For example, assuming that the domain-level event "a person is walking through the subway" lasted for 2 min, the system would continuously capture and process the data and provide its decisions at regular intervals (say 1 s). These decisions are accumulated to make an overall decision about the domain-level event.

There has been a significant amount of research on the automatic detection of various events using features and patterns obtained from low-level data. Also, some event models have been proposed by researchers. However, these event models provide only a generic perspective and do not provide clear guidelines how the models can be realized in a specific application, such as multimedia surveillance. Moreover, existing event models are neither suitable to construct a hierarchy of events at different granularities nor able to cluster the low-level (data-level) events into high-level (domain-level) events, which is an important aspect of any multimedia surveillance system.

Inspired from the aforementioned discussion, in this chapter, we present a framework that represents events from the perspective of different granularities in time and space at which they occur. Since events can be long or short, and a longer event can be comprised of several short events, it is fair to say that they constitute a hierarchy. We identify the following three hierarchical levels to represent events: transient-event level, atomic-event level, and compound-event level. We call the events represented at these three levels as *TE*, *AE*, and *CE*, respectively.

In Ref. [3], the authors have introduced the notion of atomic and *CE*s; however, they did not explicitly examine the issue of time and space granularities. Here we introduce the notion of *TE* and revisit *AE* in the context of the time period they may last for. We define *TE* and *AE* as follows:

Definition 1: *TE is an AE that is detected by the system within a minimum time period.*

Definition 2: *AE is an event in which exactly one object having one or more attributes is involved in exactly one activity over a period of time.*

Note that the definition of *CE* has been adopted from Ref. [3], which states that a *CE* is the composition of two or more different *AE*s. In addition, we introduce the notion of a *null* event (ϕ). The null event denotes that the *TE* that was detected at any given time instant is not found at the next time instant (even though the *TE* has occurred in reality). Such instances may occur due to inaccuracies in data capturing and processing, which is generally referred to as a false negative (*FN*).

In the context of the aforementioned definitions, we revisit the example of a "conference" event. The whole conference can be considered as a *CE*. Its various keynote and technical sessions can also be considered as a *CE*, which means that there could be various levels at which *CE*s may exist. The keynote address could be considered as an *AE*. In the keynote address, the event that the speaker spoke the word "multimedia" could be considered as a *TE*. It is important to note that an *AE* may also consist of various instances when there was no meaningful *TE* due to event detection inaccuracies. These inaccurate detections, which we call ϕ, are also considered the inherent part of the *AE*.

Our contribution in this chapter is a hierarchical framework that

- Represents events at different granularities
- Clusters events of a lower granularity into an event of a higher granularity and maps data-level events to domain-level events
- Determines relationships among events that help in better assessment of a situation in the surveilled environment

The remainder of this chapter is organized as follows. In Section 7.2, we comment on the related works. Section 7.3 presents the proposed event representation framework. Section 7.4 describes the use of the proposed framework in the case of airport surveillance. Section 7.5 presents the experiment to validate the proposed framework. Finally, Section 7.6 concludes the chapter with a discussion on future work.

7.2 Related Works

Recently, event modeling has gained the focus of multimedia researchers. Various researchers have proposed event models; however, most of these models are tailored to specific applications.

In general, there has been an emphasis on adopting event-centric approaches over media-centric approaches [17]. In the following, we discuss the past works on event modeling.

In the field of multimedia, an event model proposed by Vazirgiannis and Sellis [16] was among the earlier works on event modeling. In this work, authors proposed a language to model events and scenarios. Although their proposed model presents an important insight into high-level events and scenario descriptions, it fails to map them to low-level events.

There are many representative event models that have been proposed in the past decade. For instance, the system called "Medither" presented by Boll and Westermann [6] allows various applications to publish, to find, and to be notified about multimedia content in a distributed multimedia event space. Although this system is suitable for event exploration in a distributed environment, it does not elaborate on how low-level events can be clustered together to form a domain-level event. Similar to Ref. [6], a composite event detection framework was introduced by Pietzuch et al. [9]. In this work, the proposed framework was intended to be layered on the existing middleware architectures. This framework is more suited for distributed environments rather than for multimedia surveillance systems where sensor data are captured and processed at different levels. In another work, Appan and Sundaram [1] presented a formal event model; however, their model is tailored to the exploration of photos in a digital photo album and does not apply to multimedia surveillance systems. Similar to the aforementioned works, there have been many other application-specific works. For instance, Pack et al. [8] presented an event model that is suitable for multimedia representation and retrieval; Kim et al. [7] used event-centric approach to build e-chronicle systems; and Zoumboulakis and Roussos [19] presented a complex event detection method that was tuned to wireless sensor networks.

One of the recent works that is most closely related to ours is the event model proposed by Azough et al. [4]. Similar to our proposed work, their model was also designed mainly for monitoring human behavior. However, it does not explicitly exploit the relationship among events, whereas our proposed framework not only represents the events at various levels but also expresses their relationship.

In other domains, Barradas and Bert [5] and Schliecker et al. [14] introduced the formal models for the event-based systems. However, the notion of events described in these works is different from the notion of events in multimedia. While Barradas and Bert [5] presented semantics for event systems, Schliecker et al. [14] described event models for the analysis of heterogeneous multiprocessor systems.

To summarize, most of the works discussed earlier presented application-specific event models, and it is often hard to adopt them in multimedia surveillance scenarios. There are some generic models for event representation, such as the models presented by Westermann and Jain [17] and Scherp et al. [13]. However, these models only lay out the general characteristics that an event-based multimedia system should have but do not provide a practical perspective of how low-level (transient) events detected at a regular interval are clustered into high-level (atomic) events. The proposed framework* explicitly describes the finer details of mapping low-level events to high-level events in a multimedia surveillance application scenario. In contrast to the existing event detection methods that detect events in isolation, the proposed framework advocates establishing their relationships that eventually helps in better assessment of a situation in the surveilled environment.

---

* The earlier version of this work with preliminary results was published in [2].

7.3 Proposed Framework

7.3.1 Overview

As shown in Figure 7.1, the proposed framework represents events at three hierarchical levels: transient, atomic, and compound. This hierarchy is based on the granularities of time and space in which the events occur. For instance, a *TE* can occur for a few seconds, while an *AE* can occur over a period of time. An *AE* may consist of a sequence of both transient and null events, and many *AE*s can be clustered into a *CE*. Furthermore, many *CE*s can simultaneously occur in a surveillance environment. The *AE*s within a *CE* may be related to each other in various ways. In the proposed framework, we explicitly examine such relationships.

We describe the framework as follows. Let $TE_i(t)$ be the *i*th *TE* detected by the system at time instant *t*, e.g., December 25, 2009, 12:23:55 h. A *TE* is represented by a 3-tuple, as given in the following:

$$TE_i(t) = \langle O, A, L \rangle \tag{7.1}$$

where

    O is the object identifier, e.g., a person or a airplane
    A is the activity identifier, e.g., running or taking off
    L is the location identifier, e.g., school corridor or an airport

The null event ϕ is represented by the complement of a *TE*:

$$\phi(t) = \overline{TE(t)} \tag{7.2}$$

where *t* retains its early definition.

An *AE* is denoted as $AE_i(t_s, t_e)$, where t_s and t_e are the start and end times of the event. $AE_i(t_s, t_e)$ is represented by the following 3-tuple:

$$AE_i(t_s, t_e) = \langle O, A, L \rangle \tag{7.3}$$

where *O*, *A*, *L* have the same definitions as aforementioned.

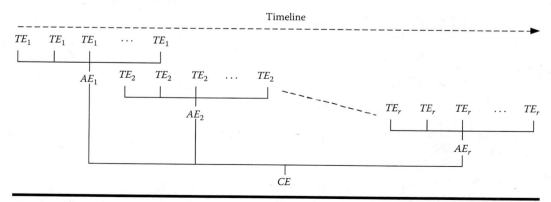

Figure 7.1 Event hierarchy and composition.

Similarly, a *CE*, $CE(t_s, t_e)$ with start- and end-time identifiers, t_s and t_e, respectively, is represented by the following 2-tuple:

$$CE(t_s, t_e) = \langle S_{AE}, R_{AE} \rangle \tag{7.4}$$

where
S_{AE} is the set representing the atomic events in the compound event
R_{SE} is the set representing the relationships among various atomic events in the compound event

In complex distributed surveillance applications that have different sets of sensors placed at different subregions or sites, there could be many *CE*s occurring simultaneously at different sites. Each *CE* usually consists of a set of two or more *AE*s. The *AE*s within the *CE* usually have three types of relationships: causal, temporal, and spatial [17].

In the following subsections, we describe how *TE*s are detected by the system, how they are clustered into *AE*s, and then how the *AE*s are composed to form a *CE*.

7.3.2 Transient-Event Detection

A typical distributed surveillance system consists of $M_1, M_2, \ldots, M_m$ sensors installed at different sites. The sensory data at a particular site are captured and processed, and then decisions about the occurrence of the *TE*s are obtained. In other words, *TE*s are detected at a regular interval by assimilating the information obtained from a set of sensors. Note that, for the detection of a specific *TE*, only a subset of sensors is used. For example, the "gunshot" *TE* may be better detected using audio sensors rather than using video cameras. Such external knowledge is provided to the system when trained.

In order to detect a *TE*, multisensory information is assimilated. Based on the set of sensors $M_1, M_2, \ldots, M_{m'}$, $m' \leq m$, the system outputs local decisions $p_{j,i(t)} = P(TE_i | M_j)$, $1 \leq j \leq m'$, about a *TE*, TE_i, at time instant t. $P(TE_i | M_j)$ represents the probability that the TE_i has occurred at time instant t. This probabilistic decision is obtained based on the jth sensor data by employing a trained classifier. When there are many sensors contributing to the evidence of the occurrence of the TE_i, their individual decisions are combined by using the assimilation method described in Ref. [3]. Further details about this method can be found in Ref. [3].

As discussed earlier, the system detects *TE*s at a regular interval. This is illustrated in Figure 7.2a for an interval of 1 s. Figure 7.2a shows two *TE*s repeatedly occurring over a few time instances, i.e., two persons walking and crossing by each other in the same surveillance environment (a subway). Note that there may be a few *FN* instances between any two *TE*s, which are denoted by ϕ in Figure 7.2a. The *TE*s are clustered together to form *AE*s, which are described in the following subsection.

7.3.3 Clustering of Transient Events into Atomic Event

As illustrated in Figure 7.2a, *TE*s may repeatedly occur over several time instances to form an *AE*. In between these events, we can also notice a few null events. For example, in the case of walking event detection, there may be a few instances when the classifier presents a decision that the person is not walking. This may happen due to many reasons, including noisy data, imperfect training, and inaccuracy of the classifiers. Therefore, an *AE* can be considered as a sequence of transient and null events.

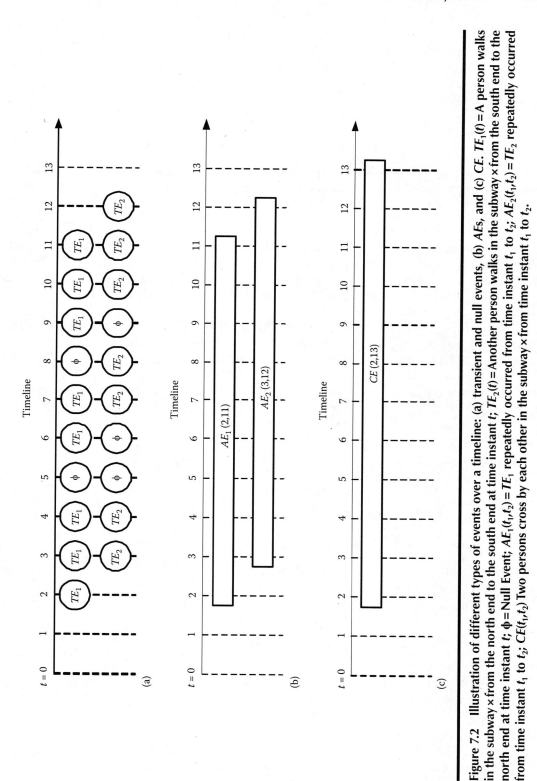

Figure 7.2 Illustration of different types of events over a timeline: (a) transient and null events, (b) AEs, and (c) CE. $TE_1(t)$ = A person walks in the subway x from the north end to the south end at time instant t; $TE_2(t)$ = Another person walks in the subway x from the south end to the north end at time instant t; ϕ = Null Event; $AE_1(t_1,t_2) = TE_1$ repeatedly occurred from time instant t_1 to t_2; $AE_2(t_1,t_2) = TE_2$ repeatedly occurred from time instant t_1 to t_2; $CE(t_1,t_2)$ Two persons cross by each other in the subway x from time instant t_1 to t_2.

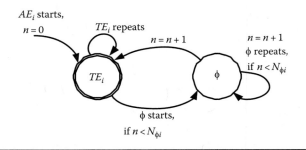

Figure 7.3 **State diagram representation of an *AE*. $N_{\phi i}$ is the number of allowable null events in a sequence for *AE_i*.**

We represent an *AE* by using a finite state model, as shown in Figure 7.3. This figure shows the relation between the *TE* and ϕ in an *AE*, AE_i. Any *AE* may consist of two states: *TE* state and null event state. The *AE* starts with the occurrence of a *TE*, which can be followed by a transient or null event. After a *TE*, a maximum of $N_{\phi i}$ number of null events can occur. Finally, the *AE* ends with a *TE*.

It is important to note that different *AEs* can have different allowable numbers of null events in a sequence. The maximum number of null events in a sequence $N_{\phi i}$ in an *AE* is part of the domain knowledge, which is input to the classifier at the time of training. Figure 7.2b shows two *AEs* denoted by $AE_1(2,11)$ and $AE_2(3,12)$. These *AEs* consist of a varying number of null events. As shown in 2a, AE_1 and AE_2 could have at most one and two consecutive ϕs, respectively.

The following algorithm (*DetermineAtomicEvent*) is used to cluster the transient and null events into an *AE*.

Algorithm 7.1: DetermineAtomicEvent

Input: A sequence of *TEs* and ϕs

Steps:

   1. $n = 0$
   2. *firstEvent* = first event from the input sequence
   3. $t_s = t_e = t(firstEvent)$
   4. while ($n \leq N_{\phi i}$) {
   5.   *nextEvent* = next event from the input sequence
   6.   if *nextEvent* = ϕ
   7. $n = n + 1$
   8. $t_e = t_e + 1$
   9. }
  10. $AE_i = TE_i$

Output: $AE_i(t_s, t_e)$

7.3.4 *Compound-Event Composition*

A *CE* is characterized by a set of *AE*s (S_{AE}), a set (R_{AE}) of the different relationships among the *AE*s in S_{AE}, and the start and end times, t_s and t_e, respectively, of the *CE*. In the following subsections, we describe how we determine these attributes of a *CE*.

There can be two or more *AE*s in a *CE*. The set of *AE*s belonging to a *CE* are determined using the following algorithm:

Algorithm 7.2: DetermineAtomicEventSet

Input: Start and end times t_s and t_e

Steps:

1. $S_{AE} = \{$All AE_i s: $t_s(AE_i) < t_s\}$
2. $t_s(CE) = Min_{\forall i} (t_s(AE_i))$
3. $S_{AE} = S_{AE} + \{$All AE_i s: $t_e(AE_i) > t_e\}$
4. $t_e(CE) = Max_{\forall i} (t_e(AE_i))$
5. $S_{AE} = S_{AE} + \{$All AE_i s: $t_s(AE_i) \geq t_s$ && $t_e(AE_i) \leq t_e\}$

Output: *AE* set S_{AE}

In the aforementioned algorithm, *AE*s are added to the set S_{AE} using a simple composition operator "+" [11] (in steps 3 and 5).

The *AE*s within a *CE* may be related to each other in various ways. The events may occur simultaneously or sequentially. In fact, an event can cause another event. Furthermore, the events occurring at two different places occurring sequentially or simultaneously may also be related to each other. Based on this, we propose the following three types of relationships among the *AE*s: temporal, causal, and spatial [17]. They are described as follows.

7.3.4.1 *Temporal Relationship*

The temporal relationship among *AE*s is based on the time they occur. Any two *AE*s can occur in parallel or in a sequence. Two parallel events could be fully parallel or partially parallel. Hence, we define three types of temporal relationships between any AE_i and AE_j: fully parallel, partially parallel, and sequential.

These three relationships are illustrated in Table 7.1. The table shows their time constraints. Two *AE*s are considered to be fully parallel if they completely overlap each other; however, one of them could be of longer duration than the other. If the two *AE*s occur in such a way that their durations of occurrences partially overlap each other, they are known to have partially parallel temporal relationship. In a sequential temporal relationship, the second *AE* occurs only when the first one has ended. However, the duration between the end of the first event ($t_e(AE_i)$) and the start of the next event ($t_s(AE_j)$) should be within a threshold δ_t. The threshold δ_t can be adjusted according to application requirements. For instance, two events occurring with a gap of 1 month may not be very interesting compared to the events that occur over an interval of a few minutes.

Table 7.1 Different Types of Relationships between *AE*s and Their Constraints

Relationship Type	Description	Constraints	Relationship Triplet
	AE_i is *fully parallel* with AE_j	$(t_s(AE_i) \geq t_s(AE_j))$ &&	
		$t_e(AE_i) \leq t_e(AE_j))\|$	(2,-,-)
		$(t_s(AE_j) \geq t_s(AE_i))$ &&	
		$t_e(AE_j) \leq t_e(AE_i))$	
Temporal	AE_i is *partially parallel* with AE_j	$(t_s(AE_i) > t_s(AE_j))$ &&	
		$t_e(AE_i) > t_e(AE_j))\|$	(1,-,-)
		$(t_s(AE_i) < t_s(AE_j))$ &&	
		$t_e(AE_i) < t_e(AE_j))$	
	Sequential—AE_i is followed by AE_j	$t_e(AE_i) - t_s(AE_j) \leq \delta_t$	(0,-,-)
Causal	AE_i causes AE_j	$P(AE_j|AE_i) > 0.5$	(-,1,-)
	AE_i and AE_j are independent	None	(-,0,-)
	AE_i and AE_j occurred in the same surveillance region	$L(AE_i) = L(AE_j)$	(-,-,1)
	AE_i and AE_j occurred in	$L(AE_i) \neq L(AE_j)$ &&	
Spatial	*different surveillance regions*	$O(AE_i) = O(AE_j)$ &&	(-,-,2)
	with the **same person**	$t_e(AE_i) > t_s(AE_j)$	
	AE_i and AE_j occurred in		
	different surveillance regions	$L(AE_i) \neq L(AE_j)$ &&	
	with *different persons*; hence, AE_i and AE_j are independent	$O(AE_i) \neq O(AE_j)$	(-,-,0)

Note: && and ‖ are logical AND and OR operators, $L(AE_i)$ denotes the location of AE_i, and $O(AE_i)$ represents the object associated with AE_i.

7.3.4.2 Causal Relationship

When the occurrence of one *AE* causes the occurrence of another *AE*, they are known to have a causal relationship between them. For example, an event AE_i "a gunshot at the public place" can cause AE_j "people are running." Alternatively, the occurrence of any two *AE*s may be unrelated or independent. For example, an event AE_i "one person walking in the subway" may not have any causal relationship with another event AE_j "another person walking in the subway." Nevertheless, these two events may also have other types of relationship, e.g., temporal or spatial.

The causal relationship and its temporal constraints are illustrated in Table 7.1. In a surveillance scenario, causality effect is usually quick, which means that the caused event takes place within a short time after the causing event has occurred. This short time is represented by a threshold δ_c in Table 7.1. If the difference of the start times of two events is greater than the threshold δ_c, they are considered independent from each other.

The important question is whether or not two *AE*s that have occurred one after the other really have a causal relationship or it is just a coincidence. We learn the causal relationship between two *AE*s based on the past history of their co-occurrences within a threshold δ_c time period. Precisely, let $P(AE_j|AE_i)$ be the probability that AE_i causes AE_j. This probability value is computed as

$$P(AE_j \mid AE_i) = \frac{N_{AE_j, AE_i}}{N_{AE_i}} \tag{7.5}$$

where N_{AE_j, AE_i} is the number of times AE_j event occurred within δ_c time of AE_i event, i.e., $t_s(AE_j) - t_s(AE_i) \le \delta_c$, and N_{AE_i} is the total number of times N_{AE_i} event has occurred.

7.3.4.3 Spatial Relationship

Spatial relationship is determined based on whether the *AE*s occurred at the same location or at different locations. Table 7.1 shows different types of spatial relationships. The events involving different persons (or objects) and occurring at the same location are automatically considered spatially related to each other. Furthermore, they may also have other types of relationships. For example, people may be walking in a subway. These walking events would have spatial relationship because they took place in the same subway. There would also be a temporal relationship as these events occurred either in parallel or in sequence.

Two *AE*s that occurred at different locations would be considered spatially related if the same person (or object) is involved in both the events. In this case, it is obvious that these two *AE*s would occur at two different times, i.e., the start of the second event ($t_s(AE_j)$) would be after the end time of the first event ($t_e(AE_i)$). For example, a person who walks through the corridor turns into adjacent corridor. Another example could be the events in which the same person is found at two different spatial locations.

Each entry in the relationship set R_{AE} consists of three values (we call this as *relationship triplet*) corresponding to three types of relationships—temporal, causal, and spatial, respectively. For each relationship, this value is shown in the last column of Table 7.1.

The R_{AE} is precisely determined using the following algorithmic steps:

Algorithm 7.3: DetermineRelationshipSet

Input: AEs AE_1, AE_2, ..., AE_r

Steps:

1. For $i = 1$ to r
2.   For $j = 1$ to r
3.   If $(t_s(AE_i) \geq t_s(AE_j)$ && $t_e(AE_i) \leq t_e(AE_j))$
4. $R_{AE}[i][j][0] = 2$
5.   Else If $(t_s(AE_i) > t_s(AE_j)$ && $t_e(AE_i) > t_e(AE_j))$
6. $R_{AE}[i][j][0] = 1$
7.   Else If $t_s(AE_j) - t_e(AE_i) \leq \delta_t$
8. $R_{AE}[i][j][0] = 0$
9.   If $P(AE_j | AE_i) > 0.5$
10. $R_{AE}[i][j][1] = 1$
11.   Else $R_{AE}[i][j][1] = 0$
12.   If $L(AE_i) = L(AE_j)$
13. $R_{AE}[i][j][2] = 1$
14.   Else If $L(AE_i) \neq L(AE_j)$
15.   If $O(AE_i) = O(AE_j)$ && $t_e(AE_i) > t_s(AE_j)$
16. $R_{AE}[i][j][2] = 2$
17.   Else if $O(AE_i) \neq O(AE_j)$
18. $R_{AE}[i][j][2] = 0$

Output: Relationship matrix R_{AE}

In event search and retrieval systems, relationships between events can be used to find events in a linked manner. Since various *AE*s in a *CE* are usually linked with each other, searching for a *CE* allows us to explore all the *AE*s associated with it. For example, for tracking a person across different locations, we may utilize spatial and temporal relationships between the corresponding *AE*s. Also, causal relationship can be used to anticipate the occurrence of an (caused) event after another (causing) event, and a precautionary action can be performed to ensure safety.

7.3.5 High-Level Situation Assessment

The proposed multilevel event representation can be used to make high-level assessment of a situation in the surveilled environment. For example, a "gunshot" *AE* followed by a "running" *AE* may imply a "terrorist attack." To make such high-level inferences, we categorize situations into two broad classes: normal and abnormal. We assume that in a normal situation, all events would be normal, e.g., in the case of walking, talking, and standing events. The abnormal situation can be further classified into two levels: *low-alert* situation and *high-alert* situation. In a low-alert situation, we assume to have at least one suspicious event such as a running event. However, if a suspicious event (e.g., gunshot event) *causes* another suspicious event (e.g., running event), the low-alert situation may turn into a high-alert situation.

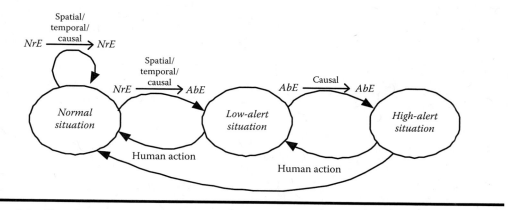

Figure 7.4 **Situation assessment.** *NrE, Normal event; AbE, Abnormal event.*

The situation model is illustrated using a state-transition diagram in Figure 7.4. It consists of three states: normal situation, low-alert situation, and high-alert situation. Initially, the situation in the surveilled environment is considered to be normal. A normal event (denoted by *NrE*) followed by another normal event having either of three relationships (spatial, temporal, and causal) with each other does not change the state. However, if a normal event is followed by an abnormal event (denoted by *AbE*) either due to the cause (i.e., causal relationship) or otherwise (i.e., spatial or temporal to relationship), situation changes from normal to low-alert situation. Furthermore, if in a low-alert situation an abnormal event causes another abnormal event, the situation is considered hazardous and is elevated to high alert. Once the surveillance system is in an abnormal situation (i.e., in low- or high-alert situation), human action is required to bring it back to normal state.

Note that this is one criteria, among many other, to design the situation in a surveillance system. It can vary depending on the requirement and application.

7.4 Use Case: Airport Surveillance Scenario

We demonstrate the use of the proposed event representation framework in a surveillance scenario at the airport. Airports are usually equipped with CCTV cameras and other sensors for observing people activities and behavior. We consider the hypothetical layout of a small airport as shown in Figure 7.5. In this scenario, there are some events that normally happen, e.g., departure of a flight. However, there could also be some unexpected or abnormal events such as a fire or a shoot-out. In the following two sections, we describe the use of the proposed framework for observing normal as well as abnormal events.

7.4.1 Case 1: Normal Events

For normal events, we assume that the following events occur.

7.4.1.1 Compound Events

At any airport, a flight departure is a common event. We can consider the event of "departure of a XYZ airlines flight" as a *CE*. Whenever a flight departure is scheduled, there are various events

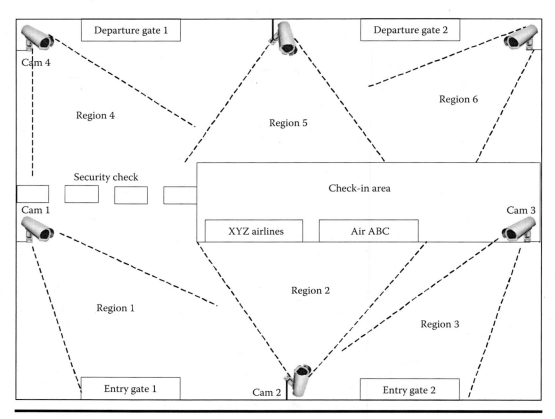

Figure 7.5 Hypothetical layout of an airport unit.

that take place, e.g., check-in baggage and boarding pass collection, security check, and flight boarding. These events are also considered to be *CE*s. It is important to note that *CE*s can exist in a hierarchical fashion. In the following, we examine these *CE*s in terms of the *AE*s (Figure 7.6).

7.4.1.2 Atomic Events

The *CE*s would consist of many *AE*s that may occur in the same or different regions on the airport premises. The regions are shown in Figure 7.5.

In the *CE* "check-in baggage and boarding pass collection," there would usually be the following sequence of *AE*s: AE_1 = "people entering through entry gate 1 or gate 2" (in region 1 or region 3), AE_2 = "people going to the check-in counter" (in region 2), AE_3 = "people staying at the check-in counter for some time for baggage check-in and obtaining the boarding pass" (in region 2), and AE_4 = "people leaving the check-in counter and moving toward the security check area" (in region 2 and region 4).

The *CE* "security check" consists of the following *AE*s: AE_5 = "people queued up at the security desks" (in region 4), AE_6 = "people are being checked by security" (in region 4), and AE_7 = "people leaving the security check area" (in region 4).

The last *CE* in this scenario is "flight boarding" that may consist of the following *AE*s: AE_8 = "people are in the waiting area" (in region 4, region 5, or region 6), AE_9 = "people are queued

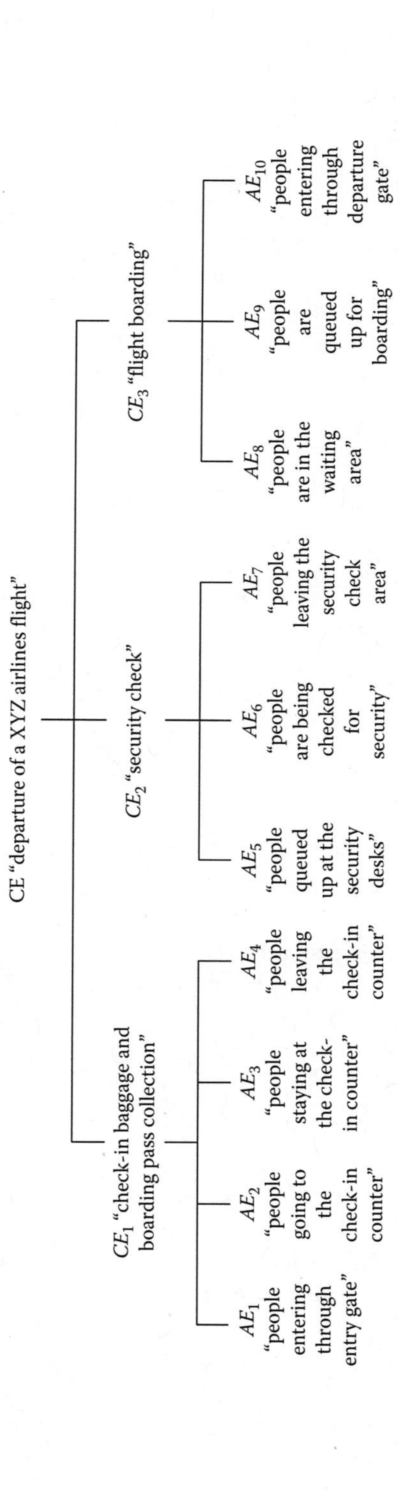

CE "departure of a XYZ airlines flight"

CE_1 "check-in baggage and boarding pass collection"

CE_2 "security check"

CE_3 "flight boarding"

AE_1 "people entering through entry gate"

AE_2 "people going to the check-in counter"

AE_3 "people staying at the check-in counter"

AE_4 "people leaving the check-in counter"

AE_5 "people queued up at the security desks"

AE_6 "people are being checked for security"

AE_7 "people leaving the security check area"

AE_8 "people are in the waiting area"

AE_9 "people are queued up for boarding"

AE_{10} "people entering through departure gate"

Figure 7.6 Hierarchy of events in airport surveillance scenario.

up for boarding" (in region 4 or region 6), and AE_{10} = "people entering through departure gate 1 or gate 2" (in region 4 or region 6).

7.4.1.3 Transient Events

Each of the *AE*s described earlier is comprised of a sequence of many *TE*s. For instance, AE_1 = "people entering through entry gate 1 or gate 2" would comprise of walking *TE*s, TE_1s through the entry gate. As shown in Figure 7.5, TE_1s should be detected from videos captured through "Cam 1" and "Cam 3" as they are covering region 1 and region 3, respectively. Similarly, for AE_2 = "people going to the check-in counter" (in region 2), video captured through "Cam 2" would be processed to detect the walking *TE*s, TE_2s. Similarly, other *TE*s can be described. We omit further discussion for brevity.

7.4.1.4 Relationships

The relationships among different *AE*s in CE_1, CE_2, and CE_3 are shown in Table 7.2 through 7.4, respectively.

Table 7.2 Relationships among *AE*s in CE_1 in the Airport Surveillance Scenario

Atomic Event	AE_1	AE_2	AE_3	AE_4
AE_1	—	(0,0,2)	(0,0,2)	(0,0,1)
AE_2		—	(0,1,1)	(0,0,1)
AE_3			—	(0,0,1)
AE_4				—

Table 7.3 Relationships among *AE*s in CE_2 in the Airport Surveillance Scenario

Atomic Event	AE_5	AE_6	AE_7
AE_5	—	(0,1,1)	(0,0,1)
AE_6		—	(0,0,1)
AE_7			—

Table 7.4 Relationships among *AE*s in CE_3 in the Airport Surveillance Scenario

Atomic Event	AE_8	AE_9	AE_{10}
AE_8	—	(0,0,1) or (0,0,2)	(0,0,1)
AE_9		—	(0,1,1)
AE_{10}			—

7.4.2 Case 2: Abnormal Events

In this case, our framework works as follows.

7.4.2.1 Compound Event

We assume that the "shoot-out" CE occurs at the airport.

7.4.2.2 Atomic Events

Let us assume that the CE called "gunshot" consists of three AEs, AE_{11}, AE_{12}, and AE_{13}, where AE_{11} = "there is a sound of gunshot," AE_{12} = "people started running," and AE_{13} = "security alarm is turned on."

In this case, AE_{11} causes AE_{12} and AE_{13}, which occur in parallel.

7.4.2.3 Transient Events

The AE_{11} may occur only for a few seconds; hence, it may consist of only a few of the TEs of the gunshot sound. For AE_{12} and AE_{13}, there could be many TEs as these two events may occur for a longer time.

7.4.2.4 Relationships

Table 7.5 shows the relationship that would exist among the AEs in "shoot-out" CE.

7.5 Experimental Validation

We validate the proposed framework by performing experiments in a multimedia surveillance environment. The objective of the experiments was to show the appropriateness of the proposed framework for detecting and representing events at different levels and how it improves the overall accuracy of event detection. We show how the TEs are detected using low-level data processing, how they are clustered into AEs, and how the AEs are then composed to form CEs.

7.5.1 Surveillance Environment and Data Collection

We collected the data using two Canon VC-C50i cameras and one USB microphone in an L-shaped corridor. As shown in Figure 7.7, the two video cameras (Cam 1 and Cam 2) and one

Table 7.5 Relationships among *AEs* in "Shoot-Out" *CE* in the Airport Surveillance Scenario

Atomic Event	AE_{11}	AE_{12}	AE_{13}
AE_{11}	—	(0,1,1)	(0,1,1) or (0,1,2)
AE_{12}		—	(1,0,1) or (1,0,2)
AE_{13}			—

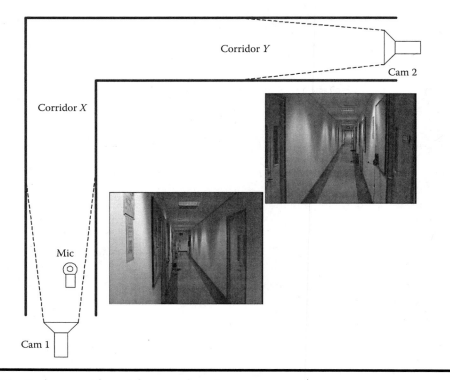

Figure 7.7 Environment layout for experiments.

microphone (Mic) were installed in the two adjacent corridors. The cameras and microphone were connected to a central PC (Pentium-IV 3.6 GHz).

In this setup, video and audio data were recorded for 6 h. The data set included normal as well as abnormal *CE*s. Normal *CE*s included "walking" (people's walking) and "conversation" (people's walking, standing, and talking). The "shoot-out" (gunshot sound and subsequent running of the people) and "abandoned baggage" (people's walking, leaving a baggage, and then walking) were abnormal *CE*s. The recorded data were later processed to detect these normal and abnormal events. Event detection and composition processes are described in the following sections. The values of the different parameters used in experiments are shown in Table 7.6.

Table 7.6 Values of Different Parameters Used

Parameter	Value
$N_{\phi i}$	2 (for walking), 5 (for talking), 1 (for running) 1 (for abandoned baggage), 0 (for gunshot sound)
δ_t	120 s
δ_c	2 s

7.5.2 Transient Event Detection

The audio and video data were processed to detect *TE*s at a regular interval of 1 s. The *TE*s of people walking, standing, running, and abandoned baggage were detected every second by processing the video data. The gunshot sound was detected using audio data.

For each camera, first, the video data were processed to model the background using an adaptive Gaussian method [15], and then the recorded video was processed to detect blobs. Blob detection was performed by first segmenting the foreground from the background by finding the difference between them on the three RGB color channels and then using the morphological operations (erode and dilation) to obtain connected components (i.e., blobs). The difference between background and foreground was determined based on a pixel value being within 2.5 standard deviations of the distribution. The blob of an area greater than a threshold was assumed to correspond to a human, and a bounding rectangle of the blob was computed. Based on the speed of the movement of blobs, a classifier was trained to categorize between the human's walking, standing/sitting, and running events. It was obvious that blobs were displaced in the image plane more in the case of a running event compared to that of a walking event. In the case of a standing event, the displacement of blobs was almost negligible. The time period of 1 s was adopted from Ref. [3].

To detect gunshot sounds, the system processed the recorded audio (of 44.1 kHz frequency). The audio data were processed every second to obtain a decision about the presence of a gunshot sound. Similar to Ref. [10], we used energy entropy and the zero-crossing rate features and used a trained classifier to distinguish between the normal situation and gunshot sound. We used audio data to detect the talking *TE*s. For this, we adopted a hierarchical (top-down) approach as described in Ref. [3].

7.5.3 Determining Atomic and Compound Events

Once all the *TE*s were detected, Algorithm 7.1 (as described in Section 7.3.3) was used to cluster them into *AE*s. The *AE*s detected by the system are detailed in Table 7.7.

From the overall data set, the system detected various meaningful normal and abnormal events at different levels. The detailed statistics of transient and *AE*s is provided in Table 7.8, while the *CE*s detected by the system are shown in Table 7.9.

The first row in Table 7.8 shows the actual number of different *AE*s *occurred* in the surveilled environment. The second row shows the total number of different *TE*s *detected* by the system. There were a total of 48 walking *AE*s detected (two less than what actually occurred) that were clustered using 1728 *TE*s. Similarly, 102 instances of standing events were clustered into two standing *AE*s. There were three instances of running detected (two more than what actually occurred) and one instance of gunshot *AE* detected that was due to the "shoot-out" event. The three running *AE*s were comprised of 25 *TE*s, whereas the gunshot event occurred for only 1 s. Note that of the two running *AE*s were false positives (*FP*s). Also, one instance of an abandoned baggage *AE* caused 123 instances of its corresponding *TE*. This was simply because the item was abandoned in the corridor for 123 s. There were a few instances of null events (φ) that occurred between the *TE*s as reported in the fourth row. We also recorded *FP*s and *FN*s at *TE* level (third row). It was observed that most of the *FN* instances (166) were for the walking event. However, most of these instances were corrected in the proposed framework by considering them as null events. Also, the running event had the most *FP* instances (12), which was due to inaccurate classification of a few of the walking events into running events. The other advantage of using the φ was observed as follows. Without considering φ, we obtained the *AE* more than what they actually occurred.

Table 7.7   *AE*s Detected by the System

Atomic Event	Description
AE_1	A person walking in corridor X
AE_2	A person walking in corridor Y
AE_3	A person standing in corridor X
AE_4	A person standing in corridor Y
AE_5	A person running in corridor X
AE_6	A person running in corridor Y
AE_7	There is a talking in corridor
AE_8	A baggage is abandoned in corridor X
AE_9	A baggage is abandoned in corridor Y
AE_{10}	There is a sound of gunshot

Table 7.8   Number of Transient, Atomic, and Null Events That Occurred and Are Detected by the System

Events	Walking	Standing	Running	Gunshot	Talking	Abandoned Baggage	Total
Actual number of *AE* occurred	50	2	1	1	2	1	57
TE detected	1728	102	25	1	23	123	1991
FP—FN at *TE* level	18–166	10–0	12–3	0–0	8–10	9–0	49–179
ϕ detected	152	0	2	0	8	0	162
AE detected with ϕ	48	2	3	1	2	1	57
AE detected without ϕ	71	2	4	1	4	1	81

Table 7.9   Details of *CE*s Detected by the System

CE	Walking	Conversation	Shoot-Out	Abandoned Baggage	Total
S_{AE}	AE_1, AE_2	AE_1, AE_3, AE_7	AE_1, AE_{10}, AE_5	AE_1, AE_5, AE_9	—
Number of *CE*	24	2	1	1	28

Table 7.10 Relationships Statistics

Relationship Triplet	Walking	Standing	Running	Gunshot	Talking	Abandoned Baggage	Total
(2,-,-)	0	2	0	0	0	0	2
(1,-,-)	4	0	0	0	2	1	7
(0,-,-)	44	0	1	1	0	0	46
(-,1,-)	0	0	1	0	0	0	1
(-,0,-)	48	2	0	1	2	1	54
(-,-,2)	0	2	1	1	2	1	7
(-,-,1)	48	0	0	0	0	0	48
(-,-,0)	0	0	0	0	0	0	0

For instance, while the actual number of walking events was 50, there were 71 detected (i.e., without considering ϕ). It was because of *FN* instances that decomposed single *AE* into more than one. Since these *FN* instances were corrected by taking null events into account, we could achieve better accuracy in terms of the number of *AE*s detected (48 with ϕ compared to 71 without ϕ).

Once all the *AE*s were detected, they were composed into *CE*s. Specifically, Algorithm 7.2 was used to determine the set of *AE*s, and the relationships between the *AE*s were found using Algorithm 7.3. Table 7.9 shows which *AE*s constitute a particular *CE* and how many *CE*s were detected by the system in all.

Different types of relationships that were determined are shown in Table 7.10. Out of 48 walking *AE*s, only four were found partially parallel (triplet (1,-,-)). This was because at four instances, two persons walked in the corridor in a temporally partially overlapping fashion. At the remaining 44 instances, the walking events were sequential, and there was no temporal overlap (triplet (0,-,-)). It can also be seen in the table that there were two instances of the standing *AE*s. At both of these instances, they were fully parallel (triplet (2,-,-)). This was because two persons stood and talked in the corridor. Furthermore, all the 48 instances of the walking *AE*s were independent (triplet (-,0,-)). This means that these events were not caused by other events.

There was only one *AE* (running) that had a causal relationship (triplet (-,1,-)) with the other event (gunshot) since the gunshot *AE* caused the running *AE*. Note that for determining the causal relationship among different events, we computed the probability $P(AE_j|AE_i)$ for all (AE_j, AE_i) pairs of events as shown in Figure 7.8. As can be seen in the figure, $P(AE_{running}|AE_{gunshot})$ was found to be very high (close to 1), while the others were quite low, which suggests that a gunshot event always caused a running event. The other pairs of events for which the probability values were significantly greater than 0 but less than 0.5 were "running causing running," "abandoned baggage causing running," and "abandoned baggage causing walking." These probability values were below the threshold (0.5) to consider any causal relationship between the corresponding events.

As far as the spatial relationship (relationship triplet (-,-,1)) is concerned, all the 55 *AE*s were found to have this relationship. At 48 instances, people walked through both of the adjacent corridors (*X* and *Y*), which caused the spatial relationship at the different locations (triplet (-,-,1)). However, seven *AE*s including standing, running, gunshot, talking, and abandoned baggage occurred in the same corridor, which resulted in a spatial relationship at the same location

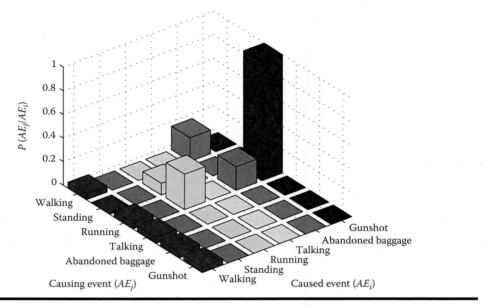

Figure 7.8 Probability values for determining the causal relationship.

(triplet (-,-,2)). Note that, in our data set, there were no spatially independent events; therefore, the last column of the table shows all zero values.

7.5.4 Illustrative Examples

Now we show two examples of "shoot-out" and "abandoned baggage" *CE*s. They are as follows.

7.5.4.1 Compound Event: Shoot-Out

Figure 7.9 shows a timeline representation of the "shoot-out" *CE*. The occurrence of different *AE*s and their corresponding *TE*s is denoted over a timeline. As shown in the figure, TE_1 (a person is walking in corridor X) was repeatedly detected from the 1st to 24th second. At the 24th second, TE_5 (gunshot sound) was detected, which lasted for only a second. After that event, the system detected a sequence of TE_{10}s (a person is running in corridor X), which occurred from the 25th to 32nd second. As shown in the figure, the pairs AE_1 and AE_5, and AE_1 and AE_{10} have temporal relationships, whereas the occurrence of AE_5 is caused by the occurrence of AE_{10}. These *AE*s (AE_1, AE_5, and AE_{10}) also have a spatial relationship, which is not shown in the figure.

7.5.4.2 Compound Event: Abandoned Baggage

For the "abandoned baggage" *CE*, the occurrence of different events at varying granularities over a timeline is shown in Figure 7.10. First, the TE_1 (a person is walking in corridor X) was repeatedly detected from beginning to the 15th second over the timeline. From the 16th to 19th second, TE_5 (a person is running in corridor X) was detected. After that, TE_8 (there is an abandoned baggage in corridor X) was detected, which lasted for 123 s. In this example, the temporal and spatial relationships that exist between *AE*s are shown in Figure 7.10.

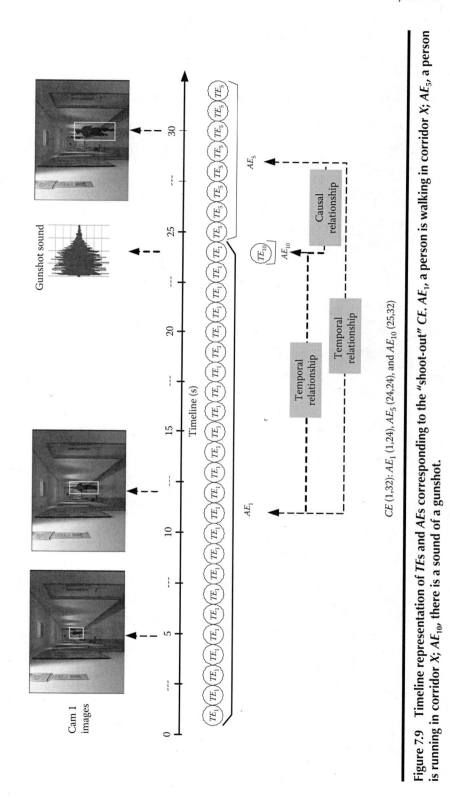

Figure 7.9 Timeline representation of *TEs* and *AEs* corresponding to the "shoot-out" *CE. AE₁,* a person is running in corridor *X; AE₁₀,* there is a sound of a gunshot.

CE (1,32); AE₁ (1,24), AE₅ (24,24), and AE₁₀ (25,32).

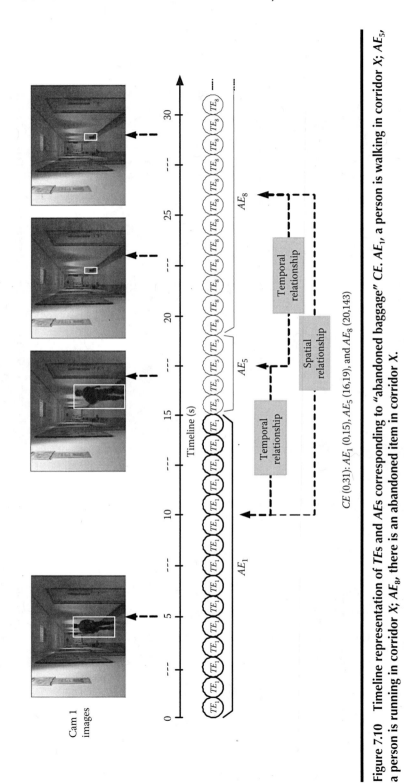

Figure 7.10 Timeline representation of *TEs* and *AEs* corresponding to "abandoned baggage" *CE*. *AE₁*, a person is walking in corridor *X*; *AE₅*, a person is running in corridor *X*; *AE₈*, there is an abandoned item in corridor *X*.

7.6 Conclusions

The framework presented in this chapter advocates for the representation of events at three hierarchical levels: transient, atomic, and compound. The proposed framework allows a mapping between low-level (data-level) events and high-level (domain-level) events. This is achieved by first clustering of *TE*s into *AE*s and then composing the *AE*s into a *CE*. Different types of relationships (temporal, causal, and spatial) between the *AE*s are explicitly determined. The use case and experiments in multimedia surveillance scenarios demonstrate the utility of the proposed framework. Future work would be to examine the suitability of the framework in other scenarios, such as e-chronicle systems.

Acknowledgment

This work was supported by the Natural Sciences and Engineering Research Council of Canada.

References

1. Appan, P., Sundaram, H. Networked multimedia event exploration. In: *Proceedings of the ACM International Conference on Multimedia*, pp. 40–47. New York City, NY, 2004.
2. Atrey, P.K. A hierarchical model for representation of events in multimedia observation systems. In: *Proceedings of the ACM International Workshop on Events in Multimedia*, pp. 57–64. Beijing, China, 2009.
3. Atrey, P.K., Kankanhalli, M.S., Jain, R. Information assimilation framework for event detection in multimedia surveillance systems. *Springer/ACM Journal of Multimedia Systems* 12(3), 2006, 239–253.
4. Azough, A., Delteil, A., Marchi, F.D., Hacid, M.S. Intuitive event modeling for personalized behavior monitoring. In: *Proceedings of the IEEE International Conference on Pattern Recognition*, pp. 1–4. Tampa, FL, 2008.
5. Barradas, H.R., Bert, D. A fixpoint semantics of event systems with and without fairness assumptions. In: *LNCS Proceedings of the International Conference on Integrated Formal Methods*, Vol. 3771, pp. 327–346. Eindhoven, the Netherlands, 2005.
6. Boll, S., Westermann, U. Medither—An event space for context-aware multimedia experiences. In: *Proceedings of the ACM Workshop Experiential Telepresence*, pp. 21–30. Berkeley, CA, 2003.
7. Kim, P., Gargi, U., Jain, R. Event-based multimedia chronicling systems. In: *Proceedings of the ACM Workshop Continuous Archival and Retrieval of Personal Experiences*, Vol. 3, pp. 1–12. Singapore, 2005.
8. Pack, D., Singh, R., Brennan, S., Jain, R. An event model and its implementation for multimedia representation and retrieval. In: *Proceedings of the IEEE International Conference on Multimedia and Expo*, Vol. 3, pp. 1611–1614. Taipei, Taiwan, 2004.
9. Pietzuch, P.R., Shand, B., Bacon, J. A framework for event composition in distributed systems. In: *Proceedings of the International Middleware Conference*, pp. 62–82. Rio de Janeiro, Brazil, 2003.
10. Pikrakis, A., Giannakopoulos, T., Theodoridis, S. Gunshot detection in audio streams from movies by means of dynamic programming and bayesian networks. In: *Proceedings of IEEE International Conference on Acoustics, Speech and Signal Processing*, pp. 21–24. Las Vegas, NV, 2008.
11. Rafatirad, S., Gupta, A., Jain, R. Event composition operators: Eco. In: *Proceedings of the First ACM International Workshop on Events in Multimedia*, pp. 65–72. Beijing, China, 2009.
12. Saini, M., Singh, V.K., Jain, R., Kankanhalli, M.S. Multimodal observation systems. In: *Proceedings of the ACM International Conference on Multimedia*, pp. 933–936. Vancouver, BC, Canada, 2008.
13. Scherp, A., Franz, T., Saathoff, C., Staab, S. A model of events based on a foundational ontology. Technical Report Number 1864–0850, Universität Koblenz-Landau, Germany, 2009.

14. Schliecker, S., Rox, J., Ivers, M., Ernst, R. Providing accurate event models for the analysis of heterogeneous multiprocessor systems. In: *Proceedings of the Sixth IEEE/ACM/IFIP International Conference on Hardware/Software Codesign and System Synthesis*, pp. 185–190. Atlanta, GA, 2008.

15. Stauffer, C., Grimson, W.E.L. Adaptive background mixture models for real-time tracking. In: *IEEE Computer Society Conference on Computer Vision and Pattern Recognition*, Vol. 2, pp. 252–258. Ft. Collins, CO, 1999.

16. Vazirgiannis, M., Sellis, T.K. Event and action representation and composition for multimedia application scenario modelling. In: *LNCS Proceedings of the European Workshop on Interactive Distributed Multimedia Systems and Services*, Vol. 1045, pp. 71–89. London, U.K., 1996.

17. Westermann, U., Jain, R. Toward a common event model for multimedia applications. *IEEE MultiMedia Magazine* 14(1), 2007, 19–29.

18. Zacks, J.M., Braver, T.S., Sheridan, M.A., Donaldson, D.I. Human brain activity time-locked to perceptual event boundaries. *Nature Neuroscience* 4(6), 2001, 651–655.

19. Zoumboulakis, M., Roussos, G. Escalation: Complex event detection in wireless sensor networks. In: *LNCS Proceedings of the European Conference on Smart Sensing and Context*, Vol. 4793, pp. 270–285. Kendal, U.K., 2007.

Chapter 8

Challenges and Emerging Paradigms for Augmented Surveillance

Francesco Flammini, Alfio Pappalardo, and Valeria Vittorini

Contents

8.1 Introduction

In modern society, the development of a territory is increasingly tied to the capability to ensure an adequate level of security to persons and infrastructures. Criminal acts, including terrorist attacks; accidents; and adverse natural events can pose a threat to homeland security (HS). In recent years, in all developed countries, the awareness about the high vulnerability of the infrastructures has increased considerably. In fact, the welfare, the quality of life, and all the vital functions of a country increasingly depend on the continuous and coordinated operation of several infrastructures, which for their importance are defined as critical infrastructures (CI). Critical infrastructure protection (CIP) has become a crucial and delicate activity, which requires the development of innovative approaches for identification, detection, and mitigation of threats, vulnerabilities, and risks.

The events of September 11, 2001, brought about a rapid expansion of CIP efforts, in particular to prevent terrorist attacks, minimize the damage, and recover from disruptive events. In all the activities concerning the specific context of the HS, information technology (IT) plays an important role, since it enables new and effective means to mitigate risks, providing early warning of threats and improving the response to disasters of various severity. As such, IT has an impact also in increasing CI's resilience. In fact, sensor-based technologies for detecting meaningful events can help in preventing unwilled situations. Traditionally, at least (digital) video surveillance and intrusion detection technologies have been employed. However, for an enhanced early warning and situation awareness (SA), the traditional technologies are not enough.

Often, the management of the security-related events is fragmented. Each event is treated separately. And many times there is a lack of an effective information sharing. The key to overcome those limitations is to synthesize data from multiple alerting systems and physical sensors. The use of distributed and heterogeneous sensorial subsystems (encouraged by the development of novel low-cost sensing devices) and their integration can lead to several levels of event correlation. On the one hand, they allow for the development of multimodal approaches for monitoring and surveillance activities. Such a solution aims at providing advanced event detection capabilities and/or at improving detection reliability.

On the other hand, information aggregation is also the key to develop the next generation of security management systems, the so-called PSIM (physical security information management) systems. PSIM systems help integrate security devices, improve efficiency and effectiveness, and produce an increased SA. One of the key factors to achieve those results is the presentation of all the relevant information into a single view, in order to provide essential decision support (DS) features.

Many infrastructures, especially transportation systems, can be spread through hundreds of kilometers and require thousands of employees for daily operations. A complete deployment of surveillance to cover a system of this magnitude requires thousands of cameras and other sensors, which makes human-based surveillance unfeasible. Detecting specific activities almost completely relies on costly and scarce human resources. Manual analysis of video as well as diverse sensor alarms (which can be false) is labor intensive, fatiguing, and prone to errors. Additionally, psychophysical research indicates that there are severe limitations in the ability of humans to monitor simultaneous signals. Thus, it is clear that there is a fundamental contradiction between the current surveillance model and human surveillance capabilities. The ability to monitor real-time footage provides dramatic capabilities to transit agencies. Software-aided real-time video analytics considerably alleviates the human constraints, which currently are the main handicap for analyzing continuous surveillance data [13]. However, though video analytics may not be considered as a novel development (in fact, computer vision research has been active since early 1980s), even recent experiences using state-of-the-art systems reported low performance in terms of false alarms and missed detections. Therefore, the redundancy and diversity of sensing technology is essential to build effective surveillance systems. That increases the number of sensing devices and—consequently—of the alarms to be integrated and managed.

In the context described earlier, the novel research must aim at

- Improving the technology of single sensors, by producing more and more performable and intelligent smart-sensing devices. This aspect is addressed in Section 8.2.
- Combining diverse sensing technologies, leading to the so-called multimedia and multimodal distributed surveillance solutions. This aspect is addressed in Section 8.3.
- Detecting threat scenarios as early as possible, providing superior SA and DS to quickly—possibly automatically—activate response-and-recovery strategies. That can be achieved by means of advanced and ad hoc information fusion (IF) techniques, as described in Section 8.4.

All those aspects contribute to what we define "augmented surveillance": an integrated concept, including technologies, capabilities, and functions, which we believe will be one of the most challenging paradigm of the CIP research in the years to come. A more detailed description of such a paradigm is provided in Section 8.5.

8.2 Smart Sensing

An effective surveillance system, regardless of its application domain, requires sensorial devices in order to monitor specific environmental parameters, to detect abnormal conditions or unwanted events, and, more in general, to capture information streams (continuous or discrete) of interest. Sensors and devices represent the basic information sources with which it is possible (or desirable) to reach the required level of situational awareness.

Each sensor is based on more or less sophisticated technologies, depending on the specific application needs, in terms of functionalities, performances, costs, suitability to changing or critical conditions on the field of installation, and so on. This is especially true in the context of CIP and HS.

The role of the new generations of monitoring and surveillance systems increasingly calls for intelligence. In fact they act not only as supporting platforms, but also as the concrete core of the data comprehension process. Since the overall system intelligence depends also on the intelligence of its sensing subsystems, most sensors should be converted into "smart" sensors.

Before defining what we mean by smart sensor, let us start from the concept of "standard" sensor. In general, a sensor is a device that is designed to measure a parameter (e.g., a physical quantity) from an object or the environment and to transform it into a signal (e.g., electrical). The logical architecture of a traditional integrated sensor includes the following basic components: sensing unit, processing unit (e.g., for signal amplifications, compensation, filtering), and power unit. Obviously, a sensor interface (e.g., wires, plugs, and sockets) for the physical connection with other electronic components needs to be provided (Figure 8.1).

The main difference between a smart sensor and a standard sensor lies in their "intelligence," that is, the capabilities provided by onboard microprocessors (or microcontrollers). In the last years, two different definitions about advanced sensors have emerged. They derive from the difference between the concepts of "smart" and "intelligent" [64]. The former is based on technological aspects, the latter on functional ones. Some definitions are reported in Ref. [60]. The distinction regards the role of the microprocessor, for example, if used for digital processing, analog to digital conversion, calculations, and interfacing functions or also to support various intelligent functions

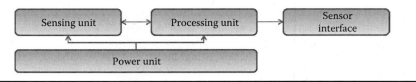

Figure 8.1   Logical architecture of a standard sensor.

such as self-diagnostics, self-adaption, self-identification, and self-calibration [37]. In some cases, it can also be used to decide when to store data or to minimize power consumption.

By leveraging recent developments in the fields of microelectronics and MEMS (microelectromechanical systems) technologies, the size of smart and intelligent sensors has decreased with time. MEMS are typically on the scale of microns (10–6 m). At the same time, mass production of MEMS and microprocessors—manufactured using VLSI (very large-scale integration) technology—for a variety of applications has significantly reduced their cost. Therefore, the production of these devices is more and more cost-effective, while the measurements methods improve as more intelligence is introduced into sensors. In the near future, the technological progress will lead to an improvement of all the other components of sensors (e.g., memory, radio transmission, batteries). As a result, there will be more capable and long-lasting devices, with reduced maintenance costs [55]. At the same time, wireless communication technologies will enable the development of low-cost and densely distributed sensing systems.

The first efforts in developing smart sensors have focused on civil engineering applications, in particular regarding structural health monitoring (SHM) and quasi real-time damage diagnostic. Today, the adoption of smart sensors is increasingly widespread and involves many different applications. Their use in the fields of security and defense is also increasing for implementing effective protection strategies. To address the issues related to HS and CIP, a great variety of technologies is required and sensors may feature several levels of sophistication.

Traditionally, the surveillance of an area to be protected was mostly based on cameras. However, a modern smart surveillance system integrates heterogeneous smart-sensing devices, made available by the physical security industry. They can be classified in different categories, representing classes of sensorial subsystems. Each category includes devices conceived for a precise functional aim, although they may differ in terms of detection technologies, computation powers, and communication facilities. In the following sections, each sensor is considered as a black box, regardless of its technological complexity, processing capabilities, and semantic level of the output information.

8.2.1 Intrusion Detection and Access Control

Intrusion detection and access control represent two different functional categories, though they are closely connected, not only logically but also physically. In fact, those subsystems have typically common control devices (junction boxes). Thus, they need an appropriate common interface toward the outside (digital contacts, serial or Ethernet ports, etc.) in order to be integrated within the surveillance systems.

Sensor systems classified as intrusion detection systems (IDS) include an entire class of electronic devices used to generate alarms upon the entry of persons into a secured area. Typical IDS devices are volumetric sensors (for motion detection), magnetic contacts (to detect illicit doors opening), glass break detectors, microphonic cables (for fence vibration detection), etc. An overview on the typologies of IDS technologies for fence line protection and open area surveillance is shown in Figure 8.2.

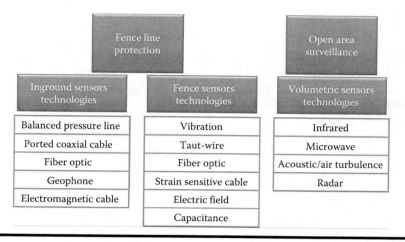

Inground sensors technologies	Fence sensors technologies	Volumetric sensors technologies
Balanced pressure line	Vibration	Infrared
Ported coaxial cable	Taut-wire	Microwave
Fiber optic	Fiber optic	Acoustic/air turbulence
Geophone	Strain sensitive cable	Radar
Electromagnetic cable	Electric field	
	Capacitance	

Figure 8.2   IDS technologies for outdoor sensors.

Moreover, to distinguish between authorized and unauthorized accesses to specific areas, it is necessary to adopt appropriate access control devices. The technologies in this field are based on one or more of the following mechanisms: possess, knowledge, and individual biometric features. Those approaches assure increasing levels of security; they can be based on several technologies (Figure 8.3). Access control systems (ACS) manage various combinations of entry, exit and/or movement through secure and controlled areas. Since ACS is used in combination with IDS, and both subsystems are integrated in a single stand-alone system, the internal interfacing between them allows for enabling access by authorized personnel (while IDS is temporary disabled) and preventing access by intruders.

Nowadays, one of the most popular ACS possess-based technologies is the RFID (radio-frequency identification). It improves and simplifies the control of accesses by means of automatic identifications, which can be faster and less invasive. Since the working principle is based on the radio-frequency transmission of a tag (i.e., a microchip of few millimeters) upon its entry

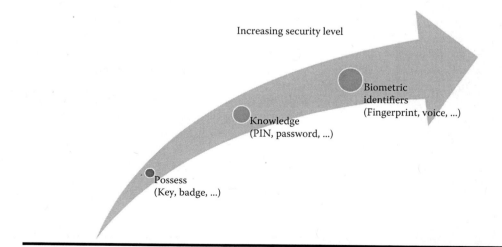

Figure 8.3   ACS working logics.

inside the electromagnetic field generated by the reader, such a technology represents a concrete alternative to the traditional personal identification approaches. In fact, RFID systems allow for hands-free recognition of people identity and motion directionality (entry or exit). The importance of RFID in the physical protection of assets or infrastructures is connected to the possibility of noninvasive tracking of authorized personnel within different areas that allows to automatically enable (or disable) protection systems, the use of a certain resource or device, and so on.

However, the level of security granted by ACS considerably increases if the accesses are granted using information on who people are, rather than what they have. Biometric technologies can be based on individual features like physiological, biological, morphological, or behavioral ones. Since related technologies are still complex and expensive, they are often used mostly for the protection of critical assets or infrastructures with high levels of risk. Some of the most commonly used biometrics, for different purposes, are fingerprint, iris, hand geometry, face, and voice recognition. Some of them are not based on contactless mechanisms, and some other can be rather invasive. Nowadays, the relationship between privacy and biometrics is an important argument for discussion; however, it is reasonable to expect that a good balance will be reached in the future. Also, from the viewpoint of the performance, the technological aspects cannot be evaluated without considering human factors. In fact, accessibility, usability, and physiological perspective play a fundamental role in determining efficiency and effectiveness of a biometric system.

Although each working logic assures a different (and increasing) security level, each technology presents a certain level of vulnerability, which is to be taken into account. As matter of fact, the effectiveness of a biometric ACS depends also on the ease in creating replicas of the biometric identifiers for malicious purposes. This is the reason why hybrid approaches that combine heterogeneous technologies (based on possess, knowledge, and biometric identifiers) are often proposed. A fingerprint cross-check (between one captured in real time and one saved in a smart card) associated with a PIN code check may represent a simple application of this principle.

8.2.2 Video Surveillance

Cameras are the most widespread devices used in surveillance and constitute the core of video surveillance systems [28,33]. The monitoring by means of a closed-circuit television (CCTV) system allows to capture relevant video in critical areas, in order to prevent theft, assault, and fraud, detect intrusion, as well as manage incidents and crowd movements. It is also used as an investigation tool for solving criminal acts, for example, to understand the dynamic of an attack and to identify the perpetrators. At the lowest level, a vision sensor may simply provide a video stream (an array of pixels at a certain frame rate). At a higher level, a vision system may be able to answer specific questions about unfolding events. The main characteristics of a camera are the following: field of view, type of acquisition, resolution of the captured scenes, nature of processed signal, and type of physical transmission interface.

Compared with the past, modern video surveillance extends the traditional CCTV systems with

- Advanced cameras with special features (high resolution, day/night capabilities, etc.)
- Digital video processing, using efficient data compression techniques (e.g., H.264*)
- Video analytics on the captured scenes, using computer vision algorithms

---

* The H.264 (also named MPEG-4 Part 10 or advanced video coding, AVC) is a compression standard, which provides superior compression ratios in comparison to existing ones. Its use leads to save storage space and bandwidth. At the same time, it is allowing a widespread adoption of megapixel cameras.

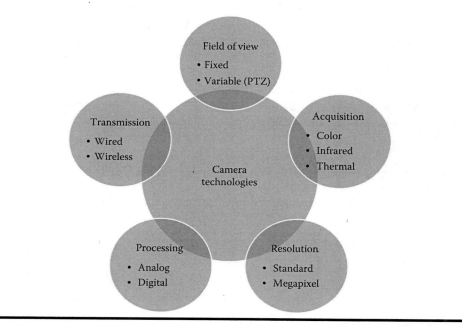

Figure 8.4 Camera technologies.

Given the main features mentioned in the preceding text, the families of camera technologies are listed in Figure 8.4. Regarding the field of view, a camera can be fixed, that is, pointed to a single direction, or it can be movable through the use of panning, tilting, and zooming, that is, moving left and right, up and down, and closer and farther away. PTZ (pan–tilt–zoom) cameras are used to cover wider fields of views, to follow objects or individuals, to zoom into areas of interest, etc.

Since the traditional acquisition of color images may fail during nighttime or in areas not adequately enlightened, the use of sensors sensitive to infrared (IR) radiation or thermal sources can solve these problems. IR cameras produce color images during the day, black and white images during the night. Each IR camera requires a source of IR light, embedded within the camera or projected by a separate lamp. On the contrary, thermal cameras don't require lighting, but they provide only outlines of objects (in addition to being expensive).

A video stream can be analog or digital. Nowadays, the trend is to move from analog cameras to digital and IP cameras. Both of them can transmit video over a computer network; however, analog cameras require the installation of specific encoders.

The transmission can be wired (via coaxial or fiber optic cable) or wireless (via radio or IR). Wired connections are typically cheaper and more reliable; however, wireless transmission can represent the only way to overcome issues like the monitoring of large and inhospitable areas, where the deployment of cables can be difficult, costly, or impossible.

Finally, the choice between a standard or higher resolution depends on the necessity (considering the application requirements) to capture more detailed images. Megapixel cameras are also used to enlarge their visual field and to zoom into the scene via software, which enables a sort of virtual PTZ (in alternative to the mechanical PTZ). Of course, high-resolution images are fundamental also to improve the performances of computer vision algorithms like face recognition.

In particular, the goal of computer vision is to automate the process of visual recognition of specific objects, persons, and behaviors within footages. Through specific algorithms, the video analytics allows for the detection of different threatening/interesting events, in order to send a warning to surveillance personnel. Due to the complexity of event recognition algorithms, only basic intelligent capabilities are usually embedded at the camera level (camera-based VCA, video content analysis) using onboard processing units.

In those cases, it is possible to detect basic events like tampering, accidental or intentional disruption, redirection, covering, and spray painting. Other important functionalities are motion detection and auto-tracking (which enables a camera to automatically follow moving objects).

In server-based VCA, it is possible to detect more complex events. Depending on the specific application, the VCA software can detect events like unattended object, line crossing, people counting, intrusion in critical areas, perimeter violation, license plate recognition, and abnormal situations and behaviors (like motionless persons, overcrowding, and aggressions). Recent researches and new efforts are going also toward the automatic detection of critical situations in crowded scenes [39]. Hybrid approaches (camera-based and server-based VCAs) are also proposed, for instance, for metadata acquisition at camera level and their analysis at server level, where metadata are compared with the rules that have been set during the programming phase of the VCA software.

Despite the continuing developments in this area, intelligent video analysis is still a technology with many limits, mainly due to the correct modeling of complex behaviors and the difficulty in evaluating them. For instance, the distinction between a suspicious behavior (e.g., person running with malicious intents) and a normal one (person running to catch a train) can be a difficult task even for humans.

Considering camera technologies, it is to remark the spread of emerging typologies of devices, like time-of-flight (ToF) cameras. ToF cameras are able to evaluate the distances, measuring the ToF of a light signal between the camera and the subject for each point of the image. The illumination unit normally uses IR light. More recently, Kinect-like cameras are becoming strategic also in robotic and surveillance applications. The device features an RGB camera, depth sensor, and multi-array microphone, which provide full-body 3D motion capture, facial recognition, and voice recognition capabilities. With respect to ToF method, Kinect-like camera actually encodes information in light patterns as it goes out, and the deformation of those patterns is what the camera looks for. In particular, when the camera starts deciphering the image, it looks for any shapes that appear to be a human body (a head, torso, and two legs and arms) and then starts calculating things like how those arms and legs are moving, where they can move, and where they will be in a few microseconds. Such a sensing technology can provide additional information to improve SA by means of a readily available and inexpensive device. In surveillance applications, these cameras can automatically detect, for example, violent motions in case of aggressions and similar behaviors.

8.2.3 Audio Surveillance

The automatic detection of abnormal or unexpected noises represents an emerging technology that can effectively support the surveillance task. By exploiting audio sensors and appropriate algorithms, it is possible to recognize automatically not only sounds which overcome specific predefined thresholds,* but also to identify shots, screams, explosions, and glass breaks [47]. Some of these events are not easily detectable by other sensors (like cameras), and even when it is possible

---

* Many camera manufacturers offer models with embedded microphones or audio input, which are able to provide this kind of audio detection.

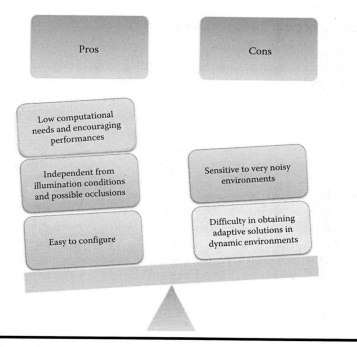

Pros

Cons

Low computational needs and encouraging performances

Independent from illumination conditions and possible occlusions

Easy to configure

Sensitive to very noisy environments

Difficulty in obtaining adaptive solutions in dynamic environments

Figure 8.5 Audio surveillance pros and cons.

to employ other technologies, the intelligent detection via microphones provides a redundancy that improves the reliability in recognizing threat events. This is especially true in crowded areas where many occlusions can hinder the visual analysis of images (both automatic and man-made) and make difficult or impossible the isolation of an individual and the tracking of his or her activities. Even where the visual analysis is possible, the audio properties are significant components of behavioral models. Generally speaking, sound constitutes a precious information to improve the detection of abnormal events and discriminate between different suspicious actions. Moreover, this approach offers further advantages such as low computational needs, independence from illumination conditions of the space to be monitored, and easy configuration. However, the acoustic surveillance implies the addressing of several issues. Pros and cons are briefly summarized in Figure 8.5.

The main criticality is the correct isolation of sounds of interest from the background in very noisy environments (e.g., areas belonging to transportation systems and passenger vehicles). This process is delicate because of its direct impact in terms reliability of the detection. Noisy environments can also highlight problems of misclassification (e.g., explosions are often recognized as gunshots). Furthermore, due to nonstationary conditions in certain environments, the process of modeling of noise should be adaptive. Therefore, some domains require the use of techniques based on the continuous update of these models, that is, learning capabilities. So the choice about the adaptation methodology becomes critical (because it may imply more phases of a certain complexity, the use of different algorithms, a high amount of input data, etc.). Despite these complications, the performance of audio sensors in detecting events like screams and gunshots encourages the use of this kind of surveillance [26,49] and the development of adaptive frameworks [48]. The main challenges in this field are the development of more efficient adaptation modules and the improvement of the detection reliability in more constrained environments (like trains, trams, or buses, where vibrations, motor noise, and external sounds complicate audio recognition [53]).

8.2.4 People Screening and CBRNe Sensors

In this section, we consider screening systems that allow the standoff detection of weapons, drugs, explosives, and chemical agents. The advantage of using these systems is twofold: on one hand, the remote detection of objects and elements of different nature (even if concealed by clothing) and, on the other hand, the adoption of innovative mass checking procedures for security reasons. The latter is a common problem in all those contexts where a solution like the security check in the airports is not really applicable or feasible. In fact, often intelligent detection systems must fulfill specific constraints, in order to allow a simple, noninvasive, and quick people screening. Obviously, the throughput is crucial in all situations where there is a passage of a high volume of people.

Therefore, the sensors used for these operations significantly extend the functions of traditional metal detectors. In particular, systems featuring CBRNe (chemical bacteriological radiological nuclear explosive) sensors can identify traces of radioactive materials and explosives, by means of a spectroscopic analysis. Thus, they constitute a powerful countermeasure for attacks carried out with the so-called *dirty bombs*. The latter consist of non-fissile radioactive material (which cannot explode), properly treated to make it very volatile. Associated with a conventional explosive charge, with low power, it can disperse the radioactive material in the environment, contaminating things and people. Many of these substances do not have an immediate contamination effect, and the symptoms may occur only several hours after the attack. This complicates its detection, without using these technologies. In case explosive detection is not integrated in this type of sensors, devices named *sniffers* are able to detect, for example, gunpowder residues on hands and clothes of the individuals.

A people screening system can be passive or active. Passive devices do not transmit any radiation to be reflected back into the device. So, there are no risks of harm (CCTV cameras are example of passive devices). Active devices transmit radiation toward target to be monitored. The reflected radiation is then captured and analyzed by the device. The main technologies for security purposes are based on millimeter waves, x-ray backscatter, and T-rays (see Figure 8.6).

Millimeter wave systems use low-energy electromagnetic waves to scan the body and detect the concealment of weapons, drugs, or explosive substances. So, they do not impose an additional pat-down (and extra staff to employ). However, millimeter wave systems can create privacy concerns. Interesting possible developments are related to the extension of the search area to several tens of meters beyond the scanning area, allowing to quickly scan a large number of people (unaware of being scanned).

Backscatter x-ray systems sense energy in the x-ray portion of the electromagnetic spectrum, which is reflected back from the target. These are active systems, but in comparison with traditional medical x-ray systems, the energy has a much lower power, in such a way to perform a screening that is not harmful to human health. However, the use of these technologies can cause privacy issues.

People Screening System Technologies			
	Millimeter Waves	Backscatter X-Rays	T-Rays
Active	✓	✓	
Passive	✓		✓

Figure 8.6   People screening system technologies.

T-rays, or terahertz, represent a form of low-power energy that all materials emit naturally, including rocks, plants, animals, and people. They allow to analyze the composition of objects (because many materials of interest have unique spectral "fingerprints" in the terahertz range) and to process images (passive imaging technology). So, T-ray systems are passive only. In the electromagnetic spectrum, terahertz rays are in the region between microwaves and IR; therefore, they are associated to a lower energy than millimeter waves and x-rays. The advantage of using T-rays lies in their capacity to pass through smoke, clouds, solids (like clothes), and, in some cases, walls. Therefore, this technology allows an effective identification of bombs, drugs, metallic and nonmetallic weapons, and explosives at much longer distances. Compared to x-ray, this technology is not harmful to health. Regarding the privacy-related issue, in comparison to the millimeter scanners, the images produced by these devices do not detect significant physical details of the screened person.

8.3 Multimodal and Multimedia Surveillance

The evolving requirements to be fulfilled in surveillance applications increasingly call for the deployment of intelligent and automated monitoring systems. Also, the growing capabilities assured by the technological progress encourage the employment of advanced surveillance systems. Although nowadays video surveillance represents the most popular form of surveillance, there are many other forms of monitoring. Hence, given the size and complexity of the sensed environments, it is easy to understand that surveillance should include multiple modalities.

Current research tends to combine and to exploit multiple modalities of monitoring, in order to create distributed surveillance solutions, including not only multi-camera systems [2], but more in general, multisensor surveillance systems [66]. The combination of traditional video surveillance with other smart-sensing technologies leads to the development of new multimedia surveillance systems [15], which collect and process different information streams (audio, video, and any output of a sensor). To that aim, a proper integration (e.g., by means of diverse algorithms) of these information is required.

Therefore, a multimodal and multimedia surveillance system combines two characteristics:

- The use of multiple sensors, possibly with overlapping sensing areas and which communicate between them through a network
- The use of heterogeneous sensors, to exploit all the information available in the monitored area

Basic forms of multimodal solutions could be, for example, only video based or audio based. Video-based approach may include the use of several typologies of cameras: PTZ and fixed, color and IR, etc. Typically, this solution is aimed at enlarging and enhancing the view of the scene, exploiting effectively redundancy and overlapping in cameras deployment.

From the functional point of view, such a camera network allows to capture further details on events detected in a wide field [28]; for example, zooming in automatically on an intruder to identify him or her, following objects and suspicious persons over extended areas, and performing a crowd analysis [65]. Specific combinations of fixed and PTZ cameras can also be used to perform, through a distributed approach, an automatic setting of deployed devices (e.g., to capture high- or low-resolution video), according to the complexity of the scenes (e.g., with more or fewer people). In this way, a PTZ is able to observe a single pedestrian at higher resolution or to track multiple pedestrians at the same time at lower resolution [57].

Also, different views of the same target can help in overcoming possible problems due to occlusions, failures, and tampering. This is a crucial point because the performances of video analytics algorithms depend also on the size of surveillance area, where, for example, the amount of occlusions has an impact on the object detection and tracking. The same consideration is valid also for face detection [36]. Therefore, it is possible to achieve an improvement in this direction and to overcome some limits of the algorithms in complex and/or crowded environments.

However, some of these benefits are counteracted by problems, like harder camera calibration. Furthermore, the correct management of available cameras is fundamental in performing functions like object tracking, in order to track an object from one camera to the next and to establish a correspondence using common reference points.

The most advanced forms of multimedia and multimodal surveillance are the answers to different needs, which are described as follows:

- The video analytics algorithms suffer from several problems. In particular, their effectiveness may be reduced by some factors: large amount of occlusions (increasing with the level of crowding), sudden changes in light conditions, reflective surfaces in the scene, objects that are camouflaged with the background, etc. So, it is necessary to overcome these limitations.
- Modern surveillance, especially in large and complex environments, cannot be performed via cameras only. Each monitored area offers different information streams, which need to be captured, evaluated, and possibly correlated. According to the specific application, an ad hoc set of heterogeneous sensing technologies is required.
- The event detection reliability is crucial in determining viability and effectiveness of surveillance systems. In particular, the probability of detection (POD) determines the effectiveness of the detection system, while the false and nuisance alarm rates determine its operational viability. Therefore, it is essential to reach a reasonable trade-off for detection and false alarm rates (FAR).
- Finally, the potential capabilities of multimedia surveillance systems are such to allow the development of advanced intelligent functions, in order to detect complex events. Considering the evolution of end-user requirements, such an aspect represents the major development toward augmented surveillance.

The integration of heterogeneous sensors within a multimedia and multimodal surveillance system is the key to address the issues described in the preceding text. Regarding the integrative approaches, they can be classified in two categories: *bottom-up* and *top-down*.

Bottom-up approaches are aimed at developing ad hoc integration algorithms whose inputs are the outputs of the sensors to be integrated. In such a case, the algorithm executed by sensors is written without using information coming from other sensors. Hence, the whole integration logic lies at a higher level of abstraction. Typically, the approach addresses the need for improving the overall performance of the surveillance system by trying to reduce FAR and to add functionalities.

Top-down approaches are aimed at developing the algorithms executed by the sensors, using the information coming from other devices. In this case, sensor output depends on the presence of other sensors and on the information they provide. Therefore, there is a part of the integration logic to be implemented in each sensing device, that is, at a lower level of abstraction. Typically, this approach is conceived to improve reliability of detection (represented by a parameter named POD). For example, in video analytics applications, the object detection and tracking performed by the single camera can be improved by means of additional information from other cameras or sensors. Some examples of advanced multimedia and multimodal surveillance are described in the following.

8.3.1 Audio–Video-Based Approaches

Audio can be auxiliary to video in solving specific problems like the tracking of people or the identification of a region of interest. By exploiting the correlation among the two modalities, the aim is to describe the observed data: (1) using unobserved audio and video or (2) using observed audio and video.

In the first case, the advantage consists of supporting the video tracking in case of occlusions by other objects. More in detail, the whole tracking activity can be the result of the combination of two stand-alone trackers: audio based and video based [59].

In the second case, the advantage can be twofold. On one hand, sound signals are used to reduce the amount of data generated by cameras (especially in situations of continuous recording of video streams). Thus, the aim is to record a video stream only when necessary. On the other hand, sound signals can be used to aim PTZ cameras toward regions of interest, in which the audio analytics has detected a sound source. In this case, the problems to solve are the identification of known sound sources (elevators, doors, etc.) and the discrimination between similar sources [35].

8.3.2 Infrared Sensors for Video Analytics Support

The integration of a multi-camera system with a wireless sensor network (WSN) is often aimed at improving the performance of video analytics algorithms. A possible application consists of using PIR (passive infrared) sensors to support the object detection and object tracking performed by the video analytics subsystem. PIR sensor working logic is based on the detection of electromagnetic radiation, emitted in the IR range from any object that has a temperature above 0 K. In particular, this kind of sensor can detect the presence of a person in its monitored area and his or her direction of movement.

The basic idea in this form of multimodal surveillance is to exploit the information from the network of PIR nodes to overcome some video analytics limitations, arising mainly from the difficulty for detecting a subject and maintaining its identity when moving. This is particularly important when the classic methods based on shape and color recognition fail because of the limited field of view of cameras or when they are deployed in places with very different lighting conditions. Thus, PIR sensors can be used to detect motion with a high accuracy (also during the night), since they are not sensitive to light conditions.

Specific problems of incorrect motion detection, for example, are due to the opening of a door inside the area monitored by a camera. If the video analytics algorithm for detecting movements is based on background changes, the door opening affects the reliability of motion detection of any cameras watching the door. However, a PIR node can be placed near the door to help the camera to discriminate between real movements of people and ordinary background updates. Furthermore, a PIR sensor can be placed in areas that cannot be fully covered by a camera (e.g., for the presence of obstacles or architectural barriers) to detect a change in the direction of a person when he or she is not viewed by the camera. In this way, it is possible to estimate the position of the subject (when not visible) with a better accuracy as well as to achieve an improved tracking (when visible again), keeping its correct identifying label. Since PIR sensors are low cost, the aforementioned issues can be addressed by deploying nodes composed by a couple of PIR sensors, in order to improve detection reliability at node level [50].

The application of these techniques can be also exploited to enhance the surveillance task in case of automatic detection of an abandoned object (e.g., luggage) to track the owner. This is especially true in some conditions, for example, when the owner passes behind a large pillar and leaves the scene without the luggage. In this case, an occlusion that lasts several seconds may complicate the tracking [34].

Another possible application is the combined use of IR barriers and cameras for intrusion detection. Typically, intrusion detection via intelligent video surveillance suffers from problems due to the camouflage of the intruder, sudden changes in light conditions, etc. A significant improvement can be achieved through the additional use of IR barriers, in order to achieve a greater overall robustness. The barriers consist of pairs of receivers and transmitters of IR radiation, which compose a sort of virtual fence. For each pair, the interruption of the beam triggers an alarm. However, it is possible to set the number (and the position) of the beams that should be interrupted in order to trigger an alarm. The use of these configurations allows to discriminate between real intrusions and ordinary (or authorized) passages. The advantage of using both IR barriers and cameras lies in capabilities like the deactivation of video analytics when required (e.g., barriers have recognized an ordinary crossing) in order to avoid the reporting of unnecessary alarms and the correlation (e.g., in "AND" logic) of the data coming from barriers and camera, in order to improve the intrusion detection reliability (i.e., triggering an overall intrusion alarm only if both systems detect an intrusion).

A railway application of IR barriers is aimed at identifying intrusions by unauthorized persons in tunnel portals. Assuming the presence of intelligent cameras and multiple IR barriers (e.g., composed by two pairs of sensors), placed at different height levels (lower, middle, higher) on the two sides of the tunnel entrance, a possible configuration of the system is the following:

- The interruption of two pairs at lower level is associated to the presence of unauthorized person walking on the tracks.
- The interruption of two pairs at central level is associated to the presence of unauthorized persons on the sidewalk of the tunnel.
- The interruption of all three barrier levels is associated to the entrance of the train in the tunnel.

By correlating the intrusion alarms detected by the IR barriers and the intelligent cameras, it is possible to alert an operator only when the intrusion is detected by both systems; another viable option is to use the two sensors in an "OR" configuration and to ask the operator (a sort of "human sensor") for a visual feedback.

8.3.3 Combined Use of Laser and Video Technologies

Laser technologies offer the possibility to support the video surveillance in several ways. For example, a sensor like the LDV (laser Doppler vibrometer) can be used to remotely capture acoustic signals like human speech. Since LDV provides contactless vibration measurement of surfaces, it can be considered like a remote voice detector. However, it is necessary to aim the laser beam at the surface of interest. The advantages are effective vibration detection within two hundred meters and the possibility to aim LDV sensors at targets that are difficult to access. Furthermore, targets are not aware of being heard.

The performance of the LDV depends on some properties of the target surface: reflectance, size, distance from sensor, etc. Performing a manual search of the best target surface can be difficult at large distances; in those cases, video surveillance can support automatic target selection. An integrated system with IR cameras, PTZ color cameras, and LDVs can represent an advanced form of multimodal surveillance for face and voice recognition systems [67]. IR cameras can detect humans and movements at long distances, while PTZ cameras are used to remotely capture video (e.g., to track a subject) and to guide the LDVs to obtain the associated audio signal by automatically selecting the best reflection surface for remote hearing [52].

Another laser-based system that comes in support to the video analysis is the LIDS (laser intrusion detection system). It can be used, for example, to protect areas from intrusions and to monitor portals and tunnels in order to detect unauthorized objects or people. By managing known profiles, which can be recognized by the system without triggering a warning, LIDS is able to reduce the rate of nuisance alarms. The insensitivity to lighting conditions, reflective surfaces, rain, and snow has a great impact on reducing the FAR with respect to video surveillance. Possible applications in railway transportation are tunnel intrusion detection, platform safety line crossing, and intrusions (accidental or malicious) onto the track. Therefore, these systems offer both an effective support for visual analysis and additional information, which can be correlated with data coming from intelligent video surveillance.

From the discussion in the preceding text, it is easy to understand that there is no general solution for adopting multimodal and multimedia surveillance sensors. The use of any smart-sensing technology has pros and cons, and the effectiveness of a solution is always application dependent. Hence, most of the design efforts should address issues related to sensing modality selection, sensor positioning, and data integration among multiple sensors. Requirements and constraints to be fulfilled include remote and adaptive sensing, coverage of possibly wide areas, high-resolution views of critical assets, and synchronization among sensors; furthermore, fundamental parameters are increase of complexity related to the integration, costs, maintenance efforts, scalability, etc. A survey on multisensor integration for wide-area surveillance is provided in Ref. [1].

8.4 Multisensor and Multisource Data and Information Fusion

8.4.1 The Need for an Overall Process Model

Multimodal and multimedia surveillance is aimed at providing complementary information and at increasing the accuracy in detecting threats and/or events of interest. Indeed, it is easy to understand that by exploiting multiple features from the monitored area, the power of event detection is greater than the one assured by a single source. However, in order to recognize in real-time complex situation patterns, to build hypotheses of unfolding situations, and to take actions in response to these situations, the overall capabilities of the surveillance system should include processing, correlation, and handling of multimedia data coming from different sources. Due to the variety of natural and malicious threat scenarios, a growing set of different sensing technologies can be required. Unfortunately, many of the recently developed innovative technologies (e.g., video analytics) do not always provide adequate reliability (see, e.g., Refs. [27,41]). Many automatic detection systems generate unnecessary warnings, which can be classified as false alarms or nuisance alarms. Especially with regard to the DS feature of surveillance systems (e.g., for triggering countermeasures), it is very important to control the rate of these alarms (see, e.g., Ref. [11]).

The integration of information coming from different sources paves the way to new generations of surveillance systems, where many different media streams contribute to provide a greater situational awareness, an improved early warning capability, and a better DS. In fact, the capabilities of the traditional systems are limited in data analysis and interpretation and hence in real-time prevention and reaction. Furthermore, since a few human operators are usually employed in security surveillance, human factors also need to be carefully addressed, including cognitive ergonomics in human–machine interaction [7,63].

Regardless the specific system to be implemented, the first objective is to model the overall integration process of heterogeneous information, in order to conceive a real-time data comprehension framework. Within the context of analysis and reasoning about dynamic situations, where application domains include HS, defense, environmental sensing, crisis management, and other information-rich domains, an active field of research is focused on IF. IF takes into account the specific aims related to the application domain, on the one hand, and the different characteristics of the available multimodal subsystems, on the other. In fact, IF may provide information at different semantic levels and in different formats, require different kinds of processing, have different reliability levels, and have a certain degree of mutual correlation (see also Ref. [4]). The complexity of such a task requires an appropriate strategy to fuse the available information. Using an efficient fusion scheme, one may expect significant advantages, such as

- Enlarging information extraction from the available sources
- Improving confidence in decisions by leveraging more information
- Increasing robustness against sensor failures and outliers in measurements (stability)

However, an important issue regarding IF is that, while using additional information is intuitively advantageous to add knowledge and to support decisions, the overall performance of the fusion process can decrease in case of additional incorrect data [18].

Other basic concepts characterizing IF systems and the models proposed in literature are described in the following.

8.4.2 State of the Art on Information Fusion

Data needs to be analyzed effectively and efficiently to provide appropriate information for intelligent decision making [61]. Hence, the power of IF is being increasingly considered in several applications. Empirical studies have shown the overall improvements of information systems based on fusion of different information sources [29]. In particular, fusion of relevant data has proven effective in reducing uncertainty (e.g., FARs), in increasing accuracy (in terms of confidence levels) in the early detection of threats, and in increasing robustness by exploiting redundant information [12]; being able to deal with data that is redundant, inconsistent, and conflicting [3] is also essential.

The basic motivation of IF is described as follows:

> exploiting the synergy in the information acquired from multiple sources (sensor, databases, information gathered by humans, etc.) such that the resulting decision or action is in some sense better […] than would be possible if any of these sources were used individually without synergy exploitation [19].

Although it is widely recognized that IF can support and enhance decision making, an information fusion system (IFS) is not concretely viewed as a decision support system (DSS) [45]. In this sense, many heterogeneous fields of research often exploit the results already available in other sectors like defense [62].

Several works have attempted to characterize IFS, but actually there is no general consensus in the literature regarding the components of an IFS; consequently, there are slightly different

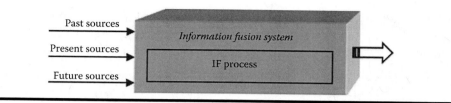

Figure 8.7   **Schematic representation of the information fusion system.**

opinions on what is required for a system to be classified as an IFS. Basically, we can say that an IFS needs to receive information from different information sources, including sensors and smart devices, human sources, or data archives (depending on the context). As shown in Figure 8.7, the sources could be classified as either past (e.g., data archives), present (e.g., sensors), or future (e.g., simulations/models) [45].

An IF process of different sources can be automated with the purpose to achieve timely, robust, and relevant assessment of unfolding situations (e.g., in terms of threats, within the context of HS) and their possible projections.

Recently, it has been acknowledged that the user could actually contribute to the IF process [9,10,12,44]. Typically an IFS involves different degrees of automation and user involvement within two extremes: "user dominant" (i.e., user is in control of the fusion process) and "machine dominant" (i.e., fully automated fusion process).

In the IF research community, different models have been proposed to have a common understanding across different applications domains which use the IF concepts. The most significant ones are presented in the following sections.

8.4.2.1 The JDL Model

The following model was created by the U.S. Joint Directors of Laboratories, hence the name "JDL." The JDL model is the most commonly used model which categorizes the fusion process. In general, the model describes how IFS transform sensor data into information which a user can employ for decision making [42].

The model is readable from left to right (see Figure 8.8), from the different sources of information to the user interface, that is, the HCI (human–computer interface). Between them,

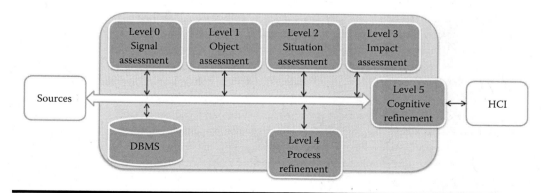

Figure 8.8   **JDL model.**

the different levels may be viewed in a hierarchical order, although the JDL model is not a process model indicating a flow. Rather, it shows different categories of functions, while the DBMS (database management system) supports the maintenance of the data used and provided by the IFS.

Only for convenience, the functions are described in their hierarchical order. In particular, levels 0–3 represent the "assessment functions," instead of levels 4 and 5, which represent "refinement functions." The latter could be considered as a sort of meta-processes, which control and refine the previous levels. More in detail, the different levels are described as follows [29]:

- *Level 0 preprocessing (signal assessment)*: This level preprocesses data at the individual sensor in order not to overwhelm the system with raw data.
- *Level 1 processing (object assessment)*: "Fusion of multisensor data to determine the position, velocity, attributes, characteristics, and identity of an entity (such as an emitter or target)."
- *Level 2 processing (situation assessment)*: "Automated reasoning to refine our estimate of a situation (including determining the relationships among observed entities, relationships between entities and the environment, and general interpretation of the meaning of the observed entities)."
- *Level 3 processing (impact assessment)*: "Projection of the current situation into the future or define alternative hypotheses regarding possible threats or future conditions." This level is also sometimes referred to as threat refinement/assessment.
- *Level 4 processing (process refinements)*: "A meta process that monitors the ongoing data fusion process to improve the processing results (namely, improved accuracy of estimated identity of entities and improved assessment of the current situation and hypothesized threats)."
- *Level 5 processing (cognitive refinements)*: "Interaction between the data fusion system and a human decision maker to improve the interpretation of results and the decision-making process."

First of all, raw data may be preprocessed (level 0—signal assessment) in order to assess the signals from the sensors and extract key information (e.g., functions such as video, audio, or signal processing). Since the information sources could refer to sensors as well as agents (human sources) or data archives, this activity should be tailored on the typology of the sources, bringing the extracted information to the same semantic level before the subsequent processing.

The second function is object assessment (level 1) and it concerns the combination of data from different sources to obtain estimates of an object's attributes or identity (e.g., classical techniques such as tracking and pattern recognition are used).

Level 2, situation assessment, is a collection of functions to interpret the different objects' relationships and their relationships with the environment (typically automated reasoning and artificial intelligence techniques are used here). The difference between the two levels is the following: level 1 involves attribute-based state estimations, while level 2 involves relation-based state estimations [31].

Impact assessment (level 3) concerns the future states and the projection of the interpreted situations, in order to assess the possible threats, risks, and impacts.

Considering Figure 8.8, level 4 and level 5 are located on the border of the fusion process. They are quite similar, although there are some distinguishing features. The main difference between them lays in the responsibility of the refinement process: in level 4, the responsible is the system itself; in level 5, it is the user who controls the process depending on the particular needs he or she has at the moment. Anyway, the incorporation of level 5 into the JDL model has not yet achieved common usage within the IF community [30]. However, the aspect related to the understanding of the active role of human information processing in IF should be carefully addressed [43]. The JDL model is under constant revision, and although other models have emerged, they have not gained the same popularity. One of the reasons for that is related to the holistic perspective provided by the model, which is usable for many purposes related to the research domain of IF systems [46].

8.4.2.2 Other Fusion Process Models

In this section, the alternative models to describe the fusion process and functions are briefly summarized. The aim is to highlight that the JDL model is not the only way of modeling the fusion process. These models include the following.

8.4.2.2.1 Dasarathy's Functional Model

Dasarathy defined a useful category of different fusion functions, based on the types of data and information processed and on the types of results obtained from the process [17]. The input and output of a fusion process can be of any level: data, feature, and decision. For this reason, the Dasarathy's functional model is also known as DFD model (see Figure 8.9).

In this way, it is easy to represent different fusion techniques. The components responsible for the fusion stages are the following:

- DAI-DAO (Data In—Data Out)
- DAI-FEO (Data In—Feature Out)
- FEI-FEO (Feature In—Feature Out)
- FEI-DEO (Feature In—Decision Out)
- DEI-DEO (Decision In—Decision Out)

where DAI-DAO corresponds to low-level fusion, FEI-FEO to medium-level fusion, DEI-DEO to high-level fusion, and DAI-FEO and FEI-DEO are included in multilevel fusion. The main contribution of Dasarathy's classification is that it specifies the abstraction level of both the input

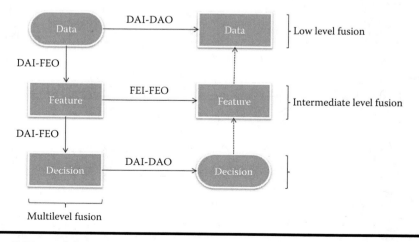

Figure 8.9 DFD model.

and the output of a fusion process, avoiding possible ambiguities. However, this functional model refers to a data driven process [31], where an overall systemic view is not provided and the user role cannot be accommodated. In Ref. [58], a mapping between Dasarathy's functional model and JDL model has been provided.

8.4.2.2.2 OODA Loop Model

Another model for IF, mainly developed in the military field, is the OODA (observe–orient–decide–act) loop. The aim of the model is to enable faster decisions by identifying both your own decisions and your opponent's ones, in order to act before your opponent. Despite the fact that the OODA loop is quite simplistic, it is the most accepted decision-making process model used within IF. The four activities considered in the process are the following (see Figure 8.10):

■ *Observe*: The environment, in order to detect an opponent
■ *Orient*: Position yourself in the environment, in a good place for the next step
■ *Decide*: Make a decision, based on previous stages
■ *Act*: Perform the decision

The model illustrates the ultimate goal of a decision maker, taking the right decision within the minimum time, where speed is a condition for winning. Although the OODA loop has its origins in the military domain, it focuses more in general in the human decision process. Besides, the only military-specific term is "*orient,*" so by replacing this term with "*interpret*" (to represent the concept of situation understanding), the model becomes more generic.

Formally, an extension of the original OODA loop model in order to improve the capacity to represent dynamic and complex situations by a modular approach is proposed with the M-OODA (modular OODA) loop [54]. It consists of four goal-oriented modules (more generic than the original four activities):

■ Data gathering (observe)
■ Situation understanding (orient)
■ Action selection (decide)
■ Action implementation (act)

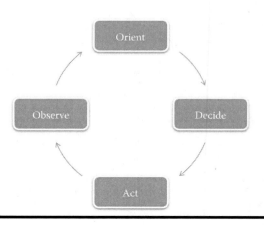

Figure 8.10   OODA loop.

In addition, each module is structured around three components: process, state, and control. The M-OODA loop incorporates explicit control elements within and across modules, enabling a bidirectional data/information flow between modules. It also includes a feedback loop within each module. Finally, it provides a basic architecture for modeling a variety of team (rather than individual) decision making, differently from the OODA loop.

8.4.2.2.3 Object-Oriented Reference Model

The object-oriented reference model represents a formal approach to fusion system design, and it shows the role of the psychology of the HCI in the system design process [38]. In fact, with this model, the human capabilities can naturally find their space. In particular, the model does not specify fusion tasks or activities; however, it provides a set of roles and specifies the relationships among them. The identified roles are as follows:

- *Actor*: Responsible for the interaction with the world, collecting information, and acting on the environment.
- *Perceiver*: Once information is gathered, the perceiver assesses such information, providing a contextualized analysis to the director.
- *Director*: Based on the analysis provided by the perceiver, the director builds an action plan specifying the system's goals.
- *Manager*: The manager controls the actors to execute the plans formulated by the director.

The proposed model perspective is such that human and computer objects are not distinct.

8.4.2.2.4 Waterfall Model

The waterfall model is an example of hierarchical architecture, described in Ref. [32]. The flow of data operates from the data level to the decision-making level, where the sensor system module (level 1) is continuously updated with feedback from the decision-making module (level 3). The intermediate level is responsible for the pattern processing. The three levels are described as follows:

- Level 1 transforms raw data to provide the required information about the environment.
- Level 2 is composed of feature extraction and fusion in order to obtain an inference about the data. The output of this level is a list of estimates with associated probabilities.
- Level 3 relates objects to events, according to the information that has been gathered, the available libraries and databases, and the human interaction.

A detailed schema of the model is proposed in Ref. [22].

8.4.2.2.5 Omnibus Process Model

This model draws together several models, taking their advantages and overcoming some of their disadvantages, presenting a general taxonomy to capture the IF process [6]. The models involved are JDL, OODA loop, DFD, and the waterfall model. Omnibus process model includes a dual perspective: system and task oriented. The decision making is considered as a computational process. It can be considered as level 4 of the JDL model and as the decide phase of the OODA loop.

8.5 Toward Augmented Surveillance

8.5.1 Basic Concepts and Requirements

In the following section, we propose a paradigm aimed at the physical protection of assets in threat scenarios. The basic idea is to collect and exploit all the means, techniques, methods, and approaches already available (and briefly described in the previous sections), in order to obtain an integrated layered platform easy to adapt to the specific application domain.

The key to achieve "augmented surveillance" is to combine and synthesize data from multiple and distributed sensorial subsystems, at different levels. First of all, technological issues, techniques and methodologies of protection, and overall fusion strategies should be viewed in a cohesive way. Furthermore, ad hoc information aggregation and management are paving the way to a new generation of PSIM. The latter should present the available (or inferred) information into a single integrated view, to increase effectiveness and efficiency in DS. In fact, traditional surveillance systems feature a fragmented management of the security-related events: each event is treated separately with a lack of an effective information sharing. Those limitations explain a certain skepticism about PSIM adoption in the industry [51]. The new-generation PSIM can significantly contribute to improvements not only in threat detection, but in several directions, such as

- *Deterrence*: To discourage the adversary from acting
- *Minimization*: To mitigate the effects of attacks
- *Response*: To enable operators to counteract the attack and to protect assets and persons
- *Recovery*: To enable the system to resume normal operations

The proposed paradigm is aimed at reaching advanced early warning capabilities, inside a general context of enhanced SA. It aims at aiding decision makers in obtaining a greater knowledge of events, factors, and variables affecting a certain environment. According to one of the first and most widely accepted definitions, SA is the perception of elements in the environment within a volume of time and space, the comprehension of their meaning, and the projection of their status in the near future [20].

SA includes also the important concept of "situation recognition," which aims at identifying a priori-defined situation patterns within an information flow, in order to support decision makers, allowing them to focus only on the most relevant aspects. Situation recognition can be considered as a pattern matching problem, where patterns represent situations of interest. In such a task, often the issue is not the lack of information, but finding the information needed when needed [21]. That requires the use of computer-based support systems, since the human operators may not be able to analyze all information properly and timely. Further background concepts specifically related to multimedia surveillance and monitoring systems are provided in Ref. [5].

From the physical security viewpoint, the a priori-defined situations of interest include the threat scenarios, which are identified during the phase of risk analysis (RA), performed for the infrastructure or the assets to be protected. They are typically composed by sequences of actions used by attackers to reach their objective. The preliminary stage of RA regards the adoption of rigorous and systematic approaches to model possibly complex threats. The aim is to identify and to model, using a certain formalism, the possible modes of attack (i.e., the threat scenarios). Each threat is typically associated to a risk index to obtain a quantitative or qualitative classification. This is essential to define a priority in the adoption of countermeasures and protection mechanisms. Therefore, for all the subsequent stages (selection of detectors, system deployment, definition of the IF strategy, etc.), an a priori knowledge about the possible threat scenarios can be assumed.

The increasing need for correlating large heterogeneous information to provide greater SA and early warning should fulfill several requirements. First of all, given a known threat and assuming that

- All the means (i.e., sensors and devices) for threat detection are available.
- Each device works properly, that is, it is in the condition to correctly detect a threats trace (data, status, event, etc.).

the detection of the threat and the report of the related alarm to the operators should be assured. In other words, given a problem, the existence of a "solution" should be assured. This affects the overall approach (e.g., correlation techniques and related models), which lies behind the detection mechanism implemented by the surveillance systems.

In addition to that, a quick data processing is required. This means that the logic which rules the behavior of the surveillance system has to be based on models sharing the requirement of (soft) real-time solvability.

The requirements mentioned in the preceding text should be fulfilled also with a certain level of reliability. In fact, the surveillance systems should assure as much as possible a high POD and a low FAR: those parameters determine the effectiveness and the viability of the system, respectively (see Section 8.5.2).

These considerations give useful indications in defining the right approach to face the detection problem. For example, artificial neural networks (ANN) represent a possible approach to solve large and computationally demanding problems. It is usually used to model complex relationships between inputs and outputs or to find patterns in data. However, ANN are also considered as nonlinear, black box, and requiring a training phase. Therefore, it is necessary to reason on more specific constraints:

1. To assure the predictability and repeatability of the behavior of the system (e.g., within an ANN, it is not possible to describe the stored knowledge base [KB])
2. To overcome the critical concern of the learning phase that can require sophisticated training techniques, long computation time, and a large set of examples
3. To fulfill the requirement related to the existence of a "solution" (e.g., ANN cannot assure problem solution since the existence of a learning algorithm, which converges, is not guaranteed.)

The preceding statements suggest using expert systems, which are not "intelligent" in the usual sense of the word, that is, in a creative way. While the deductions of expert systems are constrained by the stored KB, they can process a large amount of data very quickly, taking into account many "rules" and details that human experts cannot. One limit of this approach is that the completeness of the KB depends on the effectiveness and quality of the RA activity: threat scenarios that are not identified and translated into a model will never be detected.

This issue leads to a further reasoning on the capabilities to be provided by modern PSIM systems featuring a certain level of "augmented surveillance." The model-based threat detection approach, in fact, should also assure a certain tolerance to imperfect modeling (due to human faults), on the one hand, and to missed detections (due to device faults), on the other. The set of possible solutions includes techniques of pattern matching and similarity analysis, in order to recognize new and not (perfectly) modeled threats. The techniques based on similarity between patterns are not new, in particular in the field of computer network IDS. They are often based on the following solution: if an alert, which is the known consequence of a forerunning event, is received and the forerunning event has not been detected, then the missed event can be identified [16]. The limit of this solution lies in the fact that it cannot cope with missing events that are not linked to other events. A more effective technique should not assume that direct cause/consequence relationships exist between detected and missing events. For example, this is possible with solutions based on ad hoc metrics. With respect to traditional approaches of infrastructure surveillance, such a technique allows for earlier as well as more robust and straightforward detection of complex threat scenarios. It does not require further modeling efforts, since threat scenarios do not need to evolve completely to provide a warning: operators may receive a warning level, which is somehow proportional to the similarity index. These quantitative indications about unfolding threats can effectively help operators to quickly undertake appropriate countermeasures [24].

Innovative approaches for the design of distributed surveillance systems should aim at adding interactivity and adaptability capabilities, fulfilling the constraint of a preventive and manageable mode of reaction. Recent studies on cognitive systems (CS) help in reaching this goal. As matter of fact, automatic surveillance systems are required to emulate the cognitive capabilities of human operators in detecting and assessing possible threats. In particular, this kind of approach is increasingly used in the field of intelligent video surveillance [40], not only to understand complex activities occurring within a video stream but also to learn from them in such a way to build a KB automatically adapted to the specific environment. Recently, the cognitive paradigm has been also applied to the field of CIP [14], in order to provide a more comprehensive SA. Methods for the representation and the organization of knowledge and for the learning from experience allow a system to evaluate the state evolution and to predict "near-future events". The emerging concept of cognitive surveillance, based on this kind of researches, aims at providing these capabilities also by means of the cooperation with human agents to perform corrective actions. Regarding the cognitive cycle, discussions about the correctness and suitability of the semantic descriptions of events of interest (depending on the domain) are provided in Ref. [23].

8.5.2 Viability and Effectiveness

The human management of critical situations involving many simultaneous events is a very delicate task, which can be error prone. Integrated surveillance systems are necessary to allow the human supervision of a large number of sensors, devices, or cameras positioned inside the environment to be monitored. These systems allow to call the attention of the operators only and anytime an alarm is detected, trying to make surveillance independent from their attention level. Generally speaking, the concern is related to a quick and effective management of possible large amounts of data (e.g., events, alarms). Therefore, the first challenging goal is to support and strengthen the human capabilities without replacing them. The main motivation relies in the need for taking into account many details that a human could ignore, miss, or forget.

Since a few human operators are usually employed in security surveillance, human factors need to be carefully addressed, including cognitive ergonomics in human–machine interaction. In fact, many critical tasks are under the responsibility of human operators that cannot manage a great amount of surveillance streams in real time. Hence, it is necessary to find the best trade-off between the trend of sensing subsystems to produce a large amount of data (events, warnings, alerts) and the limited human capabilities. In the field of human factors and ergonomics (HFE), it is widely believed that highly non-stimulating and repetitive activities make human surveillance very difficult [56]. This is especially true in multimedia surveillance systems, where the operators may monitor a wide area, through a large number of sensors producing many events, warnings, and alerts.

Furthermore, modern surveillance systems typically support the undertaking of countermeasures, whose activation can be fully automatic (independent from human intervention) or partially automatic (based on human discrimination, e.g., by manual confirmation of detected alarms). The choice of the response mode may depend on the kind of countermeasure, but also on timeliness requirements and on the alarm trustworthiness.

Obviously enough, alarm systems should only detect situations that actually represent a threat. However, intelligent sensing systems may generate unnecessary warnings, which can be classified as false alarms or nuisance alarms. Therefore, with regard to the triggering of countermeasures, it is very important to take into account and to control the rate of these alarms.

False alarms are due to events that should not cause an alarm, while nuisance alarms are generated when a legitimate cause occurs, but the related alarm activation is inconvenient. As an example, nuisance alarms occur when maintenance staff enters restricted areas without prior identification. False and nuisance alarms can have a significant impact on

- Operational efficiency, due to the time wasted in evaluating and dismissing unnecessary alarms as well as in the possible deactivation of automatic countermeasures
- Vigilance level and response time, since when a large number of alarms are false, operators tend not to trust them

In other words, if the POD determines system effectiveness, false and nuisance alarm rates significantly influence its operational viability and efficiency. Therefore, it is essential to identify reasonable goals for detection and FARs and then to determine the methods to achieve them.

Considering the joint automation–human performance—and in particular, how the level of automation unreliability affects human performance—a research revealed that alarm systems should have a reliability factor of 70% [63]. At a reliability level below this threshold, the automation can be considered worse than no automation at all, nullifying its practical usefulness. The analysis also showed that performance was more strongly affected by reliability in high workload conditions, which are critical in the context of surveillance and supervision.

According to this result, when more than 30% of alarms are false or nuisance, operators waste time in discarding alarms, ignore or respond slowly to real events, and lose confidence in the surveillance system. This aspect is tied to the adverse effects of false alarms on human behavior. The rule mentioned in the preceding text is important to establish a minimum level of reliability in order to achieve a viable system.

Many approaches address the issue of nuisance alarms in a retroactive way, in particular employing self-learning engines to filter out unnecessary alarms based on human feedback. With this capability, the system can adapt to the specific conditions of each installation and learn to recognize events that are cause of false and nuisance alarms. The difficulties of this approach lie in the self-learning process, recognition strategy, and duration.

One obvious method to improve detection rates is to increase the sensitivity of the sensing subsystems; however, this will also increase the number of false alarms. Following the usability criterion mentioned earlier, the surveillance system (and/or its HMIs) should be optimized in such a way to get the highest detection rate with no more than 30 discardable alarms out of any 100 generated (on average). An improvement of alarm trustworthiness as well as system resilience can be achieved by exploiting redundancy and diversity in sensors displacement and technologies.

8.5.3 Practical Applications

In this section, a practical application of augmented surveillance is proposed. One of the basic needs is to frame in a cohesive way technologies, techniques, capabilities, and features available for distributed intelligent monitoring in order to merge the two areas of IF and DS. More in detail, in the field of IF there is a lack of the research focusing on the user's decision-making process embedded in an IFS that is essential to fully take advantage of its benefits [45]. In order to represent the overall process describing how information transforms from sensor data to information which a user can use for decision making, a general model is proposed. It is based on the JDL model, because it highlights three important aspects that are reflected in the domains of interest:

1. The possible need for preprocessing raw data coming from sensors. This aspect depends on the level of heterogeneity of the sensing subsystems (ranging from temperature sensors to intelligent cameras) and on the semantic level of the information provided by them. The issue could be addressed by the subsystems, by the PSIM which integrates them, or even before IF processing.
2. The identification of different levels of capabilities. The data combination from sources is aimed at evaluating (a) states, attributes, or identities of the monitored entities; (b) mutual relationships between monitored entities and surrounding environment; and (c) future states and projections starting from recognized situations, in order to assess threats, risks, and possible impacts.
3. The need for performing a constant refinement process, which can be automatic, user driven or hybrid. In fact, the user can effectively contribute to this process to complement the IFS [8].

An overall process for handling data from multiple sources is represented in Figure 8.11. In the figure, each source may represent a single sensor (regardless of its "intelligence"), a complex—possibly multimodal—sensing subsystem, or a human agent. Depending on the type of outputs, a preliminary processing may be required or not. The figure remarks the important aspect of

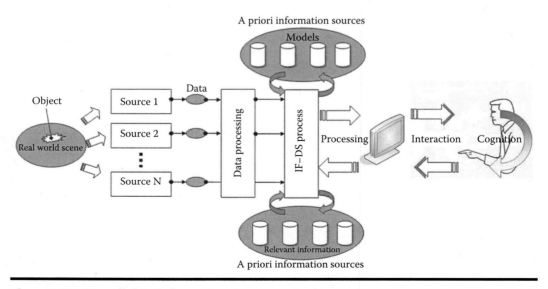

Figure 8.11 Overall data/information management process.

considering the IF and DS processes as a whole. Furthermore, it takes into account both the KB (represented by detection models) and the relevant information databases (e.g., the ones used to store the user feedbacks) as information sources, which can be updated during the fusion process. Finally, the interaction with the final user allows for understanding situations, recognizing emerging trends, and undertaking decisions and countermeasures.

From the application point of view, the augmented surveillance paradigm could be implemented by an integrated framework addressing surveillance-related information at different levels; its PSIM capabilities should include

■ The integration and interfacing with several heterogeneous sensing platforms, in such a way to solve the problem of the preliminary data processing
■ The detection of relevant events occurring in all the monitored locations
■ The warning and alarm reporting to operators in control centers, in order to support the emergency procedures and/or to activate automatic reactions

Since the PSIM may generate a large amount of alarms, which could overwhelm the personnel in charge of reacting to suspicious events, event correlation capabilities need to be integrated into the framework in order to lower the FAR and to improve threat detection reliability. The problem of event correlation has been largely studied in the scientific literature, and a wide class of potential solutions have been defined. Nevertheless, those results have been widely studied and applied to domains not related to physical security, for example, to develop intrusion detection in computer networks. In physical security applications, the capabilities of legacy systems are very limited in data analysis and interpretation and hence in real-time prevention and reaction. The lack of advanced approaches in PSIM may be motivated by the still missing light and efficient approaches to the recognition of evolving situations based on a priori knowledge of threat patterns, to be easily updated by the human operators: such an objective is far from being trivial to achieve. However, it is increasingly important to achieve early warning and SA in domains where a large number of dynamic objects are engaged in complex spatial–temporal relations.

In the assumptions that threat scenarios can be decomposed in a set of basic steps executed in a predictable sequence, model-based logical, spatial, and temporal correlation of detector outputs can be used to recognize event patterns indicating possible threats. Ideally, in order to recognize (partially) unknown threats, the detection engine should be resilient to human faults in scenario modeling and sensor faults in detecting events. One possibility that has been recently researched is to consider heuristics like similarity analysis with known event patterns (see, e.g., Refs. [11] and [24]). Finally, advanced detection capabilities should be integrated in PSIM systems in order to effectively support human operators in responding to threats, also in case of strategic distributed attacks [25].

References

1. Abidi, B. R., N. R. Aragam, Y. Yao, M. A. Abidi. 2008. Survey and analysis of multimodal sensor planning and integration for wide area surveillance. *ACM Computing Survey*, 41(1), Article 7, December 2008.
2. Aghajan, H., A. Cavallaro. 2009. *Multi-Camera Networks: Concepts and Applications*. Elsevier, Burlington, MA, 2009.
3. Akita, R. M. 2002. User based data fusion approaches. In *Proceedings of the International Conference of Information Fusion*, Annapolis, MD, pp. 1457–1462, July 2002.

4. Atrey, P. K., M. A. Hossain, A. El-Saddik, M. S. Kankanhalli. 2010. Multimodal fusion for multimedia analysis: A survey. *Springer Multimedia Systems Journal*, 16(6): 345–379.

5. Atrey, P. K., M. S. Kankanhalli, R. Jain. 2006. Information assimilation framework for event detection in multimedia surveillance systems. *Springer/ACM Multimedia Systems Journal*, 12(3): 239–253.

6. Bedworth, M., J. O'Brien. 2000. The omnibus model: A new model for data fusion. *Aerospace and Electronics Systems Magazine*, 15(4): 30–36.

7. Bisantz, A. M., R. Finger, Y. Seong, J. Llinas. 1999. Human performance and data fusion based decision aids. In *Proceedings of the International Conference of Information Fusion*, Sunnyvale, CA, July 6–8, 1999.

8. Blasch, E. 2006. Level 5 (User Refinement) issues supporting information fusion management. In *Proceedings of Information Fusion*, Florence, Italy, July 10–13, 2006.

9. Blasch, E., S. Plano. 2002. JDL level 5 fusion model "user refinements" issues and applications in group tracking. *SPIE Aerosense*, 4729: 270–279.

10. Blasch, E., S. Plano. 2003. Level 5: User refinements to aid the fusion process. In *Proceedings Multisensor, Multisource Information fusion: Archetetures, Algorithms, and Applications*, Orlando, FL pp. 288–297, April 1, 2003.

11. Bocchetti, G., F. Flammini, C. Pragliola, A. Pappalardo. 2009. Dependable integrated surveillance systems for the physical security of metro railways. In *IEEE Proceedings of the Third ACM/IEEE International Conference on Distributed Smart Cameras (ICDSC 2009)*, Como, Italy, August 30–September 2, 2009, pp. 1–7.

12. Bossé, E., A. Guitouni, P. Valin. 2006. An essay to characterise information fusion system. In *Proceedings of the International Conference of Information Fusion*, Florence, Italy, pp. 1–7, 2006.

13. Candamo, J., M. Shreve, D. B. Goldgof, D. B. Sapper, R. Kasturi. 2010. Understanding transit scenes: A survey on human behavior-recognition algorithms. *IEEE Transactions on Intelligent Transportation Systems*, 11(1): 206–224. http://www.cse.usf.edu/~mshreve/publications/ITS.pdf

14. Ciardelli, L., L. Bixio, M. Ottonello, M. Cesena, C. S. Regazzoni. 2009. Multi-sensor cognitive based approach to critical infrastructure protection. In *Third International Conference on Safety and Security Engineering (SAFE 2009)*, Rome, Italy, pp. 71–81, July 1–3, 2009.

15. Cucchiara, R. 2005. Multimedia surveillance systems. In *Proceedings of ACM International Workshop on Video Surveillance and Sensor Networks*, Singapore, pp. 3–10, November 2005.

16. Cuppens, F., A. Miege. 2002. Alert correlation in a cooperative intrusion detection framework. In *IEEE Symposium on Security and Privacy*, Oakland, CA, pp. 202–215.

17. Dasarathy, B. V. 1994. *Decision Fusion*. IEEE Computer Society Press, Los Alamitos, CA.

18. Dasarathy, B. V. 2000. More the merrier... or is it?—Sensor suite augmentation benefits assessment. In *Proceedings of the Third International Conference on Information Fusion (Fusion 2000)*, Vol. 2. IEEE, Paris, France, July 10–13, 2000, WEC3/20–WEC3/25.

19. Dasarathy, B. V. 2001. Information fusion—What, where, why, when, and how? *Information Fusion*, 2(2): 75–76.

20. Endsley, M. R. 1995. Toward a theory of situation awareness in dynamic systems. *Human Factors*, 37(1): 32–64.

21. Endsley, M. R. 2000. Theoretical underpinnings of situation awareness: A critical review. M. R. Endsley, D. J. Garland (Eds.). *Situation Awareness Analysis and Measurement*. Lawrence Erlbaum Associates, Mahwah, NJ.

22. Esteban, J., A. Starr, R. Willetts, P. Hannah, P. Bryanston-Cross. 2005. A review of data fusion models and architectures: Towards engineering guidelines. *Neural Computing and Applications*, 14(4): 273–281.

23. Fernandez, C., P. Baiget, F. X. Roca, J. Gonzalez. 2011. Determining the best suited semantic events for cognitive surveillance. *Expert Systems with Applications*, 38(4): 4068–4079.

24. Flammini, F., A. Pappalardo, C. Pragliola, V. Vittorini. 2011. A robust approach for on-line and off-line threat detection based on event tree similarity analysis. In *Eighth IEEE International Conference on Advanced Video and Signal-Based Surveillance (AVSS'11)*, Klagenfurt, Austria, August 30–September 2, 2011, pp. 414–419.

25. Flammini, F., N. Mazzocca, A. Pappalardo, C. Pragliola, V. Vittorini. 2011. Augmenting surveillance system capabilities by exploiting event correlation and distributed attack detection. In *Proceedings of 2011 International Workshop on Security and Cognitive Informatics for Homeland Defence* (SeCIHD'11), co-located with ARES'11, Springer LNCS 6908, August 22–26, 2011, pp. 191–204.

26. Gerosa, L., G. Valenzise, F. Antonacci, M. Tagliasacchi, A. Sarti. 2007. Scream and gunshot detection in noisy environments. In *EURASIP*, Poznan, Poland, pp. 1216–1220, September 3–7, 2007.

27. Goldgof, D. B., D. Sapper, J. Candamo, M. Shreve. 2009. Evaluation of smart video for transit event detection. Project #BD549–49, FINAL REPORT. http://www.nctr.usf.edu/pdf/77807.pdf (accessed March 6, 2012).

28. Gouaillier, V., A. Fleurant. 2009. Intelligent video surveillance: Promises and challenges. Technological and Commercial Intelligence Report, March 2009.

29. Hall, B. V., S. A. H. McMullen. 2004. *Mathematical Techniques in Multisensor Data Fusion.* Artech House, Northwood, MA.

30. Hall, D., B. D. Hellar, M. McNeese, J. Llinas. 2007. Assessing the JDL model: A survey and analysis of decision and cognitive process models and comparison with the JDL model. In *Proceedings of the National Symposium on Sensor Data Fusion (NSSDF)*, June 2007.

31. Hall, D., J. Llinas. 2001. *Handbook of Multisensor Data Fusion.* CSC Press LLC, Boca Raton, FL.

32. Harris, C. J., A. Bailey, T. J. Dodd. 1998. Multi-sensor data fusion in defence and aerospace. *The Aeronautical Journal*, 102(1015): 229–244.

33. Honovich, J. 2009. Security manager's guide to video surveillance. Version 3.0. IPVideoMarket.info (accessed August 2009).

34. Jing-Ying, C., H.-H. Liao, L.-G. Che. 2010. Localized detection of abandoned luggage. *EURASIP Journal on Advances in Signal Processing*, 2010, Article ID 675784.

35. Kalgaonkar, L., P. Smaragdis, B. Raj. 2007. Sensor and data systems, audio-assisted cameras and acoustic doppler sensors. In *Proceedings of IEEE Computer Society Conference on Computer Vision and Pattern Recognition (CVPR 2007)*, Minneapolis, MN, pp. 1–2.

36. Kim, T. K., S. U. Lee, H. J. Lee, S. C. Kee, S. R. Kim. 2002. Integrated approach of multiple face detection for video surveillance. In *Proceedings of the International Conference of Pattern Recognition (ICPR2002)*, Vol. 2, Quebec City, Canada, pp. 394–397.

37. Kirianaki, N. V., S. Y. Yurish, N. O. Shpak, V. P. Deynega. 2002. *Data Acquisition and Signal Processing for Smart Sensors*, 1st edn. John Wiley & Sons, Ltd., Chichester, U.K.

38. Kokar, M. M., M. D. Bedworth, K. B. Frankel. 2000. A reference model for data fusion systems. In *Proceedings of SPIE Conference on Sensor Fusion: Architectures, Algorithms, and Applications, IV*, Orlando, FL, pp. 191–202.

39. Krausz, B., C. Bauckhage. 2011. Automatic detection of dangerous motion behavior in human crowds. In *Proceedings of IEEE International Conference on Advanced Video and Signal-Based Surveillance (AVSS 2011)*, Klagenfurt, Austria, pp. 224–229.

40. Makris, D., T. Ellis, J. Black. 2008. Intelligent visual surveillance: Towards cognitive vision systems. *The Open Cybernetics and Systemics Journal*, 2: 219–229.

41. Martin, P. T., Y. Feng, X. Wang. 2003. Detector technology evaluation. http://www.mountain-plains. org/pubs/pdf/MPC03–154.pdf (accessed March 6, 2012).

42. Nilsson, M. 2007. Human decision making and information fusion: Extending the concept of decision support. Technical Report HS-IKI-TR-07–002, *Workshop on Information Technology*, Halmstad University, Sweden, 2007.

43. Nilsson, M., J. V. Laere, T. Susi, T. Ziemke. 2012. Information fusion in practice: A distributed cognition perspective on the active role of users. *Information Fusion*, 13(1): 60–78, ISSN 1566–2535, 10.1016/j.inffus.2011.01.005.

44. Nilsson, M., T. Ziemke. 2006. Rethinking level 5: Distributed cognition and information fusion. In *Proceedings of the International conference of Information Fusion*, Florence, Italy, July 2006.

45. Nilsson, M., T. Ziemke. 2007. Information fusion: A decision support perspective. In *Proceedings of the 10th International Conference on Information Fusion*, Québec, Canada, 9–12 July, 2007.

46. Nilsson, M. 2008. Mind the gap: Human decision making and information fusion. Licentiate Thesis, Örebro University, Sweden.

47. Ntalampiras, S. 2012. Audio surveillance. In *Critical Infrastructure Security: Assessment, Prevention, Detection, Response*, WIT Press, Southhampton, U.K., pp. 191–205.

48. Ntalampiras, S., I. Potamitis, N. Fakotakis. 2009. An adaptive framework for acoustic monitoring of potential hazards. In *EURASIP Journal on Audio, Speech and Music Processing*, 2009, Article no 13.

49. Ntalampiras, S., I. Potamitis, N. Fakotakis. 2009. On acoustic surveillance of hazardous situations. In *International Conference on Acoustics, Speech and Signal Processing (ICASSP'09)*, Taiwan, Taipei, April 19–24, pp. 165–168, 2009.

50. Prati, A., R. Vezzani, L. Benini, E. Farella, P. Zappi. 2005. An integrated multimodal sensor network for video surveillance. In *Proceedings of the Third ACM International Workshop on Video Surveillance & Sensor Networks (VSSN05)*, Singapore, November 6–11, pp. 95–102, 2005.

51. PSIM Deployment Statistics. Report published on November 15, 2011 available on http://ipvideomarket.info

52. Qu, Y., T. Wang, Z. Zhu. 2009. Remote audio/video acquisition for human signature detection. In *IEEE Computer Society Conference on Computer Vision and Pattern Recognition*, Miami, FL, pp. 66–71, 2009.

53. Rouas, J.-L., J. Louradour, S. Ambellouis. 2006. Audio events detection in public transport vehicle. In *IEEE Intelligent Transportation Systems Conference*, Toronto, Canada, pp. 733–738, September 2006.

54. Rousseau, R., R. Breton. 2004. The M-OODA loop: A model incorporating control functions and teamwork in the OODA loop. In *Proceedings of the Command and Control Research Symposium*, San Diego, CA, pp. 15–17.

55. Spencer, B. F. Jr., M. E. Ruiz-Sandoval, N. Kurata. 2004. Smart sensing technology: Opportunities and challenges. *Journal of Structural Control and Health Monitoring*, 11(4): 349–368.

56. St. John, M., M. R. Risser. 2009. Sustaining vigilance by activating a secondary task when inattention is detected. In *Proceedings of the Human Factors and Ergonomics Society 53rd Annual Meeting*, Vol. 53, San Antonio, TX, pp. 155–159.

57. Starzyk, W., F. Z. Qureshi. 2011. Multi-tasking smart cameras for intelligent video surveillance systems. In *Proceedings of International Conference on Advanced Video and Signal-Based Surveillance (AVSS 2011)*, Klagenfurt, Austria, pp. 154–159.

58. Steinberg, A. N., C. L. Bowman. 2001. Revisions to the JDL data fusion model. D. Hall, J. Llinas (Eds.). *Handbook of Multisensor Data Fusion*. Boca Raton, FL, CRC Press LLC.

59. Talantzis, F., P. Aristodemos, P. C. Lazaros. 2006. Real time audio-visual person tracking. In *IEEE International Workshop on Multimedia Signal Processing*, pp. 243–247, 2006.

60. Taymanov, R., K. Sapozhnikova. 2009. Problems of terminology in the field of measuring instruments with elements of artificial intelligence, *Sensors and Transducers*, 102(3): 51–61.

61. Tien, J. M. 2003. Toward a decision informatics paradigm: A real-time, information-based approach to decision making. *IEEE Transactions on systems, man and cybernetics*, Part C. 33(1): 102–113.

62. Vin, L. J. et al. 2008. Information fusion for decision support in manufacturing: Studies from the defense sector. *International Journal of Advanced Manufacturing Technology*, 35(9–10): 908–915.

63. Wickens, C., S. Dixon. 2007. The benefits of imperfect diagnostic automation: A synthesis of the literature. *Theoretical Issues in Ergonomics Science*, 8(3): 201–212.

64. Yurish, S. Y. 2010. Sensors: Smart vs. intelligent. Editorial article. *Sensors and Transducers Journal*, 114(3): I–VI.

65. Zhan, B., D. N. Monekosso, P. Remagnino, S. Velastin, L.-Q. Xu. 2008. Crowd analysis: A survey. *Machine Vision and Applications*, 19(5–6): 345–357.

66. Zhu, Z., T. S. Huang. 2007. *Multimodal Surveillance: Sensors, Algorithms and Systems*. Artech House Publisher, Boston, MA.

67. Zhu, Z., W. Li, G. Wolberg. 2005. Integrating LDV audio and IR video for remote multimodal surveillance. *IEEE Computer Society Conference on Computer Vision and Pattern Recognition*, Vol. 3, San Diego, CA, pp.10.

Chapter 9

Pervasive Surveillance System Management

Allaa R. Hilal and Otman A. Basir

Contents

The aim of this chapter is to provide an introduction to pervasive surveillance systems and discuss the needs and challenges of designing an intelligent sensor management framework for such systems. The chapter is organized as follows: a brief introduction of pervasive surveillance and its applications is given in Section 9.1. In Section 9.2, sensor management (SM), its properties, and challenges are discussed. Section 9.3 describes the different organizational architectures used to address the SM problem. Section 9.4 surveys four popular problem-solving strategies for SM. Current commercial products, as well as future research trends and directions, are summarized in Section 9.5. Finally, Section 9.6 provides some concluding remarks of the chapter.

9.1 Introduction

Recent world events have amplified the need for enhanced security against nature and man-made threats. Recognizing that modern society faces new types of threats, the concept of homeland security has endured major transformation to be able to address attacks that are directed to civilians and infrastructure. As a result, our security measurements have to go through a paradigm shift from being centralized and investigative to being distributed and preventative. This global need has instigated significant research efforts, both academic and industrial, so as to bring about solutions that can effectively address today's security threats.

Traditional surveillance systems have been used as an integral component in addressing a wide range of security threats. From a security standpoint, surveillance is the process of monitoring and interpreting the behavior of objects within a volume of interest (VOI) to construct a complete picture of the situation [1]. It involves reliable data collection and analysis, followed by a rapid dissemination of the findings. These findings are used to direct proper resources to investigate the event so as to address it and to develop strategies for preventing such events from happening in the future. Throughout the last decade, digital surveillance systems have provided the infrastructure to collect, store, and distribute data while leaving the task of threat detection exclusively to security experts. Human monitoring and analysis of surveillance data is a labor-intensive chore. The ability to hold attention and to react to rarely occurring events is extremely demanding task. Furthermore, this task is prone to human errors due to lapses in attention and subjectivity of the human decision making.

The nature, complexity, extent, and the spread of the security threats our society has been witnessing in the recent years have made it clear that smart surveillance constitutes the most effective cure as it presents a conducive framework for seamless interaction between preventative capabilities and investigative protocols [1,2]. Smart surveillance adopts automatic data analysis technologies to transform system observations into a situation-aware knowledge that is actionable [3]. However, it should be noted that smart surveillance systems are decision support systems; thus, the final decision maker must be a security expert.

The need for smart surveillance systems is equally recognized in homeland security, as well as in applications such as public safety, health monitoring, and disaster area monitoring, just to name a few. These safety-critical applications tend to spread over large geographical areas and, hence, may require remote monitoring. To meet the challenges of all these applications, a surveillance system must exhibit capabilities such as heterogeneous and self-organized behavior, multimodal data and information fusion, and collaborative resources control and management. Thus, smart surveillance systems must possess pervasive capabilities.

9.1.1 Pervasive Surveillance Systems

Latest advancements in wireless communications and electronics have enabled the development of low-cost, low-power multifunctional sensors that exploit a physical phenomenon to provide data about the state of the environment. These tiny resourceful sensors have instigated the concept of wireless sensor networks (WSNs) [4–7]. A WSN is a collection of spatially distributed autonomous sensor nodes that communicate with each other by forming a multi-hop radio network while maintaining connectivity in a decentralized manner to cooperatively monitor physical or environmental conditions, for example, temperature, sound, pressure, and/or motion [8].

Under the homeland security umbrella lies many applications that are mission-critical, time-sensitive, and distributed over large geographical areas; crisis management, border control, territory control, transportation, and critical infrastructure security, to name a few. Such applications require decentralized intelligent solutions. Hence, the distributed capabilities as well as the increased sophistication of the sensor nodes made WSNs a suitable match for homeland security applications.

Pervasive systems are the next generation of distributed sensor networks. They are composed of a heterogeneous collection of fixed and mobile sensor nodes, in which the nodes are small and often embedded as part of a larger system. Pervasive surveillance can be defined as the active monitoring of targets as they move through a large monitored area using a network of sensors [9]. Each individual sensor has a partial view of the environment, but collectively the network monitors the entire VOI. Pervasive surveillance systems monitor ongoing and emerging patterns relevant to abnormal behavior.

Pervasive surveillance systems deal with situations that are characterized by high density of targets, stochastic environments, and dynamic threats, which results in large amounts of data to be processed. This has pushed the information acquisition problem far from what can be handled by a single sensor. Hence, pervasive surveillance systems need to exhibit capabilities such as collaborative control, heterogeneity, self-organized behavior, multimodal data, and information fusion to address the system requirements. These capabilities provide additional challenges and complexities in designing pervasive surveillance systems. As a result, the research community dedicated great efforts in the development of intelligent SM approaches to increase the effective utilization of the sensor resources.

9.1.2 Pervasive Surveillance Applications

Smart pervasive surveillance systems were first used by military forces in the homeland defense applications. The homeland security domain was the first to follow the footsteps of the military applications in adapting such systems. To date, the homeland defense and homeland security

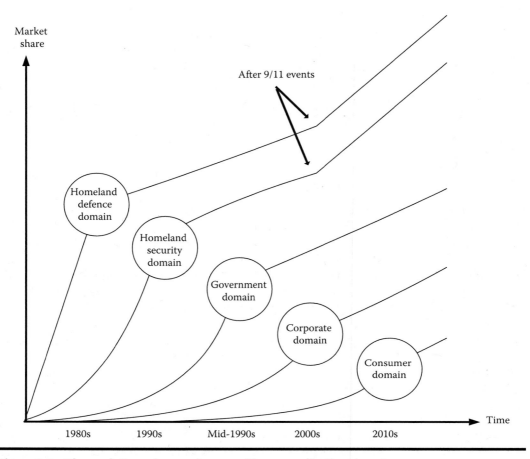

Figure 9.1   The evolution of pervasive surveillance application domain.

applications together form the majority share of the pervasive surveillance market. However, the last decade has witnessed the emergence of many smart surveillance applications. As pervasive systems become an affordable technology, different application domains have originated, as shown in Figure 9.1. For smart sensor applications, the open world market for nonmilitary sensors was expected to grow from U.S. $32.5 billion in 1998 to U.S. $50.6 billion in 2008 [10].

Figure 9.2 shows a basic categorization of pervasive surveillance applications. The largest application domain is the homeland defense domain, which includes battlefield monitoring, army bases security, and air force and navy applications surveillance, just to name a few. After the end of the cold war, homeland security paradigm started being formulated as a separate national defense [11]. Applications like crisis management, border security, and territory control are a suitable match for the use of pervasive surveillance. Subsequent to the 9/11 events, both the homeland defense and the homeland security domains have increasingly invested in the development and deployment of smart pervasive surveillance systems to address emerging asymmetric threats [11]. In addition to homeland security programs that are designed to strengthen security along national borders, the growth of this domain is further fueled by the increased concern over the effects of "crime on economy" [12]. In the mid-1990s, government applications such as environmental monitoring, historic sites and artifacts monitoring, and health monitoring have gained rapid popularity.

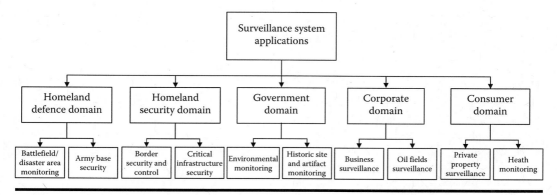

Figure 9.2 **Classification of the pervasive surveillance applications according to the application domains.**

In the 2000s, big corporations, such as oil and gas companies, have started to demonstrate interest in pervasive surveillance systems to enhance security of their businesses. Eventually, the advancement in sensor technology has led smart surveillance to be affordable enough to be used for consumer and personal applications. Although these applications still have small market share, there are numerous areas where smart surveillance systems can play an important role in our lives, for instance, pervasive surveillance of private properties is an emerging field of applications. Wireless operators in North America have already started to provide smart pervasive surveillance services in the form of home security systems.

9.2 Sensor Management

Homeland security applications may use hundreds, even thousands, of sensor nodes forming large sensor networks. Sensor networks need intelligent SM systems to coordinate the large number of sensor nodes and the large volume of data to produce relevant information that can assist in the process of decision making. In general, the world model of a multi-sensor system is only as good as the sensors that perceive it and the intelligence that process it. Single-sensor systems provide partial information of the state of the environment. To provide a global view of the surrounding environment, the network sensors have to cooperate and form a multi-sensor system. Data fusion techniques are employed to combine related data from the different network sensors to obtain better perception of the environment. This perception is then synthesized into situation awareness. The goal of a multi-sensor system is to provide a synergistic effect that enhances the quality and availability of information about the state of the VOI beyond that which would be acquired solely from one sensor.

SM refers to the process that controls and coordinates the use of the sensors in a manner that synergistically maximizes the success rate of the system in achieving its missions. The sensor manager is expected to take decisions that derive the performance of the whole system to reach its objectives. Efficient SM can significantly enhance the process of information gathering by automatically allocating, controlling, and coordinating the sensing resources [13]. SM aims to assess the situation timely, reliably, and accurately in order to collect the most complete, relevant, and accurate data from a dynamic scene. The criticality of homeland security makes intelligent management of sensory systems a necessity due to the need to deal with the high time sensitivity, large amount of information, and limited resources in these applications. However, efficient management of multi-sensor systems is a challenging task due to the spatially distributed nature of the network and the scarcity of the energy and processing resources.

9.2.1 Sensor Management and Data Fusion

Data fusion is the integration of information from multiple sources to produce the most specific and unified data about an entry. In other words, data fusion techniques combine measurements from multiple sensors, and related information from associated databases, to achieve improved accuracy data over that achieved by the use of a single sensor. As such, data fusion should be coupled with techniques for proactive or reactive planning and management of system resources, such as sensors and sensor platforms, in order to make best use of these assets [14,15]. To achieve that, SM can aid the information gathering and fusion processes by automatically allocating, controlling, and coordinating sensing and processing resources to synergetically achieve better situation awareness.

Data fusion researchers are well aware of the correlation between SM and data fusion concepts. The most popular data fusion processing model, Joint Directors of Laboratories (JDL), introduces SM as a part of the data fusion process [16], as shown in Figure 9.3. The JDL model differentiates the fusion functions into various levels; this provides a useful distinction among data fusion processes. The work in [17] has extended the functionality of the JDL data fusion model to address the SM problem in the process refinement level (level 4). The definitions of the revised JDL model levels are as follows:

- *Level 0 sub-object assessment*: Estimation and prediction of object-observable states on the basis of pixel/signal-level data association and characterization
- *Level 1 object assessment*: Estimation and prediction of entity states on the basis of inferences from observations
- *Level 2 situation assessment*: Estimation and prediction of entity states on the basis of inferred relations among entities

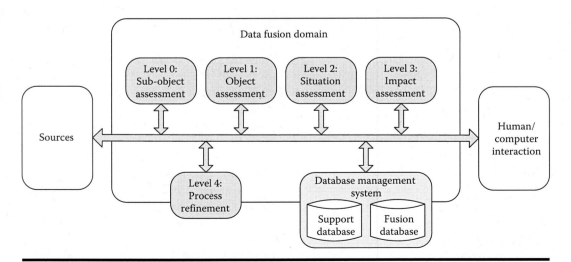

Figure 9.3 The Revised JDL Data Fusion Model. (From Steinberg, A.N. et al., *Proc. SPIE*, 3719(1), 430–441, 1999.)

- *Level 3 impact assessment*: Estimation and prediction of effects on situations of planned or estimated/predicted actions by the participants (e.g., assessing susceptibilities and vulnerabilities to predicted threat actions)
- *Level 4 process refinement (an element of SM)*: Adaptive data acquisition and processing to support mission objectives

SM provides information feedback from data fusion process to affect the sensor operations, thus representing the data fusion process as a closed-loop feedback structure [14]. The SM on level 4 uses information from levels 0 to 3 to plan future sensor actions, hence improving the data collection process. Timeliness of the management feedback is a necessary requirement for fast adaptation to environment changes. That is to say, a prompt decision on sensor functions has to be made before a change in the tactical situation has made such a decision obsolete [14]. However, since SM problem is an exhaustive one, the revised JDL data fusion model does not offer a complete solution for such complicated task. Similarly, other data fusion models, for example, DDF [18], omnibus [19], and the perceptual reasoning [20], have attempted to embed the SM into their models.

9.2.2 Sensor Management Frameworks

To address the challenges of SM, numerous researchers have directed their efforts into the development of SM framework (SMF). An SMF is the organizational control system, which seeks to manage and coordinate the use of sensing resources in a manner that improves the process of situation awareness, synergistically [21]. An SMF has to handle the overwhelming amount of information collected and adapt to the highly dynamic environments under network and system limitations. The collective performance of all the sensors dictates the performance of the whole system. Accordingly, SMF determines the overall performance and capabilities of the system.

An SMF aspires to provide an optimum sensor configuration based on predicted system performance [22]. The SMF must allocate the available sensors to the tasks that maximize the effectiveness of the whole sensing process while reducing the workload on the human operator. Moreover, SMF should result in a highly sensitive and self-calibrating system that compensates for sensor nonlinearities, thus, maximizing the information acquisition process. Furthermore, SMF manages the sensor network to rationalize the power consumption and the data link usage to increase the systems lifetime and throughput. Hence, SMFs aim to provide an intelligent system control that leads to low-cost, high-resolution sensor data and high-reasoning operations. Many research projects have proposed various SMF as a stand-alone approach to address the SM problem [13,23,24]. However, the performance comparison between these SMFs is a difficult task due to the lack of unified range of nonfunctional merits that are strived for in the design of the SMF.

9.2.3 SMF Nonfunctional Merits

The SMF nonfunctional merits are the desirable features that can characterize the system. These features have to be accounted for in the different design phases of the SMF system. Figure 9.4 offers a basic taxonomy for the SMF nonfunctional merits. The taxonomy is based on the design concept in which such merits are incorporated into the system. The design process of an SMF can be divided into three main categories: design for architecture, design for development, and design for deployment.

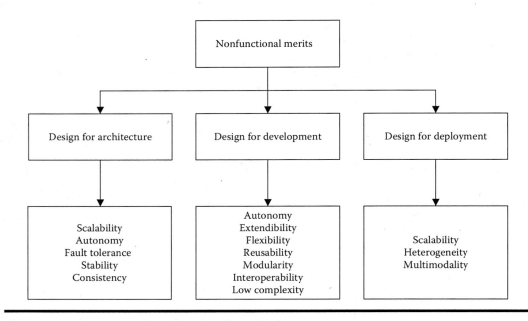

Figure 9.4   The proposed nonfunctional merits taxonomy.

The design for architecture is a phase where the specification of the system topology and communications network are identified and defined. On the other hand, the design for development is a phase related to the implementation issues and the choice of the network protocols and the software development. Finally, the design for deployment is for the specification of the system components, the functional organization, and the configuration. To establish a unified perception of the meaning of each characteristic, the following lists the different nonfunctional merits and their definitions:

■ *Scalability* is a desirable property of a system, a network, or a process, which indicates its ability to either handle growing amounts of work in a graceful manner or to be readily expanded. It is an important feature in homeland security applications due to the size and scope of such systems. From a network point of view, a scalable system has to be well designed to take into consideration the implications of the increasing number of sensors. Such implications can be in the form of increased power consumption and communication overhead due to congestion and collision. Larger number of sensors means increased management complexity, as well as a more complex programming model. Other issues like efficiency, security, throughput, and latency between nodes are trade-offs on the size of the system.

■ *Autonomy* is having the power of self-governance. An autonomous agent is an agent that can perform desired tasks in unstructured environments without continuous human guidance. Autonomy is a new trend used in homeland security applications as a result of the need to address emerging types of threats. Autonomous agents collaborate by deploying a communication network between them. Such network is used for information passing and aggregation, localization, and synchronization, to name a few.

■ *Fault tolerance* is the property that enables a system to continue operating properly in the event of the failure of some of its components. Homeland security applications have to be highly fault tolerant due to their safety-critical nature. One of the basic ways to achieve fault tolerance in networking is through redundancy; however, issues like cost, efficiency, and system utilization have to be taken into consideration.

■ *Stability* is the property of the system to operate with consistent performance over time with no changes added to the system. It is vital for homeland security applications to be stable because they are expected to run with consistent performance for long periods of time. Design for stability comes early on in the design for architecture phase. It also affects the choices of the network hardware as well as the network protocols deployed.

■ *Consistency* is the property of information and decisions to be compatible with the system information reservoirs and system objectives and goals. In applications such as homeland security, the integrity of the information is essential to the performance of the system since inaccurate information may result in failure to detect threats. Sensor measurements are collected and aggregated over the network. Reliable communication, time synchronization, as well as localization are important aspects to guarantee the integrity and correctness of information.

■ *Extendibility* is a system design principle where the implementation takes into consideration future growth. It is a systemic measure of the ability to extend a system and the level of effort required to implement the extension. System extendability is considered in the design for development phase. It is a desirable feature from the software design point of view for the homeland security applications since the nature of possible threats are ever changing. In recent years, the importance of extendable systems became more apparent as more functionalities may be added to the systems to address new types of threats.

■ *Flexibility* is the ability of a system to respond to potential internal or external changes in a timely and cost-effective manner. Flexibility is considered in the design for development phase, and it is an advantageous feature from the software design point of view to incorporate in the homeland security applications due to the dynamic nature of their environment. Wireless networks have the advantage of being flexible systems that adapt to environmental changes by route discovery and network reconfiguration.

■ *Reusability* is the property that indicates that the majority of the objects can be reused for various kinds of applications. Reusability is considered in the design for development phase. From the software design point of view, reusability is a desirable feature for the homeland security applications, especially in the private sector, because it may save a significant amount of time and money in developing other applications.

■ *Modularity* is an approach that subdivides a system into smaller parts, that is, modules, that can be independently created and then used in different systems to drive multiple functionalities. Besides reduction in cost, due to less customization and high flexibility in design, modularity offers benefits such as augmentation and exclusion. Modularity is a desirable feature from the software design point of view and also provides good programming practice. Although, modularity is not a necessity in the design of homeland security applications, it can become very beneficial in such applications due to their need to change and adapt to face the ever-changing threat.

■ *Interoperability* is a property referring to the ability of diverse systems to work together. In other words, it is the ability of systems to provide services to and accept services from other systems and to use the services exchanged to enable them to operate effectively together. The lack of interoperability can be a consequence of a lack of attention to standardization during the design of a program. Similar to modularity and reusability, interoperability is a desired feature but not a necessity in the development of homeland security applications.

- *Low complexity* is the property that is concerned with the amount of resources required to run algorithms. Due to the nature of homeland security applications, efficient algorithms need to be used to reduce the power consumption of the battery-operated sensor nodes as well as the processing time.
- *Heterogeneity* is the property of the system to support static and mobile sensors. Static sensors are the most popular type of sensors in the homeland security applications. However, the deployment of mobile sensors has received increased attention in recent years. Nevertheless, mobility adds new challenges from network points of view, such as localization, link breakage, handoff management, routing, and tunneling, to name a few.
- *Multimodality* is the property of the system to support the different types of sensors, that is, infrared, ultrasound, and video. Homeland security applications usually utilize variety of sensors to best capture the scene in the VOI. The ability of different sensors to communicate will increase the accuracy for the data fusion process; however, issues like compatibility and standardization should be taken into consideration.
- *Other merits* like availability, reliability, and support of wide range of applications.

9.2.4 SMF Functional Capabilities

SMF functional capabilities are the set of task an SMF can perform to control and manage the sensory system. This work discusses the proposed SMF functional capabilities in the literature and divides them into three main categories: sensor management, network management, and system management, as shown in Figure 9.5.

9.2.4.1 Sensor Management Tasks

Sensor management tasks are the set of tasks that manage the operation of each sensor individually. Sensor management tasks are processed locally by each sensor and lead to a decision that is carried out only by that sensor. Since sensors are autonomous devices that interact directly with the environment, the SMF has to address the following challenges:

- *Managing limited capabilities*: The SMF on the sensor level has to address the limited individual sensor capabilities. Each sensor has to minimize its power consumption, usage of memory, and cache and choose an operation mode suitable to its current resources.
- *Managing limited processing*: The SMF has to address the trade-off between the onboard processing on the sensor and transmitting the raw sensed data to a fusion node for further processing.

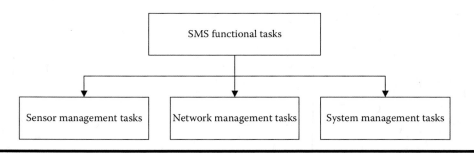

Figure 9.5 SMF functional properties categorization.

■ *Managing node failure*: Sensor nodes are cheap, small in size sensing, processing, and communicating units that are highly prone to failure. Each sensor node has to cope with its individual sensor failure that may result due to hardware limitations, software limitation, or external environmental influence.

9.2.4.2 Network Management Tasks

A WSN consists of a large number of spatially distributed autonomous sensor nodes that communicate with each other by forming a multi-hop radio network while maintaining connectivity in a decentralized manner. These properties of sensor networks lead to the emergence of a new set of responsibilities of the SMF to manage such a network. The network management tasks are the set of tasks that are responsible for managing the connectivity between the sensor nodes and the control center. The SMF must be designed to face these system challenges:

■ *Handling dynamic environments*: The SMF has to be able to cope with highly dynamic and uncertain environments. Hence, there is a need for the SMF to be highly adaptable to the fast unpredictable changes in the environment.
■ *Managing communication*: Due to the absence of global identification in sensor networks, the network management level in the SMF has to allow for different identification schemes.
■ *Performing information relay*: Sensor networks are multi-hop networks, where each node acts as both a host and a router; thus, appropriate protocols need to manage multi-hop communication. Moreover, due to the instability of the wireless link, the sensor network has to be able to quickly recover from link failures, node failures, and path breakages. Furthermore, the SMF has to provide information relay reliability.
■ *Managing insufficient resources*: Due to the broadcast nature of WSNs, bandwidth is a scarce resource that needs to be responsibly used. The limited caching of the sensor nodes is another example of a scarce resource that may affect the network performance.
■ *Handling random deployment*: The random deployment of WSN puts additional requirements on the sensor network protocols and algorithms to be self-organizing and provide distributed capabilities. Since the exact location of a particular phenomenon is unknown, distributed sensing leads to larger coverage and closer placement to the phenomenon.

9.2.4.3 System Management Tasks

After managing the framework on the sensor and the network level, many challenges still need to be handled by the SMF to manage and improve the understanding of the system on the global worldview. The SMF has to perform various tasks to handle the following system requirement:

■ *Enhance data fusion*: The SMF on a system level aims to improve the information data fusion capabilities. This can be achieved by using feedback from the data fusion algorithm to redirect the sensing resources to gather relevant data about a specific phenomenon.
■ *Task allocation*: Task allocation is the problem of allocating a set of sensor nodes to a set of sensing tasks. Task allocation has been intensively studied in literature [25,26].
■ *Cooperation*: In multi-sensor systems, the cooperation of the sensors means the harmonization by effectively unifying the information obtained from each sensor [27]. It is a joint or collaborative behavior that is directed toward improving situation awareness by sharing

information among distributed sensing resources [28]. In surveillance applications, there are two primary cooperative functions: cueing and handoff [29,30].

■ *Scheduling*: Since the lifetime of a battery directly impacts the lifetime of sensor networks, one of the key considerations in the design of sensor networks is the ability to maximize battery lifetime. Task scheduling aims to maximize the lifetime of the sensing network by minimizing energy consumption while fulfilling its requirements.

■ *Conflict detection and resolution*: Due to the distributed nature of sensor networks, simultaneous accessing of a shared resource by different sensors has to be efficiently managed and coordinated. Furthermore, if two or more sensors provide conflicting data, the SMF had to detect this inconsistency and take the necessary actions to resolve it.

■ *Control and coordination*: Control and coordination are the tasks responsible of managing and organizing the needs of the SM architecture. The main role of control and coordination is to generate actions based on the state of the resources, the sensing information, and the goals of the architecture.

■ *Synchronization*: Time synchronization is a critical piece of infrastructure for any distributed system. Distributed WSNs make particularly extensive use of synchronized time to integrate data, to localize objects, to distribute control commands, or to suppress redundant messages and information [31]. Thus, the SMF has to provide a synchronization mechanism that has unique requirements in the scope, lifetime, and precision of the synchronization achieved, as well as the time and energy required to achieve it.

■ *Selective perception*: Due to the overwhelming amount of information that must be processed and filtered to drive situation-aware knowledge, the SMF has to be able to support selective perception. Selective perception is the ability of a system to focus its resources on certain phenomena, thus minimizing the amount of irrelevant data with respect to the studied phenomena.

■ *Others*: There are many other functionalities that can be supported by the SMF depending on the application and the sensed environment, for example, focus of attention, mode control, mode switching control, emission control, failure recovery, and contingency handling.

9.2.5 Challenges of Sensor Management in Homeland Security

Designing an SMF is a difficult problem due to the significant sensory system size and complexity. Achieving efficient SM is a challenge due to the following:

■ Designing an SMF that manages hundreds to thousands of sensor nodes is, in itself, a complicated problem. The homeland security applications provide additional challenges due to their time sensitivity as well as safety criticality. The large number of sensor nodes results in a large number of sensory measurements. An SMF has to handle the overwhelming volume of information which must be processed and filtered to drive situation-aware knowledge in a time-sensitive manner.

■ The spatially distributed nature of the homeland security applications results in the use of wireless technologies. These technologies derive additional set of challenges, for example, coping with highly dynamic and uncertain environments, insufficient network resources, and addressing the information relay capability and reliability.

■ The use of limited capability sensor nodes is a corollary to the use of wireless technologies. Thus, the SMF has to address the limited individual sensor capabilities, that is, processing power, storage capabilities, battery lifetime, to name a few, in addition to coping with individual sensor failure.

■ Due to the increasing demand for high-reasoning operations, such systems are expected to exhibit intelligent behavior and provide an efficient decision support. Accordingly, the implementation of the SMF has to perform numerous functional tasks autonomously and simultaneously, for example, task allocation, scheduling, conflict detection, and cooperation.

■ Furthermore, the system has to execute an intelligent decision support algorithm that provides the security expert with accurate analysis of the scene. Decision support algorithms highly depend on the quality of information provided by the data fusion algorithm. The SM framework has to manage and improve the information data fusion capabilities of the system. However, the need to reduce the data link utilization causes the data fusion and processing of information to take place onboard the sensor.

■ The conflicting requirements for low-cost sensors that have high resolution and accuracy create new challenges for the SMF. The SMF is expected to compensate for the non-linearities in the sensed data and maximize the information acquisition process and its accuracy.

9.2.6 Border Security and Control as a Use Case

Border control deals with the problems of impeding the entrance in the national territory of unauthorized people and materials. It typically deals with illegal immigration and smuggling, but can also concern more serious items such as the incoming weapons of mass destruction [11]. The national borders are typically stretched over thousands of kilometers and are split into blue (seaside) and green (landside) borders. The green borders have designated border crossing points, which monitor millions of human and vehicle crossings.

To control the flow of people and goods not only at the crossing points but also across the entire national border, pervasive surveillance technologies must be deployed. The nature and the size of the VOI, as well as the randomness and scarcity of the events, make the border security and control a highly challenging problem. Moreover, the need to aggregate information, collect statistics, and alert security experts in case of an event has added further demands on the problem. Numerous research works have been directed to address this problem [32,33]. The organizational architecture of SMFs that address the scale and scope of the border security and control application will be further examined in the next section to shed the light on different characteristics of such applications.

9.3 Organizational Architecture

The control architecture of a system defines the organizational behavior of the nodes that comprise it and the internode communications pathways that enable control and flow of data [13]. The organization of a multi-agent system is the collection of roles, relationships, and authority structures which govern its behavior and guide the interaction between its population. The organizational design employed by an agent system can have a significant, quantitative effect on its performance characteristics. A range of organizational strategies have emerged from research, each with different strengths and weaknesses [34,35]. This section surveys the popular organizational paradigms in the context of SMFs. The advantages and disadvantages of each are discussed with reflections on the border security and control case study.

9.3.1 Centralized Architectures

The centralized strategy typically involves the classical techniques of control theory applied to the analysis and design of small-scale systems [36]. The centralized approach is one of the oldest and most popular techniques used. Significant SMF research efforts have been conducted on centralized approaches [37–45]. A centralized system is one in which most processing and control overhead are carried over one or more major central nodes. This simple approach allows a cohesive, consistent view of the world, as well as, a central decision node. Figure 9.6 shows the centralized organizational architecture.

Earlier, the centralized approach was the main architecture deployed in the homeland security applications due to its simplicity, consistency in information handling, and single-point decision operation. However, the scale and scope of homeland security applications have grown extensively in recent years. The inability of the centralized architecture to scale well as the control problem grows made it fall short in addressing such critical applications. In particular, when large-scale systems, such as border security and control, are considered, the problem becomes difficult, if not impossible, to solve using the techniques of classical centralized control theory. Furthermore, the single-point decision advantage can also be a major disadvantage as it becomes a single-point failure. The central node can also suffer from congestion and overload and can become a bottleneck to the system.

9.3.2 Decentralized Architectures

In a decentralized architecture, there are at least two nodes with two or more paths between them to provide redundant paths forming a mesh topology. The full mesh topology connects all devices to each other for redundancy and fault tolerance. Full mesh topology provides a high degree of reliability due to the multiple paths for data, as shown in Figure 9.7. In case of link failure, information can flow through other links to reach its destination. In partial mesh topology, at least one device maintains multiple connections to others without being fully meshed; a partial mesh topology still provides redundancy by having several alternative routes.

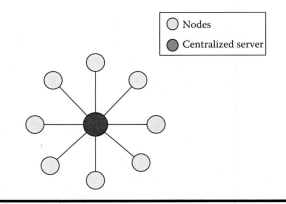

Figure 9.6 Centralized architecture.

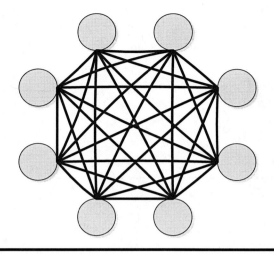

Figure 9.7   Decentralized architecture—full mesh topology.

This decentralization is the main advantage of the mesh topology since it compensates for the single-point failure disadvantage that is present when using a single device as a central node. The number of arbitrary forks in mesh networks makes them more difficult to design and implement; however, their decentralized nature makes them useful. The fully connected mesh topology is generally too costly and complex in terms of communication overhead and management for practical large-scale networks. Though, the topology can be efficiently used when there are only a small number of nodes to be interconnected.

The decentralized architecture is also unsuitable for the problem at hand, that is, border security and control, because of its lack of the necessary structure for such homeland security forces. This makes the decentralized architecture relatively robust because there is little to break, but also makes it difficult to control, which can lead to an undesirable chaotic behavior.

9.3.3 Hierarchal Architectures

The hierarchal architecture is a structured organizational design [46]. Agents are conceptually arranged in a tree-like structure, where each agent in a higher layer in the tree has higher authority over lower agents and have a larger global view than those below them. The data produced by lower-level agents in a hierarchy typically travel upward to provide a broader view, while control flows downward as the higher-level agents provide direction to those below. The hierarchy's efficiency is derived from this notion of decomposition, because the divide-and-conquer approach allows the system to use larger groups of agents more efficiently and address larger-scale problems. Figure 9.8 shows the hierarchal organizational architecture.

In hierarchies, agents are constrained to a number of interactions that is small relative to the total population size. This allows control actions and behavior decisions become more tractable, increased parallelism can be exploited, and because there is less potentially distracting data, they can obtain a more cohesive view of the information pertinent to those decisions. Using a hierarchy can also lead to an overly rigid or fragile organization, prone to single-point failures with potentially global consequences. It is similarly susceptible to bottleneck effects if the scope of control decisions or data receipt is not effectively managed. A centralized system is considered a

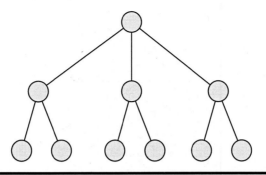

Figure 9.8   Hierarchal architecture.

flat hierarchal system, and a contract system is considered a multilevel hierarchal system. Research projects such as [44] have proposed a hierarchal SMF.

The structured control, as well as the increased parallelism of the hierarchal architecture, makes it a good candidate for the homeland security applications. The hierarchal architecture can scale gracefully for applications like border security and control due to its divide-and-conquer nature. However, being prone to single-point failures is a major disadvantage for using this architecture in such safety-critical applications.

9.3.4 *Holonic Architectures*

The holonic architecture is an organizational design that consists of a set of autonomous holons that cooperate to achieve the system objective [47]. Holons are autonomous, self-reliant units that can be a single sensor or a group of sensors. The holonic architecture possesses intermediate properties compared to both the decentralized and the hierarchal architectures. The holonic concept was first introduced by Arthur Koestler in [48] as a result of two observations. The first is that simple systems can evolve and grow to satisfy increasingly complex and changing needs by creating stable intermediate forms, which are more capable than the initial systems. The second observation is that, in living organisms and social organization, it is generally difficult to distinguish between wholes and parts in an absolute manner; almost every distinguishable element is simultaneously a whole, that is, an essentially autonomous body, and a part, that is, an integrated section of a larger, more capable body. These observations inspired Koestler to coin the term "holon" to describe the hybrid nature of sub-wholes/parts in real-life systems. Holon is derived from the Greek word "holos" meaning whole and the suffix "on" implying particle as in proton or neutron. Each holon exists simultaneously as both a distinct entity built from a collection of subordinates and as part of a larger entity. Figure 9.9 illustrates the holonic architecture.

The key properties of a holonic system, as developed in Koestler's model [48], are autonomy, cooperation, self-organization, and reconfigurability. Another important holonic concept is the notion of functional decomposition. The complexity of dynamic system can be dealt with by decomposing the system into smaller parts. Thus, recursiveness appears as a consequence of this decomposition, that is, the idea that holons can contain other holons. Koestler defines a holarchy as a hierarchy of self-regulating holons, which are groups of cooperative basic holons and recursive holons that are themselves holarchies. One of the major differences between holons and agents concerns recursiveness. A holon may be composed of other holons, while there is no recursive

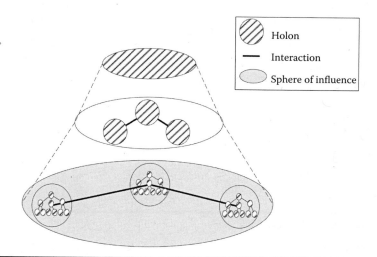

Figure 9.9 **Holonic architecture.**

architecture as such in multi-agent systems. Moreover, holons are cooperative in nature and they cannot be competitive; thus, there is no potential of gaming in a holonic architecture. In a nutshell, the holonic paradigm models different entities of the system as an autonomous holons that work to achieve local objects. Together these holons can cooperatively form a localized holarchies to achieve subsystem or system goals. One of the major disadvantages of the holonic architecture is the lack of predictable system performance due to the increased decomposition. In the recent years, few research projects have considered applying the holonic paradigm to the SM problem [13,22,49,50].

Although the application of the holonic architecture as an organizational paradigm is relatively recent, several research works have been directed to design and develop holonic SMF for homeland security applications [13,22,49]. For the border security and control application, holonic architecture can scale seamlessly; moreover, the autonomous agents can cooperate to handle increasing amounts of data. However, the holonic architecture has to be well designed to avoid the possible chaotic behavior that might result for excessive system decomposition.

9.3.5 Federated Architectures

This organizational style is modeled on the governmental system, where regional provinces retain some amount of local autonomy, while operating under a single central government, for example, the delegate. The delegate is a distinguished member of the group, sometimes called a facilitator, mediator, or broker. Group members interact only with the delegate, which acts as an intermediary between the group and the outside world. In this way, the group is provided with a single, consistent interface. Figure 9.10 demonstrates the federated architecture.

The capabilities provided by the intermediary are what differentiate a federation from other organizational types. The intermediary functions by receiving potentially undirected messages from its group members. These may include skill descriptions, task requirements, status information, application-level data, and others. Outside of the group, the intermediary sends and receives information with the intermediaries of other groups. While the intermediary must be able to interact with both its local federation members and with other intermediaries, individual

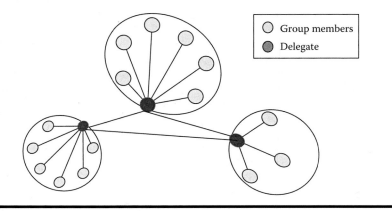

Figure 9.10 Federation architecture.

normal agents do not require a common language as they never directly interact. An intermediary reduces the complexity and messaging burden of the client, but also has the potential of being a bottleneck.

The federated architecture can lend itself to the homeland security applications due to its distributed nature with structured control. In the border security application, the use of the federated system by deploying an intermediary node allows better system scalability and hides the system complexity from the nodes within a federation. A federated system can be coupled with a cluster-based network topology, thus, utilized the fact that phenomena are usually localized. However, this architecture may suffer from the single-point failure again; nevertheless, in case of the intermediary failure, the architecture suffers only local consequences, a proficiency the hierarchal architecture lacks.

9.3.6 Market-Based Architectures

In a market-based organization, there are buying and selling agents. The buying agents may place bids for a common set of items, such as shared resources, tasks, services, or goods. Selling agents supply items to the market to be sold. Auctioneers are responsible for processing bids and determining the winner. This arrangement creates a producer–consumer system that can closely model and greatly facilitate real-world market economies. Markets are similar to federated systems in that a distinguished individual or group of individuals, for example, auctioneers, is responsible for coordinating the activities of a number of other participants. Unlike a federation, market participants are typically competitive. In addition, participants do not cede operational authority to the auctioneers; however, participants do trust the entities managing the market and abide by decisions they make. Figure 9.11 shows a market-based architecture.

It is also common for markets to operate as open systems, allowing any agent to take part so long as it respects the system's specified rules and interface. There are several drawbacks to market-based organizations. The first is the potential complexity required to both reason about the bidding process and determine the auction's outcome as the number of participants increase. The second is the communication overhead incurred as a result of communicating bids. In addition, the security issues inherent in any open system present a drawback. One must also be able to verify the validity of the auction approach itself, that is, collusion. The market-based architectures have been applied to the SM problem in [21,51].

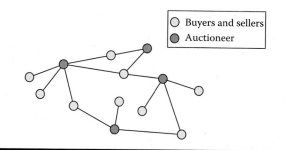

Figure 9.11 Decentralized Market-based architecture.

The market-based architecture is a highly flexible architecture that can be used in various types of applications; thus, it can be a possible candidate for the homeland security applications. Market-based applications can be used in the border security and control application; however, there is a trade of between the number of participants and the system performance and efficiency as the number of participants significantly grows. This is attributed to the auction reasoning complexity and the bids communication overhead.

9.3.7 Other Architectures

There are a number of other architectures that possess characteristics that can be used to address the SM problems in the homeland security domain; however, these architectures have not been investigated in depth for the design of the SMF in literature.

9.3.7.1 Coalitions

Coalitions in general are goal directed and short lived; they are formed with a purpose in mind and dissolve when that need no longer exists, the coalition ceases to suit its designed purpose, or critical mass is lost as agents depart [34]. They may form in populations of both cooperative and self-interested agents. Within a coalition, the organizational structure is typically flat, although there may be a distinguished "leading agent" which acts as a representative and intermediary for the group as a whole. The agents in this group are expected to coordinate their activities in a manner appropriate to the coalition's purpose. Coordination does not take place among agents in separate coalitions, except to the degree that their individual goals interact. In addition to the problem of generating coalition structures, one must also determine how to solve the goal presented to the coalition. If the population is self-interested, a division of value to be apportioned to participants once that goal has been satisfied must also be generated and agreed upon. The main advantage of coalition is the strength in number notion. However, the cost of coalition formation may outweigh its short-term benefits.

9.3.7.2 Teams

An agent team consists of a number of cooperative agents which have agreed to work together toward a common goal [34]. In comparison to coalitions, teams attempt to maximize the utility of the team (goal) itself, rather than that of the individual members. Within a team, the type and pattern of interactions can be quite arbitrary. The primary benefit of teamwork is that by acting in concert, the group of agents can address larger problems than any individual is capable of. Other potential benefits, such as redundancy, the ability to meet global constraints, and economies of scale can also be realized. However, it is the ability of the team (members) to reason explicitly about the ramifications of interagent interactions which gives the team the needed flexibility to work in uncertain environments under unforeseen conditions. The drawback to this tighter coupling is increased communication.

9.3.7.3 Congregations

Similar to coalitions and teams, agent congregations are groups of individuals who have banded together into a typically flat organization in order to derive additional benefits [34]. Unlike these other paradigms, congregations are assumed to be long lived and have a heterogeneous purpose behind each grouping. Instead, congregations are formed among agents with similar or complementary characteristics to facilitate the process of finding suitable collaborators. Individual agents do not necessarily have a single or fixed goal, but do have a stable set of capabilities or requirements that motivate the need to congregate. Agents may come and go dynamically over the existence of the congregation, although clearly there must be a relatively stable number of participants for it to be useful. Agents must also take enough advantage of the congregation so that that the time and energy invested in forming and finding the group is outweighed by the benefits derived from it. Since congregations are formed in large part to reduce the complexity of search and limit interactions, communication does not occur between agents in different congregations, although the groups are not necessarily disjoint. Although congregations can theoretically share many of the same benefits of coalitions, their function in current research has been to facilitate the discovery of agent partners by restricting the size of the population that must be searched. As a secondary effect, these groupings can also increase utility or reliability by creating tighter couplings between agents in the same congregation. The downside to this strategy is that the limited set may be overly restrictive. The main trade-off is the quality and flexibility for a reduction in time, complexity, or cost.

9.3.8 Network Considerations and Issues

Despite the numerous applications of WSNs, these networks have several restrictions, for example, limited energy supply, limited computing power, and limited bandwidth of the wireless links connecting sensor nodes. When designing a WSN, there are several practical network factors that need to be considered:

1. *Hardware constraints*: A sensor node is made up of four basic components: a sensing unit, a processing unit, a transceiver unit, and a power unit. They may also have additional application-dependent components such as a location finding system, power generator, and mobilizer. One of the most important components of a sensor node is the power unit. Power units may also be supported by power scavenging units such as solar cells. All of these subunits may need to fit into a matchbox-sized module; thus, the required size of each subunit may be smaller than even a cubic centimeter. Apart from size, there are some other stringent constraints for sensor nodes. These nodes must consume extremely low power, operate in high volumetric densities, have low production cost, be dispensable

and autonomous, operate unattended, and be adaptive to the environment. The choice of the sensor hardware defines the capabilities, functionalities, as well as lifetime of the sensor network.

2. *Production costs*: Since sensor networks consist of a large number of sensor nodes, the cost of a single node is important to justify the overall cost of the network. As a result, the cost of each sensor node has to be kept low while addressing the increased need for high-resolution, low-power, small-sized sensors.

3. *Sensor network topology*: Hundreds to several thousands of nodes are deployed throughout the sensor field. They are deployed within tens of feet of each other [6]. Deploying a high number of nodes densely requires careful handling of topology maintenance. Topology maintenance can be divided into three phases:

   a. *Predeployment and deployment phase*: Sensor nodes can be either thrown in as a mass or placed one by one in the sensor field. They can be deployed by dropping from a plane, delivered in an artillery shell, rocket, or missile, or placed one by one by either a human or a robot.

   b. *Post-deployment phase*: After deployment, topology changes may occur as a result of changes in the sensor position, reachability, available energy, or malfunctioning.

   c. *Redeployment of additional nodes phase*: Additional sensor nodes can be redeployed at any time to replace malfunctioning nodes or due to changes in task dynamics.

Consequently, WSNs have to adapt efficient network configuration and route recovery, as well as techniques to guarantee information integrity and consistency over the network in case of any failure:

4. *Environment*: Sensor nodes are densely deployed either close or directly inside the phenomenon to be observed. Therefore, they usually work unattended in remote geographic areas. They may be working in the interior of large machinery, at the bottom of an ocean, in a biologically or chemically contaminated field, in a battlefield beyond the enemy lines, and in a home or large building. These extreme environments provide additional demands on the WSNs.

5. *Power consumption*: The wireless sensor node, being a microelectronic device, can only be equipped with a limited power source (<0.5 Ah, 1.2 V) [4]. In some application scenarios, replenishment of power resources might be impossible. Sensor node lifetime shows a strong dependence on battery lifetime. In a multi-hop sensor network, each node plays the dual role of data originator and data router. The malfunctioning of a few nodes can cause significant topological changes and might require rerouting of packets and reorganization of the entire network. Hence, power conservation and power management take on additional importance. It is for these reasons that researchers are currently focusing on the design of power-aware protocols and algorithms for sensor networks.

9.4 Problem-Solving Strategies

Although the SM research field dates back to the early 1990s [52–55], it has started to receive increased attention from the research community during the last decade. Even though many research projects have investigated SM, a truly comprehensive critical study of SM methodologies is needed. Thus, this section provides a study of the latest SM problem-solving strategies proposed in the literature. These state-of-the-art algorithms can be categorized according to their underlying

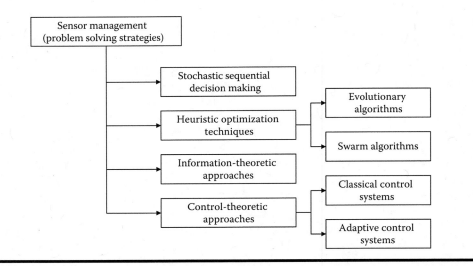

Figure 9.12 The proposed SMF categorization based on the problem-solving strategies.

techniques, as shown in Figure 9.12. In the rest of this section, each of these four strategies is explored in the context of their related SMF in literature.

9.4.1 Stochastic Decision-Making Approaches

SM can be viewed as a decision-making problem. Numerous researchers have viewed the SM problem as a stochastic decision-making one. The most popular decision-making approach, the Markov decision processes (MDP) strategy, provides a mathematical framework for modeling decision making in situations where outcomes are partly random and partly under the control of a decision maker. MDPs are useful for studying SM coupled with dynamic programming and reinforcement learning. The main drawback of such stochastic approaches is that the proposed algorithms may suffer from combinational explosion when solving moderate- to large-size problems.

Research projects such as [56,57] have applied MDP as a mechanism for decision making in SMF. Other works in [37,58–60] have modeled the SM problem as a partially observable MDP, while work in [44] adopted hierarchal MDP in solving the SM problem. A comprehensive study of the formulation of the SM problem as MDP is offered in [61].

9.4.2 Heuristic Optimization Techniques

Heuristic strategies are experience-based techniques that attempt to solve SM problems using learning and discovery. A heuristic method seeks near-optimal solutions at a reasonable computational cost without being able to guarantee either feasibility or optimality, or the quality of the found solution compared to the optimal solution. Many research projects have used heuristic optimization techniques to address difficulty and size of the SM problem.

The most popular heuristic optimization techniques are genetic algorithms and swarm optimization. Genetic algorithms are search heuristics that mimics the process of natural evolution and have been used to address the SM problem in [9] and [50]. On the other hand, swarm optimization belongs to the class of direct search methods used to find an optimal solution to an objective function in a search space. Particle swarm optimization (PSO) is one of the most popular fields of swarm optimization [62,63]. Many research studies have tried to address SM problems by using PSO techniques [23,24,64,65].

9.4.3 Information-Theoretic Approaches

In an information-theoretic problem-solving strategy, a multi-sensor system is concerned with increasing the amount of information, thereby reducing the amount of uncertainty about the state of the external world. As such, the task of the SM is to optimize the multi-sensor system process in a manner that maximizes the greatest possible amount of information obtained whenever a measurement is made.

Information-theoretic approaches use probabilistic methods to estimate the future information gain of a sensor measurement. Information-theoretic approaches have received significant attention in the last decade. The most prominent work in this field has been carried by Kastella in [66], Kolba in [39,40,41,67–69], and Kreucher in [70–79].

9.4.4 Control-Based Approaches

Control-based approaches are the algorithms that define the aggregate of responses to internal and external stimuli. These approaches can either be a predefined behavior of a control architecture or an adaptive control architecture implemented to address a specific problem in a known context.

Designing SM frameworks using classical control is a popular approach to SM. Research projects based on this approach are the ones reported in [42,80–86]. However, this approach is the least flexible and least reusable of those studied here as it is highly application dependent. On the other hand, the adaptive control systems are the next step to the predefined behavior control systems. These adaptive systems can adjust to various situations autonomously, and they mainly depend on a flexible organizational architecture for defining the interactions between the different components of the system. Works in [13,21,87] are an example of adaptive control systems.

9.5 Emerging Issues and Opportunities

This section discusses the homeland security private sector and its commercial products, then follows a brief discussion of future research trends of the pervasive surveillance and SM design in homeland security applications.

9.5.1 Homeland Security Commercial Products

The homeland security private sector is a multibillion-dollar market. Although there was a great boom in the market after the 9/11 events, the U.S. economic downturn has had an adverse effect on the 2010 private sector homeland security market. While the economic factors may have changed growth expectations in 2010, the market is positioned to recover strongly in the 2011–2014 period [88]. The work in [88] reports that there is a trend toward upgrading of the chemical industry security, smart grid security systems, cyber security, perimeter security, command, control and communication systems, IT systems, and workforce and visitors screening systems in the United States of America. Figure 9.13 shows the U.S. private sector homeland security market projection up to 2014. Over the next couple of years, the U.S. private sector homeland security market is forecasted by the authors of [88] to grow by 9.1% from $7.7 billion in 2010 to $11.2 billion by 2014.

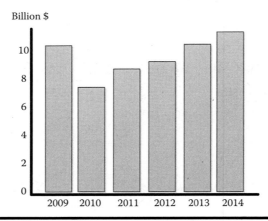

Figure 9.13 The United States of America Private Sector Homeland Security Market. (From Homeland security research, http://www.homelandsecurityresearch.com/2010/08/us-private-sector-home land-security-market-2010–2014/)

There are several players in the private sector homeland security market, the most prominent of which are the following:

■ Harris Corporation has been a key contributor to important homeland security programs for more than half a century [89]. Harris Co. has various segments that address the challenges of pervasive surveillance in homeland security. The communication systems segment presents a comprehensive range of broadcast communication systems which is further enhanced with security overlay technology. While the information processing systems segment offers an intelligent SMF that provides decision makers with the tools needed for total situational awareness, including current relevant information, accurate assessment of the situation, predictive analysis, training and reconstruction, and tailored situational awareness information.

■ L-3 Communications has various products that address the homeland security [90]. L-3 ESSCO (Wolf Coach) designs and builds technically advanced vehicles to gather, analyze, and effectively share intelligence to allow fast response by various government agencies to manage situations in real time that may be safety-critical. L-3 provides a smart SMF that aids decision makers with the tools necessary to manage critical situations. Moreover, the L-3 Global Security & Engineering Solutions division combines experienced management practices with engineering to further assist in facing intelligent threats. One of the main lines of business is knowledge and program management which offer SM techniques.

■ Raytheon is another world-leading technology company in the homeland security sector with more than 60 years of global experience in developing systems that counter existing threats and provide adaptable migration paths for future threat environments. The Raytheon Company offers complete solutions for various homeland security applications, such as Border Security, Immigration Control and Identity Management, Critical Infrastructure Protection, Transportation Security, and Cybersecurity. For applications like the Border Security, Raytheon utilizes the sensory networks and SM technologies to predict, detect, and respond to illegal border crossings between the points of entry.

9.5.2 Emerging Issues

Intelligent SM systems are an active area of research. New SM issues arise as sensor networks continue to develop and new applications emerge. Recently, prominent issues that have started gaining attention of the research community are cooperative multi-SM, energy-aware operations, and large-scale surveillance.

- *Surveillance over a large area*: The need for large area sensor networks has been recognized in applications such as wildlife preserve monitoring and natural disaster warning (e.g., for tsunami). These applications are characterized by large and remote geographic areas, which need large numbers of unattended sensor nodes to cover the VOI. Such large networks add new challenges to the SM problem, such as distributed operation with collaborative decision making, selective perception, and managing the large amounts of sensory data, to name a few.
- *Cooperative multi-SM*: The world model of a multi-sensor system can be greatly enhanced with cooperative sensing in applications where the environment dynamics rapidly change, for example, target tracking. Sensors cooperation is an essential functional property that can increase the quality of phenomenon surveillance. Cooperation can be in the form of cueing and/or handoff. These cooperative schemes use the detected information from one sensor to refine the operation of another sensor toward the same phenomenon.
- *Energy-aware operation*: The fact that sensors are typically battery-operated adds new challenges to the SM problems. Sensor networks are often randomly deployed in large number; it is often not feasible to recharge or replace the sensor nodes' batteries. These networks suffer from limited battery resources of sensor nodes; hence, the battery lifetime of these devices must be increased as much as possible. Issues such as optimizing the energy dissipation and sleep and standby periods need thorough investigation.

9.6 Conclusion

Pervasive surveillance systems are embedded systems that are composed of self-organizing sensor networks managed by an intelligent sensor framework. Pervasive surveillance has many applications in military and homeland security. More recently, we started to see pervasive surveillance emerge in various commercial and consumer applications. To achieve efficient pervasive surveillance, SM approaches have to be employed. An SMF is the organizational control system that seeks to manage and coordinate the use of sensing resources in a manner that improves the process of situation awareness. This chapter has discussed the fundamentals of SM, its nonfunctional merits, as well as its desired functional capabilities. Many challenges face the design of an intelligent SMF, for example, handling the limited node and network resources, the need of intelligent real-time operation, and managing the large number of nodes and extensive amounts of data. Thus, the SM problem is a highly complex one. Numerous research projects were dedicated to address this problem. The most promising organizational architectures were briefly surveyed. Moreover, problem-solving strategies for SM were categorized into four main categories: stochastic decision-making, heuristic optimization, information-theoretic, and control theoretic approaches, where each was briefly discussed.

References

1. K. Ball, D. Lyon, D. M. Wood, C. Norris, and C. Raab, A report on the surveillance society, The Surveillance Studies Network, Technical Report, September 2006.
2. S. Kong, C. Sanderson, and B. C. Lovell, Classifying and tracking multiple persons for proactive surveillance of mass transport systems, in *Proceedings of IEEE Conference on Advanced Video and Signal Based Surveillance*, London, UK, September 5–7, 2007, pp. 159–163.
3. M. R. Endsley and D. J. Garland, *Situation Awareness Analysis and Measurement*. Routledge, New York, 2000.
4. H. Christensen and G. Hager, *Sensing and Estimation*. Springer, Berlin, Germany, 2008.
5. C. Shen, C. Srisathapornphat, and C. Jaikaeo, Sensor information networking architecture and applications, *Personal Communications, IEEE*, 8(4), 52–59, 2001.
6. C. Intanagonwiwat, R. Govindan, and D. Estrin, Directed diffusion: A scalable and robust communication paradigm for sensor networks, in *Proceedings of the 6th Annual International Conference on Mobile Computing and Networking (MobiCom '00)*. ACM, New York, NY, 2000, pp. 56–67.
7. G. Hoblos, M. Staroswiecki, and A. Aitouche, Optimal design of fault tolerant sensor networks, in *Proceedings of IEEE International Conference on Control Applications*, Anchorage, AK, September 25–27, 2000, pp. 467–472.
8. F. Zhao and L. Guibas, *Wireless Sensor Networks: An Information Processing Approach (The Morgan Kaufmann Series in Networking)*. Morgan Kaufmann, San Fransisco, CA, 2004.
9. M. Huntwork, A. Goradia, N. Xi, C. Haffner, C. Klochko, and M. Mutka, Pervasive surveillance using a cooperative mobile sensor network, in *Proceedings of IEEE International Conference on Robotics and Automation*, Orlando, Florida, May 15–19, 2006, pp. 2099–2104.
10. N. Schroder, Sensor markets 2008, Technical Report, May 1999.
11. G. Franceschetti and M. Grossi, *Homeland Security Technology Challenges: From Sensing and Encrypting to Mining and Modeling*, Artech House, Boston, MA, 2008.
12. A. Minnaar, The implementation and impact of crime prevention/crime control open street closed-circuit television surveillance in south African central business districts, *Surveillance and Society— Special Issue on Surveillance and Criminal Justice*, 4(3), 174–207, 2007.
13. A. R. Benaskeur, H. Irandoust, P. McGuire, and R. Brennan, Holonic control-based sensor management, in *Proceedings of the 10th International Conference on Information Fusion*, Quebec, Canada, July 9–12, 2007, pp. 1–8.
14. N. Xiong and P. Svensson, Multi-sensor management for information fusion: Issues and approaches, *Information Fusion*, 3(2), 163–186, 2002.
15. B. Khaleghi, A. Khamis, F. O. Karray, and S. N. Razavi, Multisensor data fusion: A review of the state-of-the-art, *Information Fusion*, 1–17, 2011. [Online]. Available at: http://www.sciencedirect.com/science/article/pii/S1566253511000558
16. J. Llinas, C. Bowman, G. Rogova, A. Steinberg, E. Waltz, and F. White, Revisiting the jdl data fusion model ii, in *Proceedings of the International Conference on Information Fusion*, 2004, pp. 1218–1230.
17. A. N. Steinberg, C. L. Bowman, and F. E. White, Revisions to the JDL data fusion model, *SPIE Sensor Fusion: Architectures, Algorithms, and Applications III*, 3719(1), 430–441, 1999.
18. B. Dasarathy and A. Huntsville, Decision fusion strategies in multisensor environments, *IEEE Transactions on Systems, Man and Cybernetics*, 21(5), 1140–1154, 1991.
19. M. Bedworth and J. O'Brien, The omnibus model: A new model of data fusion, *Aerospace and Electronic Systems Magazine, IEEE*, 15(4), 30–36, 2000.
20. I. Kadar, Perceptual reasoning in adaptive fusion processing, in *Proceedings of SPIE Signal Processing, Sensor Fusion, and Target Recognition XI*, 2002.
21. T. Mullen, V. Avasarala, and D. L. Hall, Customer-driven sensor management, *IEEE Intelligent Systems*, 21(2), 41–49, 2006.
22. A. R. Benaskeur and F. Rhéaume, Adaptive data fusion and sensor management for military applications, *Aerospace Science and Technology*, 11(4), 327–338, 2007, COGIS '06. [Online]. Available at: http://www.sciencedirect.com/science/article/pii/S1270963807000120

23. L. Osadciw and K. Veeramachaneni, Sensor network management through fitness function design in multi-objective optimization, in *Conference Record of the Forty-First Asilomar Conference on Signals, Systems and Computers*, Pacific Grove, CA, November 4–7, 2007, pp. 1648–1651.

24. K. Krishna, H. Hexmoor, and S. Pasupuleti, A surveillance system based on multiple mobile sensors, in *Proceedings of FLAIRS*, 2004, pp. 1–6.

25. A. M. Elmogy, A. Khamis, and F. O. Karray, Dynamic complex task allocation in mobile sensor network, in *IEEE International Conference on Signals, Circuits and Systems*, Djerba, Tunisia, 2009, pp. 1–6.

26. A. M. Elmogy, A. Khamis, and F. O. Karray, Market-based dynamic task allocation in mobile surveillance systems, in *IEEE International Workshop on Safety, Security, and Rescue Robotics*, University of Denver, Denver, CO, November 3–6, 2009, pp. 1–6.

27. Q. Liu, M. Hiraki, and S. Ozono, The cooperative multi-sensor system based on belief concept, in *IMEKO-XVI World Congress*, Vienna, Austria, 2000, pp. 601–605.

28. G. P. Settembre, P. Scerri, A. Farinelli, K. Sycara, and D. Nardi, A decentralized approach to cooperative situation assessment in multi-robot systems, in *Proceedings of the Seventh International Joint Conference on Autonomous Agents and Multiagent Systems—Volume 1*, ser. AAMAS '08. Richland, SC: International Foundation for Autonomous Agents and Multiagent Systems, 2008, pp. 31–38.

29. E. Bosse and J. Roy, The Canada-Netherlands collaboration on multisensor data fusion and other Canada-NATO MSDF activities, in *Proceedings of the IEEE International Symposium on Circuits and Systems (ISCAS '98)* 31 May–3 Jun 1998, Vol. 6, pp. 561–564.

30. A. Benaskeur, A. Khamis, and H. Irandoust, Multisensor cooperation in military surveillance systems, in *IEEE International Conference on Signals, Circuits and Systems*, Djerba, Tunisia, 2009.

31. F. Sivrikaya and B. Yener, Time synchronization in sensor networks: A survey, *Network, IEEE*, 18(4), 45–50, 2004.

32. B. Marshall, S. Kaza, J. Xu, H. Atabakhsh, T. Peterson, and C. Violette and H. Chen, Cross-jurisdictional criminal activity networks to support border and transportation security, in *Proceedings of the Seventh IEEE International Conference on Intelligent Transportation Systems (ITSC2004)*, 2004, pp. 100–105.

33. H. Chen, F. Y. Wang, and D. Zeng, Intelligence and security informatics for homeland security: Information, communication, and transportation, *IEEE Transactions on Intelligent Transportation Systems*, 5(4), 329–341, 2004

34. B. Horling and V. Lesser, A survey of multi-agent organizational paradigms, *The Knowledge Engineering Review*, 19(4), 281–316, 2004.

35. D. Grossi, F. Dignum, M. Dastani, and L. Royakkers, Foundations of organizational structures in multiagent systems, in *Proceedings of the Fourth International Joint Conference on Autonomous Agents and Multiagent Systems*, ser. AAMAS '05. New York: ACM, 2005, pp. 690–697. [Online]. Available at: http://doi.acm.org/10.1145/1082473.1082578

36. M. Janssen, Centralized or decentralized organization?, in *Proceedings of the 2005 National Conference on Digital Government Research*, ser. dg.o '05. Digital Government Society of North America, 2005, pp. 247–248. [Online]. Available at: http://dl.acm.org/citation.cfm?id = 1065226.1065305

37. G. Atia, V. Veeravalli, and J. Fuemmeler, Sensor scheduling for energy-efficient target tracking in sensor networks, *IEEE Transactions on Signal Processing*, 59(10), 4923–4937, 2011.

38. M. Kolba, W. Scott, and L. Collins, A framework for information-based sensor management for the detection of static targets, *IEEE Transactions on Systems, Man and Cybernetics, Part A: Systems and Humans*, 41(1), 105–120, 2011.

39. M. P. Kolba and L. M. Collins, Sensor management using a new framework for observation modeling, in *Proceedings of the SPIE, Detection and Sensing of Mines, Explosive Objects, and Obscured Targets*, 2009, pp. 1–12.

40. M. P. Kolba and L. M. Collins, Managing landmine detection sensors: Results from application to AMDS data, in *Proceedings of SPIE, the International Society for Optical Engineering*, 2007, Vol. 6553, pp. 1–11.

41. M. P. Kolba and L. M. Collins, Information-theoretic sensor management for multimodal sensing, in *Proceeding of IEEE International Conference on Geoscience and Remote Sensing Symposium*, 2006, pp. 3935–3938.

42. I. Panella, High-level functional architecture for sensor management system, in *Proceedings of the ECSIS Symposium on Bio-Inspired Learning and Intelligent Systems for Security*, 2008, pp. 107–110.

43. M. Li, D. Ganesan, and P. Shenoy, Presto: Feedback-driven data management in sensor networks, *IEEE/ACM Transactions on Networking*, 17(4), 1256–1269, 2009.

44. D. Akselrod, A. Sinha, and T. Kirubarajan, Hierarchical markov decision processes based distributed data fusion and collaborative sensor management for multitarget multisensor tracking applications, in *IEEE International Conference on Systems, Man and Cybernetics*, 2007, pp. 157–164.

45. C. Kreucher, K. Kastella, and A. Hero iii, Sensor management using an active sensing approach, *Signal Processing*, 85(3), 607–624, 2005.

46. L. E. Montealegre Vázquez and F. López Y López, An agent-based model for hierarchical organizations, in *Coordination, Organizations, Institutions, and Norms in Agent Systems II*, P. Noriega, J. Vázquez-Salceda, G. Boella, O. Boissier, V. Dignum, N. Fornara, and E. Matson, Eds. Berlin, Germany: Springer-Verlag, 2007, pp. 194–211.

47. H. Tianfield, A new framework of holonic self-organization for multi-agent systems, in *IEEE International Conference on Systems, Man and Cybernetics*, 2007, pp. 753–758.

48. A. Koestler, *The Ghost in the Machine*, Hutchinson Publishing Group, London, U.K., 1967.

49. A. R. Benaskeur and H. Irandoust, Holonic approach for control and coordination of distributed sensors, DRDC Valcartier, Technical Report, September 2008.

50. F. Yu, F. Tu, and K. Pattipati, Integration of a holonic organizational control architecture and multiobjective evolutionary algorithm for flexible distributed scheduling, *IEEE Transactions on Systems, Man and Cybernetics, Part A: Systems and Humans*, 38(5), 1001–1017, 2008.

51. A. R. Hilal, A. Khamis, and O. Basir, HASM: A hybrid architecture for sensor management in a distributed surveillance context, in *IEEE International Conference on Networking, Sensing and Control (ICNSC)*, 2011, pp. 492–497.

52. C. F. Nche, W. H. Powell, D. J. Parish, and I. W. Phillips, A new architecture for surveillance video networks, *International Journal of Communication Systems*, 9(3), 133–143, 1996.

53. S. Musick and R. Malhotra, Chasing the elusive sensor manager, in *Proceeding of NAECON*, 1994, pp. 606–613.

54. R. Malhotra, Temporal considerations in sensor management, in *Proceeding of the IEEE NAECON*, 1995, pp. 86–93.

55. P. Rothman and S. Bier, Evaluation of sensor management systems, in *Proceeding of the National Aerospace and Electronics Conference (NAECON)*, 1989, pp. 1747–1752.

56. S. Misra, S. Rohith Mohan, and R. Choudhuri, A probabilistic approach to minimize the conjunctive costs of node replacement and performance loss in the management of wireless sensor networks, *Network and Service Management, IEEE Transactions on*, 7(2), 107–117, 2010.

57. S. Misra, R. R. Rout, T. R. V. Krishna, P. M. K. Manilal, and M. S. Obaidat, Markov decision process-based analysis of rechargeable nodes in wireless sensor networks, in *Proceedings of the 2010 Spring Simulation Multiconference*, ser. SpringSim '10. New York: ACM, 2010, pp. 97:1–97:7.

58. S. A. Miller, Z. A. Harris, and E. K. P. Chong, A POMDP framework for coordinated guidance of autonomous UAVs for multitarget tracking, *EURASIP Journal of Advances in Signal Processing*, 2009, 1–17, 2009.

59. V. Krishnamurthy and D. Djonin, Structured threshold policies for dynamic sensor scheduling—A partially observed markov decision process approach, *Signal Processing, IEEE Transactions on*, 55(10), 4938–4957, 2007.

60. Y. Li, L. Krakow, E. Chong, and K. Groom, Approximate stochastic dynamic programming for sensor scheduling to track multiple targets, *Digital Signal Processing*, 19(6), 978–989, 2009, *dASP'06—Defense Applications of Signal Processing*.

61. D. Akselrod, T. Lang, M. McDonald, and T. Kirubarajan, *Markov Decision Process-Based Resource and Information Management for Sensor Networks*. Springer, Berlin, Germany, 2010.

62. R. C. Eberhart and J. Kennedy, A new optimizer using particle swarm theory, in *Proceedings of the Sixth International Symposium on Micromachine and Human Science*, 1995, pp. 39–43.

63. J. Kennedy and R. C. Eberhart, Particle swarm optimization, in *Proceedings of IEEE International Conference on Neural Networks*, 1995, pp. 1942–1948.

64. L. Osadciw and K. Veeramacheneni, A controllable sensor management algorithm capable of learning, in *SPIE Proceedings Series Multisensor, Multisource Information Fusion: Architectures, Algorithms, and Applications*, 2005, pp. 257–268.

65. K. Veeramachaneni, L. Osadciw, and P. Varshney, An adaptive multimodal biometric management algorithm, *IEEE Transactions on Systems, Man, and Cybernetics, Part C: Applications and Reviews*, 35, 344–356, 2005.

66. K. Kastella, Discrimination gain to optimize detection and classification, *IEEE Transactions on Systems, Man, and Cybernetics—Part A: Systems and Humans*, 27, 112–116, 1997.

67. M. P. Kolba, P. A. Torrione, and L. M. Collins, Information-based sensor management for landmine detection using multimodal sensors, in *Proceedings of SPIE, the International Society for Optical Engineering*, 2005.

68. M. P. Kolba and L. M. Collins, Information-based sensor management in the presence of uncertainty, *IEEE Transactions on Signal Processing*, 55(6), 2731–2735, 2007.

69. M. P. Kolba and L. M. Collins, Sensor management for static target detection with non-binary sensor observations and observation uncertainty, in *IEEE/SP Workshop on Statistical Signal Processing*, 2007, pp. 74–78.

70. C. Kreucher, K. Kastella, and A. O. Hero, Multi-target sensor management using alpha-divergence measures, in *Proceedings of the Second International Conference on Information Processing in Sensor Networks*, ser. IPSN'03, Springer-Verlag, Berlin , Germany, 2003, pp. 209–222.

71. C. Kreucher, A.O. Hero, K. Kastella, and D. Chang, Efficient methods of non-myopic sensor management for multitarget tracking, in *43rd IEEE Conference on Decision and Control, 2004. CDC.* Vol. 1, December 2004, pp. 722–727.

72. C. Kreucher, A. O. Hero, and K. Kastella, A comparison of task driven and information driven sensor management for target tracking, in *44th IEEE Conference on Decision and Control, 2005 and 2005 European Control Conference CDC-ECC '05.* December 2005, pp. 4004–4009.

73. C. Kreucher, M. Morelande, K. Kastella, and A. Hero, Particle filtering for multitarget detection and tracking (invited paper), in *The Proceedings of the Twenty Sixth Annual IEEE Aerospace Conference*, March 2005.

74. C. Kreucher, A. Hero, K. Kastella, and B. Shapo, Information-based sensor management for simultaneous multitarget tracking and identification, in *The Proceedings of the Thirteenth Annual Conference on Adaptive Sensor Array Processing (ASAP)*, June 2005.

75. C. Kreucher, K. Kastella, and A. Hero, Multiplatform information-based sensor management, in *The Proceedings of the SPIE Defense Transformation and Network-Centric Systems Symposium*, Vol. 5820, March 2005, pp. 141–151.

76. C. Kreucher, K. Kastella, and A. Hero, Multitarget tracking using the joint multitarget probability density, *IEEE Transactions on Aerospace and Electronic Systems*, 39(4), 1396–1414, 2005.

77. C. Kreucher and A. Hero, Non-myopic approaches to scheduling agile sensors for multitarget detection, tracking, and identification (invited paper), in *The Proceedings of the 2005 IEEE Conference on Acoustics, Speech, and Signal Processing (ICASSP) Special Section on Advances in Waveform Agile Sensor Processing*, Vol. V, March 2005, pp. 885–888.

78. C. Kreucher, D. Blatt, A. Hero, and K. Kastella, Adaptive multi-modality sensor scheduling for detection and tracking of smart targets, *Digital Signal Processing*, 16(5), 546–567, 2006, Special Issue on DASP 2005.

79. C. Kreucher, A. Hero, K. Kastella, and M. Morelande, An information-based approach to sensor management in large dynamic networks, *Proceedings of the IEEE*, 95(5), 978–999, 2007.

80. Y.-C. Tseng, Y.-C. Wang, K.-Y. Cheng, and Y.-Y. Hsieh, imouse: An integrated mobile surveillance and wireless sensor system, *Computer*, 40(6), 60–66, 2007.

81. G. Wagenknecht, M. Anwander, T. Braun, T. Staub, J. Matheka, and S. Morgenthaler, Marwis: A management architecture for heterogeneous wireless sensor networks, *Wired/Wireless Internet Communications*, 5031, 177–188, 2008.

82. L. Ruiz, J. Nogueira, and A. Loureiro, Manna: A management architecture for wireless sensor networks, *IEEE Communications Magazine*, 41(2), 116–125, 2003.

83. J. Leguay, M. Lopez-Ramos, K. Jean-Marie, and V. Conan, Service oriented architecture for heterogeneous and dynamic sensor networks, in *Proceedings of the Second International Conference on Distributed Event-Based Systems*, ser. DEBS '08. New York: ACM, 2008, pp. 309–312.

84. R. Luo and W. Chang, Self managed system of sensor network an artificial ecological system, in *IEEE Workshop on Advanced Robotics and Its Social Impacts*, Hsinchu, Taiwan, 2007, pp. 1–6.

85. H. Detmold, A. Dick, K. Falkner, D. S. Munro, A. van den Hengel, and R. Morrison, Middleware for video surveillance networks, in *Proceedings of the International Workshop on Middleware for Sensor Networks*, ser. *MidSens '06*. New York: ACM, 2006, pp. 31–36. [Online]. Available at: http://doi.acm.org/10.1145/1176866.1176872

86. S. M. Jameson, Architectures for distributed information fusion to support situation awareness on the digital battlefield, in *Proceedings of the International Conference on Information Fusion (FUSION 2001)*, 2001, pp. 27–35.

87. D. Stromberg, M. Andersson, and F. Lantz, On platform-based sensor management, in *Proceedings of the Fifth International Conference on Information Fusion*, 2002, pp. 600–607.

88. Homeland security research. [Online]. Available at: http://www.homelandsecurityresearch.com/2010/08/us-private-sector-home land-security-market-2010–2014/

89. Harris corporation. [Online]. Available at: http://www.govcomm.harris.com/

90. L-3 communications. [Online]. Available at: http://www.l-3com.com/

Chapter 10

Moving from Measuring to Understanding: Situation Awareness in Homeland Security

Giusj Digioia, Chiara Foglietta, Gabriele Oliva,
Stefano Panzieri, and Roberto Setola

Contents

10.1 Introduction

While attempting to perform any homeland surveillance strategy, an essential step is to define and implement methodologies for the assessment of the actual situation, as well as its near-future evolution.

Field surveillance activities are typically based on a huge availability of sensorial data used, for instance, to determine the presence of entities in the patrolled area (e.g., ships, submarines, aircrafts), with the purpose of identifying them on the base of their behavioral characteristics, and to catalog them according to their potential intent (e.g., pirate vessel). In other terms, the surveillance activities encompass the following three questions: who, what, and why; who is inside the patrolled area, what is he or she doing (e.g., the actual situation), and why is he or she there (which is his or her intent).

This is however a nontrivial task, since any single sensor by itself usually does not allow to exhaustively answer to the aforementioned questions, especially in the presence of smart enemies, since it may provide ambiguous information. For example, the presence of an unknown object detected by a radar in a patrolled maritime area may indicate a fishing boat or a refugees' ship, rather than an attacker. Thereafter, there is the need to carefully inspect the behavior of the entities that act in the considered scenario according to multiple perspectives in order to acquire awareness on their intent and on the associated threats. Moreover, this has to be done for a reasonable amount of time, in order to assess complex behaviors. Note that, also given the challenging complexity of the task, no exact guideline can be given in this sense.

Hence, it is fundamental to provide adequate raw data aggregation methodologies in order to obtain high-level pattern or behavior detection and prediction: this is the objective of *situation awareness* (SAW) techniques.

In 1995, Endsley defined SAW as "knowing what's going on" or, more formally, as "the perception of the elements in the environment within a volume of time and space, the comprehension of their meaning and the projection of their status in the near future."

SAW is strongly related to the temporal dimension; the main idea is therefore to use knowledge acquired in the past to identify, analyze, and understand the actual situation and to forecast its evolution, with the aim to evaluate the risk.

Therefore, the field of SAW is directly connected to the data fusion problem, where multiple information sources have to be combined in order to gain insights on the situation (Hall and Llinas, 2001). Such problems arise in many contexts, for example, in the military field, in the field of environment surveillance and monitoring, in robotics, and in medical diagnosis.

In this chapter, some of the most diffused methodologies for the fusion of multiple and heterogeneous information sources will be reviewed and critically compared, having in mind the final objective to increase the awareness on the ongoing situation in a dynamic scenario characterized by nontrivial complexity.

The structure of this chapter is as follows: after describing the different paradigms for SAW, the Bayesian belief networks (BNs) and the artificial neural networks (ANNs) approaches are discussed, as powerful tools able to map sensorial information into high-level descriptions of the ongoing situation; however, these methodologies, although able to aggregate low-level data into high-level information, are not able to manage loops, since they are based on acyclic graph structures. Moreover, a nontrivial effort has to be put to set up learning procedures, in terms of availability both of large amounts of data (e.g., couples of inputs and expected outputs) and of computational effort.

To solve these issues, a further methodology, namely, Markov chain, is outlined in this chapter, as a framework where cycles are allowed.

Such an approach represents probabilistic transitions among a set of states, where the future evolution is influenced only by the actual state, without memory of past history (such a property is generally referred to as Markov property). This allows to represent behaviors as sequences of states, thus modeling dynamic situations. However, the mapping of sensorial information into these states is not a trivial task, and specific methodologies have to be implemented. To solve this issue, the evidence theory framework is discussed, as a methodology able to aggregate multiple discording and vague information sources and to map them into high-level states.

This chapter is then concluded by a case study used to highlight the characteristics and limitations of the different methodologies.

10.2 Models for Situation Awareness

The most adopted data fusion schema is the *Joint Directors of Laboratories* (JDL) model (Endsley, 1988).

The JDL is a five-layered hierarchical model, where each level is aimed to provide a more abstract, high-level, and descriptive representation of the scenario. Indeed, while proceeding from the lower to the higher levels, the degree of abstraction is increased, and the amount of information is reduced due to the aggregations performed at each level. Note that, at each level, the model theoretically provides a prediction of the expected evolution for the scenario.

Let us now describe these levels, which are defined as follows:

Level 0: Sub-object data assessment: At this layer, the single signals are taken into account. The amount of data gathered at this level can be quite relevant, hence having a very low degree of abstraction (e.g., spatial occupancy of a grid, audio/video streams). Moreover, the first identification of the objects and entities involved in the scenario, along with the first low-level prevision of their behavior (e.g., trajectory interpolation), is provided.

Level 1: Object assessment: At this layer, based on the sensorial information of the level in the following, the objects are estimated, and their behavior is predicted. In this way, it is possible to perform the tracking of the entities, eventually involving multiple sensorial information.

Level 2: Situation assessment: At this layer, the relations existing among the entities are evaluated and predicted. This is the level where complex behaviors are identified (e.g., surrounding, side attack, refueling), taking also into account the physical context (e.g., constraints in the movements due to obstacles).

Level 3: Impact assessment: At this level, the impact of situation/actions estimated at Level 2 are evaluated. Prediction of the effects is performed on entities involved in the estimated situation in order to draw inferences about enemy threats, friend and for vulnerabilities and opportunities.

Level 4: Process refinement: This level is aimed to adaptively tune the information and the insights obtained by the lower levels, based on the data acquired and on the extrapolations made from such data, in order to refine the understanding and provide a support to decisions, highlighting the impact of these decisions.

Hence, the actual assessment of the ongoing situation is mainly performed at level 2, while the prevision is mainly done at level 3. The interested reader is referred to Hall and Llinas (1997) and Endsley (1988) for a thorough discussion.

Another established SAW model is the so-called Boyd control loop (Boyd, 1987), often referred to as OODA loop, since it is composed of the four phases: Observe, Orient, Decide, and Act.

The OODA model can be partially mapped into a JDL model: The Observe phase can be compared to the JDL level 0, while the Orient phase encompasses the JDL levels 1, 2, and 3; the Decide phase is mapped into JDL level 4, but it also includes logistics and planning; the Act phase has no direct analogue in the JDL model, and it can be seen as the actual decision made based on the JDL framework. Consequently, note that the actual SAW activities are performed within the Orient phase.

The main attractiveness of the OODA model is that it closes a loop between sensing and acting, thus providing a more resilient methodology with respect to changes in the environment or in the enemy strategy. However, such an approach lacks in the ability to assess the impact of the Decide and Act phases on the other phases of the loop that is instead performed by JDL level 4.

A possible evolution is to close a loop at each level of the OODA model and to consider the interaction among these loops (Shahbazian et al., 2001).

Notice that both JDL and OODA models are not sharply defined and do not imply a unique implementation; in fact, some activities are present in multiple levels or steps. Hence, JDL and OODA should not be considered as operative procedures, but have to be treated as logical schemata that may help to better organize the information and to adequately define the steps for the extrapolation of high-level and abstract information, based on raw low-level data.

In the next sections, some of the most established methodologies to perform SAW will be described. As stated previously, a system increases users' SAW if it is capable to understand what is going on in the observed scenario and if it is capable to foresee its evolutions.

The aforementioned capabilities correspond to JDL levels 2 and 3 and to the Orient phase of the OODA model, regarding the assessment of situations and the evaluation of related threats, through situation projection. Hence, the methodologies performing SAW must be able to reason about the ongoing situation starting from observations acquired from heterogeneous sensors. With this regard, in the next sections, the following techniques will be presented:

- *Bayesian BN*: This technique is based on a probabilistic approach. It uses Bayesian nets to model hierarchical, cause–effect relationships among relevant aspects of the situation of interest. The net is characterized by probabilistic weights, and the belief related to each node is computed taking into account weights and the observations gathered from the field. Observations can be heterogeneous and can be posted at each level of the net, updating the belief of the states of the net. Evaluating the beliefs of all node of the net, the user is able to understand the ongoing situation. An extension of such a methodology is the dynamic Bayesian net that allows to compute the beliefs of the nodes of the net, in future time stamps, that is, projecting the assessed situation, and therefore, they allow also to evaluate threats.

- *Markov models (MMs)*: Also this technique is based on a probabilistic approach. It allows to model time-dependent situations, through a graph whose edges are weighted by probabilities. Once observations are gathered, it is possible to estimate the most probable path on the graph that is the most probable ongoing situation, and also it is possible to estimate which is the state of the observed situation. Moreover, according to the model, it is possible to say which is the most probable state of the graph, that is, to project situations and, consequently, to evaluate related threat.

- *Neural networks*: This approach is largely used to reason about complex situations, whose model, eventually nonlinear, is defined by learning algorithms. Within such a framework, the situation of interest is represented as a black box, which can be fed with heterogeneous observations. Even in this case, the evaluation of values of output variables, representing the situation of interest, allows user to be aware of a situation. This technique does not suit projection capability.

- *Evidence theory*: This technique is based on the theory of possibility. It allows to model knowledge about time-independent situations, thanks to bipartite graphs, correlating causes (situations of interest) to effects (observations). Evidence theory handles uncertain, heterogeneous, and eventually incomplete observations and identifies the most plausible subset of situations occurring in the observed scenario. This methodology allows also to aggregate low-level data in order to give them a semantic meaning. This meaning can be used as input to other knowledge models, eventually more complex (e.g., MMs), allowing to reason about time-dependent situations and therefore to perform threat assessment.

For what is stated before, techniques presented in this chapter can be employed to implement situation assessment and, in some cases, also threat assessment, increasing the awareness of the user.

10.3 Bayesian Belief Network

Bayesian belief networks (BNs) (Pearl, 1988) are one of the most established techniques adopted in the field of statistical inference and multi-sensor data fusion. The main idea of such an approach is to use a probabilistic representation of the relations between sets of states or behaviors (in terms of a priori and conditional probabilities) in order to quantify the "belief" of the different states/behaviors.

Note that, although the underlying structure is probabilistic, such a methodology can be applied by considering a generic information obtained, for instance, from field sensors. The information can of course be characterized probabilistically; however, in a general perspective, it may also represent certain data (i.e., a given situation actually verified) or a belief on different possibilities.

Let us now provide a definition of the key concepts of this section:

- *Evidence:* The evidence on the states assumed by a variable is an information on its numerical value (i.e., the state, the situation) based on observations (i.e., sensorial data).
- *Belief:* The belief of the state of a variable is the degree of certainty for the variable to assume a certain value (i.e., to be in a certain situation), and it is computed by taking into account the evidence so far received. Note that the term belief is a general definition that encompasses both probabilistic and subjective information.

Hence, the BN framework allows to model the causal relation existing among several variables, each characterized by different possible states or situations, based on an underlying probabilistic representation. To this end, the first step is to define the relations between the variables in terms of conditional probabilities; then, such an information will be used to compose the beliefs. Note that the use of conditional probabilities allows, from one hand, to directly highlight the dependency of a variable on the others and, from another, to invert such a relation by resorting to the rules of statistical inference. Therefore, the final objective of BNs is to determine the belief of such states based on the conditional relations existing among variables and on the observations. Indeed, if the evidence obtained from the sensors is not probabilistic (e.g., subjective beliefs), the BN framework will provide a non-probabilistic information based on an underlying probabilistic characterization of the relations existing among the variables (i.e., the conditional probabilities will be used to weight the beliefs).

Classical fields for BN applications are image recognition (Luo et al., 2005), language and speech understanding (Geoffrey and Zweig, 2003), and medical diagnosis (Nikovski, 2000). In Luo et al. (2005), the authors proposed a generic framework for semantic image understanding (e.g., the identification of an object in a frame) based on a BN, while in Huang et al. (1994), BNs are used to detect high-level traffic information such as number of cars in a highway or number of machines changing lane.

The main idea of such an approach is to consider a set of interrelated variables connected by means of a treelike structure and to characterize their relations in terms of conditional probability. Hence, the state of each node depends on the state of its parents in the tree, on the evidence obtained by the sensors, and on the state and evidence of its children nodes. Such information has to be composed, and the beliefs have to be propagated across the tree. To this end, the dependency on the parents can be directly evaluated resorting to *conditional probability tables* (CPTs), while the dependency on the children has to be obtained by reverting the conditional probabilities. Finally, the root nodes represent situations (e.g., states or behaviors) for which an a priori probability is available (i.e., a probability that does not depend on the evidence data).

The CPT can be used to compute the a priori probability $p(v_i)$ for the variable i, given the conditional probabilities $p(v_i|v_j)$ and the a priori probabilities $p(v_j)$ for each of the parents of the variable v_i. Such a task is performed by exploiting the rules of Bayesian inference:

$$p(v_i) = \sum_{v_j \in \mathcal{N}_i} p(v_i \mid v_j) p(v_j) \tag{10.1}$$

where $\mathcal{N}_i$ is the set of parents of the sate or behavior v_i.

Another interesting feature of BNs is that the conditional probability $p(v_i|v_j)$ can be reverted, using the Bayesian rule:

$$p(v_j \mid v_i) = \frac{p(v_i \mid v_j) p(v_j)}{p(v_i)} \tag{10.2}$$

Let us highlight one of the peculiarities of BN approaches. Let us suppose to adopt a BN to estimate the behavior of a ship (e.g., pirate vessel, pleasure boat, or refugee ship) based on the trajectory of the ship in terms of position, direction, and velocity. The first idea would be to assume the sensorial data as root nodes and the behavior as a leaf node (i.e., a node with no outgoing edges). However, such an approach is flawed by the inability to define a CPT (i.e., it is very hard to define the probability that the ship is a pirate vessel given the trajectory). Conversely, it would be easier to choose the behavior as root node and then to consider the sensorial information as leaf nodes. In this way, it would be perhaps possible to define the CPT that represents the probability that a ship has a given trajectory, given the probability that it is a pirate vessel. In this framework, the availability of information on a trajectory might be used to update backward the a priori probability that the ship is a pirate vessel, while the exact or probabilistic knowledge of the typology of vessel may provide insights on the actual trajectory. The choice of the link direction, therefore, might be counterintuitive and is highly dependent on the particular situation at hand and on the availability of information.

Hence, two possible applications of the BNs are possible:

- *Forward evaluation*: Given the (probabilistic or not) information about the states of the parent nodes (e.g., high-level information or sensor data, depending on the chosen link direction), it is possible to estimate the belief of the children nodes (higher-level and aggregated information or low-level data, again, depending on the link direction chosen).
- *Backward evaluation*: If some evidence on the actual state of the root nodes is available (e.g., a sensorial updated value or the detection of a high-level situation), it is possible to backward update the belief of the parents, given the a priori probability of the leaves.

Figures 10.1 and 10.2 report two examples of applications of a BN with two "cause" nodes (representing the sensors) and one "effect" node (representing the situation). Note that the links are made from the causes to the effects, that is, there is a probabilistic information on the CPT that represents the probability of a specific effect, given the a priori probabilities of the causes. Specifically, Figure 10.1 represents the case where the sensorial information is used to update the a priori probability of cause nodes, thus modifying the probabilities associated to the effect node. Conversely, Figure 10.2 represents the case where the actual effect or situation is detected (e.g., the probability is equal to one) and the probabilities of the causes are updated backward. However,

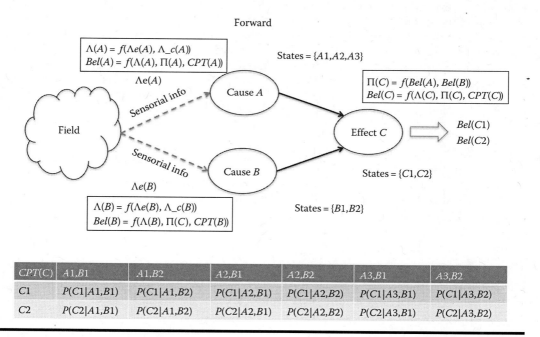

CPT(C)	A1,B1	A1,B2	A2,B1	A2,B2	A3,B1	A3,B2
C1	$P(C1|A1,B1)$	$P(C1|A1,B2)$	$P(C1|A2,B1)$	$P(C1|A2,B2)$	$P(C1|A3,B1)$	$P(C1|A3,B2)$
C2	$P(C2|A1,B1)$	$P(C2|A1,B2)$	$P(C2|A2,B1)$	$P(C2|A2,B2)$	$P(C2|A3,B1)$	$P(C2|A3,B2)$

Figure 10.1 **Example of application of a BN: The sensorial information ($\lambda_e(A)$ and $\lambda_e(B)$) is used to update the belief of the root nodes (e.g., the causes) according to Equation 10.5, and such an information is propagated to the sons to update the belief of final nodes (e.g., effects). The propagation is performed according to Equation 10.6, and in particular, $\pi_C(A)$ and $\pi_C(B)$ are modified according to the updated belief of nodes A and B, and consequently, $\pi(C)$ is updated as expressed by $\pi(C) = f(Bel(A), Bel(B))$. Finally, the belief of node C is recalculated, as a function of the CPT, and updated $\pi(C)$ and λ_C. The notation $z = f(x_1, \ldots, x_n)$ indicates that a particular variable z is function of variables $x_1, \ldots, x_n$.**

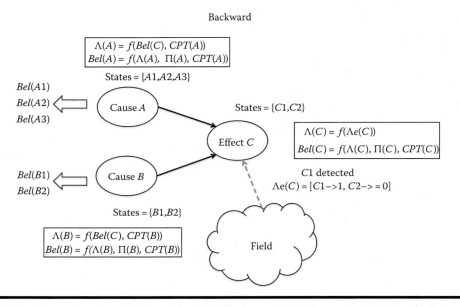

Figure 10.2 Example of application of a BN: The sensorial information $\lambda_e(C)$ is used to update the belief of the leaf nodes, *Bel(C)* (e.g., the actual situation is detected), according to Equation 10.5, and then this information is propagated to the parents, for example, in order to determine the belief of the causes. The propagation is done according to Equation 10.6, and in particular, $\lambda_C(A)$ and $\lambda_C(B)$ are modified according to the updated belief of node C, and consequently, $\lambda(A)$ and $\lambda(B)$ are updated as expressed by $\lambda(A) = f(Bel(C),CPT)$ and $\lambda(B) = f(Bel(C),CPT)$. Finally, belief of nodes A and B are recalculated, as a function of CPT, and updated π and λ. The notation $z = f(x_1, \dots, x_n)$ indicates that a particular variable z is function of variables $x_1, \dots, x_n$.

as stated before, this is not the sole possible configuration, and in the case study, the dual setting will be commented.

Let us now provide a formal definition of Bayesian BN. Many definitions are possible; however, in this section, the approach of Pearl (1988) will be adopted since it leads to a simple and powerful framework for the propagation and back propagation of the belief.

Definition (Bayesian belief network)

A Bayesian BN with n nodes is an oriented acyclic graph $G = \{V, \mathcal{E}\}$, where each variable is represented as a node v_i; $V = \{v_1, \dots, v_n\}$ is the set of all the nodes in the network; and $\mathcal{E} = \{(i, j) \mid v_i, v_j \in V\}$ is the set of the existing oriented links between the nodes of the network.

The *ith* node $v_i \in V$ of a BN is defined by the 6-tuple:

$$v_i = \{n_i, \mathrm{Bel}(v_i), \mathrm{CPT}(v_i), \pi(v_i), \lambda(v_i), \lambda_e(v_i)\} \tag{10.3}$$

where

- n_i is the cardinality of the different states associated to the node v_i (i.e., the different values that the ith variable may assume). Let v_{ij} denote the jth state of node v_i.
- $\mathrm{Bel}(v_i) \in [0,1]^{n_i}$ is the *belief vector* of node v_i that represents the belief in each of the n_i states.

- CPT(v_i) is the CPT used to update the belief based on the probability of the parents (e.g., a table that summarizes for each possible combination of the states of the parent nodes, the conditional probabilities $p(v_{ij}|v_{1a}, v_{2b}, \ldots, v_{n,h})$ used for the direct computation of $p(v_{ij})$ given the a priori probabilities $p(v_j)$ for each parent j of the ith node).
- $\pi(v_i) \in [0,1]^{n_i}$ is the total belief of the parents of node v_i computed on the base of the CPT and on the belief of the parents (i.e., the aggregation of the belief of the parents).
- $\lambda(v_i) \in [0,1]^{n_i}$ is the total belief of the children of node v_i computed by weighting the belief of the children nodes by reverting the conditional probabilities, using the Bayesian rule.
- $\lambda_e(v_i) \in [0,1]^{n_i}$ is the evidence obtained from the field for node v_i.

Note that both the forward and backward approaches may coexist at the same time: for instance, a node in a tree-structured BN may receive a sensorial information and propagate its belief backward to its children and upward to its parents.

Let us now describe the *evidence propagation algorithm* (Pearl, 1988; Subrata, 2008), used to update the beliefs when new evidence is available from the field or sensors.

Evidence propagation algorithm: During the initialization phase, for each root node, $\pi(\cdot)$ and *Bel*($\cdot$) are set equal to the a priori probabilities associated to each node, and the values of $\lambda(\cdot)$ for each node are set to a constant value, since no evidence is available from the field. For the other nodes, the initial values for $\pi(\cdot)$ are computed recursively with the following rule:

$$\pi(v_i) = \sum_{j \in \mathcal{N}_i} p(v_i \mid v_{j_1}, \ldots v_{v_{j_i}}) \prod_{k \in \mathcal{N}_i} \pi(v_k) \tag{10.4}$$

where

$\mathcal{N}_i$ is the set of parents of node v_i

$p(v_i \mid v_{j_1}, \ldots v_{v_{j_i}})$ is the matrix of conditional probabilities, that is, the CPT and $j_1, \ldots, j_i \in \mathcal{N}_i$

The belief is then set equal to the $\pi(v_i)$ vector.

When a sensorial information e_i is available to node v_i, the evidence $\lambda_e(v_i)$ is taken into account, and the values of $\pi(v_i)$, $\lambda(v_i)$, and *Bel*(v_i) are modified as follows (Pearl, 1988; Subrata, 2008):

$$\begin{cases} \lambda_{new}(v_i) = \lambda_e(v_i) \prod_{j \in \mathcal{N}_j; j \neq i} \lambda_{v_i}(v_j) \\ \pi_{new}(v_i) = \prod_{j \in \mathcal{N}_i} \pi_{v_i}(v_j) \\ Bel_{new}(v_i) = \beta \pi_{new}(v_i) \lambda_{new}(v_i) \end{cases} \tag{10.5}$$

where

β is a suitable normalizing term

$\lambda_{v_i}(v_j)$, $\pi_{v_i}(v_j)$ are the contribution of node v_j to the $\lambda(v_i)$ and $\pi(v_i)$, respectively.

Hence, the new value of $\lambda(v_i)$ (i.e., the total belief received by the children) is the product of the values $\lambda_{v_i}(v_j)$ of each children and the evidence obtained by the node v_i. The total belief received from the parents is, again, the product of the belief of each parent $\pi_{v_i}(v_j)$. Then, the belief is updated as a product of the updated π and λ.

Once the node v_i has updated its belief, the changes have to be propagated both backward and forward, that is, by providing its contribution to the λ of the parent nodes and to the π of children nodes. Specifically, the node v_i sends its updated $\lambda_{v_i}(v_j)$ to each parent node v_j and its updated $\pi_{v_k}(v_i)$ to each child node v_k. The structure of these quantities is as follows:

$$\begin{cases} \lambda_{v_j}(v_i) = \alpha \lambda(v_i) \sum_{j \in \mathcal{N}_i, j \neq i} p(v_i \mid v_{j_1}, \ldots, v_{j_{i-1}}, v_{j_{i+1}}, \ldots v_{j_i}) \sum_{f \neq j; f \in \mathcal{N}_i} \pi(v_{fh}) \\ \pi_{v_k}(v_i) = \alpha \dfrac{Bel(v_i)}{\lambda_{v_k}(v_i)} \end{cases} \quad (10.6)$$

where α is a normalization term.

Note that the term $\sum_{j \in \mathcal{N}_i, j \neq i} p(v_i \mid v_{j_1}, \ldots, v_{j_{i-1}}, v_{j_{i+1}}, \ldots v_{j_i}) \sum_{f \neq j; f \in \mathcal{N}_i} \pi(v_{fh})$ is equal to the reverse conditional probability $p(v_j|v_i)$; hence, the computation of the contribution $\lambda_{v_j}(v_i)$ that has to be provided to each parent node v_j requires the inversion of the CPT. The formula for $\pi_{v_k}(v_i)$ is obtained by dividing the belief $Bel(v_i)$ for the term $\lambda_{v_i}(v_k)$, in order to avoid to consider the contribution of node v_k to such a belief.

Let us consider the example of Figure 10.1: the CPT, as reported in the figure, contains the conditional probabilities in the form $p(C|A,B)$, that is, the probability of the states C given a particular combination of the states of nodes A and B. Let $p(v_A), p(v_B)$ be the a priori probabilities associated to the states of nodes A and B. During the initialization phase, $\pi(v_A) = Bel(v_A) = p(v_A)$ and $\pi(v_B) = Bel(v_B) = p(v_B)$, while $\lambda(v_A) = \lambda(v_B) = \lambda(v_C) = [1, \ldots, 1]^T$. The value $\pi(v_C) = Bel(v_C) = \sum_{A,B} p(v_C \mid v_A, v_B) \prod_{k=A,B} \pi(v_k)$.

If node A receives an evidence $\lambda_e(v_A)$, then $\lambda_{new}(v_A) = \lambda_e(v_A)$, $\pi_{new}(v_A) = p(v_A)$, and $Bel_{new}(v_A) = \beta \pi_{new}(v_A) \lambda_{new}(v_A) = \beta p(v_A) \lambda_e(v_A)$, while node B is unchanged.

Node C receives an updated value of $\pi_{v_C}(v_A) = \alpha(Bel_{new}(v_A)/\lambda_{v_C}(v_A)) = \alpha \beta (p(v_A) \lambda_e(v_A)/[1, \ldots, 1])$ and recalculates its belief where the product $\alpha\beta$ can be regarded as a normalizing factor.

Note that such an approach is single shot, and it is therefore suitable only for static situations, not evolving with time.

To overcome this issue, the dynamic Bayesian networks (DBNs) have been proposed in Murphy (2002), as BNs enclosing temporal information (see Figure 10.3). This extension is typically performed according to one or both of the following directions:

- All nodes of the BN are associated with a particular time step.
- Some BN nodes for a given time step may have causal dependencies on nodes from earlier time steps (in addition to the usual causal dependencies on nodes from their own time step); such dependencies are called temporal dependencies.

Let us conclude this section with some considerations on BNs.

The BNs are powerful tools to aggregate sensorial data into high-level information based on a probabilistic description of the interactions among the variables and states and considering complex

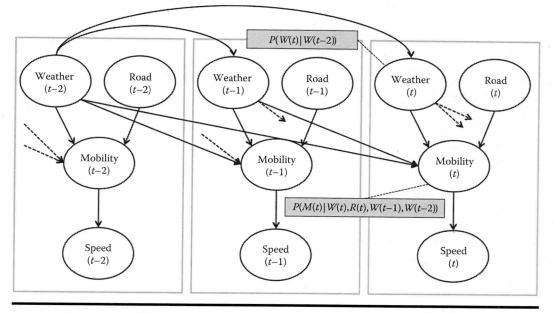

Figure 10.3   DBN example.

cause–effect relations. Hence, they represent a valuable instrument to distinguish between situations and behaviors based on a priori probabilities, intermediate states or behaviors, and multiple sensorial data.

A relevant drawback of BN approaches is that the CPTs may be not available in real-world situations and there is the need to resort to learning techniques, which are often mutated from the field of ANNs. The reader is referred to Chenga et al. (2002) and its references for the specific learning techniques tailored for BNs and to the next section, where a very general purpose learning technique will be discussed.

Another limitation is that the complexity of the approach is highly dependent on the number of nodes. These issues limit the practical applicability of this framework since there is an evident trade-off between the network size and the real-time performances. Finally, the BNs require the graph to be acyclic and hence cannot cope with feedbacks and loops.

In the following section, the ANNs will be reviewed.

10.4 Artificial Neural Networks

An ANN (Fausett, 1994; Hagan et al., 1996) is a biologically inspired computation technique aiming to reproduce the functional behavior of a neural network. To this end, sets of "neurons" or "processing elements," each with limited or local computation capability, are interconnected by means of a network topology. Similarly to their biological analogues, the functions of a neural network are exerted collectively by the neurons, with a high degree of parallelism. Moreover, mimicking the ability of biological neural networks to modify and reconfigure themselves, ANNs are typically endowed with learning mechanisms. Such mechanisms allow to reshape the network either by changing the network topology or by reinforcing the coupling among neurons (e.g., changing the weights on the links).

Such a methodology is mainly used to approximate a function, for which only a set of inputs and outputs are given. The underlying idea is to train the network with a suitable set of known inputs and associated outputs, thus influencing the network structure. The resulting trained network is then used to compute the function, in a black-box perspective.

ANNs find large application in many fields, such as modeling and identification, optimization and classification, and process control and pattern recognition (see Meireles et al., 2003 for a comprehensive survey).

Let us now discuss in detail the structure of an ANN, which is typically composed of four main ingredients:

1. The set of processing units or neurons
2. The weighted links between the processing units
3. The activation rule that converts the neuron's inputs into its outputs
4. The learning mechanisms to adjust the weights

Hence, formally, an ANN can be defined as follows.

Definition (Artificial neural network)

An ANN is a network of n interconnected neurons described by a directed graph $\mathcal{G} = \{\mathcal{V}, \mathcal{E}, W\}$, where $\mathcal{V} = \{1, \ldots, n\}$ is the set of nodes/neurons and $\mathcal{E} = \{e_{ij}\} \in \mathcal{V} \times \mathcal{V}$ is the set of links; the weight of the link e_{ij} is described by the entry w_{ij} of the adjacency matrix W.

Let us define the set of neighbors of node i as $\mathcal{N}_i = \left\{ j \in \mathcal{V} \mid e_{ji} \in \mathcal{E} \right\}$ and $x \in \mathbb{R}^p$ as the input vector of the ANN.

Definition (Neuron network function)

Each neuron i is associated with a neuron network function (NNF) $f_i(x) : \mathbb{R}^p \to \mathbb{R}$. Such a function is a composition of the other nodes' functions and has the following structure:

$$f_i(x) = K \left(\sum_{j \in \mathcal{N}_i} w_{ji} f_j(x) \right) \tag{10.7}$$

where
  $\mathcal{N}_i$ is the set of neighbors of node i
  w_{ji} is the weight of the link between node j and node i
  $K : \mathbb{R} \to \mathbb{R}$ is the activation *function*

The activation function is the function that describes the output behavior of a neuron. Typical choices for K are the step function (where the output of the neuron is 0 if the weighted sum is less than a given threshold T) or the logistic function $l(x) = 1/(1 + e^{-x})$, which has a sigmoid shape and thus provides a smooth transition.

Definition (Output of ANN)

The output $y \in \mathbb{R}^q$ of an ANN is a vector whose elements are a composition of the functions f_i of the neurons (typically a reduced set of neurons). More formally,

$$y_h = F_h(x) = \sum_{i=1}^{n} g_{ih} f_i(x), \ \forall h = 1, \ldots, q \qquad (10.8)$$

where

g_{ih} are used to compute a weighted sum
F_h is the output function whose value is y_h
$F_h(x)$ is the vectorial output function $F(x)$

Figure 10.4 shows an example of ANN with $p = 3$ inputs, $q = 2$ outputs, and $n = 7$ neurons.

Note that the network has a highly parallel structure; for instance, the functions f_5 and f_6 can be computed separately, as they depend on disjoint sets of nodes. Note further that the graph in the example is acyclic; a network with such a structure is typically referred to as feedforward. Feedforward networks are composed of multiple layers (2 in the example of Figure 10.4); each layer can be seen as an intermediate step in the computation of the output values. Obviously, the more the layers, the more sophisticated the ANN.

More complex configurations are possible, for instance, there might be loops, or a node may depend on its past values; however, these approaches are out of the scope of the present work, and the interested reader may refer to Fausett (1994) and Hagan et al. (1996) for more details.

Let us now discuss the learning procedure by which an ANN is trained. Let $\mathbb{F} = \{F(x)\}$ be a class of functions $F(x)$ and let a cost function $C : \mathbb{F} \to \mathbb{R}$. Suppose that there exists a function F^* such that $C(F^*) \leq C(F), \ \forall F \in \mathbb{F}$. The most diffused learning process, often referred to as supervised learning, is a way to find this function F^* by using a set of pairs $\{(x,y)\}$ obtained by direct observation or by means of a statistical distribution.

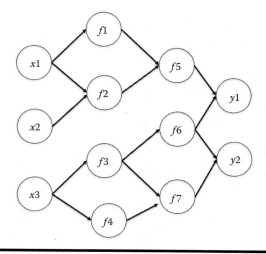

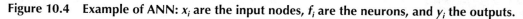

Figure 10.4 Example of ANN: x_i are the input nodes, f_i are the neurons, and y_i the outputs.

A classical approach is to find the $F^*(x)$ that minimizes the expected value

$$C = E[(F(x) - y)^2]$$

(10.9)

for pairs (x,y) drawn by a distribution $\mathcal{D}$. However, for practical computations, only a finite set of m observations are available, and the cost function is approximated by

$$\hat{C} = \frac{1}{m} \sum_{i=1}^{m} (F(x_i) - y_i)^2$$

(10.10)

If the cost function is minimized with a gradient descent technique (Avriel, 2003), the learning approach is called back propagation. The main idea is that the error between desired and actual outputs is diffused backward.

Note that the function $\hat{C}$ is obtained considering the composition of the functions f_i of the neurons. Hence, once the vector x is given a particular value, the function $\hat{C}$ can be regarded as a continuous and differentiable function of the weights w_{ij} and g_{ij}. It is therefore possible to calculate the gradient:

$$\nabla \hat{C} = \left[\frac{\partial \hat{C}}{\partial w_{1,1}}, \cdots, \frac{\partial \hat{C}}{\partial w_{n,n}}, \frac{\partial \hat{C}}{\partial g_{1,1}}, \cdots, \frac{\partial \hat{C}}{\partial g_{n,q}} \right]$$

(10.11)

The weights w_{ij} (g_{ij}) are then updated using the increment:

$$\Delta w_{ij} = -\gamma \frac{\partial \hat{C}}{\partial w_{ij}}; \quad \Delta g_{ij} = -\gamma \frac{\partial \hat{C}}{\partial g_{ij}}$$

(10.12)

where γ represents a learning constant, that is, a proportionality parameter that determines the step length of each iteration in the negative gradient direction.

In the literature, some attempts have been made to apply ANNs to situation assessment. Indeed, such a methodology can be adopted to integrate the information coming from multiple and distributed information sources, performing a sensorial data fusion.

ANNs have been successfully applied to multi-sensor data fusion (see, for instance, Bothe and Biel, 1999 and its references). Note that, for a true situation assessment, a mere sensorial data fusion is not sufficient. There is the need, besides suitably aggregating sensor data, to provide systems able to distinguish which is the actual situation or to foresee the expected evolution, in terms of high-level events. In Liang and Lai (2007), a preliminary study is performed with the aim to detect the condition of a telecommunication network, such as normal working conditions, denial of service, or buffer overflow. To this end, an evolutionary strategy is used to tune an ANN able to determine the situation by inspecting large amounts of network data. In Wang and Ye (2008), a two-layered scheme is introduced in order to assess high-level situations and to predict the next attack step in a battlefield scenario. In the context of coastal surveillance, ANNs have been adopted to identify the class of vessel based on the observation of its movement pattern (Zandipour et al., 2008). Specifically, the considered marine area was divided into a grid, and the position and velocity of the ships were assumed to belong to a reduced set of values (e.g., "slow," "fast," or "south," "southwest"); then, ANNs were trained based on a huge data set of vessel trajectories.

Analogously to BNs, however, such a technique suffers of two main drawbacks: the presence of a learning procedure and, in particular, the acyclic structure of the network. In order to address such a major drawback, MMs will be discussed in the next section.

10.5 Markov Model

MMs (Markov, 1906) are powerful instruments able to model a system that may assume discrete states, providing a prediction on the likelihood of sequences of states, that identify a pattern or behavior. The relation among the different states is represented by means of a graph structure, where the nodes represent the states and the edges represent the allowed transitions.

The main assumption of such a methodology is that, at each time step, the system evolves changing the state with a given probability, without memory of the past decisions (this property is often referred to as *Markov property*); hence, the edges are characterized by a weight that represents the transition probability. Note that the Markov property seems to imply that the behavior of the system is limited to a single step; however, since sequences of states are typically considered in such approaches, the Markov property is indeed not limitative.

The MM formalism allows therefore to calculate the likelihood of sequences of states, assessing the possible behaviors along the temporal dimension. Note that the MM formalism does not impose any constraint on the topological structure of the graph; hence, there is the possibility to model cyclic behaviors and also self-pointing edges that represent the perdurance of a given state over more time steps.

MMs find applications in many contexts. For instance, in the financial context, this instrument has been applied for the analysis of credit risk spread (Jarrow et al., 1997), while in Miller (1952), the different responses to psychological tests were modeled using MMs. Analogously to BNs and ANNs, MMs can be fed with observation, eventually noisy, acquired from the field, in order to influence the evolution of the system.

Let us now formally define an MM.

Definition (Markov model)

An MM with n states is defined as the 4-tuple $\{S, x(k), A, x_0\}$, where

- $S = \{s_1, \cdots, s_n\}$ is the set of the states.
- $x(k) = [x_1(k), \ldots, x_n(k)] \in [0, 1]^n$ is the probability vector associated to the states at time step k, that is, $x_i(k)$ represents the probability that the system at time k is in the state i. Clearly it is always verified that $\sum_{i=1}^{n} x_i(k) = 1$.
- A is the state transition matrix, whose elements a_{ij} represent the probability of passing from ith to jth state, that is, the probability $p(x_j(k) = 1 | x_i(k - 1) = 1)$. Due to the probabilistic structure of $x(k)$, the sum of transition probabilities must be 1 (i.e., the sum along each row of A is equal to 1).
- $x_0 \in [0, 1]^n$ is the initial probability vector associated to the states at time step $k = 0$. Clearly the sum of these probabilities is equal to 1.

Figure 10.5 reports an example of MM with four states. Note that the presence of self-pointing edges for the states S1 and S4 represents the probability to persist in the corresponding state.

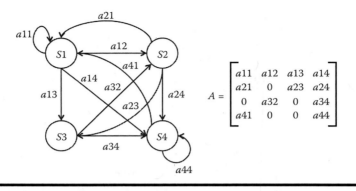

Figure 10.5 **MM example: S_i are the states, while A is the Markov matrix and is such that** $\sum_{j=1}^{n} a_{ij} = 1$ **for all i.**

Since MMs have no memory of past history, it is assumed that the transition probability for a particular couple of states is fixed; in other terms, the matrix A is stationary, and the evolution of the system is given by

$$x(k+1) = x(k)A \qquad (10.13)$$

According to the discrete-time system theory, the state transition matrix after m steps is given by A^m, and, due to the peculiar structure of the matrix (i.e., all the rows sum to one), it is always verified that $\lim_{m \to \infty} A^m$ tends to a stationary limit value, implying that the probability of the different states tends to a stationary distribution x_∞, which corresponds to the dominant or Perron–Frobenius eigenvector of the matrix A (Luenberger, 1979), in spite of the initial probability distribution x_0.

Within the standard MM framework, each state corresponds to an observable event; however, in many real cases, the states of the system are not directly observable. Instead, a set of indirect observations may be available, and these observations may be affected by noise. The exact motion of a vehicle, for instance, might not be directly observable. However, a noisy sensorial information or a witness may provide a, although vague, hint for the reconstruction of the state. In order to face the challenge of unobservable states, in the literature, the MMs have been suitably extended; the result is a hidden Markov model (HMM).

Definition (Hidden Markov model)

An HMM is described by the 7-tuple $\{S, x(k), A, x_0, O, y(k), B\}$, where $S, x(k), A, x_0$ are the same of MMs and $O, y(k), B$ are defined as

- $O = \{o_1, \ldots, o_m\}$ is the set of m types of observation.
- $y(k) \in [0, 1]^m$ is the probability vector associated to the observations at time step k, that is, $y_i(k)$ is the probability associated to the observation i; again $\sum_{i=1}^{m} y_i(k) = 1$.
- B is a $n \times m$ observation likelihood matrix, whose elements b_{ij} represent the probability of observing o_j while being in the ith state, that is, $p(y_j(k) = 1 | x_i(k) = 1)$.

The systems' dynamics of an HMM is still defined by Equation 10.13, but the state $x(k)$ is not directly observable. There is therefore the need to assess or reconstruct the state based on the observations. To this end, many techniques are possible; the first idea since $y(k) = x(k)B$ is to invert the relation by resorting to a pseudo-inverse $x(k) = y(k)B^\dagger$, leading to the system

$$x(k+1) = y(k)B^\dagger A$$

Such an approach, however, is limited to the single step and may be misleading, in particular when the observations are noisy. In the literature, the problem is formulated with the aim to identify the most probable sequence of states $\{x(1), \ldots, x(k)\}$ that is likely to generate a given observation sequence $\{y(1), \ldots, y(k)\}$. To this end, the most established approach is the *Viterbi algorithm*.

Viterbi Algorithm

Given a sequence of observations $\{y(1), \ldots, y(k)\}$, the most likely sequence of states $\{x(1), \ldots, x(k)\}$ can be computed by solving the maximization problem

$$\max_{\{x(1),\ldots,x(k)\}} p(\{x(1),\ldots,x(k)\},\{y(1),\ldots,y(k)\}) \tag{10.14}$$

that is, the maximum probability that both sequences are verified. The problem is solved recursively by considering the following variable:

$$\delta_k(s_i) = \max_{\{x(1),\ldots,x(k)\}} p(\{x(1),\ldots,x(k) = s_i\},\{y(1),\ldots,y(k)\}) \tag{10.15}$$

which is the maximum probability that a state sequence of length k ends with the state s_i. Then, the following induction principle is adopted to solve the problem:

$$\delta_{k+1}(s_j) = \max_i \left\{ \delta_k(s_i)a_{ij} \right\} b_{j,k+1} \tag{10.16}$$

where a_{ij} and $b_{j,k+1}$ are entries of matrices A and B, respectively. The algorithm is initialized by considering the probability $\delta_1(s_i)$ that a sequence of length 1 has state s_i, which is defined as follows:

$$\delta_1(s_i) = x_{i0} B_{i1} \quad \forall i = 1,\ldots,n$$

The most likely sequence is then built incrementally, keeping trace of the indices of the elements s_j associated to $\delta_k(s_j)$. The interested reader may refer to Subrata (2008) for more details.

A dual problem is to compute the likelihood of an observation sequence, given the state; to this end, the *forward algorithm* is used (see Zhao, 2007 for details).

In Damarla (2008), HMMs have been used to perform indoor human activity recognition, fusing data acquired through a multi-sensor equipped mobile robot. HMMs have also been employed in the field of image processing. In particular, in Feronand and Mohammad-Djafari (2003), the HMM approach is used to perform fusion of different processing images, related to the same object, in order to increase the awareness about the object characteristics (e.g., the inside of a suit-case). Due to their capability to model sequential patterns, HMMs have been employed for the column recognition problem in military domain, where a noncooperative military unit consisting of a sequence of objects forms a transportation column (Bjornfot and Svensson, 2000). The objective was to infer the object composition and organizational structure of the column based on noisy observations of individual objects, in combination with generic a priori information about the organizational structure of the noncooperative forces.

A further extension of HMMs is to consider a hierarchical set of interacting HMMs, where each HMM is represented as a state of a macro-model; the result is a *hierarchical hidden Markov model* (HHMM). An HHMM state, therefore, emits sequences of symbols, rather than a single one, by recursively activating one of the substates of one of the HMMs that composes the macro-network.

Finally, the *hidden semi-Markov models* (HSMMs) are HMMs where the state duration is explicitly modeled. In HMMs, it is assumed that at each time step k, the system changes its state; hence, each state is assumed to have the same duration. The representation of states of different duration can be modeled by considering a cycle from the node representing the state to itself. Analogously to HMMs, the forward and Viterbi algorithms have been suitably extended in this case (Dong and He, 2007).

In Dong and He (2007), the problem of performing diagnosis and prognosis on industrial component health is addressed and solved applying HSMM. Another application where HSMM has been used to perform fusion of data acquired from sensors and estimation of human activity is in Yu and Kobayashi (2003), where the mobility of a user in urban environment is estimated, in order to provide efficient wireless access to Internet.

Let us now provide some conclusive remarks on MMs.

These approaches are very flexible techniques and are naturally oriented to the representation of behaviors that are defined over a temporal dimension; in fact, it is possible to represent the patterns as sequences of elementary states or operations and compute their likelihood. Hence, MMs have a more compact representation, with respect to BNs, where each possible state and pattern has to be modeled by means of a node. Moreover, the cyclic nature of MMs allows to overcome many of the limitations of acyclic techniques, such as BNs and ANNs.

However, such an approach has one main drawback, in particular when a high-level set of states/observations is considered, that is, how to map a large number of often discording information sources into a suitable set of states/observations.

In order to solve this issue, the next section will describe the approaches based on the theory of evidence.

10.6 Evidence Theory

The term "Evidence Theory" was coined by Shafer (1976), reinterpreting the work of Dempster (1967) on how to represent and aggregate epistemic uncertainty.

Epistemic uncertainty and random uncertainty are usually considered as distant and antithetic concepts. Random uncertainty is generally related to variations of the physical system or the environment, for example, the variations in weather conditions or in the life of a compressor or turbine. Epistemic uncertainty, on the contrary, is mainly related to the lack of knowledge concerning the quantity, the system processes, or the environment, and is characterized by a high degree of subjectivity and vagueness. Classical example is the qualitative knowledge of a process or the lack of understanding of complex physical phenomena. However, the probability can be seen as a particular case of belief (Shafer, 1976); hence, both aspects can be captured within the framework.

Evidence theory has been applied in many contexts, like statistical inference (Dempster, 1967), fault diagnosis (Basir and Yuan, 2007; Yang and Kim, 2006), and risk analysis (Gao et al., 2008; Yang et al., 2011). Other application fields are image processing (Lin, 2008; Scheuermann and Rosenhahn, 2011) and pattern identification or recognition.

In Leung and Wu (2000), a target track identification based on a radar information has been implemented, with the aim to identify hostile flying objects. Compared to a Bayesian approach, the system proved to be more robust to perturbation and noise, but definitely more computationally expensive.

Indeed the computational complexity is the true weak point of such a methodology; nevertheless in the literature, some approaches aimed to keep the complexity down have been introduced (Smarandache and Dezert, 2009).

In the following, an example of application of such a methodology will be provided. Let $\Omega = \{\omega_1, \ldots, \omega_n\}$ be a finite set of possible values of a variable ω, where the elements ω_i are assumed to be mutually exclusive and exhaustive (e.g., different positions, different behaviors). Suppose that only vague evidence is available in order to distinguish between the different values; for instance, during a crime investigation, a witness has seen a long haired subject in the nearby of the crime scene, while another witness has heard a female voice. These two observations apply to subsets of the suspects, and there is the need to compose them in order to determine the guilty. From a set-theoretical point of view, this means that, for each observation, a value is assigned to the corresponding subset of suspects, and these values are composed for the single suspect by considering the value associated to all the subsets of the suspects that contain that specific person. Note that, in principle, all the subsets of the suspects have to be considered, and the resulting set, namely, *power set*, has a number of elements that is exponential in the number of suspects. Specifically, if the generic subset of suspects is denoted as γ_i, the power set originated by the set Ω is denoted by $\Gamma = 2^\Omega$ and is defined as $2^\Omega = \{\gamma_1, \ldots, \gamma_{|\Gamma|}\}$ and contains every subset $\gamma_i \subseteq \Omega$. In this framework, the focus is on quantifying the belief of propositions of the form: "the true value ω is contained in γ_i."

Let us now introduce a basic belief assignment, that is, a choice for the beliefs in the sets γ_i.

Definition (Basic belief assignment)

A function $m: 2^\Omega \rightarrow [0, 1]$ is called a basic belief assignment (BBA) if

$$m(\varnothing) = 0 \tag{10.17}$$

$$\sum_{\gamma_a \in \Gamma} m(\gamma_a) = 1 \tag{10.18}$$

where

γ_a is the power set Γ

$m(\gamma_a)$ is the part of belief that supports exactly γ_a, that is, the fact that the true value of ω is in γ_a

However, due to the ambiguity of the observations, there is no insight about the subsets of γ_a. The first condition reflects the fact that no belief should be committed to the empty set, and the second condition reflects that the total belief has measure one.

Note that $m(\gamma_a)$ and $m(\gamma_b)$ can be both equal to zero even if $m(\gamma_a \cup \gamma_b) \neq 0$. Furthermore, $m(\cdot)$ is not monotone under inclusion, that is, $\gamma_a \subset \gamma_b$ does not imply $m(\gamma_a) < m(\gamma_b)$.

Let us now define a belief function.

Definition (Belief function)

A function *Bel*: $2^\Omega \rightarrow [0, 1]$ is called belief function over Ω if it satisfies the following relationship:

$$Bel(\gamma_a) = \sum_{\gamma_b \subseteq \gamma_a} m(\gamma_b) \tag{10.19}$$

This function quantifies the total specific amount of belief supporting the event, and it is often taken into account in the decision-making process after data aggregation has been performed (Smets and Kennes, 1994).

The main criticism to Shafer formulation concerns the application of the Dempster–Shafer (DS) combination rule. In fact, whenever there is a strong conflict between sources to be combined, the straightforward application of DS combination rule can lead to pathological behaviors, eventually reinforcing the opinion with minimum belief (Zadeh, 1986).

To face such an issue, Philip Smets (1990) proposed the *transferable belief model* (TBM). The TBM theory, like the Shafer formulation, relies on the concept of BBA but relaxates the assumption of $m(\varnothing)=0$. This allows to explicitly take into account the level of contradiction in the information sources.

Within the TBM model, it is possible to combine different and contradictory information sources by composing the masses associated to each source, by means of the so-called Smets operator.

Definition (Smets operator $\otimes$)

In the TBM, the combination rule is defined as follows:

$$m_{ij}(\gamma_a) \triangleq (m_i \otimes m_j)(\gamma_a) = \sum_{\substack{\gamma_b, \gamma_c \\ \gamma_b \cap \gamma_c = \gamma_a}} m_i(\gamma_b) m_j(\gamma_c) \tag{10.20}$$

The fact that $m(\varnothing) > 0$ can be explained in two ways: the open-world assumption and the quantified conflict. The open-world assumption reflects the idea that Ω might not be exhaustive, that is, it might not contain all the possibilities. Under this interpretation, being the complement of Ω, the mass $m(\varnothing) > 0$ represents the modeling errors, that is, the fact that the truth might not be contained in Ω. The second interpretation of $m(\varnothing) > 0$ is that there is some underlying conflict between the sources that are combined in order to produce the BBA m. Hence, the mass assigned to $m(\varnothing)$ represents the degree of conflict.

In particular, it can be computed as follows:

$$m_{ij}(\varnothing) = 1 - \sum_{\substack{\gamma_a = \\ \gamma_a \in \Gamma}} m_{ij}(\gamma_a) \tag{10.21}$$

The main drawback of these approaches, however, is that the power set is exponential in the number of elements of Ω. Such an issue often limits the applicability of these methodologies.

Evidence theory is based on the assumption of closed world: all the interpretations considered are exhaustive for the question posed, that is, no other elements exist except those in Ω. Theoretically, such an assumption is not restrictive since one can always close any open world, adding the new elements. Another assumption made by Shafer is the third middle excluded principle, that is, the existence of the complement for any elements or propositions belonging to the power set.

10.7 Case Study

To highlight the differences and to critically compare the methodologies analyzed so far, in the following, a case study will be considered. The case study is a modification of that provided in Zandipour et al. (2008).

Consider a maritime surveillance problem, where a coastal and maritime area has to be patrolled and the behavior of the ships in the scenario has to be assessed based on sensorial information. Specifically, suppose to partition the area into a tessellation of small uniform zones of the desired size, and suppose that the position of a ship is identified by the zone where it is detected (see Figure 10.6). Suppose further that it is possible to obtain information about the velocity and direction of the ship. Let us assume that a ship may have one of the eight directions depicted in Figure 10.6, while three different velocities are considered for each direction, that is, fast (green), slow (blue), and zero (red). Finally, for the sake of simplicity, let us suppose that only one ship is present in the marine area of interest and that the possible behaviors for the ship are the following: attacker, pleasure boat, or refugees' ship. In the following, some hints on how to set up a situation assessment framework based on each of the methodologies described in this chapter are provided.

Bayesian networks: Due to the dynamic context of the problem at hand, a static BN seems not adequate to assess the behavior of the ship. Hence, a good choice is to rely on a DBN, as shown by the example in Figure 10.7. Specifically, n Bayesian networks are considered for n time steps.

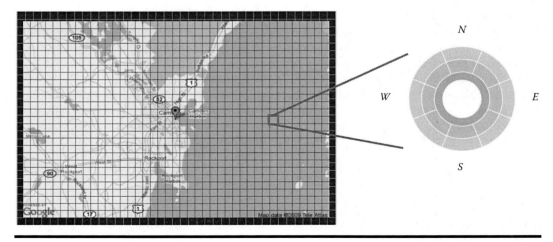

Figure 10.6   Example of maritime surveillance scenario.

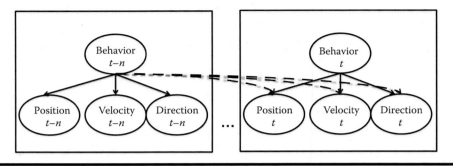

Figure 10.7   Example of DBN for maritime surveillance: the behavior of the ship is assessed based on *n* linked Bayesian network, each focusing on a particular time step (only the first and the last BNs are reported in the figure). Specifically, each BN considers the relation between position, velocity, and direction of the ship and its behavior at a given time step.

Consistently to the considerations made before on the unavailability of CPTs in a direct mapping from cause to effect, let us assume that each BN has a root node (ship behavior) and three leaf nodes (position, velocity, and direction). In order to take into account the temporal dimension, the *n* networks are interconnected, by linking the input node of each BN for time $t, t - 1, \ldots, t - n$ to the leaf nodes of the BN. Note that the complexity of this method can be overwhelming, since the number of states is indeed huge. Note further that such an approach allows both to assess the belief of a sequence of position/velocities/states given the actual behavior in a forward prospective and to determine the behavior based on the previous *n* time steps using the backward mode. However, it is not possible to handle loops in this context.

Artificial neural networks: Figure 10.8 represents an example of ANN aimed to identify the behavior of the ship. Since the setup of ANNs requires a huge availability of input/output couples, differently from the aforementioned case, it seems natural to consider an input layer containing the values of position, velocity, and direction of the past *n* steps. In the example, the network is composed of two intermediate layers of neurons and has an output layer with a node for each behavior. Although being similar to the DBN example earlier, there are some significant differences in this approach. First of all, besides the direction of the links, the input/output values need not be probabilistic; hence, the ANN framework is more general. Moreover, it is possible to consider many complex subsequent layers, without needing to assess the CPT of each node; in fact, the learning methodology for ANN assesses a reduced set of parameters with respect to BNs. Note further that the graph topology varies during the learning phase, allowing finer representations with respect to the a priori knowledge of the interaction among the layers. Finally, the value associated to the input nodes need not be a discrete value; hence, it is possible to consider more realistic data (e.g., the actual GPS position, the velocity in mph, the direction angle) without increasing the complexity of the system. Analogously to BNs, however, a learning procedure has to be set up; hence, there is the need to consider a huge set of trajectories, along with the corresponding expected behavior. Nevertheless, the complexity, in both BNs and ANNs, significantly grows with the time window considered for the input data (e.g., number of time steps), and the paradox is that a small *n* may not be descriptive of the behavior, while a big *n* may not be feasible.

Markov models: Figure 10.9 shows an example of MM and an example of HMM for the scenario at hand. Specifically, in the proposed example, a node represents a position on the grid, and the

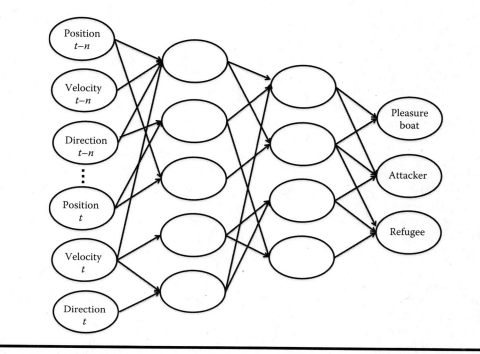

Figure 10.8 **Example of ANN for maritime surveillance: the values of position, velocity, and direction for *n* steps are used as input in order to identify the ships' behavior.**

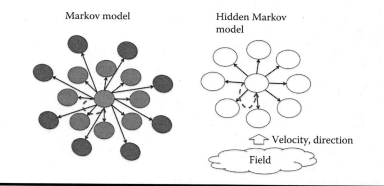

Figure 10.9 **Examples of MM and HMM for maritime surveillance. The leftmost figure represents an MM where the states are the positions in the grid. Specifically, in the figure, only the states directly reachable from the red node are represented: The light grey ones are the eight cells contiguous to the central node (i.e., reached in one step with "slow" velocity), and the dark grey ones represent a jump of two cells (i.e., "fast" velocity). The rightmost figure represents an HMM where the position information is hidden and only velocity/direction information is available.**

figure represents the neighborhood of a given node. Within the MM example, the node in red is connected to eight nodes (in blue) representing the eight cells in the grid contiguous to it (along the eight directions considered) and associated to the velocity "slow." Moreover, eight additional nodes are considered (in green) that represent a jump of two cells along the eight considered directions. The set of arcs is completed by a self-pointing link, representing the permanence in the same cell. As shown by the example, the number of states coincides with the size of the grid, but the number of links is nontrivial in this setting.

Consider the case where the position cannot exactly be assessed, but the information on direction and velocity can be obtained (e.g., by interpolating a noisy trajectory). In this case, the HMM depicted in Figure 10.9 can be considered, where the vector of states (e.g., positions) has to be assessed based on the information on velocities/directions by means of the Viterbi algorithm. In this case, the number of links can be reduced.

Note that, in both cases, a nontrivial issue is how to define the transition probabilities: If in the HMM case, it seems natural to set the probability of each of the nine outgoing edges for each node as 1/9, it is less clear how to choose the probabilities in the MM example; for instance, the probability to make a jump of two cells has to be associated with a smaller probability with respect to moving of one cell or remaining in the same cell. Note that the HMM setting may also take into account other typologies of observation; for instance, it may be possible to consider a witness that has a vague idea of the position or an audio recording that can be used to assess the size of the boat and hence the possible velocity.

Let us now provide an alternative to HMM for the assessment of high-level states by means of the evidence theory approach.

Evidence theory: Figure 10.10 reports a simple application of the evidence theory framework. Suppose that m different information sources have access to low-level or raw information and have to assess the direction of the ship. Each of the information sources has a subjective idea on how the information has to be mapped into the eight directions. In the picture, only two associations are depicted; note that the images of the combination $\{\omega_1, \omega_5\}$ partly overlap, thus leading to a

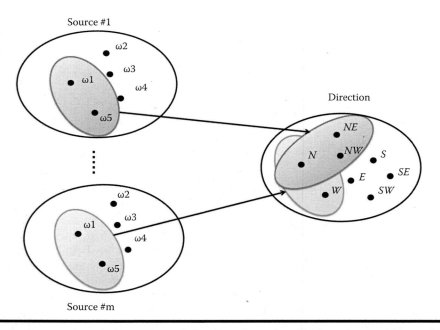

Figure 10.10 Examples of assessment of the direction of a ship based on evidence theory. In figure 10.2, out of m information sources are reported; specifically, the figure shows that the same set of information $\{\omega_1, \omega_5\}$ can be mapped differently onto the set of directions, although partly overlapping.

higher probability associated to the direction north (N). Note further that a huge set of associations might be defined and, in particular when multiple information sources are considered, the complexity may rapidly become unmanageable, since the complexity is exponential in the cardinality of the associations.

Such an approach, however, can be considered as a prerequisite for all those cases where a high-level information (e.g., the direction), although required by a situation assessment algorithm, is not directly available.

10.8 Conclusion

In this chapter, some of the most diffused models and techniques used in the context of SAW have been reviewed and compared. To this end, the problem of SAW has been discussed, along with the main theoretical approaches to such a task. Then the Bayesian networks have been described, as a powerful tool able to perform statistical inference and to determine the probability of a behavior or situation, given the probability of atomic events or the probabilistic sensorial information. A similar but more general tool, namely, ANN, has then been discussed as a methodology aimed to reproduce the computational capability of a biological neural network and typically used to approximate a function whose closed form is unknown, but for which a huge set of input/output data has to be collected. Both these approaches require the setup of learning procedures and cannot handle cycles.

To solve this latter issue, the MMs have been discussed as a compact cyclic representation aimed to represent the behaviors or situations by means of a sequence of state transitions. However, these states are often high-level states, and there is the need to implement an aggregation procedure able to cope with different and contradictory information sources: to this end, the evidence theory framework has been discussed.

The simple case study that concludes the chapter highlights that there is not a standard solution to the SAW problem and that the choice of the approach has to be carefully tailored to the particular problem at hand, to the computational requirements, and to the availability of sensorial data.

References

Avriel, M (2003). *Nonlinear Programming: Analysis and Methods*. Prentice Hall, NJ: Dover Publishing.

Basir, O. and X. Yuan (2007). Engine fault diagnosis based on multi-sensor information fusion using dempster-shafer evidence theory. *Information Fusion* 8 (4), 379–386.

Bjornfot, J. and P. Svensson (2000). Modeling the column recognition problem in tactical information fusion. In *3rd International Conference on Information Fusion, 2000*, Vol.1. Paris, France: IEEE, pp. MOD1/24–MOD1/30.

Bothe, H. and L. Biel (1999). Multivariate sensor fusion by a temporally coded neural network model. In *2nd International Conference on Information Fusion*, Sunnyvale, CA.

Boyd, J. (1987). A discourse on winning and losing. Unpublished briefing and essay, In *Maxwell AFB Lecture*, Alabama, Air University Library Document No. M-U 43947, retrieved from http://dnipogo.org/john-r-boyd.

Chenga, J., R. Greinera, J. Kellya, D. Bellb, and W. Liub (2002). Learning bayesian networks from data: An information-theory based approach. *Artificial Intelligence* 137 (2), 43–90.

Damarla, T (2008). Hidden markov model as a framework for situational awareness. In *11th International Conference on Information Fusion, 2008*, Cologne, Germany: IEEE, pp. 1–7.

Dempster, A. P (1967). Upper and lower probabilities induced by a multivalued mapping. *Annals of Mathematical Statistics* 38 (2), 325–339.

Dong, M. and D. He (2007). Hidden semi-markov model-based methodology for multi-sensor equipment health diagnosis and prognosis. *European Journal of Operational Research* 178, 858–878.

Endsley, M (1988). Design and evaluation for situation awareness enhancement. *Human Factors and Ergonomics Society Annual Meeting Proceedings* 32 (2), 97–101.

Endsley, M (1995). Toward a theory of situation awareness in dynamic systems. *Human Factors: The Journal of the Human Factors and Ergonomics Society* 37 (1), 32–64.

Fausett, L. (1994). *Fundamentals of Neural Networks*. New York: Prentice Hall PTR.

Feronand, O. and A. Mohammad-Djafari (2003). A hidden markov model for bayesian data fusion of multivariate signals. In *5th International Triennial Calcutta Symposium on Probability and Statistics, 2003,* Calcutta, India, pp. 1–14.

Gao, H., J. Zhu, and C. Li (2008, april). The analysis of uncertainty of network security risk assessment using dempster-shafer theory. In *12th International Conference on Computer Supported Cooperative Work in Design, CSCWD 2008,* Stanford, CA, pp. 754–759.

Geoffrey, G. and H. Zweig (2003). Bayesian network structures and inference techniques for automatic speech recognition. *Computer Speech & Language* 17 (2–3), 173–193.

Hagan, M. T., H. B. Demuth, M. H. Beale (1996). *Neural Network Design*. Boston, MA: PWS.

Hall, D. and J. Llinas (1997). An introduction to multisensor data fusion. *Proceedings of the IEEE* 85 (1), 6–23.

Hall, D. and J. Llinas (2001). *Handbook of Multisensor Data Fusion*. Boca Raton, FL: CRC Press.

Huang, T., D. Koller, J. Malik, G. Ogasawara, B. Rao, S. Russell, and J. Weber (1994). Automatic symbolic traffic scene analysis using belief networks. In *Proceedings of 12th International Conference in Artificial Intelligence*, Seattle, WA, pp. 966–972.

Jarrow, R., D. Lando, and S. Turnbull (1997). A markov model for the term structure of credit risk spreads. *Review of Financial Studies* 10 (2), 481–523.

Leung, H. and J. Wu (2000, April). Bayesian and dempster-shafer target identification for radar surveillance. *IEEE Transactions on Aerospace and Electronic Systems* 36 (2), 432–447.

Liang, Y. and J. Lai (2007). Quantification of network security situational awareness based on evolutionary neural network. In *Proceedings of the International Conference on Machine Learning and Cybernetics,* Hong Kong, China.

Lin, T. C (2008). Partition belief median filter based on dempster–shafer theory for image processing. *Pattern Recognition* 41 (1), 139–151.

Luenberger, D. (1979). *Introduction to Dynamic Systems: Theory, Models and Applications*. New York: Wiley.

Luo, J., A. E. Savakis, and A. Singhal (2005). A bayesian network-based framework for semantic image understanding. *Pattern Recognition* 38 (6), 919–934.

Markov, A (1906). Rasprostranenie zakona bol'shih chisel na velichiny, zavisyaschie drug ot druga. *Izvestiya Fiziko-matematicheskogo obschestva pri Kazanskom universitete, 2-ya seriya*, 15, 135–156.

Meireles, M., P. Almeida, and M. G. Simoes (2003). A comprehensive review for industrial applicability of artificial neural networks. *IEEE Transactions on Industrial Electronics* 50 (3), 585–681.

Miller, G (1952). Finite markov processes in psychology. *Psychometrika* 17 (2), 149–167.

Murphy, K (2002). Dynamic Bayesian networks: Representation, inference and learning. PhD thesis. Computer Science Division, University of California, Berkeley.

Nikovski, D (2000). Constructing bayesian networks for medical diagnosis from incomplete and partially correct statistics. *IEEE Transactions on Knowledge and Data Engineering* 12 (4), 509–516.

Pearl, J (1988). *Probabilistic Reasoning in Intelligent Systems: Networks of Plausible Inference*. Santamato, CA: Morgan Kaufmann.

Scheuermann, B. and B. Rosenhahn (2011). Feature quarrels: The dempster-shafer evidence theory for image segmentation using a variational framework. In *Computer Vision ACCV 2010*, R. Kimmel, R. Klette, and A. Sugimoto (Eds.), Vol. 6493, *Lecture Notes in Computer Science*, pp. 426–439. Berlin, Germany: Springer.

Shafer, G (1976). *A Mathematical Theory of Evidence*, Volume 1. Princeton, NJ: Princeton University Press.

Shahbazian, E., D. Blodget, and P. Labbé (2001). The extended ooda model for data fusion systems. In *International Conference on Information Fusion,* Montreal, QC, Canada, pp. FRB1-19–FrB1-25.

Smarandache, F. and J. Dezert (2009). *A Mathematical Theory of Evidence*, Vol. 3. Rehoboth, NM: American Research Press.

Smets, P (1990). The combination of evidence in the transferable belief model. *IEEE Transactions on Pattern Analysis and Machine Intelligence* 12 (5), 447–458.

Smets, P. and R. Kennes (1994). The transferable belief model. *Artificial Intelligence* 66 (2), 191–234.

Subrata, D. (2008). *High Level Data Fusion*. Norwood, MA: Artech House Publisher.

Wang, J. and L. Ye (2008). Research on prediction technique of network situation awareness. In *Proceedings of IEEE Conference on Cybernetics and Intelligent Systems,* Chengdu, China, pp. 570–574.

Yang, J., H.-Z. Huang, L.-P. He, S.-P. Zhu, and D. Wen (2011). Risk evaluation in failure mode and effects analysis of aircraft turbine rotor blades using dempster–shafer evidence theory under uncertainty. *Engineering Failure Analysis* 18 (8), 2084–2092.

Yang, B.-S. and K. J. Kim (2006). Application of dempster-shafer theory in fault diagnosis of induction motors using vibration and current signals. *Mechanical Systems and Signal Processing* 20 (2), 403–420.

Yu, S.-Z. and H. Kobayashi (2003). An hidden semi-markov model with missing data and multiple observation sequences for mobility tracking. *Journal Signal Processing* 83 (2), 235–254.

Zadeh, L. A (1986). A simple view of the dempster-shafer theory of evidence and its implication for the rule of combination. *AI Magazine* 7, 85–90.

Zandipour, M., B. Rhodes, and N. Bomberger (2008). Probabilistic prediction of vessel motion at multiple spatial scales for maritime situation awareness. In *11th International Conference on Information Fusion,* Cologne, Germany, pp. 1–6.

Zhao, H (2007). Hidden Markov models with multiple observation processes. Honours Thesis. Department of Mathematics and Statistics, University of Melbourne.

Chapter 11

Ergonomic Design and Evaluation of Surveillance Systems

Denis A. Coelho and Isabel L. Nunes

Contents

11.1 Introduction

Formal consideration of the interactions between people and their working environments can be found in writings from ancient Greece, in medieval medical accounts, and in records from Poland and Germany more than a century ago (e.g., Girault 1998; Jastrzebowski 1857a–d; Marmaras et al. 1999). The modern history of ergonomics emerges in World War II, in the early 1940s. In the United Kingdom, the ideas and expertise from different disciplines gained interest in the effectiveness of human performance (anatomy, physiology, psychology, industrial medicine, industrial hygiene, design engineering, architecture, and illumination engineering), and an emphasis on theory and methodology led to the birth of the discipline of ergonomics with two strong subgroupings: those of anatomy/physiology and experimental psychology (Wilson 2000). In parallel, the human factors profession was growing up in the United States, with strong inputs from the disciplines of psychology and engineering. In Germany, the Netherlands, and across Scandinavia, a basis for ergonomics was growing out of occupational medicine and functional anatomy, while in Eastern Europe, the growth was largely from the industrial engineering profession (Singleton 1982).

Over the last half of a century, ergonomics, a term that is used here synonymously with human factors (and jointly denoted as HFE—human factors and ergonomics), has been evolving as a unique and independent discipline. Today, HFE is the discipline that focuses on the nature of human–artifact interactions, viewed from the unified perspective of science, engineering, design, technology, and management of human-compatible systems (Karwowski 2005). Such systems include a variety of natural and artificial products, processes, and living environments. Research in ergonomics covers two broad domains (Caple 2010). The first is research on human abilities and limitations as well as human–system interactions. The second domain researches methodologies in ergonomics. These research analyses work situations for the design of more suitable technical and organizational outcomes. Transitioning research into practice is a challenge that researchers and practitioners are tackling on a day-to-day basis.

11.1.1 Review of Recent Studies in the Field of Human Factors and Ergonomics Dealing with Security and Surveillance

Many tragic incidents, like the terrorist attacks that overshadowed the world over the last decade, made concerns for ensuring the security of both people and infrastructure grow considerably. Surveillance systems are increasingly needed to provide security for citizens and infrastructures. New technologies help to complement the monitoring process, creating more powerful systems to detect dangerous situations. For this reason, intelligent surveillance systems have a crucial role for security (Castro et al. 2011). Video surveillance is the area of security where more ergonomic research has been done in recent years.

In the field of HFE, there are reports on the use of digital surveillance data to enhance forensic HFE analyses (Cohen and Cohen 2007). In another study, St. John and Risser (2009) acknowledged that people generally have difficulties sustaining vigilance tasks, such as video surveillance from remote vehicles, security operations, automation supervision, and long-distance driving, as these are highly repetitive and understimulating. It is commonplace that operators struggle to sustain vigilance for even short stretches of time. These researchers proposed a method to sustain operator vigilance by activating a cognitively demanding secondary task when inattention is detected, by monitoring operator's psychophysiology (e.g., eye movement using eye tracking systems, head nodding, percent of eye opening, and electroencephalography (EEG)).

The development of the process of visual surveillance in dynamic scenes often includes steps for modeling the environment, motion detection, classification of moving objects, tracking, and recognition of actions developed (García-Rodríguez and García-Chamizo 2011). Most of the existing work is focused on applications related to tracking people or vehicles, with a large number of potential applications such as controlling access to special areas, identification of people, traffic analysis, anomaly detection and alarm management, or interactive monitoring using multiple cameras (Hu et al. 2004).

In video-based surveillance, people monitor a wide spatial area through video sensors for anomalous events related to safety and security. The size of the area, the number of video sensors, and the camera's narrow field of view make this a challenging cognitive task. Computer vision researchers have developed a wide range of algorithms to recognize patterns in the video stream (intelligent cameras). These advances have created a challenge for human supervision of these intelligent surveillance camera networks. Morison et al. (2009) presented an approach to panoramic visualization intended to support human supervision of intelligent surveillance. This new visualization integrates video-based computer vision algorithms with control of pan–tilt–zoom cameras in a manner that supports the human supervisory role.

Figure 11.1 illustrates the positioning of surveillance systems design and evaluation based on HFE guidelines and approaches and the relationship with base science disciplines (that perform knowledge discovery, namely, in what concerns human characteristics) and applied science and technology (developing solutions, namely, for surveillance systems).

11.1.2 Definition of Aims and Description of the Remaining Parts of This Chapter

Despite aforementioned reference to some studies, HFE has played a limited role in surveillance and security systems development. The lack of recognition of the importance of human factors and the lack of expertise to address these aspects are two reasons referred by Cranor and Garfinkel (2005) for security experts having ignored usability and broad ergonomic issues.

This chapter aims to inform the design and evaluation of surveillance and security systems introducing an HFE perspective. In the remainder of this chapter, key aspects of human characteristics that must be understood to enable effective surveillance system design are summarily described. Moreover, salient aspects of human performance capacity and limitations that impinge on surveillance system design are presented. This chapter concludes with the presentation of an HFE approach to the design and evaluation of surveillance systems.

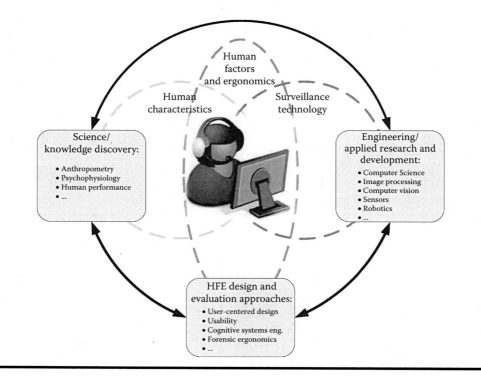

Figure 11.1 Surveillance systems HFE design and evaluation.

11.2 Human Characteristics

This section provides an initial account of the human characteristics that should be understood to enable effective surveillance system design. To this follows a review of fundamental human capacities that are called into play in the interaction of operators with current security and surveillance systems, resulting in some guidelines and recommendations for design.

11.2.1 Auditory Ergonomics

The time taken by an auditory stimulus to reach the brain is 8–10 ms (Kemp et al. 1937), while a visual stimulus takes 20–40 ms (Marshall et al. 1943). Hence, when interfaces are mainly graphical, auditory signals should be considered as a key complement to visual signals and are especially important as warning and alarm signals. Chan et al. (2007) established useful ergonomic design recommendations for human–machine interfaces that should help developing effective and user-friendly interfaces so as to improve overall system and equipment design and performance. Auditory signals for soliciting specific responses or directional attention should not be positioned in a longitudinal orientation with respect to the person. Signals placed in a transverse orientation will produce quicker and more accurate responses. For faster reaction times, auditory signals should be positioned on the right-hand side of right-handed operators. The layout of response keys on control consoles should be compatible with the hand positions of the operators. Designs requiring crossing the hands to respond should not be used. If operators are required to respond using front and rear keys on a horizontal plane, the right hand should be assigned to the rear key and the left hand to the front key. For faster reaction times, a 3 s fore-period warning should be given before signal presentation to alert the operator. This warning enables the operator to concentrate and prepare for the expected signals.

11.2.2 Depth Perception under Monocular Vision Conditions

In natural settings, monocular information about depth is very imprecise. One powerful cue for 3D layout is the so-called height in the field (Allison et al. 2009). Due to perspective projection, the retinal image of more distant objects lying on the ground plane falls nearer the horizon than the projection of closer objects. This is a compelling distance cue and can specify the relative depth order and quantitative depth between stimuli based on the vertical gap between them in an image. While investigating the relationship between monocular and binocular depth cues for judgments of spatial information and spatial instrument design, Hendrix and Barfield (1995) showed that stereoscopic viewing will not provide enhanced performance over perspective displays when the monocular depth cues in the scene are as effective as stereopsis in aiding subjects in extracting spatial information from the scene.

11.2.3 Computer Vision Syndrome

Extensive literature in ergonomics and optometry has indicated that computer use is closely associated with various visual problems, which are referred to as computer vision syndrome (CVS) in medical science. Although currently there are more computer users who work with computers for longer hours than ever before, CVS is preventable, and developing good habits for using computers is important. Researchers have suggested several preventative strategies, compiled by Yan et al. (2008).

Computer users should place the computer screen a distance of at least 50 cm (20 in.) away, as suggested by clinical optometrists. Several studies have suggested that distances of 85–100 cm may actually produce fewer complaints of visual strain. Such a relatively long viewing distance will allow the computer users' eyes to relax. A general rule of thumb is that operators should position the screen at least one full arm's length away from their eyes while seated. Operators should adjust their computer monitors to a viewing angle of around 15° lower than the horizontal level. This viewing angle will likely reduce both visual discomfort (e.g., dry eyes) and musculoskeletal discomfort (e.g., neck pain and back pain). Users should follow the 20/20/20 rule as suggested by clinical optometrists. That is, after 20 min of computer use, one should look at something 20 ft (7 m) away for at least 20 s. Frequent breaks are recommended to restore and relax the accommodative system, thereby preventing eyestrain. Computer users should carefully check the screen lighting and room lighting, including glare, contrast, brightness, reflection, and dust. Any luminous source within the computer user's field of view should not exceed three times the mean screen luminance (Sheedy et al. 2005). Operators should have a good sitting position to avoid neck ache, backache, and headache. Computer users should pay attention to room conditions (e.g., humidity and dust) that can contribute to the occurrence of CVS. For those who need corrective lenses, it is important to have regular eye exams and have good eyeglasses or contact lenses to correct visual problems. Research indicates that sometimes even very small uncorrected eye problems will cause substantial eyestrain due to the nature of long and intensive computer work (Shayler 2009).

11.2.4 Visual Acuity and Motion Resolvability

Resolution or visual acuity is defined by Stenstrom (1964) as "the angular separation between two just perceivable points." It depends on the distance from the human visual system (HVS) to an observed object and geometric and dimensional characteristics of the object (Esteve et al. 2000). Hence, visual resolution increases for close objects with low eccentricity, and vice versa. The introduction of Snellen acuity charts in 1862 as a vision standard specified that a person with 20/20 acuity has a good vision.

The motion resolvability measure quantifies the quality of an object's pose for ease of resolvability (Janabi-Sharifi and Vakanski 2011). For a general case, the motion resolvability measure depends on the object pose, motion of the observed object, motion of the observer, and motion of surrounding objects in the workspace.

Many tasks in security and surveillance systems involve operating in dynamic environments with moving objects, which require that the HVS processes moving information. Examples of such tasks are flying aircrafts, driving automobiles, or resolving moving objects on a visual display unit. Miller and Ludvigh (1962) were among the first to report a significant decrease of the visual acuity as the velocity of observed objects was increased even for modest amounts. The visual motion resolvability was called dynamic visual acuity, to distinguish it from the static visual acuity. It was reported that the correlation between the static visual acuity and the dynamic visual acuity decreases with a cubic exponential rate with the increase of the object's velocity (Morrison 1980). As a measure of visual performance of drivers, a study by Burg (1971) indicated that the motion resolvability was more significantly related to the driving record, when compared to the static visual acuity. Similar findings were published by DeKlerk et al. (1964) regarding the visual performance of pilots. Motion resolvability is an important performance criterion which should be taken into consideration for evaluation of the visual perceptibility of dynamic working environments.

11.2.5 Contrast Sensitivity and Visual Fields

Contrast sensitivity refers to the ability of the eye to detect a difference in brightness (or luminance) between an object and its background. It accounts for quality of vision, such as being able to see shadows, and it is important for the ability to discern objects in complex visual environments. When measured with the eye stationary, the extent of the visual field for one eye (i.e., monocular field) is 60° superiorly, 95°–100° temporally, 50°–60° nasally, and 70°–90° inferiorly (Long 2006). The boundaries of the visual field, especially the lateral field, decrease slightly with age as the eyeball recedes into the ocular orbit.

11.2.6 Gaze-Based Control

Among others, Bolt (1982) introduced the use of eye movements as an input modality for search-and-select tasks as early as 1982. His idea of "eyes as output" was intended to facilitate human–computer interaction (HCI). Since then, numerous studies showed that the users' gaze can be used to efficiently solve search tasks (e.g., Murata 2006). However, whereas moving the mouse cursor with eye movements is quite intuitive, it is more difficult to find a proper mechanism for performing the click operation. Most solutions today are based on so-called dwell times, that is, the user has to fixate an item for a predefined period in order to activate it. This technique faces the inherent problem of finding the optimal dwell time. If it is too short, click events will be carried out unintentionally and thus lead to errors. If the dwell time is too long, fewer errors will be made, but more experienced users will get annoyed and demotivated. Especially, in scenarios where the complexity of the provided stimuli is varying over time, there is no possibility of defining an optimal dwell time (Zander et al. 2011).

11.2.7 Gesture-Based Control

Gestures play an important role in communication. They support the listener, who is trying to understand the speaker. However, they also support the speaker by facilitating the conceptualization and verbalization of messages and reducing cognitive load (Van der hoven and Mazalek 2011). Gestures thus play an important role in collaboration and also in problem-solving tasks. In HCI, gestures are also used to facilitate communication with digital applications because their expressive nature can enable less constraining and more intuitive digital interactions than conventional user interfaces. Although gesture research in the social sciences typically considers empty-handed gestures, digital gesture interactions often make use of handheld objects or touch surfaces to capture gestures that would be difficult to track in free space. In most cases, the physical objects used to make these gestures serve primarily as a means of sensing or input. In contrast, tangible interaction makes use of physical objects as embodiments of digital information. The physical objects in a tangible interface thus may serve as representations as well as controls for the digital information they are associated with. Building on this concept, gesture interaction has the potential to make use of the physical properties of handheld objects to enhance or change the functionality of the gestures made. Researchers Van der hoven and Mazalek (2011) defined the design space of tangible gesture interaction as the use of physical devices for facilitating, supporting, enhancing, or tracking gestures people make for digital interaction purposes and outline the design opportunities in this space.

11.2.8 Information Processing

Beginning in the 1950s, cognitive psychology embraced the human information-processing approach, which characterizes the human as a communication system consisting of several distinct processes that operate on representations or codes, mediating between perception and action (Proctor and Vu 2010). In this regard, Posner (1986) stated that "because the language of information processing provides an objective and quantitative way of describing the basis of human performance, it has proven useful in applications."

The information-processing approach provides a language that allows consideration of human performance from the level of brain mechanisms up to that of complex sociotechnical systems consisting of people interacting with technology. Many developments in human factors can be seen as outgrowths of this approach.

A recent trend in cognitive psychology is a move toward cognitive neuroscience, the goal of which is to understand the biologic mechanisms that underlie human information processing. Neural activity recordings (EEGs and event-related potentials [ERPs]) and other physiological techniques (e.g., transcranial magnetic stimulation, the activation of neurons in a brain region through electromagnetic induction) are used along with experimental methods and theories from cognitive psychology to determine neural underpinnings. Contemporary cognitive theories are informed as well by these studies examining neural correlates of behavior, with many theories explaining a variety of behavioral and psychophysiological data (e.g., Harmon-Jones and Winkielman 2007).

The idea that human factors can benefit from incorporating knowledge about the human brain has been advocated using the term "neuroergonomics" (Parasuraman and Rizzo 2007). An application of neuroergonomics is adaptive automation, performing flexible allocation of tasks to automation as a function of dynamic changes in demands on an operator's information-processing capabilities (Wickens 2008).

11.2.9 Multiple Resources (Multiple Mental Entities) and Attention Resources

The theoretical construct known as mental workload (Wickens 2008) has been used to explain how humans face increasing cognitive demands associated with increased task complexity in operations where cognitive skills are more important than physical ones (Boksem and Tops 2008). Even if task complexity (defined as a function of objective task characteristics) is one of the most essential factors affecting performance, most frequently, mental workload (or cognitive load) is the term used to describe the mental cost of accomplishing task demands (Wickens 2008). Fluctuations of attentional state are also modulated by cognitive load (Tomasi et al. 2007), as the allocation of mental resources (attention) is hinged to different levels of mental workload (Wickens and Hollands 2000), and it has been shown that an increase of cognitive load involves increased attentional processing (Tomasi et al. 2007).

The multiple resources model developed by Wickens (2008) is a theoretical framework for workload assessment related to human information processing. The model provides an explanation for mental activity changes that follow after changes of the operational conditions (e.g., task difficulty, time pressure). According to the Wickens' model, attentional resources can be categorized along three dimensions: (1) input/output modalities, (2) processing codes, and (3) response execution. Accordingly, high similarity in the resource demands imposed by the task components leads to severe competition for similar resources that results in a high level of workload (Di Stasi et al. 2011). This could be the case, for example, due to high demands of perceptual or working memory processing.

11.2.10 Human Alarm Handling Response Times

The model of alarm-initiated activity (AIA) presented by Stanton (2006) distinguishes between routine events involving alarms and critical events involving alarms (Stanton 1994; Stanton and Baber 1995; Stanton and Edworthy 1999). Although the two types of events have most activities in common, critical events are distinctive by virtue of an investigative phase. It was proposed that the model of AIAs should be used to describe the stages in alarm–event handling. The term "activities" was used to refer to ensuing behaviors triggered by the presence of alarms. The main stages of AIA (Stanton 2006) are as follows (minimum and maximum response times in parentheses):

1. *Observation*: The initial detection of the alarm (1–2 s)
2. *Acceptance*: The act of acknowledging the alarm (1–8 s)
3. *Analysis*: The initial assessment and prioritization of the alarm (2–6 s)
4. *Investigation*: The activity directed at determining the underlying cause for the alarm (6–40 s)

5. *Correction*: The stage at which the system controller implements his or her response to the alarm condition (7–80 s)
6. *Monitoring*: The assessment of success of the analysis, investigation, and correction activities (variable)
7. *Resetting*: Extinguishing the alarm and returning it to its inactive state

The total response time for AIA as surveyed from literature by Stanton (2006) hence ranges from 17 to 136 s.

11.2.11 Psychophysiological Fitness for Work

Ergonomic approaches to the evaluation of operator's fitness do not assume that the functional characteristics of the operator (e.g., knowledge about task, skill level, or information-processing capacity) are invariant. These are influenced by variables such as operator mood state, sleep history, or time on task. While the requirements for professional knowledge and skills may be defined for various kinds of physical and cognitive work, the evaluation of their functional state over time needs to take into consideration psychophysiological parameters and changes of state of the human operator, especially those occurring over different periods of time (year to year, day-to-day variation, within work schedule variation, or variation produced by changing shifts). Direct or indirect measurement of psychophysiological changes enables the evaluation of the functional state of the operator, allowing prediction of individual fitness and reliability of the operator for effective work (Burov 2006).

11.2.12 Cognitive Flexibility

Cognitive flexibility can be defined as the awareness of various possible options for dealing with a situation, willingness for adaptation and flexibility in new situations, and an individual sense of self-efficacy (Martin and Anderson 1998; Martin and Rubin 1995; Martin et al. 1998). Individuals need to be aware of the alternatives and choices before they decide to adapt their behaviors to new situations; thus, they consider their own options in relation to the new situation (Bilgin 2009). The more options individuals can develop, the more flexible they are considered to be (Martin and Anderson 1998).

11.3 Human Performance Capacity and Limitations

Reliable performance is a fundamental goal in any system design for security and surveillance. Both long uneventful periods as well as continuously attention demanding long periods may take human operators to extreme performance requirements. Sudden action after a long period of inactivity, as well as constant action, and many intermediate states of arousal and vigilance need to be contextualized in light of HFE concepts so that they may be accounted for in systems design, to enhance effectiveness and reliability. This section looks at human performance and capacity limitations that impinge on surveillance system design.

11.3.1 Human Performance Depending on Arousal States

Recent studies indicate that arousal affects many cognitive activities (Storbeck and Clore 2005). In a review, Gilet and Jallais (2011) found that arousal is defined either as the intensity of an event ranging from very calming, through relaxing to highly exciting (Kensinger and Schacter 2006), or as the perception of arousal associated with an emotional experience or as a level of vigilance or activation. Lambourne and Tomporowski (2010) investigated the impact of acute exercise on cognitive task performance via meta-analytic techniques. They found that exercise-induced arousal enhanced performance on tasks that involved rapid decisions and automatic behaviors. Cognitive performance was affected differentially by exercise mode. Cycling was associated with enhanced performance during and after exercise, whereas treadmill running led to impaired performance during exercise and a small improvement in performance following exercise.

11.3.2 Human Performance and Attention

Given the predominance of automation in current systems, evaluating operator vigilance is as important as workload assessment (Parasuraman and Wilson 2008). Several vigilance studies have used transcranial Doppler (TCD) sonography to noninvasively monitor blood flow velocity in intracranial arteries in the left and right cerebral hemispheres (Tripp and Warm 2007). The results reveal a close coupling between vigilance decrement over time and blood flow. In addition, the vigilance/blood flow link is stronger in the right than in the left hemisphere, consistent with other findings indicative of right hemispheric control of vigilance (Parasuraman et al. 1998). Overall, research results indicate that blood flow represents a metabolic index of resource depletion during vigilance (Warm and Parasuraman 2007). TCD offers a noninvasive tool to "monitor the monitor." It could help in deciding when operator vigilance has declined to a point where task aiding is necessary or operators need to be rested or replaced.

11.3.3 Human Performance and Cue-Based Processing

Human beings are able to adapt to and to react quickly to stimuli in a variety of manners. This adaptability becomes apparent when people switch between different tasks in their everyday life (Lukas et al. 2010). When switching between modes of attention, cue-based stimuli have been shown to yield faster responses (Spence and Driver 1997). Auditory cues can prompt switching between processing and performance modalities, given the prevalence of the visual modality, especially in screening and surveillance tasks.

11.3.4 Human Real-Time Processing

Time pressure may be brought about by work or other activities involving the need for real-time processing. Time pressure has been described as resulting from an unfavorable ratio between the amount of time that is required to accomplish a task and the amount of time that is available (Coeugnet et al. 2011). The presence of a sanction if the task is not completed in time has also been previously seen as a main determinant of time pressure. The incidence of cross-situational contagion suggests that time pressure may extend to nearly all of an individual's activities, with detrimental effects on performance and well-being. Requirements for real-time processing hence need to be evaluated and if possible balanced with automation to decrease time pressure on operators.

11.3.5 Mental Fatigue and Related Phenomena

Mental fatigue refers to the feeling that people may experience after or during prolonged periods of cognitive activity. These feelings are very common in everyday modern life and generally involve tiredness or even exhaustion, an aversion to continue with the present activity, and a decrease in the level of commitment to the task at hand (Boksem and Tops 2008). In addition, mental fatigue has been associated with impaired cognitive and behavioral performance. Fatigue may provide the cognitive system with a signal that encourages the organism to lower present goals and to seek lower effort alternative strategies. People will only be motivated to engage in or continue activities when potential rewards for performance are high, compared to the effort required for these activities. However, when tasks have to be performed for prolonged periods of time, the amount of energy invested in performance increases compared to potential rewards, resulting in a decrease in the motivation to work for rewards that fail to be procured (Boksem and Tops 2008). The feeling of mental fatigue corresponds to a drive to abandon behavior when energetic costs continue to exceed perceived rewards of task performance.

11.3.6 Tolerance to Shift Work

Shift work induces some perceived problems, such as more frequent health problems and higher stress levels (Lac and Chamoux 2004). Shift work tolerance is a term describing the ability to adapt to shift work without adverse consequences. Saksvik et al. (2011) reviewed the literature on this issue, finding that young age, male gender, low scores on morningness, high scores on flexibility and low scores on languidity, low scores on neuroticism, high scores on extraversion and internal locus of control, and some genetic dispositions are related to higher shift work tolerance.

11.4 Human Factors and Ergonomics Design and Evaluation

In this section, selected HFE design approaches and evaluation methods are reviewed, including usability, while cognitive systems engineering is introduced as an approach to systems design that embeds both the user-centered design and the design of effective systems approaches. The set of concepts reviewed and the methods proposed with adaptations to suit the nature of surveillance and security systems form a body of knowledge and techniques that when deployed will contribute to the design of effective surveillance systems and may be used to improve existing ones.

11.4.1 Activity Theory-Based Model of Design by Research

Under the light of a framework derived from activity theory, any task, or activity, can be broken down into actions, which are further subdivided into operations. In a design context, using these categories can provide the designer not only with an understanding of the steps necessary for a person or operator to carry out tasks in collaboration with a technological system but also with the motive of the person's actions and the system's goals. The objectives and motives of any human activity, the social and material or physical perceptions, and the needs of the human determine the activity and its structure (Hydén 1981). The means for carrying out an activity include techniques and skills, procedures, and artifacts. Activity theory can be used to inform product and system development efforts. A general process underlying the conduction of studies that aim at supporting design endeavors was developed by Coelho and Dahlman (2006). Activity theory enables the decomposition of this process, considering the levels of activity, action, and operations. The process is schematically presented in Figure 11.2 together with Table 11.1, which develops on the meaning of the terms used in the figure and is adapted to the design and evaluation of security and surveillance systems. Research approaches are deemed necessary to complete the design process.

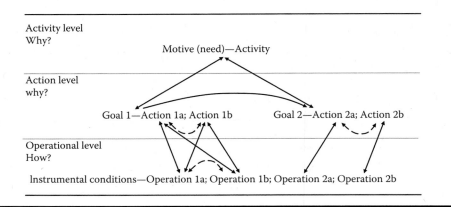

Figure 11.2 Schematic presentation of the application of activity theory to a three-level breakdown of the process of designing HFE quality systems. This figure is complemented with Table 11.1. Dashed arrows represent an interaction at the same level, the double headed arrows are used to represent feedback between levels.

The framework presented is intended to assist in guiding or directing the research parts of the combined research-design process intended for specification of human requirements and for attaining system properties.

11.4.2 Cognitive Systems Engineering

The need to better support operators in unanticipated situations led researchers to pioneer a new analytic framework that came to be known as cognitive systems engineering (Hollnagel and Woods 2005; Rasmussen 1986; Rasmussen et al. 1994; Roth and Woods 1988; Woods and Hollnagel 1987, 2006; Woods and Roth 1988). One of the major innovations of cognitive systems engineering was the development of functional analysis methods that define the goals, constraints, and affordances in a domain that constitutes the cognitive problem space confronting domain practitioners (Roth 2008). These functional analysis methods drew on concepts from systems engineering and ecological psychology and stressed the importance of analyzing the inherent characteristics and constraints in a domain to anticipate cognitive demands. The results of the functional analyses are used to develop systems that enable domain practitioners to directly "perceive" and reason about system goals, constraints, and affordances. This enables them to perform effectively under unanticipated conditions.

11.4.3 Testing and Evaluation of Systems from an Ergonomic Standpoint

Labarthe and De la Garza (2011) establish a three-class model of the integration of ergonomics in system design projects, depending on the stage of the project. (1) An "expert" integration via the specific reference systems of the area and the rules of ergonomics: This integration comes more from the advice and expertise of the human factors specialist than from the analysis (strictly speaking) of the work situation. This contribution is intended to be a guide for the design but requires subsequent evaluation and, or, comparison with the actual operation. (2) A "one-off" integration, depending on the constraints of the project (for instance, in one of the upstream phases for ergonomic recommendations adapted to project requirements or downstream for the

Table 11.1 Motive (Need), Activity, Goals, Actions, Instrumental Conditions, and Operations Depicted in Figure 11.2

Level of Analysis	Goal/Consequence	Activity	Constraints Guiding Interaction between Elements of the Activity Structure
Activity level (why?)	Motive (need)—designing effective security and surveillance systems	Activity—designing functional, useful, and usable technological systems to enable and support surveillance and security tasks	Prior to the conduction of actions 1a or 1b, it is necessary to consider the task setting (purpose of task, the level of novelty of the task in a context, the level of complexity of the environment, the level of safety criticality of the environment) delivering an understanding of the level of importance of physical, cognitive, emotional, sociological, ideological, and performance adequateness of the task.
Action level (what?)	Goal 1—understanding and satisfying human needs in relation to the technological system (physical, psychological, sociological, ideological, and performance) Goal 2 Check if needs have been satisfied (using evaluation methods)	Action 1a—generate design seeds (departing from a practice-centered perspective generating hypotheses) Action 1b—perform principle-driven design (requirements are delivered by theory) Action 2a—perform evaluation of design prototype (fielded and/or simulated) Action 2b—predict outcomes (based on application domain knowledge or across domains reported in the knowledge base)	Actions 1a and 1b (leading to operations 1a and or 1b) can both take place in a design problem or only one of them, depending on the level of development of the theoretical structures (knowledge base) and the degree of novelty of the field/product/task relationship (whether the context of application is new or it is a redesign of an existing and documented application).

(*continued*)

Table 11.1 (continued)   Motive (Need), Activity, Goals, Actions, Instrumental Conditions, and Operations Depicted in Figure 11.2

Level of Analysis	Goal/Consequence	Activity	Constraints Guiding Interaction between Elements of the Activity Structure
Operation level (how?)	Instrumental conditions prototype (product) properties, human properties	Operation 1a—transfer experiential properties (requirements) into formal product/system properties (using existing knowledge) Operation 1b—transfer experiential properties (requirements) into formal product/system properties (based on hypotheses) Operation 2a—measure/ assess response for the human (in terms of experiential properties) and the task Operation 2b—predict the response concerning human aspects and task performance	Actions 2a or 2b are carried out in sequence to actions 1a or 1b. The choice between actions 2a and 2b (leading to operations 2a or 2b) is controlled by the levels of domain complexity and domain safety criticality. The overall feedback between the lower and higher levels of the activity structure represents the enriching of theory or knowledge bases.

evaluation of a prototype): The human factors expert must have knowledge about the actual work to be able to provide recommendations based on an analysis of future user requirements and to construct relevant evaluation scenarios to evaluate the technical choices. (3) "Holistic" integration, in which the ergonomist will have increased legitimacy insofar as he or she can follow the design process overall from start to completion: This integration involves a high level of investment from the point of view of human factors skills and an association of those skills with other skills. Ergonomists will therefore have a prescriptive role and can act on the specifications during different phases of the project, based on analysis of the current situation and on evaluations made gradually. They rely on diagnoses for making forecasts that can be evaluated and enriched during the various human factor evaluation campaigns.

From the point of view of the design procedure, three additional approaches can be deployed (Garrigou et al. 2001). These approaches have different aims and involve separate ergonomic methods, consisting in a top-down approach, based on the expertise of the ergonomist and knowledge of how people operate but also knowledge from the field (e.g., operating activities in the control room) and from literature and specific studies; a bottom-up approach taking into account the variability of work situations and use of the available tools (analyses of the current situation, analysis of the requirements of future users); and a simulation approach, confronting operators with difficulties that they could encounter in future activities.

11.4.4 Usability

As one of the salient approaches from the ergonomic systems evaluation toolbox, usability is a quality or characteristic of a system (e.g., software, website, tool, machine, process) that denotes how easy this system is to learn and to use (Dillon 2001); but it is also an ergonomic approach, and a group of principles and techniques aimed at designing effective, efficient, and satisfactory products, based on user-centered design (ISO 9241-11: 1998). Usability is defined as the "extent to which a product can be used by specified users to achieve specified goals with effectiveness, efficiency and satisfaction in a specified context of use" (ISO 9241-11: 1998). It applies equally to hardware and software designs.

ISO 9241-11 emphasizes that usability of computers is dependent on the context of use, that is, the level of usability achieved will depend on the specific circumstances in which the product is used. The context of use includes users, tasks, equipment (hardware, software, and materials), and the physical and social environment, since all these factors can influence the usability of a product within a working system (Figure 11.3).

In practical terms, a product designed with the user's psychological and physiological characteristics in mind is more efficient to use (less time to accomplish a particular task), easier to learn (operations can be learned by observing the object), and more satisfying to use (Nielsen 1993). According to Nielsen, usability can be characterized based on the following five attributes: learnability, efficiency, memorability, errors, and satisfaction.

A large number of guidelines and principles have been published in literature, most of them addressing web design. The Nielsen Norman Group website (http://www.nngroup.com/) is a good source of references on usability. Many of the guidelines and principles are generic and should be adopted by developers when designing a product. Examples of such references are Jordan (1998), who enumerates 10 design principles (consistency, compatibility, consideration of user resources, feedback, error prevention and recovery, user control, appropriate transfer of technology, and explicitness), or Gerhardt-Powals (1996), who developed a different set of heuristics or

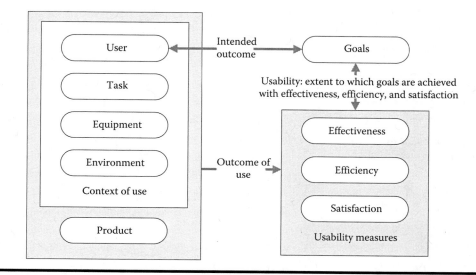

Figure 11.3   Usability framework, according to ISO 9241-11:1998.

cognitive principles, to improve performance in the use of computers (automate unwanted load, reduce uncertainty, condense the data, present new information with meaningful ways to support their interpretation, use names that are conceptually related to function, limit data-oriented tasks, include only information on the screens that the user needs at any given time, provide multiple coding of data, where appropriate, practice a judicious redundancy).

New technologies (e.g., mobile computing, touch and multitouch interfaces) introduce new usability challenges that offer the opportunity for the development of new usability guidelines and test and evaluation methods (e.g., Budiu and Nielsen 2011; Waloszek 2000).

One approach to the use of the concept of usability is user-centered design, also referred as usability engineering (Nielsen 1993). User-centered design is a structured development methodology that focuses on the needs and characteristics of users. The user requirements should be considered from the beginning of the development process in order to produce useful and easier to use products (Averboukh 2001; Nunes 2006).

According to EN ISO 13407: 1999, there are four key activities related to user-centered design, which should be planned and implemented in order to incorporate the requirements of usability in the process of software development. The activities aim to (see Figure 11.4)

- Understand and specify context of use
- Specify the user and organizational requirements
- Produce design solutions
- Evaluate design against requirements

There is a wide range of tools and methodologies for identifying and evaluating the usability of a system. There are approaches that are especially adequate for the design stage (e.g., analysis of context of use and tasks), while others are more suited to early stages of development and prototyping (e.g., competitive analysis, parallel project, brainstorming, prototyping), and others still are fit

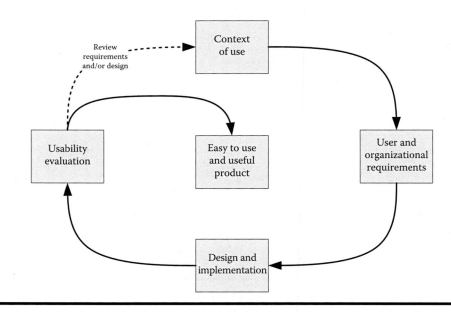

Figure 11.4 Activities of user-centered design, adapted from EN ISO 13407:1999.

for evaluation and testing (e.g., analytic and heuristic evaluations, software usability measurement inventory (SUMI), website analysis and measurement inventory (WAMMI 2011)). A set of methodologies and tools for evaluating the usability can be found in Simões-Marques and Nunes (2012).

Usability evaluation can be done through objective and subjective methodologies. Objective evaluation of performance measures the ability of users to operate the system. The subjective assessment of users' preferences evaluates how much users like the system.

ISO 9241 Part 11 states that usability is measured as a function of the degree to which the goals of the system are achieved (effectiveness), of the resources (such as time, money, or mental stress) that must be spent to achieve the objectives (efficiency), and of the extent to which users of the system find it acceptable (satisfaction). Typically, effectiveness and efficiency are evaluated based on quantitative data on user's performance (e.g., success, time, errors), while satisfaction evaluation is based on qualitative data, collected using, for instance, heuristic evaluations (Nielsen and Mack 1994) and the SUMI method (SUMI 2011).

Usability testing is not just a milestone in a project schedule. The results of usability evaluation should be carefully considered by the implementation team to set effort priorities and to improve the product based on tests' results (Nunes and Simões-Marques 2010). Therefore, usability principles are key in the design of effective surveillance systems and on the evaluation of existing ones, contributing to their improvement.

11.5 Conclusion

Very little HFE work has been done on the kinds of systems that come under focus in this chapter. This lack is in itself a threat, as it represents a significant systems engineering risk, since in order to compensate for technical performance issues, constant staffing is required (Sanquist et al. 2009). Often, new operator tasks are created to handle resolution of imperfect system output. There is a continuum of levels of human involvement in surveillance processes, as human operators can provide physical detection, decision-making verification, interpretation and classification, and context. However, human operators must be understood in multiple dimensions, considering their capabilities and limitations, in order to contribute to increased coupling with surveillance goals. It is expected that the wide literature review provided contributes to raise awareness on the impact of human limitations, capabilities, and characteristics on the operation of surveillance systems and to influence the design of future systems.

References

Allison, R. S., B. J. Gillam, and E. Vecellio. 2009. Binocular depth discrimination and estimation beyond interaction space. *Journal of Vision,* 9(1): 10, 1–14. http://www.journalofvision.org/content/9/1/10, http://dx.doi.org/10.1167/9.1.10

Averboukh, E. A. 2001. Quality of life and usability engineering. In *International Encyclopedia of Ergonomics and Human Factors*, ed. W. Karwowski, pp. 1317–1321. London, U.K.: Taylor & Francis Group.

Bilgin, M. 2009. Developing a cognitive flexibility scale: Validity and reliability studies. *Social Behavior and Personality*, 37(3): 343–354. http://dx.doi.org/10.2224/sbp.2009.37.3.343

Boksem, M. A. S. and M. Tops. 2008. Mental fatigue: Costs and benefits. *Brain Research Reviews*, 59(1) (November): 125–139. http://dx.doi.org/10.1016/j.brainresrev.2008.07.001

Bolt, R. A. 1982. Eyes at the interface. *Proceedings of the 1982 Conference on Human Factors in Computing Systems*, pp. 360–362. New York: ACM Press.

Budiu, R. and J. Nielsen. 2011. *Usability of iPad Apps and Websites: First Research Findings*, 2nd ed., Fremont, CA: Nielsen Norman Group.

Burg, A. 1971. Vision and driving: A report on research. *Human Factors*, 13(1): 79–87.

Burov, A. Y. 2006. Psychophysiological fitness for work. In *International Encyclopedia of Ergonomics and Human Factors*, ed. W. Karwowski, 2nd edn., Vols 1–3, Chapter 105, London, U.K.: Taylor & Francis Group.

Caple, D. C. 2010. The IEA contribution to the transition of Ergonomics from research to practice. *Applied Ergonomics,* 41: 731–737. http://dx.doi.org/10.1016/j.apergo.2010.03.002

Castro, J. L., M. Delgado, J. Medina, and M. D. Ruiz-Lozano. 2011. Intelligent surveillance system with integration of heterogeneous information for intrusion detection. *Expert Systems with Applications*, 38(9): 11182–11192. http://dx.doi.org/10.1016/j.eswa.2011.02.165

Chan, A. H. S., K. W. L. Chan, and R. F. Yu. 2007. Auditory stimulus-response compatibility and control-display design. *Theoretical Issues in Ergonomics Science*, 8(6): 557–581.

Coelho, D. A. and S. D. Dahlman. 2006. Ergonomic design structured through activity theory. In *Research in Interactive Design—Volume 2, Proceedings of Virtual Concept'2006 (26–30 November, Playa del Carmen, Mexico)*, eds. X. Fischer and D. Coutellier. Paris, France: Springer Verlag.

Coeugnet, S., C. Charron, C. Van De Weerdt, F. Anceaux, and J. Naveteur. 2011. Time pressure: A complex phenomenon that needs to be studied as a matter of urgency. *Travail Humain*, 74(2): 157–181.

Cohen, J. and H. H. Cohen. 2007. Enhancing forensic human factors/ergonomics analyses using digital surveillance video. *Proceedings of the Human Factors and Ergonomics Society 51st Annual Meeting—2007*, Baltimore, MD, pp. 1129–1132.

Cranor, L. F. and S. Garfinkel. 2005. *Security and Usability. Designing Secure Systems that People Can Use.* Sebastopol, CA: O'Reilly Media.

DeKlerk, L. F. W., J. T. Ernst, and J. Hoogerheide. 1964. The dynamic visual acuity of 30 selected pilots. *Aeromedica Acta*, 9(1964): 129–136.

Di Stasi, L. L., A. Antoli, and J. J. Cañas. 2011. Main sequence: An index for detecting mental workload variation in complex tasks. *Applied Ergonomics*, 42(6): 807–813.

Dillon, A. 2001. Evaluation of software usability. In *International Encyclopedia of Ergonomics and Human Factors*, ed. W. Karwowski, pp. 1110–1112. London, U.K.: Taylor & Francis Group.

EN ISO 13407. 1999. *Human-Centred Design Processes for Interactive Systems.* Genève, Switzerland: International Organisation for Standardisation.

Esteve, B., A. Aoussat, and H. Berger. 2000. Various systems for measuring a car's visibility field. *International Journal of Vehicle Design*, 24(1): 70–78.

García-Rodríguez, J. and J. M. García-Chamizo. 2011. Surveillance and human–computer interaction applications of self-growing models. *Applied Soft Computing*, 11(2011): 4413–4431. http://dx.doi.org/10.1016/j.asoc.2011.02.007

Garrigou, A., J. F. Thibault, M. Jackson, and F. Mascia. 2001. Contribution et demarche de l'ergonomie dans le processus de conception. *Pistes*, 3(2), 1–18 (online). http://www.pistes.uqam.ca/v3n2/sommaire.html

Gerhardt-Powals, J. 1996. Cognitive engineering principles for enhancing human-computer performance. *International Journal of Human-Computer Interaction*, 8(2): 189–211.

Gilet, A.-L. and C. Jallais. 2011. Valence, arousal and word associations. *Cognition & Emotion*, 25(4): 740–746. http://dx.doi.org/10.1080/02699931.2010.500480

Girault, P. 1998. Ergonomics: Not a new science. *Ergonomics in Design*, 6/2(6): 30.

Harmon-Jones, E and P. Winkielman. 2007. *Social Neuroscience: Integrating Biological and Psychological Explanations of Social Behavior.* New York: Guilford.

Hendrix, C. and W. Barfield. 1995. Presence in virtual environments as a function of visual and auditory cues. *Proceedings of the Virtual Reality Annual International Symposium '95*, pp. 74–82.

Hollnagel, E. and D. D. Woods. 2005. *Joint Cognitive Systems: Foundations of Cognitive Systems Engineering.* Boca Raton, FL: Taylor & Francis Group.

Hu, W., T. Tan, L. Wang, and S. Maybank. 2004. A survey on visual surveillance of object motion behaviors. *IEEE Transactions on Systems, Man and Cybernetics*, 34(3): 334–352.

Hydén, L.-C. 1981. *Psykologi och materialism: Introduktion till den materialistika psykologin.* Stockholm, Sweden: Prisma.

ISO 9241-11. 1998. *Ergonomic Requirements for Office Work with Visual Display Terminals (VDTs).* *Part 11—Guidance on Usability.* Genève, Switzerland: International Organisation for Standardisation.

Janabi-Sharifi, F. and A. Vakanski. 2011. Analysis of visual acuity and motion resolvability as measures for optimal visual perception of the workspace. *Applied Ergonomics*, 42(3): 473–486. http://dx.doi.org/10.1016/j.apergo.2010.09.008

Jastrzebowski, W. B. 1857a. An outline of ergonomics, or the science of work based upon the truths drawn from the science of nature. *Nature and Industry*, Part I, 29, 227–231.

Jastrzebowski, W. B. 1857b. An outline of ergonomics, or the science of work based upon the truths drawn from the science of nature. *Nature and Industry*, Part II, 30, 236–244.

Jastrzebowski, W. B. 1857c. An outline of ergonomics, or the science of work based upon the truths drawn from the science of nature. *Nature and Industry*, Part III, 31, 244–251.

Jastrzebowski, W. B. 1857d. An outline of ergonomics, or the science of work based upon the truths drawn from the science of nature. *Nature and Industry*, Part IV, 32, 253–258.

Jordan, P. 1998. *An Introduction to Usability.* London, U.K.: Taylor & Francis Group.

Karwowski, W. 2005. Ergonomics and human factors: The paradigms for science, engineering, design, technology and management of human-compatible systems. *Ergonomics*, 48(5): 436–463. http://dx.doi.org/10.1080/00140130400029167

Kemp, E. H., G. E. Coppee, and E. H. Robinson. 1937. Electric responses of the brain stem to unilateral auditory stimulation. *American Journal of Physiology*, 120: 304–322.

Kensinger, E. A. and D.-L. Schacter. 2006. Processing emotional pictures and words: Effects of valence and arousal. *Cognitive, Affective and Behavioral Neuroscience*, 6: 110–126.

Labarthe, J.-P. and C. De La Garza. 2011. The human factors evaluation program of a control room: The French EPR approach. *Human Factors and Ergonomics in Manufacturing & Service Industries*, 21: 331–349. http://dx.doi.org/10.1002/hfm.20227

Lac, G. and A. Chamoux. 2004. Biological and psychological responses to two rapid shiftwork schedules. *Ergonomics*, 47(12): 1339–1349. http://dx.doi.org/10.1080/00140130410001724237

Lambourne, K. and P. Tomporowski. 2010. The effect of exercise-induced arousal on cognitive task performance: A meta-regression analysis. *Brain Research*, 1341(23): 12–24. http://dx.doi.org/10.1016/j.brainres.2010.03.091

Long, J. 2006. Quantifying how we see the world: Visual acuity, contrast sensitivity, and visual fields. In *International Encyclopedia of Ergonomics and Human Factors*, ed. W. Karwowski, 2nd ed., Vols 1–3, Chapter 116, London. U.K.: Taylor & Francis Group.

Lukas, S., A. M. Philipp, and I. Koch. 2010. The role of preparation and cue-modality in crossmodal task switching. *Acta Psychologica*, 134(3): 318–322. http://dx.doi.org/10.1016/j.actpsy.2010.03.004

Marmaras, N., G. Poulakakis, and V. Papakostopoulos. 1999. Ergonomics design in ancient Greece. *Applied Ergonomics*, 30: 361–368.

Marshall, W. H., S. A. Talbot, and H. W. Ades. 1943. Cortical response of the anaesthesized cat to gross photic and electrical afferent stimulation. *Journal of Neurophysiology*, 6: 1–15.

Martin, M. M. and C. M. Anderson. 1998. The cognitive flexibility scale: Three validity studies. *Communication Reports*, 11(1): 1–9.

Martin, M. M., C. M. Anderson, and K. S. Thweatt. 1998. Aggressive communication traits and their relationships with the cognitive flexibility scale and the communication flexibility scale. *Journal of Social Behavior and Personality*, 13(3): 531–541.

Martin, M. M. and R. B. Rubin. 1995. A new measure of cognitive flexibility. *Psychological Reports*, 76: 623–626.

Miller, J. W. and E. J. Ludvigh. 1962. The effect of relative motion on visual acuity. *Survey of Ophthalmology*, 7(1962): 83–116.

Morrison, T. M. 1980. *A Review of Dynamic Visual Acuity.* Pensacola, FL: Naval Aerospace Medical Research Laboratory.

Morison, A. M., D. D. Woods, and J. W. Davis. 2009. How panoramic visualization can support human supervision of intelligent surveillance. *Proceedings of the Human Factors and Ergonomics Society 53rd Annual Meeting—2009*, San Antonia, TX, pp. 1136–1140.

Murata, A. 2006. Eye gaze input versus mouse: Cursor control as a function of age. *International Journal of Human–Computer Interaction*, 21: 1–14.

Nielsen, J. 1993. *Usability Engineering*. Boston, MA: Academic Press.

Nielsen, J. and R. L. Mack. 1994. *Usability Inspection Methods*. New York: John Wiley & Sons.

Nunes, I. L. 2006. Ergonomics & Usability—Key factors in knowledge society. *Enterprise and Work Innovation Studies*, 2: 87–94.

Nunes, I. L. and M. Simões-Marques. 2010. Usability study of an emergency management system. In *Proceedings of the 2010 Industrial Engineering Research Conference*, 5–9 June, eds. A. Johnson and J. Miller, Cancun, MX: CD-Rom.

Parasuraman, R. and M. Rizzo, (eds.). 2007. *Neuroergonomics: The brain at work*. New York: Oxford University Press.

Parasuraman, R., J. S. Warm, and J. W. See. 1998. Brain systems of vigilance. In *The Attentive Brain*, ed. R. Parasuraman, pp. 221–256. Cambridge, MA: MIT Press.

Parasuraman, R. and G. F. Wilson. 2008. Putting the brain to work: Neuroergonomics past, present, and future. *Human Factors: The Journal of the Human Factors and Ergonomics Society*, 50(3): 468–474.

Posner, M. I. 1986. Overview. In *Handbook of Perception and Human Performance Vol. II: Cognitive Processes and Performance*, eds. K. R. Boff, L. Kaufman, and J. P. Thomas, pp. V3–V10. New York: Wiley.

Proctor, R. W. and K.-P. L. Vu. 2010. Cumulative knowledge and progress in human factors. *Annual Review of Psychology*, 61: 623–651. http://dx.doi.org/10.1146/annurev.psych.093008.100325

Rasmussen, J. 1986. *Information Processing and Human-Machine Interaction: An Approach to Cognitive Engineering*. New York: North Holland.

Rasmussen, J., A. M. Pejtersen, and L. P. Goodstein. 1994. *Cognitive Systems Engineering*. New York: Wiley.

Roth, E. M. 2008. Uncovering the requirements of cognitive work. *Human Factors: The Journal of the Human Factors and Ergonomics Society*, 50(3): 475–480.

Roth, E. M. and D. D. Woods. 1988. Aiding human performance 1: Cognitive analysis. *Le Travail Humain*, 41: 39–64.

Saksvik, I. B., B. Bjorvatn, H. Hetland, G. M. Sandal, and S. Pallesen. 2011. Individual differences in shift work tolerance. A systematic review. *Sleep Medicine Reviews*, 15: 221–235.

Sanquist, T., T. Sheridan, J. Lee, and N. Cooke. 2009. Human factors aspects of anomaly detection systems. Committee on Human-Systems Integration National Research Council (February 12, 2009); URL: http://www7.nationalacademies.org/bohsi/048745.pdf (accessed March 5, 2012).

Shayler, G. 2009. Optometric remediation for problems caused by Visual Display Unit use. The Free Library. (2009). Retrieved October 13, 2011 from http://www.thefreelibrary.com/Optometric remediation for problems caused by Visual Display Unit use.-a0216682118

Sheedy, J. E., M. V. Subbaram, A. B. Zimmerman, and J. R. Hayes. 2005. Text legibility and the letter superiority effect, *Human Factors*, 47(4): 797–815.

Simões-Marques, M. and I. L. Nunes. 2012. Usability of interfaces. In *Ergonomics—A Systems Approach*, ed. I. L. Nunes. InTech, pp. 155–170.

Singleton, W. T. 1982. *The Body at Work*. Cambridge, U.K.: Cambridge University Press.

Spence, C. and J. Driver. 1997. On measuring selective attention to an expected sensory modality. *Perception & Psychophysics*, 59: 389–403.

St. John, M. and M. R. Risser. 2009. Sustaining vigilance by activating a secondary task when inattention is detected. *Proceedings of the Human Factors and Ergonomics Society 53rd Annual Meeting—2009*, San Antonia, TX, pp. 155–159.

Stanton, N. A. 1994. *Human Factors in Alarm Design*. London, U.K.: Taylor & Francis Group.

Stanton, N. A. 2006. Human alarm handling response times. In *International Encyclopedia of Ergonomics and Human Factors*, ed. W. Karwowski, 2nd ed., Vols 1–3, Chapter 88, London, U.K.: Taylor & Francis Group.

Stanton, N. A. and C. Baber. 1995. Alarm initiated activities: An analysis of alarm handling by operators using text-based alarm systems in supervisory control systems. *Ergonomics*, 38(11): 2414–2431.

Stanton, N. A. and J. Edworthy. 1999. *Human Factors in Auditory Warnings*. Aldershot, Hampshire: Ashgate.

Stenstrom, S. 1964. *Optics and the Eye*. Goteborg, Sweden: Butterworths.

Storbeck, J. and G. L. Clore. 2005. With sadness comes accuracy: With happiness, false memories. *Psychological Science*, 16: 785–791.

SUMI. 2011. Software Usability Measurement Inventory. http://sumi.ucc.ie/, accessed on November, 2011.

Tomasi, D., L. Chang, E. C. Caparelli, and T. Ernst. 2007. Different activation patterns for working memory load and visual attention load. *Brain Research*, 1132: 158–165.

Tripp, L. D. and J. S. Warm. 2007. Transcranial Doppler sonography. In *Neuroergonomics: The Brain at Work*, eds. R. Parasuraman and M. Rizzo, pp. 82–94. New York: Oxford University Press.

Van der hoven, E. and A. Mazalek. 2011. Grasping gestures: Gesturing with physical artefacts. *AI EDAM-Artificial Intelligence For Engineering Design Analysis and Manufacturing*, 25(3): 255–271. http://dx.doi.org/10.1017/S0890060411000072

Waloszek, G. 2000. Interaction design guide for touchscreen applications (experimental). http://www.sapdesignguild.org/resources/tsdesigngl/TSDesignGL.pdf, accessed on November, 2011.

WAMMI. 2011. Website analysis and measurement inventory. http://www.wammi.com/index.html

Warm, J. S. and R. Parasuraman. 2007. Cerebral hemodynamics and vigilance. In *Neuroergonomics: The Brain at Work*, eds. R. Parasuraman and M. Rizzo, pp. 146–158. New York: Oxford University Press.

Wickens, C. D. 2008. Multiple resources and mental workload. *Human Factors*, 50: 449–455.

Wickens, C. D. and J. G. Hollands. 2000. *Engineering Psychology and Human Performance*, 3rd edn, Saddle River, NJ: Prentice Hall.

Wilson, J. R. 2000. Fundamentals of ergonomics in theory and practice. *Applied Ergonomics*, 31: 557–567.

Woods, D. D. and E. Hollnagel. 1987. Mapping cognitive demands in complex problem-solving worlds. *International Journal of Man Machine Studies*, 26: 257–275.

Woods, D. D. and E. Hollnagel. 2006. *Joint Cognitive Systems: Patterns in Cognitive Systems Engineering*. Boca Raton, FL: Taylor & Francis Group.

Woods, D. D. and E. M. Roth. 1988. Cognitive engineering: Human problem-solving with tools. *Human Factors*, 30: 415–430.

Yan, Z., L. Hu, H. Chen, and F. Lu. 2008. Computer vision syndrome: A widely spreading but largely unknown epidemic among computer users. *Computers in Human Behavior*, 24(5): 2026–2042. http://dx.doi.org/10.1016/j.chb.2007.09.004

Zander, T. O., M. Gaertner, C. Kothe, and R. Vilimek. 2011. Combining eye gaze input with a brain-computer interface for touchless human-computer interaction. *International Journal of Human-Computer Interaction*, 27(19): 38–51. http://dx.doi.org/10.1080/10447318.2011.535752

Chapter 12

Awareness, Assessment, and Reduction of Web Application Vulnerability

David Ward and Jessica Cavestro

Contents

12.1 Overview

Web applications, more commonly considered as "applications over the net" (Internet or intranet), for example, through a portal, can be viewed as a combination of four key building blocks: a *database* (or data repository or inventory), appropriate *networking*, a *trust*(ed) environment, and *content* (management). Each one of these four blocks embodies, and is called upon to satisfy, specific social and individual user needs. The citizen (singularly or collectively) that uses them becomes the most important factor in establishing the success of a web application as well as defining truly what is vulnerable and eventually under attack (see Figure 12.1).

More importantly, web applications are now entirely embedded in our complex society so much so that the citizen is not only a key exploiter but also often the subject of abuse by third parties, especially external parties. Not surprisingly do we see a rise in the need for surveillance, protection, and, ultimately, intervention in cases of abuse (Verizon, U.S. Secret Service and Dutch High Tech Crime Unit 2012). For this reason all four building blocks need to contemplate a broader outlook, that is, technologically, sociologically, and legislatively.

In discussions on web application security and vulnerability, the emphasis is on the informatics side, that is, from a purely preventive, preparedness, and contingency plan or business–organizational perspective (Stuttard and Pinto 2008). However, understanding the subtle differences in web application use and users provides the security expert with a better awareness of what a breach might mean in practice, why it might be enacted, how and to what extent vulnerability can be reduced, and, ultimately, where legislation prevails. Indeed current web applications are characterized by four elements:

Coping and enabling information needs: That is strictly related to the content and how the content is retrieved from the database and then exploited (Norwood 1999) in the web application by the users (good or malicious). The same needs can also be seen from an incentive's perspective. Hence, identifying the needs is vital to understanding both how incentives influence the user's priorities and drive user satisfaction (Internet Security Alliance 2008, pp. 4–5).

The database: That acts as a data warehouse and is structured in such a way so as to facilitate data mining, information extraction, and/or business intelligence (Vercellis 2011) functionality.

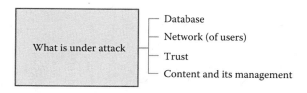

Figure 12.1 What is under attack.

The scope: That implies the foreseen usage and benefits for the end user via the exploitation of the data and information stored in the database and subsequently exploited through the portal by the user.

The user: That is either a database populator or exploiter or both. In this case the populator is the content "manager–customer" and knowledge expert, while the exploiter is the end user/consumer and decision maker.

When the previously described four blocks are perfectly matched with these latter four elements, the web application is usually a success story but also a potential treasure find and target for the attacker. Thus, when all four blocks and elements are seen from the malicious user's perspective, that same success becomes the core of the incentives to attack the web application.

Notable examples of this rule are as follows:

■ Ebay™ that has a huge database of people trading goods with customers–consumers in a trusted environment and network.
■ Google™ that has an immense index of web page content which it tries to effectively match to the customer–consumer's search words and phrases, that is, provide meaningful page content.
■ Friends Reunited™ unites old-school friends through a database and specific network.
■ Facebook™ is a very popular social networking service that provides its users with communicating and social networking tools such as personal profiles, photo albums, lists of hobbies and personal interests, contact and personal information, management of private and public communication with friends and other users, and chitchatting.
■ LinkedIn™ is a database of people in business that helps share their personal data and needs by providing linkages in a trusted environment.
■ Wikipedia™ that shares knowledge in an open and self-organized manner and managed under a peer review patronage.

Although the recognition of the previously mentioned blocks and elements is far from recent, the whole domain of web application security from a vulnerability, surveillance, and protection perspective is still incredibly in its infant stage. Victims can range from single users to complex and large organizations such as universities, large corporations, and governmental bodies (Briffaut et al. 2011, p. 1). Perhaps the reason for this is the frenzied evolution and exploitation of computer science and technologies coupled with an apparently hyper-relaxed search for overall sociological, legislative–regulatory, and technical frameworks. In other words the latter can't keep up with the former as it didn't take the lead in the first place: cloud computing (Subashini and Kavtha 2011) and cyber security (Shannon 2010, p. 55) being the most recent examples.

In this scenario the authors have opted to focus essentially on the societal–technological aspects of web application vulnerability by first providing an overview of the types of user need and the relative breaches and web application attacks (WEAs), then what "data" actually means and provides a simple example of an attack. The chapter then proceeds with an overview of the real content of WEAs and briefly summarizes each vulnerability and how malicious users (i.e., attackers) exploit them. It closes by looking at the societal and legislative aspects of web and cyber security in general.

12.2 Needs and Anti-Breach Strategies

Data are collected and distributed by organizations either to support decisions or justify them, or both. When data usage is abused, the intent is to satisfy a need by the malicious attacker (or sponsors) and this need can take many forms, from simple data viewing to deleting and/or defacing of entire records of data. In industrial informatics espionage and sabotage, the overall intent is to gain competitive advantage by the sponsors of the attack. On the other hand, when it is perpetrated by an individual, one can speak of satisfying one or more "personal" needs. Clearly from a legislative perspective, one thing is to judge industrial espionage and sabotage, and another is to tackle cases of abuse by single citizens such as piracy (European Commission 2004/48/EC 2010) and e-Stalking. Note also that the common concept of "territorial" border is irrelevant (European Commission, Enterprise and Industry Directorate-General 2010, p. 32) in breaches of web applications and cyber systems in general. Indeed Tikk et al. (2010) insist that "practical and operational cyber security solutions must be guided by and supported with comprehensive legal and policy analyses."

The importance of data security appears when it is either sensitive collectively or singularly or in batches and can consequently vary depending on the contents. For example, viewing and/or downloading the names of customers by an enterprise worker may not necessarily be a threat for the enterprise although formally it is considered a breach. Furthermore, if this breach is associated with contact details, addresses, revenues, etc., this may well constitute not only a breach in security but also worker integrity and infringement of "code of conduct," legally and socially binding contracts, etc. Hence, the sensitivity will also depend on the "value" of the data and the position in its "life" cycle (Bayer 2007), for example, stealing the personal details of a customer is one thing, while stealing the identity of the personal details of terrorists or "most wanted" criminals is another (European Commission, Enterprise and Industry Directorate-General 2010, p. 59). Note that the concept of "sensitive data" becomes subjective if it cannot be legally accounted for (such as in a contract), that is, there is an absence of an adequate jurisdictional framework. This is important because current cyber security (at an operational level) thinking focuses on vulnerability and defense but from an informatics and not jurisdictional perspective. Only when the consequences of the breach become threatening do we step into the legal domain.

In other words, operational web application vulnerability, from the informatics standpoint, focuses on the need(s) of the attacker and defendant. Hence, "defeating" the needs of the attacker and/or making it more difficult to satisfy the attacker's needs essentially reduces vulnerability. Equally by satisfying the defendant's security needs, for example, privacy, we decrease vulnerability. If this approach is backed up by adequate and updated legal thinking (which are both part of the defendant's needs), then the system is even more robust. Moreover, when a system provides a trusted and "policed" environment and allows users to act in confidence, then it provides a socially accepted and binding means of interaction. The stronger this interaction, the more the users themselves become the co-guardians of the system and can seriously and positively reduce system vulnerability.

Not surprisingly, the identification of the needs, scope, and user are all key in web application security. Hence, the human-in-the-loop view is not only key for web application usability, but it is the driver behind the reliability (security) of databases, networks, as well as trust and content management.

To this end Norwood (1999) proposes an "information needs" pyramid similar to Maslow's original hierarchy needs model (Maslow 1954) or Revich's three circle equivalent (Ward and Lasen 2009). His model describes the kinds of information that individuals seek during their daily work and life. At the most basic and lowest level, individual's needs are addressed by information that copes with situations, otherwise known as *coping* information. This information is primarily about satisfying an immediate need and thus has a very short-term time frame of application, virtually call-on-demand such as Google search and booking of train or flight tickets. It can also be intentionally malicious such as exploiting an individual's mobile phone number (as in stalking), stealing a credit card pin number, and obtaining access ID to a building.

The next level of information addresses safety, defined as "helping information" by Norwood, and satisfies a need for safety and security. Although this information can also be judged "short term" (see also online transaction processing [OLTP] and online analytical processing [OLAP] later in this chapter), it requires continuous refreshing and confirmation so as to provide reassurance such as parcel tracking, e-mail delivery while on the move, in-flight information, system monitoring such as the network icon on a PC desktop, password confirmation, and firewalling. It is possible to make a direct parallel to the Maslow and Revich models that have a sociological–psychological perspective of coping and helping information addressed by Norwood.

Individuals will also search for belongingness just as Maslow suggested with love needs and social acceptance or also the exact opposite, hate needs, social antagonism, and social exclusion. Norwood classifies this information as enlightening information and represents an individual's need to seek the development of relationships (think of social networking) or their destruction or impediment of exploitation. At the fourth level, esteem needs are represented by empowering information and concern self-worth and awareness. In the case of web application security, we can easily imagine the "dark" side of this because the attacker attempts to destroy this fourth level. Finally, people in the growth levels of cognitive, aesthetic, and self-actualization, as seen in the seven needs model (and extension of Maslow's original five needs-levels model), search for edifying information. Hence, attackers might set out to deliberately change user photos, deface CVs, make adverse claims about the enterprise, and so forth. Norwood's five-level model is shown next in Figure 12.2 and is represented as a pyramid to coincide with Maslow's original five needs-levels model; Revich's model is also reported.

Why is it necessary to consider needs in terms of web application security? For the reason that the attacker usually attempts to satisfy his or her own needs or impede other users in achieving their objectives. Hence, the question of why it (the web application) is under attack needs to be examined and is summarized in Figure 12.3.

So by starting to understand the motivation of the breach and possibly the final objective, which are both "needs" driven, one can then proceed with (better) anti-breach strategies. Such strategies should be based on the building of trust (within the community of users of the web application) and building the network in such a way that it deters the approach of malicious users in the first place. For example, only new users with referrals from current members of the web application are accepted, web application user identification is verified before becoming a member, free membership is not possible (i.e., members are also subscribers and obliged to pay for use),

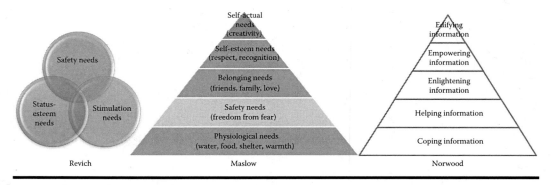

Figure 12.2 From human to information needs models.

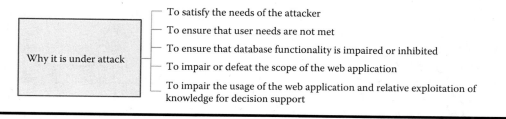

Figure 12.3 Why it is under attack.

users can only be members if their corporate mail has been accepted and screened by the web application manager, users are members of other web applications that have been accepted as being respectful, and hardware keys are necessary to access the web application.

From a legislative–regulatory perspective, it is also common to propose terms of use and/or membership rules that need to be signed and/or accepted by the user before access to online applications. Note though that the overall approach is not just legal; rather, it is also essentially regulatory (WatsonHall 2011), which tends to create a false sense of security even though the intent is to create trust between the service users and service provider. A perfect example is when you agree to share your personal data within a web application such as a social forum and mailing list, but the administration of your account is also accessible to thirds or for purposes outside your understanding of the boundary of the application. If you have agreed to the terms of use, this catapults you into the domain of policy (Google 2011), code of practice, and membership rules, which not necessarily provides "complete" protection. Indeed it is only when infringements and breaches of property–privacy rights occur with malicious intent and/or actions does legislation offer to play its role, if at all (Science and Technology Committee 2012, p. 80).

Clearly, incentives to improve security are advocated (Internet Security Alliance 2008, p. 9) by many businesses but rarely is this considered part of a competitive business plan; rather, cyber security is a consequence of a business plan direction–decision. As many enterprises consider security as a cost, it follows that it is generally enforced by external forces including the legislator and the competition. Indeed the European Union (EU) attempts to promote such an approach through specific directives (European Council—Directive 2006/24/EC 2006).

Often it is not the data or information that the attacker is after, rather the use of the derived knowledge and possibly exploitation or impediment of this knowledge with a malicious intent. Indeed when such knowledge is correctly used, the user shows wisdom; when the opposite occurs, it is either foolishness or malicious, or both: In other words, it can be constructive or destructive (Benkler 2011, p. 69). So in terms of database security, it is essential not to see content management as data alone but also information and ultimately the exploitation of the relevant knowledge within national and extranational jurisdiction (European Council—Directive 2006/24/EC 2006, p. 8). We will now take a closer look at this user "playing space."

12.3 Databases: From Data to Knowledge to Wisdom

A database is nothing else but either a data repository or, more loosely, an inventory of entities, that is, records. The term repository is from the Latin *repositorium*, that is, a container in which things can be placed and collected. Depending on how the term *repository* is used, it may be directly accessible to users or may be a place from which specific databases, systems, files, or documents are obtained for further relocation or distribution in a network (Gasson 2005). Based on its scope, a repository may have one of two outcomes, OLTP and OLAP.

It may imply or involve some ability to process data so as to selectively synthetize into information such as graphs, tables, results, reporting, billing, and wikis. The processing of the data can be conducted by the user (as in searching and browsing) or executed automatically such as in consumer billing. This is typical of what is commonly known as OLTP. In enterprises OLTP work is carried out by clerks or in general white collars.

Subsequently extract or mine knowledge with or without the aid of dedicated algorithms or tools such as text mining and descriptive or inferential statistics. If the knowledge is appropriately used in decision support (strategic, tactical, or operational), it is called wisdom, that is, knowledge is contextually exploited. This is typical of what is commonly known as OLAP. In enterprises OLAP work is carried out by the knowledge worker who supports the decision maker (Surajit and Umeshwar 1997).

A data repository may therefore be viewed as a data warehouse or single data mart in which data are stored and subsequently used for decision support, as in the case of business intelligence (Vercellis 2011, p. 3). In order to facilitate decision support, the data are usually processed so that the key features are extracted and presented in a summarized fashion, for example, graphs, presentations, reports, and listings. The summarization of the data is what is often thought of as information. The processing can be user driven and human managed or automated based on suitable algorithms and may be sophisticated or exactly the opposite, that is, very basic.

The scope is to extract knowledge, which can then be exploited to improve decisions or uncover hidden information such as the likelihood that a customer will remain faithful to a phone service provider, revenue trends for a business unit, payroll data of employees, movement of goods, and transactions. Table 12.1 summarizes some of the key features of OLTP and OLAP systems (Vercellis 2011, p. 80).

The importance of OLAP and OLTP in web application vulnerability lies in realizing that the malicious user will attempt to disrupt the contents, take control of its management, and weaken or destroy the network and/or the trust between the user(s) and the web application service provider. One of the first by-products of this in the business arena is "fear of use" since users will be reluctant to even view data (let alone buy goods) and therefore lead to loss of online sales. If the breach concerns an "informatory" type of web application such as a portal for a newspaper, association, and governmental body, the first by-product is the lowering of perceived quality combined with an overall negative impression concerning security and respect of authority.

In all cases, violating a web application emphasizes the need for a proper web application security plan and clearer responsibility.

Such responsibility will include the developers of the applications, website administrators, network managers, IT managers, security administrators, and compliance coordinators, and these actors will be absorbed in one or more of the web application performance pillars (see Figure 12.4).

Focusing on the first and fourth pillars, the scope of a database or data repository is to capture, organize, and process the data so as to provide the results (content) in a user-friendly format to satisfy a user need. Together the four pillars define the repository domain, but it is the network and trust that define the enlargement of the application. Typically this domain is where the knowledge worker or knowledge user is the prime actor and where the database and content (and management) are judgmental for the performance of the web application. However, often when web applications are attacked, it is not the content breach or database damage that hurts rather

Table 12.1 Comparison between OLTP and OLAP

Feature	OLTP	OLAP
Typical users	White collars, surfers, exploiters, etc.	Knowledge worker, trawlers, followers, etc.
Volatility	Dynamic data	Static data
Actuality	Current data	Stored (historical) data
Time base	Current	Past
Data granularity	Detailed	Aggregated and totalized data
Updating	Continuous and irregular	Periodic and regular
Activity	Repetitive	Unpredictable
Flexibility	Low	High
Performance	High	Medium
Functionality	Operative	Analytical
Usage	Transactions	Complex queries
Priority	High performance	High flexibility
Performance measure	Transaction rate	Response rate
Dimensions	Up to gigabytes	Up to terabytes
Application	Commercial	Stock control, libraries, archives
Example of typical user needs	Rapid access to up-to-date information to cope with situations	Searching and retrieving in order to be informed
Malicious user needs	Examine–exploit the contents and eventually disrupt the services or use them for malicious purposes, e.g., stealing identity and property, impersonate	Examine–exploit the contents and eventually disrupt or corrupt the search and retrieving functions or use contents for malicious purposes, e.g., stealing industrial secrets, defacing
Principal methods of attack	Active attacks. A common approach is to slow down or stop performance all together or corrupt the data so that it is no longer current and/or even wrong. In other words frustrate the user and destroy the trust in the web application by taking direct control of the database contents, performance, and relative quality	Passive attacks. A common approach is to make the search either slow or the retrieval results ambiguous or unobtainable. In other words, confuse the user and destroy the trust in the web application by working in the background. This often depletes the quality of the service as well as contents of the database

Source: Adapted from Vercellis, C.: *Business Intelligence: Data Mining and Optimization for Decision Making*. 48. 2011. Copyright Wiley-VCH Verlag GmbH & Co. KGaA. Reproduced with permission.

Web application

Figure 12.4   Database, network, trust, and content management.

the external effects because these are often the real malicious part of the attack, that is, it destroys both trust and the network itself.

In normal circumstances the exploitation of a database is found in the subsequent knowledge that is mined and extracted after which it is then used accordingly in decision support. In this second case the use of knowledge such as know-how, know-why, know-what, and who-knows-what/who (Gasson 2005) is based on an individual's insight (wisdom) and experience. Typically this domain is where the decision worker is the prime actor and who is extrarepository. This chain of action is described well by Alavi and Leidner (2001) that state "The most commonly-held view in the organizational knowledge management (KM) literature is that there is a hierarchy in which data, information, and knowledge incrementally build on each other, to construct the basis for human action ..." cited by Gasson (2005). This is depicted in Figure 12.5.

However, in practice and in abnormal circumstances, the entire chain (or part of it) is open to cracking and manipulation. So irrespective of the intent and exploitation of the data, what is becoming a critical system performance feature is the accessibility and vulnerability of such data and what can be done with it by those who steal the data. This is becoming increasingly more evident since such services are offered through web applications (Jazayeri 2007).

Jazayeri (2007) stated that "In just one decade, the Web has evolved from being a repository of pages used primarily for accessing static, mostly scientific, information to a powerful platform for application development and deployment." A perfect example of web application vulnerability is shown in Figure 12.6 subjected to an "active" attack.

The enterprise network under attack consists of a router, a firewall and switch, and a collection of servers. The servers operate at three different levels: (1) web servers, (2) a web application server, and (3) database servers. The two web servers in this enterprise are used for two different purposes: the first is for the sharing of project files such as documents and presentations, while the second is for the personal data of customers and employee profiles. In both cases certain data are more sensitive than others, for example, mobile phone numbers and benchmarking of competitors. The first web server function is provided by Sharepoint™, while the second is a purpose-designed inventory database or repository. The two sets of data are stored on separate data servers, the first being for project files or documentation, while the second stores the personal data or records of

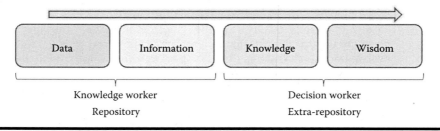

Figure 12.5   Data, information, knowledge, and wisdom.

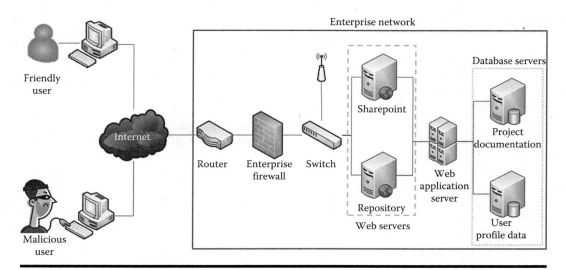

Figure 12.6 Example of a web application under attack.

Table 12.2 Example of Key WEA Steps

Step 1	The hacker finds a vulnerability in the custom web application of the enterprise and sends an attack via port 80/443 to the repository web server. He or she does this by injecting SQL command to the database that stores the personal data. The attack takes place through the Internet and therefore remotely.
Step 2	The repository web server receives the malicious code and sends this code to the web application server.
Step 3	The web application server receives the malicious code and sends this code to the database server that stores the personal data of the users.
Step 4	The database server in question executes the malicious code on the database. The database returns data from the stored "personal data" records.
Step 5	The repository web server sends the personal data back to the hacker.

"users" (customers and employees). Figure 12.6 shows a potential threat for the enterprise enacted by a hacker (see colored red border line) who goes through the following process (see Table 12.2) to steal the personal data of the users.

12.4 Web Application Attacks

The definition of WEA is rather a generic one because while WEAs are broadly classified (by the informatics experts) as either passive or active, in practice the distinction is not that clear-cut, especially from historical (Watson 2007, p. 10) and legal perspectives (Tikk et al. 2010, pp. 7–9). Also the birth of the first "web applications" in the late 1980s (e.g., web browsers, web servers) coincided with a thirst for functionalities, which have multiplied not only the vulnerabilities but

Table 12.3 Business versus Personal Attacks

Business Attacks	Personal Attacks
Enterprise operations information such as competitor benchmarking, reports, strategic and business plans, costs analysis, operations management	Stealing of identity or use of credentials and authentication without authorization
Business partner details and confidential partnership agreements (not disclosed to the public and business community)	Redirection to rogue sites for commercial and noncommercial purposes, denial of normal services, etc.
Customer data (both past and present)	Spam, junk mailing
Employee data information such as CVs, performance evaluations, medical records	Selling and/or purchasing of unsolicited goods and/or services
Product and service data such as service reports, price lists, stock status, bill of materials, testing and commissioning, design, production analysis	Hijacking of user PC, netbook, tablet content, and operation
Defacing and corruption of websites, portals, rogue	Stealing, duplication, and/or corrupting of personal data including passwords, software applications, templates
Intellectual property including patents, copyright, branding, and confidential agreements such as memoranda of understanding, secret codevelopment agreements, and letters of intent	Eavesdropping

also the types of vulnerability. Moreover, in both types of attack, the role of the user, that is, the victim or "human in the loop," is decisive.

Another way of considering WEAs is to look at the expected outcome (or malicious benefits if the attacker is successful), which we have broadly split into business attacks and personal attacks (see Table 12.3, for example).

In both cases though, the malicious user exploits one or more of the attacks normally categorized as "passive" or "active." Such attacks are defined as follows.

12.4.1 Passive Attacks

Passive attacks include the categories of interference of web applications (e.g., denial of service or DoS), information disclosure, authentication, client-side attacks, authorization, and command execution. This type of attack is initiated (accidentally and, often, unknowingly) by the victim during a browsing activity with the attacker waiting in the background to strike. These attacks are designed to corrupt the data/services of the victim's computer, involve remote intrusion, and aim to obtain information from the victim's computer or system.

Saltzman and Sharabani (2009) define a passive attack as those methods in which an attacker intercepts (views or modifies) sensitive data sent to or received by a user from the router in an "untrusted network," by deploying a man-in-the-middle (MITM) attack (using techniques such as address resolution protocol [Arp] poisoning, intercepting Wi-Fi traffic, rogue access point).

Another perspective to "passive attacks" is to take the view of the attacker type.

The attacker is *passive*, if he or she does not actively initiate malicious actions in order to disturb the functionalities of the web application. A passive attacker is often called "honest but curious" and is usually referred to as an eavesdropper.

The active attacker, on the other hand, can directly interfere with the functionalities of the web application such as by modifying routing data through the modification of protocols, by fabricating false routing information, or by impersonating other nodes (Banerjee and Swaminathan 2011, p. 440).

12.4.2 Active Attacks

Active attacks are initiated by the attacker rather than the victim; hence, the scenario is in the control of the attacker. Besides, the scope is to usually interrupt the service and/or session rather than information stripping as in a passive attack. The "active" attacker, that is, a malevolent third party, manipulates a response within a legitimate session in a way that tricks the client into issuing an unwanted request that discloses sensitive information. Once this is done, the attacker applies a regular passive attack on this information. It is important to emphasize that this is made possible by a security design flaw, not an implementation error or bug. In mobile networks the attackers target one or more specific nodes (Sudhir et al. 2011, p. 43). We describe this type of attack as "active" rather than "passive" because of two essential differences in the spirit of the attack:

1. It is initiated by the attacker rather than the victim.
2. The target is entirely controlled by the attacker, rather than being limited by the extent of the victim's browsing activity.

The rise of mobile web applications brings also forward the need to classify other types of attackers especially because of the need to detect intrusion in mobile ad hoc networks. So in addition to active and passive attackers (Banerjee and Swaminathan 2011, pp. 440–441), identify

- Static and adaptive attackers
- Computationally bounded and unbounded attackers
- Byzantine attackers or k-adversary
- Mobile attackers

As can be imagined with so many varieties of attacks, it becomes necessary to consider these from different perspectives such as the needs perspective or "school of thought" discussed previously. From an informatics "school of thought," the taxonomy interpretation seems to be predominant and three common ones are Howard's computer and network security taxonomy (Howard 1997), Álvarez and Petrović's web attacks taxonomy (Álvarez and Petrović 2003), and Jung-Ying et al. (2008), which looks at the hypertext transfer protocol (HTTP)-derived threats. All three, however, have an underlying process.

Howard's taxonomy analysis is based on the attack process of the attacker (see Figure 12.7) that results from an unauthorized access. Note that Howard does not focus on the type of intrusion that system's vulnerability allows rather on the attacker's malicious action.

Álvarez and Petrović's taxonomy (see Figure 12.8) is based on the web attack life cycle, which starts at an entry point and ends with maliciously corrupting the HTTP.

Jung-Ying et al. propose a six-step HTTP attack-based process as shown in Figure 12.9.

Figure 12.7 Howard's threat taxonomy analysis and process.

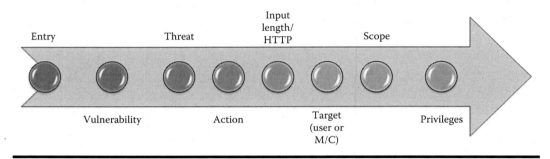

Figure 12.8 Álvarez and Petrović's threat taxonomy analysis and life cycle process.

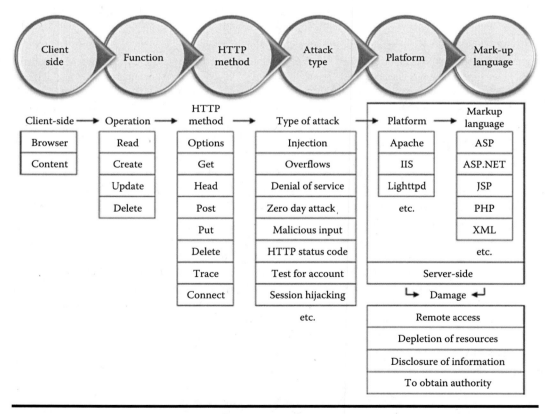

Figure 12.9 HTTP threat taxonomy by Jung-Ying et al. (Adapted from Jung-Ying, L. et al., Designing a taxonomy of web attacks, *Proceedings of the International Conference on Convergence and Hybrid Information Technology*, Daejeon, Korea, pp. 278–282, 2008.)

It is also worth mentioning the work of Bishop (1995), with his vulnerability taxonomy (for Unix), and that of Hansman and Hunt (2005) who propose a network and computer attacks taxonomy.

The approach used in this chapter is to provide an overview of passive and active attacks through which we briefly address each type of attack (see Figure 12.10). Although this work is in itself a type of taxonomy of "attacks through vulnerabilities," the objective has been to provide a "helicopter view" and thus spur a more general awareness of web application vulnerabilities.

For this reason we now take a closer look at active and passive attacks and provide a simple yet effective overview of what these are in practice. The overview (see Figure 12.10) provides an overall map and picture of the current, principle, cyber security breaches and attack methods, that is, web application vulnerability. This discussion exploits many formal and less formal sources from informatics experts, for which we acknowledge their work and patience.

Authentication vulnerability concerns the process of determining whether or not someone or something is (in reality) what he or she or it claims and declares to be. Therefore, it should be seen both from the human-in-the-loop and machine-in-the-loop perspectives. In private and public computer networks (including both intranets and the Internet), authentication is commonly performed through the use of log-on passwords and it is precisely here where the authentication vulnerability lies. Indeed passwords can be stolen, forgotten (and therefore lie dormant), or accidentally revealed to third parties, for example, writing them in diaries and mobile phone SIM cards.

An underlying concept in authentication is that knowing the log-on password justifies that the user is authentic irrespective of whether or not we are using an assigned (which is usually temporary) or a self-declared password (which is not usually temporary, at least until the user changes it). Also once the system functionality is accessed, the system remains open until either closed by the user or shut down by the system itself (i.e., when a time-out function intervenes).

To access the functionality of the system, the user must first enter and know the official password; otherwise, the system denies access. If the password is correct, then authorization by the system to proceed is given. Henceforth, authentication always comes before authorization.

Moreover, when attackers manipulate passwords or the code that manages them, the malicious intent and outcome is to deny access.

12.5 Brute Force Attacks

A brute force attack is based on an automated process to determine a password among a large number of possible passwords (WASC-11 2010, p. 21). Note that from an informatics standpoint, a password is a value, so the longer the password or value and the more characters it uses, the more likely it requires time before it is cracked, that is, the correct value is found. Indeed the fundamental reasoning behind this type of attack is the fact that the attacker knows that the user considers the likelihood of uncovering the password to be remote when in reality it is the opposite. Hence, brute force attacks exploit the fact that the entropy of the values is smaller than perceived by the authenticated user (Ugarte-Pedrero et al. 2011). In fact, an eight-character alphanumeric password (most users have shorter ones incidentally) can have up to 2.8 trillion possible values, but in practice users adopt and prefer passwords from a much smaller subset and based on user common words–terms (WASC 2011).

Therefore, from a user perspective, there is this false idea that finding passwords is protracted and haphazard when in reality it is systematic and logical with a guaranteed outcome providing

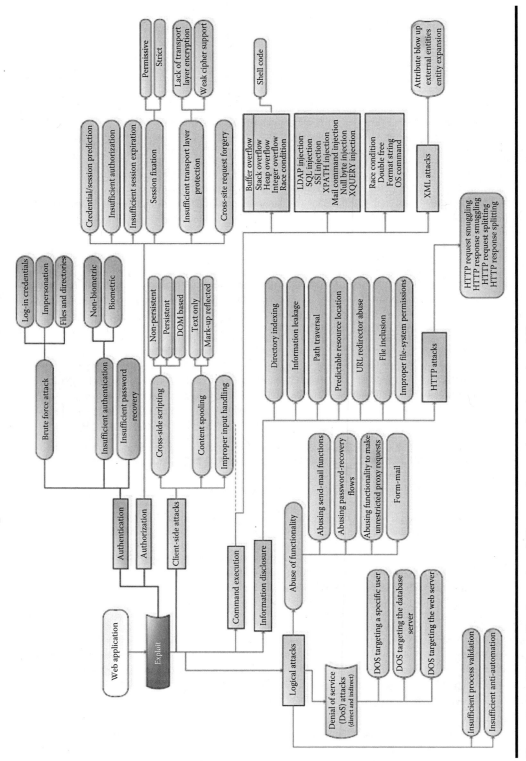

Figure 12.10 Web application vulnerability overview authentication vulnerability.

the attacker has the opportunity, time, and appropriate algorithm. Indeed modern technology not only automates this task but also accelerates it as well. That said vulnerability also lies with the user not just in terms of "excessive" trust (in the system security and incapacity of the attacker) but because human behavior tends to "ceremonize" the authentication process (Blaze 2004) making it more vulnerable. In other words if the log-in procedure is just something that "gets in the way," then it will be ritualized and made (too) short, simple, and, thus, easy to crack.

The term brute force attack is really an encompassing term for several types of cipher attack of the same nature as we will now witness.

12.5.1 Brute Forcing Log-In Credentials

The classical type of a brute force attack in web applications is an attack against log-in credentials (Singh et al. 2011). Since users need to remember passwords, they often select easy to memorize words or phrases as passwords, making a brute force attack using a suitable dictionary straightforward. Often these passwords are recycled by the user across web applications and other systems, for example, mobile phone pin numbers, credit card pin numbers, and e-mail user IDs.

The attacker attempts to log in to a system using a large list of words and phrases as potential passwords. For this reason it is often referred to as a "word list attack" or a "dictionary attack" (Fonseca et al. 2010). Attempted passwords may also include variations of words common to passwords such as those generated by replacing "o" with "0" and "i" with "1" or "-" with "_" as well as personal information including family member names, birth dates, and phone numbers. Note that an attacker may need to guess both the user password and user ID. This approach will be based on a preferred method such as the attacker might first fix the username and iterate through a list of possible passwords or fix the password and iterate through a list of possible usernames. This method therefore targets a specific user (and/or types of user).

The second type of victim is based on what is called a reverse brute force attack (Sharma et al. 2010) where the scope is to obtain the credentials of a random user. Here the intent is to disrupt the service since the attacked system locks out users after a certain number of failed log-in attempts, thus denying access.

12.5.2 Brute Forcing Session Identifiers: Impersonation of the User

Figure 12.6 illustrated a simple web application based on a collection of servers. The communication within the application is carried out by sending and receiving stateless protocols, that is, those where each server is not obliged to retain session information or the communication status as during multirequest sessions. Brute force session identifiers exploit HTTP (which is a stateless protocol) since these are needed by the web applications to ensure that a session identifier is sent by the browser with each request. The session identifier is most commonly stored in an HTTP cookie or uniform resource locator (URL). Using a brute force attack, an attacker can guess the session identifier of another user and, if successful, impersonate the user (Brown 2004, p. 86) so as to obtain personal information and perform actions on behalf of the user. Note that the attacker can simultaneously impersonate more than one user at a time as illustrated in Figure 12.11 where Bob (B) is the attacker and Veronica and Ramesh the victims. During the same session, other users (who are not being impersonated by Bob) are also present. In a two-way connection between Veronica and Ramesh, Bob the attacker is conducting the connection and communication between the two (victims). Hence, Bob can impersonate either Veronica or Ramesh within the server and web application and reroute the conversation.

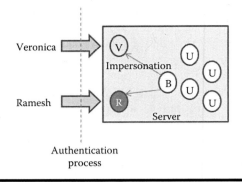

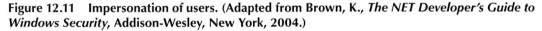

Figure 12.11 Impersonation of users. (Adapted from Brown, K., *The NET Developer's Guide to Windows Security,* **Addison-Wesley, New York, 2004.)**

What probably is not so evident is that Bob is not only conducting the "game" but also misleading trust and hence destroying the trust not just between Veronica, Ramesh, and the web application but also all the other users in the network (indicated with the letter "U" in Figure 12.11) (Brown 2004, p. 87). This is why understanding the two central pillars in Figure 12.4 is so important.

12.5.3 Brute Forcing of Directories and Files

This type of attack targets files and their directories that are served by the web server but are not linked anywhere. Accessing these files requires "knowing" their file name or value or even just their extension type such as ".bak." Therefore, in some cases, the attacker exploits the presence of those files that have been left by mistake such as a backup file or leftovers from an older version of the web application. In other cases files are intentionally left unlinked as a "security by obscurity" mechanism allowing only people who know the file names to access them.

This type of attack is based on making educated guesses by the attacker in terms of file and directory names not intended for public viewing. For example, the attacker proceeds by making an arbitrary file or directory requests, usually to publicly available web servers. The existence of a resource can be determined by analyzing the web server HTTP response codes. Although this seems a hit-or-miss approach in reality, it is easy because files/paths often have common naming conventions and reside in standard locations on a server. These include temporary files, backup files, logs, administrative site sections, configuration files, demo applications, sample files etc. These files may disclose sensitive information about the website, web application internals, database information, passwords, machine names, file paths to other sensitive areas, etc.

12.5.4 Insufficient Authentication

Would you open your front door without asking who is outside? This simple example is proof that you might want to authenticate the identification of the individual outside before opening the door, especially if you have something valuable to protect. In web applications, insufficient authentication occurs when a website permits any user to access the contents of the web application without prior and adequate authentication of the user. The attacker is obviously on the prowl for sensitive data, so to hinder or stop the unwanted access, this malicious user is required to identify him or herself. This can be done several ways, for example, through the renewal or confirmation

Biometric	Fingerprint	Face	Hand geometry	Iris	Voice
					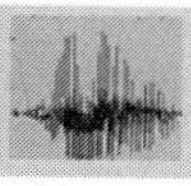
Barriers to universality	Worn ridges; hand or finger impairment	None	Hand impairment	Visual impairment	Speech impairment
Distinctiveness	High	Low	Medium	High	Low
Permanence	High	Medium	Medium	High	Low
Collectibility	Medium	High	High	Medium	Medium
Performance	High	Low	Medium	High	Low
Acceptability	Medium	High	Medium	Low	High
Potential for circumvention	Low	High	Medium	Low	High

Figure 12.12 Comparison of biometric authentication. (From Prabhakar, S. et al., *IEEE Secur. Privacy*, 33, 2004.)

of user IDs and passwords and/or through additional questions such as "what is your favorite football team?" or through tokens, that is, hardware keys. Another approach is to "hide" the specific location of access and not linking the location into the main website or other public places. This is typical of corporate e-mail or portals that rely on submersed access points within non-index pages. Needless to say, this is still "security through obscurity," which is like having a steering wheel lock on your car but that doesn't stop the thief from stealing the tires. More recent methods of user authentication are based on biometric measures (Prabhakar et al. 2004, p. 34) such as fingerprints, iris patterns, and voice (see Figure 12.12), but even these have their flaws (Matyáš and Říha 2003). These flaws are not just in the technology but also in the current national legislation (WatsonHall 2011) and policies and on a global front (Global Cyber Law Database 2012).

It is important to realize that even though a non-biometric resource (i.e., value) is most likely unknown to an attacker, it still remains accessible directly through a specific URL. The specific URL could be discovered through a brute force probing for common file and directory locations (e.g., "/admin"), error messages, referrer logs, or documentation such as help files. These non-biometric resources, whether they are content or functionality driven, need to be adequately protected.

O'Gorman (2003, p. 2024) summarized user authentication under three main headings: knowledge based, object based, and ID based. Figure 12.13 shows this summary.

12.5.5 Insufficient Password Recover Validation

Insufficient or weak password recovery validation is when an attacker is allowed to illegally obtain, change, or recover another user's password through inadequate validation by the web application administration. The "forgot password" service is provided by the administration because users, especially occasional users, tend to forget passwords, and therefore, it is an important user-expected service for the web application.

So a web application is considered to have weak password recovery when the attacker is able to easily guess or circumvent the password especially when brute force attacks, inherent system weaknesses, or easily guessed answers to secret questions are at hand or possible.

After obtaining access to a web application (which might involve the generation of a temporary password sent to the user's e-mail account), future authentication requires the user to remember the same password or sometimes a passphrase or subsequently replace it with a new password or passphrase. It is assumed that the user is the only person that knows the password although

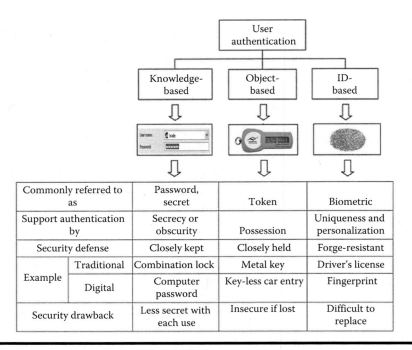

Figure 12.13 Comparison of biometric authentication methods. (Adapted from O'Gorman, *Proc. IEEE,* 91(12), 2019, December 2003.)

sometimes this might be handled by the user's delegate (e.g., secretary, spouse, colleague) or a collection of users (e.g., project team). Unless the password is easy to recall, and as time goes by, the user's ability to remember it inevitably fades (Yan et al. 2004); this is why users tend to stick with simple, short, and repetitive passwords. Indeed Yan et al. (2004, p. 29) demonstrated that randomly selected passwords are harder to crack than user-selected ones; they also suggested that users should be instructed "… to choose mnemonic-based passwords, which are as memorable as naively selected passwords but as hard to guess as randomly chosen passwords." This is especially true when the user needs to memorize several passwords for different applications.

12.5.5.1 Credential–Session Prediction

Credential–session prediction is a method of hijacking or impersonating a website user. This is possible because each time the user accesses the web application through the website, a session ID is created uniquely for that user and for the entire duration of the user's visit (see Figure 12.14). The majority of websites are designed to authenticate and track a user through log-in mechanisms, that is, when the contact is first established. By doing so user permissions can be verified before granting network access to its resources that may be specific or general. To do this, users must prove their identity to the web application, typically by providing their (confidential) credentials, that is, username/password. Rather than pass these personal credentials back and forth with each transaction (which would also increase vulnerability), websites will generate a unique "session ID" to identify and authenticate the user session. Subsequent communication between the user and the web application is tagged with the session ID as "proof" of the authenticated session. If an attacker is able to predict or guess the session ID of a user, then the system is open to attack.

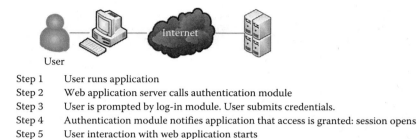

Step 1	User runs application
Step 2	Web application server calls authentication module
Step 3	User is prompted by log-in module. User submits credentials.
Step 4	Authentication module notifies application that access is granted: session opens
Step 5	User interaction with web application starts

Figure 12.14   Credential–session prediction.

The session ID can be a cookie, a URL, or a form field, and therefore, deducing or guessing the unique value it has for a specific session is within the bounds of the attacker. Since the attacker is attempting to take over the session, this type of vulnerability is also known as session hijacking and one in which the attacker issues website requests with the compromised user's privileges. There are, however, some enterprises that find authentication and authorization desirable, but not necessarily required for users to access all the resources since some of these resources may be open to the public, for example, Google images. In such circumstances guest authentication provides a more flexible approach (Guest Authentication 2011).

12.5.5.2 Insufficient Authorization

Whenever authorization procedures do not protect data and operations from unauthorized access, one speaks of insufficient authorization, for example, when an unauthorized user can transfer money from an account that does not belong to him or her or has access to data or functionalities that he or she is not allowed to use or view, more specifically an access control flaw (Noseevich and Petukhov 2011, p. 10). More formally insufficient authorization results when an application does not perform adequate authorization checks to ensure that the user is performing a function or accessing data in a manner consistent with the security policy for the web application. Critical to the reduction of this vulnerability is that the authorization procedure must enforce what a user is permitted to do and not do. This implies a hierarchy of responsibility and ownership as depicted in Figure 12.15.

12.5.5.3 Insufficient Function Authorization

The performance and acceptability of a web application seen by the user depend on the functions and therefore functionality provided. Functionality will also depend on the type of application and its scope. For example, an accountancy department will have different access permissions for "accounts payable" and "accounts receivable" because these two functions will most likely be (or need to be) accessed by different users or users with different hierarchical status. Similarly, access to read, write, or create documents will change depending on access and functionality rights the user has such as news sites, hospital records, and online database such as libraries, institutions, and wikis. Insufficient Function Authorization occurs when an application does not prevent users (malicious or otherwise) from accessing application functionality in violation of security policy and the rights the users may formally have.

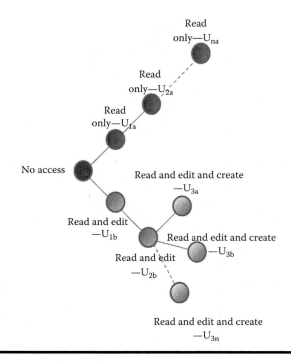

Figure 12.15 Differentiation of user authorization.

12.5.5.4 Insufficient Data Authorization

Websites are found by their addresses or URLs on the web but also their contents or data too. For example, Google has http://www.google.com, and for its images section, we have something like http://www.google.com/imghp?hl=en&tab=wi

Many web applications actually provide clear data identifiers in their URLs, for example, a medical record on a system might look like this:

http://medicalrecordexample.com/RecordView?id=12345

If the application does not ensure that the authenticated user ID has the necessary read rights, then this patient's record might be viewable by the user that this user should not see, for example, close relative or adversary of the patient.

According to the Web Application Security Consortium (WASC 2011) "Insufficient Data Authorization is more common than Insufficient Function Authorization." This is because programmers generally have a complete understanding of application functionality and services provided but not always the content (data) and its relative mapping. This is even more pronounced if the content is sensitive and subjective in nature. So while function authorization mechanisms may be well controlled by the programmer, this is not usually the case for the databases where the content is stored and retrieved.

12.5.5.5 Insufficient Session Expiration

This vulnerability is similar to session prediction except that it occurs when a web application permits an attacker to reuse former session credentials or session IDs for authorization. Insufficient

Session Expiration is possible because as seen previously, the use of the HTTP stateless protocol is commonplace by websites and cookies that store session IDs that essentially uniquely identify a user between requests. In order to reduce vulnerability (NIST 2011), each session ID must be safeguarded in order to prevent multiple users from accessing the same account. If this is not done or it is executed loosely, then the attacker can steal the session ID (since it hasn't expired) and use it to view another user's account or perform a fraudulent action–transaction. Hence, lack of session time-outs increases the vulnerability of a web application.

Two methods are possible to manage session time-outs: inactivity and absolute. In the former case, the session time-out is linked to the amount of time ensued before the session is considered invalid, that is, inactive. If the expiration time is particularly or excessively long, then several sessions may be concurrently open, hence increasing risk of attack. In the latter case, the total or absolute time is the time permitted before authentication is needed again, irrespective of use.

Note that the vulnerability works on two fronts; the first is connected to the time-out, while the second depends on the size of the pool sessions currently open and available to the attacker. Clearly the shorter the time-out, the worse for the attacker but also the user. Since modern authentication tends to automate the signing in process (see Figure 12.8 and biometric technologies in Figure 12.13), this too might render the shorter time-out more acceptable but at the same time still keep the vulnerability accidentally high.

A possible approach is to invalidate a session after a predefined idle time that is acceptable for the user and functionality being used. This would also provide the option to the user to log out as soon as a functionality is no longer needed. This is typical of public access points such as online banking, cash dispensers, and ticketing machines. This is why good web applications have log-out buttons clearly visible on-screen and allow the user to enable–disenable their session at will.

12.5.5.6 Session Fixation

This type of attack deliberately forces a user's session value; in other words, the user's session identifier value is explicitly fixed by the attacker (Johns et al. 2011). There are several ways of doing this, but all depend on exploiting the way the session is managed by the system. In general session management and therefore ID value definition can take two paths (see Figure 12.16):

- Permissive systems that allow web browsers to specify any ID, that is, an "open" or "arbitrary" approach. In this case the arbitrary ID session is maintained without interaction with the website.
- Strict systems that only accept server-side-generated values, that is, a "closed" or "systematic" approach. This second approach is better because the system requires the attacker to be periodically in contact with the website in order to avoid being timed-out because of inactivity. In other words the "trap session" has to be maintained live.

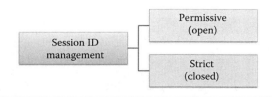

Figure 12.16 Types of session management mechanisms for web applications.

The attack works by first fixing the session identifier ID then waits for the user to log in to the application. Once this is done, the attacker uses the predefined session ID value to assume the same online identity as the user.

Since websites using session IDs for authentication are normally cookie based or URL driven or use some hidden form field, this type of vulnerability is common and easy to exploit especially the cookie-based type. This type of vulnerability is obviously attractive to the attacker because session fixation has a wider scope and opportunity for malicious purposes.

12.5.5.7 Insufficient Transport Layer Protection

Insufficient transport layer protection implies that the attacker intercepts and subsequently modifies communication traffic. To alleviate this risk, SSL or Secure Sockets Layer and Transport Layer Security (TLS) protocols (Horman aka Horms 2005) are used and these can be visualized in the HTTP script window as shown in Figure 12.17 (see text, i.e., HTTPs or the padlock graphical object next to the HTTP script).

The advantage here is that the TLS is verifying that the session certificate is valid, that it is from a trusted website, and that the site is genuine and not fake. Note, however, that such security measures require that the website be configured to use SSL/TLS; otherwise, the session is vulnerable and one is possibly running the risk of compromising the web application and/or providing an opportunity to steal sensitive information. As Rescorla (2001) states, because "…Secure Sockets Layer (SSL) is used in virtually every commercial web browser and server…it is the most widely deployed security protocol in the world" and it represents the most common secure communications protocol but also attracts the most attention from the attackers.

12.5.5.8 Lack of Transport Layer Encryption

Before you send data across a network, sensitive or otherwise, you need to make sure that you are sending it to the right machine, and while you are doing this, the data are adequately protected against prying eyes. This implies that the machine has to be identified and that the gateways and network switches do not allow intrusion by malicious users (Rhodes and Goerzen 2010, p. 87).

When the transport layer is insufficiently protected or there is a lack of protection, that is, lack of encryption, all communication between the website and client becomes insecure because it is sent in "open" text and therefore vulnerable to interception, injection, and redirection to an MITM (WASC-04 2010, p. 166).

Nahari and Krutz (2011, p. 443) discuss insecure communication and see it in two different phases, the authentication phase and the post-authentication phase.

In the first case the communication is secured by the use of SSL and TLS protocols, but after (i.e., post) this is usually not the case because of "…the performance impact of using SSL/TLS and partly as a result of complex and layered network topology." Note that this type of vulnerability is

Figure 12.17 Transport layer protection examples.

passive in nature in the sense that an attacker might passively intercept a communication including access to sensitive data like usernames and passwords. Similarly an attacker may also "… actively inject/remove content from the communication, allowing the attacker to forge and omit information, inject malicious scripting, or cause the client to access remote untrusted content." An attacker may also redirect the communication in such a way that the website and client are no longer communicating with each other but instead are unknowingly communicating with the attacker in the context of the other "trusted party" (WASC-04 2010), in other words cross-site request forgery (CSRF).

12.5.5.9 Weak Cipher Support

Thanks to better browsers and website security improvements, weak cipher support vulnerability is gradually improving; nevertheless, they lead to an increased risk in encryption compromise, MITMs, etc., because some of the older websites are configured to support weak cryptographic options for those clients that are restricted to only using weak ciphers (McNab 2007, p. 324).

So even today some websites are still configured to support outdated weak ciphers and therefore allow the attacker to force the client to downgrade to a weaker cipher during website connection, thus allowing the attacker to break this weak encryption.

12.5.6 Cross-Site Request Forgery

A CSRF is an attack that exploits the trust that a website has for a user. Once again the attack involves forcing the victim (i.e., user) to send an HTTP request to a target website without him or her actually knowing. Another possibility is that the attacker intentionally acts as the victim. In both cases this is possible because the application uses predictable URL/form actions in a repeatable way (Gallagher 2006). A typical CSRF attack is perpetrated as follows:

1. Attacker hosts web page with pre-populated HTML form data.
2. Victim browses the attacker's HTML form.
3. Web page automatically submits pre-populated form data to a site where the victim has access (and for which a trusted relationship exists between website and user).
4. Website authenticates the request (but with the attacker's form data) and considers this to come from the victim.
5. Attacker's form is accepted by the server and therefore legitimizes the user.

Note that the CSRF (or XSRF) attacks exploit the trusted relationship and can also happen when the user is on the same local network as the target website or when the user has an active session open with the target website.

12.6 Client-Side Attacks

12.6.1 Cross-Site Scripting

Cross-site scripting (XSS) is not new and dates back to the start of 2000 or earlier since it coincides with the development of the web (Sullivan 2000).

There are three types of XSS attack:

1. Nonpersistent
2. Persistent
3. Document Object Model (DOM) based

By contrast with XSRF, XSS exploits the trust that a user has for a website such as a governmental or official body website. XSS is an attack technique based on the "echoing of attacker-supplied code into a user's browser instance. A browser instance can be a standard web browser client, or a browser object embedded in a software product such as the browser within WinAmp, an RSS reader, or an email client" (WASC-08 2010, p. 32).

Nonpersistent attacks and DOM-based attacks require a user to either follow a specially crafted link laced with malicious code such as those received in spam or visit a malicious web page containing a web form, which, when posted to the vulnerable site, will subsequently mount the attack. Using a malicious form will often take place when the vulnerable resource only accepts HTTP POST requests (WASC-08 2010, p. 32).

Persistent attacks submit malicious code to a website where it is stored for a period of time. The code itself is usually written in HTML/JavaScript but may also extend to any browser-supported technology, for example, Flash and VBScript. DOM-based attacks are also known as "XSS attacks of the third kind" (Klein 2005).

12.6.2 Content Spoofing

The word "spoof" means to imitate, conduct forgery, falsify, etc., and the means or process of doing it is known as "spoofing." In web application security, an attacker that spoofs the user is simply masquerading him or her. It is also possible to spoof through programs, that is, an unlawful program spoofs a legitimate version. The act of "content spoofing" is when the attacker injects a malicious packet into the web application, which then interprets it as legitimate web application content.

There are two types of spoofing in web applications:

1. Text only content spoofing
2. Markup reflected spoofing

12.6.2.1 Text Only Content Spoofing

Rendering web pages more dynamic is commonly achieved by *passing text or portions of text* into the page via an HTTP query string value. This approach is common for error pages or sites providing latest news, bulletins, etc. The content specified in this value is later reflected into the page to provide the content for the page or pages. For example, suppose the bulletin title was "Latest GDP figures for Europe show economic slow down in the euro zone," that is, http://crc.example/news?id=123&title=Latest+GDP+figures+for+Europe+show+economic+slow+down+in+the+euro+zone

The "title" parameter or value in this example specifies the content that will appear in the HTML body for the news bulletins. If an attacker has access to the string value, then it is very easy to change its contents and willfully convey a completely different message. This is especially critical for news sites or where the user and website owner depend on up-to-date but truthful information.

Consider the true message: British prime minister considers Iraq war not an option. However, the attacker decides otherwise and writes http://crc.example/news?id=123title=British+prime+minister+considers+Iraq+war+option

The stronger the trust relationship between the website owner and user, the more likely the content will be considered legitimate and obviously more appealing for the attacker.

12.6.2.2 Markup Reflected Content Spoofing

In this second type of spoofing attack, the attacker's aim is to create *fake web pages* including log-in forms, defacements, false press releases, bulletins, and running text. Once again the attacker exploits the trust relationship established between the user and the website but this time replaces the parameter value with his or her own parameter value. This is possible because some web pages are served using dynamically built HTML content sources, for example, ⟨frame src = "http://crc.example/file.html"⟩ could be specified by a URL parameter value: (http://crc.example/page?frame_src=http://crc.example/file.html).

An attacker may be able to replace the "frame_src" parameter value with "frame_src = http://malicioususer.example/spoof.html."

Unlike redirectors, when the resulting web page is served, the browser location bar visibly remains under the user-expected domain (crc.example), but the foreign data (malicioususer.example) are cloaked by legitimate content. This type of spoofing is usually inflicted by inviting the friendly user through a malicious URL, such as those sent in spam. The more the user trusts the sender, the more likely he or she will trust the URL and obviously the contents displayed in the web page.

Indeed in the example provided, the browser location bar displays http://crc.example, when in fact the underlying HTML frame is referencing "http://malicioususer.example," thus exposing the spoofed content.

12.6.3 Improper Input Handling

According to Trustware™ (Trustware 2011), improper input handling was the second most common weakness exploited in applications in 2010 (globally). Generally, the term input handling refers to functions like validation, sanitization, filtering, encoding, and/or decoding of input data such as that from human users but also browsers and network devices, for example, switches, servers, and peripheral devices. Further, input from web applications can be transferred in various formats, for example, name value pairs, JSON, REST, and SOAP, and obtained via URL query strings, POSTed data, HTTP header fields, cookies, etc. Non-web application input can be obtained via application variables, environment variables, the registry, configuration files–tables, etc. Irrespective of the type of input, it should be considered untrusted and potentially malicious because the processing of untrusted input may lead to attacks such as buffer overflows, Structured Query Language (SQL) injection, operating system (OS) commanding, DoS, and command execution in general. This is a good example of where users are made aware of the regulatory measures–aspects of WEAs, that is, by stipulating not to open suspicious e-mails. We will now take a closer look at command execution that hijacks the control of a web application.

12.7 Command Execution Attacks

12.7.1 Buffer Overflow

Buffer overflow or buffer overrun occurs when the data that are being written to a buffer overrun the limits of buffer and overwrite partially or entirely the adjacent memory. This can occur due to a flaw in the control of the buffer and this anomaly can be accidental or malicious. The overflow is triggered by an input that then executes code or manipulates the way the program runs, thus resulting in erratic program performance and behavior. Malicious attacks usually aim at crashing the program and/or breaching the security of the application and system. Despite this risk and need to control buffer overrun, certain programming languages such as C and C++ have no built-in protection against this, for example, ensuring that data transfer stays within the limits of the buffer. As a consequence, attackers exploit this flaw in the mother language and modify portions of the target process address space (Foster 2005) with one of the following intents:

- To control the execution of the process, which is the most favored by attackers and is done by modifying the function pointer in the buffer memory
- To force the process to crash
- To modify the internal process variables

In many cases, the function pointer is repositioned to a predetermined location where malicious assembled machine-specific instructions have been placed. These instructions spawn a command-line environment, or shell, in the running process and are often referred to as "shell code." Such code leads to several buffer overflow types that can be classified and described as follows:

- Stack-based overflow (Silberschatz et al. 2005, pp. 565–568)
- Heap-based overflow (Wilson et al. 1995)
- Integer overflow (Brumley et al. 2007)

12.7.2 Stack-Based Overflow

The "stack" refers to a memory partition used to organize data associated with the connection between caller and callee through function calls, including function parameters, function–local variables, and frame and instruction pointers. The details of the stack layout are defined by the computer architecture and by the function calling convention used. A typical stack-based overflow problem is depicted in Figure 12.18.

12.7.3 Heap-Based Overflow

Heap-based memory allocation is the allocation of memory storage for use during the run time of programs in dynamic memory. Like the stack the "heap" refers to a memory partition structure used to manage dynamic memory, but it differs by the fact that programmers often use the heap to allocate memory whose size is not known "a priori," where the stack capacity is insufficient or where it is intended to be used for function calls. Heap-based overflow attacks occur when the relative allocated storage memory is deliberately overflowed by the attacker.

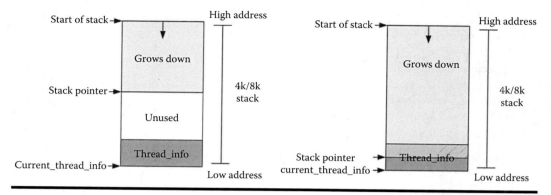

Figure 12.18 Stack-based overflow. (From Silberschatz, A., Gagne, G., and Baer Galvi, P.: *Operating System Concepts*, **7th edn. 566. 2005. Copyright Wiley-VCH Verlag GmbH & Co. KGaA. Reproduced with permission.)**

12.7.4 Integer Operations and Buffer Overflows

In general typical buffer overflows occur when the limiting value of an integer has been exceeded such as during arithmetic computation: this causes the integer operation to freeze at the maximum (or minimum) value and may cause the system to crash.

12.7.5 Buffer Overflow Defenses

The easiest and best defense against buffer overflows is to avoid them in the first place and closely evaluate how the memory is managed, especially the lower memory. Indeed one strategy could be to use higher-level languages such as Java, C#, or scripting languages because these discourage low-level memory access during common operations like using strings. In other words these are safer alternatives to C and C++ that are renowned to be prone to memory abuse.

If language choice is not an option and C or C++ must be used, it is best to avoid dangerous APIs (Application Programming Interface) whose use often leads to buffer overflows. Instead, libraries or classes explicitly created to perform string and other memory operations in a secure fashion should be used.

Another strategy is to exploit run-time protections that already exist to stop buffer overflows.

It should also be noted that many run-time protections exist for buffer overflows and that reduce this type of vulnerability (Livshits et al. 2006).

12.7.6 Format String

Format string attacks exploit the programmer's approach in reducing code such as that for printf as far as possible. For example, instead of writing printf("%f," str), the programmer writes printf(str) to save time, effort, and, *in primis*, 6 bytes of source code. However, by doing so the string is interpreted by the printf function as a format string and is scanned for special format characters such as "%f." As formats are encountered, a variable number of argument values are retrieved from the stack allowing the attacker to peek into the memory and subsequently print out these values. Such vulnerabilities and attacks occur when user-supplied data are used directly as formatting string input for certain C/C++ functions including fprintf, printf, sprintf, setproctitle, and syslog. This allows an attacker to

■ Execute arbitrary code on the server
■ Read and print values off the stack
■ Cause segmentation faults/software crashes

Format string attacks are therefore closely related to buffer overflows and integer overflows since all three allow the manipulation of the memory stack and content.

12.7.7 LDAP Injection

Lightweight Directory Access Protocol (LDAP) is a protocol used to communicate with directories that allow users to *access* their information via an industry-standard protocol also known as LDAP. LDAP Injection is an attack technique used to exploit websites and web services that construct LDAP statements from user-supplied input (Akrils 2003).

When a web application fails to properly sanitize user-supplied input, it is possible for an attacker to alter the construction of an LDAP statement. When an attacker is able to modify an LDAP statement, the process will run with the same permissions as the component that executed the command. (e.g., database server, web application server, web server). This can cause serious security problems where the permissions grant the rights to query, modify, or remove anything inside the LDAP tree. The same advanced exploitation techniques available in SQL injection can also be equally applied in LDAP Injection.

12.7.8 OS Commanding

OS Commanding is an attack technique used by an attacker to execute unauthorized OS commands. This is possible because OS Commanding permits the mixing of trusted code and untrusted data such as when an application accepts untrusted input to build OS commands. This involves accepting data that haven't been properly sanitized and/or the improper calling of external programs. It is a serious attack because the attacker's executed commands will run with the same privileges of the component, for example, database server, web application server, web server, and application, that executed the command and therefore be able to reach OS directories and files.

12.7.9 SQL Injection

SQL is a specialized language and query tool for organizing, managing, and retrieving data stored by a computer relational-type database. Among other things it allows to

■ Execute queries against a database
■ Retrieve data from a database
■ Insert new records in a database
■ Delete records from a database
■ Update records in a database

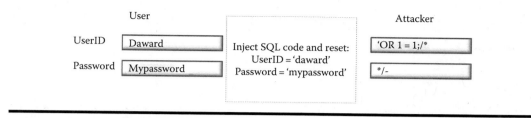

Figure 12.19 SQL injection.

The attraction of attackers to SQL manipulation through injection is therefore very high, and in general, the attacker most likely wants not only to enter the database to modify its contents but also to bypass log-ins or even shut down a MySQL server.

Many web applications often use user-supplied data to create SQL statements, and if an SQL statement is not appropriately constructed, it is possible to change the structure of the statement and launch ad hoc commands by the attacker. Clearly the attacker is masquerading the user, but the application does not realize this (see Figure 12.19). This allows the attacker to take control of all the user-accessible database resources by deliberately manipulating the SQL statements from user input such as dynamic strings and therefore change the very logic of the statement (My SQL 2012). This is why SQL injection is considered as a serious vulnerability (Clarke 2009, p. 13).

12.7.10 XPath Injection

XPath Injection is another injection attack technique, but this type instead exploits applications that construct XPath queries from user-supplied input to query or navigate Extensible Markup Language (XML) documents. The syntax of XPath bears some resemblance to an SQL query, and indeed, it is possible to form SQL-like queries on an XML document using Xpath (WASC-39 2010, p. 113).

It can be used directly by an application to query an XML document, as part of a larger operation such as applying an extensible stylesheet language transformations (XSLT) transformation to an XML document or applying an XQuery to an XML document.

12.7.11 SSI Injection

SSI (server-side include) injection is a form of attack that is used to compromise websites that contain SSI statements such as a "last modified" date that a server then places in an HTML file (WASC-36 2010, p. 101). In this case the attacker sends code to a web application that is then executed locally by the server. This is possible because during the development of the web application, the necessary sanitization measures were not in place for user-supplied data, that is, before they are inserted into a server-side interpreted HTML file.

Before sending the file to the user that requests it, the server searches the file for common gateway interface (CGI) variables and inserts the appropriate values in the places where "include" statements appear. In SSI injection, the variable values are modified by the attacker so as to add, change, or delete server HTML files. Note that the same injection technique may provide access to server resources.

12.7.12 Mail Command Injection

Communication protocols such as Internet Message Access Protocol (IMAP), POP3, Simple Mail Transfer Protocol (SMTP), and HTTP are used to properly transmit information such as e-mails, mail transfer, accessing your mailbox, and downloading e-mail. More specifically in order to deal with your e-mail, you must use a mail client to access a mail server and a suitable protocol such as IMAP and SMTP. Mail Command Injection attacks mail servers and webmail applications especially through improperly sanitized IMAP/SMTP statements from the user.

IMAP and SMTP injections are two different attack techniques, but the goal is the same, to unlawfully access a mail server from either outside the web application or within it. Recent work by Bowen (2011) shows how a suitable decoy approach can be used to improve system security and reduce IMAP/SMTP injection vulnerability.

12.7.13 Null Byte Injection

Null Byte Injection (Fonseca et al. 2010, p. 303) is an active exploitation technique used to bypass security checking filters in web infrastructure by adding URL-encoded null byte characters to the user-supplied data, that is, %00 or 0×00 in hex (WASC-28 2010, p. 83). This injection process can alter the intended logic of the application and allow the attacker to get unauthorized access to the system files.

Most of today's web applications are developed using higher-level and better protected languages such as Java, Perl, hypertext preprocessor (PHP), and active server page (ASP) but not for all the web applications, for example, at system level certain "C/C++" functions are still exploited.

In C/C++, a null byte is used to signify the end of a string and the attacker can exploit it to stop processing the string immediately. This attack technique is called "Null Byte Injection" or "Null Byte Poisoning" (WASC-28 2010, p. 83) and once found will automatically mean that the bytes that follow will be ignored. Another way of exploiting the null byte delimiter is to remove it all together so that the length of a string becomes unknown and thus cause erratic behavior (since the zero byte cannot be found) in the application.

12.7.14 XQuery Injection

XQuery Injection is a variant of the classic SQL injection attack against the XML XQuery language (WASC-46 2010, p. 122) and therefore follows the same strategy. Indeed during the authentication of the user ID and password, the relative content of HTML form goes somewhere into an XQuery as a literal string; thus, this injection is not properly sanitized. In other words the XQuery Injection exploits improperly validated data (user data in this case) that then are used in XQuery commands. Since the XQuery commands need to be executed and these have not been properly verified, the injected data are executed (van der Vlist 2011, p. 179).

12.7.15 XML Attacks: Attribute Blowup

In all modern web browsers, XML parsers convert an XML document into an XML DOM object so that it can then be manipulated with a JavaScript. The attacker targets the web application by sending malicious documents that then overload the CPU. This attack technique is possible because (1) XML parsers are not very efficient in handling XML documents and (2) numerous attributes can be included in the same XML node.

12.7.16 XML Attacks: External Entities

XML has been developed to standardize information exchange over networks and is at the core of modern web applications (Dick 2002).

This attack technique takes advantage of two features of XML, namely, that signed XML elements together with the associated signature can be copied across documents. During this process the signature is verified and documents are dynamically built at the time of processing. This affords the sharing of documents in a multiactor scenario, which is typical of business processes and satisfies prime user needs (Norwood 1999). However, from the attacker's perspective, this provides a chance to modify documents and go undetected in the process. This is possible because XML signature protects an element's name, attributes, and value but does so without protecting its position in the document. Hence, proper use of XML signatures requires a thorough understanding of the semantics (McIntosh and Austel 2005, p. 23).

According to Open Web Application Security Project (OWASP) (OWASP-DV-008 2011), the XML attack technique consists in exploiting external entities to replace the entity value with malicious data, alternate referrals, or compromise the security of the data the server/XML application has access to.

12.7.17 XML Attacks: Entity Expansion

XML DTDs (Document Type Definition) allow the creation of custom macros ("entities") within documents, but the same entity creation can also be exploited by the attacker to expand them indefinitely. In an XML entity expansion attack, the attacker recursively defines a set of custom entities at the top of a document with the intent to overwhelm the parsers that manage them.

Indeed the parsers attempt to completely resolve the entities by forcing them to iterate almost indefinitely on these "attacker implanted" recursive definitions (WASC-44 2010, p. 118).

12.8 Information Disclosure (Shows Sensitive Data to Attackers)

12.8.1 Directory Indexing

As users when we type a generic URL such as "helponline.com," an indication of the index or home page is explicitly stated in the string so the server assumes that the user wants the index or home page and therefore searches for it as if it was present. On the other hand, if it is not there, then the server will provide a complete directory list and it does this automatically (hence the term ADL—automatic directory listing) if nothing is in place to stop it. This listing will show the complete list of files, with no exceptions; it is like typing DIR in Windows.

There are two possible ways of stopping this: (1) Add an index page, even a blank page will suffice, or (2) ensure that you redirect the user to starting page irrespective of what he or she types. Clearly from the attacker's perspective, the complete listing not only provides vital insight about what you have to share but can also directly download the contents. Things are made worse when file names are self-explanatory about the contents such as files named "Productpricelist2011.pdf," "confidential.doc," and so forth.

12.8.2 Information Leakage

According to WASC Information Leakage, vulnerability is by far the most common and account for well over of 50% of all the vulnerabilities they have monitored (WASC 2012).

But the term "Information Leakage" goes far beyond than just revealing sensitive data in a business sense because in web security the information may be about the web application, for example, code or something more specific like user personal details. This implies that such sensitive data may extend also outside the target web application, for example, its hosting network and its services users. The leakage not only dents or destroys the trust between the user and web application owner but also makes it difficult to capture the real significance of the theft because the term "sensitive" is subjective, subtle, and often context driven. Note also it is not just about classical data leakage but also about accidentally leaving behind sensitive debugging code and comments during development. For example, failure to scrub out HTML/script comments may reveal information such as server directory structure, SQL query structure, and internal network information.

12.8.3 Path Traversal

The path traversal attack technique provides access to directories, its contents (files), and commands that reside outside the web document root directory, and for this reason, this attack is also known as a directory traversal attack. An attacker may manipulate a URL in such a way that the website will execute or reveal the contents of arbitrary files anywhere on the web server. Any device that exposes an HTTP-based interface is potentially vulnerable to path traversal, as shown in the example in the following (Acunetix 2011): http://test.webarticles.com/show. asp?view=oldarchive.html

Here the document root is the folder where you keep website files for a domain name and most websites restrict user access to a specific portion of the filesystem, typically called the "web document root" or "CGI root" directory. Since these directories contain the files intended for user access and the executable necessary to drive web application functionality, they are "the" target for path traversal attacks. Such attacks are based on the ability of special-character sequences to enter the paths and to guess (by trial and error) the position of the directory to attack (OWASP 2011).

12.8.4 Predictable Resource Location

Predictable Resource Location (WASC-34 2010, p. 92) is an attack technique based on brute forcing with the sole intent to uncover hidden web content and functionality by predicting file and directory names that are not intended to be viewed by non-authorized readers such as the general public.

The attacker makes educated guesses concerning file names and paths and exploits the fact that many databases follow some form of naming structure for files and paths, such as productspec/assembly/product123. The vulnerability lies in the common naming convention and the standardization of file locations. Other useful indicators to improve the guess and increase vulnerability (WASC-16 2010, pp. 126–127) are file types, for example, "*.bak," "*.tmp," "demo.*," "*.ini," "*.exe," and ".cfg." Another aspect of this vulnerability may lie in the contents of such files once opened because the contents may contain sensitive information about the website, web application internals, database information, corporate and single-user passwords, machine ID names, file paths to other restricted areas, etc.

12.8.5 URL Redirector Abuse

A URL redirector is a common website functionality used to forward an incoming request to an alternate resource (see comment on index and home pages). But URL redirectors are also used to record outgoing links and it is this use that is often exploited in phishing attacks. URL redirectors do not necessarily represent direct security vulnerability because their intention is to move the user from an old and expired URL to the new one that replaces it. However, attackers can exploit this option to take the user to a website that they want and hence is not the user-desired destination.

12.8.6 File Inclusion

Web applications take user input (such as URLs, parameter values) and pass them into "file-include" commands; such mechanisms are called "dynamic file include." However, these commands can also host malicious code, and when this occurs the attack technique is known as a Remote File Include (RFI) attack.

Since almost all web application frameworks support file inclusion commands, it follows that when a web application references an include file, the code in this file may be executed implicitly or explicitly by calling specific procedures (WASC-05 2010, p. 94) such as HTTP requests leading to RFI vulnerability. In general RFI attacks are applicable to

- Running malicious code on the server thus compromising the complete system
- Running malicious code on clients such as stealing client session cookies

12.8.7 Improper Filesystem Permissions

Users are given specific permissions to act and/or work on database contents and vary depending on their organizational position, functional position, and/or authorization level. For example, one user may have read-only permission, while another is allowed to edit the same file or other selected files. When filesystem permission control is "loose" and incorrectly managed, this poses a threat not just to confidentiality but also to the integrity and availability of a web application if it is attacked. It should also be noted that improper permissions also include access to restricted file directories and the modification and deletion of the relative contents.

The same risk is also applicable when a generic account is created for a group, for example, project team, or worse when the attacker penetrates the system and escalates the permission level, for example, from read-only to write-deletion, or targets directories outside the web root (WASC-17 2010, p. 128) for a given user.

12.8.8 HTTP Attacks: Request and Response Splitting

Response splitting is another "code injection" type of attack so once again it is when malicious code/script is injected into a program/web application from an outside source (in this case HTTP). This input field, which is provided by the web application, takes input from the end user (Patel et al. 2011, p. 199).

In HTTP request splitting, the attacker forces the browser to send arbitrary HTTP requests, inflicting XSS and poisoning the browser's cache. The objective is to manipulate one of the browser's functions to send two HTTP requests instead of one HTTP request, hence the term "splitting." For this attack to work, the browser must use a forward HTTP proxy (not all of them "support" this attack), or the attack must be carried out against a host located on the same IP (from the browser's perspective) with the attacker's machine (WASC-24 2010, p. 57).

In an HTTP response splitting attack, at least three parties are involved: a web server (where the vulnerability lies), the target, and an entity that interacts with the web server. The attack is perpetrated as follows:

The attacker sends a (single) HTTP request that forces the web server to form an output stream (thus implying a security flaw in the web server), which the target interprets as two HTTP responses instead of one, which would be the normal case. It is usually (but not always) the second response that the attacker completely controls, that is, manipulates the form of the second response from the HTTP status line to the last byte of the HTTP response body (WASC-25 2010, p. 60) by sending two requests through the target. The first invokes two responses from the web server, and the second is typically some "innocent" resource on the web server. However, the second request would be matched (by the target) to the second HTTP response controlled by the attacker. In this way the attacker tricks the target into believing that a particular resource on the web server (designated by the second request) is the server's HTTP response (server content). However, this fake and forged response carries the attacker's code through the web server, this being the second response.

12.8.9 HTTP Attacks: Request and Response Smuggling

This attack technique exploits HTTP requests between two HTTP devices and it too is a "code injection" type of attack (WASC-26 2010, p. 65). The attacker sends one set of requests to the second device, while the first device sees a different set of requests. This allows the attacker to smuggle a request to the second device "through" the first device. It has several possible exploitations, such as partial cache poisoning and bypassing firewall protection and XSS, and, in general, the technique abuses the discrepancy in parsing of non-RFC (Request for Comments) compliant HTTP requests between two HTTP devices such as a front-end proxy or HTTP-enabled firewall and a back-end web server.

HTTP response smuggling is an attack technique to "smuggle" two HTTP responses from a server to a client, through an intermediary HTTP device that expects (or allows) a single response from the server (WASC-27 2010, p. 67). HTTP response smuggling is an anti-HTTP response splitting security measure. In this case, the intermediary is the anti-HTTP response splitting mechanism between the web server and the proxy server (or web browser). Another use would be spoof responses received by the browser via a malicious website that serves the browser a page that the browser will then interpret as originating from a different (target) domain. HTTP response smuggling can be used to achieve this when the browser uses a proxy server to access both sites.

12.9 Logical Attacks (Which Interfere with Application Usage)

12.9.1 Abuse of Functionality

Abuse of Functionality is an attack technique that uses a website's own features and functionality to attack other websites (or itself) resulting in resource depletion through excessive resource consumption, dodging access controls, or leaking information.

The attacker essentially abuses the application's functionality to perform an undesirable outcome that may vary from website to website, through a combination of other attack types including

- Abusing send-mail functions
- Abusing password recovery flows
- Abusing functionality to make unrestricted proxy requests

12.9.1.1 Abusing Send-Mail Functions

This type of abuse refers to the send-mail functions, namely, From, To, CC, BCC, Subject, Body, and Attach, that are provided for the e-mail user (WASC-42 2010, p. 19). If these functions are readily attackable and there are no user restrictions, then the e-mail functions become a potential spam vehicle. Typical attractors are "e-mail this page to a friend" that provides a web form and ends up with the user getting a "visit our website" response or, worse, is taken there directly. To a certain extent the attractiveness of this type of "attack" can be mitigated by simply removing certain functions like attaching files or restricting usable e-mail directories. An example of send-mail function abuse can be found in the PERL-based web application "FormMail," which was (and in some cases still is) normally used to transmit user-supplied form data to a preprogrammed e-mail address (WASC-42 2010, p.19). The script offers an easy to use solution for websites to gather feedback but in the hands of a malicious user implies also a vulnerability because it allows remote attackers to send e-mail to any remote recipient, that is, spam users with one, single, browser web request. To exploit this vulnerability, all the attacker has to do is to simply prepare a URL to supply the desired e-mail parameters and perform an HTTP GET to the CGI, such as http://example/cgi-bin/FormMail.pl? recipient=email@victim.example&message=you%20got%20spam thus forcing the web server to act as the sender and allowing the attacker to be fully proxied by the web application.

12.9.1.2 Abusing Password Recovery Flows

A typical password recovery is one that follows the resulting three-step process or flow:

1. Ask user for username/e-mail.
2. Message the user informing that a mail has been sent to their account.
3. Send user a link allowing them to change their password.

The vulnerability stems at step 2 because here the user has entered a valid e-mail address and/or account name that is confirmed by the web application and therefore could lead to a potential leakage that the attacker exploits.

There are four potential defense strategies: (1) to request additional user knowledge data such as "my favorite football is," (2) do not reveal the username except to the user and only if needed, (3) confirm an encrypted word(s) sent shown only at the time of entering the web application (see Figure 12.20), and (4) use a random username generator software package.

12.9.1.3 Unauthorized Proxy Requests

A proxy server enables users to connect a private network or local area network (LAN) to a public network such as the web by acting as a gateway for internal client computers to the Internet. Services

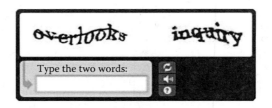

Figure 12.20 Improving password recovery flows.

such as Google Translate can be abused to act as open proxy servers and the user becomes aware that the proxy server is actually requesting web content on their behalf when it is actually disallowed.

12.9.2 Denial of Service

The objective of a DoS attack is to prevent the user from accessing and using the web application functionalities. Such attacks are usually common at the network layer although the application layer is also a potential target. The DoS attack technique essentially starves the system of vital resources or abuses the availability of functionalities such as e-mails. But it can also be a "system of systems" attack such as the DDoS (distributed denial of service) of large networks including the Internet and critical infrastructures such as ICT, water, and electricity supply networks and assets (Ward and Matuziene 2011). This is because over the last decade, critical infrastructures depend on the Internet, or ICT in general, as a means of communication (Raghavan and Dawson 2011, p. V).

In general a DoS technique attempts to consume CPU processing capacity, overload the memory, and fill disk space of the system so that once a certain minimum working system threshold is exceeded, the system will revert to a safe running mode and render a website inaccessible. In other words the system's safe (defense) mode is deliberately activated and the service denied.

12.9.2.1 DoS Targeting a Specific User

When a web application has log-in protection, the user is allowed to make a fix number of errors in entering the user ID and/or password. This limitation protects the user from abuse by non-authorized users, that is, unauthorized access. However, the same protection measure can be abused by an attacker that deliberately attempts to log in repeatedly using a wrong password until the system "locks out" the authorized user. Note that the lockout function is typical of password protection procedures, more rarely for user IDs.

12.9.2.2 DoS Targeting the Database Server

An intruder will use SQL injection techniques to modify the database so that the system becomes unusable (e.g., deleting all data, all usernames, and passwords). This attack is therefore aimed at the database server of the web application.

12.9.2.3 DoS Targeting the Web Server

An intruder will use buffer overflow techniques to send a specially crafted request that will crash the web server process, and the system will normally be inaccessible to normal user activity. This attack is therefore aimed at the web server of the web application.

12.9.3 Insufficient Anti-Automation

There are many web application functions that require the user to *manually confirm*, indicate, assign, and conduct web application tasks such as log in, indicating delivery destination, credit card details, editing and deleting files, and so forth. When an attacker is able to side step the user, the manual process is automated by the attack technique without the need for human intervention. In cases like these, the attack technique is called insufficient anti-automation (which is an automated robot program) and usually focuses on one or more of the following target categories or outcomes:

- Application log-in forms—to automate brute force log-in requests in an attempt to "guess-timate" user credentials.
- Service registration forms—to automatically generate new accounts and fictitious users.
- E-mail forms—to exploit e-mail forms and apply them as spam relays or flood a user's mailbox or annoy users with repeated message postings.
- Account maintenance—to force a DoS response by the application so as to flood it with repetitive requests to disable or delete user accounts.
- Account information forms—are exploited to bulk harvest user personal information.
- Comment forms/content submission forms—are used to send and post spam on blogs, web forums, and bulletin boards. However, they may also be used to send malware.
- SQL database query forms—are used to send mass and heavy SQL queries in a very short time period so as to provoke a DoS for the real users.
- e-Shopping/e-Commerce—are used to exploit single users who buy in small batch purchases of products and services, typically in a B2C and human-purchaser scenario. The attacker then piggy backs the requests and dramatically increases the quantities that are then "scalped" as in the mass purchase of sport event tickets, which also feeds the secondary ticket market (Drayer 2011, p. 228). In this case the vulnerability is caused by the fact that large bulk purchasing is allowed by the web application.
- Online polls—when online voting and polling systems are attacked, the objective is to change the voting or polling outcome, that is, in favor of one of the responses or candidates.
- Web-based SMS message sending—similar to e-mail spamming except that attackers hit mobile phone users by sending text message spam.

12.9.4 Insufficient Process Validation

In web applications there are two main types of processes that require validation: flow control and business logic. The former refers to multistep processes that require each step to be performed in a specific order by the user, and failure to do so will force an application integrity error. Certain processes may be lenient and allow this to happen a fixed number of times such as incorrect password entry or require a specific process such as "forgot password" and relative password recovery. At a business level multistep processes include purchase checkout, account sign-up, credit card management, shipping method choice, and shipping destination address selection that follow a specific business logic. Business logic therefore refers to the business requirements that may be customer specific and usually requires expert business process knowledge on behalf of the attacker.

Insufficient process validation occurs when a web application fails to prevent an attacker from dodging the intended flow or business logic of the application under attack. In the real business world, especially that of e-Commerce, insufficient process validation is due to ineffective access controls and protection and incorrect or lack of business process logic and leads to loss of business (permanent or otherwise) and trust between the enterprise and user (WASC-40 2010, p. 162).

12.10 Web Application Security Scanning

There are essentially two types of scanning tools or methods to assess and monitor web application security:

1. Black box scanning
2. White box scanning

Black box scanning focuses on the web application and takes the user's perspective. The main reasoning behind this method is that the site's security is assessed as a whole, which means that all the application code is working together, for example, HTML, JavaScript, and XML.

In white box scanning, the web application source code that the website runs on is assessed. This type of scanning, which the user doesn't see, provides much better insight into security flaws, suitable or suggested patches, and even up to the granularity of line by line of the code (Figure 12.21).

There is also a third approach, which is a combination of the two methods that we call "gray" box scanning. Here the combination of the best tools comes together, which improves security in general but may impact performance.

12.11 Some Further Discussion and Reflection

The reader has witnessed that the vulnerabilities in web applications go far beyond simple, single threats; it is now a multitude of threats and vulnerabilities that concern and concert together in web applications. Another aspect is that in order to reduce vulnerability, the user (friendly or malicious) needs must be clearly understood. Thus, reducing vulnerability implies supervising three domains, technology, sociological, and legislative–regulatory. This chapter focused on the informatics side and has attempted to provide an overall view of web application vulnerabilities. Such vulnerabilities are not at a specific level; rather, they are spread across several levels and between

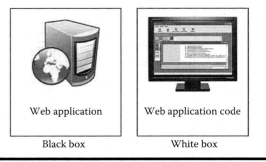

Web application | Web application code

Black box | White box

Figure 12.21 Security scanning.

web application networks as shown in Figure 12.18 (Erikson 2005). These seven levels of vulnerabilities and operability between networks and applications may be summarized as follows:

Physical level: At this level the networks are physically connected with the sole intent to exchange flows of data and, more specifically, raw bits of data.

Data connection level: Together with the bits of data, there is also the need to handle eventual flow errors and in general data flow handling tasks. At the data connection level, there is also a need to activate, conduct, and deactivate the connection.

Network level: At the network level, routing and network activities are conducted as well as functionalities across the other adjacent levels.

Transport level: The transport level provides reliability and optimization functionalities that would be difficult or less convenient to manage at network level.

Session level: At this level the correct connection (opening–conducting–closure) of the application is managed. It is an important level because of its implicit and explicit vulnerabilities.

Presentation level: The presentation of data in terms of syntax and translation is cared for at the presentation level; this includes decryption/encryption and compression/decompression.

Application level: This level takes care of the applications' requirements (Figure 12.22).

Another way of looking at web application vulnerability is to take a security perspective, that is, consider the protection of the system, which here is split into four levels (see Figure 12.23) and briefly summarized as follows:

Physical protection concerns the site (or sites) where the system or parts of it are secured and located: this view may also be classified "on-site security." *Metaphysical* or human protection concerns the user and therefore can be seen as "human" protection. At this level the users are screened including for "abuse of use" concerning their user privileges and interaction with the system.

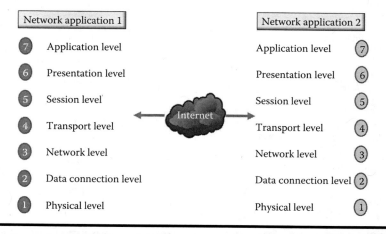

Figure 12.22 Seven levels of vulnerabilities and operability between networks. (Adapted from Erikson, J., *Hacking: The Art of Exploitation,* **2nd edn., Starch Press, Inc., San Francisco, CA, 2005.)**

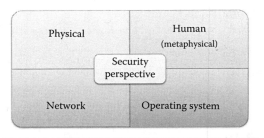

Figure 12.23 Web application vulnerability: the security perspective.

At the OS level, the objective is to protect and prevent security breaches such as those concerning DoS and code injection. At the last and fourth level, the *network security* is supervised. Depending on the preferred system setup, networking may rely on private or public data transmission networks; security breaches therefore can occur off-site.

A third and final way of reducing web application vulnerabilities is to consider the legislative aspects especially the consequences of a "security" breach (Cole 2009, pp. 105–107).

Although it is not possible to cover all legislative aspects (in view of the multitude of national variations), here we consider six different clusters of legislative domains (see Figure 12.24a) based on current U.K. and EU legislation. Figure 12.24b shows a taxonomy approach to the same discussion.

Data protection: Data protection also includes that of fraud and general investigation; hence, legislation can go from the Data Protection Act (WatsonHall 2011) to that of antiterrorism acts.

e-Commerce: Security breaches will most likely have a user protection perspective, which, in the case of commercial web applications, equates to the consumer. Here legislation can cover anything from consumer protection (WatsonHall 2011) to money laundering regulations (FATF report 2010).

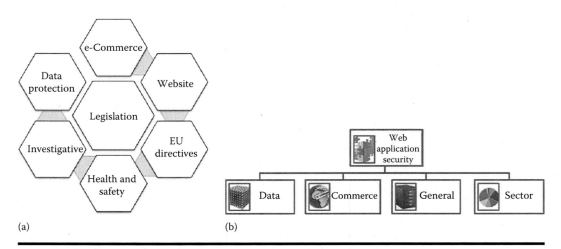

(a) (b)

Figure 12.24 Web applications, society, and legislation: (a) six legislative domains (UK and EU perspective) and (b) equivalent taxonomy of the same 6 domains.

Websites: The disclosure of information on websites will often imply considering privacy, copyright, and intellectual property in general; this is made more critical if such information (Google 2011) involves the e-Commerce of knowledge (such as publication retrieval services) or is done without authorization (http://www.watsonhall.com).

EU directives: The bewildering number of legislation at national level has inevitably provided the need to encompass a more wider and EU-level approach to web application security such as that of personal data protection and privacy (EU Directive 45/2001 on Personal Data Protection 2001).

Health and safety: Although this may seem at first a non-web application vulnerability, the site location and facilities will most certainly have some form of Health and Safety Act at the core to ensure that health and safety provisions are provided (see also physical protection).

Investigative: In this domain we intend all those aspects of data and content management that may be at the center of investigative activities such as the Police and Justice Act and Computer Misuse Act (The UK National Archives 2011).

We will conclude our discussion by briefly taking a look into the future of web applications and information technology not just to forecast change but to see their impact on security:

■ Over the last 5 years, we have seen an explosion in social fora and wireless devices all connecting to the same network, the www. This has meant people are more connected than ever and devices are now becoming active elements of the same network. At home we not only have printers, laptops, tablets, kindles, etc., but also appliances, electricity meters, mobile phones, water boilers, heating and ventilation systems, home entertainment, television, digital audio broadcasting (DAB) radios, and closed-circuit TV (CCTV): the list is lengthening not shortening. In essence we will see a dramatic increase in the number of objects in the www or subparts of it and/or interfacing with it, think of RFIDs and μProcessors. But this is only the tip of the iceberg because so far people have interacted in a passive way, accessing the web for knowledge, latest news, and services with the aim to simplify daily chores and gain time to do more and/or do better. But people will soon be (more) "active" in the web not just because of innovations such as human implants, but their interaction will be continuous, natural, and spontaneous. Barriers such as user IDs, passwords, and identification will be managed in a much more virtual way, and the arrival of cloud computing will force us to look at IT as a service rather than a physical object (Tiwari and Pratibha 2011).

■ Social fora have brought about a new security scenario, and with as little as five pieces of information, any person in the www can be identified with an accuracy of 95%. Add to this the involvement of objects and diffusion of Web 2.0 will take security to a new level and possible different interpretations. This accuracy and integration will certainly increase, as will the awareness of the importance of safeguarding people's privacy and security of such devices. In this respect we will most likely see a socio-driven need to introduce new legislation or improve the existing legislation. This will be imperative as enterprises move toward cloud computing and where machines might become the "criminal" rather than the "gun that fires the bullet."

■ The arrival of cloud computing is already changing the IT service landscape and we have already started to move from the "hosting of services." But the arrival of cloud computing will force enterprises to think security in a completely different way and accelerate the concept of complete security services outside the enterprise as well.

◼ The acquisition of McAfee™ by Intel™ (The New York Times 2010) is the perfect example of hardware–software security integration at a strategic level. If this acquisition is anything to go by, we will see others integrating security directly in their products and going beyond the current domain of system protection (McAfee DeepSafe 2011).

◼ We will also see the use of information to improve security not only for investigative purposes but also as a means of using knowledge in making the best decision. To this end we are walking toward a new paradigm in the exploitation of data; in fact, we will move from the classical data–information–knowledge triangle to one where wisdom will be imperative (see Figure 12.5). This is why there is so much interest in business intelligence even in the small medium-sized enterprise (SME) and where the onus is moving from a pure data mining school of thought to making the wisest possible decision in the shortest possible time.

◼ The push for mobile payments and relative standardization (Boer and de Boer 2009).

◼ The rise of the digital citizen (IPSC—Institute Protection Security Citizen 2012).

12.12 Societal and Legislative Aspects of Cyber Security

Addressing the societal and legislative aspects of cyber security is no straightforward task not just because of technological advances of the web but also the sheer complexity and the repercussions the Internet is having on society. As Peiravi and Peiravi (2010) quite rightly show, Internet and cyber security are a bit of a paradox because the same technological advances are also available to the cyber criminals. Further as security measures and cyber legislation get stricter and effective, privacy infringement and security, in general, become more onerous and fuzzy. Establishing a timeline to spot trends and form an idea of where the Internet and cybercrime is going is equally demanding because while it is true that enterprises and their customers were (and still are) the main victims of cybercrime, today we see much more emphasis on hitting authorities such as government and institutions as well as individuals. In this sense it is clear that cybercrime and cyber terrorism require specific addresses and boundaries. Indeed the FBI already defines cyber terrorism as any "premeditated, politically motivated attack against information, computer systems, computer programs, and data which results in violence against non-combatant targets by sub-national groups or clandestine agents" (FBI 2011). On the other hand, cybercrime is nonpolitical and has no assigned boundary or classical territorial or criminal footprint demarcation.

Understanding the impact of cybercrime is more problematic than ordinary crime because victims are often unaware of it, such as identity theft. Indeed estimates of the annual cost of cybercrime vary from 100 M to 1 trillion US$ (FBI 2011) depending what "social" good(s) and services are affected. This makes law enforcement harder because if the entity and location of the damage are prone to miscalculation and/or misinterpretation, then, assuming the criminals are caught, establishing an appropriate sentence is even harder. Further, when such "social" good(s) and services are provided increasingly more via the web and through dedicated web applications, then a whole new legal landscape unfolds (Rustad and D'Angelo 2011). Ironically, law cases involving cybercrime require the support of similar web applications to ensure the sharing of up-to-date legal litigation information sources (Lloyd's of London Litigation Database 2011).

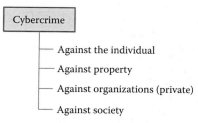

Figure 12.25 Cybercrime categorization.

Currently cybercrime is spread across four legislative categories (see Figure 12.25) with corresponding legislation, strong, weak, or nonexistent, depending on the national legislator and circumstance.

More specifically and descriptively

Cybercrime *against the individual*: E-mail spoofing, spamming, cyber defamation, harassment and cyber stalking, etc.

Cybercrime *against property*: Credit card fraud, intellectual property crimes such as patents, copyright, brands, and Internet time theft

Cybercrime *against organizations*: Unauthorized access of computers and informatics systems so as to change–delete–read–copy data, DoS, virus attacks, e-mail bombing (aimed at the employee, part or all the organization), salami attacks (i.e., when fractions of money are diverted or stashed by the criminal), logic bombing, Trojan horses, data diddling, etc.

Cybercrime *against society*: e-Forgery, cyber terrorism, web jacking, pornography (especially child pornography), indecent exposure, dissemination and sale of illegal material, trafficking, financial crimes, illegal business such as unauthorized gambling, etc.

Looking at the categorization of cybercrime helps us understand that the societal and legislative aspects of cybercrime are intimately interlaced, and therefore, a concerted action is needed if we are to improve cyber security, reduce web application vulnerability, and develop adequate policing and law enforcement approaches. Further, while the suggested categorization provides a clear statement of the classification of the techniques and vulnerabilities exploited by cyber criminals, often such criminals combine them in multifaceted ways making it much more difficult to formulate adequate legislation. In other words what is required is a general and agreed policy toward cybercrime (since "one law cannot fit all cases") and its issues, such as national legislation integration and jurisdiction agreed at an international level.

To this end the EU over the last two decades has initiated and started this legislative journey (Tikk et al. 2010, p. 100). Many governments have made progress in privacy law, individual freedom, war on piracy, etc., but only recently do we start to see an international law framework specific to cybercrimes on both a national and global stage.

Judge Schjolberg provides a set of proposals for new legal mechanisms to combat cybercrime and global cyber attacks (Schjolberg 2011). In his work, "An International Criminal Court or Tribunal for Cyberspace (ICTC)," he quite rightly states the need for an international court or tribunal to deal with the most serious cybercrimes of global and of extranational concern, for the simple reason that "many serious cyber-attacks will go unpunished" (Schjolberg 2011, p. 3). In the meantime legislators, government, law enforcement authorities, and law

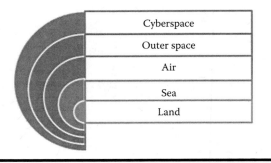

Figure 12.26 Five domains of legislation.

experts have agreed that cyberspace is the fifth legislation domain after land, sea, air, and outer space (see Figure 12.26).

Promoting cyberspace, as the fifth common domain, implies that it too should be a part of the progressive development of international law, something that the other four domains have taken centuries to build, prune, and perfect. But cyber security works on a completely different evolutionary time frame, a different playing space, and where criminals interact with their victims differently and diversely with respect to the other four domains. Indeed technology and cybercrime move at a much faster rate than ordinary crime. Moreover, both have still to show any signs of slowing down or taking a definitive direction. Further, in non-cybercrimes the same criminal cannot simultaneously rape, rob, and run off in different places, while in cybercrime this is not the case because the scene of the crime is virtual. This implies that cybercrime can be iterated simultaneously in different locations toward thousands (if not millions) of victims.

Thus, cyber criminals need to be proven to be on the "scene of the crime" to be held responsible for their acts, and for the current law this is still very much uncharted and often undefinable territory. This implies that international cybercrime policy and laws need first to have a strong legislative base and be able to tackle a wider scope of legislative issues and cases before arriving at a harmonized approach. Judge Schjolberg's words on unlikely punishment of cybercrime are echoed even in the most serious and recent global cyber attacks; the case of Estonia in 2007 is a prime example (Tikk et al. 2010, pp. 25–29). The Estonian cyber incident was shocking because of its concertedness, intensity, and wide scale, so much so that it has been likened more to cyber war (essentially between Russia and Estonia although other nationals were also apparently involved). This specific incident lasted several weeks and is estimated to have cost Estonia over 10 million euros (Tikk et al. 2010). In the Estonian incident, nobody has yet been sentenced for those acts, largely because of lack of cooperation between Estonia and Russia (Herzog 2011, pp. 50–51).

Another worrying aspect of global cybercrime is that it is increasingly involving government and key institutions and bridging into pseudo- or real cyber terrorism (Grove 2000). Recent examples of such global attacks on government institutions include: Whitehall-UK, London and New York stock exchanges, Canada and South Korean government, Australian parliament and prime minister, the EU, the French finance, economy and unemployment ministry, etc. In this latter case, this incident coincided with the French presidency of the G20 and supposedly involved the leakage of high-level information that could have threatened the economic and national security of the concerned countries. Moreover, the attack on the U.K. and U.S. stock exchanges (including National Association of Securities Dealers Automated Quotation [NASDAQ]) aimed to spread panic in leading global financial markets.

That said, cyber attacks and cybercrime are nothing new to society and legislation. Indeed Arquilla (1999) and Wingfield (2000) and, more recently, the ISA (Internet Security Alliance 2008) clearly outline that such incidents were already brewing more than a decade ago. As Rustad and D'Angelo (2011) state, "the internet has changed the legal landscape" and "the Internet is arguably the most transformative invention since the printing press" (Internet Security Alliance 2008, p. 5).

It is argued here that response has been sluggish essentially for three reasons:

1. Technological advancement is in front of legislative advancement and what can be technologically sound (or unsound) in reasoning is not necessarily enough to justify intervention by the law enforcement authorities. Things are made worse by the fact that enforcing cyber law is at its early stage and the majority of cyber attacks go unpunished. This implies that current deterrents are more technological than legislative in nature.
2. Security solutions are embedded principally at web application and organizational level and rarely take into consideration a "system of systems" or more comprehensive approach (Ward and Ward 2011, p. 70). This grossly hinders improving cyber security since the philosophy is "protect ourselves" rather than providing a comprehensive coverage. Indeed the vast majority of cyber security solutions are paid for and managed exclusively by organizations, for example, enterprises and departments.
3. Assessment of damages is very rarely quantified and made public. This has three effects: First, the real entity of potential damage is often ignored providing a false sense of security for those who haven't been damaged, that is, it fuels the "it will never happen to me" attitude and security complacency; second, in the event that the cyber criminals are caught, reimbursement of damages is ambiguous and haphazard and justifying the application of appropriate legislation is harder; and third, the evaluation of costs versus benefits for cyber security solutions is more focused on the inoperability of systems rather than the destruction of the trust in using them. This may have a serious impact on the social contract that exists between the service provider and user. Indeed from a purely social contract perspective, whenever there is a deal between entities such as in B2C, B2B, and B2G (Sampson 2008, p. 3), both entities agree to provide–exchange services and receive benefits that result in a larger and shared social good. In fact when this social contract is broken, for whatever reason, do signees realize the fallacies in the multijurisdictional and legislative systems, the effects it has on their daily life, and the economic effect on the enterprises involved in the contract. In fact in 2004, congress was informed that "There are no standard methodologies for cost measurement, and study of the frequency of attacks is hindered by the reluctance of organisations to make public their experiences with security breaches" (Cashell et al. 2004, p. 3).

This brings us to a suggested closure of this chapter, that is, one that captures the needs of the electronic society (e-Society) that the authors see as being composed of individuals, property, and organizations (private and public) who interact within a boundary where cyber law legislators and policy makers, the cyber law enforcers, cyber security operators, and cyber technologists (the innovators of cyber technologies) act to perform social good for society in general. In essence, the cyber governance of the e-Society is depicted in Figure 12.27.

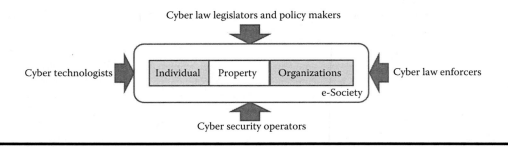

Figure 12.27   e-Society and its cyber security governance.

12.13 Conclusions

More and more people are conducting their business and relative transactions online (e.g., B2B, B2C, B2G), conducting their work over the web (e.g., video conferencing and work package sharing), storing and elaborating data and information (e.g., Google docs), publishing personal thoughts through blogs and social fora (e.g., Facebook), publicizing themselves (e.g., LinkedIn, Monster™), and fostering relationships through Skype™, Friends ReUnited, etc.

Many (new and more) threats against databases are possible because of human error that creates vulnerabilities such as flaws or bugs in OS and server software or slipups made by end users and web application administrators (NIST Guide to Server Security 2008).

Threats may involve intentional actors (e.g., attacker who wants to access information on a server) or unintentional actors (e.g., administrator who forgets to disable user accounts of a former employee.) Threats can be local, such as a disgruntled employee, or remote, such as an attacker in another geographical area.

A further observation is that there is a need to have a clear view of the taxonomies of attacks and keep these updated. Three excellent examples are represented by the works of Howard (1997), Álvarez and Petrović (2003), and more recently Jung-Ying et al. (2008). The authors of this chapter also hope that this work is in line with this train of thought and clarifies some of the less disseminated parts of this topic.

We conclude by hypothesizing that the future of web applications will most likely be shaped on five fronts:

1. The arrival of *new technologies* that will forge new more secure system architectures and take a more comprehensive view of cyber security, that is, from the single processor to the "system of systems."
2. More *people cooperation* concepts such as cloud computing and wikis.
3. New end user *tools* and their *accessibility* such as tablets and democratization–globalization of ITC and social engineering.
4. *Extension* of the Internet through Web 2.0 and extension of web-based applications. Cloud computing, for example, will transfer local applications to a remote applications not just to enhance performance by thinning down the client computing facilities and reducing costs but also to disseminate the contents and network services of both machine and man.
5. The birth of a *common and international legislative engine* that tackles the fifth legal and jurisdiction domain, that is, cyberspace.

So according to the authors of this chapter, what would be on the top of agenda reducing WA vulnerability?

- Get to know the user better so as to provide stronger authentication.
- Build and foster trust into and within the network.
- Clean up at source approach during code development, that is, minimize or eliminate the security holes in the first place. This will entail that the software developers not only are proficient in code exploitation but also understand and ethically abide by the rules that society applies in using it for social good.
- Audit the web application security following a precise scheme of thought and action.
- Think more like the attacker (or hacker) and not the victim.
- Know the needs and reasoning of the attacker as well as the non-malicious user.
- Realize that advances in technology, for example, Web 2.0, will expand the security horizons; hence, it has to be addressed at operational, tactical, and strategic levels (Ward and Trucco, Exploiting Fuzzy Cognitive Maps in Resiliency related Management Decisions 2011).
- When discussing security one should discuss it by simultaneously leveraging technological, societal, and legislative evolution (Cellary and Iyengar 2002).
- From a purely legal perspective, the terminology and the definition of the type of attack become critical. Tikk et al. (2010, p. 101) state that classifying cyber attacks as cyber war and cyber terrorism not only is misleading but may well totally derail the legal process. In other words cyber criminals and cyber terrorists are two completely different entities even though their methods and attacks may be the same.
- The societal impact of web applications and informatics is probably only at its infant stage, and one must realize that while both facilitate social inclusion, they can also expose parts of society to even more risk such as young children, ill, and elderly people.
- On a legal grounding not only is national and international collaboration essential to address ("post-attack") court cases, but also it allows the law enforcement authorities to work within a legal framework and protect society as whole from malicious attackers.
- In interorganizational information systems, such as those found in large and/or global organizations (private and public) and their web applications, the emphasis is on integration and efficiency. However, Homburg argues that "…in practice, development and use of integrated information systems that have cross organizational boundaries often result in confusing power struggles, politicking and sometimes manifest sabotage" (Homburg 2000). From a web application vulnerability perspective organizations should consider not only the security of each single organization (e.g., department, business unit) but also the whole system of organizations, not just in terms of resilience but also cyber security. He concludes that "…data ownership and incentives, rather than integration, are of vital importance for the success of inter-organizational information systems." Interestingly Homburg uses motives, conditions, and decisions as being the key driving factors of success or the lack of it (Homburg 2000, p. 13) in security.

Acknowledgments

We would like to acknowledge all those people out there that do their best to monitor, analyze, and propose solutions to real-world software security problems. Without their work we would have not been able not only to put this chapter into print but also truly grasp the impact of web application vulnerability. In particular we would like to thank all the software communities; authorities, private or public; WASC; OWASP; National Institute of Standards and Technology (NIST); individuals such as Stuttard, Pinto, and Cole; and the academia that, in spite of falling resources and lack of trust, endeavor to make this a more knowledgeable and less vulnerable world. If we have forgotten you, we can assure you that it wasn't for laziness or lack of gratitude; rather, the overwhelming task of disseminating your knowledge appropriately re-elaborated according to our thoughts. Thank you for inspiring and instilling us with the need to know and let others know.

References

Acunetix. Directory traversal attacks. 2011. www.acunetix.com (accessed June 12, 2012).

Akrils, B. *LDAP Directories Explained: An Introduction and Analysis*. Pearson Ed. Inc., Upper Saddle River, NJ, 2003.

Alavi, M. and D. E. Leidner. Knowledge management and knowledge management systems: Conceptual foundations and research issues. *MIS Quarterly* 25(1), 2001: 107–136.

Álvarez, G. and S. Petrović. A new taxonomy of web attacks suitable for efficient encoding. *Computers & Security* 22(5), 2003: 435–449.

Arquilla, J. Can information warfare ever be just? *Ethics and Information Technology* 1, 1999: 203–212.

Banerjee, U. and A. Swaminathan. A taxonomy of attacks and attackers in MANETs. *International Journal of Research and Reviews in Computer Science* 2(2), 2011: 437–441.

Bayer, R. Information life cycle, information value and data management. *Database and Expert Systems Applications: Lecture Notes in Computer Science*, 2007: 277–286.

Benkler, Y. A free irresponsible press: Wikileaks and the battle over the soul of the networked fourth estate. *Harvard Civil Rights-Civil Liberties Law Review* 46, 2011: 311–397.

Bishop, M. A Taxonomy of Unix system and network vulnerabilities. Technical report CSE-9510. Department of Computer Science, Davis, CA, 1995.

Blaze, M. Toward a broader view of security protocols. *Proceedings of the 12th Cambridge International Workshop on Security Protocols*, Cambridge, UK, 2004, pp. 121–132.

Boer, R. and T. de Boer. Mobile payments 2010: Market analysis and overview. 2009. https://www.ebaportal.eu/_Download/Research%20and%20Analysis/2010/Mobile_payments_2010_Innopay.pdf (accessed June 13, 2012).

Bowen, B. M. Design and analysis of decoy systems for computer security. Google Scholar. Columbia University, New York. 2011. http://scholar.google.com/scholar?hl=en&q=IMAP%2FSMTP+security&as_sdt=0%2C5&as_ylo=2011&as_vis=0 (accessed June 12, 2012).

Briffaut, J., P. Clemente, J. F. Lalande, and J. Rouzaud-Cornabas. From manual cyber attacks forensic to automatic characterization of attackers' profiles. 2011. http://www.univ-orleans.fr/lifo/prodsci/rapports/RR/RR2011/RR-2011-14.pdf (accessed June 10, 2012).

Brown, K. *The .NET Developer's Guide to Windows Security*. Addison-Wesley, New York, 2004.

Brumley, D., T. Chiueh, R. Johnson, H. Lin, and D. Song. Automatically protecting against integer-based vulnerabilities. 2007. http://www.cs.cmu.edu/~dbrumley/pubs/integer-ndss-07.pdf (accessed June 10, 2012).

Cashell, B., W. D. Jackson, M. Jickling, and B. Webel. The economic impact of cyber-attacks. CRS Report for Congress, Government and Finance Division, 2004.

Cellary, W. and A. Iyengar. *Internet Technologies, Applications and Societal Impact*, Vol. 104. Springer, New York, 2002.

Clarke, J. (Ed.). SQL injection attacks and defense. Syngress Publishing, Inc., Burlington, MA, 2009.

Cole, E. *Network Security Bible*, 2nd edn. Wiley Publications, Inc., Indianapolis, IN, 2009.

Dick, K. *XML A Manager's Guide. Information Technology Series*. Addison-Wesley, New York, 2002.

Drayer, J. Examining the effectiveness of anti-scalping laws in a United States Market. *Sport Management Review* 14 (2011): 226–236.

Erikson, J. *Hacking: The Art of Exploitation*, 2nd edn. Starch Press, Inc., San Francisco, CA, 2005.

EU Directive 45/2001 on Personal Data Protection. Legislation summaries. 2001. http://europa.eu/legislation_summaries/information_society/data_protection/l24222_en.htm (accessed June 12, 2012).

European Commission 2004/48/EC. Application of Directive 2004/48/EC of the European Parliament and the Council of 29 April 2004 on the enforcement of intellectual property rights. December 22, 2010. http://eur-lex.europa.eu (accessed June 12, 2012).

European Commission, Enterprise and Industry Directorate-General. Study of the industrial implications in Europe of the blurring of the dividing lines between Security and Defence: Final report. 2010. http://ec.europa.eu/ (accessed June 12, 2012).

European Council—Directive 2006/24/EC. *Data Retention Directive 2006/24/EC*. Directive, European Publications Office, 2006, 1–10.

FATF report. Money laundering using new payment methods. FATF, 2010.

FBI. The FBI Federal Bureau of Investigation. 2011. http://www.fbi.gov/stats-services/publications/facts-and-figures-2010–2011/investigative-programs#cyber_crime (accessed June 11, 2012).

Fonseca, J., M. Vieira, and H. Madeira. The web attacker perspective—A field study. *Proceedings of the IEEE 21st International Symposium on Software Reliability Engineering*. San Jose, CA, November 1–4, 2010, pp. 299–308.

Foster, J. C. *Buffer Overflow Attacks: Detect, Exploit, Prevent*. Syngress, Burlington, MA, 2005.

Gallagher, T. Finding and preventing cross-site request forgery. 2006. http://www.blackhat.com/presentations/bh-usa-06/BH-US-06-Gallagher.pdf (accessed June 12, 2012).

Gasson, S. The dynamics of sensemaking, knowledge, and expertise in collaborative, boundary-spanning design. 2005. http://jcmc.indiana.edu/vol10/issue4/gasson.html (accessed June 12, 2012).

Global Cyber Law Database. 2012. http://cyberlawdb.com/main/ (accessed June 11, 2012).

Google. Privacy Centre. 2011. www.google.co.uk/intl/en/privacy (accessed June 14, 2012).

Grove, G. D. Cyber-attacks and International Law. *Survival* (NATO) 42(3), 2000: 89–103.

Guest Authentication. 2011. www.bluecoat.com (accessed June 14, 2012).

Hansman, S. and R. Hunt. A taxonomy of network and computer attacks. *Computers & Security* 24, 2005: 31–43.

Herzog, S. Revisiting the Estonian cyber attacks: Digital threats and multinational responses. *Journal of Strategic Security* 4(2), 2011: 49–60.

Homburg, V. M. F. The political economy of information exchange: Politics and property rights in the development and use of interorganizational information systems. Faculty of Social Sciences, Erasmus University of Rotterdam, Rotterdam, the Netherlands, 2000, pp. 1–19.

Horman aka Horms, S. SSL and TLS: An overview of a secure communications protocol. *Security Mini-Conference at Linux*, Canberra, Australia, 2005, pp. 1–26.

Howard, J. An analysis of security incidents on the internet, 1989–1995. PhD thesis. Department of Engineering and Public Policy, Carnegie Mellon University, Pittsburgh, PA, 1997.

Internet Security Alliance. The cyber security social contract policy recommendations. *Report to the Obama Administration and 111th Congress*, Internet Security Alliance, 2008.

IPSC—Institute Protection Security Citizen. The digital citizen. 2012. http://ipsc.jrc.ec.europa.eu/index.php/132/0/ (accessed June 14, 2012).

Jazayeri, M. Some trends in web application development. *International Conference on IEEE Computer Society, FOSE 07 Future of Software Engineering ed.*, 2007, Lugano University, Lugano, pp. 199–213.

Johns, M., B. Braun, M. Schrank, and J. Posegga. Reliable protection against Session Fixation attacks. *SAC '11 Proceedings of the 2011 ACM Symposium on Applied Computing*, New York, 2011, pp. 1531–1537.

Jung-Ying, L., W. Jain-Shing, C. Shih-Jen, W. Chia-Huan, and Y. Chung-Huang. Designing a taxonomy of web attacks. *Proceedings of the International Conference on Convergence and Hybrid Information Technology*, Daejeon, Korea, 2008, pp. 278–282.

Klein, A. DOM based cross site scripting or XSS of the third kind. www.webappsec.org. 2005. http://www.webappsec.org/projects/articles/071105.shtml (accessed June 14, 2012).

Livshits, B., M. Martin, and M. S. Lam. SecuriFly: Runtime protection and recovery from web application vulnerabilities. Technical report, Stanford University, Stanford, CA. 2006. http://suif.stanford.edu/~livshits/papers/pdf/securifly_tr.pdf (accessed June 14, 2012).

Lloyd's of London Litigation Database. September 21, 2011. http://uniset.ca/lloyds_cases/lloyds_cases.html (accessed April 5, 2012).

Maslow, A. H. *Motivation and Personality*. Maslow Publications, New York, NY, 1954.

Matyáš, V. and Z. Říha. Towards reliable biometric authentication through biometrics. *IEEE Security and Privacy*, 1(3), 2003: 45–49.

McAfee DeepSafe. *McAfee DeepSafe Technology*. 2011. http://www.mcafee.com/us/solutions/mcafee-deepsafe.aspx (accessed January 18, 2013).

McIntosh, M. and P. Austel. XML signature element wrapping attacks and countermeasures. *SWS '05 Proceedings of the 2005 Workshop on Secure Web Services*, George Mason University, Fairfax, VA, 2005, pp. 22–27.

McNab, C. *Network Security Assessment: Know Your Network*. 2nd edn. O'Reilly Media, Inc., Sebastopol, CA, 2007.

My SQL. *My SQL*. June 2012. http://dev.mysql.com (accessed June 14, 2012).

Nahari, H. and R. L. Krutz. *Commerce Security: Design and Development*. Wiley & Sons, New York, 2011.

NIST Guide to Server Security. National institute for standards and technology. 2008. http://csrc.nist.gov/publications/nistpubs/800-123/SP800-123.pdf (accessed June 9, 2012).

NIST. National vulnerability database at NIST. 2011. http://nvd.nist.gov/home.cfm (accessed June 14, 2012).

Norwood, G. Maslow's hierarchy of needs. The Truth Vectors (Part I). 1999. http://www.deepermind.com/20maslow.htm (accessed January 18, 2013).

Noseevich, G. and A. Petukhov. Detecting insufficient access control in web applications. *SISSEC Project, 1st Project Workshop Proceedings*, Amsterdam, the Netherlands, July 6, 2011, pp. 10–17.

O'Gorman, L. Comparing passwords, tokens, and biometrics for user authentication, *Proceedings of the IEEE*, 91(12), 2003: 2019–2040.

OWASP. The web application security project. 2011. www.owasp.org (accessed June 14, 2012).

OWASP-DV-008. Testing for XML injection. The web application security project. 2011. https://www.owasp.org/index.php/Main_Page (accessed June 14, 2012).

Patel, N., M. Fahimm, and S. Santosh. SQL injection attacks: Techniques and protection mechanisms. *International Journal on Computer Science and Engineering (IJCSE)* 3(1), 2011: 199–203.

Peiravi, A. and M. Peiravi. Internet security—Cyber crime paradox. *Journal of American Science* 6(1), 2010: 15–24.

Prabhakar, S., S. Pankanti, and A. K. Jain. Biometric recognition: Security and privacy concerns. *IEEE Security and Privacy*, 1(2), 2004: 33–42.

Raghavan, S. V. and E. Dawson. *An Investigation into the Detection and Mitigation of Denial of Service (Dos) Attacks: Critical Information Infrastructure Protection*. S. V. Raghavan and E. Dawson (Eds.). Springer, New York, 2011, pp. 1–8.

Rescorla, E. *SSL and TLS: Designing and Building Secure Systems*. Addison-Wesley, New York, 2001.

Rhodes, B. and J. Goerzen. *Foundations of Python Network Programming*. Springer, New York, 2010.

Rustad, M. L. and D. D'Angelo. The path of internet law: An annotated guide to legal landmarks. *Duke Law and Technology Review* 12, 2011: 1–74.

Saltzman, R. and A. Sharabani. Active man in the middle attacks. IBM Rational Application Security Group. February 27, 2009. http://blog.watchfire.com/AMitM.pdf (accessed June 14, 2012).

Sampson, G. *Electronic Business*. 2nd edn. British Informatics Society Limited, Swindon, UK, 2008.

Schjolberg, S. Cyber Crime Law. May 2011. http://www.cybercrimelaw.net/documents/International_Criminal_Court_or_Tribunal_for_Cyberspace_(ICTC).pdf (accessed June 5, 2012).

Science and Technology Committee. Malware and cybercrime. House of Commons, U.K. Government, 2012, pp. 1–81.

Shannon, G. 2010 CERT Research Report. Carnegie Mellon University, Pittsburgh, PA, 2010.

Sharma, A., Z. Kalbarczyk, R. Iyer, and J. Barlow. Analysis of credential stealing attacks in an open networked environment. *Proceedings of the Fourth International Conference on Network and System Security (NSS)*, Melbourne, Australia, 2010, pp. 144–151.

Silberschatz, A., G. Gagne, and P. Baer Galvi. *Operating System Concepts*, 7th edn. Wiley & Sons, New York, 2005.

Singh, A.-P., V. Kumar, S.-S. Sengar, and M. Wairiya. Detection and prevention of phishing attack using dynamic watermarking. *Information Technology and Mobile Communication*, 2011: 132–137.

Stuttard, D. and M. Pinto. *The Web Application Hacker's Handbook: Discovering and Exploiting Security flaws*. Wiley Publications, Inc., Indianapolis, IN, 2008.

Subashini, S. and V. Kavtha. A survey on security issues in service delivery models of cloud computing. *Journal of Network and Computing Applications* 34, 2011: 1–11.

Sudhir, A., J. Sanjeev, and S. Sanjeev. A survey of routing attacks and security measures in mobile ad-hoc networks. *Journal of Computing* 3(1), 2011: 41–48.

Sullivan, B. XML denial of service attacks and defenses. *MSDN Magazine*. 2000. http://msdn.microsoft.com/en-us/magazine/ee335713.aspx (accessed June 15, 2012).

Surajit, C. and D. Umeshwar. An overview of data warehousing and OLAP technology. 1997. http://www.cs.sfu.ca/cc/459/han/papers/chaudhuri97.pdf (accessed June 14, 2012).

The New York Times. With McAfee deal, Intel looks for edge. *The New York Times (on-line version)*. August 19, 2010. http://www.nytimes.com/2010/08/20/technology/20chip.html (accessed June 14, 2012).

The UK National Archives. 2011. http://www.legislation.gov.uk (accessed June 14, 2012).

Tikk, E., K. Kaska, and L. Vihul. *International Cyber Incidents—Legal Considerations*. CCDCOE, Tallinn, Estonia, 2010.

Tiwari, S. and S. Pratibha. Survey of potential attacks on web services and web service compositions. *ICECT 2011 Third International Conference on Electronics Computer Technology*, Kanyakumari, India, 2011, pp. 47–51.

Trustware. Global security report. 2011.

Ugarte-Pedrero, X., I. Santos, B. Sanz, C. Laorden, and P. Garcia Bringas. Countering entropy measure attacks on packed software detection. *Proceedings of the Ninth IEEE Consumer Communications and Networking Conference (CCNC2012)*, Las Vegas, NV, 2011, pp. 164–168.

van der Vlist, E. XQuery injection: Easy to exploit, easy to prevent, *XML Prague 2011—Conference Proceedings*, Prague, Czech Republic, March 26–27, 2011, pp. 177–190.

Vercellis, C. *Business Intelligence: Data Mining and Optimization for Decision Making*. Wiley & Sons, New York, 2011.

Verizon, U.S. Secret Service and Dutch High Tech Crime Unit. 2011 Data breach investigations report. Annual report, Verizon, 2012, pp. 1–74.

Ward, D. and M. Lasen. An overview of needs theories behind consumerism. 2009. http://mpra.ub.uni-muenchen.de/13090/1/MPRA_paper_13090.pdf (accessed June 5, 2012).

Ward, D. and V. Matuziene. A Kernel view of critical infrastructure modelling. *International Journal of Decision Sciences, Risk and Management* 3(1/2), 2011: 98–128.

Ward, D. and P. Trucco. Exploiting fuzzy cognitive maps in resiliency related management decisions. *Intelligent Decision Support Systems for Managerial Decision Making*. Asers, Romania, 2011, pp. 89–143.

Ward, D. and B. Ward. Business continuity, disruptions and the fuzziness of management decisions in complex socio-technical-economical systems. *International Alternative Investment Review*, October–December edn., 2011: 64–75.

WASC. The Web Application Security Consortium. 2011. http://projects.webappsec.org/w/page/13246995/Web-Hacking-Incident-Database (accessed June 14, 2012).

WASC. Information leakage. 2012. http://projects.webappsec.org/w/page/13246936/Information%20Leakage (accessed June 16, 2012).

WASC-04. The Web Application Security Consortium. January 1, 2010. https://files.pbworks.com/download/iy1omtp7mW/webappsec/13247059/WASC-TC-v2_0.pdf (accessed June 14, 2012).

WASC-05. The Web Application Security Consortium. January 1, 2010. https://files.pbworks.com/download/iy1omtp7mW/webappsec/13247059/WASC-TC-v2_0.pdf (accessed June 14, 2012).

WASC-08. The Web Application Security Consortium. January 1, 2010. https://files.pbworks.com/download/iy1omtp7mW/webappsec/13247059/WASC-TC-v2_0.pdf (accessed June 14, 2012).

WASC-11. The Web Application Security Consortium. January 1, 2010. https://files.pbworks.com/download/iy1omtp7mW/webappsec/13247059/WASC-TC-v2_0.pdf (accessed June 14, 2012).

WASC-16. The Web Application Security Consortium. January 1, 2010. https://files.pbworks.com/download/iy1omtp7mW/webappsec/13247059/WASC-TC-v2_0.pdf (accessed June 11, 2012).

WASC-17. The Web Application Security Consortium. January 1, 2010. https://files.pbworks.com/download/iy1omtp7mW/webappsec/13247059/WASC-TC-v2_0.pdf (accessed June 10, 2012).

WASC-24. The Web Application Security Consortium. January 1, 2010. https://files.pbworks.com/download/iy1omtp7mW/webappsec/13247059/WASC-TC-v2_0.pdf (accessed June 14, 2012).

WASC-25. The Web Application Security Consortium. January 1, 2010. https://files.pbworks.com/download/iy1omtp7mW/webappsec/13247059/WASC-TC-v2_0.pdf (accessed June 14, 2012).

WASC-26. The Web Application Security Consortium. January 1, 2010. https://files.pbworks.com/download/iy1omtp7mW/webappsec/13247059/WASC-TC-v2_0.pdf (accessed June 14, 2012).

WASC-27. The Web Application Security Consortium. January 1, 2010. https://files.pbworks.com/download/iy1omtp7mW/webappsec/13247059/WASC-TC-v2_0.pdf (accessed June 14, 2012).

WASC-28. The Web Application Security Consortium. January 1, 2010. https://files.pbworks.com/download/iy1omtp7mW/webappsec/13247059/WASC-TC-v2_0.pdf (accessed June 14, 2012).

WASC-34. The Web Application Security Consortium. January 1, 2010. https://files.pbworks.com/download/iy1omtp7mW/webappsec/13247059/WASC-TC-v2_0.pdf (accessed June 10, 2012).

WASC-36. The Web Application Security Consortium. January 1, 2010. https://files.pbworks.com/download/iy1omtp7mW/webappsec/13247059/WASC-TC-v2_0.pdf (accessed June 14, 2012).

WASC-39. The Web Application Security Consortium. January 1, 2010. https://files.pbworks.com/download/iy1omtp7mW/webappsec/13247059/WASC-TC-v2_0.pdf (accessed June 14, 2012).

WASC-40. The Web Application Security Consortium. January 1, 2010. https://files.pbworks.com/download/iy1omtp7mW/webappsec/13247059/WASC-TC-v2_0.pdf (accessed June 11, 2012).

WASC-42. The Web Application Security Consortium. January 1, 2010. https://files.pbworks.com/download/iy1omtp7mW/webappsec/13247059/WASC-TC-v2_0.pdf (accessed June 14, 2012).

WASC-44. The Web Application Security Consortium. January 1, 2010. https://files.pbworks.com/download/iy1omtp7mW/webappsec/13247059/WASC-TC-v2_0.pdf (accessed June 9, 2012).

WASC-46. The Web Application Security Consortium. January 1, 2010. https://files.pbworks.com/download/iy1omtp7mW/webappsec/13247059/WASC-TC-v2_0.pdf (accessed June 14, 2012).

Watson, D. Web application attacks (part 1). *Network Security 2007* 11, 2007: 10–14.

WatsonHall. May 23, 2011. www.watsonhall.com/security (accessed June 9, 2012).

Wilson, P. R., M. S. Johnstone, M. Neely, and D. Boles. Dynamic storage allocation: A survey and critical review. 1995. http://www.cs.northwestern.edu/~pdinda/icsclass/doc/dsa.pdf (accessed June 14, 2012).

Wingfield, T. C. *The Law of Information Conflict: National Security Law in Cyberspace.* Aegis Research, Falls Church, VA, 2000.

Yan, J., A. Blackwell, R. Anderson, and A. Grant. Password memorability and security: Empirical results. *IEEE Security and Privacy*, 2004: 25–31.

Chapter 13

Distributed Framework for Cybersecurity of Critical Infrastructures

Salvatore D'Antonio, Luigi Coppolino, Michał Choraś, and Rafał Kozik

Contents

13.1 Introduction

Systems that manage and control infrastructures over large geographically distributed areas are typically referred to as supervisory control and data acquisition (SCADA) systems. A SCADA system is composed of a central core, where system information acquisition and control are concentrated and a number of remote terminal units (RTUs) equipped with limited computational resources. RTUs communicate with the center by sending to and receiving from it short real-time control messages. A typical architecture of a SCADA system is shown in Figure 13.1, where field sensors are connected to the RTU, which in turn is connected to the local supervisor through a local area network (LAN). SCADA LANs are interconnected through a wide area network.

The increasing interconnectivity of SCADA networks and the large adoption of COTS (commercial off-the-shelf) components have exposed SCADA systems to a wide range of security and resilience issues. For example, a denial of service (DoS) attack could inhibit some vital functions of a complex SCADA system, such as control data aggregation in a distributed control system or synchronization between real-time status and historical data in a SCADA backup system.

Detecting attacks is a hard task in any networked environment, since a network naturally lends itself to a distributed exploitation of its resources. In a SCADA networked system, the identification of a potential attack requires that information is gathered from many different sources and in many different places, since no locality principle (neither spatial nor temporal) can be fruitfully applied in the most general case. For these reasons, we designed a distributed framework for

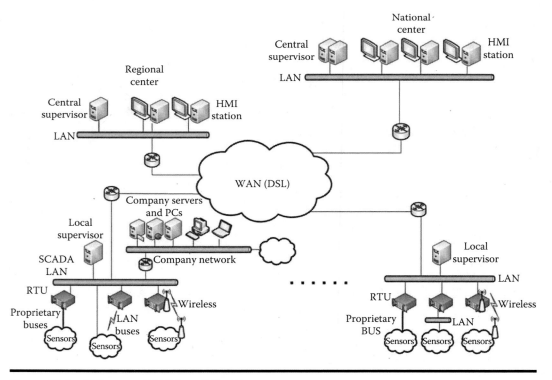

Figure 13.1   Reference SCADA architecture.

SCADA system security comprising a number of components, whose operation is orchestrated to ensure that the overall SCADA infrastructure is effectively protected. The main functions of the proposed framework, called diagnosis and remediation system (DiReS), are monitoring, detection and diagnosis, and remediation. A distributed framework allows for the separation of concerns among a well-defined set of entities, each conceived to deal with a particular aspect of the problem. As an example, the security system might need several probes sniffing traffic in crucial points of the network, as well as several detection modules, each exploiting the best fitting attack detection technique according to the system status and node location. The online part of DiReS is capable of monitoring the SCADA infrastructure being protected, collecting information from the heterogeneous components of the SCADA system, and processing such information in order to detect cyber attacks and apply remediation actions in a real-time fashion. Moreover, we also developed the off-line part (closely linked to online detection and diagnosis), namely, decision aid tool (DAT), which supports operator in threat ranking, forecasting, and risk assessment.

In this chapter, we present the overall architecture of the proposed distributed framework and provide a detailed description of both the detection and diagnosis module and the DAT. We also demonstrate the effectiveness of our framework to protect a SCADA system by showing how it can be used to secure the wireless sensors of a SCADA network from attacks exploiting routing protocol vulnerabilities.

This chapter is structured as follows: firstly, in Section 13.2, the overall architecture of the proposed framework is described. In Section 13.3, we focus on the online part, and we describe the real-time cyber-attack detection and diagnosis system. In Section 13.4, we focus on the off-line part, and we describe the DAT. Afterward, in Section 13.5, we show how the online and off-line parts of the framework cooperate to enhance the overall security of a SCADA system. In Section 13.6, we present a practical example on how our framework can be effectively used to protect the wireless zone of a SCADA network. Conclusions are given in Section 13.7.

13.2 Architectural Framework for SCADA Systems Security

In this section, a distributed framework for SCADA system security, called DiReS, is described. Such framework comprises the following main functional blocks: monitoring, detection and diagnosis, and remediation (Figure 13.2).

Monitoring is performed by different kinds of probes, such as network traffic analyzers, log parsers, and system monitors, which are spread over the SCADA infrastructure in order to collect and possibly filter out status data. To cope with the heterogeneity of the formats of such data, adaptable parsers are used to translate raw events to an intermediate format so that they can be merged in a single data stream for further processing.

Such data are processed by diagnosers that are in charge of detecting the symptoms of anomalies/intrusions, identifying the affected component of the SCADA system, and activating reconfiguration actions. A diversity-based approach to the selection of diagnosis techniques is exploited in order to improve the coverage and the accuracy of the overall security framework.

In case an intrusion or anomalous activity is detected, the diagnosis system raises an alert to the reconfiguration block that employs a policy-based approach to enforce remediation strategies aiming at mitigating the effects of the attack and isolating the target system component.

However, automating intrusion detection and diagnosis could be self-defeating if they are carried out in wrong circumstances. In some cases, the decision to perform remediation as well as

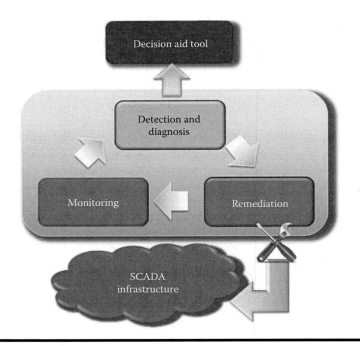

Figure 13.2   Functional blocks of the DiReS system.

the choice of the remediation strategies could be left to the human operator. For these reasons, the framework includes an off-line part, named DAT, which is in charge of

- Providing the human operator with information about the security incidents detected by the online part and about the reactions undertaken
- Supporting the human operator analysis of these incidents so that he or she can confirm or correct the decisions (detection and reaction) taken by the automatic online part

To summarize, the architecture of this framework consists of two hierarchical levels, that is, the real-time part and the off-line part, which cooperate and complement each other.

13.3 Real-Time Detection and Diagnosis of Cyber Attacks

The overall architecture of the detection and diagnosis subsystem is depicted in Figure 13.3. It comprises the following components:

1. A number of probes, which are distributed throughout the SCADA infrastructure and feed events to the event bus
2. One or more network-level detection systems, which consist of
   a. The data broker, which is in charge of gathering information from the monitoring system and distributing the collected information to one or more detection engines
   b. One or more detection engines, which receive data from the broker and decide on whether or not such information represents a potential attack pattern, based on a specific detection technique

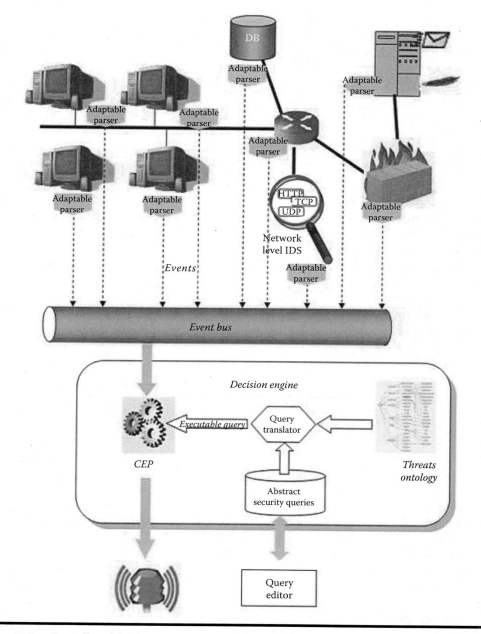

Figure 13.3 Overall architecture of the detection and diagnosis subsystem.

    c. The decision maker, which is in charge of combining information coming from multiple detection engines and analyzing diverse subsets of the source data in order to effectively detect attacks

3. The decision engine, which queries the event bus and takes the final decision on whether or not the collected information represents a potential attack

Several solutions have been proposed to increase the effectiveness and performance of an attack detection process; in particular, recently distributed architectures have been largely investigated. In [1], the authors present a scalable system for high-performance intrusion detection that relies on a cluster-based architecture. A scalable and flexible intrusion detection system is also presented in [2]. The authors propose an innovative framework that allows multiple and cooperative network-based detection systems to exchange internal state information with the goal of performing a stateful and accurate traffic analysis. In [3], the author proposes a highly configurable attack detection framework consisting of several autonomous agents that locally monitor network traffic and transfer gathered information to a centralized data fusion server. The agents are extremely flexible since they can dynamically download and install appropriate modules, signatures, and policy files from a central server.

Another agent-based detection system is proposed in [4]. The proposed system provides five different types of agents, each with a specific task, in order to analyze events from different sites and to detect attack symptoms using an anomaly-based approach.

A different approach is proposed in [5], where the authors present a parallel detection system that is capable of monitoring network traffic on a single ingress/egress point by performing discrete tasks, as data analysis, in a parallel manner.

Regardless of previous solutions, our detection and diagnosis system conjugates the main features of both distributed and parallel detection systems. In particular, our framework provides a flexible solution allowing multipoint traffic data acquisition and analysis. Several analysis approaches, for example, anomaly or misuse-based detection, can be exploited in parallel on the same traffic data set, thus improving the reliability of the overall detection process.

13.3.1 Probes

Probes are responsible for managing the process of collecting (and converting) events that are produced by a variety of data feeds. They operate at different levels of the SCADA infrastructure (network level, operating system level, database level, application level) and are implemented as adaptable parsers that are based on the concept of "grammar-based log analysis." This concept implies

- A very large degree of expressiveness
- The availability of well-known tools for the automatic processing of grammar-based artifacts
- A high level of generality and technology independence, which decouples the format definition from the underlying technology used for data processing

The format and the source of application logs must be both configurable at run time, which makes the adaptable parser completely independent of the specific characteristics of the processing infrastructure to which it is connected. Manually writing parsers for new data stream formats is not a viable solution. This strategy is slow and tedious; it often produces code that is difficult to be understood and error prone, and it is strictly tied to a specific format.

The aforementioned considerations suggested some essential principles we considered in designing the architecture of the monitoring framework:

- *Transparency.* In case a new stream is added, this should only entail integrating an external plug-in component into the framework.
- *Technology independence.* The process of extending the application with a new information source should not depend on the specific technology used to implement the application.

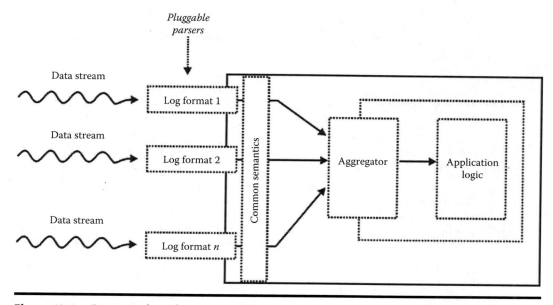

Figure 13.4   Grammar-based stream parsing.

Formats should be defined in a uniform, reusable, and technology-independent formalism.

- *Automated design.* Reliable tools for automated generation of format-dependent components should be available.
- *Streaming.* The additional components required by new formats should not alter the streamed nature of information flows, for example, by adding unnecessary synchronization points.

The resulting component is described in Figure 13.4. The availability of a common semantics that is shared by individual streams is a key factor to achieve the aforementioned presented design principles. Such common semantics (e.g., a common set of data objects that the application will extract from the various processed streams) needs to be exposed as the external, uniform application interface. The syntax and the format-specific semantics (needed, e.g., to perform particular data format conversions) are formally described in a separate element. This element is a grammar definition, which provides a suitable technology-independent formalism and also a set of associated off-the-shelf tools (such as Lex/Yacc or JavaCC) for automatic generation of processing components. Grammars are totally independent of the application logic and technology. Writing a grammar only implies knowing the common semantic interface exposed by the application. Grammar definitions are used to generate "pluggable" components, one for each data format, that are then connected to the main application through an appropriate programming interface inferred from the common semantics. The multiple streams that enter the application after the conversion can then be uniformly processed; for example, they can be aggregated into a single stream and/or analyzed for extracting common global events.

13.3.2 *Network-Level Detection System*

The detection and diagnosis system analyzes data provided by the probes for identifying attack evidences. Focusing on the network-level detection system, traffic metrics of interest need to be selected according to the traffic properties that are deemed to be able of exposing the symptoms of addressed attack types, thus making attack-related traffic flows easily separable from normal traffic. Whenever a suspicious activity is detected, the system generates an alert. Detection effectiveness depends on the technique employed for classification and on both the traffic data analyzed and the metrics chosen to represent them for the purpose of attack detection. The more accurate the classification mechanism, the more effective the overall detection process, in terms of correctly detected anomalous events and false alarms. Furthermore, the more suitable the metrics are, the more effective the separation between normal and anomalous traffic is. Another degree of freedom in the system, which could dramatically affect its performance, is the choice of the detection techniques to be employed. The proposed system exploits a diversity-based approach to the selection of detection techniques. In fact, by integrating different mechanisms for attack classification, the system increases its detection capabilities, since more accurate analysis can be performed in order to detect specific attacks. A support for reliability evaluation can be added when multiple detection techniques are used, thus allowing to evaluate the accuracy of each issued decision. In some cases, such an approach, exploiting several techniques, might require each technique to analyze different sets of monitored traffic metrics. This is because a detection process for a specific attack does not necessarily need to analyze all the network parameters provided by monitoring, but exclusively the parameters that are of interest to the specific anomaly or behavior it has been trained to detect. Therefore, a data management module, the so-called data broker, is required to properly distribute the incoming traffic metrics to different detection engines (Figure 13.5).

A multi-classification approach can be implemented either in a centralized or in a distributed fashion: the combination of multiple detection techniques can be used both locally, in order to increase the reliability of alerts raised at each detection engine, and in a distributed fashion, by combining evidences of events communicated by different detection engines to the decision maker, in order to gain a global knowledge of the overall security status of the monitored networking scenario. The network-level detection system relies on a distributed architecture in order to increase the overall system robustness and dynamicity as long as the detection reliability. Several detection engines are spread across the network, each exploiting the best suited detection

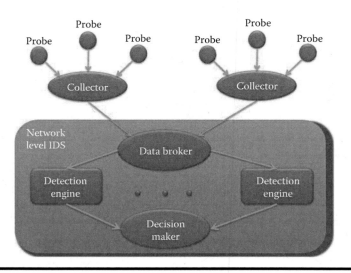

Figure 13.5 Architecture of the network-level detection system.

technique according to both system status and node location. Such a dynamically distributed system might, for instance, adapt itself at the occurrence of a distributed DoS (DDoS) attack, by appropriately placing detection engines in the most critical nodes (i.e., the nodes along the attackers' path) and by coordinating such nodes through a proper signaling protocol (e.g., a protocol for tracing back the attack). New detection modules can be dynamically integrated in the framework by means of an effective network protocol defined aside with the architecture specification. Interaction between each detection engine and the decision maker is realized using the Intrusion Detection Message Exchange Format (IDMEF) data format. IDMEF provides data formats and exchange procedures for sharing information on alerts and, in general, on detection responses between distributed components. The extensibility of IDMEF allows for the definition of new data types, formats, and procedures suitable for the interaction scenario at hand. In order to exploit the diversity of detection techniques, we necessarily need to define an effective approach for orchestrating and combining information coming from the multiple sources foreseen. In fact, a multi-classification approach bases its performance improvement on the ability of effective and secure detection of attacks by combining information coming from diverse engines, each potentially using different detection techniques, and analyzing diverse subsets of the source data. This task is performed by the decision maker that exploits several techniques, ranging from very simple majority voting to complex information fusion techniques. Such techniques are needed, which allow for combining several pieces of information, produced by different detection engines, with the final aim of improving both the accuracy of the classification process and the reliability of the decision-making process.

13.3.3 Decision Engine

The decision engine queries the event bus looking for symptoms of attacks. It relies on a complex event processor (CEP) to correlate events produced by different sources, such as application-level probes, operating system-level probes, and network-level detection systems. Complex event processing is the software technology that enables applications to monitor multiple streams of event data, analyze them in terms of key performance indicators that are expressed in event rules, and act upon threats in real time, potentially by creating derived events or forwarding raw events.

The CEP supporting the decision engine queries the bus looking for complex events sequences representative of the ongoing attack. It is driven by a threat ontology that describes relationships between vulnerabilities, threats, and attacks. The sequences to look for are obtained by translating abstract queries by applying details inferred from the threat ontology. Abstract queries refer to generic threats. In order to make such queries executable, an ad hoc tool, called query translator, is used. Such tool retrieves information related to what kind of symptoms a threat produces. The ontology allows for decoupling the threat to be monitored (abstract query) from the events giving evidence of such threat in the specific context (threat ontology). When one or more of the registered queries match a particular sequence of events, the decision engine raises an alert, providing diagnostic info. Such info is used by the remediation component in order to identify and implement the appropriate and necessary action for mitigating the effects of the ongoing attack.

13.4 Keeping the Human in the Loop: The Decision Aid Tool

Currently used tools for monitoring critical infrastructures (CIs) are not designed to provide the operator with good situation awareness. Typically, these tools are mainly experience-based solutions with a raw or tabular data presentation–user interface. Often the data volume and complexity can overwhelm the operator, making the system unsuitable as a real-time decision support system (DSS).

There are different tools available that are designed to assess hardware, applications, or information systems weaknesses. These tools typically conduct an analysis in order to gain information about a network (open ports, application fingerprints, operating systems versions, etc.). One of the most basic tools for network reconnaissance is network mapper (NMAP) [6]. It uses port scanning and fingerprinting techniques in order to indentify operating systems, applications, and their versions. By correlating this information with the data stored in vulnerability databases, such as National Vulnerability Database (NVD) [7], it is possible to indentify the threats. More advanced tools, like Nexpose [8], Nessus [9], SAINT [10], and OpenVAS [11], can automatically correlate data, and the correlation results are gathered in detailed report for the user.

There are also different risk assessment methodologies, such as those proposed by CRAMM [12] and International Organization for Standardization (ISO), that support these tools during the evaluation process. Most of such methodologies are characterized by the following steps:

1. Identify the background and understand the context.
2. Identify assets and model the system.
3. Identify the value of asset (e.g., business value).
4. Identify and rank network vulnerabilities.
5. Analyze the risk.
6. Apply countermeasures and reaction plans in order to decrease/eliminate risk.

The CSET tool [13] was developed under the direction of the Department of Homeland Security. During the evaluation process, the CSET tool uses National Institute of Standards and Technology (NIST), ISO, and North American Electric Reliability Corporation (NERC) standards. The output obtained from this tool is a list of recommendations aiming at improving the cybersecurity of the analyzed infrastructure.

Another example of security assessment tool is Microsoft security assessment tool (MSAT). It was designed to help the operator to identify security risks in IT environment. The tools aim at assessing the security posture of the analyzed system.

NSAT (network security analysis tool [14]) is an example of network vulnerability scanner. Authors state that this tool can identify 50 different services and hundreds of vulnerabilities. It relies on techniques similar to NMAP (fingerprinting, banner identification, etc.).

DAT analyzes and simulates the network layer of CIs and SCADA systems. The main goal of DAT is to handle threat detection (current system status tracking), CI configuration faults, consequences of failures, and evaluation problems [15]. The major innovation is that DAT can be used to assess various types of networks and contexts since it exploits expert knowledge maintained in the form of semantic notation (ontology). The knowledge can be modified, while the tool functionalities remain unchanged. Hereby, we use DAT to analyze communication networks supporting CIs (including SCADA).

As depicted in Figure 13.6, DAT comprises a user-friendly graphical interface that allows to identify and rank the threats found in a CI. Furthermore, DAT allows user to find security solutions for a particular threat and define an adequate countermeasure and strategy for minimizing the risk. What is more DAT allows user to perform simulation scenarios answering the question "what may happen if particular action is taken."

The tool is also equipped with a GUI that allows the user to provide security rules, which may both describe relations between particular elements or inject some additional facts about the

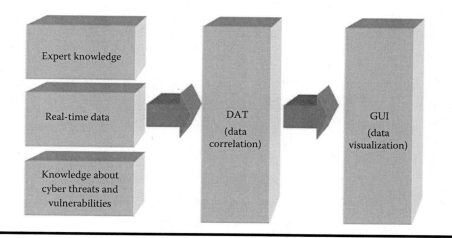

Figure 13.6 DAT information flow.

system enlarging the knowledge maintained by the tool. Moreover, the concept of human in the loop is one of the most important design concepts.

Many examples of DSSs are customized and focused on a particular branch of CIs [16–19]. DSSs are usually designed for specific kind of industry or application. On the other hand, DAT is designed to be a general solution that can be applied to various domains. Most current tools focus either on network security or on a particular domain-awareness issue, while DAT encompasses a multi-domain analysis of network security and resilience for any CI environment.

DAT task is to increase the situation awareness of the CI operators. The tool visualizes (see Figure 13.7) the network status and provides information about both historical and current network events and security incidents [20]. The tool uses data about historical network performance, information from the underlying detection and diagnosis system, and reported network events. The tool analyzes and presents the threats, provides support and guidance to the operator, and evaluates potential actions to be taken as well as decisions made by the operator. The tool also allows the operator to incorporate high-level knowledge (like business models or business value of a particular asset) about the CI by means of a semantic description. Moreover, the tool enables the operator to visually track and annotate the "footprints" of attacks and to correlate them with other network incidents in order to combine this information for further analysis.

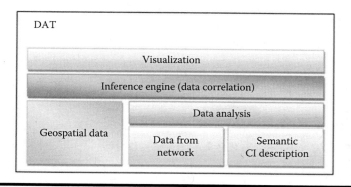

Figure 13.7 DAT functional elements.

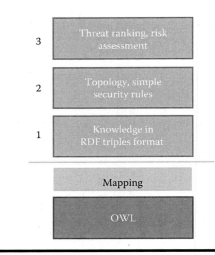

Figure 13.8 DAT knowledge logical layers.

13.4.1 Knowledge Representation

Knowledge used by DAT in the reasoning process is organized in a hierarchical way (from low-level facts to high-level ones) as shown in Figure 13.8. It is maintained as Resource Description Framework (RDF) triples. Such description allows to extract information about basic relations between elements and, particularly, to identify the root classes and instances belonging to those classes (asset, vulnerability, threat, safeguard). These concepts allow to extract the so-called root facts about the CI being analyzed, and thus, this knowledge, describing relations "asset–vulnerability–threat," provides the user with information, which is equal to that which can be found in typical vulnerability databases.

The second layer is in charge of extracting the topology of the CI being protected. Hereby information about a particular node, its connection to the network, and application it runs can be found. Such approach allows to identify additional facts about the analyzed environment (faults in elements connectivity, configuration faults, etc.). On top of this knowledge, DAT allows the user to provide security rules and acquire information about the CI. Particularly, operator has ability to assess what may happen if a particular action is taken. Let us consider the scenario where the operator plans to take down the router during the maintenance of the CI network. By using the information about the connectivity and information about business importance of the detached nodes (detached by router shut down), DAT will raise an alert informing that this may cause a serious malfunction of CI or has no impact on it. Also, the addition of a new machine to the CI may also be validated by DAT prior the physical manipulations, saving the time and possibly the money.

13.5 How Real-Time and Off-Line Tools Can Cooperate to Enhance Cybersecurity

The events coming from sensors (see Figure 13.9) are received by the DAT event-processing engine in the form of streams. It implements mechanisms that allow DAT to efficiently execute multiple queries over the data streams in order to perform event correlation. Particularly, the engine allows

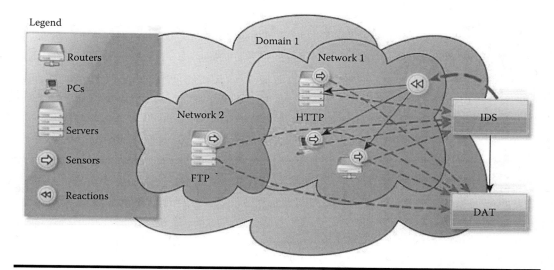

Figure 13.9 Real-time data sources.

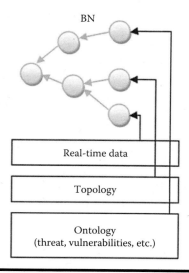

Figure 13.10 BN is fed by the facts about CI.

DAT to efficiently aggregate the same kind of events coming from multiple sources generated by particular IP addresses.

The general idea of data fusion is presented in Figure 13.10. The Bayesian network (BN) output computes the particular threat severity using observations about the CI gained from ontology.

The input is obtained from the first and second layers. First, the knowledge layer provides the network with the basic information about the threatened asset, the threat itself, the vulnerability, and the safeguard. The third layer introduces information obtained from sensors (real-time data), such as intrusion detection systems, intrusion prevention systems, anomaly detection systems, network probes, and network sensors in various layers (e.g., application logs).

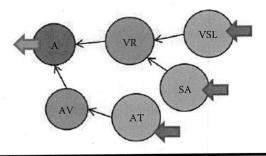

Figure 13.11 **Example of BN used for threat probability estimation. A, attack {T,F}; VSL, vulnerability severity level {h,m,l}; AV, asset value {h,m,l}; SA, safeguard applied {T,F}; AT, asset type {os,hw,app,prot,other}; VR, vulnerability risk {h,m,l}.**

The structure of the proposed BN is presented in Figure 13.11. The arrows on the right-hand side represent the input (observations), while the one on the left represents the posterior probability of the fact that the node is threatened by the attack given the asset type (AT), vulnerability risk level (VRL), and safeguard-applied (SA) observation.

Those observations are extracted by DAT using the knowledge about the CI. The AT observation represents the asset type. The information is adapted here to emphasize the fact that some assets (elements in the CI) are more valuable than others. Furthermore, the number of valuable assets also influences the total risk value. Particularly the asset value (AV) is used to increase the importance of servers, routers, and other critical elements. According to ISO standard, each network element may have vulnerabilities, which threaten the system; therefore, BN uses the vulnerability risk (VR) to evaluate the vulnerability severity. The VR and AV are combined to assess the final value of the risk probability.

Each real-time event received by DAT from the network being analyzed is considered as an attack symptom and as such is matched with knowledge obtained from ontology in order to infer the most likely attack. In other words, the probability $p(A|o_1, o_2, \ldots, o_n)$ of a particular attack (A) is estimated given the observations $\{o_1, o_2, \ldots, o_n\}$. Using the Bayesian theory, the probability can be rewritten as

$$p(A\,|\,o_1,o_2,o_3,\ldots,o_n) = \frac{p(o_1,o_2,o_3,\ldots,o_n\,|\,A)p(A)}{p(o_1,o_2,o_3,\ldots,o_n)}$$

For all known attacks and known symptoms, the problem of finding the most probable attack in practice becomes a maximum a posteriori (MAP) problem. However, assuming observation independence, it is possible to simplify the problem to that of finding maximum joint probability:

$$p(A\,|\,o_1,o_2,o_3,\ldots,o_n) = p(A)\prod_{t=1}^{N} p(o_i\,|\,A)$$

The event-observation matching process uses information retrieved from the ontology indicating which event is semantically equal or is a subclass of a particular observation.

If the event is successfully matched with observation, all possible (matching) attacks are analyzed. If the score function (joint probability $p(A|o_1, o_2, \ldots, o_n)$) is greater than a (predefined) threshold, then information about that fact is visualized to the operator in the topology diagram

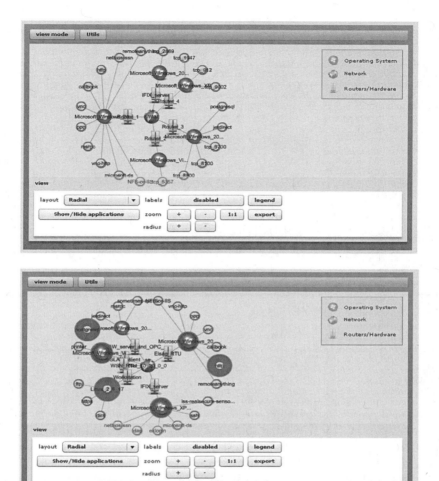

Figure 13.12   Visualizing topology and inferred threats.

(see Figure 13.12). More information about the detected threats is provided through security reports (see example in Figure 13.13).

13.6 Use Case: Detection, Diagnosis, and Remediation in the Wireless Zones of a SCADA Network

It is foreseen that wireless technology, and particularly wireless sensor networks (WSNs), will be increasingly used in critical information infrastructures for several good reasons [21–23]. One is that WSN technology has the potential of significantly improving the sensing capabilities of SCADA systems, since it provides a wide variety of low-cost sensors, which can be easily and flexibly deployed. Also, the use of WSNs may result in increased resilience of the overall SCADA architecture, thanks to the capability of sensors to build a mesh-based routing topology.

Rank	Asset	Threat	Severity level	Details
	Microsoft Windows Vista SP0	CAPEC-114	89.597	show
	Microsoft Windows Vista SP0	CAPEC-94	89.597	show
	Microsoft Windows Vista SP0	CAPEC-57	89.597	show

> AT: Windows
> AS: F
> VSL: high
> CVE Description: The DNS client in Microsoft Windows 2000 SP4, XP SP2, Server 2003 SP1 and SP2, and Vista uses predictable DNS transaction IDs, which allows remote attackers to spoof DNS responses.
> CVSS Score: 8.8
> Asset: Microsoft Windows Vista SP0
> Severity level: 89.597
> Solution: CWE-287
> Threat: CAPEC-94
> Exploits: CVE-2008-0087
> Mitigation(s): -Architecture and Design - [Use an authentication framework or library such as the OWASP ESAPI Authentication feature.]
> Motivation(s): -Data Modification
> -Privilege Escalation
> -Information Leakage

| | Microsoft Windows XP SP2 or SP3 | CAPEC-46 | 89.597 | show |

Figure 13.13 Example of security report.

Evidence is demonstrating that this increasing use of wireless communication technologies caused a dramatic increase of external-borne security incidents (while internal are basically stable, and accidental have increased only slightly). Most of the attacks against WSNs exploit the vulnerabilities affecting routing protocols in order to prevent real-time delivery of SCADA messages, which would result in the loss of monitoring information or even of the ability to control entire portions of the SCADA system. Several solutions, both centralized and distributed, for attacks detection in WSNs have already been proposed. In centralized solutions, sensor nodes send control data to a detection agent running on a host that is connected to the WSN [24,25]. The agent analyzes the data and possibly detects ongoing attacks. Since successful attacks prevent control packets from reaching the agent, in centralized approaches, the agent may get to an erroneous view of the network and ultimately fail to detect the attack. This is one of the major drawbacks of centralized approaches.

In decentralized solutions, sensor nodes are in charge of running detection mechanisms [26,27]. This means that distributed solutions are potentially more resilient to network-level attacks, since ongoing attacks can be locally detected, even in case of severe damage to the network infrastructure. Additionally, distributed solutions require for a collaborative protocol in order to allow each node to share its local view of the network with a set of neighbors. This results in consumption of additional resources, mainly due to an increased number of transmissions.

In this section, we show how the DiReS can be used to detect, diagnose, and remediate two types of attacks, that is, sinkhole attack and sleep deprivation attack, which exploit WSN routing protocol vulnerabilities. DiReS can be seen as a hybrid detection solution where any node runs a network-level detection system that is in charge of identifying suspicious nodes. Suspicious nodes are temporarily inserted in a blacklist, and an alarm is sent to the decision engine, which is in charge of making the final decision.

There is a wide variety of routing protocols for WSNs [28]. Multihop is one of the most popular WSN routing protocols. Multihop and its enhancements (e.g., Collection Tree

Protocol [CTP] [29], MintRoute [30], and MultiHopLQI [31]) use a shortest path first algorithm, which gives priority to the route to the base station having the lowest cost. The cost function can be based on either the hop count to the base station or the estimate of the link bandwidth. These parameters are used to select the parent node that is the neighbor node with the best path metric.

Multihop nodes periodically send route update messages with routing information to their neighbors. These route messages contain the expected transmission cost (EXT) to the base station and the link quality for every neighbor node. These messages can be exploited by an attacker who is able to forge packets, thus altering the expected behavior of the network. This is allowed by the fact that this routing protocol does not implement any authentication and encryption mechanisms to protect the exchange of data between WSN nodes. This is because the execution of such mechanisms is a CPU-intensive operation that can severely decrease the lifetime of battery-powered sensors.

For this use case, the following assumptions are made:

- A node in the WSN has been compromised.
- No single node can cause a partitioning of the network.
- Nodes are fixed (they cannot move around).

13.6.1 Sinkhole Attack

The center of a sinkhole attack is a malicious node that has been compromised by an intruder. We assume the presence of an attacker that can access and change the internal state of a sensor node. Attacker nodes can forge false routing packets, pretending to be very attractive for connections to the base station. In this way, the attacker (the red circle in Figure 13.14) may force the surrounding nodes to select it as parent.

At this point, the attacker is able to compromise the confidentiality of data, the integrity of messages, and the availability of sensors.

In TinyOS, that is, the operating system running on the WSN nodes, this means that the attacker claims to have a very low EXT value, since this value is used by the routing protocol as gradient to generate routes from a node to a base station. The attack may be reinforced by modifying link estimation exchange protocol (LEEP) packets in the same way, which are used by the nodes to estimate the bidirectional link quality. For robustness purposes, in CTP, that is, the

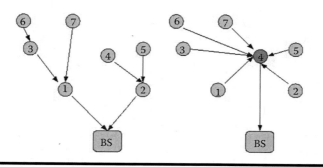

Figure 13.14 Sinkhole attack.

routing protocol for TinyOS, nodes collect a certain number of routing packets before making a change in their routing tables.

13.6.2 Sleep Deprivation Attack

The precondition for this type of attack is that a malicious user has gained control of a node (red node in Figure 13.15). Assuming that this is the case, two alternative attack techniques can be used:

■ Forwarding routed packets multiple times
■ Generating fake packets with a high frequency

By doing so, the malicious node induces two negative effects on the WSN: (1) discharge all the nodes along the route (orange node in Figure 13.15) to the base station (or neighbor nodes in routing message based attack) and (2) a DoS for those nodes (yellow node in Figure 13.15) whose path (dashed lines in Figure 13.15) intersects the attacked, overloaded one (the red one).

13.6.3 Use of DiReS to Protect a WSN from Attacks Exploiting Routing Protocol Vulnerabilities

Attack detection is performed by analyzing the attack signature matching the specific attack. As an example, in case of a sinkhole attack, the detection and diagnosis module detects the attacker based on (1) the WSN topology—inferred by the control packet received by the central agent—and (2) the list of nodes recognized as victims. A node is recognized as a victim if the ratio between sent routing packets and received routing packets has an anomalously low value. In fact, to force routing changes, the attacker sends a high number of routing packets, while other nodes keep their normal behavior and send a lower number of routing packets. Once the victims have been identified, the attacker is recognized as the parent of the victims that share the same parent.

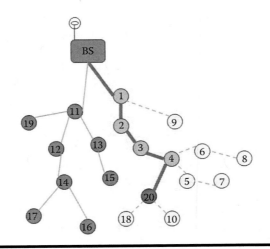

Figure 13.15   Sleep deprivation attack effects.

In general, after the detection has been performed, a further analysis of the attack is necessary in order to

- Identify the attack type.
- Identify the attacker: this action depends on the diagnosed attack. Control data are exploited to detect the malicious node.
- Evaluate the damage.

Such activities are under the responsibility of the diagnostic module.

Once the attack has been successfully detected, the proper reaction mechanism is selected and activated. The diagnosis component receives a feedback from the reaction system, and an assessment of damage is performed based on the result of reaction activities.

As for the impact (i.e., damage) of the attack, it will be evaluated based on (1) knowledge of the specific attack (what is the target of this kind of attacks? What is the expected impact?) and (2) the result of recovery actions.

Detection of sinkhole attack can be also supported by human operator using DAT. DAT can show the current topology of the WSN. Moreover, for each node of the network, traffic statistics (customized by the user according to his or her needs) can be visualized. This way, scattered data representing traffic can be visualized by single view (Figure 13.12) to show current trends and status of the network. In sinkhole attack case, the traffic ratio can be shown to the operator so that he or she can visually notice anomalous values and compare such information with the results of the detection activity performed by the underlying real-time detection and diagnosis module. Moreover, DAT can assess attack severity and its impact on organization (e.g., CI).

13.6.4 Remediation Mechanisms

In order to mitigate the effects of an attack on a WSN, the following remediation techniques have been developed:

- *Over-the-air (OTA) reprogramming of the malicious node*: Most of the sensor families allow remote reprogramming (OTAP) of the nodes. After a successful attack, a recovery action consists in reprogramming the exploited node bringing it to the initial (non-malicious) state. A successful OTAP action implies that the attacker has not disabled the OTAP feature on the exploited node.
- *Stopping the malicious node switching it in sleep mode*: The node must be able to receive a sleep command that results in disabling the radio transmission/reception function. Since this command is sent in broadcast by the base station, the node can easily recognize (based on the number of identical packets sent on multiple channels) a forged sleep packet sent by an attacker.
- *Light isolation of the malicious node according to the following steps (Figure 13.16)*: (1) The attacker node is no longer eligible as parent; (2) any node having the attacker node as parent changes its parent. This means that the node is still able to send packets to the base station.
- *Total isolation of the malicious node (Figure 13.16):* In addition to a light isolation, two further actions are taken, specifically (1) packets from attacker node are ignored and (2) all the queues are cleaned up from the attacker messages.
- Manual shutdown of the malicious node.

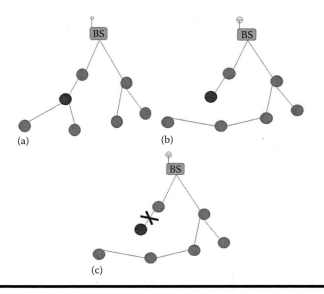

Figure 13.16   Isolation mechanism: (a) before isolation, (b) light isolation, and (c) total isolation.

13.6.5 *Implementation of Recovery Actions*

The recovery actions are intended to stop or mitigate the attack. However, since the vulnerability is an intrinsic characteristic of the system, it cannot be excluded that the attacker will be able to reproduce the attack (e.g., after the reprogramming of a node, the attacker may execute the same steps as before to gain the control of the node). Therefore, remediation actions must be undertaken in order to remove the vulnerability or reconfigure the system in a way that makes the system tolerant to further attacks.

Examples of such actions may be

- Redistribution of new cryptographic keys to exclude compromised keys
- Lowering of keys expiration time
- Usage of new longer keys (that ultimately results in a more secure system with lower performance, thus causing a graceful degradation of the system function)

13.6.6 *Simulation-Based Performance Tests*

The performance of the detection and diagnosis module of DiReS has been assessed on a simulated WSN. The simulation was performed by using TOSSIM [32]. Each simulation run was conducted with the number of nodes ranging between 100 and 250 and the following settings: (1) only one attacker, (2) nodes are stationary, and (3) a number of neighbors for each node between 5 and 10.

Experiments were conducted focusing on the sinkhole attack. We simulated two attack scenarios and carried out a performance comparison between our system and a centralized solution.

In scenario A, we assumed that the malicious node modifies sensor data, but it does not modify the control messages that are used for detection purposes. In scenario B, we assumed that the attacker is smarter, and it is able to modify all received messages (data and control packets).

The simulated network was made of a random number of sensors. We tested 100 different network topologies. Each topology has been used in 10 different simulations. In each run, a random node behaves as the attacker. The results of the simulation tests showed that the detection rates of the two approaches are comparable in scenario A, where both systems provide good performance. In particular, our system has a detection rate of 96%, while the centralized detection system achieves a detection rate of 94%. In scenario B, where the attacker is smarter, the centralized solution is ineffective (<20%), while our system still performs well and has a detection rate of 94%.

13.7 Conclusions

In this chapter, we presented a distributed framework for cybersecurity of CIs. Such a framework is composed of different functional modules capable of monitoring a SCADA system, diagnosing attacks, and performing recovery and reconfiguration actions. Security and resilience of CIs are addressed in a systemic perspective since the framework integrates both techniques for real-time protection of a SCADA system and functions for off-line security assessment of a CI. Security mechanisms have been developed to protect the entire SCADA network infrastructure, both the wired and wireless trunks. We demonstrated the effectiveness of the proposed framework by testing the detection and diagnosis module in an extensive simulation campaign. More precisely, we simulated a WSN and tested the capability of the proposed framework to detect attacks exploiting WSN routing protocol vulnerabilities. Numerical results are provided.

References

1. Vallentin, M., Sommer, R., Lee, J., Leres, C., Paxson, V., and Tierney, B. 2007. The NIDS cluster: Scalable, stateful network intrusion detection on commodity hardware, in *Proceedings of the International Symposium on Recent Advances in Intrusion Detection (RAID)*, Gold Coast, Australia, pp. 107–126.
2. Colajanni, M., Gozzi, D., and Marchetti, M. 2007. Enhancing interoperability and stateful analysis of cooperative network intrusion detection systems, in *Proceedings of the ACM/IEEE Symposium on Architecture for Networking and Communications Systems*, Orlando, FL, pp. 165–174.
3. Cai, Y. 2007. A distributed autonomous intrusion detection framework, in *Proceedings of the IEEE Globecom Workshop*, Washington, DC, pp. 1–5.
4. Boughaci, D., Drias, H., Bendid, A., Bouznit, Y., and Benhamou, B. 2006. Distributed intrusion detection framework based on autonomous and mobile agents, in *Proceedings of the IEEE International Conference on Dependability of Computer Systems*, Philadelphia, PA, pp. 248–255.
5. Wheeler, P. and Fulp, E. 2007. A taxonomy of parallel techniques for intrusion detection, in *Proceedings of the ACM Southeast Regional Conference*, Winston-Salem, NC, pp. 278–282.
6. NMAP tool, *Nmap—Free Security Scanner For Network Exploration and Security Audits*. http://nmap. org (last accessed May 17, 2010).
7. National Vulnerability Database Home, http://nvd.nist.gov (last accessed May 17, 2010).
8. Nexpose, *Vulnerability Management & Penetration Testing Software, Rapid7*. http://www.rapid7.com (last accessed May 17, 2010).
9. Nessus 5, *Tenable Network Security*. http://www.tenable.com/products/nessus (last accessed May 17, 2010).
10. SAINT, *Security Vulnerability Management, Penetration Testing, and Security Compliance Solutions from SAINT*. http://www.saintcorporation.com/ (last accessed May 17, 2010).
11. OpenVAS, *Open Vulnerability Assessment System*. http://www.openvas.org (last accessed May 17, 2010).
12. CRAMM, Siemens hompage. http://www.cramm.com (last accessed May 17, 2010).
13. CSET tool homepage, *US-CERT: Control Systems—Downloading and Installing CSET(TM)*. http://www.us-cert.gov/control_systems/csetdownload.html (last accessed May 17, 2010).

14. NSAT tool, *Network Security Analysis Tool.* http://nsat.org (last accessed May 17, 2010).

15. Choras, M., Flizikowski, A., Kozik, R., and Holubowicz, W. 2010. Decision aid tool and ontology-based reasoning for critical infrastructure vulnerabilities and threats analysis, in E. Rome and R. Bloomfield (Eds.), *Critical Information Infrastructures Security*, LNCS 6027, Athens, Greece, pp. 98–110.

16. Shankar, M., Stovall, J., Sorokine, A., Bhaduri, B., and King, T. 2008. Visualizing energy resources dynamically on earth, in *Power and Energy Society General Meeting—Conversion and Delivery of Electrical Energy in the 21st Century*, 2008 IEEE, July 20–24, 2008, pp. 1–4.

17. Xiao-Feng, D., Yu-Jiong, G., and Kun, Y. 2008. Study on intelligent maintenance decision support system using for power plant equipment, in *Proceedings of the IEEE International Conference on Automation and Logistics*, Qingdao, China, pp. 96–100.

18. Jun Lee, S., Mo, K., and Hyun Seong, P. 2007. Development of an integrated decision support system to aid the cognitive activities of operators in main control rooms of nuclear power plants, in *Proceedings of IEEE Symposium on Computational Intelligence in Multicriteria Decision Making (MCDM)*, Honolulu, HI, pp. 146–152.

19. Zhang, B., Wu, G., and Shang, S. 2008. Research on decision support system of water pollution control based on immune agent, in *Proceedings of the International Symposium on Computer Science and Computational Technology, ISCSCT*, Vol.1, Shanghai, China, pp. 114–117.

20. Amantini, A., Choras, M., D'Antonio, S., Egozcue, E., Germanus, D., and Hutter, R. 2012. The human role in tools for improving robustness and resilience of critical infrastructures, *Cognition, Technology & Work* 14(2), 143–155.

21. Bai, X., Meng, Z., Du, M., Gong, M., and Hu, Z. 2008. Design of wireless sensor network in SCADA system for wind power plant, in *Proceedings of the IEEE International Conference on Automation and Logistics*, Qingdao, China September 1–3, 2008, pp. 3023–3027.

22. Shouqiao, X., Liye, X., Guomin, Z., and Jiaxing, Z. 2010. Power supply based on small current transducer for wireless sensor in smart grid, in *Proceedings of the International Conference Electrical and Control Engineering (ICECE)*, June 25–27, 2010, pp. 3990–3993.

23. Ye, W. and Heidemann, J. 2006. Enabling interoperability and extensibility of future SCADA systems, Technical Report ISI-TR-625, USC/Information Sciences Institute.

24. Bo, Y. and Bin, X. 2006. Detecting selective forwarding attacks in wireless sensor networks, in *Proceedings of the 20th International Parallel and Distributed Processing Symposium*, Boston, MA, pp. 25–29.

25. Ngai, E. C., Liu, J., and Lyu, M. R. 2007. Comput: An efficient intruder detection algorithm against sinkhole attacks in wireless sensor networks, *Computer Communications*, 30(11–12), 2353–2364.

26. da Silva, A. P., Martins, M. H., Rocha, B. P., Loureiro, A. A., Ruiz, L. B., and Wong, H. C. 2005. Decentralized intrusion detection in wireless sensor networks, in *Proceedings of the 1st ACM international Workshop on Quality of Service and Security in Wireless and Mobile Networks*, ACM, New York, NY, pp. 16–23.

27. Krontiris, I., Giannetsos, T., and Dimitriou, T. 2008. LIDeA: A distributed lightweight intrusion detection architecture for sensor networks, in *Proceedings of the 4th international Conference on Security and Privacy in Communication Networks (SecureComm '08)*, ACM, New York, NY, Article 20, pp. 10.

28. Das, S. K. and Ammari, H. M. 2009. Routing and data dissemination in wireless sensor networks, in J. Zheng and A. Jamalipour (Eds.), *Invited Book Chapter, Wireless Sensor Networks: A Networking Perspective*, Chapter 4, Wiley-IEEE Press, Hoboken, NJ, pp. 67–144, July 2009.

29. Gnawali, O., Fonseca, R., Jamieson, K., Moss, D., and Levis, P. 2009. Collection tree protocol, in *Proceedings of the Seventh ACM Conference on Embedded Networked Sensor Systems (SenSys)*, New York.

30. Woo, A., Tong, T., and Culler D. 2003. Taming the underlying challenges of reliable multihop routing in sensor networks, in *Proceedings of the First International Conference on Embedded Networked Sensor Systems (SenSys'03)*, Los Angeles, CA, USA.

31. Fonseca, R., Gnawali, O., Jamieson, K., and Levis, P. 2006. TinyOS enhancement proposals 119: Collection. February 09, 2006. [Online] Available at: http://www.tinyos.net/tinyos-2.x/doc/html/tep119.html (last accessed June 01, 2010).

32. Levis, P., Lee, N., Welsh, M., and Culler, D. 2003. TOSSIM: Accurate and scalable simulation of entire TinyOS applications, in *Proceedings of the First International Conference on Embedded Networked Sensor Systems, SenSys '03*, Los Angeles, CA, November 05–07, 2003, ACM, New York, pp. 126–137.

Chapter 14

Modeling and Counteracting Virus Diffusion in Sensor Networks for Net-Centric Surveillance Systems

Giorgio Battistelli, Luigi Chisci, Giovanni Mugnai,
Alfonso Farina, Antonio Graziano, and Alessio Liburdi

Contents

14.1 Introduction

Following the recent rapid and tremendous advances in information and communication technology, networks of multiple sensors are nowadays widely employed in a variety of fields and with a wide range of civil as well as military applications (e.g., surveillance, network centric warfare, threat assessment). Traditional surveillance systems operate in a centralized fashion, in that peripheral sensor units gather data from the environment, locally process them, and transmit (either raw or processed) data to a central node where information fusion occurs. It is well known, however, how the presence of a central fusion node represents a weakness point of centralized architectures for several reasons. First, a fault in such a node would actually make the overall network unusable. Second, the centralized approach is not scalable since the computational complexity of the fusion node grows with the number of network nodes. Finally, for large-scale networks, it is reasonable to think that nodes are organized, from a topological point of view, according to a complex structure incompatible with the presence of a unique fusion center.

The trend of modern networked systems is toward *distributed* or *decentralized* or *net-centric* configurations, where each agent is equipped with communication, computing, and sensing capabilities and, by exchanging data with the neighboring agents, wishes to gain situation awareness about the overall system of interest without the coordination of a fusion center. While decentralization provides benefits in terms of scalability, flexibility, and fault tolerance (as it does not need any coordination infrastructure), unfortunately net-centric surveillance and monitoring systems are still prone to some deliberate threats like the attack of an informatic virus. The goal of this chapter is to analyze this issue from several points of view. First, it will be shown how to model the virus spread over a sensor network and what the effects of a virus epidemic are on a net-centric data fusion algorithm; secondly, the correlations between network connectivity, distributed data fusion performance, and virus diffusion will be investigated; finally, it will be discussed how the effects of a virus attack can be mitigated by a careful redesign of the sensor network as well as of the distributed information fusion algorithm.

The first part (Sections 14.2 and 14.3) will be devoted to describing the types of networks and distributed information fusion algorithms considered in this work. In particular, the focus will be on networks consisting of two types of nodes (namely, sensor nodes and communication nodes). All the nodes have *processing* and communication capabilities, that is, they can process local data as well as exchange data with neighboring nodes. The only difference is that the so-called SEN nodes have also *sensing* capabilities, that is, they can sense data from the environment.

As for net-centric information fusion, the considered algorithms will rely on two convenient tools, *covariance intersection* fusion [1–3] and *consensus* [4,5], which are fundamental in order to develop distributed state estimation algorithms that counteract *data incest* (the unaware reuse of the same piece of information due to the presence of loops within the network). The covariance intersection fusion rule allows to fuse estimates from multiple agents by guaranteeing that the fused estimate is consistent, that is, characterized by an overestimated (pessimistic) covariance. Consensus is a technique for distributed averaging over a network that aims to compute in each node (agent) the collective average of a given quantity by iterative regional averages, where the terms *collective* and *regional* mean *over all network nodes* and respectively, *over neighboring nodes only*.

The second part of this chapter (Section 14.4) will deal with the modeling of a virus epidemic over a sensor network by focusing both on the spreading mechanisms and on the possible effects. As for virus spreading, several models will be reviewed characterized by different levels of complexity, including *macroscopic models* [6–9] that describe the aggregate behavior of the virus epidemic through a set of ordinary differential equations and *microscopic models* [10–14] wherein all the network nodes and edges are taken into account separately. Anyway, all the considered models will be based on variants of the classical susceptible (S)–infected (I)–recovered (R) model for epidemic spreading in a population. This kind of virus diffusion models relies on a suitable homogeneous Markov chain. In particular, it is supposed that each node of the network can be in one of the following states: *S*, that is, the node is not I and not immune; *I*, that is, the node is I and can transmit the virus; *recovered* (*R*), that is, the node is not I and immune; and *dead* (*D*), that is, the node has stopped working due to the infection and can no longer transmit it. Further, it is assumed that transitions among states can randomly occur according to appropriate probabilities.

Several alternatives can also be considered to model how the virus manifests itself in the network nodes: the *noncooperative virus model*, wherein the I nodes stop taking part in the distributed estimation algorithm; the *misbehaving virus model*, wherein the I node takes part in the consensus algorithm with randomly generated data; and the *malicious virus model*, wherein the node takes part in the consensus with data carefully generated to compromise the consensus algorithm functioning. The present work deals with the noncooperative virus only.

Relationships will be established between the network topology, the possibility of a virus epidemic outbreak, and the performance of distributed information fusion algorithms. In particular, it will be shown that an important feature of all the considered virus diffusion models is the existence of an *epidemic threshold* that depends on the network topology as a function either of the *average degree* or of the *spectral radius of the adjacency matrix*. This will allow to provide meaningful measures of the *robustness of a network* to a virus epidemic in terms of some network topological parameters (*algebraic connectivity, node connectivity*, average degree, spectral radius, etc.) that, in turn, will be the basis for the proposed guidelines for sensor network design.

This chapter will be concluded by an extensive simulation study (Section 14.5) on a realistic network model so as to validate the proposed models and analysis, followed by concluding remarks (Section 14.6).

14.2 Sensor Network Model

The type of network being considered in this work is schematized in Figure 14.1. As it can be seen from the figure, the network consists of two types of nodes. Both types of nodes have *processing* and COM capabilities, that is, they can process local data as well as exchange data with neighboring nodes. The only difference is that the so-called sensor (SEN) nodes have also *sensing* capabilities, that is, they can sense data from the environment, while the other nodes,

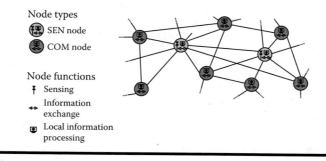

Figure 14.1 Sensor network model.

called communication (COM) nodes, do not have such an additional sensing capability. Notice that, since COM nodes do not provide any additional information, their presence is needed only to improve network connectivity.

Besides this classification between SEN and COM nodes, the network of interest is characterized by the following assumptions:

N1. The network has no *central fusion node*, that is, it has a *decentralized* or *distributed* rather than *centralized* configuration. As a consequence, all network nodes operate in the same way, that is,
- Possibly sense data from the environment (SEN nodes only)
- Receive data from neighboring nodes
- Suitably fuse sensed, received, and local data
- Transmit the fused data to neighboring nodes

N2. No node is aware of the network topology, that is, the number of nodes and the connections among them.

From a mathematical point of view, the network can be described in terms of an undirected graph $\mathcal{G} = (\mathcal{N}, \mathcal{A})$ where $\mathcal{N}$ is the set of nodes and $\mathcal{A} \subset \mathcal{N} \times \mathcal{N}$ the set of arcs, representing links (connections). In particular, (i, j) belongs to $\mathcal{A}$ if nodes i and j can exchange data. The set of nodes is partitioned into $\mathcal{N} = \mathcal{S} \cup \mathcal{C}$ where $\mathcal{S}$ and $\mathcal{C}$ denote the disjoint subsets of SEN and, respectively, COM nodes. $N_s \triangleq \mathcal{S}|$, $N_c \triangleq |\mathcal{C}|$, and $N \triangleq |\mathcal{N}| = N_c + N_s$ denote the number of SEN nodes, the number of COM nodes, and, respectively, the total number of nodes. For each node $i \in \mathcal{N}$, $\mathcal{N}^i \triangleq \{ j \in \mathcal{N} : (j, i) \in \mathcal{A} \}$ denotes the set of neighbors of node i. By definition, $(i, i) \in \mathcal{A}$, and, hence, $i \in \mathcal{N}^i$ for all $i \in \mathcal{N}$. Similarly, $\mathcal{S}^i = \mathcal{N}^i \cap \mathcal{S}$ and $\mathcal{C}^i = \mathcal{N}^i \cap \mathcal{C}$ denote the sets of SEN and respectively, COM nodes, neighbors of node i. Finally, let N_s^i, N_c^i, and N^i denote the cardinalities of $\mathcal{S}^i$, $\mathcal{C}^i$ and, respectively, $\mathcal{N}^i$.

Each node of the network is characterized by a number of parameters, including

- Geographic coordinates (in the 1D, 2D, or 3D surveillance area)
- Node type, either SEN or COM, and in case of SEN node, also the type of sensor, as the network can accommodate heterogeneous sensors
- List of neighbors

14.2.1 Network Metrics

Hereafter, the objective is to introduce some graph (network) metrics that will be useful to characterize the network in terms of connectivity. In particular, our interest is to analyze the behavior of a net-centric state estimator (to be introduced in the next section) under various connectivity conditions and thus relate estimation performance/robustness to network metrics. A further specific objective will be to analyze the effects of computer viruses on sensor networks and be able to relate the spreading of viruses to appropriate network metrics.

A significant network metric is the so-called Laplacian matrix of the associated graph [15]. Given the undirected graph $\mathcal{G} = (\mathcal{N}, \mathcal{A})$ with N nodes, its *adjacency matrix A* is defined as the $N \times N$ matrix of entries a_{ij} such that $a_{ij} = 1$ if $(i, j) \in \mathcal{A}$ or $a_{ij} = 0$ otherwise.

Further, let D denote a diagonal $N \times N$ matrix whose entry d_{ii} is equal to the degree of node i, that is, the number of nodes connected to i. Then, the Laplacian matrix, or simply Laplacian, of graph G is defined as $L \triangleq D - A$. Such a matrix L turns out to be symmetric, positive semi-definite, and singular. More specifically, the Laplacian eigenvalues $\lambda_1, \lambda_2, \dots, \lambda_N$ satisfy the inequalities:

$$0 = \lambda_1 \leq \lambda_2 \leq \cdots \leq \lambda_N$$

In particular, the second smallest eigenvalue $\lambda_2 \geq 0$ of L is called *algebraic connectivity* of the graph G. In fact, this eigenvalue represents an indicator of the graph's connectivity as the graph turns out to be connected if and only if $\lambda_2 > 0$ [16]. Actually, there are several other relationships between λ_2 and connectivity. To this end, let us introduce the *node connectivity* ν defined as the smallest number of nodes that, when removed from G, leave a disconnected subgraph or a trivial subgraph. Further, let $\in$ denote the *edge connectivity* defined as the smallest number of edges that, when removed from G, leave a disconnected subgraph or a trivial subgraph. Then, as shown in [16], it turns out that $\lambda_2 \leq \nu \leq \varepsilon$, that is, the algebraic connectivity λ_2 is a lower bound for the node connectivity ν that, in turn, is a lower bound for the edge connectivity ε.

Other interesting relationships have been found between algebraic connectivity and diameter or mean distance of a graph. In this respect, let us first define the distance $\varrho(i, j)$ between two nodes $i, j \in \mathcal{N}$ of the graph as the number of arcs composing the shortest path joining such two nodes. Then, the diameter of a graph is the maximum distance between any two nodes in the graph, that is,

$$diam(G) \triangleq \max_{i, j \in \mathcal{N}} \varrho(i, j)$$

Conversely, the *mean distance* of a graph is equal to the average of all distances between distinct nodes, that is,

$$\bar{\varrho}(G) \triangleq \frac{1}{N(N-1)} \sum_{i, j \in \mathcal{N}, i \neq j} \varrho(i, j)$$

Mohar [15] has proved the following λ_2-dependent (lower and upper) bounds on the diameter and mean distance of a graph:

$$\frac{4}{N\lambda_2} \leq diam(G) \leq 2 \left\lceil \frac{\Delta + \lambda_2}{4\lambda_2} \ln(N-1) \right\rceil$$

$$\frac{1}{N-1} \left\lceil \frac{2}{\lambda_2} + \frac{N-2}{2} \right\rceil \leq \bar{\varrho}(G) \leq \frac{N}{N-1} \left(\left\lceil \frac{\Delta + \lambda_2}{4\lambda_2} \ln(N-1) \right\rceil + \frac{1}{2} \right) \tag{14.1}$$

where $\Delta = \Delta(G)$ denotes the maximum node degree of the graph G, that is,

$$\Delta = \max_{i \in \mathcal{N}} \left\{ \left| \mathcal{N}^i \right| - 1 \right\}$$

Notice that the bounds on the diameter and mean distance in (14.1) are decreasing for increasing algebraic connectivity λ_2.

In [4,5], it has been shown that the convergence speed of consensus algorithms is related to the algebraic connectivity λ_2 of the network. Hence, the algebraic connectivity will be a fundamental graph metric in the present work as the consensus paradigm will be adopted in the considered distributed state estimation as detailed in the following section.

14.3 Net-Centric Information Fusion

In surveillance systems, a fundamental task is tracking a moving target [17], that is, estimating its kinematic state given noisy position measurements. Whenever measurements are provided by multiple sensors spread over the surveilled region and communicating among each other with the possible aid of communication nodes, a suitable distributed estimation strategy has to be adopted. Such a strategy has to satisfy the following requirements: (1) *scalability*, that is, the processing load of each node must be independent of the network size; (2) *stability*, that is, the target state estimation error must be bounded and as small as possible in each node; and (3) *robustness*, that is, the network's surveillance functionality must be preserved in presence of faulty nodes and/or viruses.

A scalable approach consists of updating local target state estimate and covariance in each node and then performing therein a regional fusion with the information of adjacent nodes. This idea represents a natural application to distributed estimation of the well-known consensus algorithms. *Consensus* is a well-known and established technique for distributed averaging over networks [4,5,18] and is widely used in distributed parameter/state estimation algorithms. The prototypal consensus problem can be defined as follows. Let node $i \in \mathcal{N}$ be provided with an estimate $\hat{\theta}^i$ of a given quantity θ. The objective is to develop an algorithm that computes in a distributed way, in each node, the average

$$\hat{\theta} = \frac{1}{|\mathcal{N}|} \sum_{i \in \mathcal{N}} \hat{\theta}^i \tag{14.2}$$

To this end, let $\hat{\theta}_0^i = \hat{\theta}^i$, then consensus algorithms take the following general iterative form:

$$\hat{\theta}_{\ell+1}^i = \sum_{j \in \mathcal{N}^i} \pi^{i,j} \hat{\theta}_\ell^j, \quad \forall i \in \mathcal{N} \tag{14.3}$$

where the *consensus weights* must satisfy the conditions

$$\pi^{i,j} \geq 0 \quad \forall i, j \in \mathcal{N}; \quad \sum_{j \in \mathcal{N}^i} \pi^{i,j} = 1 \quad \forall i \in \mathcal{N} \tag{14.4}$$

Notice from (14.3) and (14.4) that at a given consensus step, the estimate in any node is computed as a convex combination of the estimates of the neighbors at the previous consensus step. In other words, the iteration (14.3) is nothing but a *regional average* computed in node i, the objective of consensus being convergence of such regional averages to the collective average (14.2). Important convergence properties, depending on the consensus weights, can be found in [4,18].

However, it turns out that application of consensus algorithms to distributed state estimation is not a trivial issue, since stability of this approach crucially depends on the way in which the fusion is carried out. For instance, the simplest way of averaging state estimates does not ensure stability. Conversely, a more sensible distributed information fusion approach meeting the stability requirement is described hereafter. Let $\hat{x}_{t|t}^i$ and $P_{t|t}^i$ denote the target state estimate and, respectively, covariance of node i at time t recursively provided by some, possibly nonlinear, filter. Then, the following fused covariance $P_{t|t}^{f,i}$ and estimate $\hat{x}_{t|t}^{f,i}$ can be computed at node i:

$$P_{t|t}^{f,i} = \left[\sum_{j \in \mathcal{N}^i} \pi^{i,j} \left(P_{t|t}^j \right)^{-1} \right]^{-1} \tag{14.5}$$

$$\hat{x}_{t|t}^{f,i} = P_{t|t}^{f,i} \left[\sum_{j \in \mathcal{N}^i} \pi^{i,j} \left(P_{t|t}^j \right)^{-1} \hat{x}_{t|t}^j \right] \tag{14.6}$$

where $\pi^{i,j}$ are convex combination coefficients, that is, must satisfy

$$0 \leq \pi^{i,j} \leq 1, \quad \sum_{j \in \mathcal{N}^i} \pi^{i,j} = 1$$

Equations 14.5 and 14.6 provide the so-called *covariance intersection* fusion rule or equivalently a consensus step on the information matrix P^{-1} and the information vector $P^{-1}\hat{x}$. Such a step can be iterated to achieve faster consensus. As proved in [19], the strength point of the fusion (14.5) and (14.6) is that, in the linear filtering case, it guarantees stability under weak conditions, precisely whenever the network is connected and the target state is collectively observable, that is, observable from the set of measurements of all sensors.

Throughout this chapter, it will therefore be assumed that each node i of the network estimates, at each sample time $t \geq 1$, the state of the dynamical system:

$$\begin{cases} x_{t+1} = f_t(x_t) + w_t \\ y_t^i = h_t^i(x_t) + v_t^i \quad i \in \mathcal{S} \\ E[w_t w_t'] = W_t^{-1} > 0, \ E\left[v_t^i (v_t^i)'\right] = (V_t^i)^{-1} > 0, \ E[v_t^i w_t'] = 0 \end{cases} \tag{14.7}$$

by means of the following recursive algorithm, initialized from $\Omega_{1|0} = P_{1|0}^{-1}$ and $q_{1|0} = P_{1|0}^{-1}\hat{x}_{1|0}$.

14.3.1 Consensus on Information (CI) Algorithm

1. If i is an SEN node, sample the measurement y_t^i and set

$$\begin{cases} \hat{x}_{t|t-1}^i = \left(\Omega_{t|t-1}^i \right)^{-1} q_{t|t-1}^i \\ C_t^i = \dfrac{\partial h_t^i}{\partial x_t}\left(\hat{x}_{t|t-1}^i \right) \\ \bar{y}_t^i = y_t^i - h_t^i\left(\hat{x}_{t|t-1}^i \right) + C_t^i \hat{x}_{t|t-1}^i \\ \Omega_{t|t}^i = \Omega_{t|t-1}^i + \left(C_t^i \right)' V_t^i C_t^i \\ q_{t|t}^i = q_{t|t-1}^i + \left(C_t^i \right)' V_t^i \bar{y}_t^i \end{cases}$$

Otherwise, if i is a COM node, set $\Omega_{t|t}^i = \Omega_{t|t-1}^i$ and $q_{t|t}^i = q_{t|t-1}^i$.

2. Set $\Omega_{t|t}^{i}(0) = \Omega_{t|t}^{i}$ and $q_{t|t}^{i}(0) = q_{t|t}^{i}$.
3. For $\ell = 0, 1, \ldots, L-1$, perform the following consensus steps:
   - Transmit $q_{t|t}^{i}(\ell)$ and $\Omega_{t|t}^{i}(\ell)$ to all adjacent nodes $j \in \mathcal{N}^{i} \setminus \{i\}$.
   - Wait until $q_{t|t}^{j}(\ell)$ and $\Omega_{t|t}^{j}(\ell)$ have been received from all adjacent nodes $j \in \mathcal{N}^{i} \setminus \{i\}$.
   - Fuse the quantities $q_{t|t}^{j}(\ell)$ and $\Omega_{t|t}^{j}(\ell)$ according to

$$q_{t|t}^{i}(\ell+1) = \sum_{j \in \mathcal{N}^{i}} \pi^{i,j} \, q_{t|t}^{j}(\ell)$$

$$\Omega_{t|t}^{i}(\ell+1) = \sum_{j \in \mathcal{N}^{i}} \pi^{i,j} \, \Omega_{t|t}^{j}(\ell)$$

(14.8)

where the consensus weights $\pi^{i,j} \geq 0$ must satisfy $\sum_{j \in \mathcal{N}^{i}} \pi^{i,j} = 1$ for all $i \in \mathcal{N}$.

4. Compute the filtered estimate:

$$\hat{x}_{t|t}^{i} = \left[\Omega_{t|t}^{i}(L) \right]^{-1} q_{t|t}^{i}(L)$$

5. Perform the prediction step:

$$\hat{x}_{t+1|t}^{i} = f_{t}\left(\hat{x}_{t|t}^{i}\right)$$

$$A_{t} = \frac{\partial f_{t}}{\partial x_{t}}\left(\hat{x}_{t|t}^{i}\right)$$

$$\Omega_{t+1|t}^{i} = W_{t} - W_{t} A_{t} \left(\Omega_{t|t}^{i}(L) + A_{t}' W_{t} A_{t} \right)^{-1} A_{t}' W_{t}$$

$$q_{t+1|t}^{i} = \Omega_{t+1|t}^{i} \, \hat{x}_{t+1|t}^{i}$$

(14.9)

14.4 Modeling Virus Diffusion over Sensor Networks

The first question to be addressed is how virus spreading in sensor networks can be modeled. In this regard, different classes of models of different complexity have been proposed in the literature. For instance, one can consider *macroscopic models* that describe the aggregate behavior of the virus epidemic through a set of ordinary differential equations or, instead, *microscopic models* wherein all the network nodes and edges are taken into account separately. In turn, the latter can be subdivided into exact *single-Markov-chain models*, involving an exponential number of states, and simplified *N-intertwined Markov-chain models*.

Anyway, almost all the existing models are based on variants of the classical S–I–R model for epidemic spreading in a population. This kind of virus diffusion models [20] relies on the Markov chain depicted in Figure 14.2. In particular, it is supposed that each node of the network can be in one of the following states:

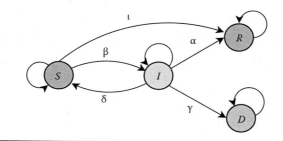

Figure 14.2 Markov-chain model for virus diffusion.

- *S*: The node is not infected and not immune.
- *I*: The node is infected and can transmit the virus.
- *R*: The node is not infected and immune.
- *D*: The node has stopped working due to the infection and can no longer transmit it.

Further, the transitions between the states are governed by the following probabilities:

- *Infection probability* β: associated with the transition from state *S* to state *I*
- *Immunization probability* ι: associated with the transition from state *S* to state *R*
- *Heal or cure probability* δ: associated with the transition from state *I* to state *S*
- *Recovery probability* α: associated with the transition from state *I* to state *R*
- *Death probability* γ: associated with the transition from state *I* to state *D*

Typically, simplified models are considered wherein some of such phenomena are neglected. For example, the *SIS model* considers nodes as being either in state *S* or *I*: susceptible node can become infected with probability β and then get healed with probability δ. Of course, this amounts to setting α = 0, ι = 0, and γ = 0 in the Markov chain of Figure 14.2. Another model that has gained special attention is the *SIR model*, obtained from the general one of Figure 14.2 by setting δ = 0, ι = 0, and γ = 0. This means that, once healed, an infected node always gets immunization from the virus by entering the terminal state *R*.

14.4.1 Macroscopic Models

Let $i(t)$ denote the fraction of infected nodes at time t. The idea upon which macroscopic models are based is that, when the network size N is sufficiently large, $i(t)$ can be seen as a continuous quantity whose time evolution can be described by a set of ordinary differential equations. For instance, for a network with average degree $\bar{k}$ and an SIS epidemic model, Kephart and White [6] proposed to represent the time evolution of $i(t)$ via the differential equation

$$\frac{di(t)}{dt} = \beta \bar{k} i(t)[1 - i(t)] - \delta i(t) \tag{14.10}$$

Such a model can be derived by supposing that for each susceptible node, the rate of infection is obtained by multiplying the infection rate per link β with the number of infected neighbors that, in turn, can be approximated as $\bar{k}\, i(t)$.

Despite its simplicity, this model is surprisingly useful in predicting the existence of an *epidemic threshold* (i.e., a condition under which the virus can take over and create an epidemic instead of quickly vanishing to zero). In fact, it can be seen that Equation 14.10 gives rise to two different behaviors depending on the value of the ratio β/δ. More specifically, when $\beta/\delta < 1/\bar{k}$, the epidemic asymptotically vanishes as $i = 0$ is an asymptotically stable equilibrium point with domain of attraction including $[0,1]$, whereas when $\beta/\delta > 1/\bar{k}$, the fraction of I nodes converges to the steady-state value $1 - \delta/(\beta\,\bar{k})$. Thus, it can be seen that for the Kephart–White model, the epidemic threshold turns out to be

$$\frac{\beta}{\delta} \geq \frac{1}{\bar{k}}$$

While the Kephart–White model (14.10) can lead to reasonable predictions for homogeneous networks wherein all the nodes have approximately the same degree, it is in general inappropriate for modeling epidemic spreading in nonhomogeneous networks. Thus, different modifications have been proposed in the literature so as to account for the network topology. For example, in [7,8], it has been proposed to use different models for the dynamics of nodes with different degrees. More specifically, let $P(k)$ be the fraction of nodes with degree k and $i_k(t)$ the fraction of such nodes that is infected at time t. Then, it is supposed that the time evolution of $i_k(t)$ can be described via the differential equation

$$\frac{di_k(t)}{dt} = \beta k \Theta(t)[1 - i_k(t)] - \delta i_k(t) \tag{14.11}$$

where $\Theta(t)$ represents the "probability that any given link points to an infected host" and is given by

$$\Theta(t) = \frac{\sum_k (k-1)P(k)i_k(t)}{\sum_k kP(k)}$$

Unfortunately, as pointed out in [9], even this topological macroscopic model is inherently inaccurate due to an implicit homogeneous mixing assumption. In fact, the variable $\Theta(t)$ "does not distinguish whether infected nodes are connected, clustered together, or scattered around the topological network" by implicitly supposing that infected nodes are uniformly distributed in the network. For this reason, as shown in [9] via an extensive simulation analysis, this kind of models tends to overestimate the propagation speed of the epidemic.

As for the SIR virus-spreading model, in place of (14.10), one can consider the two coupled differential equations

$$\frac{di(t)}{dt} = \beta \bar{k} i(t)s(t) - \delta i(t) \tag{14.12}$$

$$\frac{dr(t)}{dt} = \delta i(t) \tag{14.13}$$

where $r(t)$ and $s(t)$ denote the fraction of recovered and, respectively, susceptible nodes at time t with $s(t) + i(t) + r(t) = 1$, for all t. A first important difference between the SIR model embodied by (14.12)–(14.13) and the SIS one is that for the former, the epidemic always vanishes as time goes to infinity, regardless of the initial conditions and the infection/recovery probabilities. This means that a different notion of epidemic threshold has to be introduced. In this regard, a reasonable choice is to define the epidemic threshold as the condition under which the fraction of infected nodes $i(t)$ increases (or, better, is expected to increase) from the initial value $i(0)$. When such a definition is adopted, it turns out that the epidemic threshold depends on the initial conditions in that the *epidemic peak $max_i i(t)$* exceeds the initial value $i(0)$ if and only if $\beta/\alpha > 1/[\bar{k}\,s(0)]$. However, supposing that the network size N is sufficiently large and that, at time 0, only a few nodes are infected, one can approximate $s(0)$ with 1 and conclude that the epidemic threshold is

$$\frac{\beta}{\alpha} \geq \frac{1}{\bar{k}}$$

which is equivalent to the one for the SIS model with the heal probability δ replaced by the recovery probability α.

14.4.2 Exact Single-Markov-Chain Model

In this model, the diffusion of the virus epidemic in the network is described by a single Markov chain whose state space is represented by all the possible configurations in which the network nodes can be. As should be evident, this model involves an exponential number of possible states: 4^N states for the general model of Figure 14.2, 3^N for the SIR model, and 2^N states for the SIS model. We point out that such an exponential complexity is unavoidable in order to provide an exact representation of the virus epidemic dynamics. In fact, it is not possible to consider the network nodes as separate independent entities since, in general, the probability β_i that a susceptible node i is infected would depend on the number of infected neighbors N_i^I. For instance, supposing independence of the events, such a probability can be obtained as

$$\beta_i = 1 - (1 - \beta)^{N_i^I} \tag{14.14}$$

where β is the probability of infection from a single neighbor. For the reader's convenience, the infection probability as a function of N_i^I for different values of β is depicted in Figure 14.3.

As for the recovery probability α_i of an infected node i, in general, it depends on the elapsed time $t - T_i^I$ since the node has been infected (here T_i^I is the time of infection of node i). Typical simplified models are the *constant recovery time*, where $\alpha_i = 1$ if $t - T_i^I$ exceeds a certain threshold and $\alpha_i = 0$ otherwise, and the *geometrically distributed recovery time*, where at each discrete-time instant, the instantaneous recovery probability is constant and equal to α. Hereafter, we shall always refer to the latter model, for which the recovery time has expected value $1/\alpha$ and variance $(1 - \alpha)/\alpha^2$. Figure 14.4 depicts the probability mass function of the recovery time for different values of α. Analogous considerations can be made also on the heal probability δ_i.

In principle, the exact Markov-chain model contains all the information necessary to predict the epidemic behavior. Unfortunately, the number of states is exponential, and so application of standard Markov-chain analysis becomes computationally intractable for nontrivial networks. Nevertheless, some useful conclusions can be drawn.

Consider first an SIS virus model. Then, it is easy to verify that the Markov chain has a unique absorbing state corresponding to the configuration wherein all the nodes are susceptible. In fact, once the virus epidemic has vanished and the network has entered such a state, no other configuration changes can occur. Since all the other states of the Markov chain are transient and the Markov

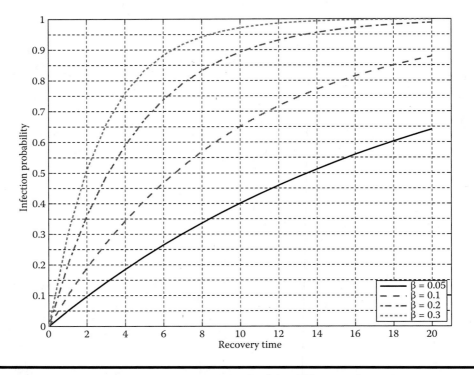

Figure 14.3 **Infection probability as a function of N_i^I for different values of β.**

chain itself is irreducible (i.e., all states are reachable from each other), then one can conclude that the Markov chain will eventually enter the unique absorbing state with probability 1 (i.e., the absorbing state is the steady state). The foregoing can be summarized as follows.

Fact: For the SIS model, there is only one absorbing state (corresponding to all nodes being in state *S*). As a consequence, the epidemic asymptotically vanishes at an exponential rate regardless of the initial conditions and the network topology.

Remark (The Metastable State Paradox). Clearly, such an asymptotic behavior represents a substantial departure from the behavior of the Kephart–White model (14.10) according to which the epidemic can be persistent under suitable conditions. It is however important to point out that, in practice, the convergence of the Markov chain to its absorbing state can be extremely slow at the point that it can be impossible to observe via simulations. In fact, as will be also confirmed in the simulation results at the end of this chapter, when the epidemic threshold conditions are satisfied, the SIS virus model exhibits an apparent steady state characterized by a persistence of the virus in the network, which is coherent with the predictions of the Kephart–White model. Such an apparent steady state is often called a "metastable state" since, despite the appearances, on a sufficiently long timescale, it is guaranteed to disappear with probability 1 [12].

The situation is quite different when a SIR virus model is considered. In fact, in this case, all the states in which none of the nodes is in state *I* are absorbing states. Thus, a total of 2^N absorbing states exist, corresponding to all the possible configurations of susceptible and recovered nodes. Since all the other states are transient and the Markov chain is irreducible, the following property follows at once.

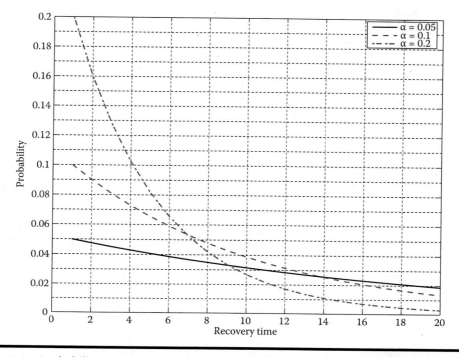

Figure 14.4 **Probability mass function of the recovery time for different values of α in the case of geometrically distributed recovery time.**

Fact: For the SIR model, there are 2^N absorbing states (corresponding to none of the nodes being in state *I*). As a consequence, the epidemic asymptotically vanishes at an exponential rate regardless of the initial conditions and the network topology.

We notice that, in this case, the asymptotic behavior of the exact Markov-chain model is in accordance with the predictions of the macroscopic model (14.12) as well as with the simulation results.

We conclude this section with a brief consideration on the epidemic threshold for the SIR model. To this end, suppose that at time 0, a single node of the network is infected, whereas all the other nodes are susceptible. Then, it is an easy matter to compute the expected number, say $\bar{I}$, of infected nodes at the following time instant. In fact, by observing that $P(k)$ represents the probability that the infected node has degree k, we can write

$$\bar{I} = \sum_k P(k)\bar{I}_k + 1 - \delta$$

where $\bar{I}_k$ is the expected number of infected neighbors of a k-degree node that, in turn, can be written as

$$\bar{I}_k = \sum_{j=1}^{k} j\binom{k}{j}\beta^j(1-\beta)^{k-i} = k\beta$$

Thus, combining the two latter equations, we have

$$\bar{I} = \sum_k P(k)k\beta + 1 - \delta = \bar{k}\beta + 1 - \delta.$$

This means that, if we adhere to the definition introduced for the macroscopic model (14.12) by imposing $\bar{I} \geq 1$, the epidemic threshold turns out to be the same predicted by such a macroscopic model.

14.4.3 N-Intertwined Markov-Chain Model

Unfortunately, due to its exponential complexity, it is difficult to draw further conclusions by analyzing the exact single-Markov-chain models. For this reason, simplified models have been proposed that, while keeping a microscopic perspective, are characterized by a moderate complexity. In particular, in this section, we shall focus on an N-intertwined Markov-chain model obtained by relying on an *independence assumption* [10]. For the sake of brevity, the model will be presented only for the SIS case even if a generalization to different virus epidemic models is possible [13]. Let $\pi_i^S(t)$ be the probability that node i is in state S at time t. Then, we clearly have

$$\pi_i^S(t+1) = [1 - \beta_i(t)]\pi_i^S(t) + \delta[1 - \pi_i^S(t)] \tag{14.15}$$

where $\beta_i(t)$ is the probability that node i is infected by its neighbors at time t. Since an exact computation of $\beta_i(t)$ would entail the solution of the exact single-Markov-chain model, the idea of [10] is to approximate it by setting

$$\beta_i(t) = 1 - \prod_{j \in \mathcal{N}_i} \{1 - \beta[1 - \pi_j^S(t)]\} \tag{14.16}$$

where, according to the independence assumption, the probabilities $\pi_j^S(t)$ are supposed to be independent of each other.

Since Equations 14.15 and 14.16 have to be repeated for each node of the network, the considered approximation gives rise to an N-dimensional nonlinear discrete-time system whose dynamics can be analyzed via classical system theory tools. For instance, the following results can be readily stated:

Fact: The state $\pi_1^S = \cdots = \pi_N^S = 1$, corresponding to the epidemic having died out, is an equilibrium point for the nonlinear system (14.15) (14.16), $i = 1, \ldots, N$.

Fact: [10] Let $\rho(A)$ be the *spectral radius* (largest eigenvalue) of the network adjacency matrix A. Then, if $\beta/\delta < 1/\rho(A)$, the epidemic asymptotically vanishes irrespective of the initial conditions and the network topology. Otherwise, the epidemic never dies out as the equilibrium point $\pi_1^S = \cdots = \pi_N^S = 1$ is not asymptotically stable.

Such results allow one to conclude that the epidemic threshold for the approximate model (14.15) (14.16) is

$$\frac{\beta}{\delta} \geq \frac{1}{\rho(A)} \tag{14.17}$$

Some remarks are in order. The first observation is that such a threshold, which can also be obtained with other approximations (e.g., mean-field theory and linearized models [11]), is in general different from the one derived via the macroscopic Kephart–White model. In fact, for a generic network, we have

$$\bar{k} \leq \rho(A) \leq k_{max}$$

where k_{max} is the maximum degree of a node in the network. Thus, the two thresholds only coincide when $\rho(A) = \bar{k}$ (this happens, e.g., when the network is regular, i.e., all the nodes have the same degree), while in the other cases, threshold (14.17) tends to be less stringent, meaning that it more often predicts an epidemic spread. For instance, for a power-law (scale-free) network, with degree distribution $P(k) \propto k^{-\eta}$, the spectral radius is, for a sufficiently large network size,

$$\rho(A) \cong \begin{cases} \sqrt{k_{max}} & \text{if } \eta > 5/2 \\ \sigma_k^2 / \bar{k} & \text{if } 2 < \eta < 5/2 \end{cases}$$

where σ_k^2 is the degree variance of the network.

Notice that the foregoing analysis can in principle be extended also to different models. For example, for the SIR case, the epidemic threshold for the N-intertwined Markov-chain model turns out to be [13]

$$\frac{\beta}{\alpha} > \frac{1}{\rho(A)}$$

However, this result is less supported by evidence and has been recently criticized [14]. As a final remark, it is pointed out that, as far as the epidemic threshold is concerned, the introduction in the SIR model of the additional absorbing state D as in Figure 14.2 would not bring any substantial modification to the described behavior. In fact, since the two states D and R play the same role, one simply has to consider $\alpha + \gamma$ in place of α.

14.4.4 Modeling the Virus Epidemic Effects

As discussed in the previous sections, several models are available to describe how a virus epidemic spreads over a sensor network. An important feature of all such models is the existence of an epidemic threshold that depends on the network topology as a function either of the average degree $\bar{k}$ or of the spectral radius $\rho(A)$. Thus, it seems natural to consider such two quantities as possible measures of the *susceptibility of a network* to a virus epidemic. However, for our purposes, this analysis alone tells only part of the story. In fact, another question of paramount importance that needs to be answered is how destructive a virus epidemic is for the proposed distributed state estimation algorithms. Of course, the answer to such a question is not unique as it depends in a crucial way on how infected nodes behave.

To complete the model of virus epidemic in sensor networks, it is therefore necessary to specify how the virus manifests itself in the network nodes. In this regard, the simplest model, also used in the simulation analysis, is the *noncooperative* one. In this model, it is assumed that, once infected, a node loses all its data, stops collecting new data, and stops taking part in the distributed estimation algorithm. Then, after recovering from the infection, the node resumes its normal behavior with the local estimate reinitialized to an arbitrary value and the local covariance reinitialized to an extremely high value.

As evident, for a noncooperative virus model, the main effect of the virus epidemic is a reduction of the network connectivity. This, in turn, implies that a virus epidemic is less destructive when the network is more robust with respect to connectivity. Thus, the topological parameters that seem most suitable to summarize the network robustness with respect to virus epidemic effects are the algebraic connectivity λ_2 and the node connectivity ν. In fact, the larger λ_2 and ν, the more difficult it is to cut a graph into disconnected components. Recalling that for a generic network we have

$$\lambda_2 \leq \nu \leq k_{\min} \leq \bar{k} \leq \rho(A) \leq k_{\max}$$

where $k_{\min}$ is the minimum degree of any node in the network, it is immediate to conclude that at least to a first approximation, the networks whose functioning is less prone to being compromised by a virus epidemic are those characterized by a small spectral radius $\rho(A)$ as well as by a small gap between the node connectivity ν (or, alternatively, the average degree $\bar{k}$) and the spectral radius $\rho(A)$. On the other hand, since the convergence of consensus algorithms, upon which all the proposed distributed state estimation algorithms are based, is faster as the algebraic connectivity λ_2 increases, possible design guidelines for a sensor network are making $\rho(A)$ as small as possible while keeping a sufficiently large value for λ_2 and ν. For example, scale-free networks are clearly not very robust with respect to virus epidemic being intrinsically characterized by a large gap $\rho(A) - \nu$. On the other hand, for regular networks, it is theoretically possible to make the gap arbitrarily small since $k_{\min} = \bar{k} = \rho(A) = k_{\max}$.

Summing up, a noncooperative virus can be tolerated provided that the network has a large algebraic or node connectivity. The situation is more problematic when other virus effects are considered. To see this, consider, for example, a *misbehaving virus model*, wherein the infected node takes part in the consensus algorithm with randomly generated data, or a *malicious virus model*, wherein the node takes part in the consensus with data carefully generated to compromise the consensus algorithm functioning. Then, in these cases, virus epidemic can be very destructive. In fact, as well known, if no countermeasures are taken, even one misbehaving node can compromise the consensus algorithm functioning [21]. Further, even taking countermeasures, few misbehaving or malicious nodes can compromise the consensus algorithm functioning. In fact, as shown in [22], a consensus network needs to have node connectivity at least equal to $2k + 1$ (resp. $k + 1$) for k malicious (resp. misbehaving) nodes to be detectable and identifiable by every well-behaving agent. Finally, even when the detection of the infected nodes is possible, the design of distributed computationally efficient algorithms to perform such a task is still an open problem. In conclusion, the epidemic of a misbehaving or malicious virus can be very destructive. If possible, the network should be designed so that the epidemic threshold is not exceeded.

14.5 Effects of Network Parameters on Virus Diffusion and Net-Centric Information Fusion

In this section, the effect of network parameters on virus diffusion and net-centric information fusion will be analyzed by means of an extensive simulation campaign over a realistic surveillance scenario. To this end, the problem of tracking a moving object over a surveillance region of 5 km × 5 km is considered. It is supposed that the object motion can be described by the kinematic nearly constant velocity model:

$$x_{k+1} = \begin{bmatrix} 1 & \Delta & 0 & 0 \\ 0 & 1 & 0 & 0 \\ 0 & 0 & 1 & \Delta \\ 0 & 0 & 0 & 1 \end{bmatrix} x_k + w_k$$

where $\Delta = 1s$ is the sampling interval and the unknown state vector is given by the position and velocity components along the coordinate axes, that is, $x = [p_x, v_x, p_y, v_y]'$. The covariance matrix of process noise has been assumed equal to $Q = Gq^2$ with

$$G = \begin{bmatrix} \Delta^3/3 & \Delta^2/2 & 0 & 0 \\ \Delta^2/2 & \Delta & 0 & 0 \\ 0 & 0 & \Delta^3/3 & \Delta^2/2 \\ 0 & 0 & \Delta^2/2 & \Delta \end{bmatrix}$$

and $q = 0.5$ m/s^2.

A total of 10 sensors is supposed to be available, providing measurements of the object position in Cartesian coordinates, that is,

$$y_k^i = \begin{bmatrix} 1 & 0 & 0 & 0 \\ 0 & 0 & 1 & 0 \end{bmatrix} x_k + v_k^i$$

The covariance matrices of measurement noise have been assumed equal to $R^i = \text{diag}(r^2, r^2)$ where $r = 20$ m.

Together with the 10 sensors, the surveillance network is composed of a certain number of COM nodes. Specifically, three different node configurations are considered characterized by 10, 40, and 90 COM nodes (the node coordinates being randomly generated in the surveillance region with uniform distribution). As for the links between the network nodes, a *geometric* link model is considered. This amounts to assuming that a connection exists from node i to node j whenever the distance between the two nodes does not exceed a given threshold r_{max}, called the network *connectivity radius*. Such a model arises from the simple consideration that, in real wireless sensor networks, the signal attenuation from node i to node j is proportional to a suitable power of their distance and node j receives properly the data transmitted by node i only if the received power is larger than or equal to a given threshold. For each node configuration, different values of the connectivity radius have been considered in order to analyze the effect of this parameter on virus diffusion. In Figures 14.5 through 14.7, the resulting surveillance networks are reported. Notice that, for the three considered node configurations (20, 50, and 100 nodes), the minimal connectivity radii ensuring that the network is connected are 2000, 930, and 780 m, respectively. From Figures 14.5 through 14.7, it is evident how the 50% increase of the connectivity radius implies a remarkably higher number of links that, on one hand, makes the network more robust with respect to the disconnection of the infected nodes but, on the other hand, also enhances virus diffusion through the network. In Figures 14.8 through 14.10, it is shown how some of the most important network parameters (namely, the adjacency matrix spectral radius $\rho(A)$,

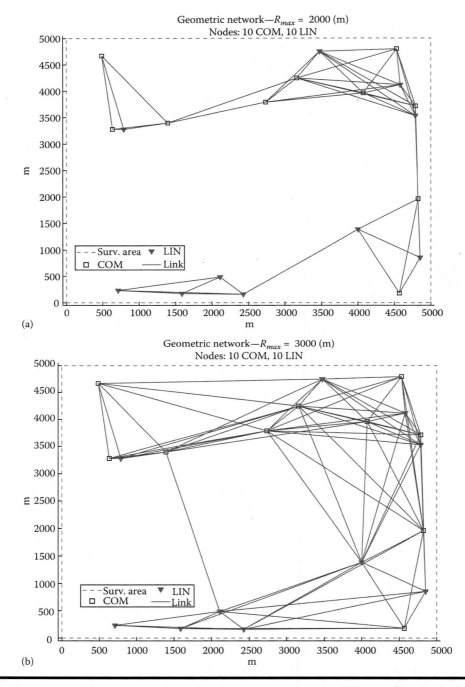

Figure 14.5 Surveillance networks with 20 nodes and two different connectivity radii, respectively, 2000 (a) and 3000 (b).

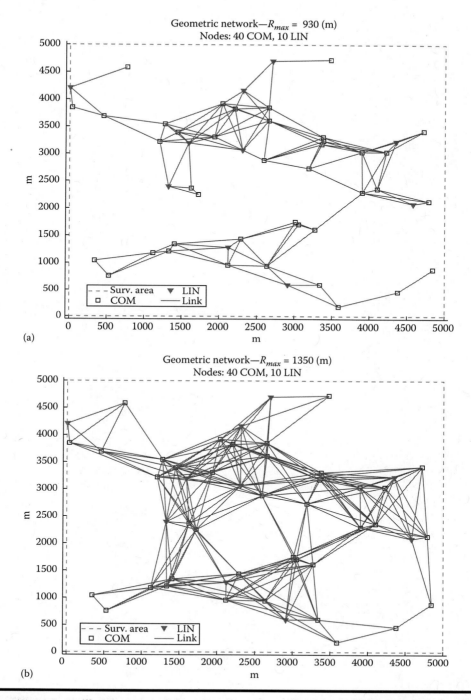

Figure 14.6 **Surveillance networks with 50 nodes and two different connectivity radii, respectively, 930 (a) and 1350 (b).**

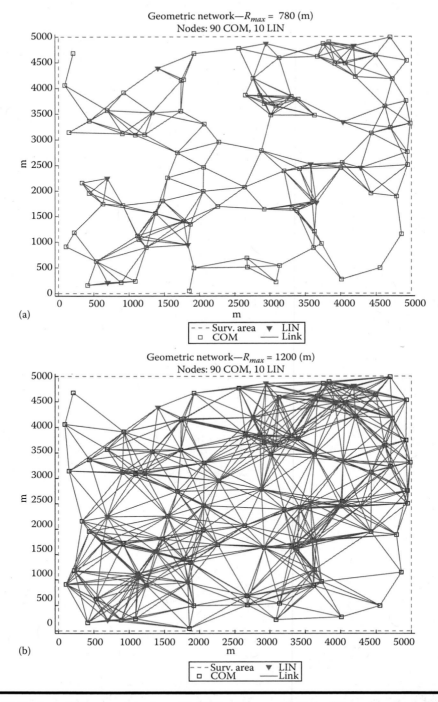

Figure 14.7   Surveillance networks with 100 nodes and two different connectivity radii, respectively, 780 (a) and 1200 (b).

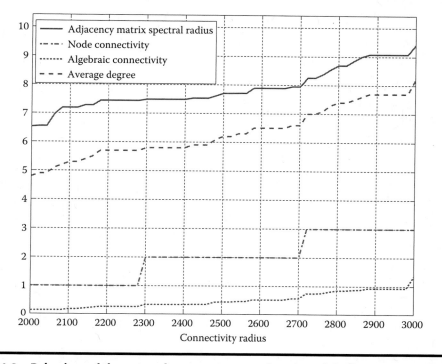

Figure 14.8 Behaviors of the network parameters as a function of the connectivity radius r_{max} in the case of 20 nodes.

the average degree $\bar{k}$, the node connectivity ν, and the algebraic connectivity λ_2) vary as the connectivity radius r_{max} increases. Notice that all parameters, as expected, are monotonically nondecreasing functions of the connectivity radius. In particular, the two curves of the adjacency matrix spectral radius and average degree are almost parallel, that is, these two parameters undergo similar variations. Further, node connectivity, which is an integer parameter, undergoes stepwise increments starting from the minimum value of 1 in correspondence of the minimum radius for network connectivity. Finally, the algebraic connectivity, which primarily characterizes the convergence speed of consensus algorithms (i.e., the diffusion of information throughout the network), is only slightly increasing with the connectivity radius for this type of random (irregular) networks.

The diffusion of a noncooperative virus in the considered surveillance networks has been simulated considering both the SIR and the SIS exact single-Markov-chain model of Section 14.4.2 with infection probability of a node depending on the number of infected neighbors according to (14.14). When not otherwise stated, the recovery probability α (SIR case) and the heal probability δ (SIS case) have been set equal to 0.01. The first part of the simulation analysis has been devoted to the empirical determination of the epidemic thresholds. The resulting behaviors are depicted in Figures 14.11 through 14.13. Some interesting conclusions can be drawn. For the two virus models, the epidemic thresholds turn out to be quite similar; in general, the theoretical epidemic threshold $1/\rho(A)$ is a lower bound on the actual one; as expected, the epidemic threshold tends to decrease as the connectivity radius increases, thus indicating that the more connected a network is, the more susceptible it is to virus epidemic. The prevalence

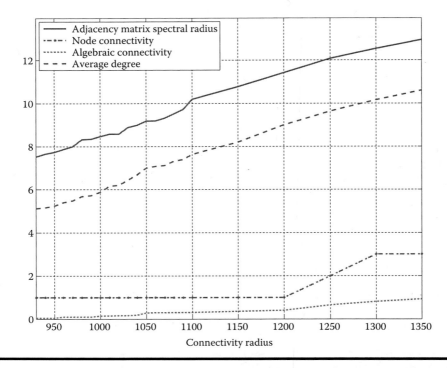

Figure 14.9 **Behaviors of the network parameters as a function of the connectivity radius r_{max} in the case of 50 nodes.**

of the virus epidemic in the different network configurations can be analyzed by looking at Figures 14.14 through 14.16 where, in each of the considered settings, the maximum percentage of infected nodes is reported as a function of the connectivity radius (the plots are averaged over 500 independent Monte Carlo trials). It can be seen that, for all the networks, an increase in the connectivity radius leads to an increase in the virus epidemic prevalence, especially for a higher value of the infection probability β. However, such an increase turns out to be more moderate for the 20-node network, which as a result turns out to be more robust with respect to virus diffusion. It will be the subject of further studies to investigate whether this observation can be generalized to conclude that less dense networks exhibit some advantages in terms of robustness with respect to virus diffusion.

For what concerns the epidemic dynamics, as anticipated, the two virus diffusion models, namely, SIR and SIS, exhibit quite different behaviors. In fact, in the SIR case, the epidemic always vanishes after a certain time interval, whereas in the SIS case, the epidemic is seemingly persistent whenever the epidemic threshold is exceeded. Typical behaviors of the epidemic dynamics are reported in Figure 14.17 (the plots are averaged over 500 independent Monte Carlo trials). Thus, one can conclude that providing the sensor network with a virus recovery capability can substantially reduce the effect of a virus epidemic. Unfortunately, in practical situations, this is not always possible since it would require the presence of some antivirus mechanism in all the nodes of the network, a requirement that might be in contrast with the limited capabilities of the available wireless devices.

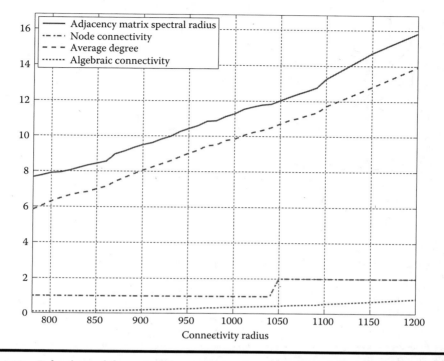

Figure 14.10 **Behaviors of the network parameters as a function of the connectivity radius r_{max} in the case of 100 nodes.**

Let us finally turn our attention to the effects of a virus epidemic on the considered distributed information fusion algorithm. To this end, some conclusions on the performance of the proposed net-centric information fusion algorithm can be drawn by looking at Figures 14.18 through 14.20, wherein the time behavior of the position root mean square error (PRMSE) is reported for different networks in the presence of a virus epidemic. The virus model is an SIS one with heal probability $\delta = 0.1$ and infection probability tuned in each network so as to achieve an epidemic prevalence equal to 30%. The corresponding values of β are reported in Table 14.1. The PMRSE is averaged over all the non-infected network nodes and over 200 independent Monte Carlo trials. Clearly, the presence of a virus epidemic in general leads to a certain degradation in the estimation performance. However, such a degradation is far less evident for the networks characterized by larger connectivity radii, while the number of nodes of the network has only a minor effect. This state of affairs can be understood by noting that an increase in the connectivity radius (i.e., higher node power) has the effect of increasing the network (algebraic) connectivity, thus making the network more robust with respect to the malfunctioning of some nodes and allowing for faster consensus convergence that, in turn, leads to better estimation performance. Of course, one has always to keep in mind the fact that, as discussed earlier, a more connective network is more prone to virus diffusion, being characterized by lower epidemic threshold and higher epidemic prevalence. In practice, the choice of the connectivity level of a sensor network has to be carefully made by taking into account these two contrasting effects, besides the relevant technological issues, so as to obtain a desired tradeoff of performance characteristics.

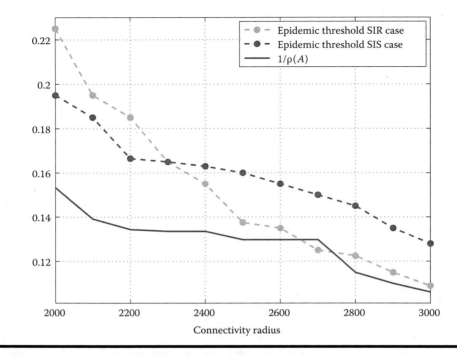

Figure 14.11 Behaviors of the epidemic thresholds (theoretical and empirical) as a function of the connectivity radius r_{max} in the case of 20 nodes.

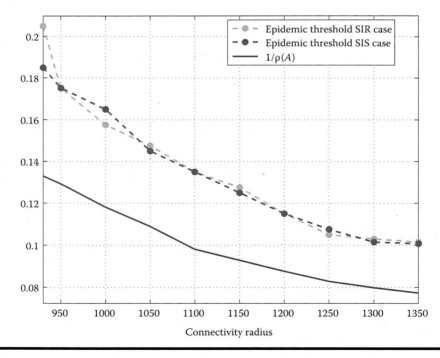

Figure 14.12 Behaviors of the epidemic thresholds (theoretical and empirical) as a function of the connectivity radius r_{max} in the case of 50 nodes.

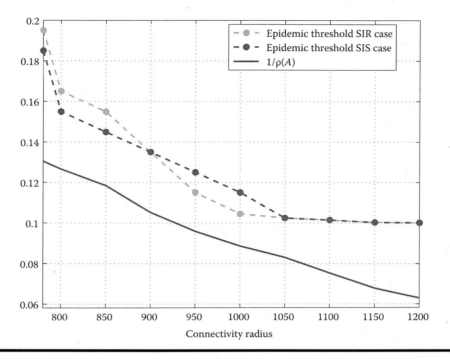

Figure 14.13 **Behaviors of the epidemic thresholds (theoretical and empirical) as a function of the connectivity radius r_{max} in the case of 100 nodes.**

14.6 Conclusions

Relationships have been established between the network topology, the possibility of a virus epidemic outbreak, and the performance of distributed information fusion algorithms. It has been shown that increasing network connectivity, especially in terms of node transmission power, has two contrasting effects: (1) making the network more robust with respect to the malfunctioning of some nodes and (2) making the network more prone to virus diffusion (lower epidemic threshold and higher epidemic prevalence). Further, it has been shown that nodes with recovery capabilities are preferable since a SIR virus epidemic has only a time-limited effect, whereas a SIS virus epidemic is almost persistent.

Results have been analyzed so far for random networks and noncooperative viruses. Future work will concern regular networks and/or misbehaving or malicious (Byzantine) viruses. Concerning the first issue, it is expected that regular networks might be less prone to the virus effects, since it may be possible to reduce the gap between the algebraic connectivity and the spectral radius of the adjacency matrix. As for the second issue, increasing connectivity might be more problematic for misbehaving/malicious viruses, since even few such nodes can seriously compromise the functioning of a net-centric information fusion algorithm. In this case, a challenging task is to develop suitable algorithms for virus detection, isolation, and accommodation in the context of net-centric information fusion.

A further perspective for future work is to validate the results discussed in this chapter by means of more realistic simulations obtained with a COM-based network simulator (e.g., NS2 or OPNET) and/or real experiments on a sensor network test bed.

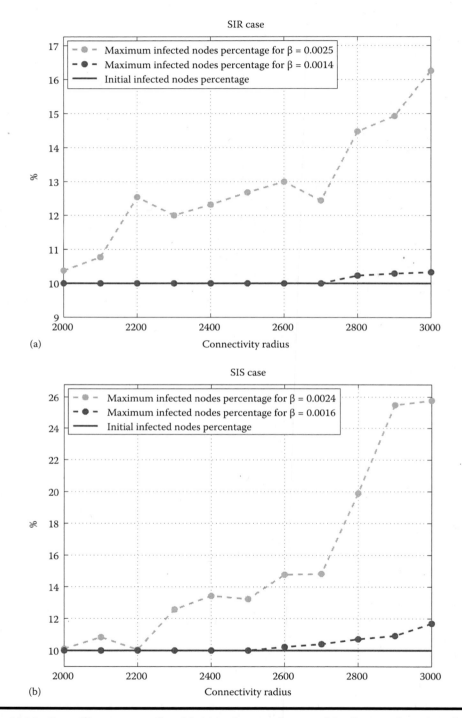

Figure 14.14 Surveillance networks with 20 nodes: maximum epidemic prevalence as a function of the connectivity radius r_{max} for SIR (a) and SIS (b) virus models.

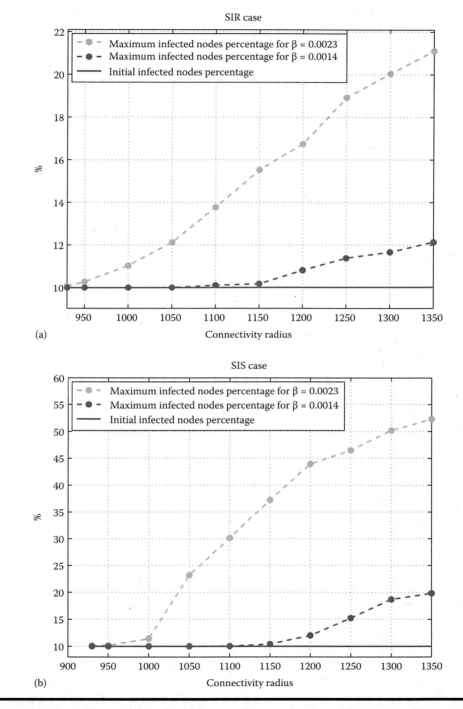

Figure 14.15 **Surveillance networks with 50 nodes: maximum epidemic prevalence as a function of the connectivity radius r_{max} for SIR (a) and SIS (b) virus models.**

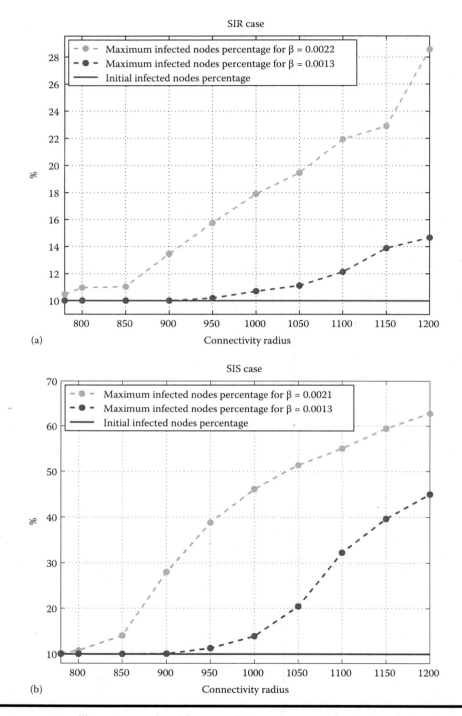

Figure 14.16 Surveillance networks with 100 nodes: maximum epidemic prevalence as a function of the connectivity radius r_{max} for SIR (a) and SIS (b) virus models.

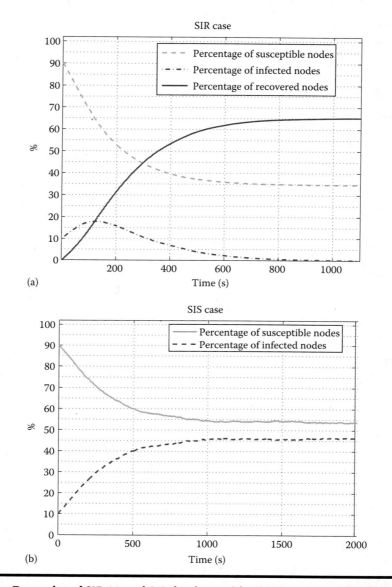

Figure 14.17 **Dynamics of SIR (a) and SIS (b) virus epidemics versus time for the network with 100 nodes. The connectivity radius r_{max} and the infection probability β are set equal to 1000 and 0.002, respectively.**

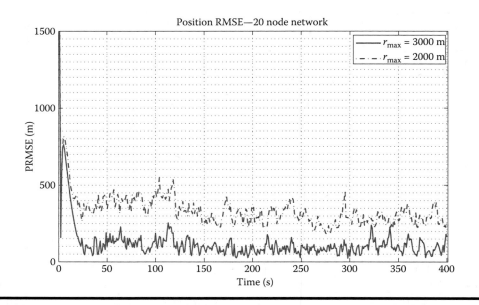

Figure 14.18 Performance, in terms of PRMSE, of the considered net-centric information fusion algorithm for the 20 node network with connectivity radii 2000 and 3000.

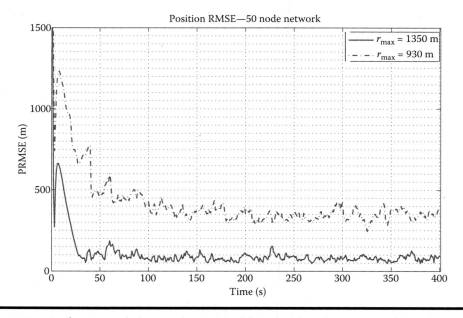

Figure 14.19 Performance, in terms of PRMSE, of the considered net-centric information fusion algorithm for the 50 node network with connectivity radii 930 and 1350.

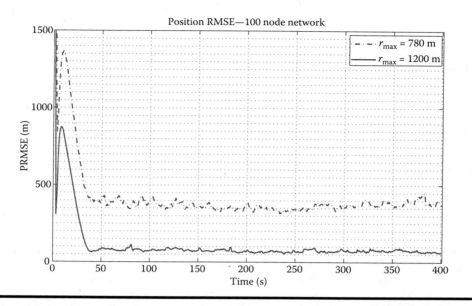

Figure 14.20 Performance, in terms of PRMSE, of the considered net-centric information fusion algorithm for the 100 node network with connectivity radii 780 and 1200.

Table 14.1 Values of β Corresponding to an Epidemic Peak of 30% Infected Nodes in the Considered Networks (δ Is Fixed at 0.1)

No. of Nodes	Connectivity Radius, r_{max}	*Infection Probability,* β
20	2000	0.052
20	3000	0.026
50	930	0.038
50	1350	0.016
100	780	0.031
100	1200	0.011

References

1. Julier, S.J. and Uhlmann, J.K. (1997). A non-divergent estimation algorithm in the presence of unknown correlations. In *Proceedings of the 1997 American Control Conference*, Albuquerque, New Mexico, Vol. 4, pp. 2369–2373.
2. Julier, S.J. and Uhlmann, J.K. (2001). General decentralized data fusion with covariance intersection. In *Handbook of Data Fusion*, CRC Press, Boca Raton, FL.
3. Chen, L., Arambel, P., and Mehra, R. (2002). Estimation under unknown correlation: Covariance intersection revisited. *IEEE Trans. Autom. Control*, 47, 1879–1882.
4. Olfati-Saber, R., Fax, J.A., and Murray, R.M. (2007). Consensus and cooperation in networked multi-agent systems. *Proc. IEEE*, 95, 49–54.

5. Olfati-Saber, R. and Murray, R.M. (2004). Consensus problems in networks of agents with switching topology and time-delays. *IEEE Trans. Autom. Control*, 49, 1520–1533.

6. Kephart, J.O. and White, S.R. (1991). Directed-graph epidemiological models of computer viruses. *Proc. IEEE Comput. Soc. Symp. Res. Secur. Privacy*, 3, 343–359.

7. Pastor-Satorras, R. and Vespignani, A. (2001). Epidemic spreading in scale-free networks. *Phys. Rev. Lett.*, 86, 3200–3203.

8. Boguna, M., Pastor-Satorras, R., and Vespignani, A. (2003). Epidemic spreading in complex networks with degree correlations. *Stat. Mech. Complex Netw.*, 625, 127–147.

9. Zou, C.C., Towsley, D., and Gong, W. (2007). Modeling and simulation study of the propagation and defense of internet e-mail worms. *IEEE Trans. Depend. Secure Comput.*, 4, 105–118.

10. Chakrabarti, D., Wang, Y., Wang, C., Leskovec, J., and Faloutsos, C. (2008). Epidemic thresholds in real networks. *ACM Trans. Inform. Syst. Secur.*, 10, 1–26.

11. Ganesh, A., Massoulié, L., and Towsley, D. (2005). The effect of network topology on the spread of epidemics. In *INFOCOM*, Miami, FL, pp. 1455–1466.

12. Van Mieghem, P., Omic, J., and Kooij, R. (2009). Virus spread in networks. *IEEE/ACM Trans. Netw.*, 17, 1–14.

13. Prakash, B.A., Chakrabarti, D., Faloutsos, M., Valler, N., and Faloutsos, C. (2010). Got the flu (or mumps)? Check the eigenvalue! *arXiv*, 1004.0060v1.

14. Castellano, C. and Pastor-Satorras, R. (2010). Thresholds for epidemic spreading in networks. *Phys. Rev. Lett.*, 105, 218701–218704.

15. Mohar, B. (1991). Eigenvalues, diameter and mean distance in a graph. *Graph Combinator.*, 7, 53–64.

16. Fiedler, M. (1973). Algebraic connectivity of graphs. *Czech. Math. J.*, 23, 298–305.

17. Farina, A. and Studer, F.A. (1985). *Radar Data Processing Vol. 1—Introduction and Tracking*. Research Studies Press LTD, Letchford, Hertfordshire, U.K.

18. Xiao, L., Boyd, S., and Lall, S. (2005). A scheme for robust distributed sensor fusion based on average consensus. In *Proceedings of the 4th International Symposium on Information Processing in Sensor Networks (IPSN)*, Los Angeles, CA, pp. 63–70.

19. Battistelli, G., Chisci, L., Morrocchi, S., and Papi, F. (2011). An information-theoretic approach to distributed state estimation. In *Preprints 18th IFAC World Congress*, Milan, Italy, pp. 12477–12482.

20. Pradip, D., Yonghe, L., and Sajal, K.D. (2006). Modeling node compromise spread in wireless sensor networks using epidemic theory. In *IEEE Proceedings of the 2006 International Symposium on World of Wireless, Mobile and Multimedia (WoWMoM'06)*, Buffalo, New York, 0-7695-2593-8/06.

21. Pasqualetti, F., Bicchi, A., and Bullo, F. (2007). Distributed intrusion detection for secure consensus computations. In *Proceedings of the IEEE Conference on Decision and Control*, New Orleans, LA, pp. 5594–5599.

22. Pasqualetti, F., Bicchi, A., and Bullo, F. (2012). Consensus computation in unreliable networks: A system theoretic approach. *IEEE Trans. Autom. Control*, 57, 90–104.

TECHNOLOGIES FOR HOMELAND SECURITY III

Chapter 15

GEPSUS GEOINT Applications for Homeland Security

Raffaele De Amicis, Giuseppe Conti, Federico Prandi,
Stefano Piffer, Daniele Magliocchetti, Alberto Debiasi,
Diego Taglioni, Andrej Škraba, and Radovan Stojanović

Contents

15.1 Introduction

Global population swell, together with increasing pollution levels caused by expanding industrialization, growing vehicle use, rising standards of living, and other anthropic activities, is cause for an unprecedented level of threat to security, both due to industrial accident and terrorist attacks.

While a significant effort has been made by many countries to protect their main infrastructures, key installations, and mass transportation systems against terror attacks, insufficient attention has been given to protect sites containing hazardous materials/pollutants that could adversely affect the environment if released. Such sites can be easy targets for terrorists seeking great loss of life, disruption to routine activities, and publicity by causing not only severe damage but possibly irreversible effects to both the population and the environment. For these reasons, Geographical Information Processing for Environmental Pollution-Related Security within Urban Scale Environments (GEPSUS) emphasis is placed on air pollution, especially caused by industry, which can be considered as point sources. Case studies are being performed using existing industrial sources of potential air pollution risks.

Release of pollutants in the atmosphere, such as fine airborne particle matter (PM2.5), is currently considered one of the top environmental public health concerns due to its many toxic, carcinogenic, and genotoxic compounds. Various pollutants have been linked to premature mortality and to a variety of cardiopulmonary diseases. In addition to natural and industrial disasters, terrorist attacks might result in the release or emission of hazardous pollutants in atmosphere which can be a major threat in densely populated urban areas.

This issue becomes critical within densely populated urban areas. Cities and megacities today are home to more than 3.3 billion people, or half of the planet's population, according to United Nations Population Fund (UNFPA). Predictions by UNFPA expect this number to rise to 5 billion, or 60%, by 2030. Planning on how to handle acute crises at the urban scale caused by exceptional air pollution levels as well as by pollutants released in atmosphere during a terrorist attack is of key importance to be able to deploy adequate countermeasures.

GEPSUS responds to the aforementioned need through a cooperative and multiagency geospatial intelligence (GEOINT) platform that can be used to manage emergency events, through improved situation awareness, as well as to identify best reaction strategies through its simulation capabilities. Most interestingly the same GEOINT infrastructure can be also used in normal operational conditions, as training tool.

GEPSUS, which is being developed in the context of the "Science for Peace and Security Program of the North Atlantic Treaty Organization (NATO)," has been engineered as comprehensive GEOINT simulation toolkit to enable users with different roles and responsibilities to access real-time data and existing plans in order to simulate emergency scenarios. This is done within a single user-friendly 3D client designed to help operators build a common situation picture. Its potential impact is significant both in social and economical terms. Providing emergency operators and decision makers with such a simulation and training tool can potentially help save lives and reduce the impact of unexpected events both in environmental and financial terms.

The aim of GEPSUS is to provide decision makers and operational staff with decision support tools, based on integration of advanced 3D simulation models within a geobrowser, based on web services, designed to manage environmental pollution-related security events within urban-scale environments and other emergency-related incidents.

The main objectives of GEPSUS are to provide the following:

- Methods and tools for detecting and presenting critical environmental hazards, for example, release of hazardous chemical material, or fire smoke, that causes, or threatens to cause, harmful effects to human, livestock, and real estate and simulates its predicted dispersion/spreading in order to support emergency management operations
- Real-time visualization of 3D dynamic and spatially distributed model results in order to provide efficient interactive decision support tools using discrete multi-criteria optimization and rule-based expert systems

- Simulation of emergency-related accidents and online risk and safety analysis, presented via a 3D geobrowser, to different system users
- Real-time decision-making and emergency intervention as support deployment of mitigation measures

To do so the GEPSUS relies on a set of web services available through a highly flexible and modular client–server architecture, based on standard protocols, connected by number of related real-time communication channels for voice and data exchange, data acquisition, interfacing to databases, geographic information system (GIS), global positioning system (GPS), and video.

15.2 Outlook

Several major accidents have tragically demonstrated the effect of inadequate preparation to such disasters. The Chernobyl nuclear reactor explosion and fire is one of the worst man-made accidents, causing a massive release of radiological pollutants. The 1984 accident at the Union Carbide plant, Bhopal, India, was a major industrial disaster caused by a substantial chemical release in close proximity to a densely urban area.

Similarly, on June 29, 2009, the train derailment in Viareggio (Italy) caused two wagons carrying liquefied petroleum gas (LPG) to explode and catch fire, causing seven fatalities and major damage in the area.

The aforementioned security problem underscores the need for new IT technologies, improved preparedness, decision-making support, and adequate management of disasters.

In particular the goal of GEPSUS is to develop an integrated system for environmental pollution-related disaster management based on a fusion of geographical information processing, computer modeling and simulation, and credible decision making. The test sites for assessment and validation of GEPSUS are all located in Montenegro.

The solution shall be based on updated information–communication–sensor technology, which has improved significantly over the last decade. In this context, the project provides an overall overview of the methodology developed, highlighting the main implications from a purely GEOINT perspective.

The first requirement is to develop mathematical simulation models of air pollution dispersion. The developed models are based on acknowledged modeling methodologies such as Lagrangian dispersion model, box model, Eulerian model, and dense gas model assuming point and lateral release of pollutants in the area.

Then using GIS data available for Montenegro (including digital terrain model (DTM) and urban plans with building heights), a 3D model of the cities (e.g., Podgorica) involved in the pilots, including local and regional topographic information, should be created. This model is to be used for the modeling stage and will take into account a mixed urban layout including low-rise buildings (the old town and newest development) and high-rise (from communist times) architectures. This will be essential to assess the effects of the 3D urban layouts on aeration conditions. For this reason, dispersion will take into account urban canyons that exist in sections of the city.

GEPSUS will deploy a pilot spatial data infrastructure (SDI) conceived as decision support systems (DSSs) and integrated with the governance process. The 3D client will allow interactive orchestration of web services delivering processing functionalities, deployed according to the OCG standard Web Processing Service (WPS), by providing the support for chaining of processing units.

Figure 15.1 Image of how the result of the simulation may look like through a 3D interactive client.

This ensures interactive access to time-dependent datasets and asynchronous processing at the server side. Three-dimensional web clients will be able to visualize results of the simulation in an intuitive way within an interactive environment, and they will provide support to tasks typical of environment monitoring, including content-based GI search, data analysis, clustering, and high-level simulation of environment phenomena (see Figure 15.1).

15.3 Related Works

The fusion of remote-sensing data, GIS technology, and precise geographic information from the GPS constellation, coupled with the increasing power and decreasing cost of computing over a network, has enabled an explosion of geospatial data across the globe. To fulfill this role, the maps should not only be properly designed according to cartographic principles. What the users really need are highly interactive, dynamic map displays that are linked to various additional instruments supporting these creative activities (MacEachren 1994, MacEachren and Kraak 1997).

In case of civil protection or homeland security, it is crucial to collect and analyze data in a collaborative and shared environment in order to be able to quickly respond to the emergency. For this reason, the technology is rapidly moving toward distributed GIS instead of desktop GIS that requires both data and geographic functionalities to be available on the user's computer (Peng and Tsou 2003).

The GEOINT community has engaged with standards development organizations to develop and mature a set of standards and specifications that will enable data and service interoperability in the context of a service-oriented architecture (SOA). Standardization efforts are bringing together diverse national and international community members to implement geospatial data standards that, through an SOA, enhance interoperability across these communities. The evolution of web services is enabling great advancements in GI technology by allowing the loose coupling of systems using standards such as XML rather than tight, inflexible proprietary interfaces. Using web services based on standards for open information exchange via vendor-neutral interfaces, organizations can reconfigure systems more quickly, reducing cost and risk. Only technology built on open standards will be able to deliver the collaboration needed to tie together information that is held and managed at central and local government levels as well as in the private sector—ensuring that the right people have the right information at the right time. However, understanding and implementing these specifications and standards are critical to true interoperability across the spectrum from data producers down to users in the field.

Within this context, the geospatial-intelligence exploitation has been proposed as the "bottom-up" approach to SDI. In particular in the United States, the National System for Geospatial Intelligence (NSG) has been created, that is, the "combination of technologies, policies, capabilities, doctrines, activities, staff, and communications necessary to produce geospatial intelligence into an integrated, multi-agency and multi-domain system" (NGA 2006). The "bottom-up" approach to the SDI is characterized, therefore, by the focus on the purpose of the system that was created to meet very specific requirements and functionalities (e.g., from prevention of hydrogeological risk to monitoring of critical areas, to homeland security problems, to support of strategic and tactical military operations). These systems are characterized by the need to integrate distributed data sources, with independent cycles of production and maintenance and, often, to carry out, from them, the processing on clients. These SDI "bottom-up" examples are, however, characterized by the presence of structural elements typical of an SDI, that is, use of web services standards, or deployment of geoportals, that guarantee interoperability.

In August 2008, the U.S. National Geospatial-Intelligence Agency (NGA) launched GEOINT Online, a "geospatial collaboration portal" intended to be a one-stop shop for the discovery and dissemination of geospatial information and products. This web-based application provides a wide variety of users, from novices to professionals, the ability to search and discover an expanding repository of geospatial information, including links to external sources, mapping applications, and most importantly the ability to collaborate with other users through the creation and use of a growing number of "communities" created by users for people with common goals and interests.

Previous works have also highlighted that not only the information sharing is fundamental but, in addition, it is needed to access to update data and to know the temporal evolution of the phenomena. In this context for the users, a deep awareness of the temporal dimension of geographic information is needed (De Amicis et al. 2011). In a more general perspective, a variety of remote-sensing, geographical data and analysis, in situ sensors generate massive amounts of data where the quantized nature of the measurements frequently leads to a time-driven data structure. Examples include sensor time series, moving objects 2D imagery, 3D image time series and x/y/z spatial cubes, and 4D x/y/z/t spatiotemporal cubes. In this sense, some previous works such as an extension to web coverage services (WCSs) which adds flexible, open-ended coverage processing capabilities to WCS will be analyzed (Baumann 2010).

In the specific context of urban and environmental modeling, having access to 3D interactive geovisual analytics applications can provide fundamental support to effectively understand complex spatial relationships between information and datasets, for example, to define the most appropriate evacuation routes or to plot an emergency plan. For this reason, 3D GIS has recently received considerable attention (Brooks and Whalley 2008). One noteworthy system, called GeoTime (Kapler and Wright 2005), proposes an interesting solution to the problem of integrating time-line events into interactive GIS. The Adelaide 3D GIS planning model (2007) is an example of a 3D GIS that provides 3D visualizations of social and environmental data within a 3D cityscape. Further research is required to explore the possibilities and constraints of 3D GIS in order to move beyond the somewhat limited scope of providing a tool for terrain fly and mapmaking.

In particular, a key requirement of homeland security DSS is to ensure support for complex geoprocessing tasks (De Amicis et al. 2010). This is essential to allow operators to automate GIS tasks (Furnas 1997). One relevant example is the geovisual analytics system developed by GraphiTech (Conti et al. 2010) that can provide access to multiple-step procedures known as workflows. The types of tasks to be automated can be potentially very complex sequences of elementary operations necessary to model and analyze complex spatial relationships. The interface can help operators perform operations on different datasets (e.g., feature class, raster, or table) and to produce a new dataset as result. The interface supports common geoprocessing tasks including feature overlay, selection and analysis, topology processing, raster processing, and data conversion.

Several authors have focused on modeling the problem of emergency decision support systems (EDSSs) (Ye et al. 2008). A comprehensive state of the art on use of agents' technologies for decision support in environmental processes has been edited by Aulinas et al. (2009). A further state of the art of decision support systems for renewable energy sources has been edited by Georgilakis (2006). A specific DSS for urban emergency has been proposed by Zhang and Li (2008). The role of networks, sensors, and emergent knowledge process in the context of network DDS (NWDSS) is discussed by Dolk et al. (2007) who present Global Information Network Architecture (GINA), a model-driven architecture for DSSs. The system allows integration data from incident-related organization to perform integrated analysis and it is built on top of CyberSIG, a digital city infrastructure service platform. A comprehensive study of EDSS for mass evacuation can be found in Javed et al. (2010, 2011a,b,c). A recent study on homeland security has focused on decision support system for dispersion of toxic agents in atmosphere (Arnold et al. 2010).

Additionally several commercial solutions or governmental packages are also available on the market including Emergency Simulation Program (ESP) by Straylight Multimedia; DisasterLAN™ Crisis Information Management System by Buffalo Computer Graphics, Inc.; Homeland Security Exercise and Evaluation Program (HSEEP) toolkit by U.S. Federal Emergency Manag. Agency (FEMA); SOftCopy Exploitation Toolkit (SOCET) Geospatial eXploitation Products (GXP®) by British AErospace (BAE) Systems or Business Intelligence; and Intergraph/Law Enforcement Automated Data System (I/LEADS) and security suite by Intergraph.

Finally, with specific regard to modeling of environmental conditions, El-Harbawi et al. (2008) present an overview of existing literature on air pollution assessment and evaluation. These methods include mathematical models, simulation modeling methodology, and simulation software. The basic technology for predicting the impact of air pollution is based on use of a variety of mathematical models including Gaussian model, Lagrangian model, box model, Eulerian model, and dense gas model.

15.4 Methodology

One of the fundamental characteristics of the proposed framework is that the proposed solution should be addressed to homeland security needs while, at the same time, it should also be as generic as possible because emergency response is transversal to several types of scenarios.

The specific risk scenarios addressed by GEPSUS require tackling several aspects connected to the use the spatiotemporal dimension of geographic information. Specific requirements include availability of services capable to perform a range of tasks, ranging from risk assessment in relation to release of pollutants in the atmosphere to assessment of weather conditions and their evolution over time to identify possible risk patterns connected to release of chemicals in the atmosphere.

For these reasons, the approach followed in order to collect the requirements for services development has been a typical user-driven approach. This means that after a detailed analysis of users' needs, a specific data and metadata model has to be developed and, according to this, the related services are developed. At this first stage, user, technological, and metadata requirements are collected together with use cases and relevant existing data available. Typical use case includes high-level functionalizations (e.g., retrieving of data from sensors or from a spatial database, plotting a chart or table) to more specific use cases dealing with emergencies (e.g., generation of automatic alerts following specific conditions, calculation of pollutant exposure risk). In this way, thanks to the variety of the scenarios, it has been possible to set up a generic data model that can be applied to various different datasets that have some specific temporal properties. In particular on the most common requirement was the possibility to retrieve information based on their temporal information. For this purpose, the typical approach based on the resource date is not sufficient. A typical example of this is the case of forecast or simulation models where the temporal information to be considered is, at least, made of two time stamps: time of running and the time the simulations or forecast refer to.

The methodology followed to deal to this huge domain has been therefore to start from the particular use case related to the pilot and generalize this to the project purpose. In this way, it has been possible to meet the user's needs and then, by generalizing this, it has been possible to obtain a useful extension capable to consider the time dimension in most common case related to the emergencies such as forecast time series, moving objects change detection, and sensors time series.

The user-driven approach has allowed also defining in very precise way to define the requirements in terms of spatiotemporal processing, highlighting that the final user in terms of processing doesn't require very complex operation but instead they need the capabilities to perform workflow of single simple operation on temporal dataset.

15.4.1 Collection of User Requirements

The "security and emergency world" currently can use a number of tools to manage security emergencies and disaster events. However, there is a crucial lack of specific and advanced tools to manage, practice, and carry out emergency responses by decision makers and senior and operational staff in a large-scale emergency disaster scenario, in which collaboration and cooperation among multiagency and multidisciplinary forces are required. One of the requirements of GEPSUS is to enable users with several levels of responsibility and authorization to deal with emergencies by having real-time information, access to database/maps, as well as simulation of scenarios, all in one system, to support centralized decision making.

GEPSUS has been designed as a system to be deployed by governments (at national, regional and local level), ministries and agencies, and security and emergency response forces. The adoption by the GEPSUS system of open internationally accepted standards ensures that services can be integrated with existing GIS technologies already in place among public administration and security/civil protection corps.

From a methodological point of view, in order to cover the requirements, the approach has been strongly user driven and therefore has been based on real used needs and practices. During the first part of each of the projects, a comprehensive analysis, carried on with extensive involvement of the final users, has brought to the documentation of well-defined use cases formalized in UML. The goal has been to identify, clearly and analytically, use cases together with the corresponding "actors" within public administrations, environmental management, and risk management agencies.

With their support, it has been possible to identify tasks that had to be performed at operational stage, for the final system to be considered as successful. UML formalization, carried on starting from feedback collected through interviews and specifically designed surveys, has been essential in order to design the functionalities required by a practically usable system.

Use cases were structured both in terms of general use cases, horizontally applicable to a variety of emergency situations, and scenario specific. General use cases have been formalized in terms of system access, management of information (e.g., data access, data storage, service management), information visualization (e.g., access to layered data, 2D and 3D visualization, and query), data creation (creation and editing of data and metadata), processing of information (e.g., feature extraction, change detection, statistic time-driven analysis), and, lastly, generation of alerts.

Scenario-specific use cases have considered specialized conditions typical of different critical situations, by defining the operational activities necessary for tasks such as emergency management, emergency service planning, resource management, and access to specific sensors. Use cases have been complemented by underpinning of requirements collected by the users involved in the projects, covering technological, operational, as well as usability issues.

A fundamental requirement emerging from the analysis was the support for intuitive access to complex geoprocessing tasks as illustrated in Figure 15.2. This is considered essential to allow operators to automate GIS tasks. Specifically there is a need to provide access to multiple-step procedures known as workflows and action procedures. The interface must support geoprocessing, that is, the automation of workflows and action procedures, by providing a rich set of tools and mechanisms to combine a series of tools into a sequence of operations using models and scripts. The types of tasks to be automated need to be potentially complex sequences of elementary operations necessary to model and analyze complex spatial relationships. The interface needs to perform operations on different datasets (such as a feature class, raster, or table) and to produce a new datasets as result. The interface must support common geoprocessing operations including geographic feature overlay, feature selection and analysis, topology processing, raster processing, and data conversion.

The GEPSUS system has extended available simulation components through a standardized open standard WPS from the Open Geospatial Consortium (OGC). This way the results of GEPSUS can be expanded to domains is very diverse in their nature, ranging, for example, from being able to predict the path of wildfires, analyzing and finding patterns in crime locations, and predicting which areas are prone to landslides to predicting flooding effects of a storm event.

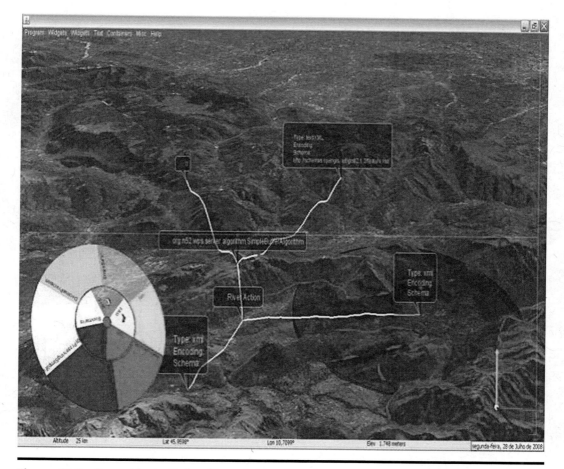

Figure 15.2 Screenshot of the 3D web-based geobrowser providing access to processing functionalities.

With specific regard to simulation models, several have been developed at the macroscopic or microscopic level of representation, depending on the purpose of the implementation in order to understand the procedures and the impacts of crisis managers' decisions. The models are applied to studies of the emergency situations at different impact scales in order to develop a proper control strategy for an evacuation process. Solutions to the mentioned models are usually obtained numerically by means of simulation. In this way one may check the validity of the model and use it for studying or controlling an emergency situation. Computing time at the performance of the simulation models usually represents important issues due to the size and complexity of the addressed problem.

A different strategy to simulate complex physical and social systems is based on system dynamics. This is a computer-based approach to simulate and experiment using specific models to design policies for management and control. In a system dynamics approach, feedback loops are the building blocks of these models and their interactions are used to represent and explain system behavior.

15.5 System Architecture

The software architecture of GEPSUS has followed a modular methodology based on a federated approach to data collection, processing, and distribution of spatiotemporal data. The entire GEPSUS architecture has been designed according to the classical multi-tier (layer) system with a communication paradigm based on open-source SOA, where each component (service), interacts with the others through a set of messages written in a standard format. With the term service, we include not only each one of the three layers but also all the components inside them, allowing the integration of several multifaceted computational units inside a unique system.

This allows creating a logical layer between existing services, exposing data and functionalities via SOAP or through OGC communication protocols such as WMS, WFS, and, WPS. The framework follows a multilevel structure. At the lowest data level, there will be the data repositories including those from several public administrations, which are already available through OGC web service (OWS). The middleware level then builds on top of these low-level OWS a number of geoprocessing services deployed as WPS.

From the conceptual point of view, GEPSUS is being based on a set of service components, to be run from one or more servers, which are made accessible via a client deployed as Java™ Web Start technology.

At the lowest data level, all the different datasets (both static and real-time) are made available within the network by the different content providers, that is, city administrations, civil protection agencies, and environmental agencies. The data repositories can be both physically separated and geographically distributed.

Moving to a higher level (from a software perspective), the so-called middleware level, GEPSUS provides a number of web services that can expose data as well as processing functionalities in an interoperable manner. The different services can be grouped into subgroups:

- Catalog services
- Ingestion services
- Simulation services
- OWSs

The lowest ensures standardized provision to data made available at the lowest level where there are WMS (Web Map Service), WFS (Web Feature Service), and WCS.

A further, more articulated layer provides simulation capabilities. In particular, services are made available via the WPS standard. This is a very flexible standard engineered to ensure generic interoperable access to processing functionalities. In other words, GEPSUS processing functionalities can be distributed over the network and retrieved by WPS-enabled clients, in a very simple and user-friendly way. These functionalities will be exposed as a WPS to ensure full interoperability. To do so, an Enterprise JavaBeans (EJB) will be developed for each software component. Each EJB communicates with other EJBs at various levels, that is, through an enterprise service bus (ESB), remote method invocation (RMI), or via a web service by coupling each EJB to a Java Servlet, exposed on the network through a servlet container. The simulation services planned within GEPSUS provide a series of WPS focused on air pollution. All the simulation models returned by the service are being implemented using matrix laboratory (MATLAB®).

From a technological standpoint, GEPSUS framework is based on a number of available R&D works already completed or due to be delivered throughout the project's duration, and it is based on a number of available technologies either made available by the project's partners or through public results of European Union (EU) projects or as free and open-source software (FOSS) initiatives. This ensures further development and processing functionalities built on top of the GEPSUS framework, to be extended by public administrations or private industries according to their specific needs. The components are discussed within the following sections.

15.6 3D Client

In order to provide to the final users with an instrument able to consume the spatiotemporal services provided by GEPSUS servers, a client application was needed.

The application is an interactive 3D environment capable to provide support to large-scale monitoring and planning activities. The application gives the user the possibility to access simulation modules through an interoperable standard (WPS). The operators could then define complex procedures, known as workflows, by creating chains of processes through a mechanism to combine a series of tools into a sequence of operations using models. The application is not only able to access to the standard OCG services but also allows exploiting the temporal dimension. The user can use a simple graphical user interface to select the required services (e.g., WMS, WCS, or WFS) and then select the particular dataset related to a specific date.

In case of sensor observations that contain a huge number of value for time series, or when accessing services or coverages that denote complex space-varying phenomenon (i.e., a geographic object with some extent whose values depend on the location and time of probing), it becomes very important to provide the user with visual tools that can help them understand the information being handled. The developed solution is able to change the scale of visualized phenomenon or modify the table of content in accordance with the values of the observed phenomenon.

Furthermore, the client interface allows the user to visualize the information provided by sensor using 2D chart or 3D visualization according to a specific temporal interval.

From an infrastructural perspective, the control room setup envisaged for GEPSUS is presented in Figure 15.3. Different operators are connected together via a protected LAN. The operator's station provides an instance of the GEPSUS application. Inside the same room, there will be a master station operator that will run the GEPSUS application, in addition to the control software of the projection system (Figures 15.4 through 15.6).

The server part consists of three different machines:

- Database server: In this server, all information coming from the sensors will be stored.
- Simulation server: Is responsible for the simulation processes.
- Testing server: Used for testing and not production services.

All these servers will be connected in the internal LAN, protected by an HW/SW firewall solution.

Another server, hosting the OWS and GEPSUS-server logical core, is also present, and this will be housed in an external server farm.

This latter solution in fact is based on the great flexibility ensured by the use of distributed web-service-based architecture. The one single underpinning of GEPSUS has been to provide web-service-based access to data and, most importantly, processing functionalities in an interoperable way through a federated software infrastructure as seen in Figure 15.7.

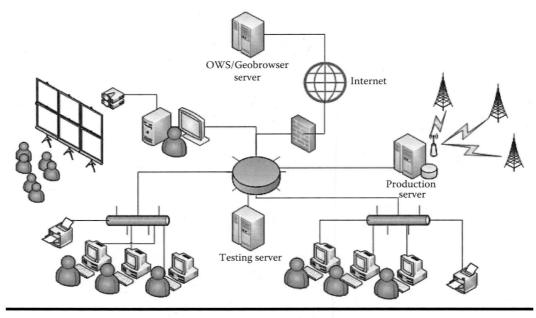

Figure 15.3 Overall overview of the GEPSUS integrated system.

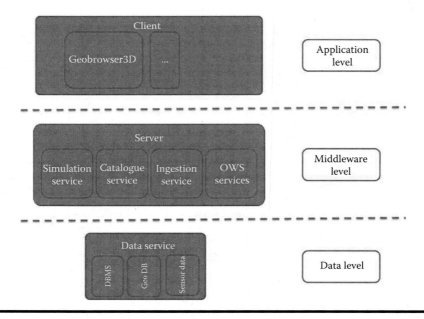

Figure 15.4 General overview of the system architecture.

Figure 15.5 Visualization of the WPS within the 3D client application.

15.7 Simulating Man-Made Disaster

In general terms, GEPSUS, as a true GEOINT system, should support emergency services to better respond to different air pollution incidents. Such a flexibility is ensured through an intrinsically distributed approach to simulation and data processing. In fact in GEPSUS, all functionalities are delivered as service and then made available to the client through interoperable protocol. This ensures that the client can be developed as very "general-purpose" software capable to connect to remote processing units. These processing units then provide specialized simulation to the client in a totally transparent way to the client that thus becomes process agnostic. This radical approach has a number of advantages: the client has to be engineered only to ensure fastest rendering and best possible user interaction, while several server components provide specialized simulation and processing functionalities as web services.

As soon as the client is started, the function available from the system of services is sent to the client. The latter then configures the interface providing reference to the various services available, data required by each of them (e.g., measurement from a sensor station), and produced output (e.g., a risk map). The user graphically selects the service available to them and logically connects them to create potentially complex simulations.

The single most important outputs of the GEOINT system are the threat zones, which are equipped with exact concentration levels, threat classes, and geolocation. Besides the threat zones, the system should be able to provide evacuation plans, essential to the rescue teams on site. It is

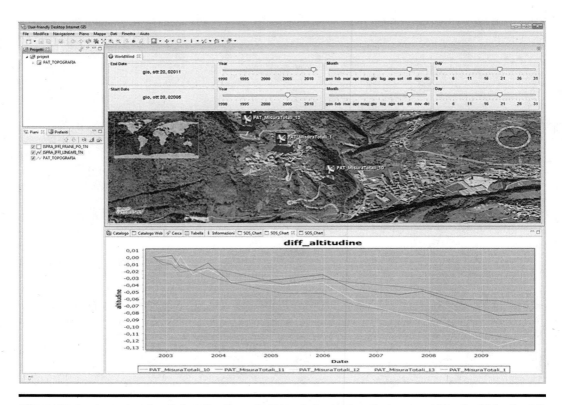

Figure 15.6 An example of visualization of sensor information that are rendered within the 3D environment and plotted as 2D chart.

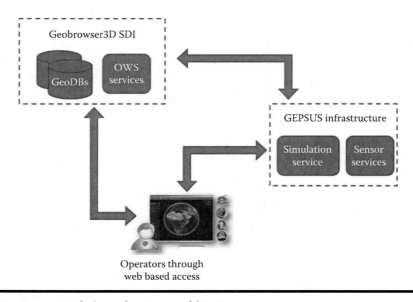

Figure 15.7 Conceptual view of system architecture.

important that the evacuation plans are preplanned based on the expert knowledge since at the time of the accident, there is not much time and the plans provided to the rescue crew should be short, concise, and precise.

The output of the systems will be provided to the handheld mobile devices, which will be used by the members of the rescue crew at the site providing better spatial awareness of the incident, which is especially important in the context of urban environments. As the final output of the system, the information about the incident will be provided to the population via SMS as well as via webGIS.

As mentioned earlier in this chapter, GEPSUS addresses well-defined use cases, all including a major release of pollutants next or within an urban area. This group of incidents includes analyzed and quantified forms of incidents that may result in substantial injury or death to people, animals, and agricultural/plant life, or destruction of goods/properties. These can have various causes such as major incidents involving oil installations and petroleum products; breakdowns during transportation, storage, or use of chemical, toxic, explosive, and radioactive substances; explosions; pollution of drinking water springs; chemical and toxic incidents; radiological incidents; combined effects of terrorism and large-scale toxic radiological and biological effects; major traffics; outages in large power plants and hydropower plants; chemical and radiological contamination; and incidents with dangerous chemical substances.

In the first scenario, a bomb explodes during terrorist attack at the *Kombinat Aluminijuma Podgorica* (KAP) (Aluminium Plant Podgorica) in Montenegro. KAP is the single most important industrial site in the whole country, and it poses serious threats to the health of those living in the nearby capital city Podgorica, due to the large amount of aluminum oxide (Al_2O_3) stored within the site, a notoriously toxic substance with potentially fatal consequences and poisoning of water reservoirs and surrounding soil. Furthermore, as visible in Figure 15.8, the vicinity of the plant to Podgorica International Airport would prevent, in case of a major accident at the plant, aids and search and rescue (S&R) teams from being flown in.

In the second scenario, as result of a road accident within Podgorica city center, a truck carrying a 35 m^3 gas tank capsizes causing a spill of flammable chemical gas. The leak causes a 2.5 cm wide circular leak at the base of the tank.

In both scenarios, the emergency operators need to identify threat zones based on the simulation of pollutants over time. Threat zones need to be plotted as function of toxic level of concern (LOC) according to acute exposure guideline levels (AEGL) to identify the areas where concentration of toxic material can be harmful or fatal. Most importantly the analysis needs to be projected at several time ranges to ensure that emergency staff and population can be moved to safe areas. In both scenarios, emergency staff need also to identify alternative routes to ensure that traffic can be rerouted through safe areas. Both scenarios require overlaying simulation data on top of geographic information available including, but not limited to, cadastral information and infrastructures to be able to assess infrastructures or population at risk.

These two scenarios have been identified through the involvement of the Ministry of Defence (MoD) of Montenegro and will be simulated within the 3D GEOINT platform developed within the project and used to improve response to terrorist attack or environmental incidents.

More in general, we can describe how the emergency activities can be managed under situations, which can be related to those kinds of use cases. A short description of the typical flow of data in the case of an emergency occurring, the operating center must immediately be activated after a hazardous event. With regard to the aforementioned use case scenarios, the analysis has brought to the identification of several UML diagrams with corresponding "actors," as shown in Figure 15.9.

Figure 15.8 Aerial view of the scenario, it shows the vicinity of the plant to Podgorica International Airport.

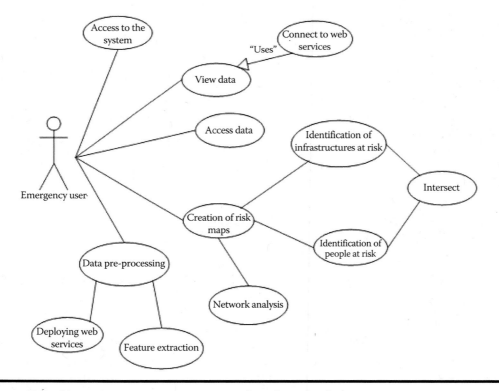

Figure 15.9 Use case on emergency response based on simulation.

The typical actors of GEPSUS, authorized to have access to the system, must be able to access—via web services—the databases storing information such as pollutant distribution, road networks, land use, and population distribution, in order to perform a number of analysis in the selected area.

After interactively selecting the area of interest and after visualizing the basic layers needed, the user can then select, from the geoprocessing library, the tools needed for emergency management or for simulation purposes.

More specifically the user can create hazardous material exposure risk maps through, for example, the intersection of pollution exposure with the main transportation networks or the urban areas.

In order to perform such simulations, the system's input consists of data coming from the following sources:

- Hydrological and meteorological service of Montenegro (*Hidrometeorološki zavod Crne Gore*, HMZCG, or the Hydrometeorological Institute of Montenegro). HMZCG provides the current state of weather and forecasting, ensuring access to data from automatic weather stations and weather simulation models. The latter are based on the weather data gathered from the weather centers in European Centre for Medium-Range Weather Forecasts (ECMWF) in Reading, United Kingdom, and aviation/global forecast system (AVN/GFS) data from Washington, United States
- Centre for Ecotoxicological Research (CETI) of Montenegro, which provides data on the toxic emissions from the automatic telemetric stations, which are positioned on strategic points in Montenegro as well as from mobile stations
- Real Estate Administration (REA) of Montenegro, which provides updated geographical information about the geospatial information of Montenegro, through survey as well as from the cadastral survey

The basic input for the GEPSUS system, which is automatic, is therefore the information on weather conditions, forecasts, and with special emphasis on wind condition. Here we should mention the different aspects of the data sampling for each of the stated automatic input. HMZCG and CETI input should be provided at 1 min intervals, while the frequency of update of other standard geospatial information should be updated monthly or only when important changes in geospatial information occur, for example, in case of definition of new urban plans.

It should be noted that HMZCG has its own simulation and modeling capabilities including a high-performance computing (HPC) center, which enables the HMZCG to generate weather forecasts for the territory of Montenegro every 3 h at a resolution of 1 km on their own developed software simulation models. In order to run the forecast models, HMZCG determines the initial and end conditions as well as other parameters from the weather centers in Washington, United States, and Reading, United Kingdom. Important information from the REA includes strategic buildings and areas such as hospitals, schools, public event areas, and other sites where large concentrations of people are anticipated.

This information is essential for adequate decision making in the case of an emergency event, where the decision makers must know which areas are most populated and should be evacuated.

Another key input for GEPSUS is the users' input, who can provide description of the pollution extent which could not be provided by automatic input, including factors such as exact location of the release (latitude and longitude), chemical emission rate, special weather condition parameters, type of emission, or release parameters. Generally speaking, the users' input should address the data which could not be reliably acquired by automatic methods including on-site visual assessment of important factors such as dimension of the release source (e.g., tank with toxic liquid) or the type of chemical in question (from the tank specifications).

This type of user's input is provided by air pollution experts, by emergency management team, as well as by the rescue crew that is on the field and provide accurate information about the incident. Since air pollution dispersion is fast, direct input to the GEPSUS system is provided via mobile handheld devices.

15.7.1 Modeling and Simulation Features

Providing a thorough description of the mathematical models developed to simulate spread of pollutant in atmosphere is beyond the scope of this chapter and can be read in detail within previous works of the authors (Stojanović et al. 2011, 2012) where detailed description of the model used for pollutant spread is presented. However, for the sake of completeness, it is worth providing an overall overview of the methodology developed, highlighting the main implications from a purely GEOINT perspective. The model has been initially implemented in MATLAB in order to allow for fast prototyping and testing, while the final implementation is being implemented as remote web service based on the interoperable standard WPS.

The model, which assumes zero point release, has been based on acknowledged methodologies including Lagrangian dispersion model, box model, Eulerian model, and dense gas model.

The greatest dangers in relation to air pollution are anticipated from forest fires, from present technical and technological disasters from industrial sources, as well as from static facilities for storage or transport of dangerous gases or liquids. Thus, the simulation system should take into consideration the following sources:

Direct: Instantaneous or continuous release of material from a point source.

Puddle: Liquid puddle of constant radius. The liquid can be either normal evaporating liquid or boiling.

Tank: This option is selected when the source is a horizontal or vertical cylinder or a spherical tank at ground level with a single hole. The tank initially contains a gas, a liquid, or a liquefied gas. The contents can change phase as a result of temperature and/or pressure changes.

Pipe: This option is selected when the source is a pressurized pipe containing gas with a single hole at ground level.

The model purpose is to highlight a toxic threat zones with confidence lines. The model developed (Stojanović et al. 2011) accounts for the following parameters: emission rate (in g/s), height of the source of emission (in mt), wind speed (in mt/s), wind direction (in degree), location of the stack assumed as source of pollution, stack layout (x and y in meters), environmental temperature (in degree Celsius), and overall weather conditions. Simulation is provided at different time intervals at 3 h difference in order to be able to predict 3D spreading of pollutant (e.g., due to changing environmental conditions) as illustrated in Figure 15.10. The model has been calibrated on past data from HMZCG to assess its reliability.

The results in terms of predicted concentrations of pollutants (see Figure 15.10) are used extract threat zones, according to specific concentration levels. A threat zone is an area where a hazard (such as toxicity or thermal radiation) has exceeded a user-specified LOC.

In particular, modeling component is designed to display up to three threat zones on a single plot. In practical terms, the various threat zones are automatically saved as KML file ready to

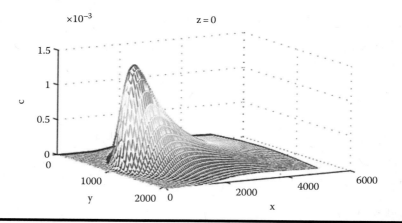

Figure 15.10 Simulation of 3D concentration for the emissions of the thermal power plant in Pljevlja, Montenegro.

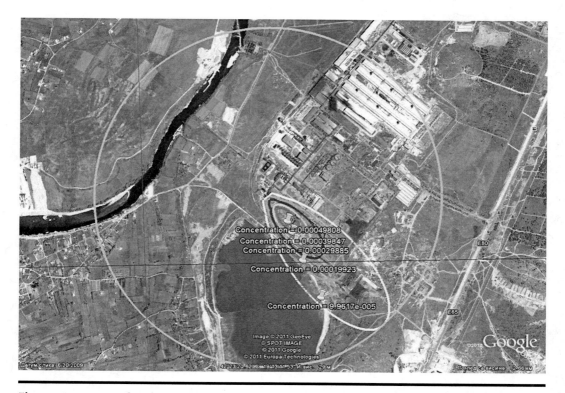

Figure 15.11 Levels of concern, case study of the Aluminium Plant Podgorica, using the GEPSUS program.

be loaded within a geobrowser (including Google Earth). As illustrated in the following picture, the inner threat zone (the innermost dark ellipse) represents the worst hazard. The threat at a point feature displays specific information about hazards at locations of interest (such as a school). The footprint of threat zones can be then appreciated within the 3D geobrowser as visible in Figure 15.11.

15.8 Conclusions

This chapter has illustrated the first results of GEPSUS. The project is bringing to the development of an interactive 3D environment capable to provide support to large-scale monitoring of critical events and planning of remedial actions. In particular the system has been designed to respond to critical events related to release in atmosphere of chemical compounds within an urban context. In particular two scenarios have been considered, the first related to a terrorist attack within an industrial plant and, the second, dealing with a release of gas within an urban environment caused by a truck carrying a gas tank.

The aforementioned security problem underscores the need for new IT technologies, improved preparedness, decision-making support, and adequate management of disasters where exceptional pollution levels may appear in or near urban, densely populated areas. In both cases, operators need to access a variety of geographical resources ranging from environmental data, through fixed or mobile stations, weather forecasts, as well as typical geographical information such as cadastral data and census data.

Through the use of GEPSUS, the users can not only access data but can also perform simulation within a comprehensive 3D client. The user can access simulation functionalities in a very user-friendly way. More specifically processing functionalities are made available at the server side as processing service through an interoperable standard (WPS). Each processing service is rendered, at the client side, as a building block that can be used to compose, in a very simple manner, complex procedures, referred to as workflows, by creating chains of processes through a mechanism to combine a series of tools into a sequence of operations using models.

In GEPSUS these workflows, in particular, have been engineered to ensure simulation of air pollutant spread, specifically addressing scenarios related to release in atmosphere of dangerous chemical compounds within urban environments. This has required a fairly complex modeling stage, which has allowed definition of very articulated mathematical models (Stojanović et al. 2011, 2012).

The system is going to be tested by staff of the Ministry of Defence of Montenegro in operational scenarios typical of a control station used to manage large-scale crisis. The achievements of the project represent a noteworthy example of how GEOINT applications can be extremely effective to improve responsiveness and preparedness in case of critical events.

Acknowledgments

The achievements described within this chapter have received funding from NATO through the Science for Peace and Security (SPS) through the project GEPSUS (n. SfP 983510). The authors are solely responsible this work which does not represent the opinion of the NATO. The NATO is not responsible for any use that might be made of information contained in this chapter.

References

Adelaide Model. 2007. Adelaide Model, retrieved October 10, 2007, from http://www.gisca.adelaide.edu.au/projects/am.html

Arnold, E., Simpson, M., Larsen, S., Gash, J., Aluzzi, F., Lundquist, J., and Sugiyama, G. 2010. Improved meteorological input for atmospheric release decision support systems and an integrated LES modeling system for atmospheric dispersion of toxic agents: Homeland security applications. Final Report for NASA Grant NNS06AA68G.

Aulinas, M., Turon, C., and Sànchez-Marrè, M. 2009. Agents as a decision support tool in environmental processes: The state of the art. In *Advanced Agent-Based Environmental Management Systems*, Eds., U. Cortés and M. Poch, Whitestein Series in Software Agent Technologies and Autonomic Computing, 2009, pp. 5–35.

Baumann, P. 2010. The OGC web coverage processing service (WCPS) standard. *GeoInformatica*, 14(4), 447–479, DOI: 10.1007/s10707–009–0087–2.

Brooks, S. and Whalley, J. 2008. *Multilayer Hybrid Visualizations to Support 3D GIS*. Amsterdam, the Netherland: Elsevier.

Conti, G., De Amicis, R., Piffer, S. et al. 2010. Multi-level service infrastructure for geovisual analytics in the context of territorial management. *International Journal of Information Technologies and Systems Approach (IJITSA)*, 3, 57–71.

De Amicis, R., Conti, G., and Prandi, F. 2010. An integrated framework for spatio-temporal data management: The project BRISEIDE—Bridging services information and data for europe. In *Proceedings of WebMGS 2010—1st International Workshop on Pervasive Web Mapping, Geoprocessing and Services*, pp. 26–27, August 2010, Como, Italy.

De Amicis, R., Prandi, F., Conti, G., and Debiasi, A. 2011. Spatio-temporal services for spatial data and metadata in civil protection context. In *Proceeding of STDM 2011 The International Symposium on Spatial-Temporal Analysis and Data Mining*, London, U.K.

Dolk, D., Anderson, T., Busalacchi, F., and Tinsley, D. 2007. GINA: System interoperability for enabling smart mobile system services in network decision support systems. In *45th Hawaii International Conference on System Sciences*, pp. 1472–1481, Maui, Hawaii.

El-Harbawi, M., Mustapha, S., and Zulkifli, A. R. 2008. Air pollution modeling, simulation and computational methods: A review. In *IERT: International Conference on Environmental Research and Technology*, Penang, Malaysia.

Furnas, G. 1997. Effective view navigation. In *Proceedings of CHI*, pp. 367–374, New York: ACM Press.

Georgilakis, P. S. 2006. State-of-the-art of decision support systems for the choice of renewable energy sources for energy supply in isolated regions, *International Journal of Distributed Energy Resources*, 2(2), 129–150, April–June 2006.

Javed, Y., Norris, T., and Johnston, D. M. 2010. A design approach to an emergency decision support system for mass evacuation. In *7th International Conference on Information Systems for Crisis Response and Management (ISCRAM)*, pp. 1–6, Seattle, Washington. Available online at: http://www.iscram.org/ISCRAM2010/Papers/199-Javed_etal.pdf

Javed, Y., Norris, T., and Johnston, D. M., 2011a. Mass evacuation support system (MESS). Validating information requirements of emergency managers. In *7th International Conference on Information Technology and Applications (ICITA)*, pp. 249–254, Sydney, Australia.

Javed, Y., Norris, T., and Johnston, D. M., 2011b. Combining naturalistic and rational decision models for designing mass evacuation support system (MESS). In *Intellect International Consortium Academic Conference*, pp. 105–116, Sydney, Australia.

Javed, Y., Norris, T., Johnston, D. et al. 2011c. Towards a framework for crisis decision support systems: Information requirements for contextual team situation awareness. *CutterIT Journal: Special Issue on IT and Crisis Management*, 24(1), 26–33.

Kapler, T. and Wright, W. 2005. Geo time information visualization. *Information Visualization*, 4(2), 136–146.

MacEachren, A. M. 1994. Visualization in modern cartography: Setting the agenda. In *Visualization in Modern Cartography*, Eds., A. M. MacEachren and D. R. F. Taylor, New York: Elsevier Science Inc., pp. 1–12.

MacEachren, A. M. and Kraak, M.-J. 1997. Exploratory cartographic visualization: Advancing the agenda. *Computers and Geosciences*, 23(4), 335–344.

National Geospatial-Intelligence Agency. 2006. *In National System for Geospatial Intelligence (GEOINT) Basic Doctrine*, Publication 1–0. Available from: http://www.fas.org/irp/agency/nga/doctrine.pdf

Peng, Z.-R. and Tsou, M.-H. 2003. *Internet GIS: Distributed Geographic Information Services for the Internet and Wireless Network*. New York: John Wiley & Sons.

Stojanović, R., Škraba, A., Lekić, N. et al. 2011. Integration of system simulation and geographical information processing for the air-pollution emergency situations control and decision making. In *Advances in Simulation-Based Decision Support*, Vol. II, Eds., M. Kljajic and G. Lasker, pp. 31–35, Canada: The International Institute for Advanced Studies in Systems Research and Cybernetics, Awarded as the best paper.

Stojanović, R., Škraba, A., Berkowicz, S. M. et al. 2012. GEPSUS: Simulation-based decision making system for air pollution accidents. In *Organizacija—Thematic Issue on Recent Advances in Systems, Decision Making, Collaborative Work and Learning*, Vol. 45(5), Eds. Kljajić, M. and Weber, G.-W., pp. 200–211, Kranj, Slovenia: Moderna organizacija.

Ye, X., Wang, Y., Li, H., and Dai, Z. 2008. An emergency decision support system based on the general decision process. In *Proceedings of the 2008 IEEE/WIC/ACM International Conference on Web Intelligence and International Conference on Intelligent Agent Technology—Workshops*, December 9–12, 2008, Sydney, Australia.

Zhang, Z. and Li, Q. 2008. An open urban emergency decision support system. *International Archives of Photogrammetry Remote Sensing and Spatial Information Sciences*, 37(3), 1123–1128.

Chapter 16

Omnidirectional Human Intrusion Detection System Using Computer Vision Techniques

Wai Kit Wong, Chu Kiong Loo, and Way Soong Lim

Contents

16.1 Introduction

Homeland security is an effort by government (normally parked under national defense department) to prevent terrorist attack in a country and reduce a country's vulnerability to terrorism [1]. The scopes of homeland security on human trespasser do include the protection of a critical infrastructure's perimeter and the border security (country border of territorial land, water, and air space). Homeland threats refer to the crimes that have an immediate and visible impact on the local community and affect citizen quality of life. Illegal immigrants with unknown identity information in Department of Citizenship and Immigration database will flush out a peaceful and economically stable country as refugees, which might bringing in thefts, smugglers terrorists threat etc. issues. Therefore, national security department and convergent security engineers will have to develop strategies and security/surveillance system to fulfill the requirement of homeland security, on trespassers' threats. This chapter proposes some homeland security systems on human intruder detection.

Intrusion detection is the act of detecting a trespasser in a guard zone. Human intrusion detection system is a system used to detect human trespasser entering a prohibited area. Conventional human intrusion detection system uses burglar alarm system (active or passive sensors), whereby modern human intrusion detection system applies computer vision techniques, both to trace out whether there is an existence of a trespasser/human being or not in a prohibited area. The main merit of modern human intrusion detection system as compared to conventional human intrusion detection system is that the image processing–based human intrusion detection system can help capture pictures. Since pictures are captured, there are more chances of the intruders being recognized and caught. The authority can wisely place security cameras in every vulnerable place of the guarded area, indoor and outdoor, that would be accessible to a human intruder. This allows the authority to stay safe inside the premise while still being able to see what is happening in the outdoor area of the premise. It also gives them more time to call for help or backup if they notice any security threat.

In general, the modern computer vision technique–based human intrusion detection system can be divided into two main categories: one is vision spectrum–based human intrusion detection system and another one is night vision/infrared (IR) spectrum–based human intrusion detection system. Vision spectrum–based human intrusion detection system applies vision spectrum range imaging tools to capture images. One problem encountered in this type of surveillance system is the change in ambient light, especially in an outdoor environment where the lighting condition varies naturally. This makes the conventional digital color images analysis task in smart surveillance system become very difficult. One common approach to eliminate this problem is to train the system to compensate for any change in the illumination [2]. However, this is generally not enough for human intrusion in the dark. It is better to apply some sort of night vision imaging tool that helps in imaging objects in the dark. Then comes the application of IR spectrum–based human intrusion detection system. Thermal camera is an excellent night vision security camera. It perceives IR radiation and does not need a source of illumination. Thermal camera is ideal for any low-light areas, not just for the nighttime. It produces an image in the darkest of nights and can view through light fog, rain, and smoke. Thermal imaging cameras make small temperature differences visible. Thermal imaging cameras are currently applied widely in many new or existing security networks.

If a single imaging tool is to monitor a single angle of a location, then for more locations in different angles of view, more imaging tools are required. Hence, it will cost more, besides complicating the surveillance network. Therefore, an omnidirectional human intrusion detection system using minimum hardware is developed to overcome the cost and network complication problems. The method applied to obtain omnidirectional images can be classified into two approaches [3]: (1) mechanical approach and (2) optical approach. Since mechanical approach leads to many problems on discontinuity and inconsistency, therefore, optical approach was favored by practitioners.

The captured omnidirectional images normally have some different properties comparing to perspective images in terms of imaging deformation. Such distortion leads to the images being difficult to be directly implemented. Thus, it is necessary to work out an efficient method to unwarp the omni-image. Unwarping, generally, is a method used in digital image processing in "opening" up an omnidirectional image into a panoramic image, hence providing the observer and image processing tools a complete wide angle of view for the surveillance area surroundings and preserving fine output image quality in a higher data compression manner. Unwarping method is actively adopted in the application of visual surveillance systems. There are currently three unwarping methods actively practiced around the world, which are the pano-mapping table method [4], discrete geometry techniques (DGT) method [5], and log-polar mapping method [6]. This chapter studies the advantages and disadvantages of each method, and their performance is compared and evaluated.

Conventional surveillance system normally employs human observers to analyze the surveillance video. Sometimes this is more prone to error due to lapses in attention of the human observer [7]. It is a fact that a human's visual attention drops below acceptable levels when assigned to visual monitoring, and this fact holds true even for a trained personnel [8,9]. The weakness in conventional surveillance system has raised the need for a smart surveillance system where it employs computer and pattern recognition techniques to analyze information from situated imaging tools and automatically detect a trespasser [10]. Two automatic human intrusion detection algorithms are discussed in this chapter; this includes partitioned region of interest (ROI) algorithm [11] and human head curve test algorithm [12,13]. With the algorithms proposed in this chapter, it is simple to detect the human intrusion of more than one location in a single view captured by the imaging tool. These monitoring and subsequent analyses of the images from the inspection can alert security personnel to take further action to either catch or hustle the trespasser effectively.

In this chapter, the fundamentals of human intrusion detection system, classical burglar alarm system (active or passive sensor system) and radar system versus computer vision technique system, vision spectrum imaging versus IR imaging system, and directional versus omnidirectional viewing, are first discussed. The algorithm and implementation of some universal unwarping methods will be discussed too, such as discrete geometric transforms (DGTs) [4], pano-mapping table method [5], and log-polar mapping method [6] proposed in transforming the captured omnidirectional images into panoramic form, providing observer or image processing tools a wide angle of view. Besides that, automatic human intrusion detection is implemented in the omnidirectional imaging systems (both in vision spectrum and in IR spectrum, respectively). The developed human intrusion algorithms are partitioned ROI algorithm [11] and human head curve test algorithm [12,13], and their design procedures will be included here. Later, some experimental results to prove the algorithms proposed for the human intrusion detection system are shown. In the last section of this chapter, we summarize the work and envy some future enhancement.

16.2 Human Intruder Surveillance System

According to tort law, property law, and criminal law [14], a human intruder is a person who commits the act of trespassing/intruding on a prohibited area, that is, without the permission of the authority. A human intruder trespasses to a critical infrastructure's perimeter and the border security is defined as "an intentional interference with the infringe onto national security that proximately will cause injury, vandalism, terrorism, theft, etc." In U.K. jurisdictions, trespassing has been codified to clearly define the scope of the remedy, and in most jurisdictions, trespassing remains a purely common law remedy, the scope of which varies by jurisdiction. Surveillance is the monitoring of the activities, behavior, or other changing information, normally with people in a surreptitious manner and at the entrance of prohibited area. Surveillance is very useful to security authority to recognize and monitor threats and prevent criminal activity.

Human intruder surveillance system can be used to help security authority guard a critical infrastructure's perimeter and the border security. It is designed to detect an intrusion, activate a warning device upon detection of an intrusion, determine crime, protect life and property, bring an appropriate response to an emergency, and enhance the apprehension of criminals. Human intruder surveillance system can be divided into three main categories, which are the conventional burglar alarm system, the radar-based human intruder detection system, and the image processing–based human intruder detection system.

16.2.1 Burglar Alarm System

Burglar (or intrusion) alarm systems are electronic alarms designed to alert the user to a specific intruder. Detection sensors are connected to a control unit via a narrowband RF signal or low-voltage wiring that is used to communicate with a response device. New construction systems are predominately hardwired for efficient, more economical hardware installation. Refurbish construction often applies wireless systems for a faster, more economical channel installation, due to need not digging wall, ceiling, and floor for rewiring. Some systems serve a single purpose of either burglar or fire protection and some combination systems provide both fire and intrusion protections. Systems range from small, self-contained noisemakers to complicated, multi-zoned systems with color-coded computer monitor outputs. Many of these burglar alarm system concepts also apply to portable alarm systems for protecting motor vehicles (cars, trucks, busses, etc.) and their contents. Burglar alarm systems (or intrusion detection systems, perimeter detection systems, perimeter security systems, perimeter protection systems, and many more terms for the identical item) are divided into many types, such as passive IR (PIR) motion detector system, ultrasonic motion detector system, glass-break detector system, photoelectric beam system, vibration sensor system, passive magnetic field detection system, microphonic system, and taut wire perimeter security system. Each of these burglar alarm systems will be briefly illustrated in the following.

16.2.1.1 Passive Infrared Motion Detector System

A PIR sensor is an electronic sensor that measures IR light radiating from objects within its field of view. PIR sensors are often used in the construction of PIR-based motion detectors. The PIR-based motion detector is one of the most common detectors found in household and small business environments because it offers affordable and reliable functionality. The term "passive" means the detector is able to function without the need to generate and radiate its own energy. This is different from ultrasonic and microwave volumetric intrusion detectors in which they are "active" in operation. If an IR-emitting object exists in the coverage area, the PIR-based motion detector is able to identify by first learning the ambient temperature of the monitored space and then detecting a change in the temperature caused by the presence of that object. Applying the differentiation principle (creating individual zones of detection where each zone comprises one or more layers) can achieve differentiation. Between the zones, there are areas of no sensitivity (dead zones) that are used by the sensor for comparison, that is, a check of presence or non-presence; PIR-based motion detector can verify whether an intruder or object is actually in place.

In a PIR-based motion detector, the PIR sensor is typically mounted on a printed circuit board comprising the required electronics used to interpret the signals from the pyroelectric sensor chip [15]. The complete assemblage is confined within a housing attached in a site where the sensor can view the area to be monitored. IR energy is able to reach the pyroelectric sensor through the window because the plastic used is transparent to IR radiation but somehow translucent to visible light spectrum. This plastic sheet also inhibits the intrusion of dust and/or insects from obscuring the sensor's field of view and, in the case of insects, from generating false alarms. Some mechanisms have been used to concentrate the distant IR energy onto the sensor surface.

The PIR-based motion detector working as a human intruder detection system has the merits of simple and lower installation cost and less sensitive to illumination changes. However, PIR-based motion detector has these demerits when working as a human intruder detection system: (1) it can be easily triggered by moving animals, blowing shrubs, etc.; (2) it cannot detect people who are stationary, thus may lead to a large number of false alarms; (3) its output is highly bursty (some commercial off-the-shelf sensors use a heuristic solution to make up for this, by ignoring detections that fall within a refractory period of an earlier event. These issues are largely ignored by the vast majority of PIR-based research by limiting their system to single-person scenarios and/or assuming people are always moving); and (4) it does not tolerate large areas or large temperature changes.

16.2.1.2 Ultrasonic Motion Detector System

The transmitter of the ultrasonic detector is radiating an ultrasonic signal into the area under surveillance. The ultrasonic sound waves are reflected by solid objects (such as the surrounding walls, floor, and ceiling) and then detected by the receiver. Since ultrasonic waves are transmitted through air, the hard-surfaced objects tend to reflect most of the ultrasonic energy, while soft surfaces tend to absorb most energy. The received frequency will be equal to the transmitted frequency when the surfaces are stationary. However, a change in frequency will occur as a result of the Doppler principle, due to a person or object moving toward or away from the detector. This event will initiate an alarm signal.

In general, ultrasonic motion detector can be categorized into two types: active and passive. Active ultrasonic motion detector emits ultrasonic sounds that are inaudible to human ear (frequencies between 15 and 75 kHz). Passive ultrasonic motion detector consists of only receivers that simply receive the emitted sounds. As these devices are one of the most sensitive among the human intruder detection systems, they are also expensive in cost.

Ultrasonic motion detector systems utilize advanced technology, but somehow under some conditions, they are prone to false alarms by stuffs like passing birds or insects, gusts of wind, or vibrations caused by airplanes passing overhead. Passive ultrasonic motion detector systems do not provide complete detection in areas with large objects, thus creating a "dead" zone. Hence, in these cases, another type of detection system may be required to work together the ultrasound system as a second detector for more accurate alarm. Due to its poor effectiveness, this technology is considered obsolete by many alarm professionals and is not actively installed.

16.2.1.3 Glass-Break Detector System

A glass-break detector is a sensor used in electronic burglar alarm systems for detecting if there is a pane of glass shattered or broken. These detectors are commonly placed near glass doors or glass storefront windows to detect whether there is an intruder trying to break the glass and enter the premises. Glass-break detectors normally apply a microphone, which monitors any noise or vibrations coming from the glass. If the vibrations exceed a certain threshold (user selectable/preset), they are analyzed by detector circuitry. Simpler detectors just simply apply narrowband microphones that tuned to frequencies typical of glass shattering and react to sound above certain threshold, whereas more complex designs will compare the sound analysis to one or more glass-break profiles using signal transforms such as discrete cosine transform or fast Fourier transform and react if both the amplitude threshold and statistically expressed similarity threshold are breached.

The glass-break detector can be applied for internal perimeter building protection. When glass breaks, it actually creates sound in a wide band of frequencies ranging from infrasonic (below 20 Hz, this frequency range is inaudible to human ear) to the audio band (20 Hz to 20 kHz that is audible to human ear) right up to ultrasonic (which is above 20 kHz and again it falls in range inaudible to human ear). There are two types of glass-break detectors in general: glass-break acoustic detector and seismic glass-break detector. Glass-break acoustic detectors are mounted in close proximity to the glass panes and listen for sound frequencies associated with glass breaking. Seismic glass-break detectors are different in that they are installed on the glass pane. When glass breaks, it produces specific shock frequencies that travel through the glass and often through the window frame and the surrounding walls and ceiling. Typically, the most intense frequencies generated are between 3 and 5 kHz, depending on the type of glass and the presence of a plastic interlayer. Seismic glass-break detectors sense these shock frequencies and generate an alarm condition accordingly.

However, glass-break detectors can only be applied at limited areas, for example, building/premises with windows. Glass-break detectors are also sensitive to environmental effect, such as water spreading/rain, insects, birds, or object hitting windows (but window not clashing) and can sometimes generate false alarm.

16.2.1.4 Photoelectric Beam System

Photoelectric beam systems detect the presence of an intruder by transmitting visible or IR light beams across an area, where these beams may be obstructed. Photoelectric beam sensors transmit a beam of IR light to a remote receiver creating an "electronic fence." These sensors are often used to "cover" openings such as doorways or hallways, acting essentially as a trip wire. Once the beam is broken/interrupted, an alarm signal is generated. Photoelectric beam system consists of two main components: a transmitter and a receiver. The transmitter uses a light-emitting diode (LED) as a light source and transmits a consistent IR beam of light to a receiver. The receiver consists of a photoelectric cell that detects when the beam is present. If the photoelectric cell fails to receive at least 90% of the transmitted signal for as brief as 75 ms (time of an intruder crossing the beam), an alarm signal is generated.

The photoelectric beam system working as a trespasser detection system has the merits of easy installation and high immunity to ambient light, and its functionality is not affected by electrical and magnetic fields. However, photoelectric beam system has these demerits when considered to be worked as a trespasser detection system: (1) high installation cost with two devices having to be mounted, wired, and adjusted and (2) detection of very small objects; this may somehow lead to a large number of false alarms due to animals, passing objects blown by winds, or even passing insects triggering an alarm.

16.2.1.5 Vibration Sensor System

Vibration sensors rely on an unstable mechanical configuration that forms part of the electrical circuit. The working operation for vibration sensor is that when movement or vibration occurs, the unstable portion of the circuit moves and breaks the current flow; this leads to an alarm. The technology of the devices is varying and can be sensitive to different levels of vibration. The medium transmitting the vibration must be correctly selected for the specific sensors as they are best suited to different types of structures and configurations.

Vibration sensors are very reliable sensors. It generates low false alarm rate in trespasser detection system and moderate in price range. However, this type of detection system must always be fence mounted. Also, vibration sensors are a new technology with an unproven record as opposed to the mechanical sensor, which in some cases has a field record in excess of 20 years. That's why it is not widely seen in the market yet.

16.2.1.6 Passive Magnetic Field Detection System

This type of buried security system is based on the magnetic anomaly detection (MAD) principle of operation. The principle of the MAD is based on the ability to sense the anomaly in the Earth magnetic field produced by the target [16]. The system applies an electromagnetic field generator powered by two wires running in parallel. Both wires run along the perimeter and are usually installed about 5 in. apart on top of a wall or about 12 in./30 cm below ground. The wires are connected to a signal processor that analyzes any change in the magnetic field. Passive magnetic field detection system has very low false alarm rate. It can be put on top of any wall and has very high chance of detecting real burglars. However, it has high interference if it is installed near high-voltage lines or radars.

16.2.1.7 Microphonic Detection System

Microphonic-based detection systems have a variety of designs, but all are generally based on the detection of a trespasser attempting to cut or climb over a chain wire fence. The microphonic detection systems are usually installed as sensor cables attached to rigid chain wire fences. One example is the microphonic fence disturbance sensor system. Microphonic fence disturbance sensors apply the signals generated by the minute flexing of triboelectric coaxial sensor cable, which are analyzed by powerful signal processors to detect the sound associated with cutting, climbing, or lifting the fence structure. The systems can also be embedded with a special audio channel that enables securities to "listen" to activity along each zone of the fence for the protection of existing fences and structures against cutting, climbing, or lifting. They can also be fitted to coiled razor wire fences.

In operation, microphonic fence disturbance sensor systems are designed to detect and analyze incoming electronic signals received from the sensor cable and then to generate alarms from signals that exceed some preset conditions. The systems offer adjustable electronics to allow installers to change the sensitivity of the detectors' alarm to suit a specific environmental condition. The tuning of the system is normally accomplished before the detection devices are put in commissioning. Microphonic fence disturbance sensor systems are very cheap in cost, easy to install, and simple in configuration. However, these systems have a high rate of false alarms because some of these sensors might be too sensitive to extreme weather, contact by large animals, badly maintained fences, and overgrown vegetation.

16.2.1.8 Taut Wire Perimeter Security System

A taut wire perimeter security system is normally a stream of tensioned trip wires usually mounted on a wall or fence. It is particularly useful for detecting climbing (on top of a wall) or where it is necessary to build up a physical barrier (fence). This system is designed to detect any physical attempt to penetrate the barrier.

Taut wire perimeter security system can operate with a variety of detectors or switches that detect movement at each end of the tensioned wires. These detectors or switches can be an electronic strain gauge, a static force transducer, or a simple mechanical contact. False alarms caused by birds and animals can be avoided by tuning the detectors to omit objects that exert small amounts of pressure on the wires. However, this type of system is vulnerable to trespassers digging under the fence. Hence, a concrete footing is installed directly below the fence to prevent such trespassing. Taut wire perimeter security systems are having very reliable sensors, low rate of false alarms, and high rate of detection. However, this type of trespasser detection system is very expensive, it is complicated to install, and the technology is quite ancient.

In general, conventional burglar alarm systems are simple and lower in installation and maintenance cost. However, they have a lower probability of detecting human intruders and high false alarm rate. This is due largely to many uncontrollable factors, such as environmental issues (rain, ice, wind, standing water), random animals, and human activities, as well as other electronic interference sources.

16.2.2 Radar-Based Human Intruder Detection System

The second category of human intruder surveillance system is radar-based human intruder detection system. Radar is radio detection and ranging, which is an object detection system that applies radio waves to determine the range, attitude, direction, and speed of an object. In human intrusion detection system, radar can be used to detect human intruder. The radar dish or antenna transmits pulses of radio waves or microwave that will bounce off any object in their path. A radar's component consists of (1) a transmitter that generates the radio frequency signal with an oscillator and controls its duration by a modulator, (2) a waveguide that bonds the transmitter and antenna, (3) a duplexer that acts as the switch among the antenna and transmitter or the receiver for the signal when the antenna is used in both situations, (4) a receiver that knows the shape of the desired received signal (so-called pulse), and (5) an electronic section that controls all those devices and the antenna to perform the radar scan ordered by software.

For the working principles of radar, the transmitter will emit radio waves (radar signal) in predetermined directions. When these signals come in contact with an object, they usually reflect/ scatter in more than one direction. The radar signals are reflected back toward the transmitter. In human detection (moving object detection), if the object is moving either closer or farther away, there is a slight change in the frequency of the radio waves. Doppler radar is one of such common perimeter monitoring systems. However, this kind of radar system required the coverage area to be clear of foliage and obstacles that might create coverage shadows and false alarm. This requirement might not suit many outdoor environments, and even though in indoor usage, it might create undesirable installation and maintenance expenses. Also, slow-moving targets sometimes might not be detected on this radar system due to low-resolution detectable Doppler shift [17]. In Ref. [17], engineers are proving that the ultra-wideband (UWB) RF can overcome the deficiencies on conventional Doppler radar. Some other recent advanced radar systems also developed for homeland security included the Reutech Radar System [18] and the HARRIER Ground Surveillance Radar (GSR) [19].

Reutech Radar System developed and launched the Spider RSR 940 in July 2009. The figure of Spider RSR 940 is shown in Figure 16.1. It is a highly mobile land-based, 360° continuous

Figure 16.1   Spider RSR 940. (From Reutech radar systems. Homeland security, http://www.rrs. co.za/products/homeland-security.html)

Figure 16.2 HARRIER GSR. (From DeTect, Inc., Security and surveillance radar systems, http://www.detect-inc.com/security.html)

scanning surveillance radar that is capable of detecting surface and air targets. It also provides sector scanning surveillance used for detection and identification of slow-moving surface-based targets such as human beings, small boats, and even helicopters. In addition to the local control station, a remote control and monitoring capability is also provided for typical application including the border control operations, monitoring of coastal traffic, coastline control, and monitoring of private and unattended airfield. The radar system has an instrumented range up to 40 km. On the other hand, DeTect's radar processing technology developed the HARRIER GSR in year 2011, as shown in Figure 16.2. HARRIER GSR uses state-of-the-art solid-state Doppler radar technology available in S-, X-, and combined S/X-band radar frequencies. Solid-state radar technology applied in HARRIER GSR offers significant increased performance, longer useful life, and lower maintenance cost over conventional magnetron-based systems. HARRIER GSR uses high-speed scanning for enhanced small target detection in high-clutter environments such as developed areas, terrain, and high sea states. It also has automatic detection and tracking capabilities and includes user-defined monitoring and alarm zones. HARRIER GSR is offered in fixed and mobile configurations and can be linearly networked to cover large areas such as border crossings and coastlines.

In general, radar-based human intruder detection system is expensive in hardware, since radar antennas (transmitter and receiver), duplexer, waveguides, and electronic tools are required to be set up, and it also requires specific operating software. Besides, the target might be detected by the radar, but their type or class is not known. It can be sometimes vehicles, animals, or moving objects, which give false alarm. Also, some narrowband radars might sometimes find difficulties in having insufficient range resolution to discriminate between a smaller nearby target and a larger longer-range target.

16.2.3 Image Processing–Based Human Intruder Detection System

The third category of human intruder surveillance system is image processing–based human intruder detection system. It is by means of using image to trace out whether there is an existence of trespasser/human intruder or not. Image processing–based human intruder detection system is widely favored by many practitioners as compared to burglar alarm systems and radar-based human intruder detection system, mainly due to these four reasons:

1. It helps capture pictures. The applied security camera is a great tool to capture a picture of the burglar/terrorist when they are trying to trespass/break into a prohibited territory. This is very important because the security camera gives the authorities something that they can use to help them identify the burglar/terrorist. Having a security system that triggers an alarm is essential, but without security cameras, the authorities will never know who or how many burglars/terrorists tried to get into their territory.

2. More chance of the burglars/terrorists being caught. When the authorities are able to view the pictures from the cameras to identify the burglars/terrorists, it provides higher possible rate for the burglars/terrorists to get caught. In many occasions when authorities arrive at their incident site, the burglars/terrorists will be long gone. Without the captured pictures, there is not much chance for the burglars/terrorists being caught.

3. Security cameras are great prevention tools. They are something that all burglars/terrorists will look through before they decide to break into/trespass a territory. Most of the burglars/terrorists will not even attempt a territory if they detect the existence of security cameras because they know that this is going to work against them and cause them to get caught. Burglars/terrorists are known for avoiding territory that has good security, especially the ones that are monitored with security cameras. The cameras pose too big of a threat for them, so they will move on to a target that doesn't have good security.

4. Security cameras can secure vulnerable areas. When authority is inside the infrastructure's perimeter and needs to see what is happening outside of the nearby building for security, security cameras are the best way to achieve that goal safely. The authority can wisely place security cameras in every vulnerable area of his or her building, indoors and outdoors, that would be accessible by a burglar/terrorist. This allows the authority to stay safe inside his or her building with his or her protected person while still being able to see what is happening in the outdoor area of the building. It also gives them more time to seek for help if they notice any security threat.

In general, the image processing–based trespasser detection system can be divided into two main categories: one is vision spectrum image processing–based human intruder detection system and another one is night vision/IR spectrum image processing–based human intruder detection system.

16.2.3.1 Vision Spectrum Image Processing–Based Human Intruder Detection System

Vision spectrum image processing–based human intruder detection system can be divided into two categories: one is analog video surveillance system and the other is the digital video surveillance system.

16.2.3.1.1 Analog Video Surveillance System

Dating back to as early as 1965, analog video surveillance was first begun with simple closed circuit television (CCTV) monitoring. The U.S. press reports suggesting police already start using surveillance cameras in monitoring public places' security. In 1969, police installed sets of surveillance cameras in New York City at the municipal building near the city hall. This practice later spreads to other cities in the United States with CCTV systems and watch by police officers at all times. CCTV is the application of video cameras to send image signal to a specific location, on a limited set of monitors. The first CCTV applied in public places was crude, conspicuous, low definition, and in black and white systems that are unable to pan or zoom into particular view. In modern days, CCTV systems apply smaller-size and high-definition color video cameras that can focus to resolve minute detail and also can link the control of the video cameras to a computer. This makes the objects to be tracked semiautomatically. This technology, the so-called video content analysis (VCA), is currently used by a large number of technological companies around the world to enable the systems to recognize whether a moving object is a walking person, a crawling person, an animal, a vehicle, etc.

However, in the mid-1990s, the emerging of digital technology has superseded the analog technology in video surveillance system. Digital makes video surveillance clearer, faster, and more efficient. Digital video surveillance has made complete sense as the price of digital recording dropped with the computer revolution. Instead of changing analog videotapes daily, the digital users could now reliably record a month's worth of surveillance contents on hard drive because of its high compression capability and lower storage cost. The digitally recorded images are so much clearer than the analog-recorded images. This leads to the recognition process immediately improving for police, private investigators, and other users that use video surveillance for identification purposes. By using digital technology, the images could also be manipulated to further improve clarity by adding light, enhancing the image, zooming in on frames, etc.

16.2.3.1.2 Digital Video Surveillance System

Digital technology is a data technology that uses discrete values [20]. Digital video is a type of video recording system applying digital technology. There is a broad range of digital video surveillance cameras available in the market:

- *Fake security cameras*: These cameras look similar to those surveillance cameras available in the market, but they are not actual cameras. They have no recording capability. These cameras can act as deterrent cameras to scare burglars/theft. If something happens, they will not have a record since they have no recoding capability.
- *Covert surveillance cameras*: These cameras look like regular items, to hide its identity as a surveillance camera, for example, a wall clock in a shop, a facing front door teddy bear, and a potted plant at the shop's corner. Each one of them could very easily embed a surveillance camera. The surveillance cameras can record the scenes anytime without anybody knowing its existence.
- *Wireless security digital cameras*: These surveillance cameras are easy to install and removed, are often small in size, have no wiring connection seen, and offer more flexibility in setup. These cameras transmit image signals wirelessly to a center hub that are shown on a monitor screen in a monitoring room.
- *Wired surveillance digital cameras*: These surveillance cameras are wired and lack flexibility in setup. They are appropriate for permanent setup. These cameras transmit image signals through a wire to a center hub that are shown on a monitor screen in a monitoring room.
- *Home surveillance cameras*: These cameras come in a package that often includes some extra features such as timers for lamps, motion sensors, and automatic gate door lock.

One problem encountered in most vision spectrum image processing–based surveillance systems is the change in ambient light, especially in an outdoor environment where the lighting condition varies naturally. This makes the conventional digital color image analysis task in smart surveillance very difficult. One common approach to alleviate this problem is to train the system to compensate for any change in the illumination [2]. However, this is generally not enough for a trespasser in the dark. It is better to apply some sort of night vision imaging tools that can help imaging objects in the dark.

16.2.3.2 Night Vision/Infrared Spectrum Image Processing–Based Trespasser Detection System

Night vision is the ability to see in a dark environment. Night vision is made possible by a combination of two approaches: (1) sufficient spectral range and (2) sufficient intensity range. Human beings have poor night vision ability compared to many animals because human eyes lack an element, so-called the tapetum lucidum. The tapetum lucidum [2] is a layer of tissue in the eye of many vertebrate animals, which lies immediately behind or sometimes within the retina. It reflects visible light back through the retina, increasing the light available to the photoreceptors. This improves vision in low-light conditions but can cause the perceived image to be blurry from the interference of the reflected light. The tapetum lucidum contributes to the superior night vision of some animals. Many of these animals are nocturnal, especially carnivores that hunt the organism at night, while others are deep sea animals.

Thermal camera is an excellent night vision security camera. It perceives IR radiation and does not need a source of illumination. Thermal camera is ideal for any low-light areas, not just for the nighttime. It produces an image in the darkest of nights and can view through light fog, rain, and smoke. Thermal imaging cameras make small temperature differences visible. Thermal imaging cameras are currently applied widely in many new or existing security networks.

16.2.4 Directional versus Omnidirectional Viewing

In spite of the availability of many modern sophisticated surveillance monitoring products in the market, majority of the systems have the limitation in the viewing angle of the camera. Omnidirectional prompts to the concept of the existence in all direction, with 360° area coverage on a single plane/axis. In imaging point of view, an omnidirectional visualization has visualization capability of a 360° field of view around the horizontal plane or with visual field that covers the entire sphere. Omnidirectional visualization system is important in areas that need large visual field coverage, such as in panoramic imaging and in robotics. A conventional imaging tool normally has a field of view with the range of a few degrees to maximum of 180°. It can capture only a semisphere image with light falling onto the imaging tool's focal point. However, on the other hand, an omnidirectional imaging tool can capture light from all directions (surrounded 360° field of view) falling onto its focal point, covering a full sphere.

Convergent security systems are security systems that integrate intrusion, holdup, fire, video surveillance, access control, and monitoring applications in physical security systems and IT infrastructures. However, the current convergent security systems apply digital CCTV monitoring systems, in which the coverage area is directional. Even they can do it in omnidirectional, but it requires more hardware. Conventional approaches to obtain panoramic (wide view) image for an omnidirectional view mainly consist of combining snapshots captured separately into a single and continuous image. This combination of images is computationally intensive sometimes. An example is by using a RANSAC iterative algorithm [21] to combine the snapshots. RANSAC is an abbreviation for "RANdom Sample Consensus." This algorithm was first published by Fischler and Boller in 1981 and found to be used in solving the corresponding problem (parts of an image correspond to parts of another image; after the imaging tool has moved, time has elapsed or the focusing objects moved around) and calculates the fundamental matrix corresponding to a pair of stereo imaging tools. RANSAC can estimate the parameters with a high degree of accuracy but with limitation that there is no upper bound on the time it takes to compute these parameters. To process an image, it is sometimes time consuming or endless. Even if an upper time bound is used (set with a maximum number of iterations), the results obtained may not be the optimal one. It may not be one that generates the image in a good way.

Besides computational intensive, the combining of images to form a panoramic image also depends on the quality and consistency of the snapshots used. The snapshot images might have a number of deficiencies that will further impair the quality of the output panoramic image. In comparison, an omnidirectional imaging tool can be used to create real-time panoramic art, without post-processing requirement, and somehow will provide much better output quality image.

In robotics and computer vision, omnidirectional imaging tools are widely used in visual odometry [22] and also help solve the simultaneous localization and mapping (SLAM) [23] problems visually. Visual odometry is the process of defining the position and orientation of a robot by analyzing the captured images from the attached imaging tools, whereas SLAM is a technique applied by autonomous vehicles and mobile robots to form a map within an unknown environment or to update a map within a known environment and in the meantime keep on tracking their current location. Due to the omnidirectional visualization's ability to obtain a 360° view, robotic and computer vision tasks can have better results for optical flow and in feature selection and matching.

Besides panoramic art, robotics, and computer vision, application of omnidirectional visualization also includes surveillance, in which it is important to cover a large visual field, and teleconferencing, in which it is of great interest to cover as many participants as possible in the same image, and yet there are unlimited applications that will be discovered in the future soon. Next section will further discuss the methods applied to acquire omnidirectional views.

16.2.4.1 Optical Approach versus Mechanical Approach

Omnidirectional visualization possesses significant application potentials in the areas such as panoramic art, mobile robot navigation and computer vision, quality control, and surveillance. The methods applied to obtain omnidirectional images can be classified into two approaches [3]:

1. *Mechanical approach*: The method of gathering images to generate an omnidirectional image
2. *Optical approach*: The method of capturing an omnidirectional image at once

In addition, they are classified into two categories by the viewpoint of the image [3]: single viewpoint and multiple viewpoints.

For the mechanical approach, the images captured on a single viewpoint are continuous. One example is the rotating camera system [24–27]. In such a system, the camera rotates around the center of the projection. It generates an omnidirectional image from a single viewpoint. The proper order of images obtained by rotation is joined together to acquire a panoramic view for the scene. An example of rotating camera is shown in Figure 16.3. A rotating motor is required to rotate the video camera in order to scan the omnidirectional view. However, since it is necessary to rotate a video camera in a full circle in order to acquire a single omnidirectional image, it is impossible to generate real-time omnidirectional image. Other disadvantages of rotating camera system are that it requires the use of moving parts and precise positioning. The image captured

Figure 16.3 Rotating camera. (From Stun-ningsales.com, Weatherproof CCD color rotating video security camera, redirecting from http://www.stun-ningsales.com/homethings/outdoor_securitycameras.htm)

at multiple viewpoints is relatively easy to construct, as shown in Figure 16.4. A single camera or many cameras are applied to gather multiple images at multiple viewpoints and combine them into an omnidirectional image. QuickTime VR system [28] adopted such technologies and has many market applications. However, the images generated by the system are not always continuous and consistent, and it also cannot capture the dynamic scene at video rate.

Since mechanical approach leads to many problems on discontinuity and inconsistency, optical approach was in use. This approach is most appropriate for real-time applications and it is of single viewpoint. This type of approach need not use motors and in the meantime it can capture omnidirectional image at once, no extra combination work required, and it is fast. Two alternatives have been proposed, namely, the use of special-purpose lens (such as the fish-eye lens [29]) and the use of hyperbolic optical mirrors [30]. Fish-eye lens, as shown in Figure 16.5, are used to replace a conventional camera lens that have very short focal length that allows the camera to view objects as much as in a hemisphere scene. Fish-eye lens have been widely used for wide-angle imaging areas as noted in Refs. [31,32]. However, Nalwa's works in Ref. [33] found out that it is difficult to design fish-eye lens that ensure that all incoming principal rays intersect at a single point to yield a fixed viewpoint. The acquired image using fish-eye lens normally does not permit the construction of distortion-free perspective images of the viewed scene. Hence, to capture an omnidirectional view, the design of optimal fish-eye lens must be quite complex and large, and therefore, they are expensive in cost. Besides, according to Ref. [34], the relative illumination for a fish-eye lens design is widely varying. In addition, the existences of distortion across the hemispherical field of view need to be in consideration when designing a good quality fish-eye lens. Since fish-eye lens are expensive and complex in design and almost provide the same reflective quality as hyperbolic optical mirror, hyperbolic optical approach is planned to adapt.

Figure 16.4 Multiple cameras system. (From Chen, S.E., Quick time VR: An image-based approach to virtual environment navigation, in *Proceedings of the 22nd Annual ACM Conference on Computer Graphics*, Los Angeles, CA, pp. 29–38, 1995.)

Figure 16.5 Fish-eye lens. (From MIR Web Development Team, Fisheye lenses and their optical properties, http://www.mir.com.my/rb/photography/companies/nikon/nikkoresources/fisheyes/)

16.2.4.2 Vision Spectrum–Based Omnidirectional Surveillance System

The proposed vision spectrum–based omnidirectional surveillance system model is shown in Figure 16.6.

In this model, omnidirectional images of an observed scene are captured using the combination of a web camera (webcam) and a specific design hyperbolic optical mirror. MATLAB® in the laptop computer will perform unwarping on the images captured into panoramic form. The human intruder detection algorithm that is programmed in MATLAB will then be used to process the panoramic images to detect the presence of human intruder. If human intruder is detected, alarm will be signaled and portions of suspected image with human intruder will be stored in a database for further identification purposes.

The surveillance camera set used in this surveillance system consists of a web camera and an attached specific design hyperbolic optical mirror as shown in Figure 16.7.

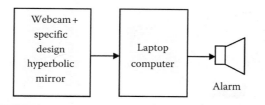

Figure 16.6 **Omnidirectional surveillance system model.**

Figure 16.7 **Surveillance camera set (web camera and specific design hyperbolic optical mirror).**

Figure 16.8 Front view of the custom-made bracket.

The web camera used in the surveillance system is E3500 Plus QuickCam by Logitech. It is a domestic web camera that captures high-quality VGA (640×480) videos and 1.3 megapixel (software-enhanced) images. The web camera is small in size and cheap compared to digital and CCTV camera with fine-resolution output. The digital control is also accomplished through the USB port connected to a laptop or personal computer (PC) via plug and play on Windows XP or Vista. It can be interfaced with MATLAB too. Therefore, it is best outfitted in omnidirectional surveillance system.

The specific design hyperbolic optical mirror used in the omnidirectional surveillance system is a small-size wide-view type, with outer diameter of 40 mm and angle of view 30° above horizontal plane manufactured by ACCOWLE VISION. The mirror can reflect a 360° view surrounded by itself, and as the web camera plugs on it, omnidirectional images within a guarded perimeter can be captured and sent to a laptop computer in a monitoring room to be processed for surveillance purpose. A custom-made bracket that is shown in Figure 16.8 is designed to attach the hyperbolic mirror to the web camera via a socket.

A laptop computer can be used for image processing of an observed room. A core 2 duo laptop computer with specs 1.83 GHz processor and 2 GB DDR2 RAM with MATLAB ver. 7.0 is chosen to be used here. MATLAB has a data acquisition toolbox interface that enables attainment of videos and images through the E3500 Plus QuickCam. A set of connecting speakers to the laptop computer sound the alarm if human intruder is detected.

16.2.4.3 Thermal/Infrared Spectrum–Based Omnidirectional Surveillance System

One problem encountered in most surveillance systems is the change in ambient light, especially in outdoor environment where the lighting condition is naturally varying. This makes the video analysis task in smart surveillance very difficult. One common approach to alleviate this problem is to train the system to compensate for any change in the illumination. However, this is generally not enough for object tracking and monitoring in the dark. In recent times, several manufacturers have come up with highly sophisticated thermal camera for imaging objects in the dark. The camera uses IR sensors that capture IR coming from different objects in the surrounding and

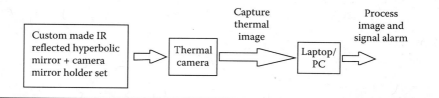

Figure 16.9 Omnidirectional thermal imaging surveillance system model.

form an IR image. Since IR radiation from an object is due to the thermal radiation, the image formation will depend on the object temperature and not on the light reflected from the object. Hence, such camera can be conveniently used for night vision. The present state of the art even allows thermal camera to capture object even from a very long distance.

If a single thermal camera is to monitor the security of a single location, then for more locations in different angles of view, more thermal cameras are required. Hence, it will cost more, besides complicating the surveillance network. The proposed thermal/IR spectrum–based omnidirectional surveillance system model is shown in Figure 16.9. This system requires a custom-made IR-reflected hyperbolic mirror, a camera mirror holder, a fine-resolution thermal camera and a laptop or PC installed with MATLAB programming (version R2007b or later), and an alarm signaling system. The alarm signaling system can be as simple as a computer's speaker.

The best shape of practical use omnidirectional mirror is hyperbolic. As derived by Chahl and Srinivasan in Ref. [37], all the polynomial mirror shapes (conical, spherical, parabolic, etc.) do not provide a central perspective projection, except for the hyperbolic one. They also show that the hyperbolic mirror guarantees a linear mapping between the angle of elevation θ and the radial distance from the center of the image plane ρ. Another advantage of hyperbolic mirror is when using it with a camera/imager of homogenous pixel density, the resolution in the omnidirectional image captured is also increasing with growing eccentricity, and hence, it will guarantee a uniform resolution for the panoramic image after unwarping.

The research group of OMNIVIEWS project from Czech Technical University further developed MATLAB software for designing omnidirectional mirror [38]. From the MATLAB software, omnidirectional hyperbolic mirror can be designed by inputting some parameters that specify the mirror dimension. The first parameter is the focal length of the camera f, in which for the thermal camera in use is 12.5 mm and the distance d (ρz plane) from the origin is set to 2 m. The image plane height h is set to 20 cm. The radius of the mirror rim is chosen t1 = 3.6 cm as modified from Svoboda's work in Ref. [39], with radius for fovea region 0.6 cm and retina region 3.0 cm. Fovea angle is set between 0° and 45°, whereas retina angle is from 45° to 135°. The coordinates as well as the plot of the mirror shape are generated using MATLAB and shown in Figure 16.10. The coordinates as well as mechanical drawing using AutoCAD are provided to precision engineering company to fabricate/ custom made the hyperbolic mirror. The hyperbolic mirror is milled from aluminum bar and then chromed. Chromium is of great interest because of its lustrous (good in IR reflection) property, high corrosion resistance, high melting point, and hardness. The fabricated mirror is shown in Figure 16.11.

The camera mirror holder is self-designed and custom made with aluminum material as shown in Figure 16.12. The thermal camera used is an affordable and accurate temperature measurement mode: ThermoVision A-20M is manufactured by FLIR Systems. The thermal camera has a temperature sensitivity of 0.10 ranging from –20°C to 350°C. However, for human detection, the temperature range is set to range from 30°C to 40°C. The thermal camera can capture thermal images with fine resolution up to 320 × 240 pixels offering more than 76,000 individual measurement points

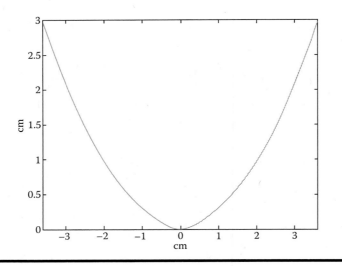

Figure 16.10 Mirror coordinates plot in MATLAB.

Figure 16.11 Fabricated mirror.

per image at a refresh rate of 50/60 Hz. The A-20M features a choice of connectivity options. For fast image and data transfer of real-time fully radiometric 16 bit images, an IEEE-1394 FireWire digital output can be chosen. For network and/or multiple camera installations, Ethernet connectivity is also available. Each A-20M can be equipped with its own unique URL allowing it to be addressed independently via its Ethernet connection, and it can be linked together with a router to form a network. Therefore, it is best outfitted for human intruder detection.

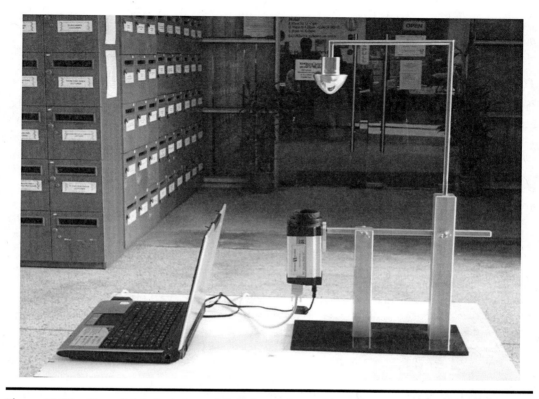

Figure 16.12 Overall fabricated omnidirectional thermal imaging surveillance system model.

A problem encountered in thermal camera selection is the existence of the haloing effect in uncalibrated ferroelectric barium strontium titanate (BST) sensors. Haloing effect is the presence of halos around objects having a high thermal contrast with the background [40]. A-20M is chosen because it uses the uncooled microbolometer FPA detector technology that does not produce the haloing effect. A laptop or PC can be used as image processor, placed either on site or in a monitoring room. MATLAB version R2007b programming is chosen to be used because it has user-friendly software for performing log-polar mapping technique to unwarp the omnidirectional thermal image into panoramic form and it can partition the panoramic thermal images easily according to each single location to be monitored and process with the trespasser and faint detection algorithm. The alarm will be triggered once a human being is detected in a tested image for human intruder detection mode. The overall fabricated system model is shown in Figure 16.12.

16.3 Unwarping Methods

The captured omnidirectional images have different properties compared to perspective images in terms of imaging deformation. Such distortion leads to the images being difficult to be directly implemented. Thus, it is necessary to work out an efficient method to unwarp the omni-image. Unwarping, generally, is a method used in digital image processing in "opening" up an omnidirectional image into a panoramic image, making the information on the image be able to be directly implemented and understood. This subsection studies three universal unwarping methods that are currently applied actively around the world in transforming omnidirectional image to panoramic image, namely, the DGT method [4], the pano-mapping table method [5], and the log-polar mapping method [6].

16.3.1 Discrete Geometry Technique Method

DGT method, by the name itself, means that this technique is used by applying one by one the geometry of the image, discretely, in order to successfully unwarp the omnidirectional image into a panoramic image. This method is practically used in transforming the omnidirectional images into panoramic images on a cylindrical surface using PDE-based resampling models [4].

In DGT method, it is required to perform the calculation of each and every pixel in the omni-image first and then check for its corresponding radius from the center of the omnidirectional image and later determine whether it should be considered or not. The calculations start from a fixed position and direction, such as from the right going counterclockwise for 360°. For a radius of 1, a circle of radius 1 will be visualized in the center of omnidirectional image, which in other words means that the circle will be in size of 3 × 3 pixels. All the pixels in this boundary of 3 × 3 pixels will be considered, and their corresponding radius will be calculated. All pixels that fall within the radius of 1, which is the radius of concern, will be considered in the conversion. Due to the pixels that are generally an area of data information, it is possible that the circle will lie in between the pixels. Therefore, a tolerance of ±½ radius is set to counter this problem. In other words, a circle of radius 1 will consider the pixels lying between radius of 0.5 and 1.4, and a circle of radius 2 will consider the pixels lying between radius of 1.5 and 2.4, and so on. An example is shown in Figure 16.13.

As soon as a pixel in the boundary is deemed to be considered or in range of the radius, it will be mapped into a new matrix of panoramic image. However, since the pixels mapped into the panoramic image must be in order so that the image will not be distorted, the image will be split into four sections of 90° each, as shown in Figure 16.14, where each section will perform the calculation based on the moving direction of the circle. For example, for a circle drawn, starting from the right in a counterclockwise direction, the pixels in the section at the upper right part will be taken and calculated one by one, from the bottom part of the section and from right to left, which will then be increased one by one, till the upper part of the section, from right to left as well. On the other hand, for the lower left part of the section, the calculation will go from the top of the section, going from left to right.

However, due to the pixels being considered for different circles of different radii that will be nonuniform, as shown in Figure 16.15, a resampling process is needed to standardize the pixels in every row of the panoramic image. Therefore, after every pixel in the whole omni-image is mapped

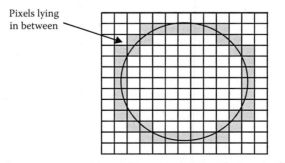

Figure 16.13 Circle lying in between pixels.

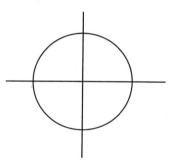

Figure 16.14   Circle being split into four sections.

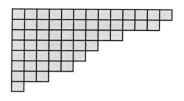

Figure 16.15   Nonuniform resolution of panoramic image.

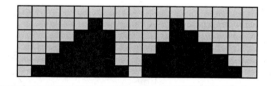

Figure 16.16   Spacing inserted in between pixels, denoted by black dots.

onto the panoramic image plane, spacing will be inserted in between pixels in every row (as shown in Figure 16.16) in order to standardize the resolution of the panoramic image for each row. This will generate a standard resolution of panoramic image. However, due to spacing that is generally empty pixels with no data information, a row with very little pixels will be hardly understandable. Therefore, the pixels will be duplicated over the spacing, instead of inserting empty pixels into it, and an understandable uniform resolution panoramic image can be generated.

16.3.2 Pano-Mapping Table Method

This method uses a table, which is so-called the pano-mapping table, to process the image conversion. Pano-mapping table will be created "once and for all," consisting of many coordinates corresponding to the coordinates taken from the omnidirectional image that will then be mapped into a new panoramic image, respectively. It is practically used in omnidirectional visual tracking [41] and the unwarping process of omni-images taken by almost any kind of omni-cameras prior to requiring any knowledge about the camera parameters in advance, as proposed by Jeng and Tsai [5] and Wu and Tsai [42].

In pano-mapping table method, it is required to select five landmark points from the omni-directional image first. These points will be taken from the same line, drawing from the center of the omni-image to the circumference of the image, which in other words is called the radius of the image. Five points in between the end of this line will be picked, and the value corresponding to their radius from the center is obtained. It is then used in order to obtain the five coefficients of a_0 through a_4 in the "radial stretching function," $f_r(\rho)$, described by the following 4th-degree polynomial function of

$$r = f_r(\rho) = a_0 + a_1\rho_1 + a_2\rho_2 + a_3\rho_3 + a_4\rho_4 \qquad (16.1)$$

where
    r corresponds to the radius
    ρ is the particular radius for the each of the five points taken
    a_0–a_4 are five coefficients to be estimated using the values obtained from the landmark points

Once the five coefficients are obtained, the pano-mapping table, T_{MN}, can then be generated. The size of the table will first be determined manually, by setting it to a table of size $M \times N$. Hence, in order to fill up a table with $M \times N$ entries, the landmark point ρ, which corresponds to the radius of the omnidirectional image, will be divided into M separated parts, and the angle θ will be divided into N parts as follows:

$$\rho_{ij} = \frac{i \times radius}{M} \qquad (16.2)$$

$$\theta_{ij} = \frac{j \times 360°}{N} \qquad (16.3)$$

and the calculation will be processed, by taking the first point where $i = 1$ and $j = 1$, which gives $\rho_{11} = radius/M$ and $\theta_{11} = 360°/N$. The value of ρ_{ij} will then be substituted into the "radial stretching function" in order to obtain the particular radius at that particular landmark point. This radius obtained will then be substituted into the equation as follows to be rounded up, in order to get the corresponding coordinates in the omnidirectional image:

$$v = r \cos\theta \qquad (16.4)$$

$$u = r \sin\theta \qquad (16.5)$$

where v and u correspond to the x- and y-coordinates of the omnidirectional image. This coordinate (u,v) obtained is inserted into the pano-mapping table $T_{MN} = T_{ij}$. The u and v will then be processed for N times by increasing j for N times to obtain different angles, θ, to later determine all the coordinates corresponding to the value of landmark point. These coordinates obtained are inserted into the table of $i = 1$ with their corresponding $j = 1$ to $j = N$, and the i will then be increased by 1, and the process is repeated for $j = 1$ to $j = N$ to determine all coordinates related to $i = 2$. This i will be repeated for M times, and a table of $M \times N$ entries with all the coordinates can be generated. The coordinates in each of the entries are taken one by one, in order to map each and every pixel in the omnidirectional image with the coordinate in the current entry, into a new panoramic image. The conversion is completed upon the end of mapping of the table.

16.3.3 Log-Polar Mapping Method

Log-polar mapping is a type of spatially variant image representation whereby pixel separations increase linearly with distance. It enables the concentration of computational resource on an ROI as well as maintaining the information from a wider view. This method is implemented by applying log-polar geometry representations. The captured omnidirectional image will first be sampled by spatially variant grid from a Cartesian form into a log-polar form. The spatially variant grid representing log-polar mapping will then be formed by i number of concentric circles with N number of samples, and the omnidirectional image will then be unwarped into a panoramic image in another Cartesian form.

This method is practically used in robust image registration [43], or in robotic vision, particularly in visual attention, target tracking, egomotion estimation, and 3D perception [44], as well as in vision-based navigation, environmental representations, and imaging geometries [45], by José Santos-Victor and Alexandre Bernardino. In log-polar mapping method, the center pixel for log-polar sampling is calculated by

$$\rho(x_i, y_i) = \sqrt{(x_i - x_c)^2 + (y_i - y_c)^2} \tag{16.6}$$

$$\theta(x_i, y_i) = \left(\frac{N}{2\pi}\right) \tan^{-1} \frac{y_i - y_c}{x_i - x_c} \tag{16.7}$$

and the center pixel for log-polar mapping is calculated by

$$x_o(\rho, \theta) = \rho \cos\theta + x_c \tag{16.8}$$

$$y_o(\rho, \theta) = \rho \sin\theta + y_c \tag{16.9}$$

where
  x_c, y_c are the center points of our original Cartesian form coordinate
  N is the number of samples in each and every concentric circle taken

The original (x_i, y_i) in Cartesian form is sampled into log-polar coordinate of (ρ, θ), as shown in Figure 16.17. The center point is calculated by using (16.6) and (16.7) to get the respective ρ and θ, which cover a region of the original Cartesian pixels of radius:

$$r_n = br_{n-1} \tag{16.10}$$

and

$$b = \frac{N + \pi}{N - \pi} \tag{16.11}$$

where
  r is the sampling circle radius
  b is the ratio between two apparent sampling circles

Figure 16.18 shows the circular sampling structure and the unwarping process done by using the log-polar mapping method [43]. The mean value of pixels within each and every circular sampling

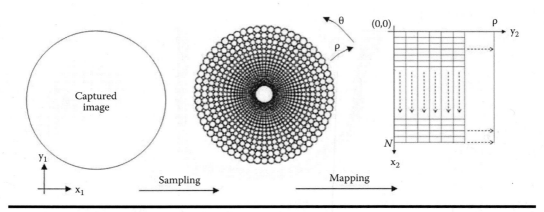

Figure 16.17   Process of log-polar mapping.

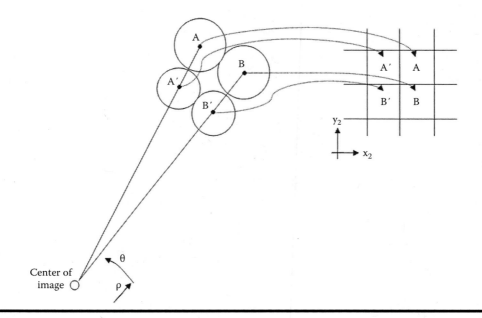

Figure 16.18   Circular sampling structure and the unwarping process.

is calculated and will be assigned to the center point of the circular sampling. The process will then continue by mapping the mean value at log-polar pixel (ρ,θ) into another Cartesian form using Equations 16.8 and 16.9, and the unwarping is done at the end of mapping.

16.3.4 Performance Evaluation

This subsection reports the performance evaluation for different unwarping methods. Few important factors are selected for the performance evaluation of the unwarping methods. These factors include resolution of the image generated, quality of image, algorithm used in perform-

Figure 16.19 Performance evaluation (a-1, a-2). Samples of omnidirectional images (b-1, b-2). Panoramic images generated using DGT method (c-1, c-2). Panoramic images generated using pano-mapping table method (d-1, d-2). Panoramic images generated using log-polar method.

ing the unwarping process, complexity, processing time, and data compression. Some captured omnidirectional images as shown in Figure 16.19 will be used to test the unwarping methods.

1. *Resolution of the image generated*: The resolution of each generated panoramic image using log-polar mapping method, DGTs, and pano-mapping table method is discussed in this subsection. The log-polar mapping method provides smaller resolution of dimension that equals to 1/4-fold of the omnidirectional image, whereas for the DGT method and pano-mapping table method, the resolution of the panoramic image produced can be as large as the length of the perimeter of the omnidirectional image, with the width equals to the radius of the omnidirectional image. However, due to the images being rescaled for viewing purposes, the difference is not obvious in this chapter.
2. *Quality of image*: Since the images are rescaled, the difference in quality is not apparent as well. However, pano-mapping table method is found to produce the highest quality of image, followed by the log-polar mapping method, and the DGT method correspondingly in descendent quality order.

3. *Algorithm used in performing the unwarping process*: In log-polar mapping algorithm, the omnidirectional image is considered in the form of a number of sectors in which each sector consists of a group of pixels that will be extracted later in sector by sector to be arranged into a rectangular form of image, whereas for the DGT method, pixel by pixel is to be extracted and arranged into a rectangular form image. These pixels will then be reproduced, or duplicated, in order to standardize the number of pixels available in each row of the panoramic image. For the pano-mapping table method, an algorithm is used whereby a table is created at initialization, to indicate the coordinates of the pixels to be extracted from the omnidirectional image. Once the table is created, it will then be used over and over again to map each of the pixel at that particular coordinate, one by one, from the omnidirectional image into a panoramic image, hence the name "once and for all."

4. *Complexity*: Table 16.1 shows the big-O complexity of log-polar mapping method, DGT method, and pano-mapping table method.

5. *Processing time*: The processing time for all the three unwarping methods to transform an omnidirectional image into a panoramic image is calculated using MATLAB function "cputime." The program is processed five times on five different images, and the average processing time is computed. It is found that pano-mapping table method has the fastest computation time, which is 1.220 s, followed by log-polar mapping method being 2.003 and 3.426 s for the DGT method.

6. *Data compression*: The generated panoramic image produced by log-polar mapping method has the resolution of 473×114; DGT method has a resolution of 1472×235 and 1146×243 for pano-mapping table method, in which the original omnidirectional image is of resolution 473×473. From the output resolution, it is clear that log-polar mapping has the highest compression, which compresses the image up to fourfold, compared to DGT method (0.65-fold image expansion) and pano-mapping table method (0.80-fold image expansion).

In terms of *resolution of the image generated*, although the image generated by DGT method and pano-mapping table methods is larger as compared to the image generated by log-polar mapping method, these two methods seem to elongate the actual size of the image. In other words, this

Table 16.1   Big-O Complexity

	DGT	Log-Polar Mapping	Pano-Mapping Table
Addition	$O(XY^2)$	$O(X^2Y^2)$	$O(Y^2)$
Subtraction			
Multiplication	$O(Y)$	$O(X^2)$	$O(Y^2)$
Division			
Logarithmic	—	$O\left(\dfrac{\log(X)}{\log(Y)}\right)$	—

X, length of the panoramic image = perimeter of the omnidirectional image taken into consideration; Y, height of the panoramic image = radius of the omnidirectional image taken into consideration.

method tends to make the objects in the image extended and "broader" than the original image. Due to this elongation, it will be harder to examine the picture and the objects, as the sense of the size had been eliminated. For log-polar mapping method, the extension is not much, and it is not as obvious as DGT method and pano-mapping table methods. In terms of *quality of image*, pano-mapping table method produces the highest quality among the three methods, followed by log-polar mapping method with a slightly lower image quality but still within an acceptable range, and lastly the blurred DGT method. In terms of *algorithm used in performing the unwarping process*, pano-mapping table method uses the simplest and easiest algorithm, followed by a slightly complex algorithm that is the log-polar method, and lastly, a complicated and complex algorithm from the DGT method. In terms of *complexity*, it is found that pano-mapping table method has the least complexity, followed by DGT method, and lastly log-polar mapping method in big-O notation. In terms of *processing time*, on average, pano-mapping table method has the fastest processing time to transform an omnidirectional image into a panoramic image, followed by log-polar mapping method and DGT method. In terms of *data compression*, log-polar mapping method has the best data compression rate compared to pano-mapping table method and DGT method. This is very good in preserving CPU's memory, as the memory available is usually very limited.

16.4 Automatic Human Intruder Detection Algorithm

Automatic human intruder detection is implemented in the proposed omnidirectional imaging system to analyze information from the position of the imaging tools and automatically detect a trespasser. Two automatic human intruder detection algorithms are discussed in this section; this includes partitioned ROI algorithm [11] and human head curve test algorithm [12,13].

16.4.1 Partitioned Region of Interest Algorithm

The partitioned ROI-based human intruder detection algorithm is summarized as follows:

Step 1: Adjust the thermal camera detection ranging from 30°C to 40°C so that object with human body temperature range can be detected.

Step 2: Unwarp the omnidirectional thermal image into panoramic thermal image using log-polar mapping technique.

Step 3: Capture images continuously from thermal camera into laptop and name it as P_x where $x = 1, 2, 3, \ldots$ is the discrete-time instant.

Step 4: Divide each image captured from thermal camera into $(m \times n)$ regions. Each region consists of equal number of pixels.

Step 5: Define a matrix M with size of $(m \times n)$ to represent the characteristic of each corresponding region.

Step 6: Define a threshold value Q. Q is the threshold value of the difference between sums of RGB value for a particular current image pixel and previous image pixel.

Step 7: Define a variable h for counting the number of pixels exceeding Q. Initially, h is set to 0.

Step 8: Define H as a minimum number of pixels with difference exceeding Q.

Step 9: Compare current taken image P_x with previous taken image P_{x-1}. For each corresponding region, find out the difference between a particular current image and previous image pixels' sum of RGB values. If the difference between sums of RGB values for a particular

Figure 16.20   Example for partitioning of ROI for trespasser detection surveillance system.

current image pixel and previous image pixel $\geq Q$, then $h = h + 1$. If $h \geq H$, mark a "1" into the corresponding element of M; else if $h < H$, mark a "0" into the corresponding element of M. An example is shown in Figure 16.20.

Step 10: Let F be the number of different elements that align vertically and continuously. Some examples of calculation of F are shown as follows:

Examples

Example 1

$$
\text{Compare } \begin{bmatrix} 0 & 0 & 0 & 0 & 0 \\ 0 & 0 & 0 & 0 & 0 \\ 0 & 0 & 0 & 0 & 0 \\ 0 & 0 & 0 & 0 & 0 \\ 0 & 0 & 0 & 0 & 0 \end{bmatrix} \text{ with } \begin{bmatrix} 0 & 0 & 0 & 0 & 0 \\ 0 & 1 & 0 & 0 & 0 \\ 0 & 1 & 0 & 0 & 0 \\ 0 & 1 & 0 & 0 & 0 \\ 0 & 1 & 0 & 0 & 0 \end{bmatrix}
$$

$F = 4$ in this example.

Example 2

$$
\text{Compare } \begin{bmatrix} 0 & 0 & 0 & 0 & 0 \\ 0 & 0 & 0 & 0 & 0 \\ 0 & 0 & 0 & 0 & 0 \\ 0 & 0 & 0 & 0 & 0 \\ 0 & 0 & 0 & 0 & 0 \end{bmatrix} \text{ with } \begin{bmatrix} 0 & 0 & 0 & 0 & 0 \\ 0 & 1 & 0 & 0 & 0 \\ 0 & 0 & 0 & 1 & 0 \\ 0 & 0 & 0 & 1 & 0 \\ 0 & 0 & 0 & 1 & 0 \end{bmatrix}
$$

$F = 3$ in this example because only three different elements are aligned vertically and continuously.

Example 3

$$
\text{Compare } \begin{bmatrix} 0 & 0 & 0 & 0 & 0 \\ 0 & 0 & 0 & 0 & 0 \\ 0 & 0 & 0 & 0 & 0 \\ 0 & 0 & 0 & 0 & 0 \\ 0 & 0 & 0 & 0 & 0 \end{bmatrix} \text{ with } \begin{bmatrix} 0 & 0 & 0 & 0 & 0 \\ 0 & 1 & 0 & 0 & 0 \\ 0 & 1 & 0 & 1 & 0 \\ 0 & 0 & 0 & 1 & 0 \\ 0 & 0 & 0 & 1 & 0 \end{bmatrix}
$$

If there are more than two groups of vertically and continuously different elements, then we will take the largest number. In this case, $F = 3$.

Step 11: Define G as minimum regions that a human being will appear on-screen.

If $F \geq G$, then alarm unknown trespasser detected.

16.4.2 Human Head Curve Test Algorithm

The human head curve test algorithm is summarized as follows:

1. *Algorithm for Trespasser Detection*

    Step 1: Acquire thermal image through hyperbolic reflector. Refer to Figure 16.21 for the example of image captured.

    Step 2: Image unwarping: Unwarp the acquired thermal image into panoramic image. Refer to Figure 16.22 for the example on resulting panoramic image.

    Step 3: Image cropping: Crop the image to obtain the thermal image of the interested area only. Please refer to Figure 16.23 for the example on the resulting cropped image.

    Step 4: Binary image conversion: Convert thermal image into purely black and white image (BW) using

$$BW(i,j) = \begin{cases} 1, & T_l \leq Temp(i,j) \leq T_h \\ 0, & \text{otherwise} \end{cases} \tag{16.12}$$

where
   temperature at point (i,j) of thermal image
   T_l and T_h are the minimum and maximum possible human body temperatures
   i,j are the pixel's row and column coordinates, respectively

    Step 5: Object identification: Identify objects inside the BW where a group of discontinuous white pixels is considered as a single object.

    Step 6: Noise filtering:

    a. Remove from BW all connected components (objects) that have fewer than S pixels.

    b. Create a flat, disk-shaped structuring element (SE) with radius, R. An example of SE is shown in Figure 16.24.

       Perform morphological closing on the BW. Morphological operation dilates an image and then erodes the dilated image using the same SE for both operations.

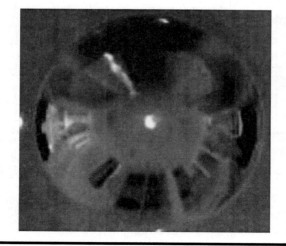

Figure 16.21   Thermal image captured through hyperbolic reflector.

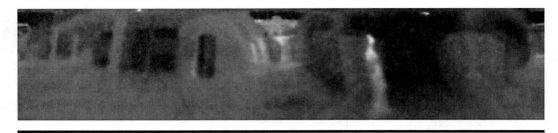

Figure 16.22 Panoramic view of the inspected scene after the thermal image is unwarped.

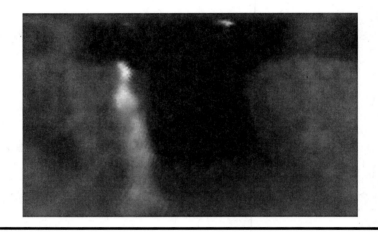

Figure 16.23 Thermal image after cropping process.

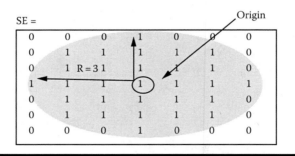

Figure 16.24 Disk-shaped SEs (e.g., R = 3).

Step 7: Boundary extraction: Find boundary line of each identified object inside BW and record it into an array of coordinates.

Step 8: Head detection: For each object's boundary, perform the head detection algorithm as explained in "Algorithm for Head Detection."

Step 9: If a human being is detected, trigger the alarm.

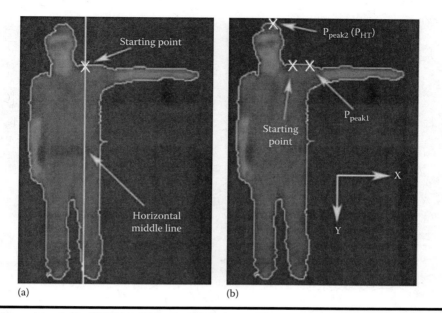

(a)   (b)

Figure 16.25 **(a) Horizontal middle line and the starting point as in step 1. (b) Detection of (c/w from starting point) and (counter c/w from starting point).**

2. *Algorithm for Head Detection*

　　Step 1: Starting point identification: Calculate the starting point for head top detection. The starting point shall be the highest point (smallest y-coordinate value) among the intersection points of the boundary with the horizontal middle line, where horizontal middle line is given by $x = x_m$ and x_m is the mean of all x-coordinates in the boundary of the object. Please refer to Figure 16.25a for better understanding.

　　Step 2: Peak point detection: From the starting point, follow the boundary in clockwise direction and search for the first peak point encountered (P_{peak1}). Again, from the starting point, follow the boundary in anticlockwise direction and search for the first peak point encountered (P_{peak1}). Peak point is defined as the point in which it has the smallest y-coordinate value compared to all the D proceeding points. D is the number of next of point to be tested. Refer to Figure 16.25b for better understanding.

　　Step 3: Head top point detection: Compare P_{peak1} and P_{peak2} obtained in step 2. Record the highest point (with smaller y-coordinate) as the head top point, P_{peak1}. For example, in Figure 16.25b, P_{peak2} is higher than P_{peak1}. Thus, $P_{peak1} = P_{HT} = P_{peak2}$.

　　Step 4: Boundary line splitting: Split the boundary into left boundary (Bl) and right boundary (Br) from the head top point toward the bottom. Take only one point for each y-coordinate to filter out unwanted information such as raised hands (refer to Figure 16.26 for better understanding):

$$Bl = \left[xl_i, yl_i \right], \quad Br = \left[xr_i, yr_i \right] \tag{16.13}$$

where

　　xl_i, yl_i, xr_i, yr_i are the pixels' y-coordinates and x-coordinates for Bl and Br, respectively

　　$i = 1, \ldots, N$ is the index number

　　N is the size of the boundary matrix (N is the number of pixels for Bl and Br)

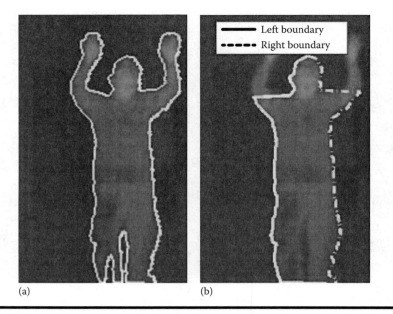

Figure 16.26 (a) Original object boundary. (b) Left and right object boundary after the splitting process (step 4).

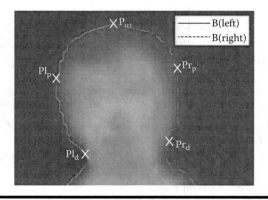

Figure 16.27 Example of points found in steps 3, 5, and 6.

Step 5: Left significant point detection: Search downward along Bl from P_{HT} for the first leftmost point encountered (Pl_p). Next, search for the rightmost point right after Pl_p which is Pl_d (refer to Figure 16.27 for better understanding):

$$Pl_p = (xl_{lp}, yl_{lp}), \quad Pl_d = (xl_{ld}, yl_{ld}) \tag{16.14}$$

where
subscript l_p is an index number of the first leftmost point
subscript l_d is an index number of the rightmost point right after Pl_p

Step 6: Right significant point detection: Search downward along Br from P_{HT} for the first rightmost point encountered (Pr_p). Next, detect the leftmost point right after Pr_p, which is Pr_d (refer to Figure 16.27 for better understanding):

$$Pr_p = (xr_{rp}, yr_{rp}), \quad Pr_d = (xr_{rd}, yr_{rd}) \tag{16.15}$$

where

subscript r_p is an index number of the first rightmost point
subscript r_d is an index number of the first leftmost point right after Pr_p

Step 7: Head symmetric test:
Define h_l = vertical distance between P_{HT} and Pl_d
h_r = vertical distance between P_{HT} and Pr_d.

Test the ratio between h_l and h_r. If h_l/h_r or $h_r/h_l > 2$, then the object is not considered as a human being and the next subsequent steps in this algorithm can be skipped and proceed with the next object. Else, if the object is possibly a human being, continue step 8 for further detection.

Step 8: Neck–body position test: Calculate Δx, which is the distance between x_c and x_m where x_c = horizontal center between Pl_d and Pr_d and x_m is obtained in step 1.
Define w_n = horizontal distance between Pl_d and Pr_d.

If $\Delta x \geq 2w_n$, then this object is not classified as a human being and the next subsequent steps in this algorithm can be skipped and proceed with the next object. Else if $\Delta x < 2w_n$, then the object is possibly a human being. Continue step 9 for further detection.

Step 9: Curve tests:
a. Top curve test
Define s_t = floor(min(l_p,r_p)/(F/2)) as the step size for top curve test.

Calculate

$$C_{tl} = \begin{cases} 1, & yl_{1+s_t*k} \leq yl_{1+S_t*(k+1)} \\ 0, & \text{otherwise} \end{cases}$$

$$C_{tr} = \begin{cases} 1, & yr_{1+s_t*k} \leq yr_{1+S_t*(k+1)} \\ 0, & \text{otherwise} \end{cases} \tag{16.16}$$

$$C_t = \sum C_{tl} + \sum C_{tr}$$

where
$k = 0, \ldots, F/2-1$
F is the step-size partition variable. F is even integer and $F \geq 2$.
For example, if $F = 6$, $s_t = 8$, then the y-coordinates tested are shown in Figure 16.28. The same concept goes for left curve test and right curve test.

Note: The symbol "*" means multiply.
b. Left curve test
Define s_l = floor(min(lp,ld − lp)/(F/2)) as the step size for left curve test.

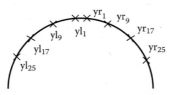

Figure 16.28   Example on top curve test.

Calculate

$$C_{l1} = \begin{cases} 1, & xl_{lp+s_t*k} \leq xl_{lp+S_l*(k+1)} \\ 0, & \text{otherwise} \end{cases}$$

$$C_{l2} = \begin{cases} 1, & xl_{lp+s_t*k} \leq xl_{lp+S_l*(k+1)} \\ 0, & \text{otherwise} \end{cases} \tag{16.17}$$

$$C_l = \sum C_{l1} + \sum C_{l2}$$

where $k = 0, \ldots, F/2 - 1$

c. Right curve test
Define $s_r = \text{floor}(\min(r_p, r_d - r_p)/(F/2))$ as the step size for right curve test.

Calculate

$$C_{r1} = \begin{cases} 1, & xr_{rp+s_r*k} \leq xr_{rp+S_r*(k+1)} \\ 0, & \text{otherwise} \end{cases}$$

$$C_{r2} = \begin{cases} 1, & xr_{rp+s_r*k} \leq xr_{rp+S_r*(k+1)} \\ 0, & \text{otherwise} \end{cases} \tag{16.18}$$

$$C_r = \sum C_{r1} + \sum C_{r2}$$

where $k = 0, \ldots, F/2 - 1$
Step 10: Human identification:
Define curve test condition:

$$C_t \geq F - 1 \tag{16.19}$$

$$C_l \geq F - 1 \tag{16.20}$$

$$C_r \geq F - 1 \tag{16.21}$$

Check conditions (16.19) through (16.21). If any two or more conditions are true, the object is verified as a human being. Else, the object is not considered as a human being.

16.4.3 Experimental Results

In this section, the application of the proposed omnidirectional human intruder detection system is briefly illustrated. An omnidirectional image captured using digital camera on the site is shown in Figure 16.29. An omnidirectional thermal image also captured using thermal camera on the site is shown in Figure 16.30. The unwarped form of Figure 16.29

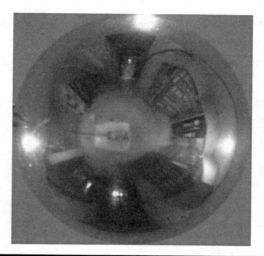

Figure 16.29   Case studies of trespasser detection (digital color form).

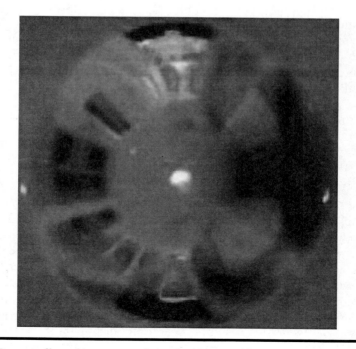

Figure 16.30   Case studies of trespasser detection (thermal image).

Figure 16.31   Unwarp form of Figure 16.29 (digital color panoramic form).

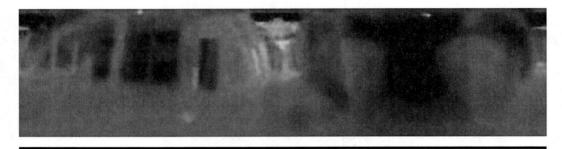

Figure 16.32   Unwarp form of Figure 16.30 (thermal image panoramic form).

(digital color panoramic form) is shown in Figure 16.31, whereas the unwarped form of Figure 16.30 (thermal image panoramic form) is shown in Figure 16.32, respectively. In Figure 16.32, the log-polar mapping process is by 4:1 reduction mapping scale, which means that 320×240 omnidirectional thermal image's Cartesian pixels are mapped to one-fourth of the thermal image Cartesian pixels (320×60) in panoramic view, with fourfold data compression compared to original omnidirectional thermal image as in Figure 16.30. The captured thermal images are tested for two trespasser faint detection algorithms as proposed in Sections 4.1 and 4.2 in the preceding text.

16.4.3.1 Experimental Results for Partitioned ROI-Based Human Intruder Detection Algorithm

In partitioned ROI algorithm for trespasser detection, there are three parameters that need to be optimized, which are Q, H, and G, where Q is the threshold value of the difference of the sum of RGB value between a particular current image pixel and previous image pixel, H is minimum number of pixels with difference exceeding Q and G is minimum regions that a human being will appear on-screen.

Since the image captured is in RGB form, the difference of the sum of RGB values between a particular current image pixel and previous image pixel is between 0 and 765. For Q parameter, 1000 sample images (with or without human being) are used to test every different point with step size of 15. The accuracy versus difference of sum of RGB values is plotted in Figure 16.33. From the plot, the optimum Q value is 345 with highest accuracy of 95.30%.

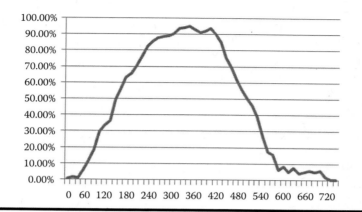

Figure 16.33 Accuracy versus difference of sum of RGB values.

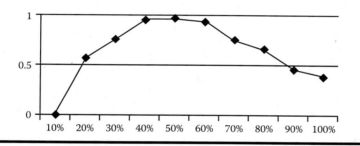

Figure 16.34 Accuracy versus number of pixel difference to total pixels in one region.

The unwarped panoramic image is partitioned into 50 regions ($m = 10$, $n = 5$) with each region consisting of equal number of pixels (384). As for H value, the algorithm with pets (hamster, cat, and dog) and human, moving toward and away from the captured region. One thousand sample images are captured. By using the sample images, we repeated the simulation with $H = 10\%$, 20%, 30%, …, 100% of number of pixel difference to total pixels in one region ratio. The graph accuracy versus number of pixel difference to total pixels in one region ratio is plotted in Figure 16.34. From the plot, the optimum H value is 50% of total pixels in a region, with the highest accuracy of 97%.

As for G value, the algorithm is tested with human moving toward and away from the captured region with minimum regions that a human being will appear on-screen, $G = 1$–5. The graph of accuracy versus minimum regions that a human being appears on-screen G is shown in Figure 16.35. From the graph, the optimum G value is 3 with highest accuracy of 93.5%.

For testing the trespasser detection performance of partitioned ROI-based trespasser detection algorithm, a total of 10,000 images with test subjects (human being or animal) roaming randomly in the test site (as shown in Figure 16.37) visible to the proposed system are taken as samples. This includes thermal images with a single trespasser, more than one trespasser, without a trespasser, and animals (cats, birds, etc., which are not counted as trespassers). The "operator perceived activity" (OPA) [46] is used and the operator will comment on the images captured,

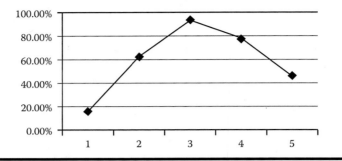

Figure 16.35 Accuracy versus minimum regions that a human being will appear on-screen.

whether there is any trespasser or not, and compare with the detected result of the surveillance system. From the total of 10,000 samples images for evaluation, 7,080 were detected perfectly (trespasser-or-not condition agreed by both observer and surveillance system), that is, with an accuracy of 70.8%.

16.4.3.2 Experimental Results for Human Head Curve Test Algorithm

The same 10,000 tested samples as mentioned in Section 16.4.3.1 are applied here. To determine optimum value for parameter T_l, a random sample image is chosen and converted into BW image using step 2 of the human head curve test algorithm with value of T_l ranging from 0 to 510 (sum of R and G components in RGB image). Perform the binary image conversion repeatedly with increasing step size of 10 for T_l and search for the optimum T_l where the noise can be minimized and the human shape is not distorted in the resulting image. Based on 1000 observable images, T_l is best suitable set at 150 in this experiment. For example, if $T_l = 130$ is used, excessive noise will be introduced. If $T_l = 170$ is used, there will be too much distortion to human being in the resulting image. Refer to Figure 16.36 for better understanding.

To determine the optimum value for parameter T_h, perform the binary image conversion repeatedly with decreasing step size of 10 for T_h and search for the minimum value of T_h that does not influence the appearance of the human object. Based on 1000 observable images, T_h is best set at 430 in this experiment. For example, if $T_h = 400$ is used, the image of human being is distorted. If $T_h = 460$ is used, there will be no improvement for the image. Lower T_h value is preferred because it will filter out more noise component. Refer to Figure 16.37 for better understanding.

Human shape's parameters S and R are approximated from 1000 testing images at a distance of 5 m from the imaging system. From those images, the human's pixels are approximately 30. Hence, S is set to 30. Larger SEs preserve larger features, while smaller elements preserve the finer details of image features. Figure 16.38 shows examples with different R values for SE selection. It is observed that when $R \geq 3$, the neck part is unidentified from the images. Since finer human head shape is of concern, R for SE is best suit to set at the minimum, which is 2, as well as with lower computational complexity.

The accuracy of the proposed algorithm is then evaluated using "OPA" in which the proposed algorithm is evaluated with respect to the results interpreted by a human observer [46]. Firstly, the panoramic images are tested using the proposed algorithm. Then, the result is

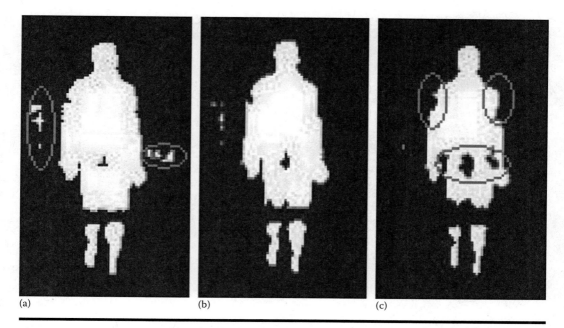

Figure 16.36 (a) $T_1 = 130$, (b) $T_1 = 150$, and (c) $T_1 = 170$.

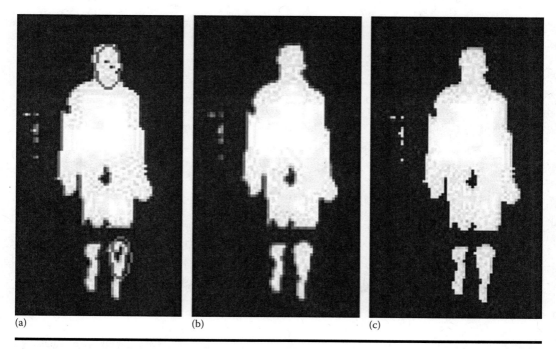

Figure 16.37 (a) $T_h = 400$, (b) $T_h = 430$, and (c) $T_h = 460$.

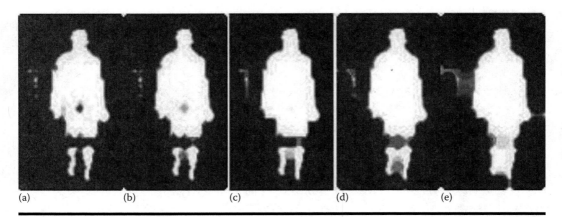

(a)   (b)   (c)   (d)   (e)

Figure 16.38 Examples with different R values for SE selection: (a) R = 1, no changes; (b) R = 2; (c) R = 3; (d) R = 4; and (e) R = 5.

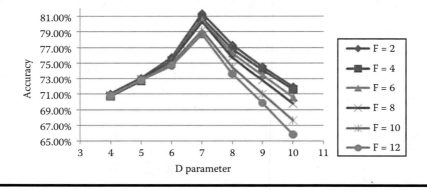

Figure 16.39 Accuracy of proposed algorithm for different combinations of D and F.

compared with the result of the human observer. The accuracy of the proposed algorithm is the percentage of interpretation (trespasser or not) agreed by both the human observer and the proposed algorithm.

To determine parameter D and F, all of the 10,000 sample images are tested with different combinations of D and F. As shown in the graph in Figure 16.39, the optimum values for parameters D and F are 7 and 2, which contribute to accuracy of 81.38%.

16.4.4 Comparison between Two Proposed Human Intruder Detection Algorithms

The first proposed algorithm that is the partitioned ROI-based human intruder detection algorithm is regional based, whereby an object that occupies more than a certain number of partitions in a panoramic image is considered as a human being and vice versa. However, the algorithm has two major concerns. First concern is the distance, in which a human being that is far away from the imaging system will not be identified as a human. The second concern is if an animal (such as cat, dog) is moving too close to the system (which occupies more than the threshold partitioned), it will be missconsidered as a human being too.

Hence, a second effective human intruder detection algorithm, which is the human head curve test algorithm with human head detection capability, is proposed. By comparing the two human intruder detection algorithms, human head curve test algorithm required complicated head symmetric test and curve test. Partitioned ROI-based human intruder detection algorithm is superseding human head curve test algorithm in terms of simplicity and lower computational time consumption (average routine time for processing one sample is 1.3 s for partitioned ROI-based human intruder detection algorithm and 2.27 s for human head curve test algorithm). However, in terms of efficiency, human head curve test algorithm with an accuracy of 81.38% is higher than partitioned ROI-based human intruder detection algorithm with an accuracy of 70.8% in the same set of 10,000 tested images.

16.5 Conclusion and Future Research Directions

This chapter presented omnidirectional human intrusion detection system using computer vision techniques. Two imaging methods, namely, vision spectrum imaging and IR imaging, are applied in computer vision–based omnidirectional human intrusion detection system. Simulation results show that log-polar mapping proposed in transforming the captured omnidirectional images into panoramic form has good quality in output image with high data compression rate and fast processing speed in providing observer or image processing tools a wide angle of view. Automatic human intrusion detection algorithms are implemented in the proposed omnidirectional imaging system, both in vision spectrum imaging and in IR spectrum imaging, respectively. The proposed human intrusion algorithm includes partitioned ROI algorithm and human head curve test algorithm. Experimental results also show that partitioned ROI-based human intruder detection algorithm is superseding human head curve test algorithm in terms of simplicity and lower computational time consumption. However, human head curve test algorithm can trace out human intruder from the panoramic images more accurately compared to ROI algorithm.

Currently, the omnidirectional human intrusion detection systems are applied in indoor building security for i-habitat (smart home), fossil power plant, etc., and prototyping for border intrusion detection, on human targets (including smugglers, illegal immigrants, or terrorists). In the future, it will be embedded with facial recognition capabilities to record and identify criminals' and suspects' identity. Also, a mobile robot can be built for moving around the surveillance site carrying such omnidirectional surveillance system. The imaging tool power is designed to be supplied by a battery instead of a power plug. It allows the robot to carry the surveillance imaging tool set without limitation of the power cables' length. By using a mobile robot, several sites can be monitored by using only one omnidirectional surveillance system. It is also a plan to employ microprocessor modules such as field programmable gate array (FPGA) and Advanced RISC Machine (ARM) for image processing and analyzing tasks instead of a computer to effectively reduce the costs and power consumption of the proposed system. These topics will be addressed in future works.

References

1. Moseley, T.M. 2006. Homeland operations. Air Force Doctrine Document 2-10.
2. Lu, C. and Drew, M.S. 2007. Automatic compensation for camera settings for images taken under different illuminants. Technical paper, School of Computer Science, Simon Fraser University, Vancouver, British Columbia, Canada, pp. 1–5.
3. Kawanishi, T., Yamazawa, K., Iwasa, H., Takemura, H., and Yokoya, N. 1998. Generation of high-resolution stereo panoramic images by omnidirectional imaging sensor using hexagonal pyramidal mirrors. In *Proceedings of the 14th International Conference in Pattern Recognition*, Brisbane, Australia, Vol. 1, pp. 485–489.
4. Akihiko, T. and Atsushi, I. 2004. Panoramic image transform of omnidirectional images using discrete geometry techniques. In *Proceedings of the 2nd International Symposium on 3D Data Processing, Visualization, and Transmission (3DPVT'04)*, Washington, DC, pp. 608–615.
5. Jeng, S.W. and Tsai, W.H. 2007. Using pano-mapping tables for unwarping of omni-images into panoramic and perspective-view images, *IET Image Processing*, 1(2), 149–155.
6. Jurie, F. 1999. A new log-polar mapping for space variant imaging: Application to face detection and tracking, *Pattern Recognition*, 32(55), 865–875.
7. Hampapur, A., Brown, L., Connell, J., Pankanti, S., Senior, A. et al. 2003. Smart surveillance: Applications, technologies and implications, *Information, Communications and Signal Processing*, 2, 1133–1138.
8. Hampapur, A., Brown, L., Connell, J., Ekin, A., Haas, N. et al. 2005. Smart video surveillance, *IEEE Signal Processing Magazine*, pp. 39–51.
9. Green, M.W. 1999. The appropriate and effective use of security technologies in U.S. schools. A guide for schools and law enforcement agencies, Research Report, Sandia National Laboratories, Albuquerque, NM, NCJ 178265.
10. Shu, C., Hampapur, A., Lu, M., Brown, L., Connell, J. et al. 2005. IBM smart surveillance system (S3): A open and extensible framework for event based surveillance, *Advanced Video and Signal Based Surveillance (AVSS 2005)*, Como, Italy, pp. 318–323.
11. Wong, W.K., Tan, P.N., Loo, C.K., and Lim, W.S. 2010. Omnidirectional surveillance system using thermal camera, *Journal of Computer Science and Engineering*, 3(2), 42–51 (ISSN 2043-9091).
12. Lee, L.H. 2008. Smart surveillance using image processing and computer vision techniques, Bachelor Degree thesis, Multimedia University, Melaka, Malaysia.
13. Wong, W.K., Chew, Z.Y., Lim, H.L., Loo, C.K., and Lim, W.S. 2011. Omnidirectional thermal imaging surveillance system featuring trespasser and faint detection, *International Journal of Image Processing, CSC Journals, IJIP-279*, 4(6), 518–538.
14. Holmes, O.W. 1881. *The Common Law*. Boston, MA: Little Brown and Co.
15. Tsai, C.F. and Young, M.S. 2003. Pyroelectric infrared sensor-based thermometer for monitoring indoor objects, *Review of Scientific Instruments*, 74(12), 5267–5273.
16. Hirota, M., Furuse, T., Ebana, K., Kubo, H., Tsushima, K., Inaba, T., Shima, A., Fujinuma, M., and Tojyo, N. 2001. Magnetic detection of a surface ship by an airborne LTS SQUID MAD, *IEEE Transactions on Applied Superconductivity*, 11, 884–887.
17. Paul, W., Herbert, F., and Soumya, N. 2003. Enhancing homeland security with advanced UWB sensors, *IEEE Microwave Magazine*, pp. 51–58.
18. Reutech radar systems. Homeland security, http://www.rrs.co.za/products/homeland-security.html
19. DeTect, Inc., Security and surveillance radar systems, http://www.detect-inc.com/security.html
20. Tocci, R. 2006. *Digital Systems: Principals and Applications*, 10th edn. Upper Saddle River, NJ: Prentice Hall. ISBN 013172.
21. Fischler, M.A. and Bolles, R.C. 1981. Random sample consensus: A paradigm for model fitting with applications to image analysis and automated cartography, *Communications of the ACM*, 24, 381–395.
22. Corke, P., Strelow, D., and Singh, S. 2004. Omnidirectional visual odometry for a planetary rover. In *International Conference on Intelligent Robots and Systems (IROS 2004)*, Sendai, Japan, Vol. 4, pp. 4007–4012.
23. Durrant, W.H. and Bailey, T. 2006. Simultaneous localization and mapping (SLAM): Part I. The essential algorithms, *Robotics and Automation Magazine*, Vol. 13, pp. 99–110.

24. Ishiguro, H., Yamamoto, M., and Tsuji, S. 1992. Omni-directional stereo, *IEEE Transactions on Pattern Analysis and Machine Intelligence*, 14(2), 257–262.

25. Huang, H-C. and Hung, Y.P. 1998. Panoramic stereo imaging system with automatic disparity warping and seaming, *Graphical Models and Image Processing*, 60(3), 196–208.

26. Peleg, S. and Ben-Ezra, M. 1999. Stereo panorama with a single camera. In *Proceedings of the IEEE Conference on Computer Vision and Pattern Recognition*, Fort Collins, CO, pp. 395–401.

27. Shum, H. and Szeliski, R. 1999. Stereo reconstruction from multi-perspective panoramas. In *Proceedings of the Seventh International Conference on Computer Vision*, Kerkyra, Greece, pp. 14–21.

28. Chen, S.E. 1995. Quick time VR: An image-based approach to virtual environment navigation. In *Proceedings of the 22nd Annual ACM Conference on Computer Graphics*, Los Angeles, CA, pp. 29–38.

29. Kumar, J. and Bauer, M. 2000. Fisheye lens design and their relative performance, *Proceedings of SPIE*, 4093, 360–369.

30. Padjla, T. and Roth, H. 2000. Panoramic imaging with SVAVISCA camera-simulations and reality, Research Reports of CMP, Czech Technical University, Prague, No. 16.

31. Oh, S.J. and Hall, E.L. 1987. Guidance of a mobile robot using an omnidirectional vision navigation system. In *Proceedings of the Society of Photo-Optical Instrumentation Engineers*, SPIE, Cambridge, CA, Vol. 852, pp. 288–300.

32. Kuban, D.P., Martin, H.L., Zimmermann, S.D., and Busico, N. 1994. Omniview motionless camera surveillance system, United States Patent No. 5,359,363.

33. Nalwa, V. 1996. A true omnidirectional viewer, Technical Report, Bell Laboratories, Holmdel, NJ, pp.25.

34. James, J.K. and Martin, B. 2000. Fisheye lens designs and their relative performance. In *Proceedings of the Current Developments in Lens Design and Optical Systems Engineering*, SPIE, San Diego, CA, Vol. 4093, pp. 360–369.

35. Stun-ningsales.com, Weatherproof CCD color rotating video security camera, Redirecting from http://www.stun-ningsales.com/homethings/outdoor_securitycameras.htm, accessed on March 2, 2012.

36. The-Digital Image.com, Fisheye lens, redirecting from http://www.the-digital-picture.com/Reviews/, accessed on March 2, 2012.

37. Chahl, J. and Srinivasan, M. 1997. Reflective surfaces for panoramic imaging, *Applied Optics*, 36(31), 8275–8285.

38. Gachter, S. 2001. Mirror design for an omnidirectional camera with a uniform cylindrical projection when using the SVAVISCA sensor, Research Reports of CMP, OMNIVIEWS Project, Czech Technical University, Prague, No. 3, 2001. Redirected from: http://cmp.felk.cvut.cz/projects/omniviews/

39. Svoboda, T. 1999. Central panoramic cameras design, geometry, egomotion. PhD theses, Center of Machine Perception, Czech Technical University, Prague, 1999.

40. Davis, J.W. and Sharma, V. 2007. Background-subtraction in thermal imagery using contour saliency, *International Journal of Computer Vision* 71(2), 161–181.

41. Huang, D.S., Wunsch, D.C., Levine, D.S., and Jo, K-H. 2008. Advanced intelligent computing theories and applications: with aspects of theoretical and methodological issues. In *Proceedings of the 4th International Conference on Intelligent Computing (ICIC 2008)*, Shanghai, China, pp. 1–8.

42. Wu, C.J. and Tsai, W.H. 2009. Unwarping of images taken by misaligned omnicameras without camera calibration by curved quadrilateral morphing using quadratic pattern classifiers, *Optical Engineering*, 48(8), 1–11.

43. George, W. and Siavash, Z. 2000. Robust image registration using log-polar transform, In *Proceedings of the IEEE International Conference on Image Processing*, Vancouver, British Columbia, Canada.

44. Traver, V.J. and Alexandre, B. 2010. A review of log-polar imaging for visual perception in robotics, *Robotics and Autonomous Systems*, 58, 378–398.

45. José, S.V. and Alexandre, B. 2003. Vision-based navigation, environmental representations and imaging geometries, In *VisLab-TR 01/2003, 10th International Symposium on Robotics Research*, R. Jarvis and A. Zelinsky (Eds.), Springer, New York.

46. Owens, J., Hunter, A., and Fletcher, E. 2002. A fast model-free morphology-based object tracking algorithm, In *British Machine Vision Conference*, Cardiff, U.K., Vol. 2, pp. 767–776.

Chapter 17

Wireless Sensor Networks and Audio Signal Recognition for Homeland Security

Marco Martalò, Gianluigi Ferrari, and Claudio S. Malavenda

Contents

17.1 Introduction

Recent years have witnessed a growing attention to the security of our daily lives, due to the recent experience of terrorist attacks. Therefore, a plethora of solutions to homeland security problems, either civilian or military [1], have been developed, from academia, national governments, and industries. One of the most critical aspects in homeland security is the requirement for noninvasiveness in security monitoring systems. To this end, Wireless Sensor Networks (WSNs) have been considered as a promising technology to increase homeland security from the very beginning, due to their low costs and the feasibility of management of hundreds of devices. Typical WSN devices are equipped with a set of sensors useful for homeland security applications, for example, audio, magnetic, movement, and light. Efficient processing and analysis of these data coming from different sensors are then required, with particular attention to the derivation of low computational complexity schemes.

In the first part of this chapter, we overview the main WSN technologies, as well as the main design issues arisen in this field. As in various homeland security applications, it is often of interest to process audio signals, for example, for surveillance of the perimeters of critical areas; in the second part of this chapter, we briefly review the main audio signal processing techniques for menace detection. In particular, we rely on time-domain processing to identify the instant of appearance of an audio signal to be detected. Moreover, we present an implementation instance of WSN-based monitoring system for homeland security applications developed by an Italian company well established in the homeland and defense business sector. This monitoring system is based on networks of Unattended Ground Sensors (UGSs), microdevices with sensors and wireless connectivity that can detect movements, magnetic fields, and audio signals and combine this heterogeneous (yet correlated) information to generate proper events and alarms.

In surveillance applications, the following problem is meaningful: detecting, with limited complexity, the presence and the pattern of an audio signal. We focus on the audio signal, since this is one of the physical quantities that can achieve high detection range, that is, cover a large zone to be detected, although with a sufficiently small signal quality obtained from transducers. The two quantities are, in fact, related by an inverse proportional relationship. For instance, high-level systems can even detect audio signals that originate from sources at 15 km [2]. The importance of audio processing in the military context is also reviewed together with some of the most important classification algorithms for this application in [3]. The data retrieved with the proposed audio recognition–based detection approach belong to a larger set of sensed data, which are properly combined by means of data fusion techniques. However, in this chapter, we limit ourselves to a detailed investigation of the audio sensor-based solution for menace recognition. We recall that our approach is not general and is "hard linked" to resources available on a real sensor node (memory, computational power, synchronization capabilities, and power consumption).

Several approaches (often computationally intense) have been proposed in the literature for audio signal pattern detection. Most of them rely on the analysis of the statistical properties of the audio signals. Unfortunately, in WSN-based surveillance scenarios, where nodes are typically battery powered, the node energy consumption is a critical issue. Therefore, in the last part of this chapter, we present a low-complexity approach, based on the combination of time- and frequency-based signal processing, to the audio recognition problem.

17.2 WSNs for Menace Detection and Area Monitoring

17.2.1 Monitoring and Menace Identification

A first important task in designing WSN-based solutions for menace detection is to face the application domain of interest. According to the application to be implemented and the type of physical data to be measured, the particular menace can be categorized. From this broader point of view, a menace can be interpreted as corresponding to a measure of the data quantity of interest out of its standard values or with an anomalous evolution during a given time period. For instance, if an area is being monitored to discover intruders, the menace will be classified as a fast physical measure variation in terms of terrain vibration or magnetic field anomaly near a sensor node. On the other hand, if a field is being monitored for agricultural purposes, the menace will correspond to an atypical increase of humidity or temperature in the area of interest. Another possible application example is traffic monitoring, where an anomaly may correspond to the increase, beyond a given threshold, of the number of cars passing by a traffic light.

Once the application of interest has been identified, one can define the physical quantity to be measured, as well as its standard (noncritical) variability range and, consequently, the level of variability, which constitutes a menace. Then, the menace has to be detected by means of proper data processing and/or fusion in order to recognize the cause of the anomalies. Let us consider the examples introduced earlier. In the intrusion detection case, data coming from different sensors have to be gathered to recognize the type of intruder (e.g., a human, a small animal, or a vehicle). In the case of field monitoring, instead, the recognition activity could aim at detecting which kind of disease is spreading in order to select the appropriate pesticide to spray.

Therefore, the operations needed to perform the menace recognition task can be summarized in the following two steps:

- During the first step, bulks of data are acquired and eventually preprocessed. The main goal of this step is to acquire data only when an event of interest occurs. Data preprocessing aims at bringing all acquired data (coming from different sensors) into a common reference system. For instance, this operation may refer to a conversion of current/voltage values in a percentage scale.
- The second step is refinement and involves the association, correlation, and combination of information obtained during the first step. The goal is to detect, characterize, and identify objects (including humans, animals, and vehicles). According to the scenario of interest, this step can be performed in a centralized or decentralized way. Algorithms should support data alignment and attribute estimation, as well as event positioning.

In the following section, we review the most important available products that, according to the design principles given earlier, have been designed and commercialized by industries for relevant applications, such as intrusion detection, infrastructure monitoring, environmental monitoring, traffic control, aeronautics, industrial control, and system automation.

17.2.2 WSN Test Beds

A large number of WSN test beds have been developed in academic environments, such as MoteLab [4] and WISEBED [5], but market-ready solutions are still not extensively available.

In fact, most of the hardware production is still limited to a few companies that sell products effectively corresponding to development boards. Moreover, the offer of these companies is usually limited: A complete WSN solution, in fact, needs not only a hardware solution but also firmware, protocols, sampling algorithm, and interface software. The different capabilities needed to develop each of these solution "ingredients" are maybe one of the major reasons behind the fact that a few market-ready and a rather small number of complete solutions exist. This is mainly due to the typically followed commercial practice, according to which the market responds to demands, rather than investing on potential solutions. The main applications fall in the agricultural field, border surveillance, and asset protection. Lately, however, urban monitoring has gained a significant attention, following the trend of formation of huge cities (only in China, e.g., there are over 170 cities populated with over a million people each).

One player with a significant impact on the definition of the standards used in the development of sensor gateways is the Internet Protocol (IP) for Smart Object (IPSO) Alliance [6]. The IPSO Alliance focuses on the standardization of the Internet of Things (IoT) technologies and promotes the IP as the networking technology best suited for connecting smart objects and delivering information from and to those objects. The goal of the IPSO Alliance is not to define technologies but to document the use of IP-based technologies defined by standardization organizations (such as the Internet Engineering Task Force, IETF) and support with various use cases.

A first interesting WSN-based solution is Tinynode [7], which is mainly focused on vehicle (trucks and cars) detection. Tinynode consists of wireless battery-powered nodes together with web-based applications. The system is claimed to yield at least 98% detection accuracy and at least 99% communication reliability. Nagios offers complete monitoring and alerting for IT infrastructures (servers, switches, applications, services, etc.) [8]. Its platform allows to monitor the entire IT infrastructure, preventing problem occurrence, becoming aware of the problems as they occur, providing security, etc. Netmagic also offers a platform for efficient infrastructure monitoring of IT systems [9]. Infrastructure monitoring enables to monitor availability and performance of IT systems so that managers can proactively take actions to maintain high uptimes: IT setup, provision of comprehensive information on the "health" of IT systems, thresholds, alerts, and reports. Advantic provides solutions for air quality, water, structural health, health monitoring, agriculture, environmental, energy efficiency, and mine monitoring [10]. In particular, the mine monitoring solution is an radio frequency identification (RFID)-based system able to locate and track personnel and machinery in mines. Finally, Libelium provides solutions in several fields such as agriculture, environment, health, industrial processes, logistics, safety and emergency, and smart metering [11]. However, most of these application fields are only considered as proof of concept of the applicability of Libelium's hardware (i.e., Waspmote) and protocol stack (Meshlium), but no practical monitoring solution has been presented. Other interesting active companies, especially in the field of smart cities and traffic control, are Urbiotica [12], Worldsensing [13], and Presto Parking [14].

In general, more and more products, from a growing number of manufacturers, are appearing in the global marketplace. Energy management is becoming the "killer application" and, thus, an efficient marketing motivation for home networking products. For instance, the KNX Association has published studies revealing how networked home and building control based on KNX allows up to 50% energy savings [15]. Interest has also been shown in energy management by other types of companies. For instance, Apple has filed patents for a device that could be used for energy management [16,17]. In particular, the device links outlets into homes via power line networking, using HomePlug technologies [18]. With this approach, every outlet in the home turns into an Internet port, also allowing efficient power supply to connected devices.

An interesting approach to the area monitoring problem is given by Disposable Sensor Networks (DSN) developed by SELEX Electronic Systems [19]. The main focus of the DSN solution is on border surveillance of large areas, and its main target is the military market. DSN possess the ability to detect the kind of intruder entering into a "hot" zone, distinguishing between human beings, animals, and vehicles. The DSN can also be configured to monitor chemical and environmental parameters. In all cases, the collected information can be routed to a fixed or mobile sink. This solution will be described in detail in Section 17.4.

To summarize, it seems that the provisioning of a commercial solution for area monitoring still requires a significant customization effort. In other words, most of the players in the WSN arena still wait for a specific customer demand to develop new solutions, rather than anticipating this demand with an offer. The difficulty in implementing effective large-scale solutions for area monitoring, also in "military" contexts, is witnessed by the cancellation of the virtual fence program after a one billion of USD investment [20]. The virtual fence was a key element of the SBInet program [21], initiated in 2006, as part of the Secure Border Initiative (SBI) [22], to develop a new integrated system of personnel, infrastructure, and technology (such as WSN) to secure land borders of the United States.

17.3 Audio Signal Recognition Techniques for Surveillance of Critical Areas

WSNs are typically equipped with a large variety of sensors, and, therefore, it is possible to monitor an event of interest from different perspectives. As a practical example of area monitoring and menace detection, let us consider the detection of the presence of an undesired user in a critical zone. In this case, this detection can be performed by resorting to very different physical quantities obtained by different sensors, for example, magnetic sensors and cameras. Video signal processing is one of the key surveillance technologies and is, since long, well established. Video processing can be used, for instance, for face human recognition [23] or to detect and prevent possible critical situations [24,25]. Real-time IP-based video processing for homeland security is proposed in [26], whereas an interesting summary of challenges is presented in [27]. The use of magnetic sensors for homeland security purposes is also attractive. In [28], the authors propose a new approach to assess the level of underwater security in civilian harbor installations, by means of the integration of a geographical information system (GIS) with acoustic and magnetic sensor models. A possible interesting approach is to identify the presence of a user by performing proper audio signal processing and determining if atypical sounds are present in the environment.

In the remainder of this chapter, we will focus on audio signal processing for surveillance of critical areas. An illustrative representation of the scenario of interest is shown in Figure 17.1. Before presenting the system model and a low-complexity energy-based time-domain processing approach, we overview related work.

17.3.1 Related Work

Sound recognition typically refers to the problem of determining which class a specific audio signal belongs to. Several approaches (often computationally intense) have been proposed in the literature, and most of them rely on the analysis of the statistical properties of the audio signals.

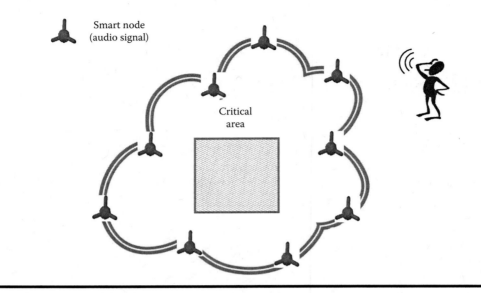

Figure 17.1 **Illustrative representation of the audio signal recognition scenario of interest.**

These approaches are typically based on the classification of some parameters of interest of the audio signals through Gaussian mixtures, hidden Markov models, or perceptron neural networks [29]. In [30], the authors propose an audio detection and classification scheme based on machine learning techniques, which can outperform classical sound recognition schemes. In [31], the authors characterize the relevant spectral peaks of different audio patterns (for health-care purposes) in order to perform the recognition task. In [32], an audio-based recognition system for gunshot detection is presented, and its robustness against variable and adverse conditions is analyzed. Different time and frequency domain metrics for audio-based context recognition systems are analyzed in [33], comparing the system performance with the accuracy guaranteed by human listeners performing the same task. Particular emphasis is given to the computational complexity of the proposed methods, since the considered application is of particular interest in resource-constrained portable devices. Other interesting approaches to audio pattern recognition are presented in [34,35].

Another interesting audio-related problem, widely studied in the literature, is the so-called *voice activity detection* (VAD) problem. Unlike the previous problem of sound recognition, in this case, one wants to detect the time intervals during which an (known) audio signal of interest (typically voice) appears, given that it will (sooner or later) appear for sure. A first possible strategy to detect the presence of an atypical audio signal, through a time-domain-based analysis, consists in evaluating the energy of the audio signal samples, as in [36,37]. Frequency domain-based VAD approaches have also been proposed through the application of the discrete Fourier transform (DFT) [38], as discussed in [39–41].

Although the performance of frequency domain processing algorithms can be better than that of time-domain processing algorithms, the price to be paid is a higher amount of computational complexity. Therefore, the use of spectral analysis for VAD purposes is not recommended in WSN-based applications. Therefore, in the remainder of this section, we focus on time-domain processing for the identification of the presence of audio signal patterns of interest. Note, however, that spectral analysis is necessary when it is of interest to classify more precisely a detected atypical audio signal. This issue will be investigated in more detail in Section 17.5.

17.3.2 System Model

The front-end of the audio sensor (i.e., the microphone) is modeled as a linear filter with response $H(f)$, at the output of which the electrical signal $x(t)$ can be written as follows:

$$x(t) = r(t) \otimes h(t) = \underbrace{s_{in}(t) \otimes h(t)}_{s(t)} + \underbrace{n_{in}(t) \otimes h(t)}_{n(t)} \tag{17.1}$$

where

$r(t) = s_{in}(t) + n_{in}(t)$ is the input signal
$s_{in}(t)$ is the atypical audio signal of possible interest
$n_{in}(t)$ is the background audio noise
$h(t) = \mathcal{F}^{-1}[H(f)]$
$\otimes$ denotes the convolution operator

The output signal $x(t)$ is then sampled with frequency f_s, and the discrete-time samples are denoted as $\{x_k\}$, with

$$x_k \simeq \begin{cases} s_k + n_k & \text{in the presence of an atypical signal} \\ n_k & \text{in the absence of any atypical signal} \end{cases} \tag{17.2}$$

where s_k is the useful signal component and n_k is the noise sample.

More precisely, n_k can be expressed as $n_k = n_{mic,k} + n_{env,k}$, where $n_{mic,k}$ is the noise generated by the microphone (on the order of 100 nV/Hz$^{0.5}$ [42]) and $n_{env,k}$ is the environmental audio noise. Typically, $n_{mic,k} \ll n_{env,k}$.

Our approach is based on per-frame processing, where a frame corresponds to a sequence of consecutive discrete-time samples. Denoting as K the number of samples per frame, the average per-frame signal-to-noise ratio (SNR) can be defined as follows:

$$\text{SNR} \triangleq \frac{E_{voice}}{E_{noise}} = \frac{\sum_{i=1}^{K} |s_i|^2 / K}{\sum_{i=1}^{K} |n_i|^2 / K} = \frac{\sum_{i=1}^{K} |s_i|^2}{\sum_{i=1}^{K} |n_i|^2}. \tag{17.3}$$

Under the assumption that the noise is ergodic, its average energy E_{noise} at the denominator in (17.3) can be estimated during an initial training phase, when the background (noisy) audio signal is sensed, but the system is still inactive for the purpose of pattern detection.

Our approach can be extended to a more general scenario where the audio signal to be detected might be subject to filtering (i.e., to the presence of convolutional noise). In other words, the recorded signal would be

$$r(t) = g(t) \otimes s(t) + n(t). \tag{17.4}$$

Under the assumption of perfect estimation of $g(t)$, considering an initial filter with impulse response $g^{-1}(t)$, at its output, one would have

$$r'(t) = s(t) + n'(t) \tag{17.5}$$

where $n'(t) = n(t) \otimes g^{-1}(t)$. The proposed detection strategy can be then applied, as its training phase takes automatically into account the statistical characteristics of $n'(t)$. In the case of unknown or time-varying channel impulse response $g(t)$, one should first consider channel estimation, but this goes beyond the scope of this chapter.

17.3.3 Training and Energy Detection

The presence of an audio signal (of interest) can be identified by the "appearance" of an energy variation with respect to the existing audio background noise. Therefore, one could first analyze the energies of consecutive audio signal frames in order to detect abrupt energy changes. This time-domain-based approach is a direct extension of typical VAD approaches. The basic principle consists in comparing the average energy of a frame with a proper threshold $E_{\text{th-initial}}$, which depends on the mean and variance of the background noise energy (denoted as μ_{low} and σ_{low}^2, respectively). Therefore, accurate estimation of the latter energy is fundamental and is the goal of the training phase.

Denoting as $N_{\text{tr-f}}$ the number of consecutive frames considered in the training phase and as $N^{\text{tr-s}}$ the number of samples per frame, the mean and the variance of the noise energy can be computed as follows:*

$$\mu_{\text{low}} \triangleq \frac{1}{N_{\text{tr-f}}} \sum_{i=1}^{N_{\text{tr-f}}} \frac{1}{N^{\text{tr-s}}} \sum_{k=1}^{N^{\text{tr-s}}} \left| x_k^{(i)} \right|^2 \tag{17.6}$$

$$\sigma_{\text{low}}^2 \triangleq \frac{1}{N_{\text{tr-f}}} \sum_{i=1}^{N_{\text{tr-f}}} \frac{1}{\left(N^{\text{tr-s}} - 1\right)} \sum_{k=1}^{N^{\text{tr-s}}} \left(\left| x_k^{(i)} \right|^2 - \mu_{\text{low}} \right)^2 . \tag{17.7}$$

Upon completion of the training phase, denoting as $\{x_k\}_{k=1}^{N^{\text{low-s}}}$ the $N^{\text{low-s}}$ samples in a generic collected frame, the following binary decision rule can be considered to determine the presence ($D_{\text{low}} = 1$) or absence ($D_{\text{low}} = 0$) of an "atypical" signal:

$$\frac{\sum_{k=1}^{N^{\text{low-s}}} \left| x_k \right|^2}{N^{\text{low-s}}} \mathop{\gtrless}_{D_{\text{low}}=0}^{D_{\text{low}}=1} E_{\text{th-initial}} \tag{17.8}$$

where $E_{\text{th-initial}} \triangleq \mu_{\text{low}} + \epsilon \sigma_{\text{low}}$, with the parameter $\epsilon > 0$ allowing to tune the sensitivity in detecting atypical signals. Our results show that $\epsilon = 1$ allows to detect significant energy variations of the input audio signal, yet limiting the probability of missed detection (MD). The impact of ϵ on the system performance will be investigated in Section 17.5.3. Note that if $D_{\text{low}} = 0$ (i.e., no significant

---

* Note that the correct unbiased estimator for small values of $N^{\text{tr-f}}$ is considered in the evaluation of the variance in (17.7). This is motivated by the fact that the number of collected frames in the training phase will be kept low, that is, $N^{\text{tr-f}} = 20$.

energy variation is detected), the average energy and the variance of the background noise can be adapted by taking into account the newly processed frame. In particular, the following adaptation rule can be used upon the reception of the ℓth frame ($\ell = 1, 2, \ldots$):

$$\mu_{\text{low}}(\ell+1) = \frac{\mu_{\text{low}}(\ell-1) + \mu_{\text{low}}(\ell)}{2} \qquad \sigma^2_{\text{low}}(\ell+1) = \frac{\sigma^2_{\text{low}}(\ell-1) + \sigma^2_{\text{low}}(\ell)}{2} \qquad (17.9)$$

where $\mu_{\text{low}}(0) \triangleq \mu_{\text{low}}$ and $\sigma^2_{\text{low}}(0) \triangleq \sigma^2_{\text{low}}$. This updating rule may be generalized considering a larger number of consecutive frames or varying the coefficients (now set to 1/2) of the linear combination in (17.9).* It can also be generalized in a decision-directed form with the smoothing parameter, which can control the adaptation speed without any additional complexity and storage need. Note that the updates (17.9) are useful especially in the presence of nonstationary noise, with highly fluctuating variance. In this case, when no atypical signal is identified in the "triggered" fine processing phase (described in Section 17.5.1), the noise characteristics can be updated to better track the environmental changes.

By using the introduced energy-based processing, one can detect the presence of an atypical energy variation. However, our problem requires also to distinguish different audio signal patterns. As an illustrative example, we consider the following two discrete-time (ideal) audio signals: (a) the audio signal emitted by an M109 vehicle (a tank) moving at a constant speed of 30 km/h, with duration equal to 235 s and sampling frequency equal to 19.98 kHz, extracted from the NOISEX-92 database [43] and (b) the audio signal of a choir singing the Handel's "Hallelujah Chorus," preloaded in MATLAB with sampling frequency equal to 8.192 kHz [44]. Note that the Handel chorus, although unrealistic in surveillance applications, will be considered in this chapter only as representative of ideal human voice signals acquired at the highest sampling frequency with a microphone characterized by very good performance. The sequences obtained with different sampling rates are downsampled to a common rate, denoted as f_s^{low}, so that they can be additively combined. For each signal, we compute the normalized energy of each audio frame. The energy normalization is expedient to make the comparison meaningful—in fact, if the average energy of one of the signals is much higher than that of the other, then distinguishing them is trivial. In Figure 17.2, the probability mass functions (PMFs) of the frame energies are shown. The number of samples in the frame, denoted as $N^{\text{low-s}}$, is set to 128. As one can see, the two audio signals (even in the presence of very accurate human voice recording) cannot be easily distinguished, since the shapes of their PMFs are very similar. This should be expected, since a VAD-inspired approach allows only to detect the time intervals where an atypical signal (e.g., the voice) is present, without giving any information about the "content" of the audio signal. Frequency domain-based approaches, typically based on the use of higher-order statistics [39], have also been proposed for VAD. However, this significantly higher complexity is spent to detect more accurately the presence of atypical audio signals. In this case as well, if the energy distributions of the two audio signals are the same, their patterns cannot be distinguished. Therefore, increasing the computational complexity in this direction is, from the perspective of the problem at hand, useless.

In Section 17.4, we present a commercial product (DSN by SELEX Electronic System) where the time-domain audio signal pattern detection algorithm described in Section 17.3 is implemented.

---

* Our results show that updating the threshold by considering two consecutive frames allows to detect significant energy variations of the input audio signal with limited complexity.

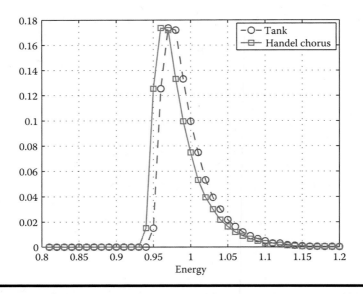

Figure 17.2 Comparison between the tank signal and the Handel chorus. In this case, the PMFs of the per-frame energies are considered.

17.4 Use-Case Example of Wireless Sensor Networks for Homeland Security

In this section, we describe an industrial example of WSN used for homeland security. As already anticipated in Section 17.2, an interesting solution to a class of homeland security problems is given by DSN produced by SELEX Electronic Systems [19]. This product family uses several customized sensor nodes in order to guarantee situational awareness and early warning. It supports force protection requirements and civil security needs, through the surveillance of target areas and the detection of hazards in different operational scenarios.

The need of situational awareness calls for advanced solutions in support of surveillance and identification in order to derive an accurate common operational picture (COP) for decision makers. This objective is currently achieved by deploying personnel equipped with expensive and sophisticated platforms. These deployments are risky, particularly for the personnel, and expensive, in terms of maintenance cost. In order to mitigate the mission risks and increase the surveillance capability, SELEX Electronic Systems has developed DSN.

17.4.1 The Architecture

DSN is an advanced solution that meets the need of low-cost, low-power consumption, and miniature sensors to ensure easy mass deployment, extended mission lifetime, and hand portability. A large quantity of sensor nodes can be deployed to cover a wide area and can routinely collect and report field information to command posts and personnel. DSN can be applied to several scenarios, by fulfilling crucial security, control, long-term monitoring, and surveillance needs, with an advanced solution that reduces system complexity and costs. The resilience of the communication is based on a set of proprietary and innovative delay tolerant networking communication protocols and asynchronous transmission, that greatly increase the battery life performing an optimal management of the limited power available on a sensor node [45]. DSN applications include battlefield and force protection, critical infrastructure protection (airports and runways, industrial sites, utilities), access and border control, and illegal activity monitoring. A possible scenario of interest is depicted in Figure 17.3. In particular, in Figure 17.3a, a military application is envisioned, namely, battlefield monitoring and army coordination. This kind of application is well known and analyzed by most of the literature in this realm. However, DSN can also be applied to a civil environment, as illustrated in Figure 17.3b, possibly integrating it with other surveillance systems, such as cameras with tracking capabilities. As an example, in Figure 17.3a, the application of interest is the control access of a civil manor. In this scenario, the ground sensor network is used together with a remote camera control, thus surrounding the civil manor with an "electronic fence." When a menace is detected from the ground sensor network, an alarm can be raised toward a home central unit in the manor itself or can be redirected toward a police station or another security agency.

Being designed to operate in both open terrain and urban areas for critical targets' detection and classification, the DSN family includes the following main functionalities.

- Detection by sensors of anomalies, with alert activation, in terms of movements, sounds, magnetic fields variations, and terrain vibrations.
- Data fusion activity and event generation performed by special nodes coordinating a given zone, denoted as "cluster head," after receiving multiple warnings from the network.
- Visualization of different alerts on the monitoring station, including georeferentiation of the occurred threat, the involved sensing capabilities, and the most likely threat classification. Together with early warning, the data fusion activity provides a support to decision makers to discriminate people, vehicles, as well as any environmental perturbation.

The standard DSN complete solution includes a network of short-range detection sensors and a central monitoring station for network monitoring and control. Default network sensing capabilities include seismic, infrared radiations, magnetic field perturbation, temperature, pressure, and acoustics, but other types of sensors with additional sensing capabilities like gas, chemical, or nuclear waste detectors can be integrated. The modular sensor node consists of a CPU, a communication board implementing a proprietary communication protocol stack, and a sensor board to be configured in order to host one or more sensing capabilities, according to the context.

Within the network, short-range sensor nodes interact with each other, thus creating an ad hoc wireless network. Nodes can automatically aggregate into clusters (short-range communication) and groups of clusters into a network (long-range communication). Within each cluster, a "cluster head" is elected and is responsible of the data fusion activity. Neighbor nodes are used as routers to convey data and information to the central monitoring station. The latter performs data acquisition from the network, as well as data processing and display of detected events, alarm generation, and threat evaluation by means of a 2D/3D GIS interface.

17.4.2 Operational Highlights

The sensor node configuration for operational awareness is based on the following detectors:

- seismic (geophones), to identify ground vibrations caused by pedestrians or vehicles;
- magnetic, to monitor movements of metal objects like vehicles;

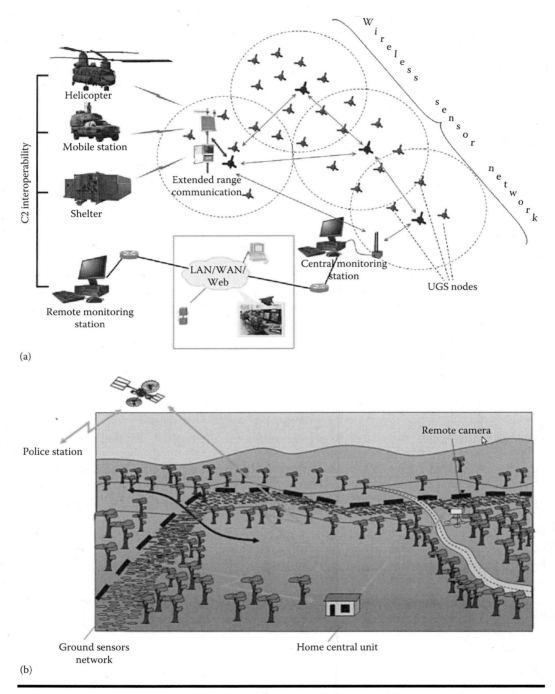

(a)

(b)

Figure 17.3 DSN in illustrative (a) military and (b) civil context environment.

- acoustic, to detect the presence of targets (human, clusters of humans, military vehicles, etc.) by means of the time-domain audio processing algorithm previously illustrated in Section 17.3.3;
- passive infrared, to detect movements of objects in a narrow field of view;
- Global Positioning System (GPS) receivers, for network geopositioning.

The main advantage of DSN with respect to other solutions on the market, is a significant menace detection performance, owing to the fusion of multisensorial data collected by several small sensors scattered across a monitored area. Moreover, from audio signal processing perspective, coherently with the main core of this chapter, it is possible to integrate into DSN more advanced audio signal processing-based classification algorithms, such as that proposed in Section 17.5, which improves the low-complexity approach of Section 17.3.3 by using spectral audio signal "fingerprints." This extension allows to distinguish different types of menace (vehicle from human, animals from humans, etc.). However, it is not possible to have a finer identification capability, for example, distinguishing a pair of adjacent humans from a single one. This is a subject of our current research activities.

DSN is available in two configurations, shown in Figure 17.4, to fit different application requirements. The first configuration is denoted as *tetrahedral*: sensor nodes have four 10 cm (or even less) long legs. In this case, the sensor nodes can be easily deployed by dropping them from aircraft, drones, or vehicles in hostile environments. The second configuration is denoted as *box*.

(a)   (b)

Figure 17.4   DSN: (a) tetrahedral and (b) box configuration.

In this case, the sensor nodes are cubes with 5 cm side, and they have to be deployed manually. This configuration is thus suitable for civilian applications.

17.4.3 Key Features

DSN brings valuable benefits to a wide range of dual-use applications. The main advantages brought by the use of DSN can be summarized as follows. First, sensor nodes can be disseminated on the ground without any specific manual intervention and, therefore, with ease of portability and deployability. This has been already observed with the tetrahedral configuration in Figure 17.4a. Moreover, the DSN architecture is highly flexible and scalable. In fact, DSN can be applied to a wide range of operational contexts demanding for enhanced protection and situational awareness. The open architecture and the use of sensor nodes lead to various scale solutions. Note also that DSN can operate in a stand-alone manner, as well as with other surveillance and identification systems, for example, closed-circuit television (CCTV), video, and unmanned aerial vehicles (UAVs) [46]. Finally, the considered processing (e.g., data fusion at cluster heads) allows to reliably avoid false alarms (FAs) from sensors, and the fault-tolerant configuration guarantees robustness and service continuity.

17.5 Low-Complexity Hybrid Time-Frequency Approach to Audio Signal Pattern Detection

While the time-domain processing approach presented in Sections 17.3 and 17.4 (from an algorithmic perspective) and Section 17.4 (from an industrial perspective) allows to detect the presence of an intruder, classifying the detected atypical audio signals requires further processing. In particular, our goal is to recognize if the detected abnormal signal belongs to a given class of interest. Referring to the homeland security problem, one possible envisioned application is to detect if a human (or a group of humans) enters a given area. Another possible application scenario consists in the detection of an unauthorized vehicle (e.g., a tank) entrance into a protected (forbidden) area. Our approach can be straightforwardly applied to other audio signals of interest (besides human and vehicles), provided that their frequency domain characteristics can be clearly identified and distinguished from those of other classes of audio signals.

In this case, VAD-inspired approaches are no longer sufficient. In this section, we apply the ideas behind speech recognition techniques [41], typically used to recognize different spoken words and to classify different audio signal patterns. In particular, our key idea is that of characterizing an audio signal frame with a spectral signature and then, through frequency domain processing, detect if the received audio signal matches with the signature.

In Section 17.5.1, the frequency domain processing is described. As the processing complexity might be very high, in Section 17.5.2, an innovative low-complexity hybrid time–frequency audio signal pattern detection algorithm is presented. Performance results are shown in Section 17.5.3.

17.5.1 Frequency-Based Audio Pattern Recognition

Upon the collection of the sequence of the samples of a single frame, denoted as $\{x_k\}_{k=1}^{N^{\text{high}-s}}$, its DFT $\{X(n)\}_{n=1}^{N^{\text{high}-s}}$ is computed:*

---

* Assuming that $N^{\text{high}-s}$ is a power of 2, it is possible to efficiently compute the DFT through a fast Fourier transform (FFT). Note also that $N^{\text{high}-s}$ might, in general, be different from $N^{\text{low}-s}$ introduced in Section 17.3.2.

$$X(n) = \sum_{k=1}^{N^{high-s}} x_k \, e^{-j\frac{2\pi}{N^{high-s}}kn} \qquad n=1,\ldots,N^{high-s}. \tag{17.10}$$

The sequence $\{|X(n)|^2\}$ is a particular instance of periodogram (in the absence of windowing between consecutive frames) associated with the sequence $\{x_k\}$ obtained by sampling the received audio signal with a sampling rate denoted as f_s^{high}. The sequence $\{|X(n)|^2\}$ thus represents an accurate estimate of the signal power spectral density [38]. Since the computation of the periodogram is computationally heavy (because of the presence of the squares of the modules of the DFT coefficients), we simply consider, as a representative "spectral shape" of the audio signal frame, the sequence of the modules of the DFT coefficients, that is, $\{|X(n)|\}$. Obviously, the spectral shape depends on the particular SNR: in fact, in the presence of high SNR, that is, high audio signal energy, the coefficients $\{|X(n)|\}$ will be large, and vice versa, for low SNR. Therefore, a "normalized" version of the spectral shape is needed to use the same spectral signature, regardless of the SNR. In particular, we propose the following normalized spectral shape:

$$|Y(n)| \triangleq \frac{|X(n)|}{\sqrt{\sum_{\ell=1}^{N^{high-s}} |X(\ell)|^2}} \qquad n=1,\ldots,N^{high-s} \tag{17.11}$$

where the normalization factor $\sqrt{\sum_{\ell=1}^{N^{high-s}} |X(\ell)|^2}$ is such that the energy of the spectral shape is unitary, that is, $\sum_{n=1}^{N^{high-s}} |Y(n)|^2 = 1$, regardless of the SNR.

The key principle of the proposed approach is to compare the normalized spectral shape of the frames of the received audio signal with a proper reference spectral *signature* (with unitary energy) of a frame of the reference audio pattern: if there is a "good agreement" between them, then the detected signal is declared of interest. In order to implement this strategy, the spectral signature and the "agreement" criterion have to be properly identified. Note that the proposed spectral signature-based approach cannot be applied if the signature is not available. The identification of the spectral signature requires the availability of a sufficiently large number of frames of the audio signal pattern of interest. However, our results show that a "coarse" characterization of the spectral characteristics of the reference audio pattern (e.g., using a few frames) is sufficient to guarantee good performance.

In the presence of nonstationary audio signals (e.g., voices), our results have shown that the best choice is to emphasize the high-energy frequency components of the reference audio pattern. To this end, the best spectral signature of an audio pattern is typically given by the *envelope* of the sequence of normalized spectral shapes of the available frames of the reference audio pattern. The envelope over n_{frame} consecutive frames can be defined as

$$\mathcal{I}^{(n\,frame)}(n) = \max_{i=1,\ldots,n_{frame}} |Y_i(n)| \qquad n=1,\ldots,N^{high-s}. \tag{17.12}$$

where $|Y_i|$ is the normalized spectral shape of the ith frame. On the other hand, in the presence of stationary signals (e.g., tank signal), an "average" spectral signature (based on the average of the FFTs of the frames) may lead to better performance. In [47], we propose an efficient (recursive)

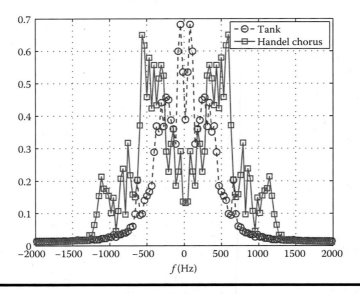

Figure 17.5 Comparison between the tank signal and the Handel chorus. In this case, the signals' spectral signatures are shown.

approach to the extraction of an envelope spectral signature. The extension to the extraction of an "average" spectral signature is straightforward.

As an illustrative example, we evaluate the (normalized) spectral signatures of the tank and the Handel chorus signals introduced in Section 17.3.2. The signatures are shown in Figure 17.5 in the case with $N^{\text{high-s}} = 128$ samples per frame (using 128-point FFT). As one can see, unlike the PMFs of the corresponding energies (Figure 17.2), the spectral envelopes are clearly different. This suggests that the two audio signal patterns may be successfully distinguished using the proposed spectral signature-based approach.

Once the spectral (envelope) signature has been extracted, upon reception of a given number of frames of an audio signal of potential interest, a partial spectral envelope can be derived and compared with the signature. In particular, one can evaluate the mean square error (MSE) between the partial spectral envelope of the received signal and the spectral signature as a function of the number of processed frames. At the mth step ($m = 1, 2, \ldots$), the MSE is

$$
\text{MSE}^{(m)} \triangleq \frac{\sum_{n=1}^{N^{\text{high-s}}} |\mathcal{I}_{\text{rx}}^{(m)}(n) - \mathcal{I}(n)|^2}{N^{\text{high-s}}} \tag{17.13}
$$

where $\{\mathcal{I}_{\text{rx}}^{(m)}(n)\}_{n=1}^{N^{\text{high-s}}}$ is the partial spectral envelope of the received signal after processing m frames. In the presence of the reference audio pattern, that is, the class of audio signals to be classified, $\mathcal{I}_{\text{rx}}^{(m)}(n)$ is an increasing function of m ($\forall n$). Provided that the spectral signature $\mathcal{I}(n)$ is representative of all possible instances of the class of audio signals of interest, that is, $\mathcal{I}(n) \geq \mathcal{I}_{\text{rx}}^{(m)}(n)$, $\forall n, m$, one can thus conclude that $\text{MSE}^{(m)}$ is a decreasing function of m: the signal is declared of interest when the MSE becomes lower than a given threshold. The following (per-frame) situations are then possible: correct detection (CD), if the MSE becomes lower than the threshold *given that* there is the reference audio pattern; MD, if the MSE does not become lower than the threshold *given that* there is the reference audio pattern; and FA, if the MSE becomes lower than the threshold *given that* there is not the reference audio pattern. The value of the MSE threshold can be chosen according to the behavior of $\{MSE^{(m)}\}$, as will be discussed in more detail in Section 17.5.3. We remark that the threshold value is a key parameter and has to be properly set in order to optimize the performance of the proposed detection algorithm.

The definition of the normalized spectral shape in (17.11) entails the use of a normalization factor with a square root and square powers. The complexity of these operations may be too high (e.g., for in-sensor applications). Therefore, we propose another heuristic normalization factor given by the sum of the modules, leading to the following simplified (still normalized) spectral shape:

$$\left|Y^{\text{simp}}(n)\right| = \frac{|X(n)|}{\displaystyle\sum_{m=1}^{N^{\text{high}-s}} |X(m)|} \quad n = 1,\ldots,N^{\text{high}-s} \tag{17.14}$$

so that the condition $\displaystyle\sum_{n=1}^{N^{\text{high}-s}} \left|Y^{\text{simp}}(n)\right| = 1$ holds. In this case as well, the partial spectral envelope of the received signal after processing m frames is

$$\mathcal{I}_{\text{rx}}^{(m)-\text{simp}}(n) \triangleq \max_{i=1,\ldots,m} \left|Y_i^{\text{simp}}(n)\right| \quad n = 1,\ldots,N^{\text{high}-s}. \tag{17.15}$$

In [47], it is shown that $\{\mathcal{I}_{\text{rx}}^{(m)-\text{simp}}(n)\}$ can be recursively updated. The performance of the detection algorithm can then be evaluated in terms of the following mean linear error (MLE):

$$\text{MLE}^{(m)} \triangleq \sum_{n=1}^{N^{\text{high}-s}} \frac{\left|\mathcal{I}_{\text{rx}}^{(m)-\text{simp}}(n) - \mathcal{I}^{\text{simp}}(n)\right|}{N^{\text{high}-s}} \tag{17.16}$$

where $\mathcal{I}^{\text{simp}}(n)$ is the simplified spectral signature. Obviously, the MLE computation has a complexity much lower than that of the MSE. It can also be shown that, provided that the simplified spectral signature $\mathcal{I}^{\text{simp}}(n)$ is representative of all possible instances of the class of audio signals of interest (i.e., $\mathcal{I}^{\text{simp}}(n) \geq \mathcal{I}_{\text{rx}}^{(m)-\text{simp}}(n), \forall n,m$), MLE$^{(m)}$ is a decreasing function of m. As in the MSE case, when MLE$^{(m)}$ becomes lower than a properly chosen threshold (different from the MSE threshold), one can declare that the detected signal is of interest. In the remainder of this chapter, the MLE threshold will be denoted as τ_{high}.

17.5.2 Hybrid Time–Frequency Algorithm

We now present a low-complexity audio recognition algorithm whose focus is to detect, with limited complexity, the presence *and* the pattern of an audio signal. In this sense, our problem is related to both VAD and sound recognition (first, presence detection and then pattern identification). In particular, we will show that our approach leads to the same performance of other approaches in the literature (e.g., that presented in [33]), but with a much lower computational complexity.

The frequency domain–based approach proposed in Section 17.5.1 does not take into account the energy content of the acquired signal, which can be evaluated in the time domain with a much lower computational complexity. In fact, when the reference audio pattern is not present in the acquired audio signal, the energy of the acquired signal coincides with that of the background noise. Therefore, one may exploit this idea to significantly reduce the computational complexity as follows. First, the *presence* of a possible atypical signal is detected, in terms of energy variation, by using the simple time-domain processing described in Section 17.3.3. Then, if an "atypical" signal is detected, its pattern is analyzed using the frequency domain processing technique described in Section 17.5.1.

Taking into account possible correlations between consecutive frames, it is expedient to consider (as often done in VAD schemes [39]) a *hangover* finite-state machine (FSM) model, shown in Figure 17.6, where the evolution between the state (F^{low}) associated with coarse processing and the state (F^{high}) associated with fine processing occurs through intermediate states. Every transition is a direct consequence of a single-frame processing. In particular, the audio signal frames have fixed duration in each processing phase. Having fixed the frame duration, we denote as $N^{\text{low-s}} = T_{\text{frame}}^{\text{low}} \cdot f_s^{\text{low}}$ and $N^{\text{high-s}} = T_{\text{frame}}^{\text{high}} \cdot f_s^{\text{high}}$ the numbers of samples per frame in the coarse and fine processing phases, where f_s^{low} and f_s^{high} are the sampling rates in the two phases, respectively. The sampling frequency f_s^{low} is low: namely, $f_s^{\text{low}} < 2 f_{\text{Nyq}}$, where f_{Nyq} is the Nyquist frequency of the audio signal at hand. This choice is not critical, since in the coarse processing phase, our goal is simply to detect abrupt energy changes but not an accurate signal reconstruction. On the other hand, f_s^{high} should be higher than $2 f_{\text{Nyq}}$. However, in the experimental results presented in the following, we will consider a microphone with a sampling frequency of slightly lower value than $2 f_{\text{Nyq}}$. Our results show that

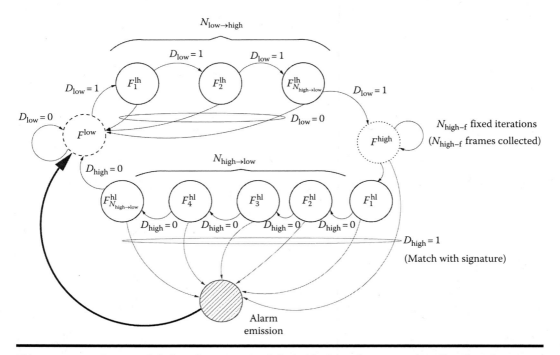

Figure 17.6 FSM model for the proposed hybrid time–frequency audio signal pattern detection scheme.

this does not hinder the performance—recall that the pattern, rather than the specific signal, needs to be detected—yet allowing to reduce the complexity.

The evolution of the proposed processing algorithm over the FSM can be described as follows. Typically, the algorithm is in F^{low}. After low-complexity processing (in time domain) of an $N^{\text{low-s}}$-sample frame, a binary decision D_{low} on the presence of an atypical signal is taken: if $D_{\text{low}} = 0$ (no atypical signal), the algorithm remains in F^{low}; if $D_{\text{low}} = 1$, the algorithm evolves to the next intermediate state, denoted as F_1^{lh}, where low-complexity processing is considered. In general, one can consider $N_{\text{low} \rightarrow \text{high}}$ intermediate states $(F_1^{\text{lh}}, \ldots, F_{N_{\text{low} \rightarrow \text{high}}}^{\text{lh}})$ to evolve from F^{low} to F^{high}. The use of the intermediate states is expedient to avoid useless and computationally intensive fine processing in the presence of impulsive noise, which may lead to short significant energy variations but, obviously, is not of interest. In the illustrative FSM model in Figure 17.6, $N_{\text{low} \rightarrow \text{high}}$ is set to 3.

If for $N_{\text{low} \rightarrow \text{high}} + 1$ consecutive frames the presence of an atypical signal is verified (i.e., $D_{\text{low}} = 1$), then the algorithm moves to F^{high}. In this state, a *fixed* number $N_{\text{high-f}}$ (to be properly selected, as discussed in Section 17.5.3) of frames, with $N^{\text{high-s}}$ samples each, is collected. After processing the $N_{\text{high-f}}$ frames in the frequency domain, as described in Section 17.5.1, a binary decision D_{high} is taken: if $D_{\text{high}} = 1$ (i.e., $\text{MLE}^{(N_{\text{high-f}})}$ is below threshold), then the signal pattern is declared of interest, a proper alarm is emitted, and the algorithm moves back to F^{low}; if $D_{\text{high}} = 0$, then the algorithm moves to an intermediate state F_1^{hl} and processes one more frame. At this point, if $D_{\text{high}} = 1$, then the algorithm moves to F^{low} and an alarm is emitted; otherwise, it moves to the next intermediate state F_2^{hl}. Eventually, if $D_{\text{high}} = 0$ for $N_{\text{high} \rightarrow \text{low}} + 1$ consecutive frames (after exiting F^{high}), then the algorithm comes back to F^{low} and no alarm is emitted: in other words, the atypical signal detected in the coarse processing phase is declared of no interest. The intermediate states $\{F_1^{\text{hl}}, \ldots, F_{N_{\text{low} \rightarrow \text{high}}}^{\text{hl}}\}$ from F^{high} to F^{low} can be interpreted as "backup" states used to collect a larger number of frames to be fine processed in order to improve the reliability of the decision on the presence of a reference audio pattern. In the illustrative example in Figure 17.6, it holds that* $N_{\text{high} \rightarrow \text{low}} = 5$. The derivation of a statistical model for the probability of FA would allow to analytically select the value of $N_{\text{high} \rightarrow \text{low}}$. However, this extension goes beyond the scope of this chapter.

We now present a comparative computational complexity analysis of the hybrid time-frequency approach proposed in this section with respect to the frequency domain-based approach presented in Section 17.5.1. To this end, suppose that the reference audio pattern is present only in a fraction α of the N_{frame} collected frames (typically, $\alpha \ll 1$). If only frequency-based processing is performed, the total computational complexity can be quantified as follows:

$$\mathcal{C}_{\text{tot}}^{\text{F}} = N_{\text{frame}} \mathcal{C}_{\text{freq}} \tag{17.17}$$

where $\mathcal{C}_{\text{freq}}$ is the computational complexity of frequency domain-based processing of a single frame. When, instead, the hybrid time-frequency approach is considered, the overall computational complexity becomes

$$\mathcal{C}_{\text{tot}}^{\text{T-F}} = \alpha N_{\text{frame}} \mathcal{C}_{\text{freq}} + (1 - \alpha) N_{\text{frame}} \mathcal{C}_{\text{time}} \tag{17.18}$$

where $\mathcal{C}_{\text{time}}$ is the computational complexity of time-domain-based processing of a frame.

Since time-domain processing requires the computation of the per-frame average energy, its computational complexity (in terms of basic operations) is on the order of $O(N^{\text{low-s}})$, where $N^{\text{low-s}}$

---

* Typically, in the VAD literature $N_{\text{high} \rightarrow \text{low}} > N_{\text{low} \rightarrow \text{high}}$ [26].

is the number of per-frame samples. In fact, the computation of the per-frame average energy involves $N^{\text{low-s}}$ square operations, $N^{\text{low-s}} - 1$ additions, and 1 division. Frequency-based processing, instead, involves the computation of the FFT of the frame and a comparison with the predefined spectral signature:

$$\mathcal{C}_{\text{freq}} = \mathcal{C}_{\text{FFT}} + \mathcal{C}_{\text{sig}} \qquad (17.19)$$

where it is well known that $\mathcal{C}_{\text{FFT}} \sim O((N^{\text{high-s}}/2)\log N^{\text{high-s}})$ [48] and $\mathcal{C}_{\text{sig}} \sim O((N^{\text{high-s}})^2)$ (because of the number of additions in (17.14)). Note that the signal power spectral density may be computed by means of the periodogram; in this case, however, no normalization is involved. Moreover, the complexity associated with this operation is negligible with respect to that of the FFT computation. At this point, one obtains

$$\mathcal{C}_{\text{tot}}^{\text{F}} = N_{\text{frame}}(N^{\text{high-s}})^2 \qquad (17.20)$$

$$\mathcal{C}_{\text{tot}}^{\text{T-F}} = \alpha N_{\text{frame}}(N^{\text{high-s}})^2 + (1-\alpha)N_{\text{frame}}N^{\text{low-s}} \qquad (17.21)$$

$$\simeq \alpha N_{\text{frame}}(N^{\text{high-s}})^2 \qquad (17.22)$$

where we have used the fact that, typically, $N^{\text{low-s}} \ll N^{\text{high-s}}$. After a few simple manipulations, the complexity reduction brought by the use of the hybrid time–frequency pattern detection algorithm is on the order of

$$\frac{\mathcal{C}_{\text{tot}}^{\text{F}}}{\mathcal{C}_{\text{tot}}^{\text{T-F}}} \simeq \frac{1}{\alpha} \gg 1 \qquad (17.23)$$

This is intuitively expected, since the hybrid approach concentrates the complexity only in the presence of an atypical signal. If the atypical signal is of interest and appears for a fraction α of the time, then the complexity reduction is on the order of $1/\alpha$.

We remark that the complexity of the frequency domain processing approach of Section 17.5.1 is comparable to other existing frequency domain-based algorithms (e.g., [33]). Therefore, the complexity reduction brought by the proposed hybrid approach holds also with respect to them.

17.5.3 Performance Analysis

17.5.3.1 "Ideal" Signals

The following setup is considered. The potential audio signals of interest are the Handel chorus and the tank sound, introduced at the end of Section 17.3.3. A "slice" of the reference audio pattern is 8 s long and is randomly additively combined with a background noisy audio signal of duration equal to 235 s and sampling frequency equal to 19.98 kHz, extracted from the NOISEX-92 database [43]. On top of the background noisy signal, a slice of another audio signal (with a spectral signature different from that of the reference audio pattern) is inserted. The two slices do not overlap: otherwise, our system would not be able to detect any of them. The training phase is carried out considering $N_{\text{tr-f}} = 20$ frames of the background noisy signal. The sampling frequencies for the coarse and fine processing phases are $f_s^{low} = 1024$ Hz and $f_s^{high} = 4096$ Hz, respectively. As anticipated in Section 17.3.3, the audio sequences (tank, Handel chorus, and background noise) obtained with different sampling rates are downsampled to $f_s^{low} = 1024$ Hz in the coarse processing phase* and to $f_s^{high} = 4096$ Hz in the fine processing phase. The numbers of samples per frame analyzed in the coarse and fine processing phases are $N^{low-s} = 16$ and $N^{high-s} = 128$, so that the frame durations in the two phases are equal to $T_{frame}^{low} \simeq 16$ ms and $T_{frame}^{high} \simeq 31$ ms, respectively. The numbers of intermediate states in the FSM have been heuristically set to $N_{low \rightarrow high} = 3$ and $N_{high \rightarrow low} = 5$. The filter that will first be considered, in our simulations, to process ideal audio signals is derived from a low-pass filter (LPF) of the commercial microphone, which will be used to collect realistic audio signals [42], as described in more detail in Section 17.5.3. In order to approximate this LPF, we use a Butterworth infinite impulse response (IIR) filter with a 3 dB bandwidth approximately equal to 2.2 kHz.

We assume that the Handel chorus is the reference audio pattern, whereas the tank audio signal is not.[†] The background noise is assumed Gaussian and white. As a first analysis step, we investigate the behaviors of the MSE and MLE (between the partial envelope of the received signal and the spectral signature) as functions of number of collected frames. To this purpose, the SNR is set to 20 dB. In order to evaluate the system performance, we perform 20 independent simulation runs (with random generation of disjoint initial time instants of the Handel chorus and tank audio signals). In Figure 17.7a, the MSE is shown, as a function of the number of processed frames. It is possible to observe that the set of curves associated with the reference audio pattern is lower than that associated with the pattern of no interest. This behavior is pronounced also for a small number of frames: for instance, after 3 frames, the signals are easily separable. In other words, the proposed spectral signature-based detection approach is effective also when a few frames are collected and analyzed. In Figure 17.7b, the MLE is considered. Although a general performance degradation (in terms of separability) can be observed (due to the simpler normalization), the reference pattern (Handel chorus) can still be distinguished from the other one (tank). From the results in Figure 17.7, one can determine the number of frames N_{high-f}, which need to be processed, in the state F^{high} of the FSM, in order to reliably recognize the identified audio pattern. Simultaneously, the corresponding value of the threshold τ_{high} can be determined as a function of the selected value of N_{high-f}. For instance, if $N_{high-f} = 5$, then $\tau_{high} \simeq 2.5$. Reducing N_{high-f}, τ_{high} should increase. However, our results show that a higher value of τ_{high} makes the probability of FA increase dramatically. Therefore, for $N_{high-f} < 5$, the best performance is obtained with a "conservative" value of τ_{high} equal to 2.5.

In Figure 17.8a, the probabilities of MD and CD are shown, as functions of the SNR, in a scenario with Handel chorus or tank as reference audio pattern and MLE-based frequency domain processing. Two possible values for N_{high-f} are considered: 1 and 5. For every value of SNR, 1000 independent simulation runs are performed in order to eliminate possible statistical fluctuations. The background audio noise is Gaussian and white. One can note that approximately the same performance can be observed for both signals of interest. In particular, for sufficiently high values of the SNR (around 8 dB), the probability of MD goes to zero, whereas the probability of CD goes to 1. One may argue that this value is too high; however, it is possible to observe that for $SNR \geq 4$ dB the probability of MD is already below 10%. Moreover,

---

* We consider a very small value of f_s^{low} in order to reduce the computational complexity, thus saving as much battery energy as possible in wireless sensor network-based applications.

† Note that similar results hold in a scenario where the tank signal is of interest and Handel chorus is not. They are not reported here for lack of space.

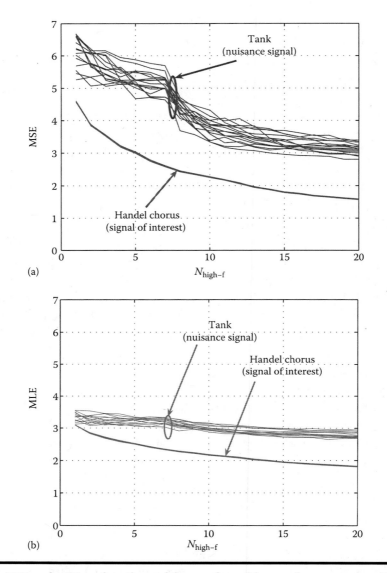

Figure 17.7 MSE and MLE, as functions of the number of frames, in a scenario with the Handel chorus as reference audio pattern.

as it will be shown in the next section, the penalty with respect to "classical" frequency-based algorithms is limited. Moreover, for low values of the SNR, increasing the number of frames in the fine processing phase allows to improve the performance. For $N_{high-f} = 5$, however, one can observe some fluctuations in the probability of CD. In this case, some false alarms, even if rare (with probability on the order of 10^{-2}), appear at intermediate SNR values and disappear for large values of the SNR. This is due to the fact that for large values of N_{high-f}, the considered value of τ_{high} may not be optimal for these intermediate SNRs. In general terms, one can consider that the detection algorithm is properly working when the probability of CD becomes significantly

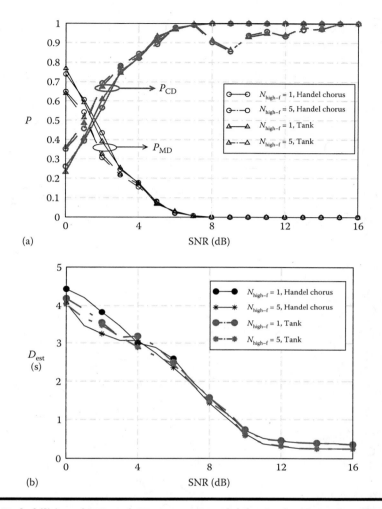

Figure 17.8 **Probabilities of MD and CD (case (a)) and delay in the presence of CD (case (b)), as functions of the SNR, in a scenario with Handel chorus or tank as reference audio pattern and MLE-based frequency domain processing. Two possible values for N_{high-f} are considered: 1 and 5.**

higher than the probability of MD. For instance, in the scenario considered in Figure 17.8, the proposed detection algorithm becomes effective for SNR ≥ 7 dB.

In Figure 17.8b, the delay (dimension: [s]) is considered. The delay is evaluated only when there is CD, since, otherwise, it would not be meaningful. In fact, when the pattern is not identified, the state of the system continuously iterates, in the FSM, between the coarse and fine processing states.* For small values of the SNR, the delay is around 4 s, and it would not be possible to detect signals with duration shorter than this maximum delay—recall that the entire duration of the signal "slice" of interest is 8 s. This is due to the large number of frames, which are processed before the presence of an atypical signal is declared in the coarse processing phase. For large values of the SNR, instead, in 0.5 s, the reference audio pattern is correctly identified, thus making the

---

* One may consider a maximum number of iterations after which the system is reset.

proposed algorithm almost real time. One can observe that the delay depends only slightly on the number of processed frames.

The limiting lower value of the delay for large values of the SNR is due to the fact that, even in the presence of correct identification, $N_{\text{low}\rightarrow\text{high}} + 1$ frames (with low sampling frequency) and $N_{\text{high-f}}$ frames (with high sampling frequency) need to be processed, thus leading to the following minimum achievable delay:

$$D_{\min} = (N_{\text{low}\rightarrow\text{high}} + 1)T_{\text{frame}}^{\text{low}} + N_{\text{high-f}}T_{\text{frame}}^{\text{high}}. \tag{17.24}$$

Expression (17.24) holds for sufficiently large values of $N_{\text{high-f}}$ (e.g., $N_{\text{high-f}} = 5$). For $N_{\text{high-f}} = 1$, instead, the delay is slightly large, since more backup frames need to be processed before a spectral match is declared (i.e., the MLE lowers below threshold). In other words, a single frame is not sufficient in F^{high}, and it may happen that the system state starts moving back toward F^{low} before declaring a match.

17.5.3.2 Experimentally Acquired Signals

We now analyze the performance of the proposed audio pattern detection algorithm in the presence of signals acquired through the realistic microphone mentioned in Section 17.3.2. We remark that this microphone is characterized by a flat frequency response and its sampling frequency is equal to 3450 Hz [42], which has been used as the sampling frequency f_s^{high} in the fine processing phase for all audio sequences. Moreover, the acquired audio sequences are further downsampled to $f_s^{\text{low}} = 1024$ Hz in the coarse processing phase. The other simulation parameters are set as described at the beginning of Section 17.5.3. The performance is analyzed either (1) considering direct use of the signal at the output of the microphone or (2) filtering the signal at the output of the filter through the front-end LPF, with cutoff frequency equal to 2.2 kHz, introduced in Section 17.3.2. The use of this LPF allows to derive preliminary insights on the impact of front-end digital filtering on the performance of the proposed detection algorithm. Further research is needed to derive the "optimal" front-end filtering technique.

The acquired speech signals used to derive the spectral signature correspond to the voices of five males (with ages between 23 and 35, at the University of Parma) reading some texts, both in Italian and in English. Since the frequency response of the real microphone between 0 and 100 Hz is not declared by the manufacturer [42], in the fine processing phase, the FFT of each frame is set to zero in the [0,100] Hz band. As nonspeech signal, we have acquired the sound emitted by the engine of a nonmoving car (FIAT Punto, 1900 cc, turbo-diesel) running at 3000 rpm. The duration of all acquired signals is around 30 s. Note that these experimentally acquired signals are recorded in very noisy environments, for example, open spaces (the university campus) or university laboratories, where these signals are mixed with different environmental noises. Therefore, these signals may be representative of signals of interest with reduced energy in surveillance applications. The spectral signature of the car engine can be uniquely extracted. On the other hand, when a speech signal is of interest, three possible approaches can be followed to extract a spectral signature: (1) compute the spectral envelope (as described in Section 17.5.1) associated with the available frames of the voice signal of the specific person to be detected, (2) compute the spectral envelope associated with the available frames of the voice signal of a person different from the one to be detected, and (3) compute the arithmetic average of the spectral envelopes associated with all persons (speaking in Italian or English). Although similar results hold for cases (1) and (2), in the following, we focus on case (3). This choice is motivated by the fact that the system should be robust against possible variations of the signals to be detected, that is, we ideally want to be able to detect all audio signals belonging to the same class (e.g., human voice) with a single spectral signature. The 8 s speech signal slices, randomly additively combined with a background white noise signal in the simulator, correspond to other people reading different scripts.

First, we analyze the impact of the presence of the front-end LPF. In Figure 17.9, the spectral signatures for speech and car engine signals are compared (a) in the presence and (b) in the absence

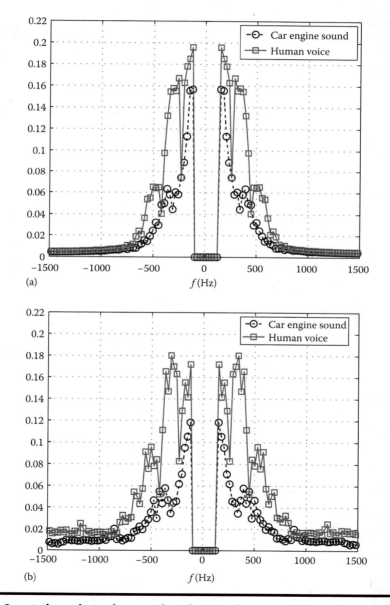

Figure 17.9 Spectral envelopes for speech and car engine signals. In case (a), the envelopes are compared in the presence of the LPF, whereas in case (b) the LPF is not considered.

of the LPF, respectively. One can observe that the presence of the LPF significantly changes the signature shape for both voice and car signals. In particular, the secondary peaks of the voice spectral signature, well evidenced in the absence of the LPF, become less evident if the LPF is considered. At this point, one could think that the use of the LPF is not beneficial, since the spectral signatures of the two audio signals seem to become less different. This, however, is not the case, as will be discussed later.

In Figure 17.10, the MLE is shown, as a function of the number of processed frames, in a scenario with SNR = 20 dB for (a) speech or (b) car engine sound as signals of interest.

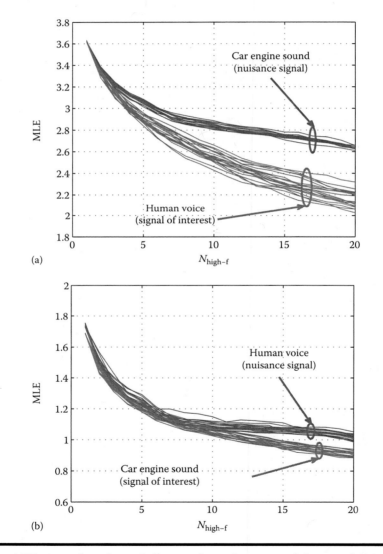

Figure 17.10 MLE, as a function of the number of processed frames, in a scenario with SNR = 20 dB for (a) speech or (b) car engine as reference audio pattern, respectively. The presence of the front-end LPF is considered.

The presence of the front-end LPF is considered, and 20 independent simulation runs are performed. In case (a), the two groups of curves are well separated: if N_{high-f} is set to 15, then the MLE threshold τ_{high} (to be used in F^{high}) can be set to 2.6. In case (b), instead, the audio pattern identification is more complicated, since the two groups of curves are not well separated. The absence of the front-end LPF leads to a performance degradation, that is, the curves associated with different classes of audio signals cannot be easily distinguished and the MLE decision threshold increases—the results are not reported here for the sake of conciseness. For instance, in the case of speech signals of interest, the optimized value of τ_{high} becomes approximately equal to 4. This seems to be in contradiction with the results in Figure 17.9, from which one may think that the absence of evident secondary peaks in the presence of the LPF would not help in distinguishing between different patterns. However, the faster convergence in the presence of the LPF allows to conclude that concentrating the energy in the primary peaks might be more beneficial for the proposed detection algorithm. As previously anticipated, the design of the "optimal" LPF is an open problem.

In Figure 17.11, (a) the probabilities of MD and CD and (b) the delay, in the presence of CD, are shown as functions of the SNR. The reference audio pattern is the speech. Both the presence and the absence of the front-end LPF are considered. On the basis of the analysis carried out in Figure 17.10, during the fine processing phase, $N_{high-f} = 15$ frames are collected and the MLE threshold τ_{high} is set, in the presence and absence of the LPF, to 2.4 and 3.9, respectively. The values of the threshold have been reduced, with respect to those predicted by the results in Figure 17.10 (i.e., 2.6 and 4, respectively), to lower the probability of FA. In general, τ_{high} should be tuned for the particular environment where the audio sensors are placed. Comparing the results in Figure 17.11a with those in Figure 17.8a, one can observe that the trends are similar. In the current scenario, the absence of the LPF is detrimental, since the probability of CD reaches 1 for larger values of the SNR. Comparing the results in Figure 17.11b with those in Figure 17.8b, the following observations can be made. Unlike in Figure 17.8b, in Figure 17.11b, for small values of the SNR, the simulated delay decreases. This is due to the fact that the number of CDs also reduces (according to the behavior of the probability of CD in Figure 17.11a). In this case, a weighted average delay between the estimated delay (in the presence of CD) and a *predetermined* maximum delay D_{max} (in the absence of CD), defined as $\bar{D} \triangleq D_{max}(1 - P_{CD}) + D_{est}P_{CD}$, is more meaningful. In Figure 17.11b, a maximum delay $D_{max} = 4$ s is considered. As expected, the $\bar{D}$ curves compare favorably with the delay curves in Figure 17.8b.

In Figure 17.12, (a) the probabilities of MD and CD and (b) the delay (in the presence of CD) are shown, as functions of the SNR, in the absence of LPF. The proposed hybrid time/frequency algorithm is compared to the frequency-based detection algorithm in [33], with spectrum quantization in eight subbands. It is possible to observe that there is a performance degradation with respect to the scenario presented in Figure 17.11, due to the fact that the spectrum is quantized with a smaller number of points. One can note that the performance loss, in terms of probabilities of FA, MD, and CD, incurred by the hybrid approach is very limited (on the order of a fraction of dB). However, the delay with the proposed hybrid approach is lower than that with the frequency-based approach. This is due to the fact that in the latter case the system spends more time processing frames without energy atypicalities, and this might delay the recognition of the pattern of interest.

We now focus on the detection of the car engine audio signal. From the analysis of the MLE behavior in Figure 17.10b, the optimized value of τ_{high} is around 1.1. However, this value leads to

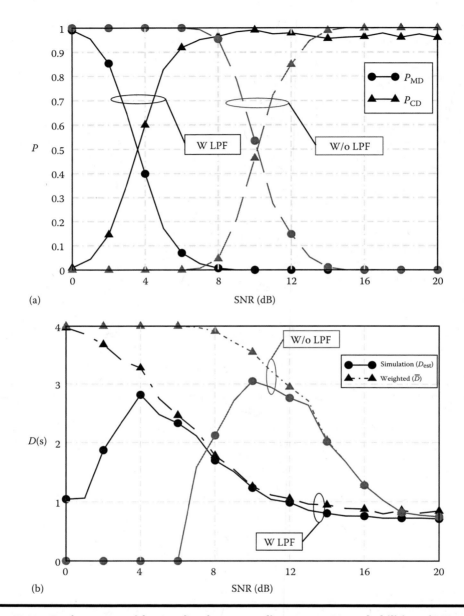

Figure 17.11 **Performance with speech reference audio pattern: (a) probabilities of MD and CD and (b) delay, in the presence of CD, as functions of the SNR. Both the presence and the absence of the front-end LPF are considered.**

a probability of FA too high, and smaller values have to be considered. If $\tau_{high} = 0.9$ is considered, P_{MD} goes to zero for increasing SNR; however, P_{FA} is too high and P_{CD} too low. Reducing τ_{high} has a beneficial impact on P_{FA}, but P_{MD} does not go to zero any longer. This dismal performance is probably due to the fact that the FFTs of the frames are set to zero in the [0,100] Hz band, where the car engine signal energy concentrates.

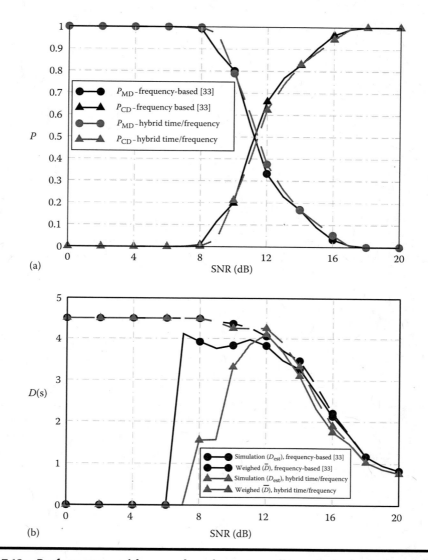

Figure 17.12 Performance with speech reference audio pattern and absence of LPF: (a) probabilities of MD and CD and (b) delay, in the presence of CD, as functions of the SNR. The frequency-based algorithm in [28] is compared to the proposed hybrid time/frequency algorithm.

We finally investigate the impact of the sensitivity parameter ε in the VAD detection. In Figure 17.13, the probability of CD is shown, as a function of ε, in a scenario with speech as reference audio pattern and absence of front-end LPF. Two values for the SNR are considered: 8 and 14 dB. As one can see, the optimum value of ε depends on the considered SNR, but it is always in the range (0,1). However, the common choice $\varepsilon = 1$ allows to obtain a performance close to the best value for all possible values of the SNR.

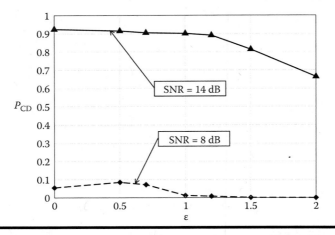

Figure 17.13 Probability of CD, as a function of ε, in a scenario with speech as reference audio pattern and absence of front-end LPF. Two values for the SNR are considered: 8 and 14 dB.

17.6 Concluding Remarks

In this chapter, we have discussed WSN-based solutions for homeland security, for example, applications like surveillance of critical areas. While we have first analyzed the main commercial WSN-based solutions for monitoring, we have then discussed one particular sensor processing for homeland security, that is, audio processing for the detection of the presence of undesired users, showing a use-case example, that is, DSN, where audio time-domain signal recognition is implemented. Finally, we have presented an innovative hybrid time–frequency audio signal pattern recognition. Our results show that the reliability of the proposed hybrid algorithm is very high, with limited computational complexity, thus making this solution suitable for WSN-based solutions for homeland security, for example, the DSN product family.

Acknowledgments

This work was funded by Elsag-Datamat S.p.A. (ED), Rome, Italy, which later became SELEX Sistemi Integrati S.p.A. We would like to thank the "SISTEMI SPECIALI" working group directed by Claudio Marchesini, its account manager Paolo Proietti, and all its management staff Luca Di Donato e Sandro Matticci for the useful discussion on audio signal processing.

References

1. Homeland Security. URL: http://en.wikipedia.org/wiki/Homeland_security, accessed on January 23, 2013.
2. HALO: Hostile Artillery Locating System. URL: http://www.finmeccanica.it/Corporate/EN/Corporate/Settori/Elettronica_per_la_Difesa_e_Sicurezza/Prodotti/HALO_Selex_Galileo/index.sdo, accessed on January 23, 2013.
3. Kaushik, B., D. Nance, and K. K. Ahuja. 2005. A review of the role of acoustic sensors in the modern battlefield. In *Proceedings of AIAA/CEAS Aeroacoustics Conference*, pp. 1–4. Monterey, CA.

4. Werner-Allen, G., P. Swieskowski, and M. Welsh. 2005. MoteLab: A wireless sensor network testbed. In *Proceedings of International Symposium Information Processing in Sensor Networks (IPSN)*, pp. 483–488. Los Angeles, CA.
5. Chatzigiannakis, I., C. Koninis, G. Mylonas, S. Fischer, and D. Pfisterer. 2009. WISEBED: An open large-scale wireless sensor network testbed. In *Proceedings of International Conference on Sensor Networks Applications, Experimentation and Logistics*, pp. 68–87. Athens, Greece.
6. The IPSO Alliance. URL: http://www.ipso-alliance.org/, accessed on January 23, 2013.
7. Tinynode: Real Life Wireless Sensor Networks. URL: http://www.tinynode.com/, accessed on January 23, 2013.
8. Nagios. URL: http://www.nagios.org/, accessed on January 23, 2013.
9. Netmagic. URL: http://www.netmagicsolutions.com/, accessed on January 23, 2013.
10. Advantic Systemas Y Servicios. URL: http://www.advanticsys.com/, accessed on January 23, 2013.
11. Libelium. URL: http://www.libelium.com/, accessed on January 23, 2013.
12. Urbiotica: The City Operating System. URL: http://www.urbiotica.com/, accessed on January 23, 2013.
13. Worldsensing: Making Smart Cities Happen. URL: http://www.worldsensing.com/, accessed on January 23, 2013.
14. Presto Parking. URL: http://www.prestoparking.com/, accessed on January 23, 2013.
15. KNX Association. Reduced energy consumption by using home and building control systems. URL: http://www.knx.org/knx/knx-applications/knx-is-green/, accessed on January 23, 2013.
16. Fadell, A. 2010. Intelligent power-enabled communications port. U.S. Patent 0007473.
17. Fadell, A. 2010. Intelligent power monitoring. U.S. Patent 0010857.
18. HomePlug Power Alliance. URL: https://www.homeplug.org/, accessed on January 23, 2013.
19. Selex Sistemi Integrati. URL: Selex Electronic Systems URL: https://www.selex-es.com, accessed on January 23, 2013.
20. Preston, J. 2011. Homeland security cancels "virtual fence" after [dollar]1 billion is spent. *The New York Times* A11.
21. Customs, U.S., and Border Protection. SBInet: Securing U.S. Borders. URL: http://www.dhs.gov/xlibrary/assets/sbinetfactsheet.pdf, accessed on July 24, 2012.
22. Customs, U.S., and Border Protection. Secure Border Initiative. URL: www.cbp.gov/xp/cgov/border_security/sbi/, accessed on July 24, 2012.
23. Chellappa, R., P. Sinha, and P. J. Phillips. 2010. Face recognition by computers and humans. *IEEE Transactions on Computers* 43(2): 46–55.
24. Trivedi, M. M., T. L. Gandhi, and K. S. Huang. 2005. Distributed interactive video arrays for event capture and enhanced situational awareness. *IEEE Transactions on Intelligent Systems* 20(5): 58–66.
25. Hampapur, A. 2008. Smart video surveillance for proactive security. *IEEE Transactions on Signal Processing* 25(4): 134–136.
26. Liu, H., C. Tang, S. Wu, and H. Wang. 2011. Real-time video surveillance for large scenes. In *International Conference on Wireless Communications and Signal (WCSP)*, pp. 1–4. Nanjing, China.
27. Maybury, M. 2009. Audio and video processing to enhance homeland security. In *IEEE Conference on Technologies for Homeland Security (HST)*, pp. 516–523. Boston, MA.
28. Caiti, A., A. Munafo, and G. Vettori. 2012. A geographical information system (GIS)-based simulation tool to assess civilian harbor protection levels. *IEEE Journal of Oceanic Engineering* 37(1): 85–102.
29. Dufaux, A. 2001. Detection and recognition of impulsive sound signals. PhD thesis, Institute of Microtechnology—University of Neuchatel, Switzerland.
30. Rabaoui, A., H. Kadri, Z. Lachiri, and N. Ellouze. 2008. One-class SVMs challenges in audio detection and classification applications. *EURASIP Journal on Advances in Signal Processing*. 2008: 14.
31. Yoo, I.-C. and D. Yook. 2008. Automatic sound recognition for the hearing impaired. *IEEE Transactions on Consumer Electronics* 54(4): 2029–2036.
32. Clavel, C., T. Ehrette, and G. Richard. 2005. Events detection for an audio-based surveillance system. In *IEEE International Conference on Multimedia and Expo (ICME)*, pp. 1306–1309. Amsterdam, The Netherlands.

33. Eronen, A. J., V. T. Peltonen, J. T. Tuomi, A. P. Klapuri, S. Fagerlund, T. Sorsa, G. Lorho, and J. Huopaniemi. 2006. Audio-based context recognition. *IEEE Transactions on Acoustics Speech and Language Processing* 14(1): 321–329.

34. Abu-El-Quran, A. R., R. A. Goubran, and A. D. C. Chan. 2006. Security monitoring using microphone arrays and audio classification. *IEEE Transactions on Instrumentation and Measurement* 55(4): 1025–1032.

35. Chu, S., S. Narayanan, and C.-C. J. Kuo. 2009. Environmental sound recognition with time-frequency audio features. *IEEE Transactions on Acoustics Speech and Language Processing* 17(6): 1142–1158.

36. Van Gerven, S. and F. Xie. 1997. A comparative study of speech detection methods. In *European Conference on Speech Communication and Technology (Eurospeech)*, pp. 1095–1098. Rodhes, Greece.

37. Tanyer, S. G. and H. Özer. 2000. Voice activity detection in nonstationary noise. *IEEE Transactions on Speech and Audio Processing* 8(4): 478–482.

38. Oppenheim, A. V. and R. W. Schafer. 1989. *Discrete-Time Signal Processing*. Englewood Cliffs, NJ: Prentice-Hall.

39. Davis, A., S. Nordholm, and R. Togneri. 2006. Statistical voice activity detection using low-variance spectrum estimation and an adaptive threshold. *IEEE Transactions on Acoustics Speech and Language Processing* 14(2): 412–424.

40. Shin, J. W., J.-H. Chang, and N. S. Kim. 2007. Voice activity detection based on a family of parametric distributions. *Elsevier Pattern Recognition Letters* 28(11): 1295–1299.

41. Junqua, J.-C. and J.-P. Haton. 1995. *Robustness in Automatic Speech Recognition: Fundamentals and Applications*. Boston, MA: Kluwer Academic Publishers.

42. Infineon SM310. URL: http://www.infineon.com/, accessed on January 23, 2013.

43. NOISEX-92, Noise Database. URL: http://spib.rice.edu/spib/select_noise.html, accessed on January 23, 2013.

44. The MathWorks—MATLAB. URL: http://www.mathworks.com/, accessed on January 23, 2013.

45. Malavenda, C. S., F. Menichelli, and M. Olivieri. 2012. Delay-tolerant, low-power protocols for large security-critical wireless sensor networks. *Journal of Computer Networks and Communications*, 2012, Article ID 863521, 10 pages, doi:10.1155/2012/863521.

46. Malavenda, C. S. 2012. Jaguar 4×4 UGV: An autonomous deployment of a wireless sensor network. In *International Symposium on Power Electronics, Electrical Drives, Automation and Motion (SPEEDAM)*, pp. 1213–1218, Sorrento, Italy, June 2012.

47. Martalò, M., G. Ferrari, and C. Malavenda. 2010. Low-complexity in-sensor audio detection with experimental validation. In *IEEE International Symposium on Industrial Electronics (ISIE)*, pp. 1674–1679. Bari, Italy.

48. Cooley, J. and J. Tukey. 2008. An algorithm for the machine calculation of complex Fourier series. *Mathematics of Computation* 19(90): 297–301.

Chapter 18

Dynamic Bayesian Multitarget Tracking for Behavior and Interaction Detection

Lucio Marcenaro, Mauricio Soto, and Carlo S. Regazzoni

Contents

18.1 Introduction

Visual tracking represents a fundamental processing step for most of the video analytics for surveillance applications where the aim is to automatically understand the action performed by the objects present in the monitored scene [1–3]. The basic tracking task consists in following a target frame by frame, labeling it, and estimating its trajectory. Although this problem has been widely investigated in the last decades, a solution is still to be found that is valid in general situations without defining tight constraints and assumptions mainly related to the complexity of the guarded scene in terms of number of moving objects and overlapping percentage between objects themselves with environmental obstacles. Crowded scenes in public unconstrained assets such as roads, railway stations, and airports represent a challenging scenario where state-of-the-art tracking algorithms are unable to correctly track each detected target. Therefore, more effective approaches (in terms of target detection and trajectory evaluation precision, object identity preservation, improved robustness to highly cluttered environments) are necessary to correctly perform the tracking task in these scenarios under different environmental conditions (e.g., light changes and nonstatic background). Moreover, research is also focusing on the development of trackers [4] able to enrich available track by including other features such as scale, pose, and shape in the object description with the aim of accomplishing advanced scene interpretation tasks. Furthermore, observation from trackers at different resolution levels can be useful to increase system performances and have a better understanding of the monitored scene.

From the methods that have been proposed in literature for visual object tracking, extended object tracking suits video surveillance applications well because it does not rely on target-specific motion and shape models, therefore allowing one to track a wide range of different objects. Extended visual object tracking can be understood as tracking a target that is represented as a group of sparse feature points that move in space and time. The main advantage of this extended representation is allowing to simultaneously track the global position and shape of the target.

Shape evolution information is especially useful in video surveillance applications because it provides meaningful cues for high-layer tasks like action and object recognition. Different algorithms for extended feature-based object tracking have been proposed in literature. These algorithms usually rely on finding correspondences of features between consecutive frames by means of featuring local information like Kanade–Lucas–Tomasi (KLT) tracker [5] or by performing matching between interest points employing local descriptors like SIFT [6] and SURF [7].

Unfortunately, matching features between frames by using only local information is a difficult and a time-consuming problem because of the amount of descriptor comparison that has to be performed and the ambiguities that can arise while finding correspondences among noisy sparse features. To alleviate this problem, feature matching should be coupled with techniques that exploit spatial–temporal coherence and consider uncertainty in the movement of the shape points in order to obtain robust and efficient algorithms.

Interestingly, it can be shown that the class of algorithms that can be designed for understanding object dynamic behaviors starting from a sparse set of features can be useful for another apparently different problem, i.e., the analysis of interactions among different objects. In this case, the configurations of the combined shape change in a less constrained way, as the two monitored entities can assume a wider set of relative apparent poses. Nevertheless, by developing appropriate hierarchical representations, similar techniques can be used to represent dynamic multitarget interactions that can rely on representation of each object as multivalued sparse features in a shared reference system. Again this approach can be demonstrated to be related with extended object tracking technique.

There are three main factors that make extended object tracking a challenging problem: (1) The state size is usually high dimensional because it is proportional to the number of tracked features and this number is usually large, (2) the observations are usually noisy due to clutter and missed detections produced by the feature extractor, and (3) there exists data association uncertainty due to possible alternative matches among sparse features in different frames.

For those reasons, coherent and consistent paradigms should be employed in order to obtain robust, reliable, and efficient algorithms. In the case of visual tracking, the application of Bayesian filtering algorithms to probabilistic graphical models (PGMs) can provide just the right tools for doing this.

PGMs [8] are able to provide an appropriate theoretical framework where object dynamics and appearance can be combined and the motion estimation problem can be efficiently solved. As a matter of fact, PGMs can represent, learn, and compute complex probability distributions by explicitly defining statistical dependencies between the elements of the probability model. Then by combining graph theory and probability theory, PGMs aim to deal with the uncertainty in problem description and the complexity in computational implementation. These capabilities have been widely exploited in many domains as computer vision, pattern recognition, and signal processing. Moreover, several technical papers and special issues in major journals have been published [9–12]. In particular in computer vision and video processing, several algorithms have been developed based on different types of PGMs such as Markov random fields (MRFs), hidden Markov models (HMMs), dynamic Bayesian networks (DBNs), and Kalman filter. The interest on the use of these mathematical tools is motivated by three main reasons:

1. PGMs enable to consistently formalize and handle the uncertainties affecting target visual observations.
2. PGMs provide a statistical framework suitable to handle complex object representation.
3. PGMs allow efficient solutions to complex problems able to meet real-time requirements.

In this context, one of the most successfully used techniques to perform the inference task is the class of PGMs that allow one to use dynamic Bayesian filtering, which provides a recursive and efficient way to update the state of the tracked object in every time step allowing to easily integrate prior information. Furthermore, the validity of the usage of the Bayesian framework for video processing applications is motivated by different studies on the human vision system where it is shown that the visual perception processes taking place in the brain have a probabilistic nature and visual ambiguities caused by occlusion and projection from 3D to 2D, among others, are resolved in the brain using prior information.

In this work, we focus on the approaches that are based on PGMs and dynamic Bayesian filtering in order to provide an overview of one of the most commonly and successfully used mathematical tools for tracking.

Results are shown that demonstrate the capabilities of the approach to develop models for object behavior and multitarget interaction analysis in surveillance applications including human action monitoring and predictions of threats in interactive environments.

18.2 Tracking as Bayesian Problem

The problem of tracking moving objects or features within a guarded scene can be modeled as a Markov process where one wants to estimate the value of a hidden state x_t from a set of observations $z_{1:t} = \{z_1, z_2, \cdots, z_t\}$ and a discrete time index t. The tracker can be considered as an extension of the one presented in [13] where the focus was the single-target tracking problem. While the proposed tracker algorithm shares with [13] the observation model, it has been significantly extended to take into account the feedback from the interaction analysis module.

In the proposed shape-based tracking approach, the state of the target x_t is the position and the velocity of the object with respect to the topological map coordinates.

The main purpose of the tracker is to estimate the distribution $p(x_t|z_{1:t})$. A recursive solution for this estimation problem is provided by the Bayesian framework. The prediction and update stages can be described as follows:

$$p(x_t|z_{1:t-1}) = \int p(x_t|x_{t-1}) p(x_{t-1}|z_{1:t-1}) dx_{t-1}$$

$$p(x_t|z_{1:t}) = \frac{p(z_t|x_t) p(x_t|z_{1:t-1})}{p(z_t|z_{1:t-1})}$$

This solution is expressed through a recursive relation assuming that the system describes a *Markov process* of order one (i.e., $p(x_t|x_{1:t-1}, z_{1:t-1}) = p(x_t|x_{t-1})$) and the observation at time step t is conditionally independent to the rest of observation given the current state (i.e., $p(z_t|x_{1:t}, z_{1:t-1}) = p(z_t|x_t)$). When these preconditions are satisfied, the estimation can be solved recursively because the posterior can be updated whenever new data become available.

A specific PGM that is known as factored DBN is used for defining the proposed technique (Figure 18.1).

In this PGM, a stochastic variable $x_t^c = (x, \dot{x}, y, \dot{y})_t^c$ can be used for modeling the position and speed of the tracked object. Similarly, a set of random variables $x_t^j, j = \{1, \ldots, n_t\}$ can be used for each point of the considered object model. Each random variable $x_t^j = (x, \dot{x}, y, \dot{y})_t^j$ represents the position and velocity of the interest point with respect to x_t^c. The quantity n_t represents the total number of model shape points at time step t. It is worth noticing that, at this point, the whole object model can be improved by adding a hidden random variable representing the center of the object. In this way, it is possible to create a model that is much closer to the stochastic structure of the problem, thus allowing a more efficient search in the factorized state space. The intraslice recursion for $p\left(x_{1:t}^c, x_{1:t}^j|z_{1:t}\right)$ can be expressed by the following equation:

$$p\left(x_{1:t}^c, x_{1:t}^{j=1:n_t}|z_{1:t}\right) = \frac{1}{c} p\left(z_t|x_t^c, x_t^{j=1:n_t}\right) p\left(x_t^c|x_{t-1}^c\right) p\left(x_t^{j=1:n_t}|x_{t-1}^{j=1:n_{t-1}}\right) p\left(x_{1:t-1}^c, x_{1:t-1}^{j=1:n_{t-1}}|z_{1:t-1}\right) \quad (18.1)$$

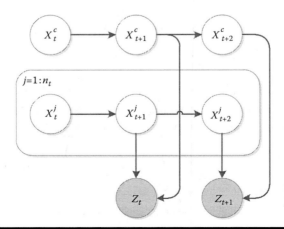

Figure 18.1   DBN graph of the proposed algorithm.

where $c = p(z_t | z_{1:t-1})$ is a constant factor ensuring that Equation 18.1 sums up to 1 being a valid probabilistic density function. In order to derive the earlier relation, it is also assumed that

$$p\left(x_t^c, x_t^{j=1:n_t} \mid x_{t-1}^c, x_{t-1}^{j=1:n_{t-1}}\right) = p\left(x_t^c \mid x_{t-1}^c\right) p\left(x_t^{j=1:n_t} \mid x_{t-1}^{j=1:n_{t-1}}\right) \tag{18.2}$$

Recent studies on human vision [14] and specifically how humans use *nonretinotopic* representations for object tracking and segmentations seem to support the assumption that was made in Equation 18.2. In visual perception studies, *retinotopic* refers to the geometry relation where neighbor points in the environment are projected to neighbor photoreceptors in the retina in a similar manner as pixels in a digital image. This phenomenon is well known and understood in the case of early visual cortical areas; however, the work from Ogmen et al. [14] shows that the representation in higher visual areas of the visual cortex occurs in a *nonretinotopic* fashion: visual perception seems to generate dynamic layers for each moving object in the scene. This representation suggests that the shape of the object and its position are marginal independent. Thus, the propagation performed by the motion model can be then formulated as

$$p\left(x_t^c, x_t^{j=1:n_t} \mid z_{1:t-1}\right) = \int p\left(x_t^c \mid x_{t-1}^c\right) p\left(x_{1:t-1}^c \mid z_{1:t-1}\right) dx_{t-1}^c$$
$$\cdot \int p\left(x_t^{j=1:n_t} \mid x_{t-1}^{j=1:n_t}\right) p\left(x_{1:t-1}^{j=1:n_t} \mid z_{1:t-1}\right) dx_{t-1}^{j=1:n_t} \tag{18.3}$$

As it can be noticed from Equation 18.3, the propagation of the shape $x_t^{j=1:n_t}$ and the position of the shape x_t^c are independent in the absence of an observation at time step t. Accordingly to this reasoning, the estimation of the new shape and the position where the corresponding object will be found with maximum probability can be disjointedly computed. On the other way, as soon as a new observation at time t is available, the state of x_t^c and $x_t^{j=1:n_t}$ is again coupled. This can be explained by considering the *explaining away* phenomenon in directed acyclic graphs (DAGs) [8]. This occurs when two causes "compete" to explain the observed data: two different random variables become conditionally dependent when their common child is observed even though they are marginally independent. In this case, the random variable $x_t^{j=1:n_t}$ interacts with the random variable x_t^c once the node z_t has been observed.

Thus, the update equation can be formulated as

$$p\left(x_t^c, x_t^{j=1:n_t} \mid z_{1:t}\right) = \frac{1}{c} p\left(z_t \mid x_t^c, x_t^{j=1:n_t}\right) p\left(x_{1:t-1}^c, x_{1:t-1}^{j=1:n_{t-1}} \mid z_{1:t-1}\right) \tag{18.4}$$

The conditional linear Gaussian (CLG) prediction models can be considered as a complementary model with respect to the one described earlier:

$$p\left(x_t^c \mid x_{t-1}^c\right) = \mathcal{N}\left(F_t^c x_{t-1}^c, Q_t^c\right)$$
$$p\left(x_t^j \mid x_{t-1}^j\right) = \mathcal{N}\left(F_t^j x_{t-1}^j, Q_t^j\right) \tag{18.5}$$

where $\mathcal{N}(A,B)$ is a Gaussian probability density function (*pdf*) with mean A and covariance B. Q_t^c and Q_t^j are covariance matrices for the motion models of x_t^c and x_t^j, respectively.

Additionally, matrices F_t^c and F_t^j in Equation 18.5 represent nearly constant velocity motion models equal to

$$F = F_t^c = F_t^j = I_2 \otimes \begin{pmatrix} 1 & \Delta t \\ 0 & 1 \end{pmatrix} \qquad (18.6)$$

If one considers the observation model of every model point, the CLG model is defined as

$$p\left(\mathbf{z}_t | \mathbf{x}_t^c, \mathbf{x}_t^j\right) = \mathcal{N}\left(H_t^j \mathbf{x}_t^j + H_t^c \mathbf{x}_t^c, R_t\right) \qquad (18.7)$$

The observation model reflects the correlation between the state of the center point $\mathbf{x}_t^c$ and the state of every model point $\mathbf{x}_t^j$. R_t is a covariance matrix that represents the uncertainty in the observation such as the uncertainty introduced by the measures of the sensor. H_t^c and H_t^j are observation model matrices for $\mathbf{x}_t^c$ and $\mathbf{x}_t^j$, respectively, equal to

$$H = H_t^c = H_t^j = \begin{pmatrix} 1 & 0 & 0 & 0 \\ 0 & 0 & 1 & 0 \end{pmatrix} \qquad (18.8)$$

In the following, the generalized Hough transform (GHT) [15] from which the observation model and message-passing algorithms are inspired is described. In particular, by using the GHT technique, it is possible to find an arbitrary nonanalytical shape in a cloud of points $\mathbf{o}^k = \mathbf{x}^{j=1:nk}$. The general algorithm consists in choosing an arbitrary reference point $\mathbf{x}_{ref}$ (e.g., the center of mass of the object) and describes each feature point of the object as a vector $\mathbf{x}_S^i$ expressing the position of the model point with respect to the object reference point (Figure 18.2).

Figure 18.2 Synthetic visual object tracking test scenario where the target is characterized with a sparse representation of interest points: feature points are obtained through the KTL [5] method.

It is possible to find the most probable position of $\boldsymbol{x}_{ref}$ in a cloud of points $\boldsymbol{o}^k$ simply by searching for the maximum in the voting space $\mathcal{V}$ where an accumulator is increased where the following constraint is verified:

$$\boldsymbol{x}_{ref} = \boldsymbol{o}^k - \boldsymbol{x}_S^i, \quad \forall i \text{ and } \forall k \tag{18.9}$$

It can be noticed that Equation 18.7 can be interpreted as the stochastic version of Equation 18.9 where $\boldsymbol{z}_t = \boldsymbol{o}^k$, $\boldsymbol{x}_t^j = \boldsymbol{x}_S^i$, and $\boldsymbol{x}_t^c = \boldsymbol{x}_{ref}$. The main difference between the traditional GHT and the current GHT-like implementation is the fact that here the priors $p\left(\boldsymbol{x}_t^c | \boldsymbol{x}_{t-1}^c\right)$ and $p\left(\boldsymbol{x}_t^{j=1:n_t} | \boldsymbol{x}_{t-1}^{j=1:n_{t-1}}\right)$ are integrated for avoiding exhaustive comparison between model and observation points (Algorithm 18.1, line 9).

Algorithm 18.1: Factored GHT-DBN $\left(\mu_{t-1}^c, \Sigma_{t-1}^c, \mu_{t-1}^{j=1:n_{t-1}}, \Sigma_{t-1}^{j=1:n_{t-1}}, \boldsymbol{z}_t\right)$

1: #γ is a gating threshold
2: $\mu_t^c = F\mu_{t-1}^c$
3: $\Sigma_t^c = F\Sigma_{t-1}^c F^T + Q_c$
4: # forward pass: find likely obs. given uncertainty $\boldsymbol{x}^c$ and $\boldsymbol{x}^j$
5: **for** $j = 1$ to n_{t-1} **do**
6:    $\mu_t^j = F\mu_{t-1}^j$
7:    $\Sigma_t^j = F\Sigma_{t-1}^j F^T + Q^j$
8:    $\hat{\boldsymbol{z}}_t^j = H\left(\mu_t^c + \mu_t^j\right)$
9:    $\boldsymbol{z}^j = \left\{\boldsymbol{z}: \left[\boldsymbol{z} - \hat{\boldsymbol{z}}_t^j\right]\left(H\left(\Sigma_t^j + \Sigma_t^c\right)H^T + R_t\right)^{-1}\left[\boldsymbol{z} - \hat{\boldsymbol{z}}_t^j\right] \leq \gamma\right\}$
10: **end for**
11: $\mathcal{V} = \iint \mathcal{N}\left(\boldsymbol{z}_k^j - \hat{\boldsymbol{z}}_t^j, \Sigma_t^j + R_t\right) d\boldsymbol{z}_t^{k=1:|\boldsymbol{z}^j|} d\boldsymbol{x}_t^{j=1:n_{t-1}} \times \mathcal{N}\left(\hat{\mu}_t^c, \Sigma_t^c\right)$
12: $\hat{\boldsymbol{x}}_t^{MAP} = argmax_{\boldsymbol{x}_t^c}(\mathcal{V})$ #find most likely value for $\boldsymbol{x}^c$
13: #backward pass: find likely obs. given $\hat{\boldsymbol{x}}_t^{MAP}$ and uncertainty in $\boldsymbol{x}^j$
14: **for** $j = 1$ to n_{t-1} **do**
15:    $\hat{\boldsymbol{z}}_t^j = \hat{\boldsymbol{x}}_t^{MAP} + H\mu_t^j$
16:    $\boldsymbol{z}^j = \left\{\boldsymbol{z}: \left[\boldsymbol{z} - \hat{\boldsymbol{z}}_t^j\right]\left(H\Sigma_t^j H^T + R_t\right)^{-1}\left[\boldsymbol{z} - \hat{\boldsymbol{z}}_t^j\right] \leq \gamma\right\}$
17:    $\left(\mu_t^j, \Sigma_t^j\right) = updatePDAF\left(\mu_{t-1}^j, \Sigma_{t-1}^j, \boldsymbol{z}_t^j, \boldsymbol{z}^j\right)$
18: **end for**
19: $\left(\mu_t^c, \Sigma_t^c\right) = updatePDAF\left(\mu_{t-1}^c, \Sigma_{t-1}^c, H\mu_t^c H^T, mean\left(\mu_t^{j=1:n_{t-1}}\right)\right)$
20: **return** $\left(\mu_t^c, \Sigma_t^c, \mu_t^{j=1:n_t}, \Sigma_t^{j=1:n_t}\right)$

In the proposed algorithm, a GHT-like procedure is performed by using a simple forward–backward sum–product passing message [8] between the two cliques $\Psi_1\left(\boldsymbol{x}_t^{j=1:n_t}, \boldsymbol{z}_t\right)$ and $\Psi_2\left(\boldsymbol{z}_t, \boldsymbol{x}_t^c\right)$ as follows:

1. During the forward pass, the variables $\boldsymbol{x}_t^{j=1:n_t}$ are eliminated by creating the factor $\delta_{1 \rightarrow 2} = \int \Psi_1\left(\boldsymbol{x}_t^{j=1:n_t}, \boldsymbol{z}_t\right) d\boldsymbol{x}_t^{j=1:n_t}$. Then the voting space $\mathcal{V}$ is obtained by creating the factor $\beta_2\left(\boldsymbol{z}_t, \boldsymbol{x}_t^c\right) = \Psi_2\left(\boldsymbol{z}_t, \boldsymbol{x}_t^c\right) \cdot \delta_{1 \rightarrow 2}(\boldsymbol{z}_t)$ and summing out $\boldsymbol{z}_t$, $\mathcal{V} = \int \beta_2\left(\boldsymbol{z}_t, \boldsymbol{x}_t^c\right) d\boldsymbol{z}_t$. This will produce

a voting space formed by a Gaussian mixture multiplied by the prior $p\left(x_t^c \mid x_{t-1}^c\right)$. Since keeping all the Gaussian components would result in an exponentially increasing time with number of components, the inference is approximated by choosing the maximum a posteriori $\hat{x}_t^{MAP} = argmax_{x_t^c}(\mathcal{V})$.

2. On the other side, with the backward pass it is possible to estimate the most likely position for each shape model as $\int \beta_1\left(x_t^j, z_t\right) dz_t = \Psi_1\left(x_t^j, z_t\right) \cdot \delta_{2\to1}(z_t)$, where $\delta_{2\to1}(z_t) = \Psi_1\left(z_t, x_t^c = x_t^{MAP}\right)$.

If the previously mentioned forward pass is considered, it can be noticed that this procedure ensures a certain robustness to missed detections and partial occlusions. In fact, x_t^c is evaluated by using the contribution of each model point x_t^j together with the observed variable z_t. The clutter is taken into account by the backward pass instead: the algorithm chooses $x_t^c = \hat{x}_t^{MAP}$, thus discarding the uncertainty associated to the random variable x_t^c when updating model points. This reduction in uncertainty can be seen clearly in line 16 of Algorithm 18.1 with respect to line 9.

Figure 18.3 shows how the Bayesian tracking approach can be successfully applied on a real moving object. Good features to track are extracted from the image at time instant t. The extracted features are used during the voting step: the GHT voting space is shown in Figure 18.3c; the maximum in this voting space indicates the most probable position for the center point x_{ref} of the tracked object. In the following time instant $t+1$ (see Figure 18.3d), the model for the shape of the tracked object is updated and new features are extracted and associated with the ones in the previous frame taking into account the votes from the GHT space.

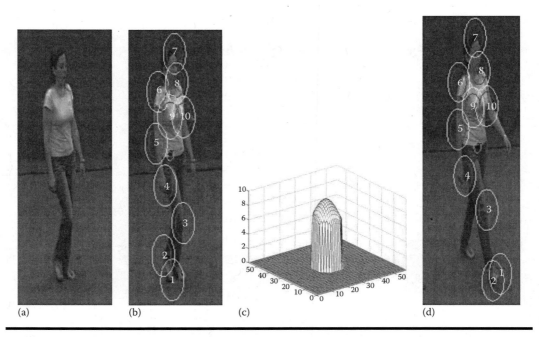

(a) (b) (c) (d)

Figure 18.3 Proposed Bayesian tracking approach on a real sequence: (a) image of the walking pedestrian at time instant t, (b) features extracted from the moving subject, (c) voting space for the GHT step, and (d) tracked subject and related features and time instant $t+1$.

18.3 Interaction Modeling and Learning

Higher-level modules of the proposed system are able to use the information from the multilayer tracking algorithm described in the previous section for detecting and recognizing interactions between moving objects in the scene. Usually, behavior understanding modules use the information produced from the tracker in an open-loop fashion (i.e., the output of the higher-level module is not used as input to the tracker to improve the tracking result). Here, on the contrary, an innovative tracking approach is proposed in which a cognitive behavior analysis module is connected to a tracker in closed loop.

Other approaches have been proposed in the past to connect a tracker with a behavior understanding module. In [13], for instance, a shape-based tracker is connected to a behavior recognition module based on the temporal shape deformation. In [16], a behavioral model that takes into account single-object motion patterns and provides feedback to the tracker by modeling a priori motion with an HMM is introduced.

Here, an interaction analysis module is able to recognize specific behaviors of the moving objects in the scene, thus improving tracker performance. This module, inspired by cognitive science research, is capable to classify the interaction occurring between two objects and to predict their positions in the future. While in the previously mentioned approaches each tracker received a feedback from a higher-level module that operated only on information provided from the tracker itself, in the proposed approach, the feedback to each tracker is produced considering the information provided by both objects in the scene. A bio-inspired learning algorithm, based on autobiographical memory (AM) [17], has been used in order to autonomously obtain probabilistic models of human interactions in the environment. Human behaviors are recognized and appropriate information about the evolution of the current scenario is supplied in real time to the tracker. Appropriate motion models are defined in order to be descriptive of a number of human-to-human interactions. These models are constituted by the conjugation of spatiotemporal information pertaining to multiple persons in an area monitored by video sensors. To understand the benefits of this approach, it is possible to refer to the example of the guard–intruder interaction that can occur in video surveillance applications. In this case it is in fact clear that, while the motion of a guard following an intruder cannot be predicted considering only the guard trajectory, it can be easily inferred considering also the trajectory of the intruder.

Some approaches can be found in literature modeling interactions in support to tracking. In [18], the a priori motion of an object from one place to another is modeled, considering parameters learned and taking into account the movement of the neighborhood objects.

This method focuses on avoiding coalescence of the trackers and therefore models only short-term low-level interactions between the objects. In [19], interactions are modeled as potential functions in a dynamic MRF. The interaction information is used as feedback to a tracking module. The approach works well; however, the optimization of the MRF requires a buffer of a number of frames (100 in the proposed experiments), which can be a drawback in some applications.

In order to obtain a manageable description of the interactions in terms of events and a regularization effect on the tracking data, the environment has been decomposed into a set of subparts or zones $Z_1, \ldots, Z_n$ using the Instantaneous Topological Map (ITM) algorithm [20]. The ITM algorithm was selected for the human behavior recognition task since it has been demonstrated that ITM is the most suitable approach for the formation of maps of state spaces whose exploration occurs along regular trajectories. In fact, since ITM is specifically designed to handle correlated data, it is therefore particularly suitable to create a map from trajectory observations. ITM does not rely upon aging or accumulative error parameters. Moreover, it does not require node adaptation (as in self-organizing maps [SOM] and growing neural gas [GNG] methods). While SOM has a rigid topology and relies on the learning rate to adjust the node position to map the input data topology, ITM has a rigid node position topology and maps the topology of input data through adaptation rules.

The elements of an ITM network are

1. A set of nodes i represented by weights w_i
2. A set of undirected edges j between them

For each input vector ξ, the adaptation of the ITM network is performed in three steps:

1. *Matching*: With respect to the input vector ξ, the nearest node (n) and the second nearest node (s) are selected.
2. *Edge update*: An edge connecting n and s is created if it does not already exist. For each node $m \in Neigh(n)$ if w_s lies inside the Thales sphere between w_n and w_m, the link between m and n is removed.
3. *Node update*: If the input vector ξ lies outside the Thales sphere through w_n and w_s, a new node y is created with $w_y = \xi$.

ITM outperforms SOM and GNG in terms of convergence speed, since each training step can produce and remove nodes or edges with no dependency to the network past history.

Given as input a set of trajectories $T_1,\ldots,T_n$, the ITM algorithm produces a map as a set of polygonal zones $\{Z_1,\ldots,Z_n\}$ whose average dimension is related to the granularity parameter τ that defines the minimum possible distance value used by the ITM algorithm for the creation of new zones. In this work, a relatively low granularity value ($\tau = 400$) has been chosen to produce a map partitioned into small zones (that can be considered roughly corresponding to $2m \times 2m$ cells in the real world) in order to provide an accurate localization feedback for the tracking algorithm (see Figure 18.4).

Exploiting the partitioning of the environment into a set of zones Z, the movement of each entity perceived in the scene can be described in terms of *events* ϵ. An event is recorded whenever an entity steps out of a zone Z_i into another zone Z_j. Events are defined by a *time label t* that records the time instant at which the zone change has been detected by the *local labels i, j* = $\{1,\ldots, n\}$ of the two neighboring zones interested by the movement of the entity (origin and destination zone) and by a *global label L* that takes into account which specific entity performed the zone change.

The proposed approach has been implemented according to a bio-inspired model of human reasoning and consciousness grounded on the work of the neurophysiologist A. Damasio [21]. Damasio's theories describe the cognitive entities as complex systems capable of incremental learning based on experience of the relationships between themselves and the external world. Two specific brain devices can be defined to formalize the earlier concept called proto-self and core-self. Such devices are specifically devoted to monitor and manage, respectively, the internal status of an entity (proto-self) and the relationships with the external world (core-self). Thus, a crucial aspect in modeling a cognitive entity following Damasio's model is represented, on the one hand, by the capability of accessing entity's internal status and, to the other hand, by the knowledge and analysis of the surrounding environment.

This approach can be mapped into a sensing framework dividing the sensors into endo-sensors (or proto-sensors) and eso-sensors (or core-sensors) as they monitor, respectively, the internal or external state of the interacting entities. With respect to the earlier description, interacting entities

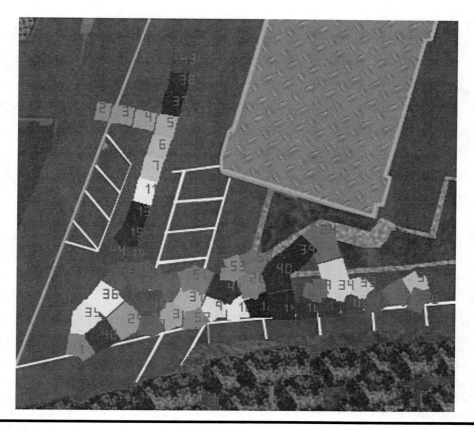

Figure 18.4 Topological partitioning of the environment.

can be represented either by a guard monitoring a critical infrastructure. For example, considering smart patrolling scenario, eso-sensors can monitor the environment from guard viewpoint, while the endo-sensors can provide information about guard's body parameters (e.g., pose and speed).

Adopting the formalism of [21], the first entity entering in the scene is labeled as the proto entity ($L = P$) and the other as the core entity ($L = C$). Therefore, if the proto entity moves from zone Z_i to zone Z_j at time t_p, the corresponding event will be recorded as $\epsilon_{t_p}^{P(i,j)}$. Similarly, if the core entity moves from zone Z_m to zone Z_p at time t_C, the corresponding event will be recorded as $\epsilon_{t_C}^{C(m,p)}$.

When more than one cognitive entity is present at the same time in the environment, the behavior of each entity can (directly or indirectly) influence the behaviors of all the other entities according to the specific interaction occurring between them.

An AM, as defined in [17], has been chosen to store the internal representation of cause–effect relationships between proto and core entities. The AM is composed by two data structures defined as *passive* memory (used to store external causes and internal effects) and *active* memory (used to store internal causes and external effects).

The cause–effect relationships, according to the neurophysiological model of *second-order neural patterns* [21], are stored in the AM as *triplets* of temporally ordered events $\left\{ \epsilon_{t_-}^{P(i,j)}, \epsilon_t^{C(m,n)}, \epsilon_{t_+}^{P(j,k)} \right\}$ (passive memory) or $\left\{ \epsilon_{t_-}^{C(m,n)}, \epsilon_t^{P(j,k)}, \epsilon_{t_+}^{C(n,p)} \right\}$ (active memory): In this way a causal relationship between two entities takes into account the internal state of one entity before the interaction

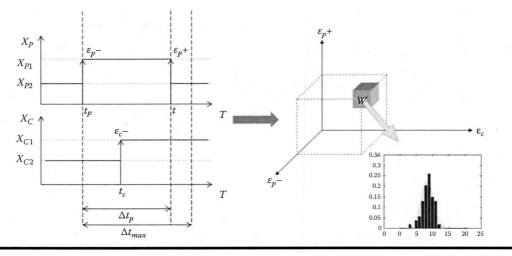

Figure 18.5 Training of the passive memory of the AM.

(proto $\epsilon_{t_-}^{P(i,j)}$ or core $\epsilon_{t_-}^{C(m,n)}$) and how this state changes $\left(\epsilon_{t_+}^{P(j,k)}, \epsilon_{t_+}^{C(n,p)}\right)$ according to external causes $\left(\epsilon_{t}^{C(m,n)}, \epsilon_{t}^{P(j,k)}\right)$.

The AM can be considered as a connection layer between the two DBNs of a cognitive entity (one for proto events and the other for core events) defined in the previous section. Specifically, each value of the AM states a weight value w for a double link between proto and core events as in Figure 18.5.

The interaction between the proto entity and the core entity in a scene can be formulated as a sequence of proto and core events $I\left(\epsilon_{t_1}^{P(i,j)}, \epsilon_{t_2}^{C(m,n)}, \epsilon_{t_3}^{P(j,k)}, \ldots\right)$ where $t_1 \leq t_2 \leq t_3 \ldots$.

The learning process of the AM is performed using a voting strategy on a training set of n_T sequences of (alternating proto and core) events representative of a set of given interactions $\Theta = \{\Theta_1, \ldots, \Theta_n\}$. Every time that a specific triplet of events $\left\{\epsilon_{t_-}^{P,C(\cdot)}, \epsilon_{t}^{C.P(\cdot)}, \epsilon_{t_+}^{P,C(\cdot)}\right\}$ occurring in a maximum time interval Δt_{max} is found in the training set, the corresponding weight w in the AM is updated.

This collection of past causal relationships between the proto entity and a core entity can be used to obtain nonparametric estimates of probability distribution functions $p\left(\epsilon_{t_+}^{P(\cdot)} | \epsilon_{t}^{C(\cdot)}, \epsilon_{t_-}^{P(\cdot)}\right)$, $p\left(\epsilon_{t_+}^{C(\cdot)} | \epsilon_{t}^{P(\cdot)}, \epsilon_{t_-}^{C(\cdot)}\right)$. These probability distributions can be obtained by normalizing the weight w of occurrence of each triplet over the last event $\epsilon_{t_+}^{P,C(\cdot)}$ in the AM.

Speed information is extracted during the training process. The temporal occurrence of the events is stored for each triplet to derive temporal conditional probability distributions (CPDs).

The time from the latest event performed by the same entity is memorized into a time histogram (i.e., $\Delta t^{P,C(\cdot)} = t_{t_+}^{P,C(\cdot)} - t_{t_-}^{P,C(\cdot)}$) if the triplet is $\left\{\epsilon_{t_-}^{P,C(\cdot)}, \epsilon_{t}^{C.P(\cdot)}, \epsilon_{t_+}^{P,C(\cdot)}\right\}$.

These two temporal distributions are necessary to represent the reaction time of one entity to an action of the other interacting entity, and they are modeled with Gaussian mixture models (GMMs), i.e.,

$$p\left(\Delta t^P | \epsilon_{t-t^P}^{P(i,j)}, \epsilon_{t-t^C}^{C(m,n)}, \epsilon_{t}^{P(j,k)}\right) = \sum_{i=1}^{N_m} \pi_i N\left(\Delta t^P | \mu_i, \Sigma_i\right) \qquad (18.10)$$

$$p\left(\Delta t^C \middle| \epsilon_{t-t^C}^{C(m,n)}, \epsilon_{t-t^P}^{P(i,j)}, \epsilon_t^{C(n,p)}\right) = \sum_{i=1}^{N_m} \pi_i N\left(\Delta t^C \middle| \mu_i, \Sigma_i\right) \tag{18.11}$$

where N_m is the number of modes of the GMM.

18.3.1 Situation Assessment

Each triplet of events $\left\{\epsilon_{t_1}^{P,C(\cdot)}, \epsilon_{t_2}^{C,P(\cdot)}, \epsilon_{t_3}^{P,C(\cdot)}\right\}$ in the current interaction is evaluated according to the probability distributions in the AM in order to obtain a distance measure $\mu^i\left(\epsilon_{t_1}^{P,C(\cdot)}, \epsilon_{t_2}^{C,P(\cdot)}, \epsilon_{t_3}^{P,C(\cdot)}, \Theta_i\right)$ of the likeness of association of the current triplet to each interaction model Θ_i stored in the AM. Then an incremental online classification is performed for each interaction, by evaluating separately all the triplets of core–proto–core and proto–core–proto events. The measure $\mu^i(t)$ is computed every time a new event $\epsilon_{t^P}^{P(j,k)} \epsilon_{t^C}^{C(n,p)}$ is detected at time t:

$$\mu^i(t) = \mu^i(t - t^C) + p\left(\epsilon_{t-t^P}^{P(i,j)}, \epsilon_{t-t^C}^{C(m,n)}, \epsilon_t^{P(j,k)}, \Delta t^P \middle| \Theta_i\right) \tag{18.12}$$

$$\mu^i(t) = \mu^i(t - t^P) + p\left(\epsilon_{t-t^C}^{P(m,n)}, \epsilon_{t-t^P}^{P(j,k)}, \epsilon_t^{C(n,p)}, \Delta t^C \middle| \Theta_i\right) \tag{18.13}$$

where $\mu^i(t - t^C)$ and $\mu^i(t - t^P)$ are the measures computed at the time of occurrence of the previous proto and core events and the expression $p\left(\epsilon_{t-t^P}^{P(i,j)}, \epsilon_{t-t^C}^{C(m,n)}, \epsilon_t^{P(j,k)}, \Delta t^P \middle| \Theta_i\right)$ indicates the likelihood that the observed triplet of events, whose intrinsic velocity is Δt^P, belongs to the ith interaction model Θ_i. This quantity can be obtained by multiplying the value of $p\left(\epsilon_{t-t^P}^{P(i,j)}, \epsilon_{t^C}^{C(m,n)}, \epsilon_t^{P(j,k)} \middle| \Theta_i\right)$ stored in the passive memory of the AM with the probability density of Equation 18.10 that represents the speed of the proto entity between events $\epsilon_{t-t^P}^{P(i,j)}$ and $\epsilon_t^{P(j,k)}$. A specular procedure is applied for core entities for which $p\left(\epsilon_{t-t^C}^{C(m,n)}, \epsilon_{t^P}^{P(i,j)}, \epsilon_t^{C(n,p)} \middle| \Theta_i\right)$ addresses the active memory of the AM, and Equation 18.11 is used.

Given a set of accumulative metrics μ^i, $i = 1, \ldots, n$ representative of interaction models $\{\Theta_1, \ldots, \Theta_n\}$, at each time t, a classification result for the current interaction can be obtained according to

$$i_t^* = arg \max_i \mu^i(t) \tag{18.14}$$

Thus, a scenario can be classified while it is currently evolving by using the considered distance measure.

18.3.2 Event Prediction

The interaction Θ_i is projected into the future in order to assess possible evolutions of the current situation. In this way, ongoing events concerning the movement of entities in the environment can be predicted according to Algorithm 18.2. The prediction is the most probable couple of ongoing events $\left(\epsilon_{t^P++}^{P(i,P^*)}, \epsilon_{t^C++}^{C(i,C^*)}\right)$ given a couple of current events $\left(\epsilon_{t^P}^{P(i,j)}, \epsilon_{t^C}^{C(m,n)}\right)$ and the label of the current interaction Θ_i. The parameter p_{conf} accounts for the global confidence value of the prediction. In this way, the most probable destination zones for the proto entity (ZP^*) and for the core entity (ZC^*) can be available in real time to the tracker.

Algorithm 18.2: Future event prediction $\left(\epsilon_{t^P}^{P(i,j)}, \epsilon_{t^C}^{C(m,n)}, p_{conf} = 1, \Theta_i \right)$

1: Generate the proto vector v_p of each possible subsequent proto event $\epsilon_{t^P++}^{P(j,P^*)}$ with probability
$$p\left(\epsilon_{t^P++}^{P(j,P^*)} \Big| \epsilon_{t^C}^{C(m,n)}, \epsilon_{t^P}^{P(i,j)}, \Theta_i \right)$$

2: **for** $\forall \epsilon_{t^P++}^{P(j,P^*)} \in v_p$ **do**

3: Generate the core vector v_C of each possible subsequent core event $\epsilon_{t^C++}^{C(n,C^*)}$ with probability
$$p\left(\epsilon_{t^C++}^{C(n,C^*)} \Big| \epsilon_{t^P++}^{P(j,P^*)} \epsilon_{t^C}^{C(m,n)}, \Theta_i \right)$$

4: **end for**

5: Select the most probable couple of events
$$\epsilon_{t^P++}^{P(j,P^*)}, \epsilon_{t^C++}^{C(n,C^*)} = \max_{\epsilon_{t^P++}^{P(j,P^*)}, \epsilon_{t^C++}^{C(n,C^*)}} \left[p\left(\epsilon_{t^C++}^{C(n,C^*)} \Big| \epsilon_{t^P++}^{P(j,P^*)} \epsilon_{t^C}^{C(m,n)}, \Theta_i \right) \cdot p\left(\epsilon_{t^P++}^{P(j,P^*)} \Big| \epsilon_{t^C}^{C(m,n)}, \epsilon_{t^P}^{P(i,j)}, \Theta_i \right) \right]$$

6: Update p_{conf}:
$$p_{conf} = p_{conf} * p\left(\epsilon_{t^C++}^{C(n,C^*)} \Big| \epsilon_{t^P++}^{P(j,P^*)} \epsilon_{t^C}^{C(m,n)}, \Theta_i \right) \cdot p\left(\epsilon_{t^P++}^{P(j,P^*)} \Big| \epsilon_{t^C}^{C(m,n)} \epsilon_{t^P}^{P(i,j)}, \Theta_i \right)$$

18.4 Object Tracking with Interaction Analysis

This section presents a tracking methodology that exploits the prediction of future events provided by the interaction analysis module. The tracker can be considered as an extension of the one described before that was significantly extended to take into account the feedback from the interaction analysis module.

As previously described, the tracking problem can be seen from a Bayesian perspective as the process that is able to recursively calculate some degree of belief in the state of the targets x_t at time t, given the observations $z_{1:t}$ up to time t. In the proposed shape-based tracking approach, the state of the target x_t is the position and the velocity of the object with respect to the topological map coordinates. When two interacting objects are in the field of view, a joint approach to tracking is used. In this case therefore the state is the joint state of the proto and core objects $x_t = \left\{ x_t^P, x_t^C \right\}$. The observations at time t are the x,y positions of the N interest points detected in the frame at time t using an interest point detector: $z_t = \left\{ z_t^n \right\}$ $n = 1, \ldots, N$.

To perform the tracking, it is assumed that the initial *pdf* of the joint state vector $p(x_0)$, which is also known as the prior, is available. Moreover, it is assumed that the interaction analysis module is receiving the state estimate and providing new event prediction.

Then, in principle, the posterior *pdf* $p(x_t | z_{1:t-1})$ may be obtained, recursively, in two stages: prediction and update. Supposing that the *pdf* $p(x_t | x_{t-1})$ and a model for the target dynamics $p(x_t | x_{t-1})$ are available at time $t-1$, the prediction stage is performed through the Chapman–Kolmogorov equation:

$$p(x_t | z_{1:t-1}) = \int p(x_t | x_{t-1}) \, p(x_{t-1} | z_{1:t-1}) \, dx_{t-1} \tag{18.15}$$

At time step t, a measurement becomes available, and this may be used, via the likelihood function, to update the prediction:

$$p(\boldsymbol{x}_t|\boldsymbol{z}_{1:t})=c\cdot p(\boldsymbol{z}_t|\boldsymbol{x}_t)p(\boldsymbol{x}_t|\boldsymbol{z}_{1:t-1}) \tag{18.16}$$

where c is a normalizing constant, which depends only on the likelihood function. To use the Bayesian framework, the dynamic model and the likelihood function have to be defined.

18.4.1 Target Dynamic Model

The dynamic model takes into account both objects own dynamics and proto–core interactions. The model is defined as follows:

$$p(\boldsymbol{x}_t|\boldsymbol{x}_{t-1})=(1-\alpha)p_d\left(\boldsymbol{x}_t^P|\boldsymbol{x}_{t-1}^P\right)p_d\left(\boldsymbol{x}_t^C|\boldsymbol{x}_{t-1}^C\right)+\alpha p_c\left(\boldsymbol{x}_t^P,\,\boldsymbol{x}_t^C|\epsilon_{t^P++}^{P(j,P^*)},\epsilon_{t^C++}^{C(n,C^*)}\right). \tag{18.17}$$

In the proposed model, each object has a specific dynamics that is modeled using a nearly constant velocity model represented with the $p_d(\cdot)$ term. The cognitive term $p_c(\cdot)$ predicts the position the agents will have considering the interaction analysis. It is possible to model this term as

$$p_c\left(\boldsymbol{x}_t^P,\boldsymbol{x}_t^C|\epsilon_{t^P++}^{P(j,P^*)},\epsilon_{t^C++}^{C(n,C^*)}\right)=cU\left(\boldsymbol{x}_t^P\in Z_t^{P^*}\right)\cdot cU\left(\boldsymbol{x}_t^C\in Z_t^{C^*}\right) \tag{18.18}$$

where
  $U()$ is 1 when its argument is true and 0 otherwise
  c is a normalizing constant that assures that, on the considered space, $p_c()$ is a *pdf*

The quantity α in Equation 18.17 is a value that can change the behavior of the a priori model. With $\alpha = 1$, the position hypotheses are propagated taking into account only the motion of each tracker. Increasing the value of α produces the effect of propagating more position hypotheses in the zones predicted by the interaction analysis model. The value of α can be changed dynamically during the tracking.

18.4.2 Target Observation Model

The goal of the likelihood function is to compute the probability that the observations have been generated by the tracked object, given a hypothesis on the state. It tries to exploit the temporal continuity of the shape of the tracked object and tries to explain the observations at time k using a shape model that exists on the image plane and that was learned during the past time steps.

In the proposed method, the likelihood of the proto and core targets is considered as independent given the state and is therefore factorable. To avoid repeating the same formula for the proto and core objects, only the likelihood of the proto object will be derived.

The shape of each target, which is compared with the observations, is composed by a set of M discrete points. Each model point has coordinates $\Delta^{p,m}$, expressed in a reference system centered on a reference point that corresponds to the base of the object's bounding box.

The coordinates of the mth model point on the image can be expressed in the following way: $pos^m\left(\boldsymbol{x}_t^P\right)=\Delta^{p,m}+I\left(\boldsymbol{x}_t^P\right)$ where $I()$ is an operator that transforms the map position coordinates $\boldsymbol{x}_t^P$ to the image coordinates. The likelihood of the observations is therefore defined as

$$p\left(z_t \mid x_t^P\right) = c \sum_{n=1}^{N} \sum_{m=1}^{M} K_{motion}\left(\|\, z_t^n - pos^m\left(x_t^P\right)\|\right) \tag{18.19}$$

where

$K_{motion}()$ is a function, which is 0 if its argument is greater or equal than a threshold *th* and
1 otherwise

c is a normalization constant

The function $K_{motion}()$ takes into account the possible distortions of the shape, which might occur from frame to frame and the observation noise. If only exact matches with respect to the model are allowed, *th* is set to 0 and only observations, which are exactly in the predicted position, are taken into account in the likelihood. It is worth noticing that the proposed likelihood function is a Bayesian formalization of the GHT, thus leading to the same results described in the first section about tracking in this chapter. In particular, the shape model can be learned during the tracking process. At each time step, after the position of the object $\hat{x}_t$ has been estimated, each observation point is put in correspondence with the model points projected on the image space using $\hat{x}_t$. Only associations, which are nearer than *th*, are considered as valid. Model points, which have a match with an observation, are updated so that their new position Δ^m is the position of the nearest observation. Model points have not been in correspondence with observations since a number of frames are removed from the model. If there are observations that were not in correspondence with model points, new model points are added in the position of the observations. The estimate $\hat{x}_t$ is then sent to the interaction analysis module as the next position of the proto and core agents.

18.5 Experimental Results

The proposed tracking Bayesian framework method is compared to the *retinotopic* (baseline) counterpart, i.e., methods in which the image features are independently tracked in the image plane as represented with the graphical model of Figure 18.6.

The experiments are performed on a synthetic video sequence featuring a walking person where the ground truth shape points were manually collected.

It is worth noticing that no appearance information such as descriptors are used while performing the experiments in order to measure the influence of the chosen PGM and observation model on the final result.

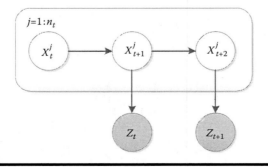

Figure 18.6   DBN representing the retinotopic approach.

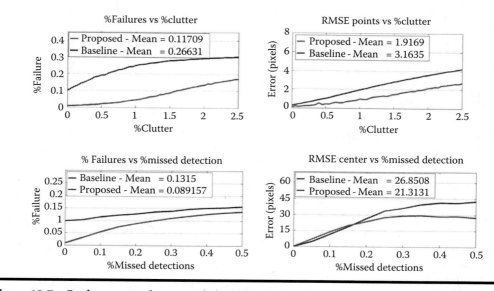

Figure 18.7 **Performance of proposed algorithm under clutter (normalized by number of model points and minimum bounding box area) and missed detections. In the graphs, percentage axis is normalized to 1 (1 = 100%).**

The only difference between chosen parameters of the proposed method and its counterpart is the value of motion model covariance matrix Q.

Its value is set to $Q = Q^c + Q^j$ in order to account for uncertainty in the motion of the object and uncertainty in the motion of the model points with respect to the center. These experiments are summarized in Figure 18.7.

They intend to assess the improvement of the proposed algorithm with respect to known problems in feature tracking such as clutter and missing detections.

Since the missing detection and clutter have been synthetically added with pseudorandom number generators, the figures are the result of averaging 100 runs for each parameter value in order to obtain significant outcomes.

Three important aspects are compared: (1) robustness, (2) accuracy, and (3) processing time. Robustness is compared by measuring the percentage of failures in tracking. Failure in tracking is defined as the loss of track of any model point due to coalescence between model points or when the position of a model point is outside of the error covariance of the associated random variable. Accuracy is compared by using the root squared mean error (RSME) between the ground truth and the estimated position. Finally, processing time is compared in Table 18.1.

Table 18.1   Comparison of Average Processing Time in the Presence of Clutter and Missed Detections

Method	Missed Detections (ms)	Clutter (ms)
Baseline	5	29
Proposed	14	49

Figure 18.7 clearly shows that the proposed algorithm is especially robust at dealing with clutter and missed detections while having better accuracy and robustness. The increase in robustness and accuracy comes at the expense of an increase in processing time as evidenced in Table 18.1.

The experimentation on real data has been performed on the public PETS2006 dataset. The video sequence has 1166 frames with 720×576 pixel resolution and presents a typical surveillance scene in a train station. The color histogram, in both the proposed algorithm and the well-known MeanShift tracking algorithm, is calculated in the RGB space with $8 \times 8 \times 8$ bins. The sequence is specially challenging for the proposed method because (1) it contains out-of-the-plane rotations of the target, (2) there is a split of targets when the main tracked object leaves an abandoned backpack in the middle of the sequences, and (3) there is a rapid change of velocity of the target that passes from standing still to running out of the scene in few frames.

In Figure 18.8, the presented method is compared to the traditional MeanShift. It is possible to see that both objects are successfully tracked by the proposed method, while MeanShift fails for the target going toward the top of the image. In particular, it can be seen that the MeanShift drifts by the distraction of a person that passes in the background and finally loses all track from the target. Specifically, the RMS error of the MeanShift is equal to 114.9 *pixels*, while the presented method is able to achieve only 24 *pixels*.

The AM has been trained using a generator of synthetic trajectories (based on data collected from real videos) that is intended to simulate the complete context evolution through a statistical engine in order to create realistic tracks descriptive of different behaviors Θ_i. The motion of the entities in the scene is simulated according to a linear Gaussian dynamic model such that $x_t = x_{t-1} + v_{t-1} \cdot T + a_{t-1} \cdot T^2/2$ where x_t is the map position and v_t and a_t are, respectively, the Gaussian random speed and acceleration. The entrance of entities into the scene is randomly determined according to a Poisson distribution. The training of the AM has been performed using training sets composed by $n_T = 1000$ trajectories for each considered behavior.

While in this case synthetically generated trajectories have been used, it is also possible to use a mixed approach in which the AM is initialized synthetically and new interaction data are added

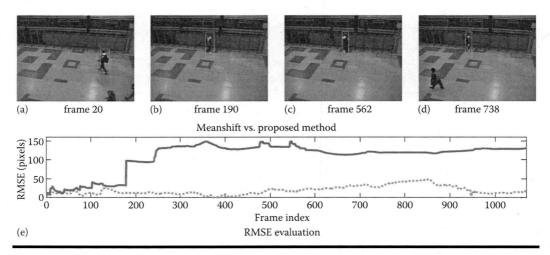

Figure 18.8 Comparison of the proposed method against MeanShift tracker. The darker bounding box (solid line RMSE) is from the MeanShift while the lighter one (dotted line RMSE) is from the proposed method. (a) frame 20, (b) frame 190, (c) frame 562, (d) frame 738, and (e) RMSE evaluation.

(possibly online) using real data from the trackers. The test sequences are real sequences in which some actors interacted in a realistic fashion according to the plot that has been assigned to them. The proto and core trackers are manually initialized when they enter in the scene. Considering that some time steps are required to allow the interaction module to provide a prediction, it is assumed that each object is tracked independently without the help of the interaction module (i.e., $\alpha = 0$ in (18.17)) till the first interaction prediction is available. At this point, α is set to a value greater than 0 (in our experiment 0.3) to spread the hypotheses in the interaction zones. A dynamic approach is used to set the value of α. If the likelihood (18.19) in correspondence of the predicted position is below a threshold, it is a symptom that the predicted position is not correct or that there is an occlusion. In this case, the value of α is increased (to 0.5 in our experiment) to give more credit to the interaction analysis model. To avoid that the shape model of the tracked object is destroyed during the anomaly, also the shape model update is stopped. Two different interactions have been tested in our experiments: the "guard–intruder" and "motion" interactions. In the guard–intruder interaction, an intruder walks freely in the parking lot while a guard patrols the zone. When the guard sees the intruder, it starts to chase the intruder. When the intruder sees the guard, it starts to run away. The fact that the agents can see each other only from specific cells is naturally modeled in the AM using historical data. In the "motion" interaction, two individuals walk in the scene each one independently from the other. An example of a guard–intruder tracking scenario is provided in Figure 18.9 where the trajectories have been depicted both on the image from the camera and on the topological map. Some points are highlighted on the map. The squares identify the positions of the objects when the agents started to interact, while the circles identify the positions where the first prediction was provided by the module. It is possible to see that the AM can understand that a guard–intruder interaction is taking place when one of the agents diverts from the original path and starts to run away from the other agent. After this point the AM predicts the positions of the guard and the intruder using the learned model.

An example of zone prediction is shown in Figure 18.10. In this figure the current and future trajectories for both the proto and core trackers are plotted using different lines. The same zones are projected on the camera image.

Finally, to test the improvement in tracking provided by the proposed algorithm, three sequences of each interaction have been tested. The results are provided in Table 18.2 showing the number

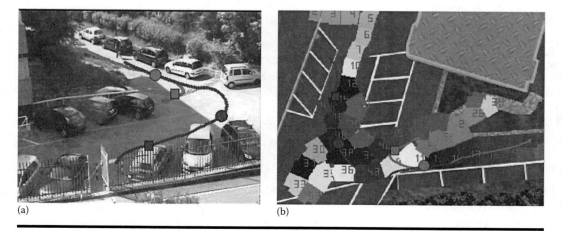

(a)   (b)

Figure 18.9 Guard–intruder interaction example. Trajectories of the guard (darker) and of the intruder (lighter) are shown using solid lines. (a) Camera view and (b) map view.

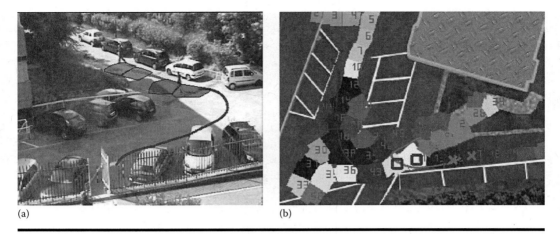

(a)   (b)

Figure 18.10 Guard–intruder interaction example. Predicted zones of the guard (darker) and of the intruder (lighter) are shown on the images. Trajectories are shown using solid lines. The scene each one. (a) camera view and (b) map view.

Table 18.2   Tracking Performances

Sequence	P_{time}	P_c	L	$L_{\alpha=0}$
Guard–intruder 1	99	1	128	120
Guard–intruder 2	105	1	200	153
Guard–intruder 3	122	1	200	185
Motion 1	90	1	270	261
Motion 2	112	1	192	192
Motion 3	80	1	190	98

of time steps required to perform the prediction P_{time}, correctness of the estimated interaction P_c (computed as the ratio between the number of times the correct interaction is provided and the number of times a prediction is available), length of the track for the proposed method L, and length of the track in case the prediction is not used for the tracker $L_{\alpha=0}$. This last result is obtained by fixing the value of α to 0 for all the sequences. As it is possible to see by comparing the L and $L_{\alpha=0}$ parameters, the track length is increased if interaction information is used. This is particularly true if the objects go in the upper part of the image where the measurements are less due to the small size of the objects.

In this zone in fact, the shape update is sometimes stopped and the a priori spread of the position hypotheses in the predicted zones is beneficial to avoid loss of track. If in fact the likelihood is high in a zone, which is not occupied by the object due to false measurements, the hypotheses, due to the tracker dynamic motions and likelihood, start to converge to the clutter and the track cannot be recovered. If some hypotheses are maintained in the predicted zones, the probability of maintaining tracks is higher. Other useful results are the P_c values that show that the interaction is always recognized by the module and the P_{time} that shows that some time is required to let the module understand the interaction.

18.6 Conclusions

An algorithm for visual object tracking using sparse features has been described. The method is inspired by *nonretinotopic* visual human perception and the GHT under the Bayesian and PGM frameworks. It has been shown that the proposed method copes well with clutter and missed detections while being more robust and accurate than its *retinotopic* counterpart. In the second part of the chapter, the proposed tracking technique was extended for a joint human tracking and human-to-human interaction recognition. This approach fuses the predictions provided by a bio-inspired module that has been trained using historical data with the shape-based tracker. The results show that the interactions between the humans in the scene are correctly classified and, at the same time, that the tracker process is improved.

References

1. V. Ramesh, Real-time vision at Siemens Corporate Research, in *Proceedings of the IEEE Conference on Advanced Video and Signal Based Surveillance*, Como, Italy, September 15–16, 2005.
2. A. Hampapur, R. Bobbitt, L. Brown, M. Desimone, R. Feris, R. Kjeldsen, M. Lu, C. Mercier, C. Milite, S. Russo, C.-F. Shu, and Y. Zhai, Video analytics in urban environments, in *Proceedings of the Sixth IEEE International Conference on Advanced Video and Signal Based Surveillance (AVSS '09)*, Genova, Italy, September 2–4, 2009.
3. N. Krahnstoever, P. Tu, T. Yu, K. Patwardhan, D. Hamilton, B. Yu, C. Greco, and G. Doretto, Intelligent video for protecting crowded sports venues, in *Proceedings of the Sixth IEEE International Conference on Advanced Video and Signal Based Surveillance (AVSS '09)*, Genova, Italy, September 2–4, 2009.
4. A. Dore, M. Soto, and C. Regazzoni, Bayesian tracking for video analytics, *IEEE Signal Processing Magazine*, 20(5), 46–55, 2010.
5. J. Shi and C. Tomasi, Good features to track, in *Proceedings of the IEEE Computer Society Conference on Computer Vision and Pattern Recognition (CVPR '94)*, Seattle, WA, June 21–23, 1994.
6. D. G. Lowe, Distinctive image features from scale-invariant keypoints, *International Journal of Computer Vision*, 60(2), 91–110, 2004.
7. H. Bay, T. Tuytelaars, and L. Gool, SURF: Speeded up robust features, in *Proceedings of the Ninth European Conference on Computer Vision (ECCV 2006)*, Graz, Austria, May 7–13, 2006.
8. D. Koller and N. Friedman, *Probabilistic Graphical Models*, The MIT Press, Cambridge, MA, 2009.
9. J. Rehg, V. Pavlovic, T. Huang, and W. Freeman, Guest editors' introduction to the special section on graphical models in computer vision, *IEEE Transactions on Pattern Analysis and Machine Intelligence*, 25(7), 785–786, 2003.
10. Q. Ji, J. Luo, D. Metaxas, A. Torralba, T. S. Huang, and E. B. Sudderth, Guest editors' introduction to the special section on probabilistic graphical models, *IEEE Transactions on Pattern Analysis and Machine Intelligence*, 31(10), 1729–1732, 2009.
11. J. Candy, Bootstrap particle filtering, *IEEE Signal Processing Magazine*, 24(4), 73–85, 2007.
12. P. Djuric, J. Kotecha, J. Zhang, Y. Huang, T. Ghirmai, M. Bugallo, and J. Miguez, Particle filtering, *IEEE Signal Processing Magazine*, 20(5), 19–38, 2003.
13. F. Monti and C. Regazzoni, A joint approach to shape-based human tracking and behavior analysis, in *Proceedings of the 13th Conference on Information Fusion (FUSION)*, Edinburgh, U.K., July 26–29, 2010.
14. H. Ogmen and M. Herzog, The geometry of visual perception: Retinotopic and nonretinotopic representations in the human visual system, *Proceedings of the IEEE*, 98(3), 479–492, 2010.
15. D. H. Ballard, Generalizing the hough transform to detect arbitrary shapes, *Pattern Recognition*, 13(2), 111–122, 1981.
16. J. Berclaz, F. Fleuret, and P. Fua, Multi-camera tracking and atypical motion detection with behavioral maps, in *Proceeding of the European Conference on Computer Vision (ECCV)*, Marseille, France, 2008.

17. A. Dore, M. Pinasco, and C. Regazzoni, A bio-inspired learning approach for the classification of risk zones in a smart space, in *Proceedings of the IEEE International Conference on Computer Vision and Pattern Recognition (CVPR)*, Minneapolis, MN, 2007.

18. S. Ali and M. Shah, Floor fields for tracking in high density, in *Proceedings of European Conference on Computer Vision (ECCV)*, Marseille, France, 2008.

19. B. Yao, L. Wang, and S. Chun Zhu, Learning a scene contextual model for tracking and abnormality detection, in *Proceedings of the International Conference on Computer Vision and Pattern Recognition (CVPR)*, Anchorage, AK, 2008.

20. J. Jockusch and H. Ritter, An instantaneous topological mapping model for correlated stimuli, in *Proceedings of the International Joint Conference on Neural Networks*, Washington, DC, 1999.

21. A. Damasio, *The Feeling of What Happens—Body, Emotion and the Making of Consciousness*, William Heinemann, London, 1999.

Chapter 19

Imaging Tunnels and Underground Facilities Using Radio-Frequency Tomography

Lorenzo Lo Monte, Francesco Soldovieri, Danilo Erricolo, and Michael C. Wicks

Contents

19.1 Introduction

This chapter examines the remote detection of underground and tunnel facilities, which is a special case of the problem of surveillance of covert targets. Detecting underground and tunnel facilities is critical for the protection of natural borders and sensitive areas. In addition, success in the remote detection of underground and tunnel facilities will also impact the detection of targets inside buildings, under tree canopies, and contraband activities.

The requirements of an effective remote-sensing technology include providing the decision maker with persistent, intelligible, and actionable information characterizing the underground scene, ideally in real time. Moreover, the deployment of sensors and supporting equipment must be prompt, with minimal human intervention, and applicable over relatively wide areas of interest, from the near-surface shallow region to many meters belowground, where hostile facilities may be located. Unfortunately, at the present time, information on underground cavities is typically retrieved using seismic sensors, or multisensor integration, although none of them complies with the previous requirements. To satisfy these requirements, an alternative approach, based upon radio-frequency (RF) tomography, is considered [1].

This RF tomography–based remote-sensing methodology utilizes a set of low-cost, randomly deployed transponders. Transmitters radiate coherent ultra-narrowband signals belowground, eventually impinging upon a dielectric and/or conducting anomaly (representative of the target) that excites a scattered field. Receivers collect these scattered fields and relay this information to overhead base stations (see Figure 19.1). Using the principles of inverse scattering, a scheme for belowground imaging of anomalies via scattered field data is presented, thus detecting, locating, and imaging difficult targets under cover. This methodology is based upon a *multiview* and

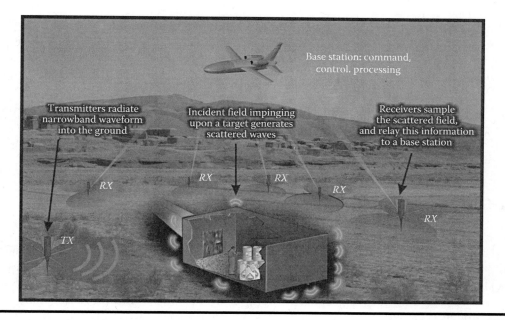

Figure 19.1 Pictorial representation of a system using RF tomography for imaging belowground areas of regard.

multistatic configuration where greater *view* diversity (associated with multiple distributed transmitters) and *observation* diversity (associated with the multiple distributed receivers) increase the information concerning the scene. By exploiting view and observation diversity, the spectral content (bandwidth) of the illumination signals may be significantly narrowed. In principle, even with a monochromatic waveform, highly resolved images may be obtained.

19.2 Problem of Tunnel Detection

Tunnels have been used since early history, for example, as an escape route to avoid capture, such as in the case of the Roman siege on Fidenae (435 BC), or to hide activities. Discovery of underground facilities (UGFs) has proven to be a very difficult problem, often resolved only by chance or human intelligence. Projects involving tunnel and UGF detection are active worldwide, but, notwithstanding many efforts, only few (if any) tunnel detection systems are reliable enough for defense and/or homeland security [2].

UGFs have been developed in recent years to conceal border-crossing passageways and military assets. During the Vietnam War, Viet Cong underground tunnels (e.g., Củ Chi) were considered major command and control posts, where militia planned and executed attacks. Camouflage of adits or point of entrance was impeccable, and discovery of UGFs could only occur via intelligence.

The birth of modern tunnel detection technology can be traced to the discovery, in 1974, of the first tunnel under the Korean Demilitarized Zone (DMZ), linking North to South Korea, and large enough to allow the transit of a regiment of troops and heavy artillery. The South Korean government believed the tunnel was being built for a surprise attack or insertion of agents for destabilization.

Tunnels have been used also across borders to smuggle drugs and weapons, kidnapping, human trafficking, clandestine entry by terrorist organizations, and spying of foreign embassies.

Tunnels are increasingly employed as a means to infiltrate into territories in order to execute terrorist attacks against civilians, for example, sophisticated terrorism-related tunnels have been found in all regions of conflict, in particular in the Gaza Strip, Afghanistan, Pakistan, and other disputed territories.

Underground facilities used as command and control posts, for the manufacture and storage of weapons of mass destruction and for leadership protection, are also posing threats for homeland security. More than 100 UGF have been developed by over 20 rogue nation leaders to conceal military assets [3].

The military has increasing need for localization and monitoring of man-made tunnels, bunkers, weapon caches, and UGF over relatively wide and deep regions of interest, for both cooperative and noncooperative (denied) terrains. In combat zones, the pursuit of "situational awareness" for the decision maker is paramount for successful dominance of the battlefield scene, especially for battle damage assessment prior and after strike, or reconnaissance/discovery of UGF shafts or adits. Other imminent threats include assailants entering military fortifications by burrowing under barricades and buildings, detonation of high-grade explosives below foundations of high-security facilities, or high-level prisoners escaping detention centers through simple tunneling techniques. Real-time monitoring of the ground surrounding prisons across the country is a desired solution to this problem. Therefore, a reconnaissance and surveillance system of the scene belowground is extremely beneficial for detention center surveillance, military bases, airports, banks, high-security storage, nuclear facilities, and any further sensitive area.

On the civilian side, localization of underground cavities is paramount for mining safety and underground search and rescue missions, disaster response, and relief activities, such as for building collapse due to natural disasters (e.g., earthquakes, avalanches, and landslides) or attacks, to search and rescue victims. In exploratory geophysics, before embarking on any mining operation, it is essential to locate the subsurface bodies, as well as their types, structures, and distributions; particularly, it is advantageous to locate these subsurface bodies with a relatively high resolution prior to actual mining to properly plan mining activities and reduce hazards, which in turn increases efficiency and productivity [4]. Nonintrusive underground surveys are desirable in many aspects of civil, urban, and environmental engineering. Many subsurface voids might raise engineering concerns, such as washouts, settlement gaps beneath roadways, floor slabs, vaults, natural limestone karsts, incipient sinkholes, or soil pipes: The presence of undiscovered cavities may cause the collapse of buildings, bridges, or other structures. Further applications include the monitoring of environmental contamination (buried waste) and the construction of viable tunnels, highways, and railways, especially during the geotechnical assessment phase of the project.

An overview of current tunnel detection capabilities follows. Each method is corroborated with a detailed pros/cons analysis, leading to the justification of using RF tomography for the problem under consideration: The method is devised for a defense/homeland security audience, where minimal human intervention and inaccessible terrains are considered the norm.

19.3 Existing Methodologies

Subsurface imaging is accomplished using a variety of data, such as seismic, gravity, magnetic, and electrical measurements. Methods and apparatuses that have been employed are currently used or may be potentially exploited for underground void detection and imaging that are listed hereafter.

19.3.1 Dog Training

Void detection was pioneered during the Vietnam War, when sensing technology was in a primordial stage, and no reliable tunnel detector was available. Due to the extreme urgency of finding enemy caches, the first reliable protocol for void detection has been the ground deployment of highly trained dogs [5]. Finding tunnels using trained dog has been used for several years with acceptable results and relatively low false alarms [6]. However, detailed surveys showed that dogs were not able to detect all tunnels within the area of investigation, while geophysical technology was slowly emerging as a more reliable solution. Therefore, dog-sniffing tunnel detection has slowly been abandoned, shifting toward more scientific and methodological methods.

19.3.2 Cosmic Ray

A suggested technique for tunnel detection is the detection of in situ anomalies of rock density [7] via cosmic rays. This method is based on the dependency of cosmic-ray intensity on the average rock density above the detector. Because the intensity is also directional, one can determine with an appropriate detector the average rock density in a specific direction.

Latest available works on cosmic-ray tomography are dated late 1980. Since then, no disclosed information concerning this technique has been found, probably due to the high randomness of cosmic particles detected at the receiver together with its relatively high cost.

19.3.3 Passive Sensing

Construction of underground structures can be detected by passively sensing dynamic activities. In the literature, three main passive approaches are presented:

- *Seismic Triangulation*: With a proper implementation of triangulation procedure, seismic reflection can be used to properly locate remote point-like seismic scatterers. A set of geophones can be implanted into the ground, and by using triangulation techniques, it is possible to localize sources of seismic noise into the ground [8]. By inspecting the seismic signature, it is also possible to establish the type of source of the signal (human made, drilling, explosion, etc.) [9].
- *Laser Interferometry*: A coherent laser signal is sent in a closed-loop fiber optic encompassing the area of regard. Vibrations due to the excavation of a tunnel are detected via interferometry, due to phase shift of the laser signal when external forces perturb the shape of the fiber [10].
- *50–60 Hz Sensors*: This particular sensing technique can detect tunnels and underground complexes even when the human activity is limited, because electric current machineries and power lines are usually kept operative.

These passive tunnel detection techniques require some activity inside the tunnel; otherwise, no signal will be detected. Therefore, these techniques may be useful for monitoring sensitive areas, but they are generally not applicable to the broader range of cases where tunnels or facilities are already present at the moment of the survey. Passive sensing is further complicated by the topographical, geological, infrastructure, and natural or man-made noise environment of the surrounding area [11].

50–60 Hz passive sensing has been extensively analyzed in [12] for detection of tunnels: Unfortunately, multiple phantom tunnels are detected, because metamorphic processes in geologic formations create high-electrical-conductivity layers insulated by lower-conductivity layers. These conductive channels guide leaking currents from nearby power distributions for many kilometers. The current flow generates observable electromagnetic (EM) fields that can be detected by sensitive 50–60 Hz receivers. Therefore, 60 Hz sensor cannot be considered a reliable strategy.

19.3.4 Microgravity

Underground cavity detection can be accomplished by invoking principles of *gravimetry* [13]. In fact, the "missing" mass of the cavity creates small perturbations in the Earth's gravitational field, called microgravity with the magnitude of the disturbance directly proportional to the volume of the cavity [14,15]. A suitable and properly calibrated gravimeter may be able to measure the gravity deviation, thus revealing the depth and dimension of the cavity. Unfortunately, the major limitation is that the gravimetric deviation is extremely low. When combined with other limitations, microgravity is not yet ready to be exploited for underground void detection.

19.3.5 Electrical Resistivity Tomography

Electrical resistivity tomography (ERT), sometimes also referred to as electrical resistivity imaging (ERI), is another geophysical technique for imaging subsurface structures from electrical measurements made at the surface or by electrodes placed in one or more boreholes. It is closely related to the medical imaging technique electrical impedance tomography (EIT), and, mathematically, it is formulated in a similar way. ERT involves injecting current into the ground between two electrodes and measuring the voltage difference between two other electrodes. Instead of using direct current (DC), the injection of low-frequency (below 10 Hz) modulated current signal, which propagates deeply inside the Earth, is technically more convenient.

Disadvantages of ERT for underground imaging include (1) the lack of capability to distinguish between cavities and competent rocks, since they are both highly resistive; (2) limited range of operation for highly resistive soils; (3) precision that decreases as the inverse square of the distance between electrodes; and (4) the use of a multitude of cables, which are unpractical for military purposes or prompt search and rescue operations.

19.3.6 Electrical Impedance Signature

According to this methodology, a dipole working in the antiresonance region is used to transmit power into the ground. When a tunnel is located underneath the dipole, standing waves change the total input impedance measured at the feeds of the dipole. This effect is amplified when the dipole is operating in the antiresonance region. However, a device must be physically above the area under examination, and the maximum impedance variation is only oscillating around 6–7 Ω, according to ideal computer simulations [16]. This suggests that this method is still at a very early stage and may not be implemented in the real world for the near future.

19.3.7 Magnetic Methods

The major limitation of ERT or ERI methods is that DC cannot penetrate through resistive formations. The EM induction methods, based on transient EM fields, overcome this difficulty because a transient field can easily propagate through resistive materials (like a radio wave propagates the air). At the same time, a transient EM field provides information not only about the resistivity of the rocks but also about the magnetic permeability μ and the dielectric permittivity ε.

Natural variations in the Earth's magnetic field induce *magnetization* and associated *telluric currents* under the Earth's surface [17]. The induced magnetization field is directly proportional to the intensity of the ambient field and to the ability of the material to enhance the local field, a property called *magnetic susceptibility*. Underground cavities create a small deviation of the normal Earth's magnetic field, which could be measured and processed to compute images of the magnetic susceptibility [15].

19.3.7.1 Passive Magnetometry

For UGF detection, the magnetic survey is a logically chosen technique because the presence of man-made ferrous objects, such as tools, rock bolts, liners, and rails, would be expected to produce large magnetic anomalies [8]. Hence, by a proper design of a magnetometer, it may be possible, at least in principle, to detect a UGF. In the case of a nonmetallic air-filled cavity, such as a tunnel in limestone, granite, or other nonmagnetic rock, little influence is expected on the existing magnetic field. As a result, passive magnetic techniques would be appropriate only when man-made metals are present. Experiments were made in Vietnam and South Korea, but the rate of failures led to the abandonment of the project [18,19].

19.3.7.2 Magnetotellurics

Magnetotellurics (MT) attempts to measure the electrical properties of the underground, in particular the *impedance tensor*, through concurrent measurements of orthogonal components of the electric and magnetic fields at the surface. The frequency range spanned by MT systems is typically from 0.001 to 500 Hz. Because of the skin effect phenomenon that affects EM fields, the ratio at higher-frequency ranges gives information on the shallow earth, whereas deeper information is provided by the low-frequency range. The ratio is usually represented as MT-apparent resistivity and phase as a function of frequency. Recent advances in hardware and MT data processing, modeling, and interpretation have led to many successes in geophysical exploration.

19.3.7.3 Controlled-Source Magnetotellurics

MT still suffers from certain inherent limitations including low signal strength in the 0.1–1 Hz region. To overcome these limitations, geophysicists have employed artificial sources to generate large amplitude EM fields that can be measured in a manner similar to the traditional MT method. This technique, a variant of the MT method, is known as controlled-source MT (CSMT), and the sources are typically long grounded dipoles or large loops of wires that are energized with alternating currents to induce EM fields in the earth. CSMT methods surmount the problems with low signal levels, noise, and the deadband, but unless very large sources and field generators are used, the penetration depths for CSMT are limited to a few kilometers at best.

A controllable EM source that could generate sufficiently strong signals that appeared locally as plane waves would be of special interest for subsurface imaging since it would overcome the limitations of the traditional MT and CSMT methods. Geophysicists [20] have exploited the transmitter used for the High Frequency Active Auroral Research Program (HAARP): By controlling its modulation, EM waves can be generated at the frequencies needed for geophysical exploration of the shallow subsurface. The potential advantages of using a source like the HAARP are that since the observed signals would appear locally as plane wave, one could use the much simpler and faster analysis and modeling codes developed for the MT method and that HAARP transmitter does not suffer from the typical deadband encountered in common MT.

19.3.7.4 Magnetotellurics Using Gradiometer Antennas

MT measurement at VLF/ELF frequencies is improved when a particular design of the receiver is considered [2]. In fact, underground cavities illuminated by a plane wave generate a back-propagation secondary wave that is cylindrical. By using a gradiometer antenna [21,22], that is, an antenna able to discern the difference (gradient) of the magnetic field, the detection of presence of cavities is improved. Among the low-frequency/magnetic-based techniques, gradiometry is considered the most reliable (in terms of false alarm and probability of detection) for tunnel detection.

19.3.7.5 Disadvantages of Magnetotellurics Methods

All MT methods described in this section experience several issues:

- Very low frequencies are involved; thus, very low resolution is expected [23].
- In the extremely low frequency, naturally occurring noise is extremely high, thus limiting the effectiveness of such methods.
- An analysis of sensitivity and resolution performed using synthetic data indicates that tunnels need to be at a depth to diameter ratios of approximately 3:1 in order to be detectable by surface EM method [20]. This is a severe limitation that restricts the use of MT methods only for very shallow targets.
- The device is required to be on top of the area under investigation.
- Currently, the technology is still experimental (e.g., there is only one HAARP facility in the world) and has not matured to a stage where tomographic principles can be implemented: Studies have shown only the capability of void detection, without giving exact information regarding its location, shape, and/or depth.

19.3.8 Radio Imaging Method

In the early 1980s, EM wave transmission experiments in coal seams confirmed Wait's [24] expectation of natural waveguides in the stratified earth. Whenever lower-conductivity layers are surrounded by high-conductivity layers, only quasi-transverse EM (quasi-TEM) waves are observable in the far field of an underground radiating antenna: Higher-order modes of propagation vanish with distance into the far field. The rediscovery of Wait's waveguides led to the development of LF/MF band continuous wave *radio imaging method* (RIM) in-mine and cross-well transmission instrumentation for detection and imaging of anomalous geologic structure in the coal seam waveguide and mineralized ore bodies [12].

Essentially, a primary TEM wave probes the ground, and with the hypothesis that tunnels' EM properties are similar to conducting cylinders, the long wavelength scattering limit [25] holds; thus, the incident and scattered field spreading wave front are diverse, and their relative phase shift is proportional to the depth. Therefore, an inversion theory that relates the properties of the scattered wave with the depth location of voids can be constructed. In particular, the cancellation of the primary wave (i.e., incident field) contribution is performed by using gradiometer antennas [21], thus allowing the user to properly measure the contribution due to the scattered field only.

The RIM is still facing several challenges:

■ RIM requires exceptionally high amount of power at MF/LF band, which currently is only provided by experimental systems. Furthermore, the primary field source must be located kilometers away from the region of investigation in order to generate a locally TEM wave front.

■ Additionally, the primary TEM wave must impinge the hypothetical scatterer perpendicularly; hence, an a priori knowledge of its orientation is mandatory: For cross-border passageways, target orientation is presumably well estimated, but in the general case of UGF detection, this awareness is ordinarily unavailable.

■ The theory is based on the detection of a perfect metallic cylinder normal to the plane of investigation: This condition implies that the operator has a priori knowledge of the orientation of the underground facility, particularly that roofs and ceilings are coplanar with the air–earth interface. Any other UGF orientation may not be accurately detected. Furthermore, the phase difference between primary and secondary field decreases with the size of the UGF: Paradoxically, larger underground entities may be less detectable than small ones.

■ At the present time, there is no algorithm that constructs an underground image from the collected data.

19.3.9 Seismic Waves

Seismic methods for underground imaging of tunnels and UGFs have appeared [26–28], mostly because of their popular use in exploration geology and petroleum engineering. Seismic methods use the information carried by scattered seismic waves (i.e., vibrations) to estimate the properties of the Earth's interior. Seismic methods for void detection range from classical *reflection seismology* to the more sophisticated *borehole seismic imaging* and *seismic tomography*. Seismic methods usually require a controlled seismic source of energy, such as dynamite explosion and air gun vibrators (i.e., large trucks that shake a vibrating pad through a known frequency band). The seismic receivers, that is, the *geophones*, record echo signal reflected from deep targets on the surface. The spatial structure of a seismic signal depends on the velocity of elastic wave propagation, which is a function of physical parameters of rocks. By logging the time undertaken by a reflection wave to arrive at a receiver, depth and features of underlying structures can be estimated. If multiple geophones are emplaced on the area of interest, a tomographic reconstruction returns highly resolved images.

Before introducing the disadvantages of using seismic methods, a brief taxonomy on waves is given. For any seismic source excitation, four classes of seismic waves can propagate (i.e., are solutions of the seismic wave equation):

■ *P waves (compressional)*: Corresponding to the longitudinal wave of propagation, they are usually the main contribution to the total seismic field.
■ *S waves (shear)*: Corresponding to the transverse waves.
■ *R waves (Rayleigh)*: Excited at the air–earth interface.
■ *L waves (Love)*: Excited between two different layers.

In conventional void detection, only P (mainly) and S (rarely) waves are generally considered, because they represent the fundamental modes of underground seismic propagation, and are recorded easily by classical geophones.

Underground imaging systems based on seismic waves are subject to the following drawbacks:

- *Weathering*: Seismic sensing, albeit affected by relatively low attenuation, becomes virtually ineffective when weathered soil (or stratified layers) is present.
- *Soft terrains*: Seismic sensing fails when soil is not compact, such as desert terrains, due to the poor sound propagation.
- *Void target*: A void target reflects nearly all power backward, since the difference between the intrinsic impedance of the rock and the one of the vacuum is several orders of magnitude higher. Therefore, targets beneath a void formation (e.g., a second floor in an underground facility) cannot be detected.
- *High noise*: Naturally occurring microseismic events, ordnance detonation, and traffic created a continuous stream of false-positive detection events. Advanced threshold detection and discrimination algorithms have been developed, but they are not able to properly differentiate between real threats and ordinary noise [12]. Experiments aimed at comparing different tunnel detection methodologies revealed seismic sensing outputs that are noisy and inconsistent [29,30].
- *Wave transformations*: Another phenomenon that limits the reliability of measurements is the evidence that naturally generated R and L waves may transform in P and S waves at the receiver, and vice versa, thus noticeably altering the data logging.
- *Polarization and pattern*: Differently from EM sensing, in seismic sensing, it is generally not possible to exploit the polarization or the antenna pattern diversity in order to discern between scattered field and background (unwanted) field.
- *Coarse resolution*: Systems that are based on *seismic waves* employ very low-frequency audio spectrum. Generally, the resolution is in the order of tens of meter or even greater, which is generally too coarse for detecting small voids such as tunnels or weapon caches [31]. Even when tomography is implemented to increase the resolution, high noise still affects the image quality.
- *Geophone resonance*: Additional complications are introduced by geophone-to-ground or geophone-to-formation coupling. Seismic phase and amplitude are highly distorted upon approaching resonant frequencies. The usable seismic frequency band must then remain well below the frequency peaks introduced by coupling to the formation. These formation coupling effects do exist also in the borehole. In this case, the geophone becomes part of the larger downhole tool, which can, in combination with the formation, give rise to formation coupling resonances. With presently available commercial tool designs, coupling resonances have been observed to fall into a frequency range as low as 18–30 Hz.
- *Environmental impact*: Reflection seismic experiments may impact the Earth's natural environment. On land, conducting a seismic survey may require the building of roads in order to transport equipment and personnel. Even if roads are not required, vegetation may need to be cleared for the deployment of geophones. If the survey is in a relatively undeveloped area, significant habitat disturbance may result.

19.3.10 Ground-Penetrating Radar

The previous subsection clearly shows how seismic methods are affected by environmental problems, low resolution, high noise, and shallow penetration; hence, EM methods should be preferred. The most common EM method for underground target detection is the ground-penetrating radar (GPR), which uses radar pulses to image the subsurface. Classically, GPR uses EM radiation in the microwave band (UHF/VHF frequencies) of the radio spectrum and detects the reflected signals from subsurface structures. GPR can detect objects, changes in material, and voids and cracks; therefore, it is suited for detection of shallow tunnels, bunkers, or caves [32,33].

In its usual configuration, GPR uses two distinct transmitting and receiving antennas or only one performing both functions. The transmitting antenna radiates short pulses of the high-frequency radio waves into the ground. When the wave hits a buried target or a boundary with different dielectric constants, the receiving antenna records variations in the reflected return signal. The principles involved are similar to reflection seismology, except that EM energy is used instead of acoustic energy.

The depth range of GPR is limited by the electrical conductivity of the ground, the transmitted center frequency, and the radiated power. As conductivity increases, the penetration depth decreases. This happens because the EM energy is more quickly dissipated into heat, causing a loss in signal strength. Higher-frequency waves do not penetrate as far as lower frequencies but result in better resolution. Good penetration is also achieved in dry sandy soils or massive dry materials such as granite, limestone, and concrete.

The depth of penetration for pulsed radar applications has been improved by using higher-power transmitters and by using data acquisition techniques, which involve point measurements and data stacking. These modifications have resulted in the acquisition of successful profiles in areas that previously were not amenable to GPR exploration, which used lower-power transmitters and dynamic profiling methods [34].

Ground penetration through radar systems encounters several challenges when applied to the problem of void detection. Some critical flaws are:

■ *Shallow application*: GPRs are intrinsically shallow systems. The typical GPR minimum frequency of operation is of the order of tens of MHz: At these frequencies, losses due to the material limit severely the depth that an echo signal can be revealed. Currently, state-of-the-art commercial systems routinely advertise 10 m of penetration, with some experimental equipment able to detect up to 40–50 m in favorable conditions [35], which is not adequate for our operations.

■ *Air–earth discontinuity*: The presence of the air–earth discontinuity causes several issues discussed later. Basically, less power is injected into the ground (i.e., shallower penetration), and rays are refracted at the interface (i.e., limiting the reconstruction process by creating blurring and aberrations).

■ *Wide band*: GPR is based on pulses and echo detection, and the resolution is proportional to the size of the probing pulse: The smaller the pulse, the wider the bandwidth.

■ *Azimuthal resolution*: Common GPR provides a blurred image of the targets in azimuth: The data are displayed in the so-called radargram, and only the operator's expertise can determine the approximated azimuthal extent of the target by inspection of the width of the hyperbolas in the radargram.

■ *Blind region*: Similarly to any radar system, common monostatic GPR experiences the *blind region* effect, in which the receiver is impeded to catch the echo signal until the transmitter completes the propagation of the pulse. This problem can be solved by invoking suited modulation techniques, such as linear frequency modulation (LFM), at the expenses of increased complexity and cost of the system.

■ *Radargram*: The output of a GPR system, as well as the output of any reflection-based device, is an unintelligible image, and the interpretation is generally attributed to the operator's personal experience and/or expertise. Prior knowledge of the soil characteristics is needed to properly retrieve information concerning the underground.

■ *Target inclination*: When the target is not perfectly parallel to air–earth interface, ray theory suggests that the backscattered power is generally reflected to an oblique direction; therefore, the echo path is not back propagating toward the GPR receiver, and a great amount of energy is lost. Theoretical studies [36] and experiments [37] have shown that an angle greater than 45° is effectively obscuring the target.

19.3.11 Need of Lower Frequencies

GPRs are intended for EM sounding of shallow depths. For our scopes, the depth of penetration needs to be significantly higher compared to what commercial GPRs achieve today. Typically, two ways to increase the depth of penetration are amenable:

■ Increase the radiated power.
■ Lower the frequency of operation of the system.

The former solution is not suggested, since increasing the radiated power undermines the cost and complexity of the final system. Therefore, the latter option is investigated. Qualitatively, two contrasting options must be balanced.

Advantages of using higher frequencies are listed as follows:

■ The range resolution is inversely proportional to the frequency of operation. Therefore, in order to obtain an accurate image, higher frequencies are desired.

■ Lower frequencies generate less scattered field than higher frequencies, increasing the dimension of the smallest detectable object. Therefore, higher frequencies should be preferred.

■ At lower frequencies, the Helmholtz equation responsible for the wave behavior of the field becomes a Laplace's equation, since the wave number becomes very small. Therefore, the field behaves diffusively, that is, the scattered power is not radiating uniformly to all directions, and the *back* scattered field is dramatically reduced [38].

■ Although the thermal noise is independent from the frequency, the external (atmospheric) noise is generally frequency dependent, and in our range of interest, it decreases when the frequency increases.

■ At higher frequencies, the antenna efficiency increases. In fact, for electrically small antennas, there is a linear relation between the current impressed at the feeding point and the radiated electric field. Therefore, at higher frequencies, more electric field is radiated toward the ground.

Conversely, lower frequencies are preferable for the following reasons:

- Attenuation sharply increases with the frequency of operation. Therefore, in order to monitor a large extent of region, lower frequencies are desired.
- In tomographic algorithms, an important approximation (called Born approximation) to linearize the image reconstruction problem (see next section for details) is adopted. Born approximation is invalidated when a quantitative reconstruction of the objects large compared to the probing wavelength is required. Therefore, for an accurate image reconstruction that involves Born approximation, the frequency of operation should be kept low.
- At lower frequency, the air–earth interface appears to be relatively smoother; thus, the theoretical formulations presented in this work are better approximating the real case.
- The EM clutter due to weathered soil is noticeably reduced at lower frequency, since the size of the cluttering objects become smaller compared to the probing wavelength.
- If the wavelength becomes too short, phase errors on the sampled received field become proportionally higher. Furthermore, the inaccuracies in the positioning of the antenna system are exacerbated when the probing frequency is high.
- The use of higher frequency implies the implementation of fast-rate analog-to-digital converter (ADC) and generally may overload the cost of production.

Unfortunately, a mathematical demonstration that determines the optimal frequency of operation for a given requirement on the depth of penetration is yet to be developed, mostly because there are many parameters playing active role in this decision. Nevertheless, the appropriate range of frequencies can be inferred heuristically, for example, by inspection of previous geophysical surveys for objects of comparable size of tunnels and similar conditions.

The experiences described in [39–41] [12] suggest a frequency range of 0.5–15 MHz is needed to surveil object up to 100 m depth. The U.S. Air Force Research Lab described an experiment in the range of 6–66 MHz, in which they reached 60 m of penetration and 1.5 m of resolution [42], although some observations have reduced this range to 3–15 MHz [43]. Lower frequencies in the MF range for EM tomography have been experimented [44,45]. In this frequency band, EM waves tend to diffuse rather than propagate as waves through the earth: Although penetration depths of more than 100 m are possible at these low frequencies, the diffusional behavior of the fields dramatically reduces the resolution.

Low-frequency GPRs have been used for the detection of the DMZ tunnels: Results have been promising by using a 20–100 MHz GPR, reaching in some instances penetrations of 100 m [46], or by using a cross-well 3–30 MHz instrumentation, successfully used for the detection of the fourth tunnel crossing the DMZ [12].

Based on these evidences, an adequate *range of frequency is* 0.5–15 MHz, where the lower bound is suited for deep targets and the upper band is preferred for close-in sensing.

19.3.12 Need of Close-Contact/Buried Sensors

In the last decade, underground imaging devices have been installed on airborne platforms. In fact, having a GPR on an airborne platform facilitates the data acquisition from different viewpoints (enabling wide areas of survey), and it minimizes the human intervention by providing a safe standoff distance, since the GPR could be mounted on UAVs.

Attempts have been made to remote probing the underground using elevated airborne GPR/synthetic aperture radar (SAR) platforms (both for underground complex and land mine detection) [42,43]. In this case, the GPR transmitter unit is located on the center plane, while the receiver unit is generally positioned on the tail or sometimes on the "bird," that is, flying a few hundred meters behind the planes.

Two Defense Advanced Research Projects Agency (DARPA) projects, the Low-Altitude Airborne Sensor Systems (LAASS), and the Airborne Tomography using Active Electromagnetics (ATAEM), performed measurement campaigns in order to proof the feasibility of underground sensing from airborne platforms.

However, deep tunnel detection by aerial remote-sensing methods has proven to be not completely effective [8]. The main causes of this inefficiency are expressed as follows:

1. Ground foliage, canopies, objects, and other imperfections reduce the depth of penetration.
2. Mechanical vibration and UAV-generated noise are altering the measured quantities.
3. Snell's principle suggests that ray paths are deviated at the interface; therefore, the collected data can be shifted in phase (depending on the location of the scatterer and the height of sensors from the ground), and if this phenomenon is not accounted for in the model, the reconstruction could be affected by blurring and aberrations [47].
4. Ground penetration via airborne devices is challenged by the excessively high path loss of the probing wave field. In fact, ground mismatch between air and earth reduces injected power into the ground; thus, the penetration is expected to be shallower. More exactly
    a. For a downward propagating wave, the transmission coefficient at the air–earth interface regulates the amount of power flowing inside the ground: Transmission loss greater than −5 dB is not uncommon.
    b. The upward propagating scattered wave is (again) subject to the reflection at the interface, thus further reducing the power directed toward the receiver.
5. High amount of ground-reflected power travels upward and couples with the receiver, thus masking the weak signal scattered from buried targets.

Conversely, placing sensors on top of the air–earth interface, or slightly burying them into the ground, further enhances the received power. In fact

1. Ground foliage, canopies, and other sources of clutter are virtually eliminated.
2. Once the sensor penetrates the ground, there is no mechanical vibration that can disturb the measurement.
3. Buried sensors experience a slight gain in power because of the coherent in-phase added contribution to the total field due to the inner reflection at the interface, both at the transmitter and the receiver side.

19.3.13 Need of Geometric Diversity

Up to this point, the presented methods are meant to *detect* anomalies below the ground. However, the problem of *imaging* the targets belowground is yet to be tackled. For the purposes of tunnel, bunker, or UGF detection, the actual target shape reconstruction is not imperative, but tracing their extensions inside domain of investigation is useful, especially for uncovering concealed adits or storage rooms. *Imaging* the underground can be performed by collecting several data at different location and then performing a suitable image reconstruction algorithm. Previously introduced techniques are basically monostatic, meaning that the signal is transmitted and received at the same geometrical location. This is clearly a loss of information, since the underground scene is not probed by different viewpoints.

To increase this information, an important diversity, called *geometric diversity*, needs to be exploited. Geometric diversity, both in the form of *view diversity* and *observation diversity*, represents the physical distribution of sensors arbitrarily in the area of regard. In this work, the view diversity refers to the concept that multiple transmitters are used in different locations, while the observation diversity is associated with the different position of multiple receivers.

Geometric diversity has been a challenge until recent years, with the advent of precision global positioning and timing systems. Another key advantage of using view and observation diversity is that the spectral content of the waveform illuminating the target can be drastically reduced. In principle, even when only a single frequency is used, high-resolution images can be reconstructed.

19.4 RF Tomography

RF tomography [1] offers a method for imaging high-contrast dielectric/conducting targets embedded in complex environments, based upon multiple observations of the EM fields due to different source/receiver locations, and under different frequencies and different polarizations.

From a system perspective, a set of low-cost, configurable, automated, EM transmitter/receivers are placed on top, above, or into the ground at *arbitrary* positions, including random deployment, as pictorially represented in Figure 19.1. During a preliminary calibration stage, sensors accurately identify their position, orientation, and time reference. Once the calibration phase is concluded, a predetermined transmitter radiates a known waveform (generally a monochromatic tone) using a suitable polarization. When the probing wave impinges upon a dielectric/conducting target, a scattered field is generated. Distributed receivers collect samples of the total field, suppress noise, clutter, direct path, and store the information concerning only the scattered field. In the next iteration, a different transmitter is activated, or different waveforms/polarizations are used. The collected data are relayed to the command and control post for processing and imaging, for example, an overlying base station or an unmanned aerial vehicle. The system operates using ultra-narrowband, adaptive waveforms, thus ensuring low interference, dispersion, thermal noise, and affordable cost. In inaccessible zones, sensors may be compounded into existing payload of earth-penetrating weapons or could be ejected by an aircraft and delivered aboveground or installed on top of moving ground vehicles, low-altitude airborne platforms, existent radio-link towers, etc. The image reconstruction algorithm shall envisage the eventual failure or obstruction of transponders, by weighting or neglecting corrupted sensors.

Advantages of using RF tomography for belowground imaging include, but are not limited to the following:

- *Minimal human intervention*: RF tomography is well suited for remote probing without direct involvement of human resources. A dangerous area, where human lives would be in peril, could still be surrounded with transponders, or in the event that the scene is completely inaccessible (e.g., an adversary territory), sensors can be launched and disseminated from airborne vehicles.
- *Spectral dominance*: RF tomography features the highest number of diversities among any other imaging systems, comprising *frequency, polarization, code, modulation, antenna pattern, view* (transmitter location), and *observation* (receiver location) diversities. In this

chapter, RF tomography performance is investigated using monochromatic waveforms, leaving studies on complex modulations/codes to future activities. With monochromatic tones, the required instantaneous bandwidth is ultranarrow, yielding ultralow signal-to-noise ratio, insignificant dispersion and spurious frequencies, and negligible interferences. Clearly, ultra-narrowband RF tomography is suited for spectrally cluttered environments.

■ *Resolution*: RF tomography theoretically guarantees *subwavelength* and *range-independent* resolution, provided that adequate numbers of transmitters and receivers are located in a proper position. This permits the use of even lower operating frequencies, thus reducing timing, positioning, and phase field estimation errors.

■ *Wide area/deep range*: Due to the exploitation of spatial diversity, this technique allows much lower operating frequencies, thus facilitating penetration deep into the ground. The multistatic geometry associated with the proposed forward model enables the possibility of the sensors residing in the near field of the targets, thus allowing larger investigation areas, from very near/shallow to very far/deep regions.

■ *Affordability*: The design, manufacturing, testing, and mass production of ultra-narrowband transponders in the low-frequency range (i.e., electrically small radiators) are relatively simple and inexpensive, and precise location, timing, and phase coherence can be guaranteed by the well-established, standardized, and low-cost GPS technology. Furthermore, the ultralow instantaneous bandwidth enables the use of high-resolution ADCs, yielding large dynamic ranges at low cost.

■ *Adaptability*: RF tomography allows the location of sensors to be arbitrary, including random placement. Random sensor position does not severely degrade the system operability: At most, if sensors are poorly arranged in the ground, a graceful degradation of the reconstructed image may result. In fact, randomization of the sensor locations could be beneficial, reducing image side lobes in a manner analogous to the reduction of grating lobes, through random arrangement of elements in antenna arrays.

■ *Modularity*: RF tomography is intrinsically modular, that is, the addition/removal of active sensors is easily implemented: There is no prior requirement of the number of active sensors, and the image quality is somewhat directly related to their number, in addition to their location. This implies that the failure of a set of transponders does not compromise the overall system but may only affect the accuracy and resolution of the reconstructions.

■ *Persistent sensing*: The peculiar distributed sensing in RF tomography provides the user with profound situational awareness of the scene. Particularly, the persistence is guaranteed by the multitude of sensors, and the unintentional (obstruction) or intentional (sabotage) failure of some Tx/Rx units does not preclude the overall image reconstruction process.

RF tomography for tunnel and UGF detection has been pioneered in the last decade by the U.S. Air Force Research Laboratory [43,48], attaining favorable results. The underlying theory was based on scalar wave equation, homogeneous space, and relatively trivial signal processing. To fully recover information concerning targets, more accurate forward and inverse models have been devised. The following sections introduce an imaging procedure based upon recently developed models for both the forward and the inverse problems. Specifically, the forward model has been extended to include the vector nature of the EM field, the possibility of using magnetic dipoles, and the accurate description of the air–earth interface [38]. For the inverse model, advanced regularized methods are addressed [49], followed by recent sparse regularization schemes [50].

19.5 Forward Model

The technique of *RF tomography* discussed in this chapter derives from the theory of EM inverse scattering. From an EM perspective, the problem of localizing and characterizing target underground is equivalent to retrieve location and shape of dielectric/conducting anomalies with respect to a dielectric/conducting background, assumed known, based upon remote measurement of scattered EM fields due to different EM sources.

In this section, 3D position and direction vectors are expressed in Cartesian coordinates. A generic position vector representing the *observation* point in the space (i.e., the point in which the field is evaluated, measured, or computed) shall be referred to as $\mathbf{r} = x\hat{\mathbf{x}} + y\hat{\mathbf{y}} + z\hat{\mathbf{z}}$, and a generic *source* position vector shall be represented with $\mathbf{r}' = x'\hat{\mathbf{x}} + y'\hat{\mathbf{y}} + z'\hat{\mathbf{z}}$.

To ensure sufficient earth penetration by EM waves, the operating frequency for RF tomography is generally in the 0.1–15 MHz range. Hence, the corresponding elementary transmitters and receivers can be effectively modeled as electrically short ($\lambda/50 \sim \lambda/5$, where λ denotes the probing wavelength) electric (for dipoles) or magnetic (for loops) dipoles.

In general, a set of $n = 1, \ldots, N$ field measurements are collected: A distinct nth measurement is obtained by either varying

- Transmitter position $\mathbf{r}_n^a$
- Transmitter direction $\hat{\mathbf{a}}_n$ (unit norm)
- Receiver position $\mathbf{r}_n^b$
- Receiver direction $\hat{\mathbf{b}}_n$ (unit norm)
- Angular frequency $\omega_n = 2\pi f_n$

Targets reside only within a volumetric region D named *investigation domain*. A generic point inside D shall be represented with the position vector $\bar{\mathbf{r}}$. Within this region D, the background conductivity is represented by the function $\sigma_D(\bar{\mathbf{r}})$ and the background relative dielectric permittivity by the function $\varepsilon_D(\bar{\mathbf{r}})$, while the background magnetic permeability is constant and equal to μ_0, that is, the one of the free space. The electric field $\mathbf{E}$ (V/m), magnetic field $\mathbf{H}$ (A/m), electric current density $\mathbf{J}$ (A/m²), and magnetic current density $\mathbf{M}$ (V/m²) are all expressed in phasor form using the $\exp(-i\omega t)$ convention: All other capitalized bold quantities represent matrices. Capitalized, bold, and underlined quantities describe dyadics, which are represented by 3×3 matrices as described in [51]. Lowercase bold variables represent vectors, and circumflexed vectors are real valued with unitary norm, generally representing directions (Figure 19.2).

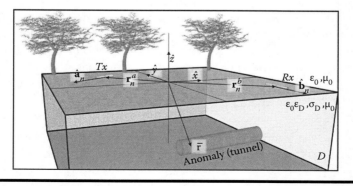

Figure 19.2 Symbols used to describe the theory of RF tomography explained in this chapter.

19.5.1 Incident Fields

Consider the electric current distribution $\mathbf{J}(\mathbf{r}')$ having support distributed in a finite volume R, outside the investigation domain D, accounting for the region where an active transmitter resides. The corresponding radiated electric field $\mathbf{E}^{Inc}(\mathbf{r})$, the *incident* field (i.e., the field in the investigation domain in absence of the scattering targets), can be expressed with an integral equation:

$$\mathbf{E}^{Inc}(\mathbf{r}) = i\omega\mu_0 \iiint_R \mathbf{\underline{G}}_{ee}(\mathbf{r},\mathbf{r}') \cdot \mathbf{J}(\mathbf{r}') d\mathbf{r}' \tag{19.1}$$

where the dyadic $\mathbf{\underline{G}}_{ee}$ is called *electric Green's function of electric type*. Physically, this quantity relates electric currents to radiated electric fields, and it depends upon the EM properties of the background environment. Mathematically, $\mathbf{G}$ is a dyadic, which can be represented as 3×3 matrix function having two juxtaposed orthogonal vectors:

$$\mathbf{\underline{G}}(\mathbf{r},\mathbf{r}') = \begin{bmatrix} G_{xx}(\mathbf{r},\mathbf{r}')\hat{\mathbf{x}}\hat{\mathbf{x}} & G_{xy}(\mathbf{r},\mathbf{r}')\hat{\mathbf{x}}\hat{\mathbf{y}} & G_{xz}(\mathbf{r},\mathbf{r}')\hat{\mathbf{x}}\hat{\mathbf{z}} \\ G_{yx}(\mathbf{r},\mathbf{r}')\hat{\mathbf{y}}\hat{\mathbf{x}} & G_{yy}(\mathbf{r},\mathbf{r}')\hat{\mathbf{y}}\hat{\mathbf{y}} & G_{yz}(\mathbf{r},\mathbf{r}')\hat{\mathbf{y}}\hat{\mathbf{z}} \\ G_{zx}(\mathbf{r},\mathbf{r}')\hat{\mathbf{z}}\hat{\mathbf{x}} & G_{zy}(\mathbf{r},\mathbf{r}')\hat{\mathbf{z}}\hat{\mathbf{y}} & G_{zz}(\mathbf{r},\mathbf{r}')\hat{\mathbf{z}}\hat{\mathbf{z}} \end{bmatrix} \tag{19.2}$$

Dot multiplying a dyadic with a vector returns a vector; for example,

$$\mathbf{G} \cdot \mathbf{J} = \begin{bmatrix} G_{xx}\hat{\mathbf{x}}\hat{\mathbf{x}} & G_{xy}\hat{\mathbf{x}}\hat{\mathbf{y}} & G_{xz}\hat{\mathbf{x}}\hat{\mathbf{z}} \\ G_{yx}\hat{\mathbf{y}}\hat{\mathbf{x}} & G_{yy}\hat{\mathbf{y}}\hat{\mathbf{y}} & G_{yz}\hat{\mathbf{y}}\hat{\mathbf{z}} \\ G_{zx}\hat{\mathbf{z}}\hat{\mathbf{x}} & G_{zy}\hat{\mathbf{z}}\hat{\mathbf{y}} & G_{zz}\hat{\mathbf{z}}\hat{\mathbf{z}} \end{bmatrix} \cdot \begin{bmatrix} J_x\hat{\mathbf{x}} \\ J_y\hat{\mathbf{y}} \\ J_z\hat{\mathbf{z}} \end{bmatrix} = \begin{bmatrix} (G_{xx}+G_{yx}+G_{zx})\hat{\mathbf{x}} \\ (G_{xy}+G_{yy}+G_{zy})\hat{\mathbf{y}} \\ (G_{xz}+G_{yz}+G_{zz})\hat{\mathbf{z}} \end{bmatrix} \begin{cases} \hat{\mathbf{x}}\cdot\hat{\mathbf{x}}=\hat{\mathbf{y}}\cdot\hat{\mathbf{y}}=\hat{\mathbf{z}}\cdot\hat{\mathbf{z}}=1 \\ \hat{\mathbf{x}}\cdot\hat{\mathbf{y}}=\hat{\mathbf{x}}\cdot\hat{\mathbf{z}}=\hat{\mathbf{y}}\cdot\hat{\mathbf{z}}=0 \end{cases}$$

$$\tag{19.3}$$

Dyadic analysis, algebra, and important theorems are discussed in [51]. Explicit analytical expressions for the dyadic Green's function $\mathbf{\underline{G}}_{ee}$ are available only for a very limited set of canonical geometries: Expressions for a homogeneous space and for a two-layered media (half-space and air–earth) are provided in [52,53], since these two cases are the most significant for the problems under consideration. Multilayered media are also described in specialized texts, including [52,54,55]. Nonplanar geometries require a numerical computation of $\mathbf{\underline{G}}_{ee}$: A recent paper is [56]; otherwise, numerical Green's functions can be computed using commercial EM software.

In this application, the nth active transmitter can be modeled as a delta distribution of the type $\mathbf{J}(\mathbf{r}') = I_n l_n \delta(\mathbf{r}' - \mathbf{r}_n^a)\hat{\mathbf{a}}_n$, where I_n is the current flowing into the dipole and l_n is its length; hence, the corresponding *incident* electric field observed at a generic point inside D is

$$\mathbf{E}^{Inc}(\overline{\mathbf{r}}) = i\omega_n\mu_0 I_n l_n \mathbf{\underline{G}}_{ee}(\overline{\mathbf{r}},\mathbf{r}_n^a) \cdot \mathbf{a}_n \tag{19.4}$$

At the same time, the incident electric field directly impinging upon the nth receiver (direct coupling between the transmitting and receiving antennas) is

$$E_n^{DP} = E_n^{Inc}(\mathbf{r}_n^b) = i\omega_n\mu_0 I_n l_n \hat{\mathbf{b}}_n^T \cdot \mathbf{\underline{G}}_{ee}(\mathbf{r}_n^b,\mathbf{r}_n^a) \cdot \hat{\mathbf{a}}_n \tag{19.5}$$

where the superscript T denotes the operation of transposition. This quantity is referred to as *direct-path* field and represents an undesired contribution to the measured field that is unavoidable when working with monochromatic waveforms. A later section is later devoted to the description of some techniques for the removal of this quantity in order to achieve a reliable estimation of the scattered field.

Similarly, the magnetic field can be expressed in terms of electric current sources as

$$\mathbf{H}^{Inc}(\mathbf{r}) = \iiint_R \underline{\mathbf{G}}_{me}(\mathbf{r},\mathbf{r}') \cdot \mathbf{J}(\mathbf{r}')\, d\mathbf{r}' \tag{19.6}$$

Here, $\underline{\mathbf{G}}_{me}$ is the *magnetic dyadic Green's function of electric type* and relates electric currents to magnetic fields. In particular, for the nth active Tx dipole, the magnetic field inside D is

$$\mathbf{H}_n^{Inc}(\bar{\mathbf{r}}) = I_n l_n \underline{\mathbf{G}}_{me}\left(\bar{\mathbf{r}},\mathbf{r}_n^a\right) \cdot \hat{\mathbf{a}}_n \tag{19.7}$$

and the direct-path contribution is

$$H_n^{DP} = H_n^{Inc}\left(\mathbf{r}_n^b\right) = I_n l_n \hat{\mathbf{b}}_n^T \cdot \underline{\mathbf{G}}_{me}\left(\mathbf{r}_n^b,\mathbf{r}_n^a\right) \cdot \hat{\mathbf{a}}_n \tag{19.8}$$

Similar expressions can be derived for magnetic currents using the duality principles. Equivalent magnetic currents are helpful in describing electrically small loops, since $M_n l_n$, the magnetic dipole moment, is related to the electric current flowing into the electric loop sensor as

$$M_n l_n = -i\omega_n \mu_0 I_n N_n^c A_n \tag{19.9}$$

while the direction $\hat{\mathbf{a}}_n$ is chosen according to the right-hand rule.

In a similar way, the incident fields due to equivalent magnetic currents are

$$\mathbf{E}^{Inc}(\mathbf{r}) = \iiint_R \underline{\mathbf{G}}_{em}(\mathbf{r},\mathbf{r}') \cdot \mathbf{M}(\mathbf{r}')\, d\mathbf{r}' \tag{19.10}$$

$$\mathbf{H}^{Inc}(\mathbf{r}) = +i\omega\varepsilon_0 \iiint_R \underline{\mathbf{G}}_{mm}(\mathbf{r},\mathbf{r}') \cdot \mathbf{M}(\mathbf{r}')\, d\mathbf{r}'. \tag{19.11}$$

For delta-source magnetic dipoles, Equations 19.10 and 19.11 simplify to

$$\mathbf{E}_n^{Inc}(\bar{\mathbf{r}}) = M_n l_n \underline{\mathbf{G}}_{em}\left(\bar{\mathbf{r}},\mathbf{r}_n^a\right) \cdot \hat{\mathbf{a}}_n$$

$$\mathbf{H}_n^{Inc}(\bar{\mathbf{r}}) = i\omega_n \varepsilon_0 M_n l_n \underline{\mathbf{G}}_{mm}\left(\bar{\mathbf{r}},\mathbf{r}_n^a\right) \cdot \hat{\mathbf{a}}_n \tag{19.12}$$

and the corresponding direct-path field contributions are

$$E_n^{DP} = E_n^{Inc}\left(\mathbf{r}_n^b\right) = M_n l_n \hat{\mathbf{b}}_n^T \cdot \underline{\mathbf{G}}_{em}\left(\mathbf{r}_n^b,\mathbf{r}_n^a\right) \cdot \hat{\mathbf{a}}_n$$

$$H_n^{DP} = H_n^{Inc}\left(\mathbf{r}_n^b\right) = i\omega_n \varepsilon_0 M_n l_n \hat{\mathbf{b}}_n^T \cdot \underline{\mathbf{G}}_{mm}\left(\mathbf{r}_n^b,\mathbf{r}_n^a\right) \cdot \hat{\mathbf{a}}_n \tag{19.13}$$

In these equations, $\underline{\mathbf{G}}_{mm}$ is the *magnetic dyadic Green's function of magnetic type* (relating magnetic currents to magnetic fields), and $\underline{\mathbf{G}}_{em}$ is the *electric dyadic Green's function of magnetic type* (relating magnetic currents to electric fields).

19.5.2 Scattered Fields

Under the action of the incident field, within the investigation domain D, a difference in dielectric permittivity or conductivity w.r.t. the background generates scattered fields. An anomaly inside D exhibits an actual relative dielectric permittivity $\varepsilon_r(\bar{\mathbf{r}}) = \varepsilon_D(\bar{\mathbf{r}}) + \varepsilon_{Tar}(\bar{\mathbf{r}})$ and conductivity $\sigma(\bar{\mathbf{r}}) = \sigma_D(\bar{\mathbf{r}}) + \sigma_{Tar}(\bar{\mathbf{r}})$: In some sense, the "anomaly quantities" ε_{Tar} and σ_{Tar} represent the electrical properties of the target under observation. Since the main focus is merely to determine the presence/absence of a target in $\bar{\mathbf{r}}$, the following dimensionless quantity, having the same properties of a relative dielectric permittivity, will be used to describe the target:

$$V(\bar{\mathbf{r}}) = \varepsilon_{Tar}(\bar{\mathbf{r}}) + i\frac{\sigma_{Tar}(\bar{\mathbf{r}})}{\omega\varepsilon_0} \tag{19.14}$$

The function V is named *contrast function*: It embodies the combined deviation of the relative dielectric permittivity and the conductivity from the background values and represents the mathematical description of the anomaly to be imaged. In fact, when there is no anomaly at the point $\bar{\mathbf{r}}$, the value of the contrast function V is zero. The equivalent electric current distribution due to the presence of a $\mathbf{E}^{Tot}$ total electric field impinging upon a dielectric/conducting target at point $\bar{\mathbf{r}}$ can be expressed as

$$\mathbf{J}_{eq}(\bar{\mathbf{r}}) = -i\omega\varepsilon_0 V(\bar{\mathbf{r}})\mathbf{E}^{Tot}(\bar{\mathbf{r}}) \tag{19.15}$$

The scattered electric field $\mathbf{E}^{Sca}$ at a generic point r due to a distributed anomaly (described by the contrast function V) inside D is then

$$\mathbf{E}^{Sca}(\mathbf{r}) = i\omega\mu_0 \iiint_D \underline{\mathbf{G}}_{ee}(\mathbf{r},\bar{\mathbf{r}})\cdot\mathbf{J}_{eq}(\bar{\mathbf{r}})d\bar{\mathbf{r}} = k_0^2 \iiint_D \underline{\mathbf{G}}_{ee}(\mathbf{r},\bar{\mathbf{r}})\cdot\mathbf{E}^{Tot}(\bar{\mathbf{r}})V(\bar{\mathbf{r}})d\bar{\mathbf{r}} \tag{19.16}$$

This equation is generally named *scattering integral equation*. This equation is nonlinear w.r.t. $\mathbf{E}^{Sca}$, because the scattered field is present both in the left- and in the right-hand sides, since $\mathbf{E}^{Tot} = \mathbf{E}^{Sca} + \mathbf{E}^{Inc}$. The nonlinearity makes the retrieval of V from Equation 19.16 challenging. Hence, a simplification is needed by means of an approximation that transforms the nonlinear inverse problem into a linear one. A suitable approximation is to assume the total field in the integrand in (19.16) to be equal to the incident field. Accordingly, Equation 19.16 is rewritten as a Lippmann–Schwinger equation in its *operator form*. By letting

$$\Theta = \iiint_D (\ );\Psi = k_0^2 V(\mathbf{r})\underline{\mathbf{G}}(\mathbf{r},\mathbf{r}')\cdot(\ ) \tag{19.17}$$

the operator form of (19.16) is

$$\mathbf{E}^{Sca} = \Theta\Psi\mathbf{E}^{Tot} \Rightarrow \mathbf{E}^{Tot} = \Theta\Psi\mathbf{E}^{Tot} + \mathbf{E}^{Inc} \Rightarrow \mathbf{E}^{Tot} = [\mathbf{I} - \Theta\Psi]^{-1}\mathbf{E}^{Inc} \tag{19.18}$$

where I represents the vector identity. The previous expression can be expressed in terms of the geometric series (Neumann series)

$$\frac{1}{1-\Theta\Psi} = 1 + \Theta\Psi + \Theta\Psi\Theta\Psi + \cdots \tag{19.19}$$

The convergence is guaranteed when the norm of the operator $\Theta\Psi$ is less than unity. Under this assumption,

$$\mathbf{E}^{Tot} = \mathbf{E}^{Inc} + \Theta\Psi\mathbf{E}^{Inc} + \Theta\Psi\Theta\Psi\mathbf{E}^{Inc} + \cdots \tag{19.20}$$

and the total electric field can be rewritten as

$$\mathbf{E}^{Tot}(\mathbf{r}) = \mathbf{E}^{Inc}(\mathbf{r}) + k_0^2 \iiint_D \mathbf{G}_{ee}(\mathbf{r},\bar{\mathbf{r}}) \cdot V(\bar{\mathbf{r}})\mathbf{E}^{Inc}(\bar{\mathbf{r}})d\bar{\mathbf{r}} + \mathbf{z}(\mathbf{r}) \tag{19.21}$$

where $\mathbf{z}(\mathbf{r})$ represents the contribution due to higher-order (multiple scattering) EM interactions. If $\mathbf{z}(\mathbf{r})$ is neglected, the resulting approximation is called *Born* approximation. In simple terms, Born approximation states that $\mathbf{E}^{Tot} \cong \mathbf{E}^{Inc}$ inside the integral in (19.16), meaning that the internal scattered field terms are small compared to the impinging incident field. Born approximation linearizes the relation between scattered field and dielectric anomalies, since the integral operator on V in (19.21) is indeed a linear operation.

19.5.3 Linear Forward Model

Under Born approximation and using (19.4) as the incident electric field, the electric field measured at receiver $\mathbf{r}_n^b$ directed along $\hat{\mathbf{b}}_n$, due to an electric dipole located at $\mathbf{r}_n^a$ and directed along $\hat{\mathbf{a}}_n$, operating at frequency ω_n, is given as the contribution of the direct path and the scattered field:

$$E\left(\mathbf{r}_n^a, \mathbf{r}_n^b, \hat{\mathbf{a}}_n, \hat{\mathbf{b}}_n, \omega_n\right) = i\omega_n\mu_0 I_n l_n \hat{\mathbf{b}}_n^T \cdot \mathbf{G}_{ee}\left(\mathbf{r}_n^b, \mathbf{r}_n^a, \omega_n\right) \cdot \hat{\mathbf{a}}_n$$

$$+ i\omega_n\mu_0 I_n l_n k_{0n}^2 \iiint_D V(\bar{\mathbf{r}})\hat{\mathbf{b}}_n^T \cdot \mathbf{G}_{ee}\left(\mathbf{r}_n^b, \bar{\mathbf{r}}\right) \cdot \mathbf{G}_{ee}\left(\bar{\mathbf{r}}, \mathbf{r}_n^a\right) \cdot \hat{\mathbf{a}}_n d\bar{\mathbf{r}} \tag{19.22}$$

where $k_{0n}^2 = \omega_n^2\sqrt{\mu_0\varepsilon_0}$. Similar conclusions can be made for the case of magnetic fields and magnetic currents. Derivations are omitted, and only the final results are reported. The measured magnetic field due to an electric dipole source is

$$H\left(\mathbf{r}_n^a, \mathbf{r}_n^b, \hat{\mathbf{a}}_n, \hat{\mathbf{b}}_n, \omega_n\right) = I_n l_n \hat{\mathbf{b}}_n^T \cdot \mathbf{G}_{me}\left(\mathbf{r}_n^b, \mathbf{r}_n^a\right) \cdot \hat{\mathbf{a}}_n$$

$$+ I_n l_n k_{0n}^2 \iiint_D V(\bar{\mathbf{r}})\hat{\mathbf{b}}_n^T \cdot \mathbf{G}_{me}\left(\mathbf{r}_n^b, \bar{\mathbf{r}}\right) \cdot \mathbf{G}_{ee}\left(\bar{\mathbf{r}}, \mathbf{r}_n^a\right) \cdot \hat{\mathbf{a}}_n d\bar{\mathbf{r}} \tag{19.23}$$

The equivalent electric current due to a dielectric anomaly irradiated by a magnetic source is

$$\mathbf{J}_{eq}\left(\bar{\mathbf{r}}\right) = -i\omega_n\varepsilon_0 M_n l_n V\left(\bar{\mathbf{r}}\right)\underline{\mathbf{G}}_{em}\left(\bar{\mathbf{r}},\mathbf{r}_n^a\right)\cdot\hat{\mathbf{a}}_n \qquad (19.24)$$

where the magnetic dipole moment is given in (19.9). Therefore, the measured magnetic field due to a magnetic dipole (Hertzian loop) source is

$$H\left(\mathbf{r}_n^a,\mathbf{r}_n^b,\hat{\mathbf{a}}_n,\hat{\mathbf{b}}_n,\omega_n\right) = +i\omega_n\varepsilon_0 M_n l_n \hat{\mathbf{b}}_n^T\cdot\underline{\mathbf{G}}_{mm}\left(\mathbf{r}_n^b,\mathbf{r}_n^a\right)\cdot\hat{\mathbf{a}}_n$$

$$-i\omega_n\varepsilon_0 M_n l_n \iiint\limits_D V\left(\bar{\mathbf{r}}\right)\hat{\mathbf{b}}_n^T\cdot\underline{\mathbf{G}}_{me}\left(\mathbf{r}_n^b,\bar{\mathbf{r}}\right)\cdot\underline{\mathbf{G}}_{em}\left(\bar{\mathbf{r}},\mathbf{r}_n^a\right)\cdot\hat{\mathbf{a}}_n d\bar{\mathbf{r}} \quad (19.25)$$

and the electric field due to a magnetic dipole (loop) source is

$$E\left(\mathbf{r}_n^a,\mathbf{r}_n^b,\hat{\mathbf{a}}_n,\hat{\mathbf{b}}_n,\omega_n\right) = M_n l_n \hat{\mathbf{b}}_n^T\cdot\underline{\mathbf{G}}_{em}\left(\mathbf{r}_n^b,\mathbf{r}_n^a\right)\cdot\hat{\mathbf{a}}_n$$

$$+k_{0n}^2 M_n l_n \iiint\limits_D V\left(\bar{\mathbf{r}}\right)\hat{\mathbf{b}}_n^T\cdot\underline{\mathbf{G}}_{ee}\left(\mathbf{r}_n^b,\bar{\mathbf{r}}\right)\cdot\underline{\mathbf{G}}_{em}\left(\bar{\mathbf{r}},\mathbf{r}_n^a\right)\cdot\hat{\mathbf{a}}_n d\bar{\mathbf{r}} \quad (19.26)$$

19.5.4 Discretization

Upon inspection of (19.22) and (19.23) and (19.25) and (19.26), the generic nth measurement may be expressed as

$$F_n\left(\mathbf{r}_n^a,\mathbf{r}_n^b,\hat{\mathbf{a}}_n,\hat{\mathbf{b}}_n,\omega_n\right) = L_n\left\{V\left(\bar{\mathbf{r}}\right)\right\}\left(\mathbf{r}_n^a,\mathbf{r}_n^b,\hat{\mathbf{a}}_n,\hat{\mathbf{b}}_n,\omega_n\right) + p\left(\mathbf{r}_n^a,\mathbf{r}_n^b,\hat{\mathbf{a}}_n,\hat{\mathbf{b}}_n,\omega_n\right) \quad (19.27)$$

where
  F_n represents the field measurement (either E_n or H_n),
  L_n represents a linear operator acting on V
  p_n accounts for the direct path between Tx and Rx

Nonlinear effects, model errors, and noise are accounted as deviations of F_n from the true value. To solve (19.27), the entire region D is discretized in M equal-size cubes (voxels), each one having volume Δ^3 and centered at location $\bar{\mathbf{r}}_m$, as shown in Figure 19.3. Hence, for a given $\bar{\mathbf{r}}_m$, the following approximation holds:

$$L_n\left\{V\left(\bar{\mathbf{r}}_m\right)\right\} \cong L_{nm}V\left(\bar{\mathbf{r}}_m\right) = L_{nm}V_m \qquad (19.28)$$

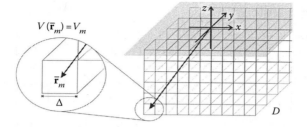

Figure 19.3 Symbols used in the discretization of the investigation domain *D*.

where L_{nm} is the value of the integral operator in (19.27) when $V(\bar{\mathbf{r}}_m) = \delta\,(\bar{\mathbf{r}} - \bar{\mathbf{r}}_m)/\Delta^3$. Hence, Equation 19.27 can be recast as a discrete system of equations:

$$
\begin{bmatrix}
F_1 = \displaystyle\sum_{m=1}^{M} L_{1m} V_m + p_n \\
\vdots \\
F_N = \displaystyle\sum_{m=1}^{M} L_{Nm} V_m + p_N
\end{bmatrix}
\tag{19.29}
$$

The set of equations in 19.29 can be conveniently expressed using a matrix equation of the form

$$
\mathbf{m}_{[N\times 1]} = \mathbf{L}_{[N\times M]} \cdot \mathbf{v}_{[M\times 1]} + \mathbf{p}_{[N\times 1]}
\tag{19.30}
$$

or equivalently

$$
\mathbf{s} = \mathbf{m} - \mathbf{p} = \mathbf{L}\mathbf{v}
\tag{19.31}
$$

In (19.30) and (19.31), **m** is the *measurement vector* and corresponds to the total field values actually measured at the receiver points; **p** is the *direct-path* vector and corresponds to a bias on the measurements due to the presence of a direct path (generally in line of sight) between any transmitter/receiver pair. The vector **s** represents the *scattered field vector*, and it is the data of the linear system in (19.31). The vector **v** is the *contrast vector*, representing the discretization of the area where the target is located, and it is the unknown in this discretized forward model. Finally, **L** is the *theory operator* in matrix form, linking the image domain (e.g., **v**) with the data domain (e.g., **s**). Equation 19.31 represents the linearized–discretized version of the Born model in RF tomography. The objective is to estimate the unknown contrast (in terms of location and shape of the targets) vector **v** given **s** from measured data and **L** from numerical computation.

19.6 Inversion Models

The objective of an inversion model consists of solving Equation 19.31, that is, estimating **v** starting from the scattered data **s**. This task is in general not trivial for the following reasons:

- The inverse problem is underdetermined and ill-conditioned, meaning that infinite solutions exist, and small errors in **s** may lead to large deviations in **v**.
- Data vector **s** can be severely affected by error, since the measurement vector is itself affected by error, model errors are present, and exact removal of the direct path is difficult.
- Unknown vector **v** is sparse (i.e., having a number of nonzero entries much smaller compared to its dimension), since the volume comprising the targets is in general small compared to the whole scene.

In this section, only three main inversion methods will be presented: *Tikhonov* regularization method, *truncated singular value decomposition (SVD)* method, and recently introduced *sparse regularization* methods. Iterative methods, such as conjugate gradient or *Landweber* methods, are still good options but are not described here since their results are similar to direct methods, where the number of iterations plays the role of the regularization parameter [49]. Minimization methods based on complicated stabilizers are also utile but are not described here because of their complexity. Specific information regarding these methods is found in [15,57–59]. In this section, bold small letters represent vectors, bold capital letters represent matrices, and circumflexed quantities represent estimations.

19.6.1 Tikhonov Regularization

Since the problem is underdetermined, infinite solutions can be found, and a formal inverse of L does not exist. In these cases, a *pseudoinverse* should be computed [60], as the solution that minimizes the ℓ_2 norm of v, that is, $\|\mathbf{v}\|_2$ subject to the condition that $\mathbf{Lv} - \mathbf{s} = \mathbf{0}$ (for a definition of ℓ_p norms, see [60]). Those conditions yield a purely analytical solution of the form $\hat{\mathbf{v}} = \mathbf{L}^H(\mathbf{LL}^H)^{-1}\mathbf{s}$, where the superscript H denotes the Hermitian operation (conjugate transposition). However, this solution can be very sensitive to small errors on the collected data. The most obvious case occurs when $(\mathbf{LL}^H)^{-1}$ does not exist; however, even if it does exist, it might still be ill-conditioned, that is, small errors in data vector **s** yield large deviations in the unknown vector **v**: In these cases, the solution would be unstable. To overcome these difficulties, the minimization scheme shall include a metric enforcing some "physical constraints" on the final solution. Accordingly, the Tikhonov regularization method seeks a solution as the global minimum of the following minimization problem:

$$\hat{\mathbf{v}} = \arg\min \|\mathbf{Lv} - \mathbf{s}\|_2^2 + \beta \|\mathbf{v}\|_2^2 \tag{19.32}$$

In (19.32), β is the *regularization* parameter that needs to be appropriately selected. The addition of the $\beta \|\mathbf{v}\|_2^2$ constraint physically means that among all possible solutions, the one with minimum ℓ_2 norm, that is, minimum energy, is selected. By manipulating (19.32), an analytical solution is obtained:

$$\hat{\mathbf{v}} = \left(\mathbf{L}^H\mathbf{L} + \beta\mathbf{I}\right)^{-1}\mathbf{L}^H\mathbf{s} \tag{19.33}$$

The earlier estimation is generally named Tikhonov-regularized solution [57]. A more complete expression for Tikhonov regularization can be obtained by solving analytically the following minimization problem [15]:

$$\hat{\mathbf{v}} = \arg\min \left\| \mathbf{W}_s \mathbf{L}\mathbf{v} - \mathbf{W}_s \mathbf{s} \right\|_2^2 + \beta \left\| \mathbf{W}_v \mathbf{v} - \mathbf{W}_v \mathbf{v}_0 \right\|_2^2 \tag{19.34}$$

where
    $\mathbf{W}_s$ is a symmetric matrix that properly weights the data entries
    $\mathbf{W}_v$ is a symmetric matrix that weights the voxels
    $\mathbf{v}_0$ is an a priori model for the contrast function

By expanding (19.34) and taking the derivative with respect to $\mathbf{v}$ and $\mathbf{v}^H$, the following expression is obtained:

$$\hat{\mathbf{v}} = \left(\mathbf{L}^H \mathbf{W}_s^2 \mathbf{L} + \beta \mathbf{W}_v^2 \right)^{-1} \left(\mathbf{L}^H \mathbf{W}_s^2 \mathbf{s} + \beta \mathbf{W}_v^2 \mathbf{v}_0 \right) \tag{19.35}$$

The optimal selection of the weighting matrices depends on the problem under consideration, generally to enforce particular features in the final solution, usually known a priori. However, this information is rarely available, and, accordingly, the proper weighting matrices are $\underline{\mathbf{W}}_v^2 = \text{diag}\left(\underline{\mathbf{L}}^H \underline{\mathbf{L}} \right)$ and $\underline{\mathbf{W}}_s^2 = \text{diag}\left(\underline{\mathbf{L}}\underline{\mathbf{L}}^H \right)$ (i.e., enforcing equal sensitivity to each data point and voxel), or simply $\mathbf{W}_v = \mathbf{I}$ and $\mathbf{W}_s = \mathbf{I}$.

19.6.2 Back Propagation

The Tikhonov regularization is computationally expensive, and questions arise for the optimal choice of the regularization parameter. To overcome these difficulties, a simple method is introduced, requiring only a phase conjugation on the received data in order to obtain an estimate of $\mathbf{v}$. This method is usually referred to as "migration" in geophysics, as "matched filtering" in signal processing, and as "back propagation" in image processing. The basic principle relies on selecting a very large value for β in the Tikhonov operator, obtaining

$$\hat{\mathbf{v}} = \left(\mathbf{L}^H \mathbf{L} + \beta \mathbf{I} \right)^{-1} \mathbf{L}^H \mathbf{s} \cong (\beta \mathbf{I})^{-1} \mathbf{L}^H \mathbf{s} \cong \beta^{-1} \mathbf{L}^H \mathbf{s} \quad \beta \gg \| \mathbf{L} \|_2^2 \tag{19.36}$$

where $\|\bullet\|_2$ is the ℓ_2 norm of a matrix (see [60] for a definition). Therefore, the inversion becomes simply a (fast) multiplication with the adjoint $\mathbf{L}^H$ and a scaling factor β^{-1} that can be neglected if qualitative shape reconstructions are sought. The reliability of the inversion by means of the adjoint matrix holds theoretically when the condition number of $\mathbf{L}^H\mathbf{L}$ is very close to unity. Unfortunately, the condition number $\kappa(\mathbf{L}^H\mathbf{L})$ equals to $\kappa(\mathbf{L})^2$, meaning that in order to properly use back propagation, $\kappa(\mathbf{L})$ should be exceptionally low, that is, a well-conditioned problem.

19.6.3 Truncated Singular Value Decomposition

Another important regularized inversion method is the truncated SVD (TSVD) method [49,61]. Basically, **L** can be decomposed in its singular values as

$$\mathbf{L} = \mathbf{U}\mathbf{S}\mathbf{V}^H \tag{19.37}$$

where **U** and **V** are unitary matrices and **S** is a diagonal matrix containing the *singular values* of **L** sorted in descending order.

The matrices **U** and **V** are both orthogonal (i.e., $\mathbf{U}^H\mathbf{U} = \mathbf{I}$, $\mathbf{V}^H\mathbf{V} = \mathbf{I}$) and complete (i.e., $\mathbf{U}\mathbf{U}^H = \mathbf{I}, \mathbf{V}\mathbf{V}^H = \mathbf{I}$). The diagonal values of S, normalized w.r.t. the first (largest) singular value s_1, are referred to as *pseudospectrum*, usually expressed in dB. In many inverse scattering problems including the one at hand, the pseudospectrum exhibits a plateau for large values (with null or low dynamical range), followed by a sharp decay for small indices, but rarely equaling the zero value due to numerical approximations. Singular values that are very small compared to s_1 represent the sensitive directions of **L**: Along these directions, small amount of noise or clutter in the sampled field leads to a large (undesired) deviation of **v**.

When the SVD is performed on **L**, an ideal matrix structure occurs:

$$\mathbf{L} = \begin{bmatrix} \mathbf{U}_\Gamma \mathbf{U}_0 \end{bmatrix} \begin{bmatrix} \mathbf{S}_\Gamma & 0 \\ 0 & 0 \end{bmatrix} \begin{bmatrix} \mathbf{V}_\Gamma^H \\ \mathbf{V}_0^H \end{bmatrix} \tag{19.38}$$

where

Γ is the number of singular values that are nonzero
$\mathbf{U}_\Gamma$ and $\mathbf{V}_\Gamma$ are the collected eigenvectors that are spanned by the singular values in $\mathbf{S}_\Gamma$
$\mathbf{U}_0$ is made of vectors that do not belong to the range of **L**
$\mathbf{V}_0$ is made of vectors belonging to the null space of **L**

Through the SVD of **L**, the Born approximation of the scattered field is related to the contrast function as follows:

$$\mathbf{s} = \mathbf{U}_\Gamma \mathbf{S}_\Gamma \mathbf{V}_\Gamma^H \mathbf{v} \tag{19.39}$$

By exploiting the properties of U and V, inverting (19.39) becomes simply

$$\hat{\mathbf{v}} = \mathbf{V}_\Gamma \mathbf{S}_\Gamma^{-1} \mathbf{U}_\Gamma^H \mathbf{s}. \tag{19.40}$$

The strategy commonly referred to as TSVD consists simply of *selecting* the singular values to be retained in $\mathbf{S}_\Gamma$: Generally, in the TSVD, the singular values to be retained are related to the signal-to-noise ratio [49].

The SVD is helpful also for the fast computation of the Tikhonov regularization scheme. In fact, by decomposing (19.33) in its singular values, one obtains

$$\hat{\mathbf{v}} = \left(\mathbf{L}^H \mathbf{L} + \beta \mathbf{I} \right)^{-1} \mathbf{L}^H \mathbf{s} = \left(\mathbf{V}\mathbf{S}^H \mathbf{U}^H \mathbf{U}\mathbf{S}\mathbf{V}^H + \beta \mathbf{V}\mathbf{I}\mathbf{V}^H \right)^{-1} \mathbf{V}\mathbf{S}^H \mathbf{U}^H \mathbf{s}$$

$$= \mathbf{V}\left(\mathbf{S}^H \mathbf{S} + \beta \mathbf{I} \right)^{-1} \mathbf{S}^H \mathbf{U}^H \mathbf{s} = \mathbf{V} \operatorname{diag}\left(\frac{s_i}{s_i^2 + \beta} \right) \mathbf{U}^H \mathbf{s} \tag{19.41}$$

The interesting feature is that the optimal selection of v by varying the parameter β is obtained just by a relatively fast matrix multiplication, rather than a formal matrix inversion.

19.6.4 Optimal Regularization Parameter

Finding the optimal regularization parameters β or Γ is generally a hard task. A conventional approach is to plot the so-called *L-curve* [57]: For the Tikhonov method, the value $\log\left(\left\|\mathbf{W}_s\mathbf{L}\hat{\mathbf{v}}_\beta - \mathbf{W}_s\mathbf{s}\right\|_2^2\right)$ is plotted in the abscissa, where $\hat{\mathbf{v}}_\beta$ is the solution obtained by using the particular value of β and the value $\log\left(\left\|\mathbf{W}_v\hat{\mathbf{v}}_\beta - \mathbf{W}_v\mathbf{v}_0\right\|_2^2\right)$ is plotted in the ordinate. For the TSVD method, the values $\log\left(\left\|\mathbf{L}\hat{\mathbf{v}}_\Gamma - \mathbf{s}\right\|_2^2\right)$ and $\log\left(\left\|\hat{\mathbf{v}}_\Gamma\right\|_2^2\right)$ are plotted, respectively. The resulting plots generally resemble an *L*-shaped curve. The optimal value of β or Γ is found at the point in which the curve changes direction, that is, at the corner of the *L*-curve.

19.6.5 Resolution Analysis

In both Tikhonov and TSVD methods, a concept of resolution can be defined and used. By calling $\mathbf{L}^\dagger$ the inverse operator obtained either using Tikhonov or TSVD, one can calculate the difference between the predicted and observed fields:

$$\hat{\mathbf{s}} = \mathbf{L}\mathbf{v} = \mathbf{L}\left(\mathbf{L}^\dagger\mathbf{s}\right) = \mathbf{L}\mathbf{L}^\dagger\mathbf{s}$$

$$\Delta\mathbf{s} = \hat{\mathbf{s}} - \mathbf{s} = \left(\mathbf{L}\mathbf{L}^\dagger - \mathbf{I}\right)\mathbf{s}$$

(19.42)

where the matrix $\mathbf{L}^\dagger$ represents the operation of inversion of $\mathbf{L}$ that depends on the method selected for the image reconstruction.

The square matrix $\mathbf{L}\mathbf{L}^\dagger$ is called *resolution matrix*, and if it is an identity matrix, then the prediction errors are zero. Therefore, the inversion procedure generates well-resolved outputs when $\mathbf{L}\mathbf{L}^\dagger \to \mathbf{I}$. The resolution matrix gives also an insight of the blurring effect of the system: Only when $\mathbf{L}\mathbf{L}^\dagger$ is an identity matrix, the blurring is reduced to zero. In particular, the row of the matrix $\mathbf{L}\mathbf{L}^\dagger$ shows how well the neighboring data can be independently predicted or resolved. The diagonal elements of the data resolution matrix indicate how much weight a datum has in its own prediction [15].

A similar definition of resolution is to check retrospectively how accurate the estimate $\hat{\mathbf{v}}$ fits compared to the true value $\mathbf{v}$:

$$\Delta\mathbf{v} = \hat{\mathbf{v}} - \mathbf{v} = \mathbf{L}^\dagger\mathbf{L}\mathbf{v} - \mathbf{v} = \left(\mathbf{L}^\dagger\mathbf{L} - \mathbf{I}\right)\mathbf{v}$$

(19.43)

In this case, the resolution matrix is $\mathbf{L}^\dagger\mathbf{L}$. This quantity is a generalization of the *point spread function*, usually encountered in radar and imaging communities. Clearly, the closer $\mathbf{L}^\dagger\mathbf{L}$ is to the identity matrix, the better the resolution in the image domain is.

19.6.6 Sparse Minimization

The solutions provided by both Tikhonov and TSVD are unique and known in closed form; they are achieved on the constraint that solutions have minimum norm. Alas, the minimum energy assumption may not be reasonable for the problem at hand. In fact, reconstructions based on ℓ_2 norm minimization penalize large values of the entries of $\mathbf{v}$, so the resulting solution contains many small coefficients. In other words, the ℓ_2 minimization returns generally smooth images and presents high side lobes, artifacts, and poor resolution, especially when the number of samples of the data vector $\mathbf{s}$ is low. To increase the image quality, one can exploit some prior knowledge of $\mathbf{v}$, such as

■ In tunnel and UGF detection, the entries of $\mathbf{v}$ should be either 0 or the value of the dielectric anomaly, given by the difference between the background and the air ones.
■ Since targets into the scene are sparse, the nonzero elements of v should be a few, although one cannot know a priori the exact number of nonzero elements.

To promote the sparsity on the estimation of v, solving the following problem should be attempted:

$$\hat{\mathbf{v}} = \arg\min \|\mathbf{v}\|_0 \quad \text{subject to:} \quad \|\mathbf{L}\mathbf{v} - \mathbf{s}\|_2^2 < \delta \tag{19.44}$$

where the ℓ_0 norm of a vector returns just the number of nonzero elements. Unfortunately, such minimization is of the type *NP*-hard and practically impossible to solve for the dimension of our problem. The intractable ℓ_0 norm can be replaced with a similar norm that has lower computational complexity. A good candidate is the ℓ_1 norm, that is,

$$\hat{\mathbf{v}} = \arg\min \|\mathbf{v}\|_1^1 \quad \text{subject to:} \quad \|\mathbf{L}\mathbf{v} - \mathbf{s}\|_2^1 < \sigma \tag{19.45}$$

This particular minimization is called *quadratically constrained ℓ_1*. The positive valued σ can be estimated on the basis of the noise level on data. The case of $\sigma = 0$ corresponds to the classical *basis pursuit* minimization, although it is not adequate for noisy problems.

Alternatively, one can set up a similar minimization procedure as follows:

$$\hat{\mathbf{v}} = \arg\min \lambda \|\mathbf{v}\|_1^1 + \|\mathbf{L}\mathbf{v} - \mathbf{s}\|_2^2 \tag{19.46}$$

where $\lambda > 0$ is a parameter that needs to be opportunely chosen. This minimization is called *basis pursuit denoising* (BPDN). Similarly, another minimization procedure can be instated

$$\hat{\mathbf{v}} = \arg\min \|\mathbf{L}\mathbf{v} - \mathbf{s}\|_2^1 \quad \text{subject to:} \quad \|\mathbf{v}\|_1^1 < \tau \tag{19.47}$$

This kind of minimization is called *least angle shrinkage and selection operator* (LASSO) [62].

Mathematically, these three problems are all different ways of arriving at the same set of solutions. In fact, the solution to any one of these problems is characterized by a triplet of values (σ, λ, τ), which renders the same $\hat{\mathbf{v}}$, although finding the values that return the same image is not trivial. Reconstructed images using sparse regularization usually are too "peaky," reducing extended objects into points or missing small dielectric perturbations. To overcome these problems, two extensions of sparse regularization algorithms will be introduced:

ℓ_1 and ℓ_2 norms using fast iterative shrinkage-thresholding algorithm (FISTA).

A more effective minimization scheme leading to enhanced image quality is

$$\hat{\mathbf{v}} = \arg\min \left\| \mathbf{Lv} - \mathbf{s} \right\|_2^2 + \alpha \left\| \mathbf{v} \right\|_1^1 + \beta \left\| \mathbf{v} \right\|_2^2 \tag{19.48}$$

In fact, the earlier minimization problem incorporates both the energy-stabilizing effect due to the ℓ_2 penalty (which encourages extended targets) and the sparsity-promoting effect due to the ℓ_1 penalty (which reduces the number of required samples and decreases side lobes and artifacts). This minimization scheme could be solved using more classical methods [63,64]. Here, a faster minimization procedure is introduced, based on the FISTA [65]. In fact, (19.48) can be easily recast in the following form:

$$\hat{\mathbf{v}} = \arg\min \left\| \begin{bmatrix} \mathbf{L} \\ \sqrt{\beta}\mathbf{I} \end{bmatrix} \mathbf{v} - \begin{bmatrix} \mathbf{s} \\ \mathbf{0} \end{bmatrix} \right\|_2^2 + \alpha \left\| \mathbf{v} \right\|_1^1 \tag{19.49}$$

where 0 is a zero-padding vector. Like many sparse regularization algorithms, FISTA converges faster if the input matrix has the norm of the column close to the unity. To achieve this goal, one shall use the following substitutions:

$$\begin{bmatrix} \mathbf{L} \\ \sqrt{\beta}\mathbf{I} \end{bmatrix} \mathbf{M}_\beta = \mathbf{N}_\beta; \quad \begin{bmatrix} \mathbf{s} \\ \mathbf{0} \end{bmatrix} = \mathbf{g}; \quad \mathbf{M}_\beta = \left(\frac{1}{\sqrt{\text{diag}\left[\begin{bmatrix} \mathbf{L}^H & \sqrt{\beta}\mathbf{I} \end{bmatrix} \cdot \begin{bmatrix} \mathbf{L} \\ \sqrt{\beta}\mathbf{I} \end{bmatrix} \right]}} \right) \mathbf{I}; \quad \mathbf{w} = \mathbf{M}_\beta^{-1}\mathbf{v} \tag{19.50}$$

The columns of $\mathbf{N}_\beta$ have now unitary norm, and the minimization problem becomes

$$\hat{\mathbf{v}} = \mathbf{M}_\beta \left[\arg\min \left\| \mathbf{N}_\beta \mathbf{w} - \mathbf{g} \right\|_2^2 + \alpha \left\| \mathbf{w} \right\|_1^1 \right] \tag{19.51}$$

Equation 19.51 has all the desired properties to be computed using the classical FISTA.

19.5.6.1 Total Variation and ℓ_1 Norms Using Çetin Algorithm

Another relevant minimization procedure for RF tomography is stated as follows:

$$\hat{\mathbf{v}} = \arg\min \left\| \mathbf{Lv} - \mathbf{s} \right\|_2^2 + \alpha \left\| \mathbf{v} \right\|_{1S} + \beta \left\| \mathbf{v} \right\|_{TV}$$

$$\text{subject to: } \tau_{\min} \leq \left| (\mathbf{v})_i \right| \leq \tau_{\max} \quad i = 1, \dots, K \tag{19.52}$$

where
   α, β are the regularization parameters
   $\tau_{\min,\max}$ is the minimum/maximum absolute value that the contrast function can have
   $[\![\mathbf{v}]\!]_i$ is the ith element of v

In (19.52), the operators $\|\bullet\|_{1S}$ and $\|\bullet\|_{TV}$ are the smoothed ℓ_1 norm and the smoothed total variation norm, respectively, both differentiable, defined as

$$\|\mathbf{v}\|_{1S} = \sum_{i=1}^{K} \sqrt{[\![\mathbf{v}]\!]_i^2 + \delta^2} \quad \|\mathbf{v}\|_{TVS} = \left\| \sqrt{\left(\nabla|\mathbf{v}|\right)^2 + \delta^2} \right\| \quad \delta^2 > 0 \tag{19.53}$$

The use of differentiable penalty functionals allows us to take advantage of simple and fast-converging algorithms, such as the one described in this section. Note that the gradient operator can be opportunely defined as a matrix operator acting on v, that is, $\nabla|\mathbf{v}| \cong \mathbf{D}|\mathbf{v}|$; for details, see [66]. The minimization problem in (19.52) incorporates several advantages:

- The total variation penalty promotes solutions that are clustered and not fragmented. The addition of δ relaxes the minimization problem.
- The ℓ_1 penalty promotes solutions having a small number of nonzero elements.
- The condition on the elements of v guarantees realistic values of the contrast functions and distributes the energy of the image to weaker voxels.

The solution of (19.52) is obtained by implementing the Çetin algorithm [66] with minor adjustments; for details, see [50].

19.6.7 Algorithm Comparison

A simulation based on finite-difference time-domain (FDTD) scattered field data has been performed to compare the behavior of different reconstruction algorithms for a typical underground scenario. The scene represents an irregular terrain, modeled as two-layered media with a rectangular box placed on top of the lower medium (see Figure 19.4). The lower medium has relative dielectric permittivity of $\varepsilon_r = 10$ and conductivity $\sigma = 5 \times 10^{-4}$; the box has the same properties of the ground. Five transmitters and five receivers are placed on top of the box. The range of frequencies used spans from 3 to 7 MHz, with intervals of 0.5 MHz. The target is an L-shaped tunnel having radius of 1 m, located at depth of 20 m, as shown in Figure 19.4. The investigation domain D is divided in cubical voxels of size $\Delta = 1$ m. The scattered fields are produced using the freeware FDTD code GprMax, available at www.gprmax.org. Note that the direct path is not included in this simulation. The theory operator $\mathbf{L}$ is computed using numerical Green's functions, using a complex procedure not described here, but that follows the same principles described in this chapter. Reconstructions are shown in Figure 19.5 using the methods described in this section. Figure 19.5a shows the reconstruction using back propagation: As expected, due to the high condition number of $\mathbf{L}$, the back-propagation method is unable to retrieve actionable information from measured data. Figure 19.5b and c shows reconstructions using minimum ℓ_2-norm methods: Images present the typical smearing/blurring effect due to the smooth distribution of energy in the image. To render spiky images, quadratically constrained ℓ_1 reconstruction scheme is applied and shown in Figure 19.5d; however, the "connectedness" of the target is lost, since the algorithm is optimized to retrieve information assuming point-like targets. To ameliorate the reconstruction, the modified FISTA algorithm is implemented and result is shown in Figure 19.5e: With a proper balance of ℓ_1-norm and ℓ_2-norm penalties, a clearer reconstruction of the original target is obtained. To further improve the quality of the image, at expenses of longer computational time, the modified

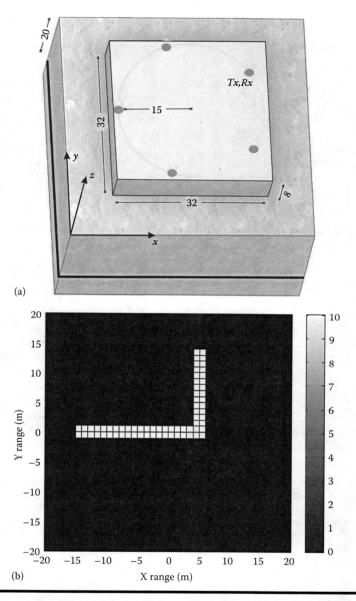

(a)

(b)

Figure 19.4 Geometry used for the simulations: dimensions of the irregular terrain (in m) (a) and shape of the discretized tunnel at depth − 20 m (b).

Çetin algorithm is implemented and shown in Figure 19.5f: Reconstruction is superlative but very sensitive to the balance between ℓ_1-norm and total-variation-norm penalties.

19.7 Direct-Path Mitigation

The two main contributions to the field measured at the receiver are the (desired) field originated from scatterers and the direct-path link between Tx and Rx (see Figure 19.6). Direct-path field is

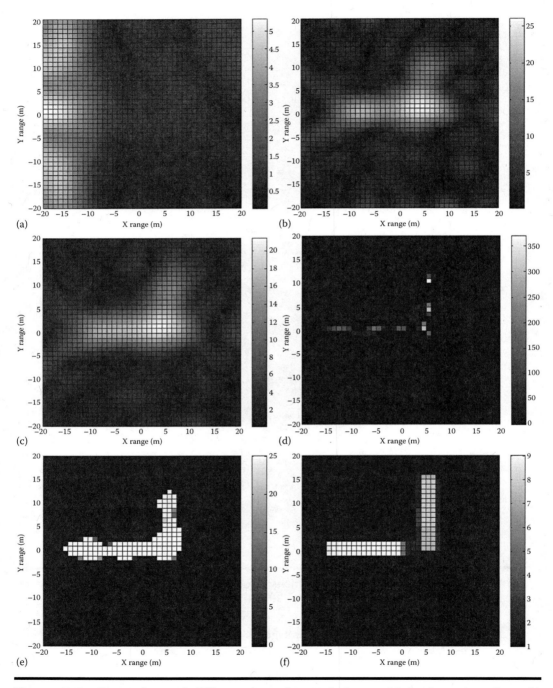

Figure 19.5 Comparison of different inversion techniques: (a) back propagation, (b) Tikhonov regularization, (c) *SVD*, (d) quadratically constrained ℓ_1, (e) modified FISTA, and (f) modified Çetin.

Figure 19.6 **Direct-path coupling between a transmitter/receiver pair. The direct-path contribution at the receiver can be several orders of magnitude higher than the scattered field from targets.**

in general several orders of magnitude stronger than scattered field. The purpose of this section is to show several strategies aimed at reducing or properly characterizing the direct-path contribution from the measured data, so that the inversion procedure can be carried out with lower error.

Recalling the discretized forward model $\mathbf{m} = \mathbf{L}v + \mathbf{p}$, the estimation of v can be performed as $\hat{\mathbf{v}} = \mathbf{L}^{-1}(\mathbf{m} - \mathbf{p})$, where $\mathbf{L}^{-1}$ represents the linear operator that in some sense relates the data domain to the image domain. Clearly, m is affected by errors (noise, clutter, or nonlinear scattering), indicated with $\Delta\mathbf{m}$. The same occurs with the contribution p: Although theoretically predictable, its real value is in general different, and its error can be indicated with $\Delta\mathbf{p}$. Since p is several orders of magnitude higher than the s, the approximation $\mathbf{m} \cong \mathbf{p}$ holds. More exactly

$$\hat{\mathbf{v}} = \mathbf{L}^{-1}\left(\mathbf{m} + \Delta\mathbf{m} - \mathbf{p} - \Delta\mathbf{p}\right) = \mathbf{L}^{-1}\left(\mathbf{m} - \mathbf{p}\right) + \mathbf{L}^{-1}\left(\Delta\mathbf{m} - \Delta\mathbf{p}\right) \tag{19.54}$$

where $\mathbf{m} - \mathbf{p} \ll \Delta\mathbf{m} - \Delta\mathbf{p}$. In other words, a small error in the estimation of the direct path can still be several orders of magnitude higher than the difference $\mathbf{m} - \mathbf{p}$, which inevitably compromise the inversion. Even assuming that the estimation of p is performed with no error, practical receiver design is challenged by the very high dynamic range in play. For example,

- The ADC may not have enough dynamic range to properly sample both the value of interest $\mathbf{m} - \mathbf{p}$ and the value p.
- The practical dynamic range of the amplifiers may not be enough for handling both signals $\mathbf{m} - \mathbf{p}$ and p in the linear region.

Although the earlier two problems could be overcome by using dithering, oversampling, and extremely long averages, practical systems designs restrict their effectiveness up to some dB.

For these reasons, the simple estimation of $\mathbf{p}$ and its subsequent subtraction from the collected measurements does *not* represent a good strategy to remove the direct path. Optimal strategies shall minimize the value of p *before* it reaches the amplifiers and/or the ADC, so that $\mathbf{m} - \mathbf{p}$ and p have comparable magnitude or preferably $\mathbf{m} \gg \mathbf{p}$ element wise.

19.7.1 Vector Transmitters and Vector Receivers

Some direct-path mitigation strategies presented here require the use of vector transmitters and vector receivers (or vector sensors). A vector sensor is a device that is able to measure instantaneously

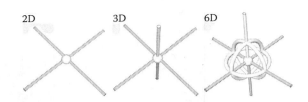

Figure 19.7 Examples of vector antenna. The 2D-vector antenna is composed by two orthogonal, colocated dipoles; the 3D-vector antenna is composed by three orthogonal, colocated dipoles; and the 6D-vector antenna is composed by three orthogonal, colocated dipoles and three orthogonal, colocated loops.

and at the same position the various components of both E and H fields. Each orthogonal direction represents a dimension, so its mathematical description can be represented with a q-dimensional vector. Vector sensors can be constructed using q-dimensional vector antennas: For instance, a simple dipole or a simple loop can be considered as a *1D*-vector antenna, while three orthogonal colocated dipoles having three separated channels can be considered a *3D*-vector antenna. A full *6D*-vector sensor is a device that is able to measure the 3D components of both electric and magnetic fields. Such sensors are recently being constructed [67]. Similarly, a vector transmitter is a device that is able to radiate electric currents and/or magnetic currents oriented in any arbitrary direction in space: This is accomplished using q-dimensional vector antenna whose channels are independently fed with predetermined current values. Only the 2D- and 3D-vector transmitters are of practical interest: Mathematically, a vector transmitter can be described with the unit-norm direction $\hat{\mathbf{a}}$ being complex valued. The usefulness of vector antennas is twofold:

- With a single q-dimensional vector sensor, q times more data can be collected.
- By properly combining a q-dimensional vector transmitter to a single channel using appropriate amplitude and phase weights, one can electronically steer transmitting dipoles and loops to arbitrary directions. The same principle applies to vector sensors (Figure 19.7).

19.7.2 Direct-Path Removal before ADC: Null Steering

With the understanding that electronic rotation of transmitting/receiving electric/magnetic dipoles can be performed using vector antennas, the proposed strategy properly steers the Tx dipole/loop and Rx dipole/loop in order to minimize the incident field measured at the receiver side. The field radiated underground is not severely affected, since radiation nulls are located only along the direct-path single direction (i.e., no side lobes). The null steering theory is discussed here only for 3D-vector antennas [68]: This theory can be easily extended/reduced to a different q-dimensional vector.

For a given measurement n, the electric/magnetic field due to an electric/magnetic dipole located at $\mathbf{r}_n^a$ and directed along the vector $\hat{\mathbf{a}}_n$ measured by an electric/magnetic receiver positioned at $\mathbf{r}_n^b$ and directed according to the vector $\hat{\mathbf{b}}_n$ is proportional to

$$
E_n \propto \hat{\mathbf{b}}_n^T \cdot \begin{bmatrix} \underline{\mathbf{G}}_{ee}\left(\mathbf{r}_n^b, \mathbf{r}_n^a\right) \\ \underline{\mathbf{G}}_{em}\left(\mathbf{r}_n^b, \mathbf{r}_n^a\right) \end{bmatrix} \cdot \hat{\mathbf{a}}_n \qquad H_n \propto \hat{\mathbf{b}}_n^T \cdot \begin{bmatrix} \underline{\mathbf{G}}_{me}\left(\mathbf{r}_n^b, \mathbf{r}_n^a\right) \\ \underline{\mathbf{G}}_{mm}\left(\mathbf{r}_n^b, \mathbf{r}_n^a\right) \end{bmatrix} \cdot \hat{\mathbf{a}}_n \qquad (19.55)
$$

The goal is to find the appropriate complex value of $\hat{\mathbf{a}}_n$ such that the corresponding received field is minimized. Mathematically, this problem can be solved by setting up a constrained minimization procedure. In particular, for each Tx and Rx pair, the following problem can be solved:

$$\hat{\mathbf{a}}_n^{opt} = \arg \min \left\| \underline{\mathbf{G}}_{ee,me,em,mm}\left(\mathbf{r}_n^b, \mathbf{r}_n^a\right) \cdot \hat{\mathbf{a}}_n \right\|_2^2 \quad \text{subject to:} \quad \hat{\mathbf{a}}_n^H \cdot \hat{\mathbf{a}}_n = 1 \quad (19.56)$$

Note that minimizing $\underline{\mathbf{G}}\left(\mathbf{r}_n^b, \mathbf{r}_n^a\right) \cdot \mathbf{a}_n$ returns the smallest value of the magnitude of the direct-path field at $\mathbf{r}_n^b$, while the constraint $\hat{\mathbf{a}}_n^H \cdot \hat{\mathbf{a}}_n = 1$ guarantees that the trivial solution $\mathbf{a}_n = \mathbf{0}$ is discarded.

In Lagrangian form, Equation (19.56) becomes

$$\Lambda_n\left(\hat{\mathbf{a}}_n, \lambda\right) = \hat{\mathbf{a}}_n^H \cdot \underline{\mathbf{G}}^H\left(\mathbf{r}_n^b, \mathbf{r}_n^a\right) \cdot \underline{\mathbf{G}}\left(\mathbf{r}_n^b, \mathbf{r}_n^a\right) \cdot \hat{\mathbf{a}}_n - \lambda\left[\hat{\mathbf{a}}_n^H \cdot \hat{\mathbf{a}}_n - 1\right] \quad (19.57)$$

By imposing $\nabla \Lambda_n = 0$:

$$\underline{\mathbf{G}}^H\left(\mathbf{r}_n^b, \mathbf{r}_n^a\right) \cdot \underline{\mathbf{G}}\left(\mathbf{r}_n^b, \mathbf{r}_n^a\right) \cdot \hat{\mathbf{a}}_n = \lambda \hat{\mathbf{a}}_n \quad (19.58)$$

Therefore, the $\hat{\mathbf{a}}_n^{opt}$ direction that minimizes the power at a desired location is the eigenvector associated with the *smallest* eigenvalue of the matrix $\underline{\mathbf{G}}^H \underline{\mathbf{G}}$.

Similarly, this minimization can be applied at the receiver side. Defining the vector

$$\begin{Bmatrix} \mathbf{E}_{\min} \\ \mathbf{H}_{\min} \end{Bmatrix} = \underline{\mathbf{G}}\left(\mathbf{r}_n^b, \mathbf{r}_n^a\right) \cdot \hat{\mathbf{a}}_n^{opt} \quad (19.59)$$

as the measured field obtained when $\hat{\mathbf{a}}_n^{opt}$ is given, possibly according to (19.56), a second minimization problem can be formulated as

$$\text{minimize} \left\| \hat{\mathbf{b}}_n^H \cdot \begin{Bmatrix} \mathbf{E}_{\min} \\ \mathbf{H}_{\min} \end{Bmatrix} \right\|_2^2 \quad \text{subject to:} \quad \hat{\mathbf{b}}_n^H \cdot \hat{\mathbf{b}}_n = 1 \quad (19.60)$$

The minimization is achieved when $\hat{\mathbf{b}}_n$ is chosen to be the eigenvector corresponding to the smallest eigenvalue of the outer product (matrix) $\mathbf{E}_{\min} \cdot \mathbf{E}_{\min}^H$ or $\mathbf{H}_{\min} \cdot \mathbf{H}_{\min}^H$.

Null steering could be even more beneficial if multiple transmitters are activated simultaneously: In this way, the interference pattern can be controlled to place field nulls in space, exactly where the active receiver is located. The theory becomes more complex, since the minimization problem cannot be solved analytically, but the solution is still unique, since the solution can be found using convex optimization techniques [69] (Figure 19.8).

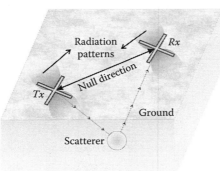

Figure 19.8 Pictorial representation of the technique of null steering in RF tomography. The "equivalent" dipoles can be electronically steered so that their respective null directions are aligned. This in turn guarantees a relatively low direct-path field contribution at the receiver.

19.7.3 Direct-Path Removal after ADC: Generalized Range Profiling

Two strategies to remove the direct path after data collection are presented. The first one is based upon least-squares estimation of the direct path along a predetermined Tx–Rx pair and its subsequent elimination. This theory can be considered a natural generalization of the range profiling used in the radar community [70]. Let $\tilde{\mathbf{m}}$ be the portion of the m vector due to a Tx–Rx pair, simply identified by the vectors $\mathbf{r}^a, \mathbf{r}^b, \hat{\mathbf{a}}, \hat{\mathbf{b}}$. Hence, $\tilde{\mathbf{m}}$ contains measured data at different frequencies $\omega_1, \dots \omega_F$. Accordingly, $\tilde{\mathbf{m}} = \tilde{\mathbf{s}} + \tilde{\mathbf{p}}$. Let $\hat{\tilde{\mathbf{p}}}$ be a direct-path vector estimate; for instance, in the case of electric field due to electric current, the estimate would be

$$\hat{\tilde{\mathbf{p}}}\left(\varepsilon_D\left(\overline{\mathbf{r}}\right), \sigma_D\left(\overline{\mathbf{r}}\right)\right) = \begin{bmatrix} i\omega_1\mu_0\mathbf{b}^T \cdot \underline{\mathbf{G}}_{ee}\left(\mathbf{r}^b, \mathbf{r}^a_b, \omega_1, \varepsilon_D\left(\overline{\mathbf{r}}\right), \sigma_D\left(\overline{\mathbf{r}}\right)\right) \cdot \hat{\mathbf{a}} \\ \vdots \\ i\omega_F\mu_0\mathbf{b}^T \cdot \underline{\mathbf{G}}_{ee}\left(\mathbf{r}^b, \mathbf{r}^a, \omega_F, \varepsilon_D\left(\overline{\mathbf{r}}\right), \sigma_D\left(\overline{\mathbf{r}}\right)\right) \cdot \hat{\mathbf{a}} \end{bmatrix} \tag{19.61}$$

The vector is purposely described as a function of the background electrical properties. Then, one can measure how well the direct-path estimate fits the data, by using least-squares approach:

$$g = \left(\hat{\tilde{\mathbf{p}}}^H \hat{\tilde{\mathbf{p}}}\right)^{-1} \hat{\tilde{\mathbf{p}}}^H \tilde{\mathbf{m}} \tag{19.62}$$

If $g \to 1$, then the direct-path estimate matches the data; otherwise, the estimate is a poor candidate. In general, $\hat{\tilde{\mathbf{p}}}$ may not be a very good estimate, since the electrical properties of the ground are guessed. Therefore, a more effective approach is to create P several candidate estimates for the direct path, by varying the dielectric permittivity $\varepsilon_D(\overline{\mathbf{r}})$ and conductivity $\sigma_D(\overline{\mathbf{r}})$ into the dyadic Green's function. Mathematically, this process can be recast in terms of a matrix:

$$\mathbf{P} = \begin{bmatrix} \left(\hat{\tilde{\mathbf{p}}}_1^H \hat{\tilde{\mathbf{p}}}_1\right)^{-1} \hat{\tilde{\mathbf{p}}}_1^H \\ \vdots \\ \left(\hat{\tilde{\mathbf{p}}}_P^H \hat{\tilde{\mathbf{p}}}_P\right)^{-1} \hat{\tilde{\mathbf{p}}}_P^H \end{bmatrix} \tag{19.63}$$

The corresponding fitting function becomes a vector $\mathbf{g} = \mathbf{P}\tilde{\mathbf{m}}$. Clearly, the best estimate $\hat{\tilde{\mathbf{p}}}_{max}$ is the row of P returning the maximum value of g, that is, g_{max}. Once g_{max} and $\hat{\tilde{\mathbf{p}}}_{max}$ are found, a good estimate for the scattered field for the Tx–Rx pair is

$$\hat{\tilde{\mathbf{s}}} = \tilde{\mathbf{m}} - g_{max}\hat{\tilde{\mathbf{p}}}_{max} \tag{19.64}$$

19.7.4 Direct-Path Removal after ADC: Frequency Difference

Due to the difficulty in properly estimating background electrical properties for the computation of (19.64), a second algorithm will be presented next. This algorithm is derived from the geophysical community interested in finding oil reservoirs, where very low frequencies are used. Let us consider a measurement m_n obtained by selecting a Tx–Rx pair and a frequency f. A strong but acceptable approximation of a generic forward model is

$$m_n\left(\mathbf{r}^a, \mathbf{r}^b, \omega_n\right) \cong \overbrace{K_n^1 \exp\left(+ik_{0n}\left\|\mathbf{r}^b - \mathbf{r}^a\right\|\right)}^{\text{Direct-path wave traveling in the air}} + \overbrace{K_n^2 \exp\left(+ik_{Dn}\left\|\mathbf{r}^b - \mathbf{r}^a\right\|\right)}^{\text{Direct-path wave traveling in the ground}}$$

$$+ \overbrace{K_n^3 \iiint_D V\left(\bar{\mathbf{r}}\right)\exp\left(+ik_{Dn}\left(\left\|\mathbf{r}^a - \bar{\mathbf{r}}\right\| + \left\|\bar{\mathbf{r}} - \mathbf{r}^b\right\|\right)\right)d\mathbf{r}'}^{\text{Scattered field coming from targets in the ground}} \tag{19.65}$$

where $K_n^{1,2,3}$ are some generic complex constants. Let us consider then a second measurement m_{n+1} taken w.r.t. the same Tx and Rx pairs but at a frequency that is slightly different from the measurement m_n, and let us compute the difference between $m_{n+1} - m_n$. The corresponding forward model is

$$m_{n+1} - m_n \cong K_n^1 e^{+ik_{0n+1}\left\|\mathbf{r}^b - \mathbf{r}^a\right\|} + K_n^2 e^{+ik_{Dn+1}\left\|\mathbf{r}^b - \mathbf{r}^a\right\|} - K_{n+1}^1 e^{+ik_{0n}\left\|\mathbf{r}^b - \mathbf{r}^a\right\|} - K_{n+1}^2 e^{+ik_{Dn}\left\|\mathbf{r}^b - \mathbf{r}^a\right\|}$$

$$+ \iiint_D \left[K_n^3 e^{+ik_{Dn+1}\left(\left\|\mathbf{r}^a - \bar{\mathbf{r}}\right\| + \left\|\bar{\mathbf{r}} - \mathbf{r}^b\right\|\right)} - K_{n+1}^3 e^{+ik_{Dn}\left(\left\|\mathbf{r}^a - \bar{\mathbf{r}}\right\| + \left\|\bar{\mathbf{r}} - \mathbf{r}^b\right\|\right)}\right] V\left(\bar{\mathbf{r}}\right) d\mathbf{r}' \tag{19.66}$$

For a particular small variation of the frequency, the following approximations hold:

$$K_n^{1,2} \cong K_{n+1}^{1,2}; \quad e^{+ik_{0n}\left\|\mathbf{r}^b - \mathbf{r}^a\right\|} \cong e^{+ik_{0n+1}\left\|\mathbf{r}^b - \mathbf{r}^a\right\|}; \quad e^{+ik_{Dn}\left\|\mathbf{r}^b - \mathbf{r}^a\right\|} \cong e^{+ik_{Dn+1}\left\|\mathbf{r}^b - \mathbf{r}^a\right\|} \tag{19.67}$$

while

$$K_n^3 \neq K_{n+1}^3; \quad e^{+ik_{Dn}\left(\left\|\mathbf{r}^a - \bar{\mathbf{r}}\right\| + \left\|\bar{\mathbf{r}} - \mathbf{r}^b\right\|\right)} \neq e^{+ik_{Dn+1}\left(\left\|\mathbf{r}^a - \bar{\mathbf{r}}\right\| + \left\|\bar{\mathbf{r}} - \mathbf{r}^b\right\|\right)} \tag{19.68}$$

Hence, the forward model obtained by subtracting two measurements taken at slightly two different frequencies becomes

$$\Delta m_n = m_{n+1} - m_n \cong \iiint_D \left[K_n^3 e^{+ik_{Dn+1}\left(\left\|\mathbf{r}^a - \bar{\mathbf{r}}\right\| + \left\|\bar{\mathbf{r}} - \mathbf{r}^b\right\|\right)} - K_{n+1}^3 e^{+ik_{Dn}\left(\left\|\mathbf{r}^a - \bar{\mathbf{r}}\right\| + \left\|\bar{\mathbf{r}} - \mathbf{r}^b\right\|\right)}\right] V\left(\bar{\mathbf{r}}\right) d\mathbf{r}' \tag{19.69}$$

Note that the frequency difference needs to be properly chosen: If the frequency difference is too small, then (19.68) becomes equalities, whereas if the frequency difference is too large, then (19.67) becomes inequalities. The correct choice depends upon the geometry at hand, and it is generally performed heuristically.

Recalling $\Delta \mathbf{L}$, the matrix obtained by discretizing the forward model in (19.69), one obtains the relation $\Delta \mathbf{m} \cong \Delta \mathbf{L} \cdot \mathbf{v}$. This method is valid only in some predetermined frequency differences that need to be opportunely discovered.

19.8 Conclusions

RF tomography has been presented for underground exploration for homeland security applications, but it could also be used for other applications, including search and rescue of civilians in case of natural disasters. The theoretical development of RF tomography requires an EM scattering model, based on Born approximation, which was developed with the aim to linearize the relation between the contrast function and the scattered field. Scattered field values are then processed to produce images of the underground scenario according to various methods. Among them, the most promising is based on sparse minimization methods. RF tomography is a complex system that faces various challenges, and one of them is the removal of the direct-path contribution, which was addressed. Future developments include the improvement of the forward model to account for multiple scattering phenomena, the improvement of inversion algorithms, and measurement campaigns to assess the limits of performance of the system in actual scenarios.

Acknowledgments

This work was sponsored by the U.S. Air Force Research Laboratory, Sensors Directorate, RYMD Branch, and U.S. Air Force Office of Scientific Research.

References

1. L. Lo Monte, D. Erricolo, F. Soldovieri, and M. C. Wicks, Radio frequency tomography for tunnel detection, *IEEE Transactions on Geoscience and Remote Sensing,* 48(3), 1128–1137, March 2010.
2. L. Stolarczyk, Detection and imaging of underground structures by exploiting ELF/VLF radiowaves, Hanscom, MA, 2000.
3. L. E. Freeman and A. C. Cogbill, A catalog of underground detection technology test sites, Non proliferation and National Security Office R&D, 1999.
4. P. Mukhopadhyay, Three-dimensional borehole radar imaging, PhD dissertation, University of Cape Town, Cape Town, South Africa, 2005.
5. Army Concept Team in Vietnam, 60th Infantry Platoon (Scout Dog) (Mine Tunnel Detector Dog), Department of Army, San Francisco, CA, December 1969.
6. E. Carr-Harris, *Mine, Booby-Trap, Tripwire and Tunnel Detection*, U.S. Army Limited War Laboratory, Aberdeen, MD, 1970.
7. A. Celmins, *Feasibility of Cosmic Ray Muon Intensity Measurements for Tunnel Detection*, U.S. Army Laboratory Command, Aberdeen, MD, 1990.
8. R. F. Ballard, *Tunnel Detection*, U.S. Army Engineer Waterways Experiment Station, Vicksburg, MS, 1982.
9. J. M. Descour, Source signature—An experimental approach, in *Fourth Tunnel Detection Symposium on Subsurface Exploration Technology*, Golden, CO, 1993.
10. M. Cathcart, *Optical Sensing and Shallow Tunnel Detection*, SGU, Baltimore, MD, 2006.

11. S. A. Ketcham, J. R. McKenna, R. J. Greenfield, and T. S. Anderson, *Seismic Propagation from Activity in Tunnels and Underground Facilities*, U.S. Army Engineer Research and Development Center, Hanover, NH, November 2006.
12. L. Stolarczyk, Detection of clandestine tunnels, bunkers and weapon cache with first interface reflection suppression ground penetrating radar, in *Proceedings of 2008 Meeting for the Military and Sensing Symposia (MSS), Specialty on Battlespace Acoustic and Seismic Sensing, Magnetic and Electric Field Sensors*, Laurel, MD, 2008.
13. A. A. Kaufman and R. O. Hansen, *Principles of the Gravitational Method*, Vol. 41, Elsevier Science, Amsterdam, the Netherlands, 2007.
14. N. C. Crawford, L. A. Croft, G. L. Cesin, and S. Wilson, Microgravity and electrical resistivity techniques for detection of caves and clandestine tunnels, in *Proceedings of American Geophyiscal Union— Fall Meeting*, Baltimore, MD, 2006.
15. M. S. Zhdanov, *Geophysical Inverse Theory and Regularization Problems*, Vol. 36, Elsevier, Amsterdam, the Netherlands, 2002.
16. J. P. Donohoe, J. R. Fairley, and L. N. Lynch, Underground object detection using antiresonant antennas, in *Proceedings of URSI General Assembly*, Chicago, IL, 2008.
17. Eastern Research Group, *Use of Airborne, Surface and Borehole Geophysical Techniques at Contaminated Sites: A Reference Guide*, Environmental Protection Agency, Lexington, MA, 1993.
18. Army Concept Team in Vietnam, *Evaluation of the Tunnel/Cache Detector—Portable Differential Magnetometer*, Department of the Army, San Francisco, CA, September 12, 1970.
19. Army Concept Team in Vietnam, *Evaluation of the Tunnel Explorer Locator and Communicator System (TELACS)*, Department of the Army, San Francisco, CA, September 1973.
20. R. L. Mackie, *Imaging of Underground Structures Using HAARP*, Air Force Research Laboratory, San Francisco, CA, February 1999.
21. D. A. Hill, Gradiometer antennas for tunnel detection, in *Proceedings of Fourth Technical Symposium on Tunnel Detection*, Golden, CO, pp. 479–496, 1993.
22. L. G. Stolarczyk, Gradiometer antennas for detection of tunnels by scattered electromagnetic waves, in *Proceedings of Fourth Tunnel Detection Symposium on Subsurface Exploration Technology*, Golden, CO, 1993.
23. A. Witten, I. J. Won, and S. J. Norton, Subsurface imaging with broadband electromagnetic induction, *Inverse Problems,* 13, 1621–1639, 1997.
24. J. R. Wait, The possibility of guided electromagnetic waves in the earth's crust, *IEEE Transactions on Antennas and Propagation,* 11(3), 330–335, May 1963.
25. R. F. Harrington, *Time Harmonic Electromagnetic Fields*, McGraw Hill, New York, 1961.
26. R. D. Lewis, J. Koester, D. Sykora, and R. J. Greenfield, Seismic location of small explosions and shot hole drilling at the Colorado school of mines' edgar mine, in *Proceedings of Fourth Tunnel Detection Symposium*, Golden, CO, pp. 115–130, 1993.
27. R. D. Rechtien, R. J. Greenfield, and R. F. Ballard, Cross-borehole seismic signatures of tunnels, in *Proceedings of Fourth Tunnel Detection Symposium*, Golden, CO, pp. 131–146, 1993.
28. W. Silva, C. Stark, and F. Ruskey, Location of a tunnel boring machine (TBM) using seismic wavefield analyses, in *Proceedings of Fourth Tunnel Detection Symposium*, Golden, CO, pp. 147–178, 1993.
29. I. J. Won, Electromagnetics for detecting shallow tunnels, in *AGU Meeting*, Baltimore, MA, 2006.
30. R. F. Ballard, *Dynamic Techniques for Detecting and Tracing Tunnel Complexes*, U.S. Army Engineer Weterways Experiment Station, Vicksbourg, MO, December 1977.
31. A. Witten and W. King, Acoustic imaging of subsurface features, *Journal of Environmental Engineering,* 116(1), 166–181, 1990.
32. D. J. Daniels, *Ground Penetrating Radars*, 2nd edn., Institution of Electrical Engineers, London, U.K., 2004.
33. R. J. Chignell, Sixteen channel ground-probing radar detection and imaging of tunnels and other subsurface features, in *Fourth Tunnel Detection Symposium on Subsurface Exploration Technology*, Golden, CO, 1993.
34. W. M. Roggenthen, Pulsed GPR detection of voids in layered geologic materials, in *Fourth Tunnel Detection Symposium on Subsurface Exploration Technology*, Golden, CO, 1993.

35. L. T. Dolphim, R. L. Bollen, and G. N. Oetzel, An underground electromagnetic sounder experiment, *Geophysics*, 39(1), 49–55, 1974.

36. M. L. Moran and R. J. Greenfield, Radar waveforms from a three dimensional tunnel, in *Fourth Tunnel Detection Symposium on Subsurface Exploration Technology*, Golden, CO, pp. 71–84, 1993.

37. T. J. Alleman, C. P. Cameron, and H. D. Mac Lean, PEMSS response of rock tunnels to in axis and other nonperpendicular antennae orientations, in *Proceedings of Fourth Tunnel Detection Symposium on Subsurface Exploration Technology*, Golden, CO, pp. 19–44, 1993.

38. T. Hansen and P. Johansen, Inversion scheme for ground penetrating radar that takes into account the planar air-soil interface, *IEEE Transactions on Geoscience and Remote Sensing*, 38(1), 496–506, January 2000.

39. A. Pralat and R. Zdunek, Electromagnetic geotomography—Selection of measuring frequency, *IEEE Sensors Journal*, 5, 242–250, April 2005.

40. J. Cook, Radar transparencies of mine and tunnel rocks, *Geophysics*, 40(5), 865–885, October 1975.

41. O. Dorn, E. Miller, and C. Rappaport, A shape reconstruction method for the electromagnetic tomography using adjoint fields and level sets, *Inverse Problems*, 16, 1119–1156, 2000.

42. W. Aubry, R. Bonneau, R. Brown, E. Lynch, M. Wicks, R. Schneible, A. George, and M. Krumme, Airborne sensor concept to image shallow-buried targets, in *IEEE Proceedings Radar Conference*, Long Beach, CA, pp. 233–236, 2002.

43. J. Norgard, M. Wicks, and A. Drozd, Distributed/embedded sub-surface sensors for imaging buried objects with reduced mutual coupling and suppressed electromagnetic emissions, in *Proceedings of International Conference on Electromagnetics and Advanced Applications*, Turin, Italy, pp. 427–430, 2007.

44. L. D. Alumbaugh and F. H. Morrison, Theoretical and practical considerations for crosswell electromagnetic tomography assuming a cylindrical geometry, *Geophysics*, 60, 846–870, 1995.

45. B. M. Spies and T. M. Habashy, Sensitivity analysis of crosswell electromagnetics, *Geophyisics*, 60, 834–845, 1995.

46. C. P. Cameron, K. D. Mitchell, K. C. Shin, and B. W. Walker, PEMSS characterization of metamorphic environments in the central Korean peninsula, in *Fourth Tunnel Detection Symposium on Subsurface Exploration Technology*, Golden, CO, pp. 45–64, 1993.

47. I. Catapano, L. Crocco, Y. Krellmann, G. Triltzsch, and F. Soldovieri, A tomographic approach for helicopter-borne ground penetrating radar imaging, *IEEE Geoscience and Remote sensing Letters*, 9(3), 378–382, 2012.

48. M. C. Wicks, J. D. Norgard, and T. N. Cushman, Adaptive tomographic sensors for below ground imaging, *IEEE Aerospace Electronic Systems Magazine*, 25, 24–28, 2010.

49. M. Bertero and P. Boccacci, *Introduction to Inverse Problems in Imaging*, Institute of Physics Publishing, London, U.K., 1998.

50. L. Lo Monte and J. T. Parker, Sparse reconstruction methods in RF tomography for underground imaging, in *IEEE Waveform Diversity and Design Conference*, Niagara Falls, ON, pp. 28–32, 2010.

51. C. T. Tai, *Generalized Vector and Dyadic Analysis*, IEEE Press, Piscataway, NJ, 1991.

52. W. C. Chew, M. S. Tong, and B. Hu, *Integral Equation Methods for Electromagnetic and Elastic Waves*, Morgan & Claypool, San Rafael, CA, 2009.

53. W. Chew, J. Jin, E. Michielssen, and J. Song, *Fast and Efficient Algorithms in Computational Electromagnetics*, Artech House, Norwood, MA, 2001.

54. W. C. Chew, *Waves and Fields in Inhomogeneous Media*, IEEE Press, New York, 1995.

55. K. A. Michalski and D. Zheng, Electromagnetic scattering and radiation by surfaces of arbitrary shape in layered media, part I: Theory; part II: Implementations and results for contiguous half-spaces, *IEEE Transactions on Antennas and Propagation*, AP-38, pp. 335–352, 1990.

56. L. Lo Monte, F. Soldovieri, D. Erricolo, and M. C. Wicks, Imaging below irregular terrain using RF tomography, *IEEE Transactions on Geosciences and Remote Sensing*, 50(9), 3364–3373, 2012.

57. P. C. Hansen, *Rank-Deficient and Discrete Ill-Posed Problems*, SIAM, Philadelphia, PA, 1998.

58. M. S. Zhdanov, *Geophysical Electromagnetic Theory and Methods*, Vol. 43, Elsevier Science, Amsterdam, the Netherlands, 2009.

59. C. T. Kelley, *Iterative Methods for Linear and Nonlinear Equations*, SIAM, Philadelphia, PA, 1995.

60. T. K. Moon and W. C. Stirling, *Mathematical Methods and Algorithms for Signal Processing*, Prentice Hall, Upper Saddle River, NJ, 2000.
61. P. Hansen, The truncated SVD as a method for regularization, *BIT Numerical Mathematics*, 27, 543–553, 1987.
62. R. Tibshirani, Regression shrinkage and selection via the LASSO, *Journal of the Royal Statistical Society*, 58, 267–288, 1996.
63. S. Boyd and L. Vanderberghe, *Convex Optimization*, Cambridge University Press, Cambridge, U.K., 2004.
64. D. W. Winters, B. D. Van Veen, and S. C. Hagness, A sparsity regularization approach to the electromagnetic inverse scattering problem, *IEEE Transactions on Antennas and Propagation*, 58(1), 145–154, January 2010.
65. A. Beck and M. Teboulle, A fast iterative shrinkage-thresholding algorithm for linear inverse problems, *SIAM Journal on Imaging Science*, 2, 183–202, 2009.
66. M. Cetin and W. C. Karl, Feature-enhanced synthetic aperture radar image formation based on non-quadratic regularization, *IEEE Transactions on Image Processing*, 10(5), 623–631, April 2001.
67. M. R. Andrews, P. Mitra, and R. deCarvalho, Tripling the capacity of wireless communications using electromagnetic polarization, *Nature*, 409, 316–318, 2001.
68. L. Lo Monte, D. Erricolo, F. Soldovieri, and M. C. Wicks, RF tomography for below-ground imaging of extended areas and close-in sensing, *IEEE Geoscience and Remote Sensing Letters*, 7(3), 496–500, July 2010.
69. L. Lo Monte, L. K. Patton, and M. C. Wicks, Mitigation of coupling in RF tomography with applications to belowground sensing, in *IEEE Radar Conference 2010*, Washington, DC, pp. 215–219, 2010.
70. M. Richards, *Fundamentals of Radar Signal Processing*, McGraw-Hill, New York, 2005.

Chapter 20

Surveillance Framework for Ubiquitous Monitoring of Intermodal Cargo Containers

Yogesh Varma, Monte Tull, and Ronald D. Barnes

Contents

If the U.S. authorities find themselves having to turn off the maritime-container-trade spigot, we will have effectively self-imposed a blockade on our own economy.

Stephen Flynn
Senior Fellow, Council of Foreign Relations
Testimony to Senate Government Affairs Committee

20.1 Introduction

Approximately 85% of the world's cargo moves by ships, and the majority of goods are transported in intermodal containers. Each year, around 200 million containers are transported between the world's seaports. Securing containerized cargo movement through the international supply chains that service commerce across the globe is critical to the security of any national infrastructure. After the terrorist attack on September 11, 2001, container security issues were raised, particularly in the United States. The U.S. government proposed and implemented several measures, such as Customs-Trade Partnership Against Terrorism (C-TPAT) [1] and Container Security Initiative (CSI) [2], to improve security systems. The safe, efficient, and uninterrupted operation of the nation's transportation modes, ports, and intermodal terminals requires the effective examination and tracking of container contents. Additional initiatives were taken by C-TPAT [1] to inspect, seal, and monitor containers at the originating seaports of major U.S. trade partners around the globe. The global containerized cargo monitoring initiatives require a ubiquitous container tracking system. The success of a ubiquitous cargo contents monitoring and tracking system hinges upon balancing compelling socioeconomic threats and opportunities.

A container terminal at seaport is a critical node in the containerized cargo transportation network. The existing intermodal cargo container inspection operations in a typical container terminal are lacking in several aspects. Improper and inefficient inspection operations generally cause a container terminal inspection center to become a throughput bottleneck. The potential for inspection bottlenecks causes a questionably large number of cargo containers to pass through the seaport security without a thorough inspection. This inattention raises a major security threat. The issue of the insufficiency of inspections is further magnified by the fact that during its journey from source of produced good to the destination consumer nation, the containers may pass through several seaports. Each seaport may follow its own unique container inspection protocol, and the intelligence generated by such inspections is often proprietary. The absence of a global containerized cargo tracking system makes it impossible to efficiently share the cargo condition and safety intelligence.

The inefficiencies of the containerized cargo supply chain remain the most critical issues of concern in implementing container security measures. The design complexity of such system can grow rapidly, especially when factoring in the key socioeconomic issues affecting the policy. The intermodal cargo containers generally carry bulk or volume goods; therefore, the social impact of an overly conservative surveillance policy may be mainly in form of economic stress due to the delays in cargo processing. In the intermodal containerized cargo shipment business, quick screening of containers is essential to maintain the economic viability of the containerized cargo transport system.

The new continuous surveillance model proposed here requires initial capital investment in container instrumentation and continuous monitoring systems. Discounted insurance under-writing premiums and tax incentives could be used to offset capital investments and operating costs, respectively. The proposed system is designed with consideration of the available technology, radio-frequency (RF) spectrum, and containerized cargo environment in all modes of transporta-tions. Finally, the industry-regulator alliance intrinsic to the proposed framework is likely to drive mass adaptation of a well-designed ubiquitous global system.

This chapter first discusses the intermodal containerized cargo transportation process and the factors that make it the favorite mode of transportation for intercontinental trade. In Section 20.3, the global and American cargo security initiatives that necessitate continuous cargo moni-toring are discussed. Section 20.4 outlines the critical factors for a successful intermodal cargo surveillance system followed by a three-layer model of the proposed ubiquitous cargo monitoring framework and enabling technologies in Section 20.5.

20.2 Containerized Freight Transportation Process

Containerized freight shipping is a specialized process that is highly adapted to meet the needs of intercontinental trade in a very-high-paced seaport environment using gigantic freight liners that serve multiple ports and follow a strict time schedule. World trade is dependent on these intermo-dal liner ships. Local economies depend on the efficiency of the container transport system that includes ships, seaports, and the rail, water, road, and air corridors that distribute the goods. Ports are typically located in heavily populated areas (e.g., Los Angeles, New York City, Long Beach, CA) and are designed for high cargo throughput connecting the vessel docks to significant manu-facturing or distribution installations using railways and highways. These characteristics make ports a strategic target for terrorist attack. Cargo surveillance in a fast-paced environment creates a security dilemma because an efficient surveillance system must strike a good balance between sea-port security and continuity of commerce. This section will first discuss some details of intermodal shipping process and then highlight key factors affecting efficient seaport surveillance.

20.2.1 Intermodal ISO Containers and Liner Ships

A vast majority of the intermodal shipping containers are International Organization for Standardization (ISO) rated. The term intermodal refers to the transport of freight in one ship-ping container by two or more modes of transportation, such as truck and rail or rail and ship. Containers are 2,438 mm (8 ft) wide by 2,438 mm (8 ft) high and generally are 6,058 mm (20 ft), 12,192 mm (40 ft), 14,630 mm (48 ft), or 16,154 mm (53 ft) long. A common unit cargo capac-ity is based on the standard container length of 20 ft and is called a twenty-foot equivalent unit or TEU. One TEU is thus approximately equivalent to the cargo capacity of one $20 \times 8 \times 8$ ft^3 container. Containers are made out of steel and have reinforced corner posts fitted with special lifting brackets in the top and bottom corners. The strong corner posts allow ISO containers to be stacked on top of each other. When transported on ships, containers are typically both stored in the shipping vessel's hull and stacked above the deck up to 23 units high. A common way to move intermodal containers out of the seaport is to double stack them on railcars. The containers can be surface transported by a flatbed truck trailer, rail, large and small container ship, or presumably on a military airplane. This chapter will interchangeably use the terms "intermodal trade," "intermodal cargo," or "intermodal commerce" to mean "intermodal containerized cargo transport using container ships."

According to the latest World Shipping Council statistics, containerized cargo transports about 85% of the world's manufactured goods using some 4000 freight liner ships. A chart produced from the data collected by the United Nations Conference on Trade and Development (UNCTAD) [3] in Figure 20.1 shows the growth trend of fastest growing countries by Liner Shipping Connectivity Index (LSCI) for years 2007–2011. The data are derived from Containerization International Online, and North America, Europe, China, and Japan are excluded from the chart. The index values are normalized to China's 2004 index value as 100. It should be noticed that some small countries with less-than-secured seaport infrastructures rank in the top connected ports.

The current largest liner ship can carry over 13,000 TEUs [4]. The global containerized trade demand has paved way for a shipbuilding industry trend of making ultra large container ships* with Samsung Heavy Industry's 16,000 TEU and STX Shipbuilding's 22,000 TEU vessels planned next. These megacapacity intermodal container ships are the most energy efficient and environmentally friendly mode of intercontinental transportation. The largest ship can be manned by as few as 15 crew members and yet a fully loaded megaship can be loaded or unloaded within one 8 h work shift. The large ships not only offer economies of scales but also make global distribution of a variety of perishable and food supplies possible. Many of these ships carry refrigerated containers, known as reefers, which must follow very strict timeline to get to their destination. The societal impact of inefficiencies in this economic global food-distribution chain will be extremely undesirable and almost inconceivable in today's interdependent world order. These strict time schedules create a severe throughput pressure for the ports (Figure 20.2).

20.2.2 Typical Flow of Goods in Intermodal Trade

In a typical scenario, the goods are loaded in an ISO container at the manufacturing facility or the exporter's warehouse. Next, this containerized cargo is moved by surface transportation to the port of origination. By definition, an intermodal container may be transported by the means of road trucks, railroads, or waterways. In this process, the main points where the container experiences a major change of status are the places where it may have been stationary for a substantial amount of time. In most cases, the containers are stationary at a point in the supply chain where a transition in the mode of transportation takes place—for example, from railroad to ship or from ship to truck. A generalized view of intermodal container transportation along with transitions points is depicted in Figure 20.3.

Figure 20.3 also shows the just-in-time (JIT) nature of production and inventory management in which manufacturing firms cut costs and improve efficiencies through a build-to-order strategy, which dramatically reduces their inventories. The ship liners also match their schedule to meet the requirements of the seasonal and regional demand–supply patterns. This new world trade practice provides many benefits to shippers, but it also presents complex security challenges, including little or no tolerance to delays and extremely high port throughput demand in holiday seasons.

---

* An ultra large container ship (ULCS) is defined as greater than 10,000 TEU capacity.

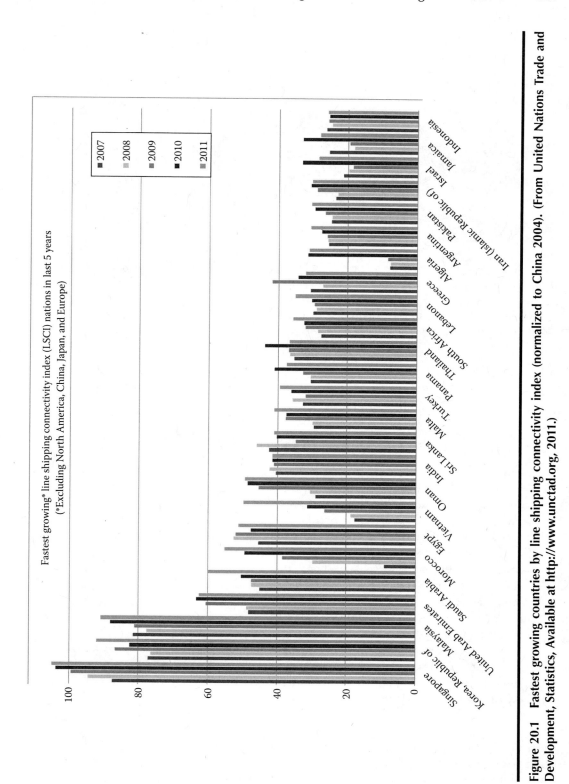

Figure 20.1 Fastest growing countries by line shipping connectivity index (normalized to China 2004). (From United Nations Trade and Development, Statistics, Available at http://www.unctad.org, 2011.)

Figure 20.2 ULCS CMA CGM Christophe Colomb Carries 13,344 TEU. (Image Courtesy of H. Uet; Uet, H., CMA CGM Christophe Colomb 01.jpg, Wikimedia Commons, Available at http://commons.wikimedia.org/wiki/File:CMA_CGM_Christophe_Colomb_01.jpg, 2012.)

Another notable property of intermodal containerized cargo flow is that the containers themselves are treated as a fungible commodity. There is no guarantee that a container leaving a particular shipping port will return to the port of origination.

20.2.3 *Vulnerability and Threats in Intermodal Cargo Transport*

The intermodal cargo transport chain is a complex system with numerous security vulnerabilities. Key vulnerabilities in the intermodal trade chain can be classified as cargo, vessel, people, and environment. These vulnerabilities are further complicated by a large variety of trade participants, multitude of legal frameworks, diversity of transportation facilitators, and versatility of geographical locations that characterize the intermodal trade system. A large number of smaller participants in this system, such as shippers, forwarding agents, and port service provider, have limited resources and motivation for surveillance, for example, a small freight forwarder may not be able to foresee impact that a minor security oversight may have at a destination half a world apart. Noticeably, despite the gigantic amount of intermodal trade volume, there is no central agency to organize and regulate the cargo transport channel.

The vulnerabilities inherent in the maritime and intermodal cargo transport pave the way for potentially severe threat scenarios including exploitation by terrorist, rogue state, and weapon traffickers. Specific threats include use of an intermodal container as a chemical, biological, nuclear, or radiological weapon; contamination of food on a large scale; and the creation of economic adversity through the disruption of the supply chain.

The key methods to secure intermodal cargo transport channel can be classified as cargo scanning and/or inspection, container integrity, channel integrity, cargo tracking, and enforcing quality of participant intelligence. These methods have a varying degree of effectiveness; moreover, the cost and practical applicability of these measures may also vary widely. Table 20.1 summarizes the key vulnerabilities and threats in intermodal cargo transportation and security measures to address them.

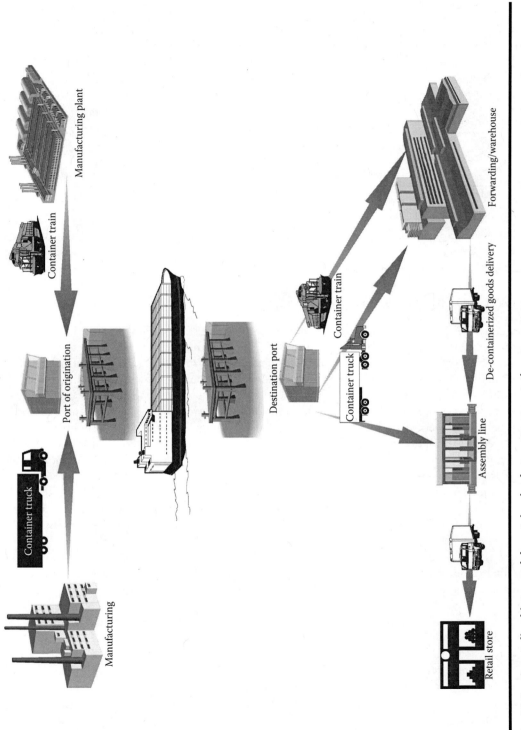

Figure 20.3   Generalized intermodal containerized cargo transportation process.

Table 20.1 Summary of Intermodal Trade Vulnerabilities, Threats, and Security Measures

Vulnerability	Security Measures	Potential Threats
Cargo Container Vessel	Scanning and inspection Container integrity	Weapons and human trafficking, biological/chemical/nuclear warfare Food supply contamination Supply-chain disruption Cyber warfare against vessel, cargo or container sensors, E-seals, and participant databases
Environment	Channel integrity, tracking	
People	Automation of participant identification, information collections, and dissemination	

The framework proposed in this chapter is expected to provide an effective and practical surveillance measure, which has salient features of cargo and channel integrity, and tracking methods and extensibility to ensure the quality of participant background by gathering and disseminating the participant intelligence through a shared repository system.

20.2.4 Legacy Cargo Monitoring Solutions

Currently, there is no standard or generally accepted technique for instrumentation of an ISO container. A variety of container tracking transponders have been tested in pilot projects carried out by various different state transportation departments [6]. However, the extent of instrumentation on containers is usually limited to the electronic identification of the vehicle using radio-frequency identification (RFID) transponders. Current container instrumentation techniques are aimed at the automated vehicle tracking and identification. There are two main methods of automatic vehicle tracking, namely, Automated Vehicle Location (AVL) and Automated Vehicle Identification (AVI). A third variation of AVI that has been specifically targeted at intermodal ISO containers on highways, railroads, and ports is known as automatic equipment identification, and it links an RFID to the individual container's unique identification number [7].

AVL means the continuous tracking of a vehicle using a satellite-supported Global Positioning System (GPS). The GPS method of AVL is expensive to implement because it needs a satellite receiver and a wireless wide area network (WWAN) communication channel transceiver. The GPS receiver receives a signal containing date and time information from three or more satellites. The receiver then calculates its own location by triangulating the distance from these satellites, based on the time it took for the broadcast signal to travel to the receiver. The role of transceiver subsystem is to periodically report the location information to a central data server. This reporting can be achieved via a subscription-based cellular, or a satellite-based communication network. Examples of the commercial AVL solutions for intermodal containers are InterLink Logistics' CargoTracs, Savi's WhereNet, GE Security's CommerceGaurd CSD, and ICC Korea's ConTracer.

The second method, AVI, is relatively simpler, practical, and inexpensive. This method involves detection of the container by sensor equipment installed at various critical waypoints along its normal route. The AVI-based monitoring using the critical tracking point sensors that can be implemented using a variety of wireless or wired technologies. The most reliable and popular choice is the use of RFID transponders on the vehicle carrying the container, with RFID tag readers installed at the tracking points. Certain frequencies of the RFID technology can accurately and dependably identify containers even at a reasonable high speeds as demonstrated in [7]. Large numbers of competing RFID products are available for container detection. Electronic toll collection is an example of the common use of such technology for vehicle identification. The railroads can also be covered for railcar detection using RFID tags. For example, Zebra Inc.'s WhereNet offers an RFID product called WhereTag IV that tracks vehicles in their wireless network [8]. The network utilizes a Cisco Wireless Location Appliance that operates in open standard ISO/IEC 24730-2 with IEEE 802.11. Similarly, RFID Inc. offers Extend-a-Read and Extend-a-Read2 products that utilize 433 MHz active and semiactive tags and extend their capabilities using GPS and general packet radio service (GPRS) networks [9].

Electronic seal (E-Seal) is an RF technology–based electromechanical lock that secures the container or the trailer doors. If an attempt to tamper with the seal is made, it stores this event in its internal memory and later reports it upon communication with an electronic reader.

Several commercial implementations of the E-Seal exist in the industry. Some of the leading vendors of E-Seals are E.J. Brook (formerly eLogicity), Hi-G Tek, Savi, Telematics Wireless, GE Security, and ICC Korea's i-Seal. Most of the E-Seals have onboard memory that can be read and written to by handheld readers and/or over-the-air (OTA) road/rail side readers. The container ID is the most common information stored in E-Seals. This feature allows the E-Seal to double as a container identifier. Heightened security alert levels have elevated the requirements for the capabilities expected from an E-Seal.

By design, E-Seals can be either low-cost disposable units or easily reprogrammable and reusable devices. Therefore, these seals may be more practical, economical, and acceptable to the industry than the permanent container tags. E-Seals also provide more useful information than container tags, such as the status (secured or tampered) of the seal. Most contemporary E-Seals can record the date and time of tamper and authorized entry and reseal events [6]. Some advanced E-Seals or door tags, such as ICC Korea's i-CON or Savi's SensorTag 676, also have built-in container sensors or interfaces for additional cargo integrity sensors.

Deployment of automated E-Seal systems in the supply chain not only expedites the container identification process but also improves the quality of cargo integrity and monitoring information. However, the global deployment of E-Seals has been marred by radio spectrum compatibility issues. Standards try to address technical protocols, interfaces, and frequencies, and the RF issues are closely related to standard issues. There are a large number of these cargo container-monitoring products that have been deployed on intermodal container or carriers by some major logistics industry stakeholders.

20.3 Containerized Cargo Security Initiatives

In this section, we describe the various maritime trade initiatives with special attention to the most popular and vulnerable intermodal containerized cargo trade safety. After the terror attacks of September 11, 2001, several of these initiatives were taken by the United States of America and were adopted by United States' global trade partners. Since 9/11, the United States has taken several initiatives to ensure safety of its trade channels, and it is a pioneer in intermodal cargo antiterrorism technologies. Aside from the ill-fated terror attacks of 9/11, there is also a statistical reason for United States' leadership in intermodal cargo safety initiatives.

The chart in Figure 20.4 shows the container port throughput of the top-ranking ports measured in TEUs for years 2008–2009. Chart data are collected by the UNCTAD [3]. The chart shows that in terms of containerized cargo throughput, the United States of America ranks highest

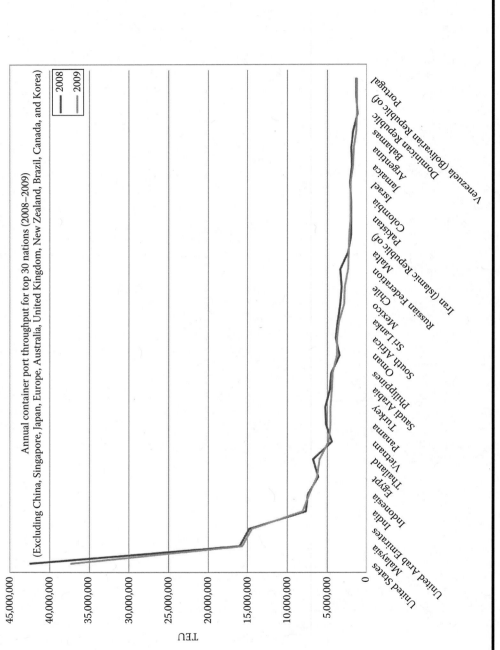

Figure 20.4 Containerized cargo throughput (in TEU) for years 2008–2009. (From United Nations Trade and Development, Statistics, Available at http://www.unctad.org, 2011.)

among the developed economies. More than 11 million cargo containers are offloaded at the U.S. seaports each year [10]. Some of the advanced ports such as China, United Kingdom, Europe, Australia, and New Zealand that are perceived as safe are excluded from the chart to highlight the rising throughput of other less secured ports.

The data in Figure 20.1, read in conjunction with Figure 20.4, reveal the fact that statistically it is very probable that liner ships provide a direct connectivity between United States' seaports and some of the vulnerable seaports with high LSCI. An important point here is that even if the exporting port of origination is safe and seals the container, there could be intermediate seaports with very poor security practices where liner ships make a routine stop before arriving to one of the busy U.S. seaports, from where the intermodal containers are quickly forwarded within the United States by mode of railway or highway for distribution of goods.

Due to busy ports and a slow screening process, only about 2% of the containers that arrived at ports in the United States in 2001 were subject to thorough screening [11]. Unscreened intermodal freight poses a severe threat to the U.S. national safety; this was a drastic situation that called for drastic measures. After September 2001, a series of immediate actions and long-term initiatives were taken to improve seaport and maritime trade security in the United States. Some of these included a series of Coast Guard operations, U.S. Customs and Border Protection (CBP) Agency's, CSI, C-TPAT, International Customs Zones (ICZ), Non-Intrusive Inspection Technology, and cargo-related intelligence databases.

20.3.1 U.S. Container Security Initiative

In January 2002, the U.S. CBP Agency launched the CSI that seeks to prescreen containers at a CSI participant port of origination with the help of the local port authorities and thereby avoid the need for thorough screening when the containers arrive at a port in United States. A team of local customs or port authorities and U.S. CBP officials at the port of origination decide which containers to screen before loading. If a container is shipped from a non-CSI port, the container may be screened at the port of arrival. CBP's 58 operational CSI ports now prescreen over 80 percent of all maritime containerized cargo imported into the United States [12]. A prequalification for a port to be included in CSI is to have regular, direct, and substantial container traffic to United States; however, the LCSI data show that container traffic via smaller intermediate ports that may tolerate a breach in security poses an equally serious threat.

A core element of the CSI is to use technology to automatically target and identify high-risk containers, as well as fast nonintrusive screening using large-scale x-ray and gamma ray scanners. However, without efficient information sharing with the non-CSI ports, scanning remains a key screening process, which is inherently a slow process. The information sharing by all the stakeholders including the manufacturer is a key to efficient surveillance. Additionally, CSI prompted discussion about smart boxes or IT-enabled containers, but as of 2011, no concrete developments have been made on that front.

20.3.2 U.S. Customs-Trade Partnership Against Terrorism (C-TPAT)

C-TPAT is the second major voluntary supply-chain security initiative announced by the United States. C-TPAT works with the shipping industry to improve end-to-end international supply-chain security. C-TPAT extends the CBP partnership offer to all the major stakeholders in the international supply chain, including small and large manufacturers, importers, carriers, consolidators, and licensed customs brokers. The C-TPAT partners are expected to conduct a comprehensive self-assessment of supply-chain security in accordance with C-TPAT guidelines in lieu of "fast-track" status to the C-TPAT participants' containers at U.S. ports of arrival. The partners are expected to invest in securing the physical integrity of their own premises but also ensure that their trading partners do so as well. C-TPAT participation could be a very costly affair, and yet it does not guarantee any better results than CSI. The only fundamental difference between CSI and C-TPAT is that besides origination port and custom authorities, other private sector participants are included in the scope of the C-TPAT program. C-TPAT has been a touted as a successful program by CBP in its 2007 survey of program participants in which over 91% of 1756 responding companies expressed their satisfaction with the program. More than 50% of the respondent companies also indicated that although they had to incur additional costs, mainly in terms of C-TPAT security compliance staff, the benefits outweighed the costs. The fast-lane status by C-TPAT increased predictability in the cargo transport for the participants, as the number of inspections at U.S. ports went down by 50% [13]. Increased employment and competitive advantage may be seen as a social effect of these homeland security measures. In spite of its wide acceptance, C-TPAT does not offer any specific technological standards to ensure proper security and monitoring of cargo; nor does it collect or share any cargo intelligence such as cargo tracking or cargo condition with the supply-chain partners. A standards-based system to collect and disseminate cargo intelligence will be discussed later in this chapter.

20.3.3 SAFE Port Act of 2006 (United States)

The Security and Accountability For Every Port Act (or SAFE Port Act) of 2006 strengthened CSI and C-TPAT by giving them legislative authority. In 2009, the SAFE Port Act finalized a consolidated strategy to enhance international supply-chain security by providing an overreaching framework to facilitate secure cargo flow and plans for specific supply-chain segments [14].

20.3.4 International Cargo Security Initiatives

The global initiatives for maritime trade security against the threat of terrorism are far and few between. A commonly referred framework is the International Ship and Port Facility Security (ISPS) Code by the International Maritime Organization. The ISPS is a comprehensive framework that provides a standardized, consistent framework for managing risk and permitting the meaningful exchange and evaluation of information between contracting governments, companies, port facilities, and ships [15]. The main purpose of the code is to provide a uniform framework for shipping and port risk assessment, rather than a standardized system for risk detection and alleviation.

The European Union (EU) and the U.S. Department of Homeland Security signed an agreement in year 2004 committing both parties to cooperate on CSI and related matters. The European Commission (EC) announced that the EC–U.S. Joint Customs Cooperation Committee (JCCC) has adopted several measures aimed at enforcing the security of maritime container transport. Among these measures are the creation of an information exchange network, the identification of best practices in security controls, and an agreement on minimum requirements applicable for European ports participating in the CSI. In 2009, U.S.–EU JCCC, cochaired by the commissioner of CBP and the director general of the Taxation and Customs Union Directorate (TAXUD) of the EC, unveiled a road map toward mutual recognition of trade partnership programs [16]. One road map item is to establish an expert-level working group to develop an information technology (IT) platform to conduct information exchanges as well as identify various IT needs to enable a fully automated data exchange, which is a work in progress. Eventually, the U.S.–EU JCCC road map is likely to lead to a standards-based information gathering and sharing system.

20.4 Key Success Factors for Efficient Intermodal Cargo Surveillance

The previous sections described the salient features of tools and infrastructure for intermodal trade and the global maritime trade safety initiatives. The U.S. and international initiatives for intermodal trade security are based upon extensive experience in handling cargo safety without disrupting the flow of trade; in order to be efficient, any proposed system must leverage upon the frameworks.

This section lists the key factors that must be considered in designing an efficient system for continuous and global monitoring of all aspects of intermodal trade. Based on the discussion of infrastructure, the following points shall serve as the design parameters of an efficient intermodal trade surveillance system:

■ *Global coverage*: Intermodal commerce is truly global in the sense that the liner ships ferry around several seaports during the course of goods delivery. This parameter warrants a joint effort by all trade partner seaports around the globe. Global coverage also requires RF compatibility within different locale's available radio spectrum. The cargo sensor node's networking interface must be able to interoperate within and with a variety of heterogeneous local area network (LAN)/wide area network (WAN) interfaces.

■ *Intermodal nature*: Containers may travel locally on railways, waterways, or highways. In order to insure end-to-end monitoring, the surveillance system must provide coverage along all modes of transportation. An added commercial benefit of the local coverage, after the port of arrival, could be the condition monitoring for sensitive cargo. This intermodal nature requires that the sensor node must be able to interact with a variety of heterogeneous networks.

■ *Low sensor node cost*: Since intermodal containers are treated as fungible, it is necessary that the sensor nodes either are easily removable or have an inexpensive fixed module that can be expanded with a variety of sensors as needed. In an automated high-throughput container-handling environment, the ability to remove the complete node may be undesirable and will likely cause severe slowdown. A standards-based modular sensor node design is more likely to succeed, since at the final destination the recipient can handle removal of expensive add-on sensors and return them to the supplier of goods.

■ *Time criticality*: The most efficient megaliner ships operate on a tight schedule, ports have limited capacity and throughput, and goods can be both seasonal and highly perishable. These three factors together put immense demand on any surveillance and monitoring system. In order to be efficient, the system must not disrupt the flow of goods. The current noninvasive screening systems are inadequately slow. This parameter requires changes in the surveillance process and technology. In order to minimize possibility of any adverse socioeconomic effects, the surveillance system must be able to handle very large volumes of cargo at a very fast pace.

■ *Diversity of stakeholders*: The list of stakeholders in intermodal cargo transport is very diverse, including shipbuilders, waterway, railway, highway and airway carriers, seaport authorities, customs, border security agencies, logistic firms, freight forwarders, manufacturers, distributors, and customers. Several of the trade participants are major stakeholders, and their participation is critical to an effective surveillance system design. In order to ensure participation by all key stakeholders, the system shall consider capturing and sharing of relevant intelligence with respective participants.

- *Legal considerations*: The vast coverage of the surveillance system subjects it to several local, states, federal, and global authorities' jurisdiction. These authorities shall participate in deciding the scope of the cargo and seaport intelligence gathering. The system shall insure that it does not violate any local law and share relevant information with respective authorities.
- *Investment and revenue sharing*: For the economic viability of a project of this scale, the system must attract both public and private investment. It shall also create operational revenue by charging for cargo intelligence. A central revenue collector and distribution authority may be formed as a consortium of key global intermodal trade players. The system adaptability will increase by insuring its compatibility with some of the existing legacy cargo monitoring sensor nodes (AVL/AVI). A standards-based modular approach will be required for legacy compatibility.

20.5 Framework for Global Ubiquitous Cargo Monitoring

Based on the success factors listed in the previous section, this section describes the design framework for an efficient cargo monitoring system. An introduction to the concept of tracking points is followed by a detailed description of the proposed framework's interfaces as a layered model. Finally, the technologies, protocols, and radio spectrum frequencies that enable the proposed surveillance model are discussed.

A global ubiquitous system can be efficient only if it does not interfere with the cargo transport process. The global cargo security initiatives are also designed around the doctrine of least interference. The key criterion for the framework design is to

1. Cause no disruption in intermodal trade flow seen in Figure 20.3
2. Keep the surveillance process in line with the CBP CSI doctrine

In accordance to the essence of the CSI core elements, it is proposed to secure containers at the port of departure after due-diligence inspection. In the proposed framework, the cargo is containerized and electronically sealed, either at the manufacturer's site or at a forwarding warehouse. The E-Seal on the container is then monitored for integrity at each storage or transportation mode change point. These possible points are marked as "tracking point" in Figure 20.5.

It should be noticed that there is no change in the secured cargo flow as it was depicted in Figure 20.3. Containerized cargo might be stored at its original location for a few days. Hence, it must be monitored periodically after being sealed. The container is then moved to the port of origination and is staged until it is loaded on a cargo ship. Therefore, the cargo shall be monitored at each port including where it is originally loaded on ship, moved from one ship to another, or unloaded at the final destination port. Even after being unloaded from the ship, obtaining security clearance by port authorities, and being transported using another form of transportation, the cargo may still be monitored for commercial purposes.

The proposed framework aims at monitoring containers mainly at specific points of storage and during change of transportation modes. These points are marked as the "tracking points" in Figure 20.5. This process provides a reasonable monitoring capability since once the container

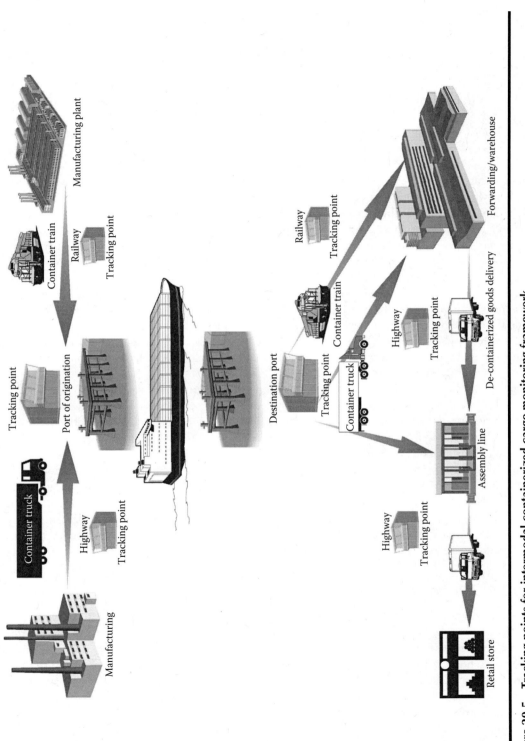

Figure 20.5 Tracking points for intermodal containerized cargo monitoring framework.

reaches a tracking point, it will transfer its historical status data, including any alarm signals. Based on the historical status data, a decision for further screening can be made.

The vitality of the proposed framework lies in the fact that, in addition to the electronically sealing the container, the same module will also be usable to gather a variety of cargo condition intelligence. Cargo integrity and conditioning information are transmitted together over a common network link and will populate a common cargo intelligence repository. At the repository level, web-based data distribution applications can be deployed to authorize different stakeholders to utilize the relevant cargo intelligence on the need to use basis. A high-level system diagram of the proposed framework is shown in Figure 20.6.

Once sealed, containers will be tracked using a wireless sensor networks during their entire transportation. However, these wireless sensors may not be accessible in certain storage situations, such as when the container is buried in a multilevel stack or in holdings beneath the deck of the ship. From a practical point of view, such situations are considered low risk. However, the sensor module on the container will continue to monitor all system events such as seal status, battery or power status, and online status and record the seal and sensor data in its local memory. If any alarm condition occurs, then the sensor module will send that information to the next available tracking point. The upper-level system layers shall provide high-level algorithms that can parse these events to detect any perceived tampering threat. Suitable remedial actions shall be prescribed depending upon severity of events, such as a thorough, invasive inspection. In order to avoid cloning of the device, a low-power cryptographic hashing algorithm utilizing the media-access identification (MAC ID) of the wireless node may be used to store the data locally on the node. The proposed system is a decision support system and will help human operators in identifying a wide range of threat conditions.

At the design implementation level, the proposed system must be provisioned for flexible combination functionalities at each of the system layer. Each system layer shall also provide for nonproprietary standards-based interfaces to allow for true plug-and-play functionality. The system can be ubiquitous only if it is capable of utilizing a variety of communication interfaces ranging from ad hoc mesh networks to cellular or satellite. The networking system will have to provide for a seamless transition of the container node between the communication channels. Similarly, the cargo intelligence data gathered by container nodes shall also be treated with respect to the reporting periodicity. In order to analyze the complex and somewhat competing demands of such ubiquitous system design, the framework provides a layered decomposition of the subsystems in Table 20.2, which also lists some of the standards and protocols that can facilitate needed flexibility and interoperability.

20.5.1 Information Capture (Sensor Node) Layer

The information capture or sensor node layer of the framework provides key functionality of interfacing a variety of cargo condition and surveillance sensors and monitors these sensors for any alarm condition. The sensor node would ideally be a network-capable low-power microcontroller board that hosts an IEEE 1451 compatible sensor interface module and provides uplink connectivity interface to a TCP/IP network. Normally, the sensor data transfer shall take place when the sensor host is queried by the networked reader; however, it shall initiate transmission of an alarm signal sensor parameters across a preset threshold. The host must also provide local storage for sensor readings that it shall periodically transfer to the information processing layer. The host shall also monitor its own battery and may optionally preserve and recharge the battery by working on a duty cycle as well as using energy harvesting [17].

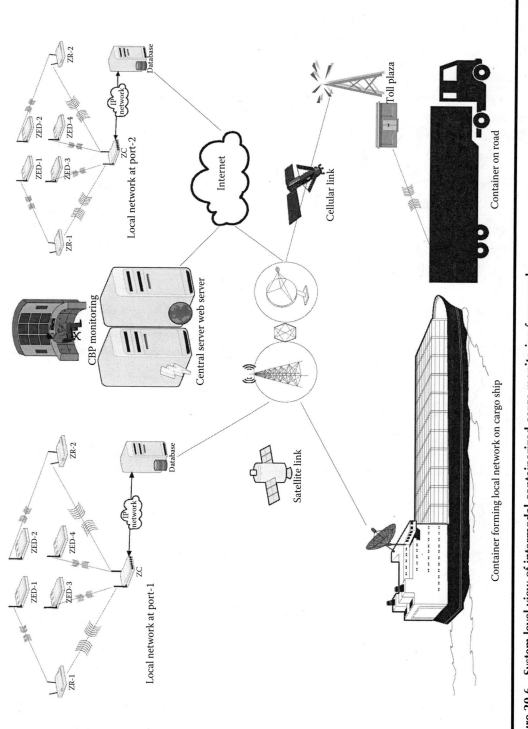

Figure 20.6   System level view of intermodal containerized cargo monitoring framework.

Table 20.2   Layered Decomposition of Cargo Monitoring Framework

Basic Functions	Additional Features	Enabling Technology
Information Capture (Sensor Node) Layer		
Insure cargo safety	Periodically read sensors	ISO 18185
Provide sensor interface	Wired/wireless sensors support	IEEE 1451
Monitor cargo sensors	Trigger data transfer on alarm	Low power motes
Store sensor data	Monitor and preserve battery	Energy harvesting
Send alarm signal	Fast readout	Active RFID
Information Communication (Network Link) Layer		
Respond to data query	Ad-hoc networking	IEEE 802.15.4 (LRWPAN)
Transfer sensor data	Ubiquitous connectivity	LAN/WAN, satellite, cellular
Provide cargo location	Interoperability	IP based geolocation
	Data security	AES encryption
Information Processing and Dissemination (Data) Layer		
Store cargo data	On demand data dissemination	Geospatial visualization
Generate locale alarms	Decision support tools	Data mining
Disseminate select data	Threat pattern identification	Relational database analytics

20.5.2 Information Communication (Network Link) Layer

The main functionality provided by the information communication or network link layer is to periodically transmit the sensor node layer data to the data layer when queried by the tracking point reader or prompted by the sensor node layer in an alarm condition. The network link layer will also insure interoperability with in and across the networks by providing standard TCP/IP connectivity. Additionally, the location of the cargo at the time of data transfer can also be determined by an IP-based geolocation service.

20.5.3 Information Processing and Dissemination (Data Repository) Layer

As the name suggests, the data repository layer gathers sensor data from a large number of sensor nodes via different network links and stores data for dissemination to various stakeholders. This layer would ideally be a geographically distributed and networked cluster of databases equipped with sophisticated software algorithms for locale-based threat detections and related decision support analysis. This layer may utilize sensor web enablement (SWE) standards.

20.5.4 Enabling Technologies, Protocols, and Standards

A future ubiquitous cargo monitoring networked sensor system is envisioned as an interoperable, vendor-neutral system for seamless sensor deployment over heterogeneous network media and hierarchical sensor data access using web interface in real time. Such a system will not only provide open sensor access to the privileged stakeholders but also provide a rich feature set encompassing control, integration, analysis, exploitation, and visualization of the sensor data derived from multiple repositories. The key success factors in terrorism-threat detection are the system's ability to correlate sensor intelligence in conjunction with the human factor as may be exposed by the cargo and crew manifest. Only a global ubiquitous system with a vast data repository, advanced data mining, processing, and geospatial analysis capabilities can perform real-time detection and assessment of a range of chemical, biological, radiological, nuclear, and other explosive terror plots and accidental hazards. The proposed global information collection and dissemination (data layer) shall also provide distributed access and alerts to all the participating intermodal commerce stakeholders with appropriate multilevel privileges. An IEEE 1451 smart transducer interface with geospatial SWE framework and availability of the wireless RF spectrum form the core of such global cargo monitoring framework. These elements are discussed next.

20.5.4.1 IEEE 1451 Smart Transducer Interface Standard

The proposed framework is based on the fundamental premise of standards-based sensors deployment and networking. IEEE 1451 is a standard for plug-and-play smart transducer interface for sensors and actuators that inherently support multiple networks and protocols. The IEEE 1451 family of standards specifies a set of common interfaces for connecting transducers to instruments, microprocessors, or field networks, covering digital, mixed-mode, distributed multidrop, and wireless interfaces, including Wi-Fi, ZigBee, and RFID. At the core of the standard is the smart transducer object model that provides encapsulation for two interfaces of a networked sensor node, namely, transducer hardware and network protocols. A key concept of the standard is Transducer Electronic Data Sheet (TEDS), which provides vendor data sheet for the sensor to self-identify on the sensor host or the upstream network. A brief overview of IEEE 1451 family of standards is presented in Figure 20.7. For a detailed discussion, the reader should refer to the standard documentation [18]. The ability to seamlessly deploy any legacy sensor over a heterogeneous network is a critical success factor for a ubiquitous cargo monitoring framework, and the IEEE 1451 standard is the enabling technology for this key feature.

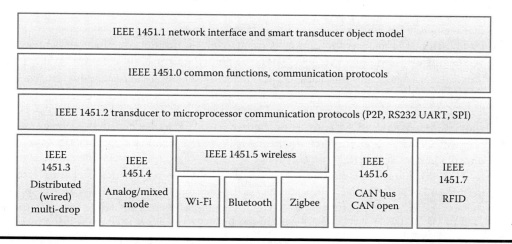

Figure 20.7 IEEE 1451 family of standards. (From NIST, IEEE 1451 smart transducer interface standards, Available at http://www.nist.gov/el/isd/ieee/ieee1451.cfm, 2011.)

20.5.4.2 Open Geospatial Consortium's Proposed Sensor Web Enablement Framework

The second critical success factor for a global ubiquitous cargo monitoring framework is the ability to analyze and disseminate the captured sensor data to geographically distributed stakeholders with a disparate set of privileges. The ability to generate real-time threat alerts from a very large dataset utilizing the local, regional, and global intelligence requires advanced collaboration, data mining, and geospatial algorithmic data analysis capability. A platform-independent mechanism to push an alert to all the relevant authorities in the geozone under threat is an equally important element in the efficient handling of a potential act of terror.

In an initiative called SWE, members of the Open Geospatial Consortium (OGC) are building a framework of open standards for exploiting web-connected sensors and sensor systems [19]. The SWE envisions that the sensor data will be discoverable using standard encoding comprehensible to humans and geographically disparate networked systems, and the sensors' observations will be accessible in real time using web interfaces [20]. A detailed discussion of SWE framework is beyond the scope of this chapter, and the readers are referred to the OGC for more information [21].

20.5.4.3 Radio Spectrum Availability and Related Standards

As previously mentioned, intermodal containers are treated as a fungible commodity. This means that if a container is instrumented with cargo monitoring and tracking sensors, it must work in all nations across all ITU zones. An efficient global supply-chain surveillance framework must utilize a globally, freely available, and consistent radio spectrum frequency. There are several existing freight identification (ISO 10374), E-Seal (ISO 18185), and comprehensive item management (ISO 18000) standards that prescribe usage of available local RFs. However, there is no single frequency available for Asia, Europe, and North America. An overview of standards in the supply-chain applications area is given in the following:

- ISO 10374 is the existing standard for automatic RF identification of freight containers. The standard includes a container identification system, data coding systems, description of data, performance criteria, and security features. It is a dual-frequency passive read-only standard that includes 850–950 and 2400–2500 MHz radio bands [7].
- ISO 18185 is a recent application standard for electronic container seals developed by Technical Committee ISO/TC 104, freight containers, Subcommittee SC 4, and Identification and Communication. ISO 18185-1:2007 is used in conjunction with the other parts of ISO 18185. It applies to all E-Seals used on freight containers, operating in 433 MHz and 2.45 GHz RF bands and covered by ISO 668, ISO 1496-1 to ISO 1496-5, and ISO 8323. ISO 18185 consists of the five parts [7], namely, 18185-1 communication protocol, 18185-2 application requirements, 18185-3 environmental characteristics, 18185-4 data protection, and 18185-5 physical layer.
- ISO 18000 defines the parameters to be determined in any standardized air interface definition in the ISO/IEC 18000 series [7]. The different parts of ISO/IEC 18000 provide the specific values for definition of their interface parameters for a particular frequency or type of air interface. It is (currently) a seven-part standard that describes parameters for air interface communications below 135 kHz, 13.56 MHz, 2.45 GHz, 5.8 GHz, 860–960 MHz, and 433 MHz and for globally accepted frequencies. Table 20.3 provides a summary of global RF band availability and standards [7,22,23].

Table 20.3 RFID Seal and Transponder Frequency Summary

Frequency (MHz)	ISO Standards Status	Acceptance
315	Agreed for use under tri-frequency active protocol, ISO 18185	Most of Asia
433	Agreed as stand-alone active protocol and as part of tri-frequency active protocol, ISO 18185 and ISO 18000-7	Europe and North America; parts of Asia
915	Agreed as stand-alone active protocol and as part of tri-frequency active protocol

Covered in passive protocol, ISO 18185, ISO 10374, part of ISO 18000-6 | North and South America |
| 862–928 | Agreed for the passive protocol under ISO 18185, part of ISO 18000-6 | Global approval for passive RFID logistics applications |
| 2450 | Part of the existing container read-only standard, ISO 10374. Part of ISO 18000-4

Approved as IEEE 802.15.4 ZigBee radio | Globally unlicensed industrial, science and medical (ISM) band |

Source: ITU, Ubiquitous network societies—The case of RFID, in *ITU Workshop On Ubiquitious Network Societies*, Geneva, Switzerland, p. 38, 2005.

Once the E-Seal communicates with a base module using short-range RF technology, the data can be further transmitted using a globally available unlicensed ISM 2.4 GHz frequency band.

For a comprehensive discussion about ISO 18000 and 18185 is the readers are advised to refer to the relevant standards [7,22–24] for a comparative analysis of the radio spectrum selection.

20.6 Conclusion

The design criterion for a global seamless containerized cargo monitoring system with a minimal socioeconomic impact together with relevant protocols and standards was discussed in this chapter. A global monitoring system for the continuous online monitoring of the intermodal cargo containers is required to eliminate seaport-inspection-system bottleneck and fragmentation of the cargo intelligence. A new paradigm for the containerized cargo monitoring is proposed by prescribing a continuous monitoring and intermittent reporting model to replace the current inspection only at the seaport terminals practice. The proposed framework utilizes globally accepted standards and frameworks for sensor deployment, networking, and data sharing. An integrated network that allows the existing intermodal trade partners to utilize their existing resources and leverage advanced geospatial threat detection using collective global data is expected to be much more robust. A detailed system diagram of our proposed system is presented in Figure 20.8.

The proposed global cargo monitoring framework is more feasible compared to alternative intermodal cargo trade security systems due to the versatility of its information capture and an information communication layer across a wide RF spectrum. Moreover, the proposed framework is designed to include many of the existing monitoring subsystems. The data are globally shared by the information processing and dissemination layer, which can also be adapted to comply with

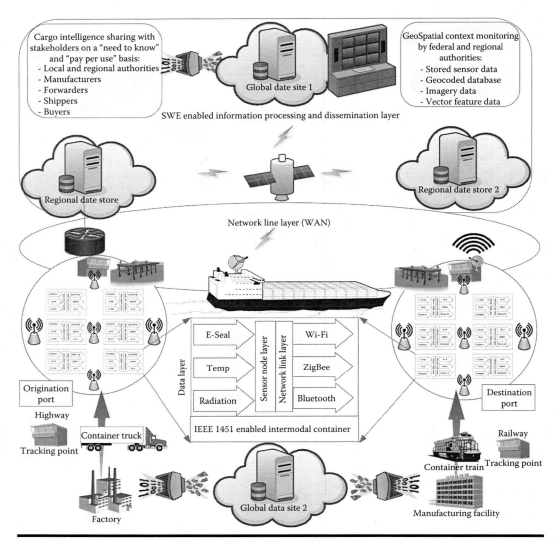

Figure 20.8 Ubiquitous cargo monitoring network based on proposed framework.

the local laws. A global standard body may ensure compliance of existing monitoring subsystems with the requirements of the proposed framework.

The model for global containerized cargo surveillance system is founded on the premise of

- Adaptability of the proposed system in the existing intermodal cargo commerce flow
- Globally feasible ad hoc wireless sensor LAN using a global ISM frequency 2.4 GHz band and the IEEE 802.15.4 (ZigBee) protocol
- Seamless deployment of sensors on nodes utilizing IEEE 1451 standard framework
- Creating an SWE-standards-based hierarchical shared data repository that provides access to selective relevant information by all interested parties
- Insuring system's economic viability by revenue generated by licensing cargo intelligence usage rights to the rightful stakeholders on a per-use basis

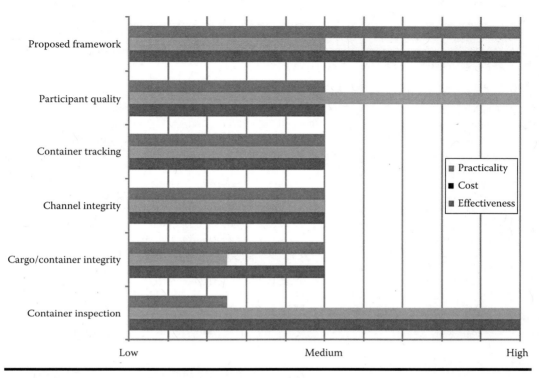

Figure 20.9 **Comparison of intermodal trade security measures.**

The containerized cargo transportation plays a pivotal role in the global commerce and distribution of manufactured and produced goods. Security of intermodal cargo containers and ports is essential for protecting nations against potential terror threats. A standards-based ubiquitous monitoring system designed for fast-paced intermodal cargo trade is expected to have a minimal socioeconomic impact while providing effective surveillance.

In the current era of highly interdependent global economy, a trade channel disruption would translate into substantial economic and social effects. A comparative evaluation of proposed framework in terms of cost, effectiveness, and implementation practicality with other security measures is presented in Figure 20.9. Alternative systems may be ineffective in preventing potential disruption of the containerized cargo supply chain, which could lead to major trade adversity. The cost of implementing the proposed system is only a small fraction of the cost of trade transport and an even smaller insurance to protect against ominous social and economic damage that it helps avoid.

References

1. C-TPAT, http://www.cbp.gov/xp/cgov/trade/cargo_security/ctpat/. [Online]. Available: http://www.cbp.gov/xp/cgov/trade/cargo_security/ctpat/. Accessed: February 12, 2012.
2. CSI, http://www.cbp.gov/xp/cgov/trade/cargo_security/csi/. [Online]. Available: http://www.cbp.gov/xp/cgov/trade/cargo_security/csi/. Accessed: February 12, 2012.
3. United Nations Trade and Development (UNCTAD), Statistics. [Online]. Available: http://www.unctad.org. Accessed: October 11, 2011.

4. J. Tiedemann and J. Svendsen, The big boats are coming, 2006 [Online]. Available: http://www.containership-info.com/misc_newjumbos.pdf. Accessed: January 15, 2013.

5. H. Uet, CMA CGM Christophe Colomb 01.jpg, Wikimedia Commons. [Online]. Available: http://commons.wikimedia.org/wiki/File:CMA_CGM_Christophe_Colomb_01.jpg. Accessed: July 09, 2012.

6. TransCoreElectronic Container Seals Field Operational Test Project—Technology Review Report—Final, September 15, 2003. [Online]. Available: http://depts.washington.edu/trac/tracuw/freight/pdf/eseal/NWITCPhase2TechnologyReviewReport_F.pdf. Accessed: January 15, 2013.

7. ISO, *ISO Standards Handbook—Freight Containers*, 2006 [Online]. Available: http://www.iso.org/iso/freight_06.pdf. Accessed: January 15, 2013.

8. Zebra, Inc., WhereTag IV datasheet, 2011 [Online]. Available: http://www.zebra.com/us/en/products-services/location-solutions/wherenet/wheretag.html. Accessed: January 15, 2013.

9. RFID, Inc, Extend-a-read data sheet, 2011 [Online]. Available: http://www.rfidinc.com/extenda.html. Accessed: January 15, 2013.

10. C-TPAT Program Information, Securing the Global Supply Chain, 2004 [Online]. Available: http://www.cbp.gov/xp/cgov/trade/cargo_security/ctpat/ctpat_program_information. Accessed: January 15, 2013.

11. A. Baker and J. Sullivan, A nation challenged—Cargo port of entry now means point of anxiety, *New York Times*, New York, December 23, 2001.

12. U.S. Customs and Border Protection—Trade. [Online]. Available: http://www.cbp.gov/xp/cgov/trade/cargo_security/ctpat/. Accessed: October 13, 2011.

13. W. K. Talley, *Port Economics*. Routledge, New York, 2009.

14. USDOT, America's container ports—Freight hubs that connect our nation to global markets, June 2009 [Online]. Available: http://www.rita.dot.gov/bts/sites/rita.dot.gov.bts/files/publications/americas_container_ports/2009/index.html. Accessed: January 15, 2013.

15. P. Crist, Security in maritime transport—Risk factors and economic impact, July 2003 [Online]. Available: http://www.oecd.org/sti/transport/maritimetransport/18521672.pdf. Accessed: January 15, 2013.

16. JCCC, Abridged external partner version of the U.S.–EU joint customs cooperation committee roadmap towards mutual recognition of trade partnership programs, January 2009 [Online]. Available: http://ec.europa.eu/taxation_customs/resources/documents/customs/policy_issues/customs_security/roadmap_abridged_en.pdf. Accessed: January 15, 2013.

17. C. Park and P. Chou, AmbiMax: Autonomous energy harvesting platform for multi-supply wireless sensor nodes, in *2006 3rd Annual IEEE Communications Society on Sensor and Ad Hoc Communications and Networks*, Reston, VA, 2006, pp. 168–177.

18. NIST, IEEE 1451 smart transducer interface standards. [Online]. Available: http://www.nist.gov/el/isd/ieee/ieee1451.cfm. Accessed: October 15, 2011.

19. C. Reed, M. Botts, J. Davidson, and G. Percivall, OGC® sensor web enablement: Overview and high level architecture, In *2007 IEEE Proceedings on Autotestcon*, September 17–20, 2007, pp. 372–380.

20. K. B. Lee and M. E. Reichardt, Open standard for homeland security sensor network, *IEEE Instrumentation & Measurement Magazine*, 14–21, 2005.

21. OGC, Open geospatial consortium. [Online]. Available: http://www.opengeospatial.org/. Accessed: October 15, 2011.

22. M. Wolfe, Electronic cargo seals—Context, technologies, and marketplace, 2002 [Online]. Available: http://www.hsdl.org/?view&did=444589. Accessed: January 15, 2013.

23. ITU, Ubiquitous network societies—The case of RFID, in *ITU Workshop On Ubiquitous Network Societies*, Geneva, Switzerland, 2005, p. 38.

24. Y. Varma and M. P. Tull, Inter-modal container instrumentation techniques, *Systems Engineering*, 2007. [Online]. Available: http://www.iyogee.com/inter-modal-container-instrumentation-techniques/76/. Accessed: October 15, 2011.

Chapter 21

Model-Based Control of Building Evacuation Using Feedback from Sensor and Actuator Wireless Networks

Paolo Lino, Bruno Maione, and Guido Maione

Contents

21.1 Problem of Evacuation

In recent years, researchers and practitioners have devoted considerable attention to the problem of safe evacuation of a large number of individuals from buildings or open-air environments. The growing interest is certainly due to some accidents and disasters that emotionally struck the public opinion, after natural or deliberate threats. Consequently, researchers and engineers have identified problems and errors in the design of buildings and entertainment places (i.e., stadiums, theaters, and cinemas) and in the necessary evacuation procedures. According to many recent studies, a lot of people got injured or lost their lives following a chaotic crowd motion, running in every direction, and trying to reach a better position to follow the event or to escape the danger (Schreckenberg and Sharma 2002). Moreover, in many cases, a better crowd management or a different evacuation strategy could have saved many lives. Surely indeed, a better strategy should consider the particular conditions and people behavior. Unfortunately, however, fixed prescriptive norms and regulations concerning building characteristics (e.g., distances, number of exits, and exit and route widths) and establishing predetermined evacuation procedures do not consider people behavior in emergency conditions.

For this reason, all the world over, current researches focus on managing evacuation by adapting strategies to changing real scenarios. Hence, the aim of this chapter is to describe a model-based control of the egress dynamics that takes into account the current evolution of the emergency. To enter into more details, the total time for evacuation, since the threatening event occurs, is the sum of three contributions: the time to recognize the emergency, the time needed to process sensorial information, and the time necessary to direct the crowd to safety zones. The main objective of the proposed control system is to minimize the third contribution, by safely driving the dynamic egress of the crowd. This is achieved by real-time adaptation of escape routes, according to the prediction of the egress time through some monitored areas and the estimated residual available time. The ultimate goal is to evacuate as many people as quickly as possible.

The control of evacuation is supported by a wireless networked control system. Namely, control actions are coordinated to reduce egress times and guarantee a safe dynamics of the crowd, by using feedback from wireless sensors and commands to the distributed actuators.

Sensing and communication technologies offer the opportunity for measuring variables that indicate emergency and/or crowded places and, at the same time, for communicating actions for a safe egress. If present, trained staff involved in rescue operations may use personal digital assistants (PDAs) for receiving instructions and GPS information on the event evolution from the control center. The presence of security operators can improve control system performances, making it possible to decentralize decisions on actions to be performed for a safe egress, also coping with possible communication disservices.

In particular, sensors could be not only the classical fire, smoke, and toxic gas (NO_x, CO, CO_2, etc.) detectors but also devices (e.g., cameras) counting and monitoring people and foreseeing congestion in specific places. In particular, feedback is necessary about the distribution of individuals in the different parts of the environment (e.g., rooms of a building); the availability of doors, exit points, and transit ways; flows in critical points; and detection of overcrowding effects and blocking, congestion, and deadlock conditions, especially close to exit points, doors, and transit points. Actuating messages can be directed to all people by using distributed actuators (monitors, flashing lights, automatically opening doors, acoustic signals and alarms, etc.) or to expert and equipped agents (firefighters, safety officers, etc.) that help and direct groups of people to a safe exit.

A suitable model describing egress dynamics is the core of the developed evacuation control. Namely, a reliable model of collective motion improves the evacuation performances, for three main reasons. Firstly, a better knowledge of the crowd dynamics can be obtained, and the parameters of the collective motion can be identified or estimated (e.g., average speed of individuals as a function of density, characteristics of inflows and outflows from doors and bottlenecks, and overcrowded and congested areas). Secondly, the model provides useful data for comparative analysis of alternative escape plans and for evaluating the effectiveness of evacuation control strategies. Thirdly, the model supports the real-time management of evacuation and allows timely actions that influence the evacuation process (controlling signs, sending signals or special audible alerts to the crowd, automatic closing or opening of doors, driving security officers, etc.).

In this chapter, we develop a discrete-event system (DES) and queuing network-based approach that represents the crowd behavior in complex buildings by assembling simple modules. In particular, the crowd in different zones of a building is modeled by an elementary queue, whose parameters depend on simplifying assumptions about main human behavioral characteristics. The proposed model is a trade-off between accuracy in representing dynamics of evacuation and modularity and simplicity necessary for real-time evacuation.

However, the state-dependent queues make it difficult to obtain a closed form solution for the proposed model. Hence, the model has been implemented by the discrete-event simulation tool SimEvents in MATLAB®/Simulink® environment. Due to lack of suitable experimental data, model validation is performed by comparing simulation results provided by SimEvents with those obtained from a highly detailed simulation model developed by the buildingEXODUS software package (Galea et al. 2006), which is assumed as a reliable representation of the details of the evacuation process. The derivation of a control law from these models is not straightforward. For this reason, the evacuation control algorithm development is assessed with reference to a different graph model. This approach allows to simplify the design and tuning procedure, making it possible to adapt existing routing algorithms based on the optimization of paths. As for the control method, two different approaches are combined, that is, the maximum flow and the quickest flow. According to the first, the flow from each door is monitored so that people gathered near overcrowded areas are redirected toward less crowded doors with a quicker outflow (number of evacuees/time). The second approach identifies the shortest path minimizing the overall evacuation time. More in details, we developed a new systematic control method by suitably modifying the Dijkstra's algorithm to take into account the peculiarities of the evacuation process and the characteristics of crowd motion.

This chapter is organized as follows. Firstly, the modeling approaches of the egress dynamics are described. Then, some practical issues concerning the wireless network of sensors and actuators are considered. Finally, after giving details on the integrated control strategy for management of the evacuation process, simulation results are given concerning both validation of models and of control strategies for a practical case study and the measured performance indices.

21.2 Theoretical Models of the Egress Dynamics

21.2.1 Background

Scientific literature reports flow-based models using graphs, cellular automata representations, and agent-based systems in which each agent represents an individual, activity-based models including sociological and behavioral aspects (see Cao et al. 2012; Kuligowski and Peacock 2005; Lino and Maione 2010; Pizzileo et al. 2011; Santos and Aguirre 2004; Schreckenberg and Sharma 2002; Waldau et al. 2007; and references therein). Sometimes, the flow-based models exploit the carrying capacity to predict the evacuation dynamics, by considering the topology of the location in which the emergency occurs, and the evacuation policies (Schreckenberg and Sharma 2002). In Cao et al. (2012), based on the Lighthill–Whitham–Richards flow model, a fractional order model of crowd dynamics is proposed. Some models also consider the human response, thus including psychological or sociological factors and detailing individual reactions (Galea et al. 1996, Klüpfel et al. 2000, Schadschneider et al. 2009). The two approaches differ for a macroscopic or microscopic point of view, respectively. Macroscopic models are usually employed to statically plan escape routes, by solving an optimization problem for achieving the *quickest flow* or the *maximum flow*; resulting escape plans cannot be modified during emergency by taking into account the feedback from real scenario. Also microscopic models cannot be adapted in real time, because a dynamic optimization of escape routes and flows requires too much computational resources and time. Moreover, a detailed microsimulation requires information that cannot be acquired during emergency.

Since models are application oriented, none of them have absolute validity. Models that differ for complexity and accuracy can be defined to take into account the main phenomena at various accuracy levels. Mathematical modeling in a control framework requires to trade-off between accuracy in representing the dynamical behavior of the most significant variables and the need of reducing the complexity of controller structure and design process. On the other hand, using accurate microscopic models allows characterizing crowd dynamics, evaluating and validating the effects of operative conditions, and setting model parameters. Nevertheless, despite of good prediction capabilities, models obtained in such a way are useless for designing a control law, as they are not in the form of mathematical equations. A suitable choice consists in using different models, with different level of details, developed by means of different design tools, to optimize the design of the control systems and suitably evaluate its performance.

21.2.2 Modeling Approaches

The aim of this work is to control evacuation by redirecting crowd flows through appropriate signs, lights, acoustic signals, and other commands. Therefore, the available feedback information from the real scenario is very important. It typically consists of discrete collected data generated by the sensors distributed in the emergency area. Then, if one considers discrete nature of feedback data, of the signals produced by actuators, of the controlled variables, and of the events in emergency situations and events that realize the control law, it is easy to understand and justify the necessity of a DES model for analyzing and controlling the evacuation dynamics.

Following the DES formalisms (Ramadge and Wonham 1987), each individual in a collective motion can be considered as an entity receiving/sending events from/to other individuals or the environment. He or she is subject to discrete events coming from the environment or messages from other individuals. At the same time, he or she may trigger events causing a state change in the environment or messages. Then, events are randomly generated in the evacuated environment (variation or interruption of available escape routes, blocking of doors and ways out, overcrowding of specific areas, elevators out of service, etc.) or be determined by the individual reactions (panic, urge to go and save relatives or socially linked people, etc.) or produced by expert agents (firefighters, policemen, safety personnel, etc.) in routing people toward emergency exit or automatically provided by distributed actuators executing an evacuation policy. Both information detected by sensors and control actions can be adapted to this DES framework. As a macroscopic model, this approach has the advantage of simplifying controller design.

A well-established modeling and analysis tool for DES is provided by queuing networks (Kleinrock 1975), which easily describe precedence relations, parallelism, synchronization, and modularity. More specifically, they can be adopted to statistically represent the decisions and actions affecting the evacuated crowd behavior. A probabilistic approach may take into account several decision parameters, depending on the current system state and on sociological and psychological factors. Namely, humans take decisions after elaborating the perceived signals and information, not simply after a causal reaction to *stimuli*. For example, consider the case in which some individuals interact to form groups or individuals try to rescue relatives going in opposite direction to the crowd or the influence of leaders, expert agents, firefighters, and so on. The approach considers an individual perspective to a certain extent. Moreover, escape routes can be easily recognized, and minimum time/shortest length paths can be identified.

To represent flows of individuals during egress (Lino et al. 2009a,b, 2011), the authors defined a queuing network, which is suitable for designing and testing evacuation control strategies. The queuing network model results from assembling simple modules, consisting of elementary queues, each one representing basic components of the building.

The modeling outputs are useful for different purposes. In this work, they are used to identify motion parameters, to verify simplifying assumptions, and to provide an estimation of the performance of the evacuation control algorithms. Also, they will allow the optimization of escape routes by minimizing an objective function, which depends on the model parameters.

However, even if the proposed model represents the main aspects of the evacuation process, it does not provide a closed form solution giving the steady-state probabilities of the network. Yet, it is useful that the real-time management of evacuation takes advantage from the knowledge of the transient dynamics. Thus, we developed a queuing network simulation model in the MATLAB/Simulink environment providing a tool suitable for implementing and validating evacuation strategies. In particular, we exploited the DES toolbox SimEvents, which is able to represent complex DESs by a network of queues. Validation of the model represents a crucial step of the developing process, as it guarantees that the model is accurate enough in representing the dynamical behavior of the most significant variables. The main problem to be faced during the validation process is the lack of suitable experimental data. In many cases, existing data refer to specific situations and cannot be generalized due to the unpredictability of the human behavior. Moreover, economic and feasibility reasons make it difficult to organize reliable experiments. A solution for the validation problem consists in developing a microscopic simulation model by a domain-specific tool, which is assumed as a reliable model of the evacuation process. Analysis of performance of the proposed model can be achieved with reference to the detailed model output. To this aim, the buildingEXODUS software package (Galea et al. 2006) is used in this chapter. This tool has been internationally recognized as a commercial software able to simulate a microscopic model for building evacuation. It has been widely used in the literature to validate models or to develop evacuation scenarios for planning the location of the more suitable exits (Schreckenberg and Sharma 2002, Waldau et al. 2007). However, if one uses it for verifying the effectiveness of a proposed evacuation control strategy, he or she would encounter a major problem: it is not possible to modify the trend of the simulation after the crowd attributes and the building geometry have been defined. For this reason, the proposed DES model is used to evaluate the effectiveness of evacuation control strategies. Finally, the control algorithm development is assessed with reference to a macroscopic graph model. This approach allows to simplify the design and tuning procedure, making it possible to adapt existing routing algorithms based on the optimization of paths. In the following, after introducing physical considerations concerning the human behavior and characteristics during motion, details on different models used in the design process are given.

21.2.3 Motion Parameters

Tuning evacuation models require a proper setting of some parameters related to physical characteristics of motion. These parameters are the average free walking speed on a flat terrain, the up–down and down–up average free walking speeds on stairs, flow rate across exits and transit points, and density-dependent travel speed across corridors, doors, and stairs.

The free walking speed (i.e., the speed each individual exhibits in an open space) mainly varies with age and sex and can be greatly influenced by the physical disabilities, the trip purpose and conditions (e.g., the need to hurry or the wish to dawdle), the carry of baggage, and the gradient of walking area (Fruin 1971). Based on about 150 literature references, Weidmann (1993) found a mean value of $s_0 = 1.34$ m/s and a standard deviation of 0.26 for the normal distribution related to the motion of a mean population on a flat terrain in a free area. However, the crowd density affects the walking speed, as people adapt their speed to the available space. Observations and experiments demonstrate that the average speed $s(\rho)$ nonlinearly decreases as traffic density ρ increases (impeded traffic), in terms of number of persons per unit area P/m² (Fruin 1971). In particular, density has almost no influence for values lower than 0.27 P/m² (Fruin 1971), whereas forward movement is halted at about 5 P/m² (i.e., a crowded immobile queue) (Fruin 1971, Jain and Smith 1997). The latter can be considered as the maximum capacity of a unit space. For densities within the range [0.3, 2] P/m², the speed decreases almost linearly. The empirical relationship between density and flow speed is described by the *fundamental diagram* (see Fruin 1971 and Schreckenberg and Sharma 2002 for details).

Here, we assume the motion of individuals in rooms and corridors as described in Mitchell and Smith (2001), according to the following formula (impeded actual speed):

$$s(\rho) = s_0 e^{-[(N-1)\beta]^{\gamma}} \tag{21.1}$$

where
N is the number of individuals occupying the area
β and γ are scale and shape parameters depending on the geometry of the area and on average walking speed when $\rho = \{2,4\}$

Similar considerations hold for motion on stairways. Apart the previously mentioned parameters, people walking on stairways exhibit normally distributed free horizontal speeds (i.e., the horizontal component of the speed vector), with an average speed that depends on the stair geometry (angle and height of riser). Moreover, differences exist between short and long stairways (see Fruin 1971, Kretz et al. 2008, and references therein). In particular, sometimes speeds going up can be larger than speeds going down in short stairways (people accelerating when going up), while in long stairways the contrary always occurs. With reference to the case study, we assume that long stairways are traveled in the down–up directions, while short stairways can be traveled in both directions. A 0.423 m/s average speed for long stairways and 0.780 and 0.830 m/s up–down and down–up, respectively, average speeds for short stairways are used (Kretz et al. 2008).

Moreover, it is shown that interaction among individuals increases with traffic density, more evidently near bottlenecks, where physical interaction generates interpersonal friction forces

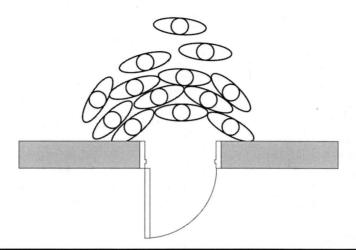

Figure 21.1   Door overcrowding due to the faster-is-slower effect.

(Helbing et al. 2000). This phenomenon is more significant when individuals wish to move faster than current speed, which is a typical behavior in panic situations. In particular, archlike blockings can be found at doors (see Figure 21.1), if desired walking speed overcomes a critical value equal to the free walking speed (Helbing et al. 2000; Parisi and Dorso 2007).

These blockings produce inefficient outflow and delays, and the consequent increase of desired speed reduces the egress speed. This *faster-is-slower* effect determines two different outflow regimes depending on the desired speed s_d. The first one implies that the faster individuals want to move, the faster they evacuate, so that the outflow depends almost linearly on s_d. The second one implies a nonlinear decrease of evacuation efficiency with s_d due to interaction forces.

21.2.4 *Modeling the Egress Dynamics as a Queuing Network*

As it is well known from established literature (Kleinrock 1975), a queuing system is the basic building block of queuing networks. Moreover, it can be used to represent many DESs. A queuing system receives clients to provide them a certain service, by means of servers and a queuing space, which has a limited capacity, and by using a queuing rule to order the arriving clients. In our context, each person in the evacuated building is a client, servers are associated to the resource spaces people compete for (i.e., doors, passages, corridors, etc.), and the rooms or available spaces are the queuing space where people wait. The system can be considered as a DES in which the standard events are the arrival of a person to the queue, for example, when it gets to the exit or to a room door, or the departure of a person, when it leaves the occupied space. The state of the system is obviously associated to the number of people in queue, and it is affected by the cited events or by the control policies that help to route people and keep queues manageable.

If time is considered, the DES dynamics is further specified and depends on the timed sequence of events, and the consequent states can also be associated to a time (i.e., the time when the state is reached or the time the condition associated to the state lasts). This helps quantitative performance evaluation, for example, by means of Markovian networks made by different queuing systems with exponentially distributed service times. Even if this last assumption is not realistic in most practical cases, it helps designing the system due to computational efficiency of Markovian networks. However, simulation is essential to validate, modify, and finely tune the design.

The method proposed in this chapter is based on the integration of different modules, each associated to a space of the environment (rooms, corridors, stairs, doors, exits, etc.). The parameters of the modules depend on statistical characteristics of crowd motion. The modules play the role of servers; the people using them are the clients. Then, each client is evacuated to the exit by waiting for and passing through a sequence of servers.

The queuing network is made by linking nodes (the servers associated to space resources) to respect the flow sequence. The number of clients entering and using an open network is not fixed, as people may enter and exit the system. The network state is defined by the states of the nodes. Referring to Markovian queues, the state is a vector $\mathbf{X} = [X_1, X_2, \ldots, X_M]$, where X_i is the random discrete variable specifying the individuals occupying resource R_i, for $i = 1, \ldots, M$, with M number of distinct space resources. Each resource R_i is further characterized by its capacity C_i, that is, the maximum number of occupants, and the queuing rule used to select the next individual to host. In a Markovian network (arrival Poisson processes, exponentially distributed service times to cross spaces, random routings), usually three main processes are assumed as Poisson: the process of leaving a resource by an individual (which is an input process for the next resource), the composition of individuals from different spaces in the same unique space, and the decomposition of a crowd in groups of individuals.

The crowd behavior in different zones of a building is modeled by an elementary queue, whose parameters are derived by physical considerations related to the human behavior and characteristics (according to Kendall's notation, Kleinrock 1975). Two different queue modules are used: the first is for rooms, corridors, and stairways, and the second is for doors, exits, entrances, and gateways.

As in Jain and Smith (1997), simple queues represent corridors. The same representation is applied to rooms and stairways, by properly considering the differences in the crowd behavior. Each queue is composed of a queuing space characterized by a capacity equal to 0 and a number of servers equal to the capacity C of the associated area. Given the maximum capacity of a unit space equal to 5, the capacity of the area of length L and width W is $C = 5 \cdot W \cdot L$. Then, the queue fills up if the number of individuals occupying servers matches the area capacity. The service time depends on the speed of individuals, which is determined by (21.1). In more details, we assume that the service time is normally distributed, with a mean value $1/\mu(\rho) = L/s(\rho)$, where μ is the average service rate. Note that different service times can be obtained for rooms, stairways, and corridors by considering the relevant free walking speeds. Finally, the arrival process follows an exponential distribution. To sum up, according to the Kendall notation (Kleinrock 1975), the resulting queue is a state-dependent M/G/C/C queue, which is characterized by an exponential distribution of arrivals (M), by a general distribution of service times (G) (as the service rates strictly depend on the number of individuals in the area), by fixed number of servers (C), and by a limited capacity queuing space (C).

To represent bottlenecks (i.e., doors, exits, entrances, and gateways), a queue with a queuing space of null capacity and a number of servers equal to its capacity is used. In this case, a capacity of $W P/m$ is assumed. If some individuals completely occupy the passage for the time needed to cross it, the preceding queue associated to a room, corridor, or stairway is blocked.

The queue service rate μ is determined by taking into account the faster-is-slower effect, as described in the following. First of all, we suppose that the desired walking speed of individuals crossing a bottleneck varies as proposed by Helbing et al. (2000):

$$s_d(t) = s_d^{max} + \left[1 - \frac{s_d^{max}}{s_d(0)}\right] \bar{s}(t) \tag{21.2}$$

where
  $s_d(0)$ is the initial desired speed
  s_d^{max} is the maximum desired speed
  $\bar{s}(t)$ is the average speed of individuals in the crowd

Then, we compute the queue desired service rate $\mu_d(t) = W \cdot s_d(t)$ and the average service rate $\bar{\mu}(t) = W \cdot \bar{s}(t)$, being W the passage width. Finally, the actual service rate $\mu(t)$ is normally distributed with an average value given by Wang et al. (2008):

$$E[\mu \mid \mu_d] = \begin{cases} \mu_d & \text{if } \mu_d \leq \mu_c \\ 1 - e^{\alpha/(\mu_d - \mu_c)} & \text{if } \mu_d > \mu_c \end{cases} \tag{21.3}$$

where
  $E[\mu \mid \mu_d]$ is the expected value of the service rate μ
  μ_c is the flow capacity of the passage
  α is a negative constant

To sum up, firstly, μ_d is computed and compared to μ_c, and then $E[\mu \mid \mu_d]$ is used to generate μ.

The relationship between desired speed and average speed given by (21.2) is depicted in Figure 21.2. It shows that when the average speed $\bar{s}(t)$ reduces below a certain threshold, the desired speed overcomes the maximum allowed exit speed $s_c = \mu_c/W$, and the faster-is-slower effect occurs. Figure 21.2 points out that the faster-is-slower effect holds if the desired speed is within the interval $\left[s_c, s_d^{max}\right]$.

21.2.5 Graph Model Used for Routing

As previously recalled, graph theory is used to develop network flow models (Ahuja et al. 1993). To this aim, graph models usually depict the spaces available and the links between them. Namely, a graph is defined by a pair $G = (V,E)$ where $V = \{v_1, \ldots, v_n\}$ is a nonempty finite set of nodes or

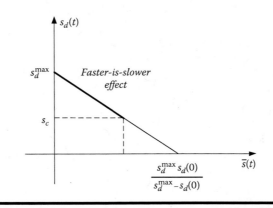

Figure 21.2 Relationship between desired speed and average speed when crossing bottlenecks.

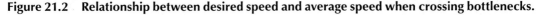

vertices and $E \subseteq V \times V$ is a nonempty finite set of arcs or edges. We use nodes to represent some significant locations in the building where people are directed to or pass by or are grouped in. These locations can be inside the building or can lead to the external environment. On their turn, arcs represent the possible paths that could be used to route people. Structural relations between nodes and arcs are modeled by the adjacency or incidence matrices.

Nodes are characterized by the capacity attribute, that is, the maximum number of people who can simultaneously occupy that space. The arcs might be characterized by certain attributes too, like the traveling time, which could depend on the crowd density and the hazard level. Moreover, dynamic changes are possible; namely, connections could fail or be missing at a certain time because of a blocking due to fire, smoke, toxic gas, or a high hazard level. Then, the arcs defined by these links are temporary and may even not exist. Since all the previously mentioned attributes change with time, a dynamic network extends the static model and is preferred. Therefore, the time-based dynamic network is defined as $G = (V_t, E_t)$, as a function of time t. On this basis, we may develop a macroscopic model for building evacuation, which includes a certain degree of adaptation. In this sense, to complete and integrate the graph model and to help in planning the evacuation, a so-called *dynamic severity matrix* (Hamacher and Tjandra 2002) is defined to represent both the hazard level and people motion. Namely, it contains the available information, such as geometrical features of the building, knowledge of the safest destinations, details about behavior of people and their distribution, and characteristics of the hazard like location and propagation. Only the geometry is statically fixed, whereas all the other data are parameters that dynamically change and can only be collected by wireless sensors. Obviously, the higher is the number of factors considered in the severity matrix, the more reliable will be the evacuation planning even if more computationally intensive. However, we may here mainly consider and focus on the cited four factors.

The geometry of the building is usually well known in advance. Then, we may define the static graph $G = (V, E)$ that depicts it. To this aim, we may classify the n nodes in V as external, that is, leading to the external safe environment (like exits), and internal, that is, strictly belonging to the evacuated spaces. Then, let n_e and $n_i = n - n_e$ be the number of external and internal nodes, respectively.

Moreover, each arc in E is denoted as $e_{ij} = (v_i, v_j)$, and it is directed from v_i to v_j and depicted by an arrow with tail at v_i and head at v_j. Node v_i is termed the parent and v_j the child. Let e denote the number of arcs that are then ordered. If every possible arc exists, the graph is said to be *complete*. If $e_{ij} = (v_i, v_j) \in E$ implies that also $e_{ji} = (v_j, v_i) \in E$, for each i and j, then the graph is said to be *undirected*; otherwise, it is *directed* and commonly termed a digraph. The edges can be represented by an *adjacency* or *connectivity* matrix $\mathbf{A} = [a_{ij}]_{n \times n}$, with $a_{ij} = 1$ if $(v_j, v_i) \in E$ or $a_{ij} = 0$ if $(v_j, v_i) \notin E$, and $a_{ii} = 0$ (no self-loop). For an undirected graph, $\mathbf{A}$ is symmetric.

A graph is further described by the *incidence* matrix $\mathbf{B} = [b_{ij}]_{n \times e}$, with $b_{ij} = 1$ if the node v_i is the head of the jth arc, $b_{ij} = -1$ if the node v_i is the tail of the jth arc, and $b_{ij} = 0$ otherwise. As previously stated, the dynamic graph G_t is a simple time extension of the static graph G.

Since the time required to move from a node to another depends on the distance between the two nodes and on crowd density level, we adopt an approach based on dynamic networks and graphs with density-dependent travel time (Schreckenberg and Sharma 2002). To this aim, we define the matrix $\mathbf{D} = [d_{ij}]_{n \times n}$ containing the Euclidean distances between each pair of nodes. Moreover, $\boldsymbol{\rho} = [\rho_{ij}]_{n \times n}$ is the matrix of densities, where ρ_{ij} is the crowd density in the link associated to arc e_{ij}, and $\mathbf{S} = [s_{ij}]_{n \times n}$ is the matrix of speeds to move between each pair of nodes. Impeded actual speed given by formula (21.1) can be applied to each arc e_{ij} to obtain

$$s_{ij} = s_0 e^{-[(N-1)/\beta]^\gamma} \tag{21.4}$$

where s_0 is the average free walking speed, with values previously specified in Section 21.2 for a flat terrain or for long and short stairways. This last relation implies that if the density ρ_{ij} on an arc tends to the maximum allowed level ρ_{max}, then the associated speed s_{ij} tends to be zero, while $s_{ij} = s_0$ if the density $\rho_{ij} = 0$.

The hazard characteristics associated to fire, smoke, toxic gases, and other dangerous phenomena and materials dynamically change and vary according to the specific case study. More specifically, hazard levels allow classification of spaces, so that some parts of the building are preferred to others. These preferred parts are considered with priority to achieve the safest evacuation. See, for example, the multiple objective approach (Hamacher and Tufekci 1987) that assigns priority levels to the different evacuation regions. This kind of approach allows to define a cost for every arc. The cost becomes very high for those arcs and then the associated connections that are characterized by a high level of risk. In particular, if t' is the time when the arc e_{ij} becomes not affordable, the cost c_{ij} associated with e_{ij} is updated as follows (Hamacher and Tjandra 2002):

$$c_{ij}(t) = \begin{cases} c_{ij}(t) & \text{if } t \leq t' \\ H & \text{if } t > t' \end{cases} \tag{21.5}$$

with H being an increased cost value. The matrix $\mathbf{C} = [c_{ij}]_{n \times n}$ contains the costs to move between each pair of nodes.

If the cost is given by the time needed to cross an arc, an increased value takes somehow into account the fact that the time grows based on the crowd density, the gases concentration, the heat and temperature, etc. If the cost is the crossing time, it holds

$$c_{ij} = \frac{d_{ij}}{s_{ij}} \tag{21.6}$$

Then the cost becomes larger as speed decreases. Moreover, we have to relate the cost to the hazard level. Therefore, we may introduce a *mobility parameter* (Galea et al. 2006), which is inversely proportional to the hazard level. Namely, let us define by m_i and m_j the mobility attributes of the nodes v_i and v_j, respectively, with $m_i, m_j \in [0,1]$, based on the hazard level associated with the production of smoke, gases, heat, and high temperatures. A mobility value close to zero means that the desired speed of people is almost reduced to zero because of the high level of hazard. Thus, we may define a matrix $\mathbf{M} = [m_{ij}]_{n \times n}$ containing the mobility between each pair of nodes. If a certain tolerance level "*tol*" is fixed, it holds

$$m_{ij} = \begin{cases} \dfrac{m_i + m_j}{2} & \text{if } m_i \text{ and } m_j > tol \\ m_j & \text{if } m_j \leq tol \end{cases} \tag{21.7}$$

which indicates that the mobility across an arc is the average between the values associated to the two nodes, if these nodes are safe, that is, if their mobility is bigger than a minimum threshold given by "*tol*." Otherwise, if the head of the arc has a very low mobility, although it could be still high for the tail, we assume that the mobility across the arc is low as well, to inhibit the use of the link represented by the arc. By these assumptions, the speed in Equation (21.4) can be modified as follows:

$$s_{ij} = s_0 \cdot m_{ij} \cdot e^{-[(N-1)/\beta]^{\gamma}} \tag{21.8}$$

and applied into formula (21.6) to compute the cost. In this way, the real speed depends not only on the crowd density but also on the hazard level affecting the mobility parameter.

21.3 Simulation Models of the Egress Dynamics

21.3.1 SimEvents Model

SimEvents is a MATLAB/Simulink toolbox for simulation of DESs. Just like other software tools like Arena, Extend, and Witness, it allows the representation of complex discrete-event systems by a network of queues. Moreover, the integration with MATLAB and Simulink simplifies the modeling process of hybrid dynamical systems, which include continuous-time, discrete-time, and discrete-event subcomponents, such as sensor networks and distributed control systems.

Figure 21.3 depicts the block scheme of the queue, which models rooms, corridors, and stairways. We assume the flow in one direction.

The main elements of the scheme are a FIFO queue representing the queuing space and the *Servers* block, consisting of a number of servers matching the available capacity. The function *service time computation* computes the service time depending on the area congestion. It consists of two functions: the first derives the current speed from (21.1) by considering the number of people crossing the area; the second computes the service time as the path length divided by the speed. The *block/release* element prevents individuals to enter area, if the maximum capacity has been reached.

The block scheme implementing bottlenecks like doors is represented in Figure 21.4, and it suitably models the *faster-is-slower effect*.

The model is composed of a *FIFO queue* and a *Servers* block with as many servers as the individuals that can cross the bottleneck at the same time. The service time is determined by (21.2) and (21.3), provided that an estimate of the average service rate is available. If Δt is the time

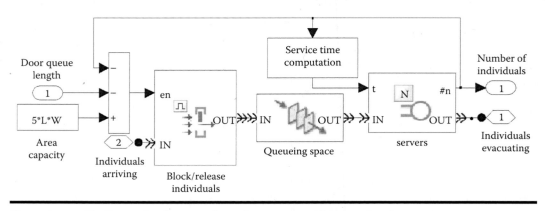

Figure 21.3 SimEvents implementation of rooms, corridors, and stairways.

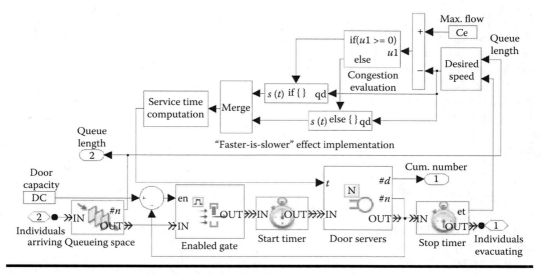

Figure 21.4 SimEvents implementation of bottlenecks.

interval taken by the last individual to cross the door, as measured between blocks *Start Timer* and *Stop Timer*, its reciprocal $\mu = 1/\Delta t$ represents the current service rate. Thus, since the number N of individuals waiting to be served has a zero service rate, the overall average service rate can be computed as

$$\bar{\mu} = \frac{\sum \mu_i}{N+1} = \frac{1}{(N+1) \cdot \Delta t} \tag{21.9}$$

Then, the *Desired speed* block calculates $s_d(t)$ according to (21.2). If the resulting value overcomes the door maximum flow capacity, a congestion occurs. Finally, the *Service time computation* block outputs a service time obtained from a normal distribution with a mean equal to the reciprocal of the service rate. To simulate the behavior of individuals leaving the queue in front of a door, the queuing space is connected both to queue servers and to different queuing spaces, with a routing probability depending on the wish of individuals to leave the queue.

When rooms/corridors and doors share the same queuing space, we must guarantee that the number of individuals in the system does not overcome the overall capacity. Then, the door queuing space capacity is set equal to the room/corridor capacity. So, after connecting the elementary submodels, the number of individuals waiting in front of the door is used to reduce the number of available servers in the room/corridor. To implement this condition, the signal *door queue length* representing the number of individuals in the door queue is fed back (see Figure 21.3).

21.3.2 *buildingEXODUS Model*

The software buildingEXODUS was developed by the Fire Safety Engineering Group at the University of Greenwich to simulate the evacuation of a large number of people from multifloor buildings. A detailed description of the buildingEXODUS model is beyond the scopes of this work; thus, only the parameters setting procedure will be briefly introduced in the following.

In buildingEXODUS, behavior and movement of individuals are based on heuristic or flexible rules operating in submodel levels (Galea et al. 1998). More in details, the *occupant submodel* defines physical and psychological attributes of people; the *behavior submodel*, which can be defined as normal or extreme, determines people response (initial response, conflict resolutions, overtaking, etc.), whose decision is then passed to the *movement submodel*; finally, the *toxicity and hazard submodels* define the evolving of the risk associated with fire, smoke, gases, heat, and people reaction (Gwynne et al. 2005).

Making the buildingEXODUS simulation realistic requires the proper setting of a number of varying attributes (*drive*, location, and response time of occupants and exit flow, to mention a few). The main attributes affecting the crowd behavior are *patience*, *response time*, and *drive*. Since normal evacuation conditions are considered in this chapter, the *patience* attribute, which represents the time before individuals recommit to another course of action, was not set. Similarly, the *response time*, that is, the time elapsed before individuals start to evacuate, was set to 0. Finally, conflict resolution depends on the difference between *drive* attributes of individuals; simulations have been carried out considering competitive conditions; thus, an equal *drive* has been set for each individual, aiming at reproducing the faster-is-slower behavior close to doors.

21.4 Wireless Sensors and Actuators

The evacuation management system is sketched in Figure 21.5. The main topic of this chapter is the evacuation control system design, which is represented by the "Routing Control System" block. A general overview on the evacuation management system will clarify the interaction between each subsystem and will show the constraints imposed by the network of sensors and actuators on the control system. A detailed description of technical implementation of the network of sensors and actuators is beyond the scope of this chapter.

The evacuation management system is composed of a Central Management Unit (CMU); a Communication, Sensor, and Actuator System; an Input Data Processing Unit; an Evacuation Management Unit; and a Routing Control System.

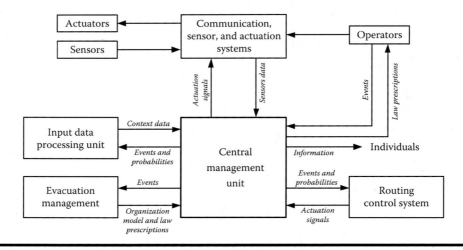

Figure 21.5   Evacuation management system block scheme.

The Central Management System (CMS) plays the role of a hub of information exchange between the subsystems. In particular, it periodically analyzes information coming from the real scenario, providing the status of sensors and actuators and a visual representation of sensor data (e.g., trend graphs, panel controls, map representations showing crowd distribution, position of security operators, and gas concentrations), managed by the Communication, Sensor, and Actuator Systems. Based on the Data Processing Unit, the CMS automatically or semiautomatically alerts external security operators (e.g., police and firefighters), which receive information on emergency situation and instructions on procedures, provided by the Evacuation Management Unit. In particular, CMS specifies intervention areas and position of sensors that detected an abnormal situation, together with a map showing position of emergency tools (e.g., fire extinguishers). Moreover, it sends sensor data to the Routing Control System, receiving actuator signals to control the evacuation process.

The communication framework included in the *Communication, Sensor, and Actuator* subsystems is organized over several hierarchical levels. The lowest level is represented by a sensor network that communicates with the upper level consisting of a wireless LAN; it is connected to the main network, servers, and overall system management unit.

The peripheral network nodes are of two types, that is, detection nodes, which are equipped with sensors, and implementation nodes, which include actuators (signs, light panels, etc.).

The network architecture includes a set of mobile nodes, whose position within the scenario is always known. They consist of PDAs equipped with GPS devices available for security operators involved in the rescue operations and position sensors allowing to identify position of individuals within the evacuation scenario with respect to georeferenced fixed nodes.

The feedback to the control system consists of three types of information collected from real-world scenario through a network of sensors: distribution of individuals in the building to be evacuated, temperature in different environments, and concentration of harmful substances.

Information on the distribution of individuals is used to estimate flows through the critical points, to detect congestion situations, and to assess the risk level associated with each path. The distribution and number of individuals in the building are determined using two different systems. The former extrapolates the position of individuals from images captured by cameras with computing capability; the second consists of a radio-localization system that allows to estimate the relative position of mobile nodes (associated with the individuals) with some appropriate radio-frequency identification (RFID) tags.

The estimation of available time to complete a safe evacuation is assessed by monitoring the temperature and heat flow dynamics in each area of interest. To this end, an optimal distribution of temperature sensors within the environment has been considered, also allowing a timely detection of fire ignition.

As stated before, escape routes are determined by taking into account the level of risk related to phenomena that may inhibit or reduce the ability of movement, in particular the presence of a fire and the spread of toxic gases and smoke. The effect of harmful gases, smoke, and temperature on health and individual mobility has been investigated to properly select sensors to be included in the network that monitors the building. In particular, based on the so-called fractional effective dose (FED) model, monitoring the concentration of CO, HCN, O_2, CO_2, SO_2, and NO_2 and temperature variation can assist in determining the time remaining before the individual has a significant reduction of his capacity motion (Purser 1988). Before reaching some threshold values, associated with death, movement is inhibited and there are effects on the health that can be permanent. In this case, we monitor the real-world scenario and evaluate the level of risk associated with each path during the evolution of the emergency and the evacuation events, with regular updating of the risk situation. Based on this information, a network of sensor nodes is built up. Each of these nodes can be equipped with up to five sensors for measuring gas concentrations as well as temperature and humidity sensors.

Finally, the control action is applied by driving proper actuators to identify suitable escape routes. In particular, small LED displays are installed close to each door/exit, showing pictograms of simple interpretation (five symbols with three different colors); large LED panel actuators, for displaying alphanumeric messages and graphs, are arranged in strategic locations. In the presence of trained personnel involved in rescue operations, the use of PDAs, equipped with a GPS receiver, is also expected in order to facilitate the communication of instructions and information on the dynamics of the event from the operations center.

The operation of the evacuation management system can be summarized as follows. Under normal conditions, sensors detect data from the scenario with a sampling period higher than emergency to save batteries of sensor nodes; the actuators provide unvarying information related to optimal escape routes. When sensors detect abnormal values of monitored variables, the communication system sends an alert to CMU and reduces sensor sampling time. After receiving alert signal, the CMU inquires the Input Data Processing Unit, which estimates the probability of an emergency condition on the base of sensor data, and eventually suggests to start the evacuation procedure. Based on this information, the CMU contacts evacuation management and eventually starts evacuation by enabling the Routing Control System, which updates escape routes at fixed time steps depending on the current situation, and provides control signals for actuators through the CMU. Information from evacuation management and optimal escape plans are also sent to security operators through the CMU.

Number and position of sensor nodes are chosen to allow prompt identification of emergency situation, on the basis of the requirements of the American standard National Fire Protection Association (NFPA) fire. In particular, distribution of sensors takes into account temperature variations to estimate the alarm intervention time interval, so that a reasonable amount of time for evacuation is guaranteed. Some design parameters have to be set for adequate sensor displacement. Main parameters are minimum expected ceiling temperature, maximum distance between flammable material and ceiling, fire growth rate (depending on the materials and fire evolution), temperature threshold for triggering the alarm, delay between fire ignition and alarm intervention, distance between sensor nodes (which is chosen considering the worst case, i.e., the maximum distance from the ignition point), and response time index (RTI) of the sensors.

To evacuate all the occupants before the so-called *flashover condition* (during which the fire becomes generalized), a timely alarm intervention has to be guaranteed, which depends on sensor distribution. The optimal sensor distribution can be determined by means of an iterative procedure, after estimating the flashover start time t_f and the total evacuation time interval t_e and by imposing that the alarm intervention time instant has to satisfy the condition $t_a < t_f - t_e$. The flashover start time can be computed as $t_f = \sqrt{Q_f / k}$, where $Q_f = 750 A_{vent} \sqrt{h_{vent}}$, with h_{vent} and A_{vent} as height and overall surface of opened doors and windows, respectively, k as a positive constant, while the time needed to evacuate the building is estimated by means of the developed dynamical models. Assuming an initial choice of parameters as noted earlier, it is possible to determine the heat flow at the detection instant as $Q_a = k \cdot t_a^2$; then, iteratively the maximum distance between nodes is determined in order to guarantee the temperature at the ignition detection time instant. It comes that the number of sensor nodes to be included in the network is in inverse relation with the requested intervention time and proportional to the height to which they are located. Thus, after choosing the desired minimum intervention time, it is possible to determine the optimal distribution of sensor nodes.

21.5 Feedback-Based Dynamic Strategies: Algorithms for Evacuation Control

The macroscopic integrated model of evacuation dynamics based on queuing networks and graph theory, which was previously presented in Section 21.2, can be adopted as the first step in the design of the supervisory controller.

In particular, the controller employs a routing algorithm that is based on the defined graph tools. The aim is to route people along the best paths that allow the maximum number of people saved in the minimum time, to reduce the risk of injuries and death. To achieve a quick flow as much as possible and then to minimize total egress time, a shortest path problem must be solved. Several methods and algorithms exist (Hamacher and Tjandra 2002). We apply the Dijkstra's algorithm (Dijkstra 1959) since it gives a solution by finding the shortest path from a node i to a node j in terms of a defined cost function. The algorithm is reasonably fast, with a running time of $O(|n|^2)$ for complete graphs and $O(|e|^2 + |n|\log|n|)$ for sparse graphs.

Obviously, the time required to evacuate is a function of the distances but also of the density of people, which inevitably causes interactions and conflicts.

Based on information stored by the building graph matrix and by the severity matrix, the algorithm estimates the evacuation time associated to each path, by eliminating overcrowded or dangerous ones. Namely, for each node, the algorithm identifies the shortest traveling time paths toward exit nodes, by updating the matrices associated with the paths and the weights. The weights depend on the estimated densities after rerouting individuals toward the selected paths. The procedure is reiterated on the basis of any further information gathered from the scenario.

We modify the Dijkstra's algorithm to consider human behavior during evacuation, as follows. Since an arc can be traveled just in one direction (Helbing et al. 2000), we change the algorithm in such a way that all the found shortest paths will never overlap with arcs in opposite directions. To this aim, one could fix a certain path (and consequently the direction of certain arcs), update the matrix **A**, and iterate computation of remaining unfixed paths with the same procedure. Even if the obtained solution does not lead to the shortest absolute paths, it provides the shortest paths that avoid conflicts between people going in opposite directions. However, a problem arises by using this approach: which path should be selected first? In other words, which path should be less penalized by this iterative approach? Intuitively, one would think that the longest out of the initially selected paths should be less penalized. This is because if we decide to give priority to the shortest out of all the selected paths, an already relatively long path could become too long to still maintain a safe level of evacuation.

To maximize flow, that is, the number of evacuated people, an online feedback about the current state of exits is needed. Namely, a given exit could be safe from hazard (i.e., no smoke or fire affects it), but it could be better avoided because of a very slow flow rate u_i, for example, due to an overcrowding of people competing to use it. Thus, u_i is a very important indicator of the state of the ith exit, and people are routed toward exits with higher values of u_i. Moreover, an exit is considered if and only if $P_i(t) > 0$, where $P_i(t)$ is the number of people to direct and it is computed as follows:

$$P_i(t) = \begin{cases} t_r(t) \cdot u_i(t-1) - \eta_i(t) & \text{if } \eta_i(t-1) > 0 \\ t_r(t) \cdot u_{max} - \eta_i(t) & \text{if } \eta_i(t-1) = 0 \end{cases} \quad (21.10)$$

where $t_r(t)$ is the residual time for evacuation, with $t_r(t) = t_a - t$, t_a being the maximum available time for a safe evacuation (Lino et al. 2009b), $u_i(t)$ is the flow rate through exit, with $u(t) = \left[u_1(t), \ldots, u_{ne}(t) \right]^T \in \mathbb{R}^{n_e \times 1}$, u_{max} is the maximum flow rate, that is, two occupants for a door of a unitary width (Fruin 1971), and finally $\eta_i(t)$ is the number of people close to that door. In any case, if $P_i(t) \leq 0$, then the ith exit is made unavailable and is considered as an internal node at time $t+1$. This represents a sort of feedback from the system.

The algorithm was proven to be reliable and able to produce an online solution for the evacuation problem, which can be obtained in a reasonable time.

21.5.1 Routing Algorithm for Building Evacuation

The routing algorithm for building evacuation can now be described as an iterative procedure in the following:

> *Step 0.* Fix the initial sets of nodes (internal and external) and the matrices **A**, **B**, and **D**. Estimate the total available time t_a for a safe evacuation (Janssens 2000). Set $t=0$.
>
> *Step 1.* Compute the matrices **M**, ρ, **S**, and **C** and the vectors η and u.
>
> *Step 2.* Fix the set of n_i internal nodes as the union between the initial set and the not available exits, that is, those with $P_i(t) \leq 0$, as obtained from (21.10). Fix n_e external nodes as the set of available exits, that is, those with $P_i(t) > 0$, as obtained from (21.10).
>
> *Step 3.* Initialize counter $i = 1$.
>
> *Step 4.* Apply Dijkstra's algorithm to find the shortest path from the internal to external nodes.
>
> *Step 5.* Apply (21.10). Fix the direction of the longest out of all the paths from an internal to an external node and modify its cost to zero (so that it will not be the longest path in next iterations). Update **A** and **B**.
>
> *Step 6.* If $i < n_i$, update $i = i + 1$ and go back to step 4. Otherwise, go to step 7.
>
> *Step 7.* Find the not available exits, that is, those with $P_i(t) \leq 0$.
>
> *Step 8.* If $t < t_a$, update $t = t + 1$ and reset **A** and **B** to the same values defined in step 0. Go back to step 1.
>
> *Step 9.* If $t = t_a$, end.

The network characteristics influence control system performances within certain limits. Thus, some details are given on the interaction between the routing control system and the sensor and actuator network, with reference to the algorithm implementation steps.

The definition of the building graph model is assessed referring to topology of the network of sensors and actuators; in fact, the supervisory control is based on the knowledge of current situation in the neighbors of each node, in terms of people distribution and hazard level, and on the capability of the actuator system to influence the choice of a specific path. It requires the presence of sensing elements able to count the number of individuals and to detect the noxious gas concentrations in the area associated to each node and the existence of an actuator suggesting the best direction. This choice must take into account the building topology (junctions between corridors, rooms, and stairways; distribution of bottlenecks; etc.) but is influenced by the available resources. It is worth to note that unavailability of sensors and actuators in a specific area makes monitoring and controlling crowd behavior unfeasible; thus, it is useless to associate nodes to areas uncovered by the sensor and actuator network. Moreover, even though a large number of nodes guarantee a more precise routing strategy, it increases the number of actuators and the probability of generating escape plans, which are difficult to be followed.

After defining fixed sensor and actuator distribution, it is possible to build the G graph and then **A**, **B**, and **D** matrices. In presence of fires, a measure of temperature variations allows to estimate residual egress time t_a, which concludes step 0 of the control algorithm. As previously shown, a suitable choice of sensor distribution determines a timely detection of the fire event and increases the available egress time (increasing the number of sensor nodes reduces the detection time, resulting in an earlier start of the evacuation process). Clearly, the network of sensor and actuator design deeply influences control system performances; however, it must to be remarked that individual reaction times largely overcome data transmission time. Conversely, a precise knowledge of the number of people in nodes is essential for a proper functioning of the control system. For this reason, two different systems have been considered to detect the position of individuals in the building, the first one based on video monitoring and second one based on radio localization.

Information collected by the network of sensors regarding temperatures and noxious gases, as well as on crowd distribution in the building, is used to build the mobility matrix **M** according to (21.7), ρ matrix (density of individuals), and η vector (number of people close to doors) and thus to compute the walking speed matrix **S** by means of (21.8) and the **C** matrix (costs assigned to arcs) by means of (21.6). An estimate of elements of vector u is obtained by computing density variations during egress; however, technical solutions exist to directly measure outflows from exits and doors. Elements of matrix **M** are determined considering the hazard level, that is, temperature values and noxious gas concentrations, according to the previously cited FED model. The *routing algorithm for building evacuation* operates in discrete time, as information transmission occurs during regular time intervals, which are sensibly smaller than the gas propagation time constants: it comes that control system performances are not affected by the measurement and data transmission process.

Problem definition is completed at step 2 by computing P_i. In particular, information on people density close to doors and on doors outflows, as derived from sensor output, is used to choose exit nodes, that is, possible destinations where to drive individuals.

For each node, a suitable path is then calculated by the Dijkstra's algorithm at steps 3–6, and then the process is repeated. Actuation signals are sent to the network of actuators at the end of step 7. The main elements of the actuator system are small LED displays and large alphanumeric LED displays, which are placed at graph nodes; a set of messages and images (pictograms) are properly coded into actuators and associated with specific control signals. The control system output consists in a sequence of nodes and arcs forming the escape route. The information on escape routes is then provided to evacuees by showing an arrow on small LED displays, which indicates the suggested direction. LED displays are also used to redirect individuals toward less overcrowded doors and bottlenecks (by means of a directional arrow) or to discourage the arrival of individuals (by means of a flashing directional arrow); the availability of the passage is properly indicated by showing a different image (e.g., a green disk). Finally, security operators in the scenario directly receive a map of escape routes generated by the control system on PDAs, making actuator of control action more effective.

21.6 Case Study and Simulation Results

As a case study, we consider the area of large lecture rooms at Technical University of Bari. It consists of five lecture rooms and a great hall, all connected to a main corridor (Figure 21.6).

More specifically, it is assumed that only one room is provided with sensor and actuator network and monitored for managing evacuation. The room is 294 m² large, with a maximum capacity of 270 persons. Sitting desks are vertically distributed from a lower to an upper level, an internal corridor separates desks in two columns, and two more external corridors are available.

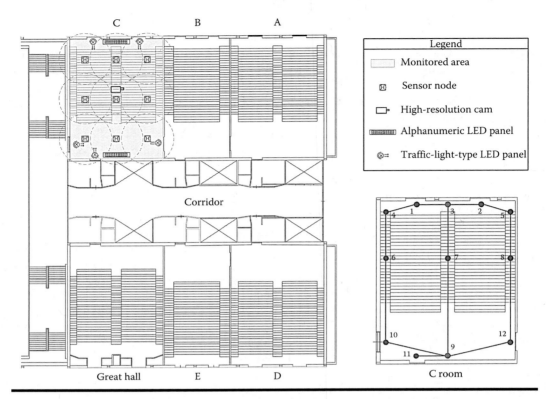

Figure 21.6   The case study: graph model and distribution of sensor nodes.

The room has three access/exit points at the lower level (1.6 m wide, maximum flow of two persons at a time) and two access/exit doors at the upper level (2.3 m wide, maximum flow of two persons at a time). In particular, the lower-level central door links the room to a main corridor and is barely used. The main and natural flow of students during evacuation is through the upper doors, otherwise through the corridor, especially the ones sitting in the first lines of desks. The teaching staff can use lower exit doors. By following the design approach described in the previous section, an optimal distribution of sensor nodes within a 9 × 9 grid is determined (see Figure 21.6), which guarantees a timely alert when emergency conditions arise.

Tuning and validation of the SimEvents model for the case study are obtained by comparing results with output of the buildingEXODUS model. More in details, three variables have been analyzed and compared, that is, people flow rate across the exits, average throughput, and total evacuation time distribution, by considering the average built upon a bench of 25 simulation runs as a result. The SimEvents model for the case study divides the room into three main areas, representing the lecturer (lower), the desks (middle), and the exit (upper) areas, respectively. The exit area consists of a landing space receiving individuals from stairways and includes two exits. Then, four queues are associated to the lower area, six queues to the middle area (considering two different flow directions on the stairways, i.e., toward upper and lower exits), and three to the last area, that is, two for exits and one for the landing space. As initial condition, an average population of 100 individuals occupies the room, mainly distributed in the desks area, while the lower and upper areas are sparsely populated. It is assumed that individuals occupying the desk and upper areas mainly evacuate from upper exits. Table 21.1 depicts the average number

Table 21.1 buildingEXODUS and SimEvents Average Evacuation Times for the Case Study

| | Evacuation Time (s) | | | |
| | buildingEXODUS | | SimEvents | |
	P	Time	P	Time
Upper-left door	34	68	34	68
Upper-right door	32	68	29	67
Lower-left door	10	40	11	42
Lower-right door	13	35	13	39

Table 21.2 Comparison of the Average Throughput for the Case Study

| | Average Throughput (P/s) | |
	buildingEXODUS	SimEvents
Upper-left door	0.50	0.50
Upper-right door	0.43	0.47
Lower-left door	0.26	0.25
Lower-right door	0.43	0.40

of individuals evacuated and overall evacuation time from each exit in buildingEXODUS and SimEvents simulations.

It is evident that only few of them try to evacuate from lower exits because routing probabilities depend on the familiarity; for this reason, results concerning the central lower exit are not represented, as it is barely used. Similar distribution of individuals between doors and comparable overall evacuation times are obtained. Also, throughput values in Table 21.2 are in good accordance.

Results about people flows across exits have been compared in Figure 21.7, showing the good prediction capabilities of the SimEvents model. Cumulative numbers of individuals increase almost linearly in all cases, being the door capacities sufficient to handle the traffic.

Finally, simulation tests were performed by implementing the *routing algorithm for building evacuation* described in Section 21.5, considering an appropriate selection of nodes and arcs in the graph as represented in Figure 21.6. A large number of nodes would lead to a more accurate routing strategy, but it would require a large number of actuators to drive the evacuation along selected paths. Therefore, a small number of nodes are chosen to reduce implementation costs and to simplify information delivered to evacuees. In Figure 21.6, three kinds of nodes have been used, denoted by blue, red, and green color, respectively: internal (intermediate places, which lead to the exits), external (the exits), and directional nodes (strategic places to locate the actuators). The graph is chosen not complete, leading to a smaller computation time, since some arcs are not necessary or physically existing, depending on characteristics of the room (stairs, seats, and desks).

Simulation results related to the controlled system are shown in Figure 21.8.

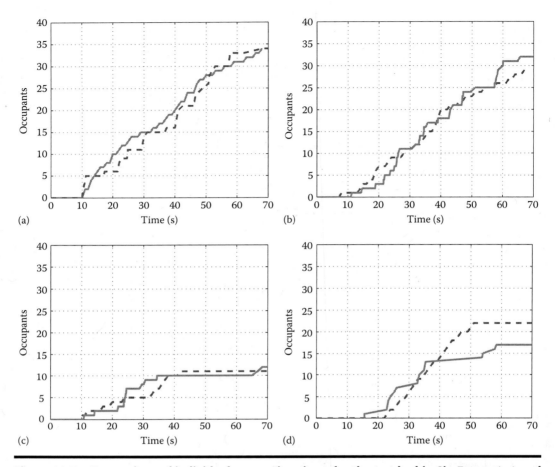

Figure 21.7 **Comparison of individual evacuation times for the test bed in SimEvents (—) and buildingEXODUS (- -): (a) upper-left door, (b) upper-right door, (c) lower-left door, (d) lower-right door.**

It is supposed that individuals are initially uniformly distributed in desks area, while lower and upper areas are empty. When simulation starts, all people try to exit the room simultaneously due to alarm. During evacuation, the network dynamic updating is discrete, also because the time required for updating data has a lower bound due to the equipment limitations. Data about density, speed of people (toward internal and external nodes), and their mobility are determined by the discrete-event model. In the test bed, these data are measured in real time and supplied by the wireless sensor network.

After defining the adjacency $\mathbf{A}$ and the incidence $\mathbf{B}$ matrices, matrix $\mathbf{M}(t)$ is randomly generated; matrices $\boldsymbol{\rho}(t)$, $\boldsymbol{\eta}(t)$, and $u(t)$ are computed by means of the DES model, while the distance matrix $\mathbf{D}$ is statically fixed. The matrices $\mathbf{S}(t)$ and $\mathbf{C}(t)$ are computed by using (21.8) and (21.6). The initial direction of traveling along a path is unknown; then we set the graph as undirected, which generates a symmetric $\mathbf{A}$ matrix. However, just before step 7 of the algorithm in Section 21.4, $\mathbf{A}$ will be not symmetric anymore. This reflects a more realistic situation of people evacuating through specific directions (Helbing et al. 2000).

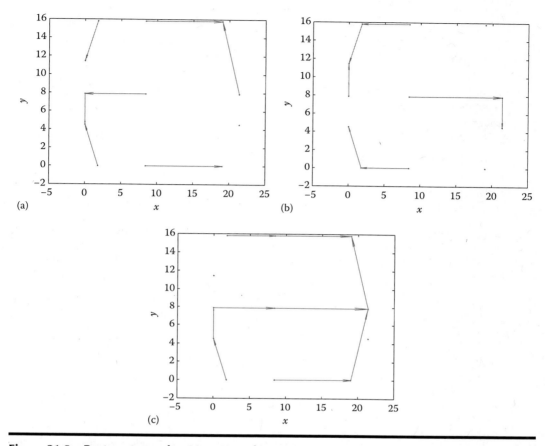

Figure 21.8 **Best route results: (a) $t = 20$ s; (b) $t = 40$ s; (c) $t = 55$ s.**

According to these results, the proposed algorithm found the quickest paths from every internal node to the safe exits. Some of these results are shown in Figure 21.8. The preferred use of the doors will be so displayed in PDAs and/or associated to pictures and paths to be provided at strategic points like the directional nodes.

21.7 Conclusions and Future Work

In this chapter, the development of a control system for managing egress from buildings in normal/emergency situations is assessed, which uses information collected from the real scenario by means of wireless network of sensors and actuators to update escape routes during evacuation. Firstly, a discrete-event model describing the evacuation dynamics from buildings has been presented, which is suitable for designing and testing control strategies. The model has been implemented in the MATLAB/Simulink environment, by using the discrete-event simulation toolbox SimEvents, and validated by comparing results with those obtained using the commercial tool buildingEXODUS. Then, an integrated macroscopic modeling approach and a routing algorithm have been proposed for managing building evacuation, by driving proper actuators to identify suitable escape routes, consisting of small LED displays and large LED panel actuators and giving instructions to trained personnel involved in rescue operations holding PDAs. Simulation results over a case study showed that the algorithm can produce a reliable and promising solution with a very small computational effort.

As future development, the algorithm will be applied to a conclusive experimental test in a real scenario simulating egress in presence of fire. Moreover, the inclusion of different kinds of actuators is under investigation, considering the use of acoustic signals, actuated doors (in order to block inaccessible or overcrowded paths), etc. Finally, the effectiveness of actuation signal system with respect to individual choices and crowd behavior is under investigation.

References

Ahuja, R.K., T.L. Magnanti, and J.B. Orlin. 1993. *Network Flows: Theory, Algorithms, and Applications.* Englewood Cliffs, NJ: Prentice Hall.

Cao, K.C., C. Zeng, D. Stuart, and Y.Q. Chen. 2012. Fractional order dynamic modeling of crowd pedestrians. In *Proceedings of the Fifth Symposium on Fractional Differentiation and Its Applications*, Nanjing, China, May 14–17, 2012.

Dijkstra, E.W. 1959. A note on two problems in connection with graphs. *Numerische Mathematik* 1: 269–271.

Fruin, J.J. 1971. *Pedestrian Planning and Design.* New York: Metropolitan Association of Urban Designers and Environmental Planners, Inc.

Galea, E., S. Gwynne, M. Owen, P. Lawrence, and L. Filippidis. 1998. A comparison of predictions from the buildingEXODUS evacuation model with experimental data. In *Proceedings of the First International Symposium on Human Behaviour in Fire*, Belfast, Northern Ireland, August 29–September 2, 1998, pp. 711–720.

Galea, E., P. Lawrence, S. Gwynne, L. Filippidis, D. Blackshields, and D. Cooney. 2006. *BuildingEXODUS v4.06 User Guide and Technical Manual.* Fire safety engineering group, London, U.K.: University of Greenwich.

Galea, E., M. Owen, and P. Lawrence. 1996. The EXODUS evacuation model applied to building evacuation scenarios. *Journal of Fire Protection Engineering* 8(2): 65–86.

Gwynne, S., E. Galea, M. Owen, P. Lawrence, and L. Filippidis. 2005. A systematic comparison of buildingEXODUS predictions with experimental data from the Stapelfeldt trials and the Milburn house evacuation. *Applied Mathematical Modelling* 29(9): 818–851.

Hamacher, H.W. and S.A. Tjandra. 2002. Mathematical modelling of evacuation problems: A state of the art. In *Pedestrian and Evacuation Dynamics*, eds. M. Schreckenberg and S.D. Sharma, Berlin, Germany: Springer-Verlag, pp. 227–266.

Hamacher, H.W. and S. Tufekci. 1987. On the use of lexicographic min cost flows in evacuation modeling. *Naval Research Logistics* 34: 487–503.

Helbing, D., I. Farkas, and T. Vicsek. 2000. Simulating dynamical features of escape panic. *Nature* 407: 487–490.

Jain, R. and J.M. Smith. 1997. Modeling vehicular traffic flow using M/G/C/C state dependent queueing models. *Transportation Science* 31(4): 324–336.

Janssens, M. 2000. *An Introduction to Mathematical Fire Modelling.* Lancaster, U.K.: Technomic Publishing Co. Inc.

Kleinrock, L. 1975. *Queuing Systems: Volume I—Theory.* New York: Wiley Interscience.

Klüpfel, H., T. Meyer-König, J. Wahle, and M. Schreckenberg. 2000. Microscopic simulation of evacuation processes on passenger ships. In *Proceedings of the Fourth International Conference on Cellular Automata for Research and Industry: Theoretical and Practical Issues on Cellular Automata*, Karlsruhe, Germany, October 4–6, 2000, eds. S. Bandini and T. Worsch, London, U.K.: Springer-Verlag, pp. 63–71.

Kretz, T., A. Grünebohm, A. Kessel, H. Klüpfel, T. Meyer-König, and M. Schreckenberg. 2008. Upstairs walking speed distributions on a long stairway. *Safety Science* 46(1): 72–78.

Kuligowski, E.D. and R.D. Peacock. 2005. A review of building evacuation models. NIST Technical Note 1471. Washington, DC: U.S. Government Printing Office.

Lino, P. and G. Maione. 2010. Applying a discrete event system approach to problems of collective motion in emergency situations. In *Pedestrian and Evacuation Dynamics 2008, Part II Simulation and Modeling*, eds. W.W.F. Klingsch, C. Rogsch, A. Schadschneider, and M. Schreckenberg, Berlin, Germany: Springer-Verlag, pp. 465–477.

Lino, P., B. Maione, and G. Maione. 2009a. A discrete event simulation model for the egress dynamics from buildings. In *Proceedings of the Sixth International Conference on Informatics in Control, Automation and Robotics (ICINCO 2009)*, Milan, Italy, July 2–5, 2009, eds. J. Filipe, J. Andrade-Cetto, and J.-L. Ferrier, Setúbal, Portugal: INSTICC Press, pp. 84–91.

Lino, P., B. Maione, and G. Maione. 2009b. Modeling and simulation of crowd egress dynamics in a discrete event environment. In *Proceedings of the 2009 IEEE Multi-Conference on Systems and Control (MSC 2009): 18th IEEE International Conference on Control Applications (CCA 2009)*, San Petersburg, Russia, July 8–10, 2009, pp. 843–848.

Lino, P., B. Pizzileo, G. Maione, and B. Maione. 2011. Tuning and validation of a discrete-event model of the egress dynamics from buildings. In *Proceedings of the 18th IFAC World Congress 2011 (IFAC WC 2011)*, Milan, Italy, August 28–September 2, 2011, eds. S. Bittanti, A. Cenedese, S. Zampieri, pp. 8743–8748.

Mitchell, D.H. and J.M. Smith. 2001. Topological network design of pedestrian networks. *Transportation Research Part B* 35: 107–135.

Parisi, D.R. and C.O. Dorso. 2007. Morphological and dynamical aspects of the room evacuation process. *Physica A* 385(1): 343–355.

Pizzileo, B., P. Lino, G. Maione, and B. Maione. 2011. A new algorithm for controlling building evacuation by feedback on hazard level and crowd distribution. In *Proceedings of the 37th Annual Conference of the IEEE Industrial Electronics Society (IECON 2011)*, Melbourne, Australia, November 7–10, 2011, pp. 387–392.

Purser, D.A. 1988. Toxicity assessment of combustion products. In *The SFPE, Handbook of Fire Protection Engineering*, ed. DiNenno, P.J., Quincy, MA: National Fire Protection Association, pp. I-200–I-245.

Ramadge, P.J. and W.M. Wonham. 1987. Supervisory control of a class of discrete event processes. *SIAM Journal on Control and Optimization* 25(1): 206–230.

Santos, G. and B.E. Aguirre. 2004. A critical review of emergency evacuation simulation models. In *Proceedings of the NIST Workshop on Building Occupant Movement during Fire Emergencies*, Gaithersburg, MD, June 10–11, 2004, eds. R.D. Peacock, E.D. Kuligowski, Washington, DC: NIST SP 1032, U.S. Government Printing Office, pp. 27–52.

Schadschneider, A., W. Klingsch, H. Klüpfel, T. Kretz, C. Rogsch, and A. Seyfried. 2009. Evacuation dynamics: Empirical results, modeling and applications. *Encyclopedia of Complexity and System Science*, ed. R.A. Meyers, Berlin, Germany: Springer.

Schreckenberg, M., and S.D. Sharma. 2002. *Pedestrian and Evacuation Dynamics*. Berlin, Germany: Springer-Verlag.

Waldau, N., P. Gatterman, H. Knoflacher, and M. Schreckenberg. 2007. *Pedestrian and Evacuation Dynamics 2005*. Berlin, Germany: Springer-Verlag.

Wang, P., P.B. Luh, S.C. Chang, and J. Sun. 2008. Modeling and optimization of crowd guidance for building emergency evacuation. In *Proceedings of the Fourth IEEE Conference on Automation Science and Engineering*, Key Bridge Marriot, Washington, DC, August 23–26, 2008, pp. 328–334.

Weidmann, U. 1993. Transporttechnik der Fussgänger-Transporttechnische Eigenschaften des Fussgngerverkehrs (in German). Technical Report, Institutfüer Verkehrsplanung, Transporttechnik, Strassen—und Eisenbahnbau IVT an der ETH Zürich, n. 90.

Index